ANNOTATED
INSTRUCTOR'S EDITION

WRITING PARAGRAPHS AND ESSAYS

Integrating Reading, Writing, and Grammar Skills

- **Joy Wingersky**
  Glendale Community College, Arizona

- **Jan Boerner**
  Glendale Community College, Arizona

- **Diana Holguin-Balogh**
  Front Range Community College, Colorado

Wadsworth Publishing Company
ITP™ An International Thomson Publishing Company

English Editor: Angela Gantner
Assistant Editor: Lisa Timbrell
Editorial Assistant: Kate Peltier
Production Services Coordinator:
  Debby Kramer
Production: Rogue Valley Publications
Printer Buyer: Karen Hunt

Permissions Editor: Bob Kauser
Designer: Wendy Calmenson
Copy Editor: Melissa Andrews
Cover: Ellen Pettengel
Compositor: Thompson Type
Printer: Courier Companies, Inc.
Cover Printer: Phoenix Color Corporation

Credits: pp. 160–162 ''Building a Better Home'' by John K. Terres. Copyright 1987 by the National Wildlife Federation. Reprinted by permission from the April/May 1987 issue of *National Wildlife* magazine. pp. 225–228 ''Courtship Through the Ages'' from *My World and Welcome to It* by James Thurber, Harcourt Brace Jovanovich, Inc. Copyright © 1942 James Thurber; copyright © 1970 Helen Thurber and Rosemary A. Thurber. Reprinted by permission of Rosemary A. Thurber. pp. 283–284 ''Why Don't We Complain?'' by William F. Buckley, Jr., *Esquire*, January, 1961. © 1960 Esquire. Renewed. Reprinted by permission of the Wallace Literary Agency, Inc. pp. 323–325 ''The Strategy of Futureness'' from *Future Shock* by Alvin Toffler. Copyright © 1970 by Alvin Toffler. Reprinted by permission of Random House, Inc.

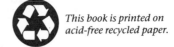

This book is printed on acid-free recycled paper.

For more information, contact:

Wadsworth Publishing Company
10 Davis Drive
Belmont, California 94002

International Thomson Publishing
Berkshire House 168-173
High Holborn
London, WC1V7AA
England

Thomas Nelson Australia
102 Dodds Street
South Melbourne 3205
Victoria, Australia

Nelson Canada
1120 Birchmount Road
Scarborough, Ontario
Canada M1K 5G4

International Thomson Publishing GmbH
Königwinterer Strasse 418
53227 Bonn
Germany

International Thomson Publishing Asia
221 Henderson Road #05-10
Singapore 0315

International Thomson Publishing - Japan
Hirakawacho Kyowa Building, 3F
2-2-1 Hirakawacho-cho
Chiyoda-ku, 102 Tokyo
Japan

1 2 3 4 5 6 7 8 9 10—99 98 97 96 95

Library of Congress Cataloging-in-Publication Data

Wingersky, Joy.
  Writing paragraphs and essays : integrating reading, writing, and grammar skills / Joy Wingersky, Jan Boerner, Diana Holguin-Balogh.—2nd ed.
      p.   cm.
  Includes index.
  ISBN 0-534-21972-1
  1. English language—Rhetoric.   2. English language—Grammar.   3. College readers.   I. Boerner, Jan.   II. Holguin-Balogh, Diana.   III. Title.
PE1408.W6188   1994
808'.042—dc20   94-10584
                                                                        CIP

CONTENTS

U N I T 3	**BEING A SENSITIVE WRITER**	**91**

U N I T 4	**ORGANIZING IDEAS AND WRITING THEM CLEARLY**	**131**

UNIT 7   MAKING IDEAS FLOW CLEARLY

*New Selection

In the second edition of *Writing Paragraphs and Essays*, we continue to integrate reading, writing, and grammar skills to teach students to write well. We use reading to help students generate ideas and to serve as strong models for their writing. We use extensive writing instruction with many suggested writing assignments. The section titled "Something to Think About, Something to Write About" in Units 2–8 includes writing assignments that are based on the reading in each of these sections. We also include material on the grammar skills necessary to students for writing effective paragraphs and essays. Students learn to integrate this material and to generate effective paragraphs and essays.

Changes in this second edition include:

■ Additional strong student and professional models

■ Vocabulary study following student and professional models

■ Discussion of computers in composition

■ Collaborative learning

  Explanation of collaborative learning
  Collaborative learning exercises (End of Part I in each Unit)

■ New exercises and examples

■ Greatly expanded section on confusing words (Appendix A)

■ Expanded teaching package

We have written a simple yet challenging text that students can understand and can assimilate with the guidance of their instructors. We separate each step of the writing process into thinking skills needed by students as they work toward becoming successful writers. In this way, students gain confidence because they find success in doing simple steps correctly, and ultimately they have a better chance of succeeding in more complex writing assignments.

At the same time, the book is thorough because we do not wish to present a developmental book with too little information that leaves a gap between the material covered in a lower-level course and the material covered in a freshman-level composition book. Instead, we bridge the gap for developmental students by presenting all of the skills necessary for mastering both paragraphs and short essays complete with effective introductions, support paragraphs, and strong conclusions. We then show the students how they can apply these skills to more complicated essays.

Our motivation in writing the second edition of this book was, once again, to provide students and teachers with a text that

- integrates reading, writing, and grammar skills
- is self-contained because it

  explains the writing process clearly yet simply

  includes grammatical concepts aimed at improving writing skills

  includes writing by students and professionals to illustrate the concepts taught throughout the book

- contains selections by professionals for generating ideas for writing
- discusses rhetorical modes

We have kept simple diction so that students coming from diverse backgrounds can understand the concepts presented in the text. Likewise, we used explanations that are intended to be encouraging and motivating. The text has been extensively class tested and revised to make it as advantageous for instruction as possible.

Each unit, particularly in the writing section, models the thinking processes that students must practice to accomplish particular tasks. Each unit also provides exercises that require the students to think through and master the concepts taught in that unit.

Features of the Book

Self-Contained Text

Students need only one textbook, yet they still have access to the writing, reading, and grammar concepts normally found in a combination of texts. Instructors have access to a full range of teaching concepts and may choose to use whichever they feel are most important for their own course needs.

The logical progression of the text facilitates instruction in an integrated approach. The book starts with simple writing, reading, and grammar concepts and progresses to more sophisticated modes of writing.

Step-by-Step Approach

The information on writing process is presented in a clear step-by-step approach that builds confidence as students see how the individual writing steps fit together to create a coherent paragraph or essay. This text focuses on the development of the paragraph and short essay by helping students generate and support one main idea. Students concentrate on topic sentences with support and on thesis sentences with support so that they can transfer these skills to more sophisticated strategies, either in this course or in college-level composition courses.

In addition, this text reduces instructor and student frustration by setting up realistic goals for developing writers. The text is divided into eight units. Units 2 through 7 are divided into four parts:

1. Writing instruction

2. Reading to generate thinking

3. Writing examples to analyze (from both students and professionals)

4. Concepts of grammar

Units 2 through 8 have two sets of writing suggestions with special emphasis on the skills covered in that unit.

Explanation and Modeling of the Writing Process

Part I of Units 2 through 8 focuses, one at a time, on steps of the writing process. Part I in these Units begins with a list of skills that are covered in that part. After these skills are explained and modeled, the students are asked to apply them by working through exercises that reflect the kind of thinking that student writers have to do in composing, revising, and editing. They are also given collaborative exercises that encourage interactive learning.

Reading Selections by Professionals for Generating Ideas for Writing

Part 2 of each unit contains a "Something to Think About, Something to Write About" section that includes a high-interest article written by a professional. These articles are used to generate ideas that students can use for their writing assignments. These selections cover a range of topics, including childhood memories, personal problems that have been overcome, values held by college students, volunteerism, women in engineering, the roles of computers, and a challenge issued to students by a college professor.

Examples of Writing by Students and Professionals

In Part 3 of each unit, writing examples by both students and professionals are provided for illustration, discussion, and/or analysis. The writing examples that illustrate the concepts taught in each unit have been strengthened. The authors of these selections have a range of writing experience and come from diverse backgrounds; thus their writing appeals to students of different ages, gender, and ethnic backgrounds.

Grammar Exercises Aimed at Improving Writing

The exercises in the grammar section of each unit (Part 4) go beyond drill and practice to include thinking exercises such as sentence combining and paragraph editing. Many exercises for in-class and out-of-class work are provided. Half of the answers are provided in Appendix D, and all of the answers are in the Annotated Instructor's Edition. As a result, teachers can have the students check their own exercises, or they can be used as homework and handed in to be graded by the instructor.

Unit on Rhetorical Modes

The unit on rhetorical modes is self-contained and includes fully developed essays illustrating how one topic can be developed into many different types of essays by using different modes. The text begins with illustration, a strategy with which students are familiar, and progresses through comparison/contrast, classification, definition, cause/effect analysis, process, and argument.

Appendixes

- Appendix A, Confusing Words (expanded)
- Appendix B, Keeping a Journal

  Discussion of Journal Writing
  Suggestions for Entries
- Appendix C, Irregular Verbs
- Appendix D, Answers to Odd-Numbered Exercises

Teaching Aids

- **Instructor's Manual** (included in Annotated Instructor's Edition) The Instructor's Manual includes our philosophy about teaching, unit notes, writing assignments, sample syllabus, suggestions for a final exam essay, two versions of nine skill-building tests, answers to tests, sample journal entry and journal log, and transparency masters.

- **Test Items**
  Multiple-choice, fill-in-the-blank, and sentence and paragraph editing questions test the skills and concepts taught in the book.

- **Computerized Testing**
  Computerized Testing will allow you to generate exams easily from the Test Items provided on disk. You can choose from the test items provided, edit them for classes, and create new questions on the computer. Computerized Testing is available for IBM-PC and compatibles.

- **Adaptable Courseware**
  Wadsworth Adaptable Courseware program allows instructors to create their own customized course materials. With Adaptable Courseware, they can select and custom publish the chapters in *Writing Paragraphs and Essays* that they want to cover. Instructors can also mix and match their

own information, activities, syllabi, etc., with chapters from the book. For more information, contact Wadsworth Publishing Company or a local Wadsworth representative.

Content Designed to Prepare Students for Proficiency Testing

Writing Paragraphs and Essays provides instruction that will prepare students to perform well on proficiency tests. For example, it covers basic grammar and usage: subject-verb agreement; consistent verb tense; fragments, run-on sentences, and comma splices; consistent point of view; and a thorough review of punctuation. The text encourages development of revision skills needed by students to pass proficiency tests. In addition, Appendix A is an expanded version of commonly confused words, such as *their, there,* and *they're.*

Writing Paragraphs and Essays provides practice in the skills students need in varied writing situations, including writing and revising essays for proficiency tests. In addition, students draft, revise, and edit both paragraphs and multi-paragraph essays. Because variety in sentence structure is one of the major criteria used to evaluate student essays, *Writing Paragraphs and Essays* also includes instruction in sentence combining to achieve sentence variety. Furthermore, the book includes a unit on rhetorical modes, which provides the skills students need when they are asked on a proficiency test to write an essay using a specific mode.

ACKNOWLEDGMENTS

We wish to thank our colleagues at Glendale Community College, Estrella Mountain Community College, and Front-Range Community College for their suggestions which arose out of several semesters of in-class testing. Other people that we specifically wish to thank include Conrad Bayley, Avis DeBrey, Dave Grant, Pat Haas, Margaret Hawks, Phil Moloso, and Nancy Seifer, all of whom gave us continual support.

We sincerely thank Linda Coble, Shyrl Emhoff, Pat Haas, Bob Hartman, Eva Montoya, Alicia Ottenberg, Jerry Palmer, Jim Reed, and Dean Terasaki, the professionals whose thought-provoking and varied articles strengthened our text. We also thank Lorena Acosta, Kathy Bagby, Brian Barnes, JoAnn Baugh, Eric Beach, Steve Bostrom, Dominique Charpentier, Nancy Chandler, Jeff Collins, Tim Darcy, YoungMi Dauer, Bill Devere, Terry M. Donaldson, Michael Gaspar, Andrea Gonzales, Muriel Gray, Jason Herrington, Phyllis Hilding, Charles Marchbanks, Joseph Mata, Joy Osterberg, Maria Palomino, Joan Papke, Jenefer Radas, Marlene Reed, Renee Robbe, Jan-Georg Roesch, John Schulz, Cynthia Vinzant, and Kristi Von Aspen, our students whose fine models provide enrichment for *Writing Paragraphs and Essays.*

We gratefully thank Angie Gantner, Lisa Timbrell, Myrna Engler, and Mary Douglas for their enthusiastic direction and support while we were revising this text. We thank the reviewers—Mary Earp, University of Alaska, Fairbanks; Michael Erickson, Monroe Community College; Joan Mathis, Paris Junior College; Dee Ann Ward, Weatherford College; Paul Wardzinski, Western Piedmont Community College—all of whom suggested valuable revisions of our text.

Most of all, we wish to thank our families for their patience, support, and sense of humor when the book took priority over other events.

UNIT 1

Introduction to Writing

ABOUT WRITING

Writing is a way of gaining control over your ideas and getting them down on paper. There is nothing mysterious about this process, and you can learn to write effectively and feel confident about your writing if you are willing to put in time and effort.

Many people find it necessary to write at one particular place or with a certain color of ink or a special type of keyboard. Having these things may help you write, but more important than these is developing the ability to concentrate. Sometimes it will be necessary to tune out everyone and everything in order to reflect inwardly and re-create incidents that you have read or heard about, experienced, or observed. With total concentration, you can "replay" these incidents and share them with your reader. For instance, if you want to remember that first day of school long ago when you were six years of age, all you have to do is close your eyes until a mental picture enters your mind. That room, that teacher, that moment of fear, happiness, or excitement can be a video played in your mind. And from your "mind's video" you can write your thoughts on paper to share with your reader.

Ways to Help Yourself Become a Better Writer

What experiences have you had with writing? Have you had good experiences or bad experiences? How do you feel about yourself as a writer? How important is writing to you? If your feelings and experiences about writing have been negative, the best thing you can do for yourself is to try to put those impressions behind you. You need to be willing to take a risk, be receptive, and be yourself.

Being Willing to Take a Risk

Being willing to take a risk might be the most difficult task you have ever had to do. Even though writing is often a personal experience, you can improve your writing if you relax and concentrate on what you have to say, rather than worrying about what your instructor or classmates will think.

Being Receptive

Along with being willing to take a risk, try to be receptive to your instructor's suggestions for improving your writing. As your instructor works with you on your paper or as you work in peer editing groups, keep an open mind about their comments. These comments are not intended to offend you personally; rather, they are directed toward helping you achieve your writing goals.

Being Genuine

Being genuine means being your real self. When you write, it is not necessary to try to impress anyone with an artificial vocabulary. On the other hand, you do want to write on a level that is appropriate for the particular purpose you have for each writing situation. The goal of writing should be to communicate with the reader simply and sincerely.

■ **Benefits of Becoming a Better Writer**

Maybe you are asking yourself questions like these: ''Why is becoming a better writer so important?'' ''How can writing help me?'' ''Will improving my writing skills bring me money, self-worth, opportunities, or friends?'' If you spend time on this valuable skill, your writing can improve. Writing well will bring many rewards your way.

You can become more successful in school, whether you write essays, do research papers, or take essay exams.

You can become more competent in your job.

You can help your children with their schoolwork.

You can bring satisfaction to yourself in personal journal writing or letters to friends.

You can defend yourself if you have been treated unjustly and have no recourse other than a letter to someone who has the power to correct the situation.

You can make writing a professional career.

THE WRITING PROCESS

Writing is a process through which you discover, organize, and write your thoughts to communicate with a reader. When you speak, you have tone of voice and facial expressions to help you get your point across. You also have the chance to clarify miscommunications quickly. When you write, you have only words and punctuation to form your message, but you do have the opportunity to organize your thoughts and words until you are happy with the finished product. The writing process gives you a chance to compose, draft, rethink, and redraft to control the outcome of your writing.

The general steps in the writing process include prewriting, organizing ideas, drafting, revising, editing, and making a final draft. If you use these steps when you have a writing assignment, you will give yourself an opportunity to make the most of your time and get your best ideas on paper. At times, you may repeat a particular step. When you become more comfortable with the writing process and become a more experienced writer, you may be able to do some steps in your mind, but skipping important steps is not advisable when you are learning the writing process.

Each step has different activities that will help you get the ideas from your mind to the paper in an organized fashion. **Prewriting** is a way of generating ideas, narrowing a topic, or finding a direction. **Organizing** involves sorting ideas in a logical manner to prepare to write a draft. **Drafting** is the part of the writing process in which you compose sentences in paragraph form to produce the first copy of your essay. **Revising**, one of the most important steps in writing a paper, involves smoothing out your writing, adding more detail, and making other changes that will help you say what you want to say in the best way. Checking for mechanical problems and correcting them is **editing**. **Making a final draft** and deciding it's ready for your intended audience is a step that takes patience and judgment. Being patient gives you a chance to take a sincere look at your paper and decide if the essay is in its best form. If not, more revision needs to take place.

Each of the steps of the writing process will be illustrated, beginning with prewriting.

Prewriting

Prewriting is the first major step in the writing process. As the following chart shows, prewriting can be accomplished in several ways.

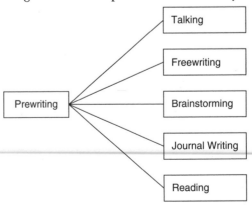

4

The prewriting chart lists some useful activities to help you begin a writing project. Five activities are offered, and you may find some more useful than others. All the prewriting approaches are designed to help you get started because at times starting can seem difficult. Starting a writing project means becoming actively involved in one or more of the activities listed above. The objectives are the same for each activity; however, each offers a different approach. You may want to try all of them to find out which ones work best for you.

Talking

One simple way to relieve anxiety and start the writing process is to talk about a subject with fellow students, instructors, family members, and knowledgeable people who can provide the inspiration you need to begin writing. Talking assists you in expressing ideas that can later be put onto paper. You might want to begin jotting down ideas that occur to you as you talk to others.

Talking to Find a Topic The following conversation could very well be an actual dialogue between two students who are using talking to begin an assignment.

''What are you writing about?''

''I'm not sure. The teacher wants a pet peeve or a pleasure. I'm not sure what a pet peeve is, so I guess I'll do pleasure.''

''A pet peeve is something that constantly irritates you, like not being able to do what you would like to do.''

''If that's what it is, I have lots of those, like never having any free time.''

''Well, why don't you dump your girlfriend then?''

''It's more than just my girlfriend. I have to rush to work right after class. And then I work so many hours that I don't have much time to do my homework or see my girlfriend.''

''Well, why don't you write about that problem — not having enough time to get everything done?''

''Maybe I will. That's it! That's what I'm going to write about — too many things to do and not enough time to get them done. At least this gives me a start on something to write about.''

Keep in mind that it is not advisable to do only talking as a prewriting activity. Talking, unlike freewriting or brainstorming, is not on paper, and ideas can be lost unless you take notes as you go along. But talking is a good starting point, and this student decided that he could write about the impact of his heavy work load on college and his personal life. Now that a subject for the writing assignment has begun to take shape, the student could talk to someone else to gather even more ideas.

Talking with Direction: The Informal Interview The student wanted to talk to someone who had graduated from college and who, he thought, had had a similar experience. After deciding on interviewing one of his instructors, he wrote out questions he felt would be useful for giving him some ideas for his paper. Here are some of the questions he prepared. Other questions that came to mind during the interview are also included.

''You have graduated from college. Did you work while you were going to college?''

> 1. ''No, I didn't have to work.''

''Did you have plenty of time to get your homework done?''

> 2. ''Yes, I did. I rode the bus, so I was able to get my homework done on the bus.''

''Did you have to ride the bus because you didn't have a car?''

> 3. ''You're right. I had to do without some things, and a car was one of those luxuries.''

''Even though you had to do without things, why do you think it's better not to work?''

> 4. ''I wouldn't have gotten through in four years. My sister did, though. She worked for two years before she started college so she could have enough money to get through college.''

''Did she make more money after she graduated than she did before she went to college?''

> 5. ''Oh yes, and she loved her job after she graduated.''

''Would you do it differently?''

> 6. ''No, because I wanted to make good grades. I appreciated the time I had to do my schoolwork.''

This informal interview gave the student a different point of view, one that he might not have considered before. After the informal interview the student needed to analyze the information to see what could be used for a paper. Here's how the student analyzed the responses he got.

Ideas Gathered from Talking	Possible Use of Ideas
1. ''No, I didn't have to work.''	gives a new perspective of not working while going to school
2. ''Yes, I did. I rode the bus, so I was able to get my homework done on the bus.''	provides an advantage for new perspective of not working
3. ''You're right. I had to do without some things, and a car was one of those luxuries.''	offers support for a new slant
4. ''I wouldn't have gotten through in four years. My sister did, though. She worked for two years before she started college so she could have enough money to get through college.''	shows a different view; could be another paragraph

5. "Oh yes, and she loved her job after she graduated." — offers additional support for the new idea

6. "No, because I wanted to make good grades. I appreciated the time I had to do my schoolwork." — shows a good reason for not working

Once you have enough information after interviewing one or more people, you might go on to the next step: organizing. If you do not have enough information to write a paper, you will need to interview more people or go on to freewriting, brainstorming, journal writing, or reading to generate information that can be used for writing. Next, examine freewriting.

Freewriting

Like other prewriting strategies, freewriting is intended to help you generate ideas. **Freewriting** is writing anything that comes to mind about your topic. It is writing without stopping to correct spelling or other mechanical errors. If you can't think of anything to write, just start with anything on your mind at that moment, even if it's just repeating the assignment. Ideally one idea leads to another, and soon your page will be filled with many different ideas. You are not expected to stay with any one idea; as a matter of fact, freewriting should bring out many different thoughts. This prewriting technique can be used when you are trying to find something to write about or are trying to get more ideas about a chosen topic.

Freewriting involves writing ideas in sentence form. Freewriting has three basic steps:

1. freewriting for a topic and direction
2. deciding on a topic
3. freewriting with direction

Examine these steps more closely.

Freewriting for a Topic and Direction Look at the following example of freewriting by a student who did not have a topic for a paper and who did not use talking as a prewriting aid. The freewriting that he did was done without regard to correct mechanics and spelling.

Well, I have to write for ten minutes on anything that I can think about. I'm not sure what I am interested in. I wish the other people in this room weren't writing so much. I wonder what they are writing about. I need to get my work done so I can get to work. I didn't get all of my work finished last night. I left the place in a mess. I hope my boss didn't notice. He is pretty nice most of the time. (1) Sometimes that place gets to me. I don't have enough time to get my school work done. Maybe dad was right. (2) I should try to cut down on my work hours so I can spend more time on school. (3) At this rate I won't ever get through. Rob is almost ready to graduate and I only have one year behind me. If I could just take more courses I could get through and get the job I really want. But then I wouldn't have money to take my girlfriend out. (4) <u>She is a pretty nice girl</u>. Maybe she would understand if I quit my job. If she broke up with me over that I guess she wouldn't be a very good girlfriend anyhow. (5) <u>There are lots of things we could do that don't cost a lot of money</u>. There is always something going on at school. (6) <u>Her brother is a lot of fun</u>. We enjoy playing racquet ball with him and his sister. I bet we could find lots of things to do. (7) <u>I could get through school faster</u>. Let's see, what should I write about. I wonder if anyone will think that what I wrote is dumb. I hope we don't have to read this in class. I guess if I have to I will. Cheee, that guy next to me has a whole page filled up. I wonder if he is going to stop pretty soon. Oh well, I guess I will just have to keep writing.

Much of the content in this freewriting probably will not be used, but it has served the purpose of warming up. After you finish freewriting, go back and see if there is anything that looks interesting enough to write about. With close reading, you can find ideas that can be turned into possible topics for further development. Here is an example of one way to analyze this freewriting to find a topic and direction.

Freewriting Idea	Possible Topic and Direction
1. "Sometimes that place gets to me."	negative aspects of my job
2. "I should try to cut down on my work hours. . . ."	educational benefits of cutting back on work hours
3. "At this rate I won't ever get through."	obstacles I face in finishing college
4. "She is a pretty nice girl."	neat traits of my girlfriend
5. "There are lots of things we could do that don't cost a lot of money."	enjoyable, low-cost recreational activities my girlfriend and I could do
6. "Her brother is a lot of fun."	her brother's personality
7. "I could get through school faster."	benefits of completing college as soon as possible

Deciding on a Topic   After you have finished freewriting, sort through your ideas. Decide which idea seems the most interesting, which you know the most about, and which you could write about most easily. The idea you choose may also suggest the direction for you to take.

Freewriting with Direction   After you have decided on the topic and direction, you need to freewrite again, this time with direction. This writing is generally easier because it concentrates on one topic. Usually most of the information that comes out in this freewriting is usable because a focus has been established, and this information can become support for a main idea. In the example, the one idea that the student has chosen to freewrite with direction is "what would happen if I cut down on my work hours?" His next step was to freewrite with direction on that idea. Here is what he wrote:

What would happen if I cut down on my work hours? I would have (1) more time to go see my girlfriend, but I would have to do without money. That means I (2) would have to give up some things that are important to me like my car. That would be rough. I wonder if my girl would find a new boyfriend. If she did, I guess she wouldn't care about our future. I (3) could study in the afternoons without having to worry about getting to work on time. (4) At night I wouldn't be too tired to go out, but then I wouldn't have any money to go out. Of course, (5) if I graduated from college, I could get a good job that I like and that pays well. (6) Dad would like that. He would be unhappy now because he is tired of supporting me. (7) My boss is going to be unhappy because he is counting on me to work forty hours a week and he is going to have to hire another employee. Of course he only pays me $4.25 an hour. He might even fire me, but I have to decide what is most important for me. If I just cut down on my work hours, dad would be happy because I was still making some money and I would be happy because I could take more courses.

Once you have completed your freewriting with direction, reread it and find any information that can be used in writing your paper. Here is how the student analyzed this freewriting:

Results of Cutting Work Hours	Interpretation of Results
1. "More time to see my girlfriend . . ."	helps my social life
2. "Would have to give up some things . . ."	may mean a sacrifice
3. "Could study in the afternoons . . ."	allows time to study
4. "At night I wouldn't be too tired to go out. . . ."	increases energy but not money
5. "If I graduated from college . . ."	could get better job later
6. "Dad would like that."	pleases dad
7. "My boss is going to be unhappy. . . ."	not too important

This list shows many writing options for the student writer. The student may choose to write on the advantages of cutting work hours, the disadvantages of cutting work hours, or just the results of cutting work hours.

If you feel you have enough information to write a paper, go on to the part of the writing process called organizing. If not, you might need to freewrite further or try brainstorming. If you were to write a longer paper, your next step would be to group together the ideas that would make separate paragraphs. (This is covered in detail in Unit 4, "Organizing Ideas and Writing Them Clearly.")

Brainstorming

Brainstorming is writing words or phrases that occur to you spontaneously. This free association can be done individually or in a group. Brainstorming and freewriting are similar in that they both produce ideas. If your teacher gives you a topic, you can begin by brainstorming to get some direction. If not, you will need to brainstorm to find a topic. You may find it easier to brainstorm for a topic than to freewrite, but others may find freewriting easier. When you are brainstorming for a topic, you will probably create a list of very general words that interest you.

Brainstorming to Find a Topic   When a student who did not have a topic was asked to brainstorm to find a topic, he responded with this list:

music	school	politics
fears	cities	homes
sports	family	vacation

As this list illustrates, the topics generated can be very broad. Because of this, it is necessary to brainstorm again, this time for direction.

Brainstorming for Direction   The student decided on "school" as a topic and brainstormed again. Here is what he wrote this time:

Topic: School

1. fun—social activities
2. not enough time to get work done
3. hate English and writing
4. tired and confused
5. enjoy school when there
6. money—where to get it
7. want to spend time with friends
8. still a freshman
9. why working hours should be cut
10. finish in four years or two years

The list shows some alternative topics for writing a paragraph. The possible topics in the list above are still general, so you need to decide which one seems the most interesting and brainstorm again. When you brainstorm again on the chosen topic, a new list of more focused topics will result.

Brainstorming with Direction   The student looked at the list of topics and decided that "why working hours should be cut" would be a good topic for him to select because it was important to him. He decided to find out what all the results would be if he cut his work hours. Here is the list he produced while brainstorming on this more focused topic:

more time to read assignments

making decisions is frustrating

boss will be unhappy

more time to study

more time to get help

less spending money to have on weekends

less money to spend on my girlfriend

can spend time with friends without worrying about studying

would miss the feel of money in my pocket

hate bad grades

could take more classes and graduate from college sooner

dad will be unhappy

At this point, if you have enough information to write a paragraph, move on to the section on organizing. If not, try talking, freewriting, or brainstorming again — or you could begin keeping a journal for ideas.

Journal Writing

Journal writing is recording information in a notebook of your daily inner thoughts, inspirations, and emotions that are usually consistently recorded in a relaxed writing atmosphere. Writing in this manner can provide you with an opportunity to connect with important inside thoughts, analyze your life environment, relieve writing anxiety, and practice spontaneous writing. Journal writing can provide ideas that you might be able to use in later writing assignments, and it can even help you find a starting place for new writing assignments.

The following brief excerpt is taken from two pages of a journal in which the student wrote about the frustrations he was feeling. This segment shows his frustration at working and going to school at the same time. He found this part when he was skimming through material he remembered writing about his job. (Journal entries are written for content, so they often contain spelling and grammar errors. This is permissible.)

> I am tired. I don't think I can every keep this up. There is so much to worry about. Sometimes I wish I didn't have to grow up. Maybe I could just quit school for a little while and get a job. I don't want to work at a hamburger dump. Pa thinks I should work as a plumber, but I'm sick of working in the ditch. Last year I could tell the time of day by the flow of the sewer. I always knew it was noon because everyone was flushing toilets and the stuff began to flow fast and furious. No way — I want to get through with school. Maybe pa wouldn't bitch too much if I could just hurry up and get through school. One semester I took twelve hours and got through ok. *If I quit work I could take even more hours and then get a good job.* [emphasis added]

Sometimes you will want to look through your journal to find a topic and a direction; other times you will already have your topic and direction and will simply be looking for ideas already expressed about your topic.

Much of this excerpt of journal writing is not appropriate for a paragraph, but the student found one sentence that would support his idea, and he also realized that because he had spent so much time writing about this subject, it must be important enough to write about.

Reading

Reading in magazines or newspapers can also help you get started with your writing. For instance, browsing through a magazine like *Time* or *Newsweek*, whether you are in the library, at home, or at the doctor's office, can spark an idea for a topic. More thorough reading will help you become more informed about your topic so that you can write intelligently about important issues.

Reading can also help you get ideas to support your paragraph or essay. This might be necessary if you do not have enough firsthand information about your topic. Some papers, especially those concerning political issues or social problems, require reading for factual information that can be used in your writing. Unit 8, "Composing with Effective Alternate Patterns," illustrates how additional reading can give you the information you need.

Summary of Ways to Get Started Writing

Talking:	informal conversation about a subject or topic
Freewriting:	writing (in sentences) anything that comes to mind without stopping
Brainstorming:	listing words or phrases as they come to mind
Journal writing:	recording your own thoughts in a notebook
Reading:	browsing through materials that might be used for writing

---

■ Organizing

Organizing is the second major step in the writing process. After you have completed one or more of the prewriting activities, it's time to think about organizing these ideas into a rough outline that includes a main idea and supporting ideas.

Before you actually start using the ideas from your prewriting to compose your paragraph or essay, you need to decide which details support the main idea and in what order these ideas need to be presented. As you sort these details into groups, you are organizing your information. Logic and a sense for putting together similar ideas can help you perform this step quickly and easily. This step in the writing process, which involves putting similar ideas into groups, is called **grouping**. It is one of the most important steps in the writing process and is covered again in detail in Unit 2, "Writing Sentences and Paragraphs," and in Unit 4, "Organizing Ideas and Writing Them Clearly." Here is how grouping can help you organize ideas for writing.

Grouping

Here is the list generated by the student who brainstormed his topic "school" with respect to "cutting work hours":

more time to read assignments

making decisions is frustrating

boss will be unhappy

more time to study

more time to get help

less spending money to have on weekends

less money to spend on my girlfriend

can spend time with friends without worrying about studying

would miss the feel of money in my pocket

hate bad grades

could take more classes and graduate from college sooner

dad will be unhappy

The task now is to organize the list into meaningful groups of related ideas, which will eventually become paragraphs. Grouping related ideas is easy if you stop and ask yourself the following very specific questions. These questions are intended to help you see how certain material can be put together to form one paragraph.

1. What phrases are similar or seem to be about the same idea?
    Group 1
    > more time to read assignments
    > more time to study
    > more time to get help
    > could take more classes and graduate from college sooner

    Group 2
    > boss will be unhappy
    > less spending money to have on weekends
    > less money to spend on my girlfriend
    > dad will be unhappy
    > would miss the feel of money in my pocket

2. In what way is each group alike?
    > The first grouping shows the *advantages* of cutting work hours.
    > The second grouping shows the *disadvantages* of cutting work hours.

3. What ideas don't seem to fit anywhere?
    > making decisions is frustrating
    > hate bad grades
    > can spend time with friends without worrying about studying

4. What general word or phrase could be used that would represent each group?
    > The general phrase for Group 1 could be "educational advantages."
    > The general word for Group 2 could be "disadvantages."

5. Are there other general words or phrases that would group the items differently?
    financial matters
        less spending money to have on weekends
        less money to spend on my girlfriend
        would miss the feel of money in my pocket
    social aspects
        less spending money to have on weekends
        can spend time with friends without worrying about studying
    personal considerations
        making decisions is frustrating
        boss will be unhappy
        hate bad grades
        dad will be unhappy

Remember, each group represents one paragraph. If a group has only two ideas, you may want to brainstorm again for additional ideas.

Outlining

Outlining involves identifying a word or phrase that represents a group of related ideas and then arranging these words or phrases in the order in which you want to discuss them. Notice that in answering questions 4 and 5 earlier, you have already grouped related ideas and found a general word or phrase that represents all of the ideas in the group, so you have made a rough outline that could be followed in writing your paragraph.

The student chose the group on "educational advantages." Here is one outline he could make:

Educational advantages
    more time to read assignments
    more time to study
    more time to get help
    could take more classes and graduate from college sooner
    bring up my grade point average*
    more time to use the library*

The general word or words will be made into a topic sentence, and each idea listed under these general words will become a support sentence.

Drafting

After you have organized your ideas in the form of an outline, you are prepared to write a first draft. **Drafting** involves taking the information that you have generated and organized and patiently writing a paragraph or an essay in

---

*These are new ideas that occurred to him as he studied the group.

which you consciously start with the main ideas and add supporting ideas that flow smoothly. You can feel confident about starting your draft because you have laid the foundation through prewriting and organizing your information. Try to write the ideas without worrying about spelling or other mechanical errors. In the first draft, you are simply interested in communicating content or meaning to the reader.

If you are writing a paragraph, look at the general word or phrase that represents the ideas in that group. Begin your draft with a sentence that includes this general word or phrase or a variation of it. Using the grouping done earlier, "educational advantages," the student wrote the following first draft of a paragraph. (Note that this and future "topic sentences" have been highlighted for you by using bold type.)

If I cut down at work I could have more time to spend on my education. By having more time to spend on school I could bring up my grade point average. Plus, I could probably have more time to do my work. I could spend as much time as I needed to get my assignments done and still have time to spend with my girlfriend. I could go to class and study in the afternoons without having to worry about getting to work on time. At night I wouldn't be too tired to go out. Tutoring is offered free of charge at school and I wouold have time to get a tutor. I could take more classes and still do well in all of them. I often have to go to the library but really don't have the extra time. It takes even more time to go to work and then have to drive back to campus on Saterdays to do my research. My car is not running right and this adds to my problems. Just as I am getting the material that I need it is time for the library to close or I begin to get tired.

After you finish your first draft, put it away for a while, if possible, so that when you come back to it, you will be able to see it from a fresh point of view. This new perspective will help you revise the draft.

Revising

Revising means making changes to clarify wording and organization. The revision of a paragraph should be done several times, until you are satisfied that it is the best you can do. It is all right, even recommended, that you let other people read your paper and make suggestions for change. It is not all right, however, to have other people actually make the changes for you. Your major objective is not to produce just one excellent paper but to have the ability to write many excellent papers, even when you may not have anyone to help. Here are some possible questions to ask yourself when you are revising:

1. Is the general word or phrase (or a similar one) from the group in the first sentence?

2. Are there words, phrases, or sentences that are not related to the main idea in the first sentence?

3. Does the paragraph make sense to you and to someone else?

4. Have you covered all ideas in the group?

5.   Can some words be changed for clarity?

6.   Are any words excessively repeated?

7.   Does the last sentence give a sense of closure to the paragraph?

As you begin to learn how to revise, it is easier to read for one or two kinds of changes at a time. Notice in the following examples that only two or three questions are asked and that only those revisions are made in the next draft.

First Revision

The first revision is based on questions 1 and 2:

1.   Is the general word or phrase (or a similar one) from the group in the first sentence?

2.   Are there words, phrases, or sentences that are not related to the main idea in the first sentence?

If I cut down at work I could have more time to spend on my **education**. By having more time to spend on school I could bring up my grade point average. Plus, I could probably have more time to do my work. I could spend as much time as I needed to get my assignments done and still have time to spend with my girlfriend. I could go to class and study in the afternoons without having to worry about getting to work on time. At night I wouldn't be too tired to go out. Tutering is offered free of charge at school and I wouould have time to get a tutor. I could take more classes and still do well in all of them. I often have to go to the library but really don't have the extra time. It takes even more time to go to work and then have to drive back to campus on Saterdays to do my research. My car is not running right, and this adds to my problems. Just as I am getting the material that I need it is time for the library to close or I begin to get tired.

Second Revision

The second revision is based on questions 3 and 4:

3.   Does the paragraph make sense to you and to someone else?

4.   Have you covered all ideas in the group?

If I cut down at work I could have more time to spend on my education. By

having more time to spend on school I could bring up my grade point average.

I would have more time to do my homework because
Plus, I could probably have more time to do my work. I could spend as much time

as I needed to get my assignments done. I could go to class and study in the

every day
afternoons without having to worry about getting to work on time. Tutering is

offered free of charge at school and I wouold have time to get a tutor. I could take

more classes and still do well in all of them. I often have to go to the library. It

takes even more time to go to work and then have to drive back to campus on

Saterdays to do my research. *If I could take five courses instead of three I could finish college almost twice as fast. I bet I would be more interested in it because that is all I would have on my mind.*

Notice that smaller script type has been used to indicate new ideas added to the draft.

Third Revision

The third revision is based on questions 5, 6, and 7:

5. Can some words be changed for clarity?
6. Are any words excessively repeated?
7. Does the last sentence give a sense of closure to the paragraph?

If I cut down at work I could have more time to spend on my education. By

having more time to spend on school I could bring up my grade point average.

Also,
~~Plus,~~ I would have more time to do my homework because I could spend as much

After class I could concentrate on studying
time as I needed to get my assignments done. ~~I could go to class and study~~ in the

afternoons without having to worry about getting to work every day. Tutering is

work with someone.
offered free of charge at school and I wouold have time to ~~get a tutor. I could take~~

but
~~more classes and still do well in all of them.~~ I often have to go to the library. ~~It~~

really don't have enough time. If I cut down at work, I would have time to go to the
~~takes even more time to go to work and then have to drive back to campus on~~

library after class as well as on   Also, if
Saterdays ~~to do my research.~~ ~~If~~ I could take five courses instead of three I could

Cutting my working hours would give me more
finish college almost twice as fast. ~~I bet I would be more interested in it because~~

time to concentrate on my studies.
~~that is all I would have on my mind.~~

So, here is how the revised draft would look before editing:

If I cut down at work I could have more time to spend on my education. By having more time to spend on school I could bring up my grade point average. Also, I would have more time to do my homework because I could spend as much time as I needed to get my assignments done. After class I could concentrate on studying in the afternoons without having to worry about getting to work every day. Tutering is offered free of charge at school and I wouold have time to work with someone. I often have to go to the library but really don't have enough time. If I cut down at work, I would have time to go to the library after class as well as on Saterdays. Also, if I could take five courses instead of three I could finish college almost twice as fast. Cutting my working hours would give me more time to concentrate on my studies.

■ Editing

Before you consider your paper finished, check for any problems in mechanics. When you are learning the writing process, content comes before mechanics and grammar, but correct mechanics and grammar will be expected as you master the writing process. The following list contains some of the items you want to find and check.

spelling

punctuation

capitalization

grammar usage

errors in sentence structure

consistency in verb tense

consistent point of view

abbreviations and numbers

You will not be expected to have all of these editing skills at first. But you will acquire these skills through writing your paragraphs and essays. To make this mechanical review easier, you might want to learn to use a good word processor that includes a spell checker and other writing aids. This is also a good time for peer editing groups to help in polishing drafts.

The student took the time to make one final check before turning in the paper. Here is how the latest draft looked after editing:

work, I

If I cut down at work~~ I~~ could have more time to spend on my education. By

school, I

having more time to spend on ~~school I~~ could bring up my grade point average.

Also, I would have more time to do my homework because I could spend as much

time as I needed to get my assignments done. After ~~class I~~ *class, I* could concentrate on

studying in the afternoons without having to worry about getting to work every

day. ~~Tutering~~ *Tutoring* is offered free of charge at ~~school and I wouold~~ *school, and I would* have time to work

with someone. I often have to go to the library but really don't have enough time.

If I cut down at work, I would have time to go to the library after class as well as

on ~~Saterdays~~ *Saturdays*. Also, if I could take five courses instead of ~~three I~~ *three, I* could finish college

almost twice as fast. Cutting my working hours would give me more time to

concentrate on my studies.

Here is how the edited draft that is ready to be turned in would look:

> **If I cut down at work, I could have more time to spend on my education.** By having more time to spend on school, I could bring up my grade point average. Also, I would have more time to do my homework because I could spend as much time as I needed to get my assignments done. After class, I could concentrate on studying in the afternoons without having to worry about getting to work every day. Tutoring is offered free of charge at school, and I would have time to work with someone. I often have to go to the library but really don't have enough time. If I cut down at work, I would have time to go to the library after class as well as on Saturdays. Also, if I could take five courses instead of three, I could finish college almost twice as fast. Cutting my working hours would give me more time to concentrate on my studies.

Now that you have seen a finished paragraph produced, review the major steps in the writing process.

Steps in the Writing Process

Prewriting: gathering ideas

Organizing: grouping and ordering details

Drafting: writing the first copy of a paragraph or essay

Revising: changing wording and organization

Editing: making mechanical changes

The writing process can prove to be a challenging but fulfilling venture, just as you learned many years ago when you first tried to ride a bike. The first time you learned to ride a bike, you had to take a risk that you would look silly as you wobbled down the street, or that you would fall and get hurt, or that you would get upset because others were moving faster than you were. However, you had more to lose by not trying, and if you had never taken that risk, you would never have learned to ride the bike.

Learning the writing process is similar to that experience. But writing is also a skill that requires many thinking activities, and you must use them all to produce an effective piece of writing. Just as you didn't give up in your bicycle experience, don't give up on the writing process, and you will experience a new pride and confidence whenever you face a writing task.

USING COMPUTERS

Computers are becoming so important that knowing how to use them is quickly becoming a basic skill for employees and for students. Becoming familiar with the world of computers or expanding your use of them may be necessary if you want to get a job or be promoted. You may also need computer skills if you want to use the resources your college has. When you register for classes, use the library, or perhaps communicate with other students and instructors worldwide, you will need to use a computer. You probably will even have to earn credits in a computer class before you can graduate from college. However, the most pressing need for you right now might be just to complete the assignments for your English class.

If you have access to computers in your English class, you have a wonderful tool to help you with your writing assignments. This technology can make all parts of the writing process easier and more effective whether you are working on a first draft or polishing a last draft. Working on a computer may allow you to progress at your own pace and revise your papers thoroughly until you are happy with the results. You can move, add, and delete text easily. In addition, you will have access to special features like a spell checker, a thesaurus, or a grammar checker. If spelling is a challenge for you, the spell checker becomes an excellent aid for finding and correcting misspelled words or just simple typos. A printer will turn out a finished copy, saving you the work of retyping a polished draft. At times, you will be working in a group and can end the session by making a hard copy for all group members to study and work on individually before coming back together as a group. A further bonus is that during the writing process, you may also have more chances to have one-on-one coaching from your instructor.

Whatever your current writing skills are, if you have access to word processing software on a computer, the process of planning, drafting, and completing writing assignments will be much easier and more positive for you.

Collaborative Project: Working and Learning Together

Bring in a sample of your writing that you would like to share with a small group. It may be a letter, a poem, a grocery list, a journal entry, a job résumé, or a school assignment. Based on what you know about the writing process, discuss your sample writing. Answer the following questions as a group.

1. How did you get started?

2. What steps did you take to do the writing?

3. What kinds of things slowed you down?

4. How did you get started again?

5. Were there periods of time when writing was easy? Why did it seem easy?

Be prepared to share your ideas with the rest of the class.

UNIT 2

Writing Sentences and Paragraphs

PART 1

PARTS TO WHOLE: TOPIC SENTENCES AND PARAGRAPHS

OBJECTIVES

The Topic Sentence

- Recognize the parts of a topic sentence.
- Expand topics into topic sentence ideas.
- Recognize suitable topic sentences.
- Recognize the topic sentence within a group of related sentences.

The Paragraph

- Identify the parts of a paragraph: topic sentence, support sentences, and concluding sentence.
- Practice the steps in the process of writing a paragraph:

  Prewrite to generate ideas.
  Group ideas to find a direction and a focus for developing a topic sentence.
  Name a general word that describes the group.
  Outline (list from the group) the topic sentence and the support sentences that will go into the paragraph.
  Add to the list a concluding sentence to finalize the main idea.

- Recognize the four elements of a good paragraph: completeness, logical order, unity, and coherence.
- Write a paragraph that demonstrates completeness, logical order, unity, and coherence.

When you can write clear sentences, you can make yourself understood by others. You can express any idea, feeling, opinion, or belief that you desire. No matter how long, short, simple, or complicated your subject may be, you must write your ideas in sentences. The sentence, then, is the basis for almost all writing.

Most of your college writing, of course, involves not just one sentence, but several, because you probably will have to explain or discuss many details to make your meaning clear. The person reading your ideas, however, will not be able to understand the overall meaning of your sentences unless you group them in a logical way. This group of related sentences is called a **paragraph**.

Following specific steps is necessary for writing good paragraphs. Before you study this step-by-step process in depth, however, it is important for you to recognize and understand the parts of a well-written paragraph.

The Topic Sentence

Parts of a Topic Sentence

A good paragraph contains several related sentences that support *one main idea*, which is limited to and focused in one sentence. This sentence helps guide your reader through the related sentences in the paragraph. This vital sentence serves as a commitment for the writer to provide an explanation or illustration of this main idea. The term used to identify this main idea is **topic sentence**.

A topic sentence has two parts:

a topic (key word or phrase)

a direction or general word, which may be a conclusion, an opinion, or a statement *about* the topic

For example, the following sentences could be topic sentences:

Doing housework can be very boring.

Browsing in a library is an exciting experience.

My trip to the botanical garden taught me a lot.

You could use each one of these sentences as a topic sentence because each main idea is limited to and focused into two essential parts: a **topic** (key word or phrase) and a **general direction** (conclusion or opinion) about the topic:

Topic	Direction or General Word
Doing housework	is very boring.
Browsing in a library	is an exciting experience.
My trip to the botanical garden	taught me a lot.

The following exercise will help you practice recognizing the parts of topic sentences.

EXERCISE 1

In each sentence below, identify the topic *(key word or phrase) and the* direction *or general word (the conclusion or opinion) about the topic.*

Example:

Owning a small business can be exhausting.

Topic: _____Owning a small business_____   Direction: _____can be exhausting_____

1. Doing well in college requires organization.

   Topic: _____Doing well in college_____   Direction: _____requires organization_____

2. Trying to buy a house is sometimes frustrating.

   Topic: _____Trying to buy a house_____   Direction: _____is sometimes frustrating_____

3. School board meetings inform parents about the school.

Topic: *School board meetings*   Direction: *inform parents about the school*

4. Buying furniture can be challenging.

Topic: *Buying furniture*   Direction: *can be challenging*

5. Enrolling in college can be a surprising experience.

Topic: *Enrolling in college*   Direction: *can be a surprising experience*

6. Traveling to a foreign country is enlightening.

Topic: *Traveling to a foreign country*   Direction: *is enlightening*

7. Riding in an airplane can be stressful.

Topic: *Riding in an airplane*   Direction: *can be stressful*

8. Going to a high school reunion can bring back many memories.

Topic: *Going to a high school reunion*   Direction: *can bring back many memories*

9. Walking to school in the spring saves money.

Topic: *Walking to school in the spring*   Direction: *saves money*

10. My family enjoys summer fishing trips.

Topic: *My family*   Direction: *enjoys summer fishing trips*

11. Going out to eat can be a cultural experience.

Topic: *Going out to eat*   Direction: *can be a cultural experience*

12. Riding a bicycle takes coordination.

Topic: *Riding a bicycle*   Direction: *takes coordination*

13. The birthday party was a great success.

Topic: *The birthday party*   Direction: *was a great success*

14. A healthy body can be achieved through exercise.

Topic: *A healthy body*   Direction: *can be achieved through exercise*

15. Character can be built through studying karate.

   Topic: *Character* _____   Direction: *can be built through studying karate*

16. Good students often receive encouragement from family members.

   Topic: *Good students* _____   Direction: *often receive encouragement from family members*

17. Owning a car can be expensive.

   Topic: *Owning a car* _____   Direction: *can be expensive*

18. Airline attendants have demanding jobs.

   Topic: *Airline attendants* _____   Direction: *have demanding jobs*

19. Writing a research paper takes preparation.

   Topic: *Writing a research paper*   Direction: *takes preparation*

20. Children enjoy playing in the mud.

   Topic: *Children* _____   Direction: *enjoy playing in the mud*

   To help you become more familiar with the parts of topic sentences, do the following exercise for expanding simple topics into full topic sentences.

EXERCISE 2

Complete each topic below by writing a statement *(conclusion or opinion) about it.* You will be focusing the topic by adding a **direction** *(your opinion or conclusion).*

Example:

San Diego *is a good place for windjamming.* _____

1. The pizza restaurant *provides wholesome food for a family.*

2. Cars *make people's lives easier.* _____

3. My sister *makes my life difficult.* _____

4. Jeeps *can be dangerous. / can be useful for ranchers.* _____

5. A nature hike *educates children.* _____

6. Baby-sitting *develops responsibility.*

7. Working on my car *requires patience. / can be expensive.*

8. Pine trees *provide habitat for small animals and birds.*

9. Reading the newspaper *can be educational.*

10. I saved my money to *prove to my parents that I am responsible.*

11. Melanie *enjoyed the special olympics last year.*

12. A family reunion *can be boring. / can be enriching.*

13. To attend major league ball games *can be expensive.*

14. Repairing old radios *makes his retirement enjoyable.*

15. Relatives *make great counselors. / can create problems.*

16. Going on vacation *can be relaxing.*

17. Making a quilt *can release creativity.*

18. Rebuilding an engine *is a time-consuming challenge.*

19. Crossword puzzles *provide mental stimulation.*

20. To go to college *can be exciting. / can be frightening.*

As you can see, a topic sentence is limited to or focused on one main idea. At the same time, a topic sentence is *general* in nature because it sums up the information or details that you will present to make your writing believable for your reader. Thus, even though a topic sentence is limited, it is the most general statement in the paragraph.

Distinguishing Topic Sentences from Simple Facts

Because the **topic sentence** is general, it cannot be just a simple fact. The following sentences would *not* be suitable topic sentences:

Susan paid $3.95 for her new blouse.

The living room contains an Early American desk.

Two of my friends went on Star Tours four times.

Study the following pairs of sentences. The first sentence in each pair is a simple fact that could not be developed into a paragraph. The second sentence in each pair shows how the simple fact has been changed into a more general idea that could be used as a topic sentence for a paragraph.

> *Fact:* Susan paid $3.95 for her new blouse.
>
> *Topic sentence:* Susan loves to shop for bargains.

> *Fact:* The living room contains an Early American desk.
>
> *Topic sentence:* The living room is furnished in authentic Early American style.

> *Fact:* Two of my friends went on Star Tours four times.
>
> *Topic sentence:* My friends and I had an exciting day in Disneyland.

The second sentence in each pair would be a suitable topic sentence because each contains a *general* word or phrase — the **direction** for the topic:

loves to shop for bargains

is furnished in authentic Early American style

had an exciting day in Disneyland

Each of these broader statements would suggest details that you could name — examples of bargains, examples of Early American furniture, and examples of activities and events in Disneyland. It is important to understand that the topic sentence in a paragraph is a general idea that is also focused in one direction or on one opinion. However, it is just as important to keep the topic sentence from being so general that it cannot be developed in one paragraph. For example, it would take much more than one paragraph to fully develop the idea in a sentence like this: "The causes of war are many."

Just remember that a topic sentence must be more than a simple fact because a simple fact cannot be expanded into a fully developed paragraph.

The following exercise will help you identify sentences that could be used as topic sentences.

EXERCISE **3**

Study each sentence below and decide if it is a simple fact (fact), too broad to be developed in one paragraph (broad), or a more general but focused statement that could be used for a topic sentence (TS).

Examples:

___*fact*___ **The birds ate all of the figs on the tree.**

___*TS*___ **The birds are enjoyable to watch.**

___*broad*___ **The evolution of birds is complex.**

_TS_   1. The Mayan Indians of South America contributed many common food products.

broad   2. Native American cultures are varied.

broad   3. The causes of world hunger are complicated.

fact   4. The ball game is scheduled to start at 7:00 P.M.

broad   5. Many varieties of aquatic life can be found in the ocean.

fact   6. The cocker spaniel rushed into the room.

_TS_   7. Ralph's room is a disaster.

fact   8. The English computer lab is open twelve hours a day.

broad   9. Children are a mystery.

_TS_   10. Our neighbors expect us to be good citizens.

_TS_   11. Swimming provides great exercise.

broad   12. The Vietnam War caused many problems in the United States.

_TS_   13. Yard work can be fun.

fact   14. The temperature is 87 degrees outside.

fact   15. My math book is on the floor.

_TS_   16. Howard found it hard to save money for car repairs.

fact   17. Three fish share the aquarium.

fact   18. The Vietnam War lasted over five years.

broad   19. Pollution causes many environmental problems.

_TS_   20. An afternoon at the park can be enjoyable.

Additional practice in thinking about how sentences relate to each other will help you write better topic sentences.

The following exercises will help you distinguish general sentences from more specific, factual statements.

EXERCISE 4

Study each group of related sentences. Underline the most general statement that could be a topic sentence.

Example:

The red oleanders have finally started to bloom.

The daisies have filled the side yard with white.

The peach trees are covered with pink blossoms.

<u>Many beautiful flowers have begun to bloom this spring.</u>

The path to the back door is edged with blue alyssum.

1. Fans can be installed.

   Some shade screens reduce the sun's glare by 20 percent.

   Large trees on the west side shield a house from the afternoon heat.

   Insulation in attics helps keep a house cool in the summer.

   <u>Tips for keeping a home cooler in the summer heat are helpful.</u>

2. <u>Putting together a newsletter requires much effort.</u>

   Interesting articles need to be written.

   Gathering information takes time.

   Typing news items requires skills.

   Proofing and correcting copy is necessary.

3. Contrasts in landscape range from beautiful deserts to majestic mountains.

   Native American and Hispanic cultures are reflected in the architecture of many cities in New Mexico.

   Carlsbad Caverns is a breathtaking sight to take in.

   <u>As the license plate boasts, New Mexico is the "Land of Enchantment."</u>

   The weather is varied but not extreme.

4. Dogs need to be trained by their owners.

   Dogs' food must be nutritious and balanced for their size.

   People should groom their pets.

   <u>A good pet owner has several responsibilities to meet.</u>

   The owner must provide a clean and comfortable place for the pet to sleep.

5. Cleaning up after the puppies is a never-ending job.

   Seeing that they are all fed is a major responsibility.

   <u>Raising puppies is time consuming.</u>

   Finding good homes for them is also a part of the job.

   Housebreaking them takes patience.

   Playing with them keeps the owners busy.

6. Athletes from many countries live together in the same quarters.

   They respect customs of other people.

   Athletes understand that people from other countries have similar goals and aspirations.

   The Olympic games can promote international goodwill.

   They return home with fond memories of friends from other countries.

7. He appointed his wife to chair a national health care task force.

   President Clinton made several important decisions in his first days as president.

   He nominated the first woman attorney general to take charge of national law enforcement.

   He proposed economic reforms.

8. Tamales are made with delicious red chili, pork, and masa.

   Biscochitos are wedding-type cookies with anise that will delight any sweet tooth.

   Posole is a hominy and pork soup served generally on New Year's Eve.

   Christmas in a Mexican home offers many unique foods.

9. Some people fear flying.

   Phobias are varied.

   Acrophobes get nervous when they are looking down from great heights.

   Agoraphobia causes people to withdraw and remain indoors for years.

   People who feel anxiety in closed spaces are claustrophobic.

10. Canoes can be rented at the lagoons.

    Many miles of quiet paths are reserved for walking or jogging.

    Tennis players can use the lighted courts for a few coins in the meter.

    In one corner of the park is an Olympic-sized swimming and diving pool.

    The beautiful public park offers many inexpensive outdoor activities for the city.

11. Small cars are easy to park.

    Many advantages result from owning and operating small cars.

    Small cars usually run on three or four gallons of gas per week, depending on the miles driven.

    Cleaning small cars does not take much time.

    Small cars are easier to drive in traffic.

12. Cowboys have a subculture all their own.

    Cowboy hats, Levis, and boots identify authentic cowboys.

    Country and western music represents the values of a unique group of people.

    Western ranchers usually love to eat barbecued spareribs and chili beans and drink strong coffee.

    Pronunciation of certain words easily identifies people who belong to the cowboy culture.

13. Many types of jobs are usually available.

   Entertainment can be found in many places.

   <u>Living in a city has advantages.</u>

   Medical facilities are readily available.

   Shopping centers provide a variety of stores.

14. Journal entries must be turned in.

   Five short papers are assigned.

   <u>The class has many requirements.</u>

   Five long papers are assigned.

   Ten grammar tests must be passed.

15. Richard really likes Philip Marlowe.

   The Maltese Falcon is one of his favorites.

   <u>Richard enjoys American detective fiction.</u>

   He has read several of Raymond Chandler's books.

   Of current writers, he enjoys Robert B. Parker and Tony Hillerman.

   He especially likes Ross Macdonald's detective stories.

The Paragraph

Parts of a Paragraph

Now that you have learned about topic sentences, you are ready to study the full paragraph. Becoming familiar with the parts of strong paragraphs will help you when you begin to write your own paragraphs.

A paragraph has three parts:

1. **a topic sentence**

2. **support sentences**

3. **a conclusion**

Read the following example of a paragraph that has these three parts.

> **My blind date last night was a disaster.** I got wet because just as I stopped to pick up my date, it started raining, and she borrowed my raincoat. At dinner, she ate so much that I had to use my next day's lunch money to pay for her meal. I had a terrible time because she could not dance. To make matters worse, I had a cut on my lip that hurt when I kissed her. **That's the last blind date I will ever have.**

The topic sentence (main idea) and the conclusion are in bold type so that you can easily identify them. All the other sentences, which contain details that explain why the blind date was a disaster, are support sentences. All parts of the paragraph work together to express the main idea clearly so that the reader can understand and appreciate the writer's disappointing blind date.

The Paragraph Writing Process

Now that you can identify and develop topic sentences, it's time for you to practice writing so that you can improve your ability to express your ideas in an organized way. There is no one right way to write a paragraph, but if you learn the process one step at a time, you will find writing to be both simplified and rewarding. In this part you will see the writing process illustrated again so you can practice prewriting, organizing, and drafting. An example of the step-by-step process as done by a student is given so that you can see how it works. Getting enough ideas and information to put into a paragraph is not something that just happens, and you may need some patience with yourself during each step of the process. The place to begin is to choose a topic.

Choose a Topic Choose a simple topic. (Choose from what your instructor suggests for topics, or follow the directions your instructor gives you for choosing a topic. You might choose a topic listed in Exercises 1 or 2 in this chapter.) Suppose the student selected "recreation" from a list provided by the teacher.

Prewrite Use one or more of the prewriting activities explained in Unit 1: **talking**, **freewriting**, or **brainstorming**. Don't worry about spelling or grammar or having complete ideas. Just let your mind produce ideas that have some connection with your topic.

A sample brainstormed list for the topic "recreation" might look something like this:

Recreation

jet skiing on weekends	fishing
reading mysteries	needlepoint
making quilts	good fishing spots
fishing equipment	cooking light meals
aerobics for fitness	stamp collecting

The student now has more specific topics from which to find direction for one main idea. The student chose "fishing" for the topic.

Brainstorm for Direction Brainstorm to generate more ideas that can be grouped into details that seem to have something in common. As you might recall, this group of related ideas will suggest your focus or direction for the paragraph. You probably will have more than one group from which to choose your focus or direction. Here is what the student's brainstorming produced:

Fishing

My fishing license has expired.

quiet stream or lake

Grandpa likes it.

the smell of fresh pine

It's disappointing if you don't catch anything.

Last time I went it was raining.

quiet, peaceful, relaxing

Family outings are fun.

Some think it's only for old people.

I'm afraid to get a fish hook in my back.

Mosquitoes are usually buzzing around.

close to nature

Mom usually doesn't go.

Corn is a good bait.

Once I caught seven trout.

What a thrill!

Name General Words to Describe the Group of Ideas Notice that some ideas in the brainstorming about "fishing" are positive aspects of fishing. A **general word** that represents the ideas in this group might be "enjoyment." This grouping of details that have something in common has been marked in the above example. It is helpful to list them separately (and possibly add more).

quiet stream or lake

the smell of fresh pine

Family outings are fun.

close to nature

Once I caught seven trout.

quiet, peaceful, relaxing

What a thrill!

Some of the ideas have something negative in common. These could form another group that might be described by other general words: the "hazards" or "frustrations" of fishing.

I'm afraid of getting a fish hook in my back.

Last time I went it was raining.

It's disappointing if you don't catch anything.

Mosquitoes are usually buzzing around.

This group could be developed into a separate paragraph.

Finally, some of the items in the list introduce different ideas that might not fit anywhere.

Grandpa likes it.

My license is expired.

Mom usually doesn't go.

Some think it's only for old people.

Corn is good bait.

Choose Direction for the Topic Sentence To find your focus and to be able to write your topic sentence, select the general word you want to use to represent your group: "enjoyment" or "frustration."

The student decided to focus on the "enjoyment of fishing."

Think About the Topic Sentence Your next step is to develop your topic sentence. Remember that it must have two parts: a topic and a statement about the topic that includes a general word to represent your group. The topic sentence should also be broad enough to include all of the items in the group you have selected as the direction of your topic.

Here are some *unacceptable* topic sentences for this group:

It is fun to tie flies.

Fishing is peaceful.

These two topic sentences do not contain the general word "enjoyment," and "It is fun to tie flies" is not broad enough to include all of the details in the group. "Fishing is peaceful" would make a good topic sentence, but not for this group of ideas.

Write the Topic Sentence The next step is to write the topic sentence. You might say, "Fishing is enjoyable," "Fishing is an enjoyable activity," or "Fishing is an enjoyable leisure-time activity." Choose the version of the topic sentence that works best for you.

Outline the Paragraph After you have written your topic sentence, it is time to list the supporting details and include a concluding (or summary) thought for the end of the paragraph. Put all the sentences into an outline form, just as the student did in the following example. (If more support details occur to you as you make the outline, include them.)

Topic sentence	Fishing is an enjoyable leisure-time activity.
Support idea	quiet stream or lake
Support idea	I love the smell of fresh pine.
Support idea	Family outings are fun.
Support idea	close to nature
Support idea	Once I caught seven trout. What a thrill!
Support idea	quiet, peaceful, relaxing
Concluding idea	Fishing will always be a positive experience for me.

All the supporting ideas are the ''proof'' given to the reader for the topic sentence. You will be able to write a strong paragraph if you develop a rough outline similar to this one.

Draft the Paragraph   The next step is to write the first version or draft of your paragraph. If new, *related* details occur to you, include them because they may help you clarify your main idea. You may want to put the ideas into a different order when you draft your paragraph. As you draft, add whatever is needed to make the sentences flow smoothly and help the reader understand the experience.

Here is the student's draft, with the topic sentence and concluding sentence in bold type:

> **Although I have several hobbies, fishing is my most enjoyable leisure-time activity.** When I am fishing, this is the time I feel closest to the natural elements. The sunrise, the quiet stream or lake, the green pine scent, and the one-on-one experience with nature relax me more than any other activity. In this peaceful scene, there is also the thrill of conquering a bit of the wilderness. For years, I will remember the seven big trout I caught on a fishing trip several years ago. It was one of the greatest experiences I have ever had. **I am convinced that fishing will always be a positive experience for me.**

Notice that the supporting ideas have been expanded in the drafting process and give a clear and convincing picture of the main idea suggested by the topic sentence. They also clarify the idea of being ''close to nature.'' The sunrise, the stream or lake, and the green pine scent all help complete the ''picture.''

The following exercises will help you practice the steps in prewriting, organizing, and drafting. Even though you have improved these three skills in this unit, they are not the only important parts of the writing process. Revising and editing, which were introduced in Unit 1, are also important parts of the writing process.

EXERCISE 5

Brainstorm either the topic "children" or the topic "rainstorms." Find your direction.

Topic: _____

Brainstorm for direction:

_____   _____

_____   _____

_____   _____

_____   _____

_____   _____

State the direction you have chosen:

_____

_____

Brainstorm with direction:

_____

_____

_____

_____

_____

_____

_____

Make a new list of all the ideas that support the direction you have chosen:

_____

_____

_____

_____

_____

_____

_____

_____

Write a general word that represents the group you have chosen: _____

Write a possible topic sentence: _____

_____

_____

Write another possible topic sentence: _____

_____

_____

Select one of the topic sentences. Using your new list of ideas that support the direction of this topic sentence, list each idea in a rough outline. Add a concluding thought.

Topic sentence: _____

_____

Support idea: _____

Support idea: _____

Support idea: _____

Support idea: _____

Support idea: _____

Concluding idea: _____

_____

You now have ideas that can be used in a first version of a paragraph about your chosen topic.

EXERCISE 6

Using the information you have generated about your chosen topic, write a paragraph for practice.

_____

_____

_____

_____

_____

_____

_____

_____

_____

Elements of a Strong Paragraph

You have learned to recognize the topic sentence, the support sentences, and the conclusion in a paragraph. You have also learned to generate the ideas that you need to write a paragraph. Now you are ready to study the four elements of strong paragraphs:

completeness

logical or sensible order

unity

coherence

All these elements work together to make the paragraph clear and effective. Study each of these and learn how to master them in your writing.

Completeness A paragraph must have enough information in it to give the reader a clear picture or a full discussion of its main idea (the topic sentence). A paragraph without details or examples will be vague and unconvincing. A paragraph that does not have enough information is called **incomplete** or **undeveloped**.

The following first version of a paragraph about dancing has a main idea but very little specific information. This draft is an incomplete or undeveloped paragraph, and, therefore, it needs more specific details that can be generated through talking, freewriting, brainstorming, looking through your journal, or reading. Then another draft can be composed.

> **Dancing can be good exercise.** It can be entertaining. It can be lots of fun as well. **Dancing can be very beneficial for everyone.**

This paragraph has a topic sentence and a conclusion, but it has only two very general statements about dancing. In fact, the "support" statements are neither details nor examples. The sentence "It can be lots of fun as well" could even be another main idea. What does "good exercise" really mean? Specific answers to this question are not in the paragraph. You can see, then, that this paragraph needs more information to explain what "good exercise" means. The reader could only guess at the meaning suggested by the topic sentence.

Here is a revised draft of this paragraph about dancing that contains more information:

> **Dancing can be good exercise.** The constant arm and leg movements are like aerobics. They can be a really good workout if the dance lasts long enough. If the dance requires lots of quick movements, many calories can be used up, and more fat will be burned. Some dances require movements that are like stretching, so flexibility and muscle tone will be increased. **Dancing can help maintain weight and can be beneficial exercise for everyone.**

There is no "correct length" for an effective paragraph, but four to eight support sentences can make a strong paragraph if they contain supporting details. When you are judging the completeness of a paragraph, look for details and examples that make the topic sentence clear.

EXERCISE   7

Revise the following paragraphs for completeness. Underline the topic sentence and the conclusion in each paragraph. Then add two or more sentences that support the topic sentence.

Example:

Hawaii is fun to visit on a vacation. I can sample fresh pineapples served by friendly Hawaiians. I can scuba dive in the ocean. Having the chance to enjoy different activities in Hawaii could mean a great vacation.

Each island offers different
sights and activities.

Hawaii is fun to visit on a vacation. ∧ I can sample fresh pineapples

Close by, I can browse in a
variety of interesting shops.

served by friendly Hawaiians. ∧ I can scuba dive in the ocean

I can join in native Hawaiian dances.

∧ Having the chance to enjoy different activities in Hawaii

could mean a great vacation.

Paragraph 1

Customer service is very important in building a successful business. Customers who are treated

well often return to the store. Customers know defective merchandise can be returned for refund or

exchange. Customers like to know apparel that does not fit can be returned. All in all, satisfied

customers spread the word about consumer-friendly stores.

Paragraph 2

Visiting a dentist can be an uncomfortable experience. X-ray tooth frames cut into gums. Lights

in a person's eyes are annoying. Most people would rather do anything than go to the dentist.

Paragraph 3

Living in an apartment requires having consideration for others. Renters should remember to

keep the music volume down. Also, if they have pets, they should keep them quiet. People living in an

apartment should enter and exit quietly at night. If residents have a car, they should use their own

designated parking space. Mutual respect for neighbors makes living in an apartment pleasant.

Paragraph 4

Some parents try to buy their children's love by giving them presents. They think that giving a

child a new doll or a new toy car every month or so will make up for not paying much attention to the child. Children probably need fewer material objects and more affection and real communication if parents want their love returned.

Paragraph 5

Planning a vacation to Japan means that you have to have money saved. Airfare and hotel rooms, for example, require a lot of money. You have to decide if you can do without some things to save money for that special vacation to Japan.

Logical Order You have learned that all the sentences in a strong paragraph relate to one main idea and that there should be enough supporting details to make the main idea clear. A second element that strong paragraphs have is **logical** or **sensible order**. All the support sentences should be in clear, logical order.

Sometimes the order of these supporting details does not matter. Other times, however, it does matter because if sentences are not in logical order, the reader misses the main point of the paragraph.

To start thinking about how to put sentences together in logical order, read the following sentences. Notice how they relate to each other but are *out* of logical order.

I opened the front door of my house and went inside.

I walked up the front steps to my front door.

These sentences are out of logical order because the person would have to walk to the door before it could be opened. This example shows what "logical" or "sensible" order is. The sentences should be in this order:

I walked up the steps to my front door.

I opened the front door of my house and went inside.

Here is another example of illogical order:

Henry washed the mud off his dog.

Henry made sure he put warm water in the big tub.

He dried the dog with a towel.

These sentences are not in logical or sensible order because they are not *in the order in which the actions would be done*. Here is the logical order:

Henry made sure he put warm water in the big tub.

Henry washed the mud off his dog.

He dried the dog with a towel.

Here is another example of logical order:

At noon today, the engineers met at a special luncheon.

The luncheon ended at two o'clock.

These sentences are in logical order because of the *time signal* in each sentence. "Noon" comes before "two o'clock."

Another kind of order exists in describing a place, such as a room in a house. The details are described or "seen" in the order in which they really exist in the room.

When you enter the living room, you see a couch on the left and a chair and table next to that. Walking straight ahead into the room, you see at the end of the dining room a fairly large table and four chairs. To the right of this large table is the door into the kitchen.

When several details flow together in a paragraph, it is important for the reader to be able to follow the ideas in a clear order. Sometimes—as in the previous example—the natural physical movement from one place to another will determine the order of the sentences.

One final example might help clarify this idea of order in a strong paragraph. In the following paragraph about sea turtles, the support sentences are in a clear, logical order. The ideas in bold type should not be rearranged because they show a logical order of what the scientists did.

American scientists are working hard to gather facts about sea turtles called leatherbacks. **The observers work**, no matter what the weather is like—on clear days or in pouring rain. **They count the turtles** as they come ashore. When the turtles lay their eggs, **the scientists walk up and down** the beaches for many hours at a time. **They count the eggs** in the sand. Then, later, **they count the eggs that hatch**. These biologists know that they are collecting information that will someday be important to other scientists.

The actions are described in the normal, natural order in which they occur.

Note Other ways of clarifying the logical order in a paragraph concern *coherence*, which will be explained later.

The following exercise will help you practice arranging sentences in logical order.

EXERCISE 8

Study the following sets of sentences and decide what their logical order would be in a paragraph. Number the sentences in the order in which they should logically appear.

Example:

    _2_   **She made plane reservations.**

    _1_   **Sara decided to go to Atlanta, Georgia.**

1. _1_   The roof on Frank's house leaked.

    _2_   He called a roofer to have it fixed.

2. _2_   Charlie planted the lettuce seed in early spring.

    _1_   He spaded his garden carefully and worked in fertilizer.

3. _1_   Sammy and his mother bought dog food at the store.

    _3_   Sammy put the food down for his puppies at three o'clock.

    _2_   Sammy got the food ready with his mom's help.

4. _3_   Kenita turned in her essay at the beginning of class.

    _1_   Kenita typed her assignment on the computer.

    _2_   Kenita wrote her name carefully at the top of the essay.

5. _3_   Ruth attended classes.

    _2_   Ruth paid her registration fees for two classes in the fall.

    _1_   Ruth took a hundred dollars from savings for her fees.

6. _4_   On the way to the door, he put on his sunglasses.

    _1_   Felix took a few precautions to prevent overexposure to the sun.

    _2_   After he showered, he applied SPF 20 sunblock to his face and arms.

    _3_   After dressing, he chose a wide-brimmed hat from his closet.

7. _4_   Harry deposited his paycheck in the bank.

    _2_   Harry walked to the personnel office to pick up his paycheck.

    _1_   Harry cleared his desk for the day at 4:30.

    _3_   Harry filled out the deposit slip on the way to the bank.

8. _4_   Mehri filled out the application for the mechanic's job.

    _1_   Mehri checked the jobs advertised in the local paper.

    _5_   Mehri waited patiently to be called for an interview.

    _3_   Mehri went to Robinson Motor Company the next morning.

    _2_   Robinson Motor Company was advertising for a mechanic.

9. __4__ Tosha removed the old filter and put in the new one.

__2__ She bought oil and an oil filter from the automotive store.

__3__ Tosha drained the oil from her car.

__5__ Tosha put the new oil in her car.

__1__ Tosha decided to change the oil in her car.

10. __4__ Finally, dinner was served.

__2__ Peanuts were brought around to all of the passengers for a mid-morning snack.

__5__ A current movie was presented after dinner.

__1__ To begin the international flight to Taiwan, flight attendants served orange juice.

__3__ Lunch consisted of a sandwich.

Unity All sentences in a good paragraph relate to the topic sentence (main idea). When any idea doesn't relate specifically to the topic sentence, then that paragraph lacks **unity** or is not unified. Look again at the paragraph about giant sea turtles. This draft has one main idea and several support sentences that help to explain the general word(s) expressed in the topic sentence.

> **American scientists are working hard to gather facts about sea turtles called leatherbacks.** The observers work, no matter what the weather is like—on clear days or in pouring rain. They count the turtles as they come ashore. When the turtles lay their eggs, the scientists walk up and down the beaches for many hours at a time. They count the eggs in the sand. Then, later, they count the eggs that hatch. **These biologists know that they are collecting information that will someday be important to other scientists.**

This paragraph shows the three parts of a good paragraph—topic sentence, support sentences, and concluding sentence (or conclusion). Now check to see if the paragraph has the important element of **unity**.

To check for unity, first separate the topic sentence into its two parts:

Topic: American scientists

Direction or general word(s): are working hard to gather facts about sea turtles called leatherbacks.

Second, check each support sentence against the topic sentence. Each supporting idea is a specific fact or detail that explains what the scientists actually do to work hard to gather information. In this case, all the sentences after the topic sentence must explain how the scientists are working hard to gather facts about sea turtles. So that you can judge the supporting sentences better, they are listed below.

Topic Sentence

American scientists are working hard to gather facts about sea turtles called leatherbacks.

Support Sentences

The **observers work, no matter what the weather is like** — on clear days or in pouring rain.

They count the turtles as they come ashore.

. . . the **scientists walk up and down the beaches for many hours** at a time.

They count the eggs in the sand.

Then, later, **they count the eggs that hatch**.

Notice that the bold words in each support sentence make reference to the main idea in the topic sentence.

This paragraph has unity because all the information clearly and directly relates to the general idea in the topic sentence. All you have to do to check a paragraph's unity is to see if each sentence gives details that explain the main idea in the topic sentence. Similarly, the best way to write good, unified paragraphs is to make all the sentences between your topic sentence and the conclusion explain your main idea.

Now read the following draft of the preceding paragraph. Look for the sentence that does not explain the topic sentence. This sentence breaks the unity of the paragraph.

American scientists are working hard to gather facts about sea turtles called leatherbacks. The observers work, no matter what the weather is like — on clear days or in pouring rain. The leatherback is the only kind of turtle that can live in the cold North Atlantic Ocean. They count the turtles as they come ashore. When the turtles lay their eggs, the scientists walk up and down the beaches for many hours at a time. They count the eggs in the sand. Then, later, they count the eggs that hatch. These biologists know that they are collecting information that will someday be important to other scientists.

The sentence that breaks the unity is "The leatherback is the only kind of turtle that can live in the cold North Atlantic Ocean." This sentence tells about the turtles; it does not directly relate to how the observers work to get their information. Consequently, this sentence spoils the paragraph's unity.

The following exercise will help you identify sentences that do not support a topic sentence. Being able to identify such unrelated sentences will help you preserve the unity in the paragraphs you are writing.

EXERCISE 9

Study each group of sentences. Identify the sentences as follows:
TS = a possible topic sentence
S = a support sentence
U = an unrelated sentence

_TS_ **Elderly people enjoy outdoor activities.**

_U_ **Children swim in the pool next to the shuffleboard court.**

_S_ **Elderly people play shuffleboard.**

1. _S_ George bought a Ford.

   _TS_ George admires American cars.

   _U_ He needs a new lawn mower.

2. _TS_ The puppies loved to play running games in the house.

   _U_ The puppies ate a lot.

   _S_ Chokka dashed headlong under the bed.

3. _TS_ Raising children can be a wonderful experience.

   _S_ Cathy has three children.

   _U_ Clothes for both boys and girls can be costly.

4. _S_ This fashion trend is reflected in increasing sales.

   _TS_ Afro-American clothing is becoming increasingly popular in the United States.

   _U_ People enjoy shopping.

5. _TS_ The football training program is strenuous.

   _U_ The quarterback is an education major.

   _S_ The runningbacks have to run many wind sprints.

6. _U_ My guinea pig has not learned when to stop eating.

   _S_ The chimps have been taught to associate the picture of a ball with a real ball.

   _TS_ Animals are very intelligent beings.

7. _S_ The librarian ordered fifteen new American novels.

   _TS_ The library has an extensive collection of American literature.

   _U_ The library's art collection is outstanding.

8. _TS_ Going to college and having a job may leave little time for recreation.

   _U_ Gerald forgot to do his math homework.

   _S_ Gerald could not go to the movies last weekend.

9. _S_ John wrote a research paper for Biology 101.

   _TS_ The biology class required several lab and writing assignments.

   _U_ John missed two biology lectures.

10. _TS_ Owning a business requires many skills.

   _S_ Being able to predict profits and expenses is essential.

   _U_ Sheryl wanted to own her own business.

11. _S_ The rose quartz was one of the best pieces displayed.

   _U_ Kim liked to go rock hunting on weekends.

   _TS_ The school library had a special rock and gem collection.

12. _S_ A monkey can turn pages of a book for the owner.

   _U_ Monkeys are often brown.

   _TS_ A monkey can aid handicapped people.

13. _S_ The dishes need to be done.

   _U_ I finally hired a gardener to do the yard work.

   _TS_ Housekeeping can be a never-ending job.

14. _TS_ Robert Patton has been actively involved in the environmental movement in the United States.

   _S_ He has donated $150,000 to preserve the Gila National Reserve.

   _U_ He plays golf every Sunday morning.

15. _TS_ Swimming provides an excellent source of exercise.

   _S_ Swimming develops upper-body muscle tone.

   _U_ Many cities offer swimming classes during the summer.

16. _S_ Richard thought he was Superman after he took steroids.

   _U_ Lifting heavy weights builds muscles.

   _TS_ Psychiatrists are finding that taking steroids can cause psychological problems.

17. _U_ John wants to run for public office.

   _S_ Two or three hours a day can be spent giving speeches.

   _TS_ Running for public office can be demanding.

18. _TS_   Community-college graduates perform well at universities.

_U_   Alicia received financial aid while attending college.

_S_   Alicia, a community-college graduate, earned an A average during her first year at the university.

19. _U_   Michael Jackson has his own private Ferris wheel on his estate.

_TS_   Eli Bridge Company is America's foremost builder of Ferris wheels.

_S_   The company has built approximately 1,400 Ferris wheels.

20. _TS_   Swimming is good physical therapy.

_U_   Many of my neighbors wonder why I swim at 6:00 A.M. every day.

_S_   Paraplegics increase muscle tone in the swimming pool at Saint Luke's Hospital.

EXERCISE 10

Check the following drafts for **unity**. *Underline any sentences that do not support or explain the main idea in the topic sentence.*

Paragraph 1

Adult reentry students often have special needs. They may have time restraints caused by families and jobs as well as by school. Reentry students are willing to put in the extra time to be successful. Since they sometimes work more slowly than younger students, they may require more time to complete tasks. As adults grow older, their vision is not as keen, so classrooms need excellent lighting with little glare. They have more experiences than younger students. Also, reentry students may experience hearing problems, making it hard for them to hear everything that is said in the classroom. These problems, although serious, do not need to be a barrier to education.

Paragraph 2

Visiting the eastern part of the United States for the first time can be a shock to someone born and raised in a desert climate. The whole landscape in the East is green with grass and trees. The mountains in the West are rocky and craggy, with trees only at higher altitudes. There are also many rivers and streams there. The houses, too, are different. Frequently, they are two-story homes, very close together, sometimes with no space at all between them. Another difference is the short travel distances between states. However, there are many exciting places to visit in the East. The eastern part of America can be a real surprise to someone used to deserts and open spaces.

Paragraph 3

People from other countries have different reasons for wanting to come to live in the United States. For example, some might want higher-paying jobs than they can get in their own countries.

Some want the freedom to change jobs or professions. Some might want the chance to get more education for themselves and their families. Church groups often sponsor people coming to America. Perhaps one of the most important reasons would be the desire to own and operate a business. Many people wait a long time for the chance to live in the United States. Every year, regardless of the reasons, many more people come to live in America.

Coherence   One of the most important considerations in writing a paragraph is **coherence**—the way all the sentences should be clearly connected to each other. Without connecting words or phrases, supporting ideas may be hard to follow and sometimes may even seem to be unrelated to the topic sentence and to each other. In those cases, the sentences sound like a list.

The following paragraph has the coherence it needs:

> When Sue was a child, she learned from her dad how to be a hard worker. For example, she always helped in the yard. Many times they mowed the lawn together. Sue emptied the grass catcher (which her dad did not overfill), and he did the heavy part by lifting the barrels full of grass. Working together, they did not quit until the job was done. She and her dad worked even after the sun was gone, making sure that the edges of the lawn were neat. In this way, Sue learned to stay with a job until she had done it well and could feel proud of her effort.

This paragraph shows **coherence** because *at least one* of the key words or phrases—or variations of them—is repeated either directly or indirectly *in each sentence.*

Key Words or Phrases	Variations of Key Words
Sue	she
learned	learned
her dad	he
Sue and her dad	they, together
hard worker	job, helped in the yard, did the heavy part, lifting, work, working, didn't quit until the job was done, making sure, stay with a job, effort

Each sentence in the paragraph is *clearly* (obviously) connected to the one before it by a clear pronoun or a clear example of a key word.

Other words or phrases also help set the scene or provide time signals in order to clarify the experience for the reader:

Other Words or Phrases That Provide Coherence

always

many times

even after

A very important signal to the reader — "for example" — occurs near the beginning of the paragraph. This phrase tells the reader to watch for specific details that will clarify the topic sentence. It helps to signal to your reader when you begin to put in your support sentences.

At the end of the paragraph, the most important connecting words "in this way" introduce the concluding sentence. This phrase points back to all the examples that help make the main point clear.

Making clear connections between two consecutive sentences is very important. Do not assume that your readers know what you are talking about. Try to emphasize the relationship between sentences. The extra effort is well worth it. (You will learn more about coherence in Unit 7.)

The following exercise will help you understand and practice giving paragraphs coherence.

EXERCISE 11

Read each paragraph below. Underline the topic sentence. Circle the key words or phrases in the topic sentence that could be used to add coherence. Revise each paragraph below and put in connecting words and phrases to show clearly how sentences relate to each other and to the topic sentence. Use the key words or variations of them. Put in "time signal" words like "then" or "next" or "later." Use "for example" to introduce specific examples. You may combine ideas if necessary to make each paragraph flow more smoothly. Finally, make sure that the concluding sentence clearly refers to the main idea in the topic sentence.

Example:

When they went in, they
~~Carol and Bev~~ had a good time at the movie. ~~Carol and Bev~~ decided to sit

to   *They liked the movie because the*
in the back ~~where~~ they could relax and have lots of room. ~~The music was~~

exciting and the   *During the show, they*
~~exciting.~~ The story was suspenseful. ~~They~~ ate popcorn and drank a soft

The best part of all was watching the   *in front of them. All of these*
drink. ~~There were lots of~~ good-looking guys ~~there. They enjoyed~~

things added up to an enjoyable
~~their~~ afternoon at the movies.

NOTE: *Answers to this exercise will vary.*

Paragraph 1

(Jason) (enjoys) (card games). He learned to play when he was a child. He likes solitaire. He likes gin

rummy. He plays fifty-two-pickup with his four-year-old brother. Jason does not like to gamble. He

would rather play for fun and relaxation.

Paragraph 2

Renting videos has many advantages over going to the movies. Videos are approximately one-third the price of a theater movie ticket. Convenience is a factor. Videos can be rented from many different stores at convenient times, and selection is good. Control over the explicit nature of the movie is something many people do not realize they have. Inappropriate scenes can be avoided by using the fast-forward button. More and more people are watching movies at home rather than going to movie theaters.

Paragraph 3

My favorite birthday present was a trip through the zoo. I was ten years old. My mom took three friends and me to the zoo. My sister went, too. We made a lot of noise when we saw the snakes. My mom said she liked tigers. We saw birds and monkeys at the zoo. I took pictures of everybody with a new camera. We had a picnic lunch. They gave me presents. We had hot dogs, ice cream, and soda pop. We had a great time at the zoo.

■ Collaborative Project: Working and Learning Together

Option 1

Break into groups of three or four. Using Exercise 2 (found in Part 1) discuss and write topic sentences for three of the topics. In each group, work on three different topics. Decide which topic sentence (for each group) you think is the best, and write it on the board for the class to see. Be prepared to discuss the topic sentences as a class.

Option 2

Read the student examples by Hilding, Gaspar, Roesch, and Donaldson. In groups of three or four, evaluate these paragraphs according to the statements given in the following chart. Rate each element on a scale of 1 (low) to 5 (high). Then share the results with the rest of the class, and be prepared to defend your scores.

The topic sentence focuses the paragraph.	The paragraph has a logical order of ideas.	The paragraph has sufficient support.	The paragraph links ideas together.
Hilding _____	_____	_____	_____
Gaspar _____	_____	_____	_____
Roesch _____	_____	_____	_____
Donaldson _____	_____	_____	_____

Topic sentence test is available in the instructor's manual in the back of the annotated edition, pp 28-29.

PART 2

SOMETHING TO THINK ABOUT, SOMETHING TO WRITE ABOUT

Sometimes reading a scholarly article can make you stop and think about the world in which you live. Articles of this type can be about political or social issues that directly affect you. They could also make you think about your past or future. By reading these articles, you can get information about the world as well as ideas that you can use in your writing. They may trigger something in your memory that you can put into your writing.

The following article may make you reflect upon events that happened early in your life or events that are going on right now as a result of your past. These events, then, can become a valuable resource for your writing.

Read the following article and then work through one or more of the suggested writing assignments that require memory of past events. If you cannot remember your past, then maybe you could focus on something that you have experienced recently.

Childhood

Dr. Linda Coble, *therapist and psychologist*

1 Do you remember what you were doing and how you were feeling in the first grade? Who was your teacher in kindergarten? Can you remember what you were doing before starting school? How far back can you reach into your past? Can you recollect your first experience of emotional awareness? What was it? fear? security? warmth? The answers to these questions can be extremely valuable to therapists working with their clients. Some people may think pulling out long-past, ancient detail is impossible, but Adlerian therapists and clients are doing it every day. In fact, a very important aspect of many psychotherapy approaches is to gather details from clients about their early history, for these early experiences may have an important impact on the clients' personality development.

2 Adlerian theory, a popular counseling approach, calls these events "early recollections." Clients are asked to recall incidents from as far back as they are able. Experiences can be both positive and negative. Therapists gather these memories. As they sort the information, they pay attention to the age of the person at the time of the recollection, the specific details of the occurrence, and the feelings the client experienced. The therapist, upon gathering several of these recollections, will use them in analyzing the client's goals and attitudes.

3 Birth order is also considered by Adlerian therapists to be an important influence on personality development. First interactions with people are within the family structure, and the position in the family may have set up certain expectations from significant family members. Children, in their effort to achieve a sense of belonging, will take on roles in the family. Commonly, the oldest children adopt the role of being responsible, serious, and dependable. The middle child is in the uncomfortable position of following the firstborn and will often experience pressure in her/his attempt to catch up with the older sibling(s). If the second-born feels a struggle, she or he may develop opposite traits from those of the older brother or sister. The youngest child is often a charmer who struggles with being taken seriously. Of course, these are generalizations, and many combinations of

the family structure can be more accurately analyzed by a qualified therapist. No doubt, however, this position in the family, as well as an understanding of how the child interpreted early family situations, provides valuable insight for the therapist.

4   In some extreme cases, a therapist may find that a client has had an unusually traumatic experience. Perhaps a serious fire, a prolonged illness of a family member, a death of a parent, or an early encounter with alcoholism may have affected a child's perception of family life, consequently affecting the child's view of the world. In this case, the therapist tries to help the client to explore the event. A therapist may use simulated drama, dialogue, simulated confrontation with conflicting family members, or writing to shed the negative feelings and "clean the slate" for the client. By reexposing the details of negative occurrences and accepting the help of a therapist to put the events to rest, so to speak, the client experiences a cathartic relief and can have a healthier, more positive outlook.

5   Early recollections and birth order are effective beginning places for therapists; however, what is done with the information once it is obtained is equally important. Even though such beginnings provide an insight into what may be the cause of the problem, the strategies for new directions or solutions provided by therapists are what make the total therapeutic process worthwhile for the client.

Understanding Words

Briefly define the following words as they are used in the above essay.

1. psychotherapy *using psychoanalysis to treat mental disorders*
2. sibling *brother or sister*
3. simulated *imitated, pretended to be like*
4. cathartic *related to alleviation or release of fears*

Something to Write About

Now that you have read the article, write a paragraph that addresses one of the following topics:

1. How did it feel to be the oldest child? middle child? youngest child? only child?
2. Describe a place that gave you a feeling of warmth or security as a child.
3. Describe the most negative or ugly place you remember as a child.
4. Describe the most beautiful object you remember seeing.
5. What responsibilities did you have growing up?
6. What qualities should a good parent possess?
7. Which people influence a child the most?
8. What types of problems do working parents encounter?
9. What are the advantages of being a working parent?
10. How can parents minimize conflicts in a family?

After you draft your paragraph, do each of the following:

Revise it so it has a clear topic sentence.

Include four to six supporting sentences.

Include a closing sentence.

Check for unity and a smooth flow of ideas.

PART 3

PARAGRAPHS FOR DISCUSSION AND ANALYSIS

Summer at Aunt Clara and Uncle Frank's Farm

Phyllis J. Hilding, *student*

My favorite memories from my past have to be the summers I spent on my Aunt Clara and Uncle Frank's farm. From the time I was ten years old until I turned sixteen, at which age I had to get a job, I spent every summer on the farm, along with at least eighteen other nieces and nephews. My aunt and uncle had no children of their own, and so, my cousins and I, plus other assorted kids, became their children for the summers, to work and play, and have the best times of our young lives. We all did the chores, household chores and farm chores alike. We girls did cooking, cleaning, and washing, while my boy cousins helped my uncle with the bulk of the heavier farm work. All of us fed and watered the farm stock, milked cows, and mucked out the pig and cow stalls, the last of which was never on the top of anybody's list of things to do. We had fun while we did our chores like riding the big boar called Pinky, squirting milk into the mouths of at least a dozen cats lined up at milking time, and shucking corn; it was all fun to me. We made friends with the neighboring farm kids, some of whom I still keep in contact with. We, including the real farm kids and my city cousins, had "parlor" parties, went on picnics and hay rides, went to county fairs and auctions, and even participated in barn-raisings where farm people got together and helped rebuild other farmers' burned-down barns. Every evening, after the farm chores were done, we all piled into the back of my uncle's old beat-up pickup and drove the mile or so to Bird Lake where we all jumped into the lake and rejoiced in the cool water, pleased with the day's work and happy with being young, healthy, and alive. There was a camaraderie among us that I haven't experienced since those long ago summers on my aunt and uncle's farm. I'll always remember those idyllic summers I spent on the farm, the good and wonderful people I met and got to know, and the feelings of love and friendship I felt then.

Understanding Words

Briefly define the following words as they are used in the above paragraph.

1. mucked *removed dirt and manure*
2. boar *male pig*
3. camaraderie *warm feelings and rapport among friends*
4. idyllic *having natural charm, simple and pleasant*

Questions on Content

1. Why did the author spend summers on the farm?
2. Who was Pinky?
3. What were the lasting effects of these summers on the author?

Questions on Form

1. In what way did the author use logical or sensible order?
2. What makes the paragraph complete?
3. How does the concluding sentence add to the paragraph?

My Grandmother and Grandfather's House

Michael Gaspar, *student*

The corner of my grandmother and grandfather's house is not an ordinary corner of a house but a very special place to me. As a young child, I could feel the warmth of the blankets and the sound of gas seeping out of the burner keeping me warm. The floor was so soft, and my brother's back against mine was reassurance that nothing could harm me. I could gaze up at the ceiling and watch the candle's reflection dancing as if to entertain me. Most of all, I could hear a very subtle breathing sound as if it were singing to me. The love in that place made me get the chills if not a slight tear to my eye. I go back once in a while to see this place, and you know, it is still the same, and I miss it dearly.

◼ **Understanding Words**

Briefly define the following words as they are used in the above paragraph.

1. reassurance *security*
2. subtle *slight*

◼ **Questions on Content**

1. What made the author get the chills?
2. Where was the special place?
3. What danced on the ceiling?

Questions on Form

1. What is the topic sentence?
2. Does the paragraph stay with the main idea?
3. What details can you name?

Concentration Camp

Jan-Georg Roesch, *student*

My visit to the concentration camp was a frightful and thoughtful experience. In the 1930s and 1940s under the regime of Adolf Hitler, this place ended many innocent people's lives. The building looked as unwelcoming as a graveyard by night. The heavy iron door, which slowly gave way to the pulling force, creaked as it was opened. Each footstep echoed through the chamber as each individual slowly pondered and walked from one end of the room to the other. Every unconscious mumble could be heard clearly. The smell was so sharp and distinct, yet I could not identify it with anything explicable. The glaring light which lit the room was unbearable, and for many it was the last sight of daylight before entering the execution room. The major impact this place had on me was that even the most negative thought could not describe the coldness of this place.

◼ Understanding Words

Briefly define the following words as they are used in the above paragraph.

1. concentration camp *a place of confinement for those considered dangerous to the regime, as in Nazi Germany*
2. regime *a system of government or rule*
3. pondered *thought*
4. explicable *understandable*

◼ Questions on Content

1. When was this concentration camp used?
2. What does the author compare this place to?
3. What was the overall feeling the author experienced at this place?

Questions on Form

1. Which senses does the author use?
2. What makes the topic sentence effective?
3. State the concluding sentence.

Fort Leonard Wood

Terry M. Donaldson, *student*

The first view of Fort Leonard Wood is very foreboding when seen from an incoming airplane. It appears to be a land decimated by war! The ground, pitted with craters, looks barren and lifeless. Scattered about the terrain are the remnants of the life it once held. The skeletal remains of a few trees stand like twisted spikes driven into the earth. Others lie rotting on the ground. All are victims of the constant volley of exploding shells. The solitary building has big holes in the walls, and a large part of the structure has been reduced to a pile of rubble. The burned-out shells of military vehicles are scattered about. A couple of dump trucks, a jeep, and farther off, what is left of an army tank are still there. The only movement is the parched sand blowing in the wind. Though only a grenade and ballistics firing range, this scene exposes the senseless devastation and vicious brutality of any war.

◼ Understanding Words

Briefly define the following words as they are used in the above paragraph.

1. foreboding *predicting something harmful*
2. decimated *destroyed*
3. ballistics *the science dealing with the motion of bullets*

Questions on Content

1. What is the author's first impression of Fort Leonard Wood?
2. What killed the trees?
3. What is the only movement?
4. What is the author actually describing?

Questions on Form

1. What makes the paragraph effective?
2. Why are the supporting details so effective?
3. What is effective about the closing sentence?

Munich

John Schulz, *student*

The most exciting city I have ever visited was Munich. There was always something going on. I think that they had a festival for just about everything. There were Maifests, Weinfests, and Oktoberfests, to name only a few. When they weren't going on, I had a lot of other sights to see, such as a castle, a palace, or a brewery. The majority of the places I visited stayed pretty crowded, but they still offered a lot of excitement. And if all else failed, I went shopping at the "Marktplatz," which consisted of a street that stretched for two or three miles and had stores, restaurants, and cafes. I plan on returning to Munich in the near future.

Questions on Content

1. Why did he enjoy Munich?
2. What did he do when all else failed?
3. How far did the Marktplatz stretch?

Questions on Form

1. Does the paragraph contain a topic sentence, support sentences, and a concluding sentence?
2. Is the topic sentence clear? In what way?

An Eyewitness Account of the San Francisco Earthquake
Excerpt from article in *Collier's* (1906) by **Jack London**

On Wednesday morning at a quarter past five came the earthquake. A minute later the flames were leaping upward. In a dozen different quarters south of Market Street, in the working-class ghetto, and in the factories, fires started. There was no opposing the flames. There was no organization, no communication. All the cunning adjustments of a twentieth-century city had been smashed by the earthquake. The streets were humped into ridges and depressions and piled with debris of fallen walls. The steel rails were twisted into perpendicular and horizontal angles. The telephone and telegraph systems were disrupted. And the great water mains had burst. All the shrewd contrivances and safeguards of man had been thrown out of gear by thirty seconds' twitching of the earth-crust.

Understanding Words

Briefly define the following words as they are used in the above paragraph.

1. ghetto *a section of a city where a particular group of people are forced to live*
2. perpendicular *at right angles to a given line*
3. shrewd *clever*
4. contrivances *devices or plans*

Questions on Content

1. What could be done about the earthquake?
2. What damage did the earthquake do?
3. At what time did the fire start?

Questions on Form

1. Do all the examples support the topic idea?
2. How is the topic idea stated?
3. Does the concluding sentence echo the topic idea?

Martin Luther King

Excerpt from *Martin Luther King* by **Rae Bains**

In Atlanta and other parts of the South, blacks were not treated the same as whites. For example, a white person who wanted to ride a bus simply got on, paid the fare, and took a seat. But a black person got on, paid the fare, got off again, walked to the rear door of the bus and got on there. Blacks could only sit in the back of the bus. If all the seats became filled, the blacks had to give up their seats to white people who got on.

Questions on Content

1. Where did blacks sit on a bus?
2. What did blacks do when the bus was full and a white person got on?
3. What part of the country is the author talking about?

Questions on Form

1. Does the idea of blacks sitting in the back support the topic sentence?
2. Where is the topic sentence stated?
3. How is the topic sentence supported?

Making a World of Difference

Excerpt from an essay in the Spring/Summer issue of *Experienced Engineer*

Coming to terms with limited technology is one thing; acclimating to foreign living conditions and social customs is another. Though the Peace Corps makes sure its volunteers have adequate language and cultural training programs, there were a few cultural hurdles [Melissa] Lang had to overcome on her own — one of which was food. ''The first week was really hard. It was the hot season, and I had serious doubts I could make it because I thought there's nothing I could eat. It was one tricky thing to face a dish of rice for breakfast. I lived with a family for the first few months, and there were many times I'd leave the breakfast table with my mouth burning.'' In retrospect, Lang found that the food was the easiest thing to get used to in Thailand.

■ Understanding Words

Briefly define the following words as they are used in the above paragraph.

1. acclimating *getting used to a new climate or place*
2. retrospect *a looking back or thinking about things past*

■ Questions on Content

1. What volunteer agency is mentioned in the paragraph?
2. What food does she remember eating?
3. What was the easiest thing to get used to in Thailand?

Questions on Form

1. Where is the topic sentence stated?
2. How does the example relate to the topic sentence?
3. Are the sentences in logical order?

Subway Station

Excerpt from *Talents and Geniuses* by **Gilbert Highet**

Standing in a subway station, I began to appreciate the place—almost to enjoy it. First of all, I looked at the lighting: a row of meager electric bulbs, un-screened, yellow, and coated with filth, stretched toward the black mouth of the tunnel, as though it were a bolt hole in an abandoned coal mine. Then I lingered, with zest, on the walls and ceiling: lavatory tiles which had been white about fifty years ago, and were now encrusted with soot, coated with the remains of a dirty liquid which might be either atmospheric humidity mingled with smog or the result of a perfunctory attempt to clean them with cold water; and, above them, gloomy vaulting from which dingy paint was peeling off like scabs from an old wound, sick black paint leaving a leprous white undersurface. Beneath my feet, the floor was a nauseating dark brown with black stains upon it which might be stale oil or dry chewing gum or some worse defilement; it looked like the hallway of a condemned slum building. Then my eye traveled to the tracks, where two lines of glittering steel—the only positively clean object in the whole place—ran out of darkness into darkness about an unspeakable mass of congealed oil, puddles of dubious liquid, and a mishmash of old cigarette packets, mutilated and filthy newspapers, and the debris that filtered down from the street above through a barrel grating in the roof. As I looked up toward the sunlight, I could see more debris sifting slowly downward, and making an abominable pattern in the slanting beam of dirt-laden sunlight. I was going on to relish more features of this unique scene: such as the advertisement posters on the walls—here a text from the Bible, there a half-naked girl, here a woman wearing a hat consisting of a hen sitting on a nest full of eggs, and there a pair of girl's legs walking up the keys of a cash register — all scribbled over with unknown names and well-known obscenities in black crayon and red lipstick; but then my train came in at last, I boarded it, and began to read. The experience was over for the time.

Understanding Words

Briefly define the following words as they are used in the above paragraph.

1. meager *small amount*
2. zest *relish, enthusiasm*
3. perfunctory *done in a careless or mechanical way*
4. leprous *characterized by ulcers, white scaly scabs*
5. defilement *filth*
6. dubious *doubtful*
7. mishmash *mixture*
8. abominable *hateful and disgusting*

Questions on Content

1. What did the author enjoy at first?
2. In spite of the negative details, what was his reaction as he stood and looked at the place?
3. What was the only "positively clean object in the whole place"?

Questions on Form

1. State the topic sentence.
2. What makes the paragraph effective?
3. How does the paragraph conclude?

Birds of an Old Farm

Excerpt from *A Naturalist Buys an Old Farm* by **Edwin Way Teale**

Secretiveness is part of the nesting season for many of our birds. We notice how silent and furtive the bluejays become, how our chickadees and tufted titmice disappear entirely from around the house while they are raising their broods. Once, when a crow passed us carrying a stick to add to its nest, it saw that we were looking up. It realized it was observed. Immediately it dropped the stick and veered away in another direction. Similarly toward evening during the first week of July, a red-eyed vireo, near my writing cabin among the juniper and aspen on the other side of the pond, sought, in a transparent ruse, to deceive me and conceal the fact it was carrying food to nestlings. When I caught sight of it — and it caught sight of me — it was carrying a small white butterfly to its nest. It abruptly changed its course, alighted on a twig, peered at me intently for some time. When I remained standing, watching it, it swallowed the butterfly and then flew away, apparently convinced I had been misled.

Understanding Words

Briefly define the following words as they are used in the above paragraph.

1. furtive *acting in a sneaky way*
2. tufted *having a group of feathers growing closely together*
3. titmice *small birds with dull colored feathers*
4. vireo *small song bird with green or gray feathers*
5. ruse *trick*

Questions on Content

1. What was a red-eyed vireo carrying in its mouth?
2. What did the crow do when it saw the author?
3. What did the chickadees do while they were raising their baby birds?

Questions on Form

1. What is the topic sentence?
2. What gives the paragraph a sense of closure?

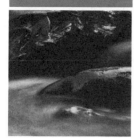
THE WRITER'S TOOLS: BASIC SENTENCE SKILLS

OBJECTIVES

- Identify prepositional phrases to avoid confusing them with subjects.
- Identify subjects and verbs in sentences.
- Recognize sentence-structure errors.
- Maintain subject-verb agreement in sentences.
- Maintain consistent verb tense in paragraphs or essays.

Having a paragraph that focuses on one idea and stays with that one idea is the most important part of writing. Sometimes, however, the effectiveness of a paragraph is diminished because of simple grammatical errors. These grammatical problems distract the reader from the ideas in the paragraph.

After writing your paragraph and making sure that all the information supports the topic sentence, you will need to do some editing. In this section, you can review prepositional phrases, subjects, and verbs. You will also be able to review basic sentence-structure errors. Emphasis is then placed on identifying subjects and verbs within a paragraph to make sure that they are both singular or both plural (subject-verb agreement). Emphasis is also placed on how to check the verbs in a paragraph to see if they are all in the present or all in the past time (consistent verb tense).

However, before you can edit your paragraph for sentence-structure errors, subject-verb agreement, and consistent verb tense, you must be able to identify subjects and verbs in sentences. **Subjects** are words that function as nouns or pronouns; however, sometimes the nouns or pronouns in prepositional phrases are mistaken for the subject of a sentence. Because this is true and because prepositional phrases are easy to identify, you will find it easier to locate subjects if you identify prepositional phrases first. One of the most common problems students face in finding the subject of a sentence is to mistake an object of a preposition for the subject of the sentence.

Finding Prepositional Phrases

Generally, prepositional phrases are phrases that begin with a preposition and end with a noun or pronoun. The noun or pronoun that ends the phrase is called the **object** and can never be the subject of a sentence. The object of a preposition can be identified by asking a question consisting of the preposition and "what":

    prep.   *obj.*
    by the rider   (by what?)

    prep.   *obj.*
    with careful training   (with what?)

prep. obj.
into water   (into what?)

prep.   obj.
to the other   (to what?)

- **A prepositional phrase may show location.**

  The mother bird quickly hopped *from one baby to the other*.

  ("From one baby" and "to the other" show the location of the mother.)

- **A prepositional phrase may show exclusion.**

  The baby birds had nothing on their minds *except food*.

  ("Except food" shows what was excluded.)

- **A prepositional phrase may show ownership or identification.**

  This spring a mother sparrow *with her two young sparrows* ventured forth.

  ("With her two young sparrows" shows that the young sparrows belong to the mother.)

- **A prepositional phrase may show time.**

  The mother sparrow and her babies ventured out *for the first time*.

  ("For the first time" shows when they ventured out.)

- **A prepositional phrase may have more than one object.**

  The mother sparrow and her babies searched *for food and water*.

The best way to learn to identify a prepositional phrase is to look for a pattern that always includes the preposition and its object. It also includes any word(s) that come between the preposition and its object.

prep.   obj. (noun)
in high esteem

prep.   obj. (pronoun)
by no one

prep.   obj. (noun)
of the young boys

prep.   obj. (pronoun)
to the pretty one

prep.   obj. (noun) obj. (noun)
for his bow and arrow

Now, refer to the following list of prepositions until they become easy to recognize.

Prepositions

aboard	beyond	onto
about	but	out
above	by	out of
across	concerning	outside
after	down	over
against	during	since
along	except	through
along with	for	throughout
among	from	to
around	in	toward
at	in favor of	under
because of	inside	underneath
before	in spite of	until
behind	into	unto
below	like	up
beneath	of	with
beside	off	within
besides	on	without
between	on account of	

Study the following paragraph and notice the prepositional phrases. The preposition is printed in bold italic type, and the rest of the prepositional phrase is in italics.

Many nineteenth-century Native Americans were expert horse trainers. *After a wild horse catch*, trainers often were able to tame a horse *in one day*. They wrapped the lasso *around the horse's nose* and guided the horse *into water*. There one *of the young boys* mounted it. The horse, of course, began bucking, but after getting its head *under water* a few times, soon quit. Native Americans *from some tribes* also trained special horses *for the buffalo hunt*. *With careful training*, these horses could be guided *to the left or right by the rider* who applied pressure *with his knees*. As a result, the hunter had both hands free *for his bow and arrow* and could shoot the buffalo *with ease*. Other horses were trained as war horses and were ridden *by no one except the trainer*. Sometimes these horses were so well trained that *during battle* they would strike the enemy *with their hoofs*. Consequently, Native Americans held their horses *in high esteem*.

To check your ability to identify prepositional phrases, work through the following exercises. In the first exercise, the sentences are isolated so that you can identify the prepositional phrases more easily. In the second exercise, paragraphs are used to help you see how prepositional phrases are a natural part of writing.

EXERCISE 1

Identify the prepositional phrases in the following sentences by placing parentheses ( ) around each phrase.

Example:

Baskets (of all sizes and shapes) covered the shelves.

1. The Florida Everglades have a wide variety (of beautiful birds.)
2. Ron liked all the exhibits (except the first one.)
3. Jill went home early (because of the rain.)
4. (Beside the lake) is a wonderful place.
5. Jim leaned (against the table) (for support.)
6. The trees (beside the lake) provide homes (for many insects, birds, and animals.)
7. The participant (in the Iron Man contest) continued (beyond human limits.)
8. I like the butterflies (on display.)
9. (Without thinking,) the man spent his entire paycheck.
10. (For two years,) the young couple stayed (within the limitations) (of their income.)
11. (During the winter) we enjoy traveling (to a warmer climate.)
12. Flight attendants constantly check (for potential problems) and offer extra comforts (to their customers.)
13. We floated (down the river) (on an inner tube.)
14. The six puppies ran (beyond the little child's reach.)
15. One (of my favorite sights) is the Arizona sunset.
16. They walked (around the track) (for two hours.)
17. The child (behind the tree) is looking (for her kitten.)
18. (In spite of the rain,) they drove their jeep (off the main road) (onto a side road.)
19. The children staying (at the lake) preferred swimming (in the pool.)
20. The information (concerning graduation) can be found (on the table) (inside the door.)

EXERCISE 2

Identify the prepositional phrases in the following paragraphs by placing parentheses ( ) around each phrase.

Paragraph 1

Parenting requires major changes (for young couples.) They must take the responsibility (for someone) (besides themselves.) Staying (at home) and caring (for a new infant) twenty-four hours a day are two major changes. Parents are required to spend their money (on the child's needs) rather than (on their own needs.) They must be able to function (on less sleep) and be prepared to get up several times each night to feed, change, and comfort a small one. This commitment continues (for many years.)

Paragraph 2

A person who wants to earn a living (by crabbing) (in Chesapeake Bay) must learn (about crabs and their varying market value.) A Jimmy or male bull crab sells (for the most money.) It is large and provides a generous supply (of sweet, white meat.) A sook or full-grown female crab is next (in size) (to the Jimmy.) She sheds her shell, becomes soft, mates, and rehardens. She then becomes a mature crab. At this point, she is a fairly large crab, but she cannot compete (with the bull crab) (for equal market value) because she is a bit smaller. A young female crab also lacks the size needed (for the market.) Crabbing can be a profitable business if a person learns (about crabs,) especially (from a good crabber.)

Finding Subjects and Verbs

Once you are skilled at finding prepositional phrases, it is easier to identify subjects and verbs. Learning to edit for certain grammar problems is usually easier if you are able to identify subjects and verbs.

Subjects

A **subject** is the word that answers "who" or "what" to the main verb in the sentence. Some sentences have a simple subject, and other sentences have a compound subject. *Only* a word that functions as a noun or a pronoun (except the noun or pronoun in a prepositional phrase) may be the subject of a sentence.

- **A simple subject is a word that functions as a noun or pronoun and is what the sentence is about.**

  Here are two sentences in which a noun is the subject:

  Ron gave me a great idea.   (Who gave me a great idea?)
  The **flowers** in the vase fell on the floor.   (What fell on the floor?)

  Here are two sentences in which a pronoun is the subject:

  He gave me a great idea.   (Who gave me a great idea?)
  Others were planted yesterday.   (What was planted yesterday?)

- **The compound subject is two or more words that the sentence is about.**
  Trisha and **Sam** are late.   (Who are late?)
  Ron and **Carrie** gave me a great surprise.   (Who gave me a great surprise?)

- All sentences *must* have a main subject and a verb. However, when a command is used, the subject is understood to be "you."

  v
  Close the door.

  v
  Water the plants.

  v   v
  Come in and sit down.

  s   v
  (You) close the door.

  s   v
  (You) water the plants.

  s   v   v
  (You) come in and sit down.

- "Here" and "there" can never be the subject of a sentence.

  v   s
  Here are the books.

  v   s
  There are five pages to complete.

Study the following paragraph. The subjects have been underlined once; prepositions are in bold italic type and the rest of the prepositional phrases are in italics. Notice how much easier it is to identify the subject(s) of a sentence once the prepositional phrases have been identified.

Many nineteenth-century <u>Native Americans</u> were expert horse trainers. *After a wild horse catch*, <u>trainers</u> often were able to tame a horse *in one day*. <u>They</u> wrapped the lasso *around the horse's nose* and guided the horse *into water*. There <u>one</u> *of the young boys* mounted it. The <u>horse</u>, of course, began bucking, but after getting its head *under water* a few times, soon quit. <u>Native Americans</u> *from some tribes* also trained special horses *for the buffalo hunt*. *With careful training*, these <u>horses</u> could be guided *to the left or right* *by the rider* who applied pressure *with his knees*. As a result, the <u>hunter</u> had both hands free *for his bow and arrow* and could shoot the buffalo *with ease*. Other <u>horses</u> were trained as war horses and were ridden *by no one* *except the trainer*. Sometimes these <u>horses</u> were so well trained that *during battle* they would strike the enemy *with their hoofs*. Consequently, <u>Native Americans</u> held their horses *in high esteem*.

To check your ability to identify subjects and prepositional phrases, do the following exercises. In the first exercise, the sentences are isolated so that you can identify the prepositional phrases more easily. Then paragraphs are used for further practice.

EXERCISE 3

In each of the following sentences, enclose all prepositional phrases in parentheses. Then underline the subject(s) once. Some sentences will have simple subjects, and others will have compound subjects.

Example:

<u>Women</u>, <u>children</u>, and <u>men</u> (of all ages) enjoy holidays.

1. The pizza, bread sticks, and salad were her favorite meal.

2. (During the movie,) the man and his daughter ate popcorn and drank pop.

3. The little girl (on the tricycle) ran (into the rose bushes.)

4. Here are the books (for you.)

You   5. Please close the door.

You   6. Please come back later (in the evening.)

7. The man and his wife discussed the various tours (of China.)

8. The children are leaving (for Disneyland.)

9. The young woman took her book (off the shelf) and read it.

10. Two (of my friends) left (for vacation) (at the same time.)

11. The dog and the cat are playing together.

12. The members (of the committee) left (at 6:00) (in the evening.)

13. The students (in the classroom) brought paper and pencils (to class.)

14. Jana was late (for the meeting.)

15. Josh is the smartest person (in the world.)

16. The wedding took much planning and work.

17. The bride and groom had a wonderful day.

18. Flying internationally, one can meet people (with very interesting backgrounds.)

19. The water (in the swimming pool) is clear and blue.

20. There is nothing (in the house) (for the children) to do.

EXERCISE 4

Master for transparencies is in the Instructor's Manual.

Identify prepositional phrases in the following paragraphs by enclosing them in parentheses. Underline the subject of each sentence.

Paragraph 1

Libraries have many activities (for children) (in the summer.) Many offer movie schedules (with educational, nonviolent classics.) (Because of donations) (from public and private organizations,) reading programs that award prizes can also motivate young readers. (For excitement,) goals are made, and prizes can be won. (In most cases,) everyone is a winner. (During many hot days,) happy children are found browsing (through books,) looking (at special displays,) or watching fish (in the library aquarium.) Cool, quiet learning environments (in a library) can be appealing (to children.)

Paragraph 2

This spring a mother sparrow (with her two young sparrows) ventured (out of their nest) (in search) (of food and water) (for the first time.) As the trio bounced along, it was easy to pick out the baby birds (from the mother) because the young sparrows fluttered their wings and opened their beaks. Then the mother sparrow inserted a crumb (of bread) or a little bug (into the tiny gaping beaks.) (In her effort) to feed both babies, she quickly hopped (from one) (to the other,) attending (to both) (of them.) She then slowly drank (from a small rain puddle.) The babies, however, had nothing (on their minds) (except food.) It was a pleasant sight to see.

Verbs

A **verb** is what the subject of the sentence does. The verb may show action—"run" or "hit"; it may be a form of "be"—"is" or "am"; or it may be "state of being"—"appears" or "sounds."

> *Action:* Ralph **ran** through the woods.
>
> Sara **hit** the car broadside.
>
> *Nonaction:* form of "be"
>
> Ralph **is** in the woods.
>
> Sara **was** in her car.
>
> state of being
>
> Ralph **appears** cool and strong.
>
> Sara **sounds** confident and impressive.
>
> The ice tea **tastes** good.

- **The verb may consist of one word or several words.**

The simple verb is one action verb or nonaction verb that tells what the subject does. The simple verb may be this one action or nonaction word alone or may be combined with a helping verb.

Here are some helping verbs:

be (all forms)	does	might
can	had	shall
could	has	should
did	have	will
do	may	would

> *Action:* Todd **blew** his horn.   (action verb)
>
> Todd **did blow** his horn.   (helping verb + action verb)
>
> *Nonaction:* form of "be"
>
> Todd **is** my brother.   (nonaction verb)
>
> Todd **has been** my brother.
>
> (helping verb + nonaction verb)

state of being

Todd **appears** happy.   (nonaction verb)

Todd **does appear** happy.

(helping verb + nonaction verb)

Sometimes forms of *do (do, does, did)* and *have (have, has, had)* are the main verb in a sentence; other times these forms are used with another main verb to form the simple verb.

Main verb: Todd **did** his homework.

Helping verb: Todd **did finish** his homework.

- **Compound verbs are two or more verbs that tell what the subject does.**

The man **looked** down and **found** a diamond ring.

The camel **ate** the apple and then **snorted**.

The following paragraph can help you understand how subjects, verbs, and prepositional phrases appear in writing. In the paragraph below, which you studied earlier, the verbs are underlined twice, the subjects are underlined once, and the prepositional phrases are in italics.

Many nineteenth-century Native Americans were expert horse trainers. *After a wild horse catch*, trainers often were able to break a horse *in one day*. They wrapped the lasso rope *around the horse's nose* and guided the horse *into water*. There one *of the young boys* mounted it. The horse, of course, began bucking, but after getting its head *under water* a few times, soon quit. Native Americans also trained special horses *for the buffalo hunt*. *With careful training*, these horses could be guided *to the left or right by the rider* who applied pressure *with his knees*. As a result, the hunter had both hands free *for his bow and arrow* and shot the buffalo *with ease*. Other horses were trained as war horses. These horses were also well trained. Sometimes they would even strike the enemy *with their hooves*. Consequently, Native Americans held their horses *in high esteem*.

Recognizing Sentence-Structure Errors

Learning to identify subjects and verbs in a sentence is a skill that can help you edit your writing. For example, you can find and revise sentence problems so that your ideas are expressed in clear and complete sentences. Examine three sentence-structure errors: sentence fragments, comma splices, and run-on sentences.

Sentence Fragments

To be complete, a sentence needs a subject and a main verb that together form a completed idea. If one or more of these parts are missing, then the sentence is a **fragment**. Consider the following example of a complete sentence:

People with loyalty for their country voted.

However, if you left out the verb, you would not have a complete sentence:

People with loyalty for their country.

Leaving out "voted" makes the idea a **fragment**. In all honesty, your readers could get some meaning, but they would not know the completed thought you wanted to express.

Likewise, if you left out the subject, "people," you would again have a fragment instead of a complete sentence:

With loyalty for their country voted.

Here are other examples of incomplete thoughts that would not work as sentences because one or more parts are missing:

Being honest and being loyal to each other.

Without these qualities for a friendship.

To make complete sentences out of these ideas, you could revise so that each idea has a subject and a verb and, therefore, is a completed thought.

Being honest and being loyal to each other are necessary for two people to be close friends.

Without these qualities for a friendship, two people might not be close friends.

Here is another kind of sentence fragment that would have to be recognized and revised:

When we first met in high school.

People who are loyal to their country.

"When we first met in high school" may sound all right because it has a subject and a verb, but the idea is still a fragment because "when" leaves the thought incomplete. The reader expects an explanation of what happened "when we first met in high school." Revised and completed, the thought might sound like this:

When we first met in high school, we did not think of each other as friends.

In the second sentence, "who" makes the sentence a fragment because the reader wants to know what happens when "people are loyal to their country." The completed thought could sound like this:

People who are loyal to their country probably vote.

Note This is a quick discussion of sentence fragments. Unit 4 provides more detailed help, including exercises.

You may have two other kinds of sentence problems that need to be eliminated: comma splices and run-on sentences.

Comma Splices

Comma splices are two complete sentences with just a comma to mark the end of one sentence and the beginning of the next.

The speed skater raced across the frozen lake, he ignored the thin ice.

Revised to indicate the end of the first sentence and the beginning of the next, the separated sentences would look like one of these:

The speed skater raced across the frozen lake. He ignored the thin ice.

The speed skater raced across the frozen lake, and he ignored the thin ice.

Note Unit 4 provides additional help and exercises to eliminate comma splices.

Run-On Sentences

Run-on sentences are two or more complete ideas with no punctuation or connecting words to mark the end of one sentence and the beginning of the next one.

The speed skater raced across the frozen lake he ignored the thin ice.

To eliminate the confusion of two ideas run together, you could mark the end of the first sentence with a comma and a connecting word, or you could use a period and start a new sentence with a capital letter. You might also use a semicolon if you are familiar with its use.

The speed skater raced across the frozen lake, and he ignored the thin ice.

The speed skater raced across the frozen lake. He ignored the thin ice.

The speed skater raced across the frozen lake; he ignored the thin ice.

Note Unit 4 provides additional help and exercises to eliminate run-on sentences.

These three kinds of sentence problems will cause confusion for your reader. Sometimes they are hard to find in your own writing, but reading aloud or getting some feedback from another reader will help you identify and eliminate these confusing sentence-structure errors.

■ Maintaining Subject-Verb Agreement

Test covering subject-verb agreement p. 30 in Instructor's Manual.

In addition to revising to eliminate sentence-structure problems, you will need to check for subject-verb agreement errors. All sentences must have both a subject and a verb that agree in number. In other words, they must both be singular (one) or must both be plural (more than one).

For example, consider the following sentences:

_S   _V
The dog likes to play in the sprinkler.

_S   _V
The dogs like to play in the sprinkler.

In the first sentence, "dog" (which is singular) agrees with "likes" (which is also singular). In the second sentence, "dogs" (which is plural) agrees with "like" (which is also plural).

Forming Plural Nouns

Most nouns are made plural by adding an *-s*. When in doubt about how to make a word plural, check your dictionary.

Singular	Plural
dog	dogs
book	books
car	cars
rock	rocks
plate	plates

Forming Plural Verbs

Adding *-s* to a noun makes it plural; however, adding *-s* to a verb makes it singular. Singular verbs should be used when the subject is a singular noun or one of the pronouns *she, he,* or *it.*

_S   _V
Incorrect: The book seem interesting.

_S   _V
Correct: The books seem interesting.

_S   _V
Correct: The book seems interesting.

_S _V
Correct: It seems interesting.

EXERCISE 5

In the following sentences, put parentheses ( ) around the prepositional phrases. Then underline the subject once and fill in the blank with the verb that agrees in number with the subject.

Example:

The lions (at the zoo) _____*sleep*_____ **peacefully. (sleep, sleeps)**

1. The flowers (in the vase) ___*need*___ water. (need, needs)

2. Many desert plants ___*grow*___ here. (grow, grows)

3. The lady at the information booth usually ___*knows*___ the answers. (know, knows)

4. The student fine arts magazine often ___*receives*___ many awards. (receive, receives)

5. The circus ___*brings*___ enjoyment (to all.) (bring, brings)

6. The kittens (in the box) ___*sleep*___ all day long. (sleep, sleeps)

7. The leader (of the group) ___*speaks*___ (at 7:00) tonight. (speak, speaks)

8. The girls ___*have*___ plans to visit Korea. (has, have)

9. The parents (of young children) ___*have*___ many responsibilities. (have, has)

10. The author (of the novel) ___*is*___ well known. (is, are)

11. All phases (of production) ___*are done*___ (by the students.) (is done, are done)

12. The dean (of students) ___*enjoys*___ the students. (enjoy, enjoys)

13. Steve ___*enjoys*___ going (to the lake.) (enjoy, enjoys)

14. The blue book (on the shelf) ___*illustrates*___ many home projects. (illustrate, illustrates)

15. The president (of the college) ___*speaks*___ (at 6:00) tonight. (speak, speaks)

16. The shirt (with silver stars) ___*belongs*___ to Sonia. (belong, belongs)

17. The puppies ___*play*___ (with each other.) (play, plays)

18. There _____*are*_____ many <u>tasks</u> to complete today. (is, are)

19. The <u>bags</u>(of groceries) *need* to be put away. (need, needs)

20. The <u>telephone</u> *rings* many times each day. (ring, rings)

EXERCISE 6

Put all prepositional phrases in parentheses ( ). Underline the subject once and the verb twice. Then change both the subject and the verb from singular to plural form.

Example:

geese   *bring*
The <s>goose</s> (with golden feathers) <s>brings</s> him fortune.

Geese swim
1. A <s>goose</s> <s>swims</s>(in the pond.)

cars appear
2. The <s>car</s> <s>appears</s> to be(out of gas.)

elephants   *eat*
3. The <s>elephant</s>(at the circus)<s>eats</s> hay.

men   *arrive*
4. The <s>man</s>(at the bank)<s>arrives</s> early every day.

men   *donate*
5. The <s>man</s>(at the counter)<s>donate</s>s many extra hours(of work.)

Pairs   *need*
6. A <s>pair</s>(of scissors)<s>needs</s> to be sharpened.

children   *listen*
7. The <s>child</s>(in the classroom)<s>listens</s>(to instructions.)

sheep graze
8. The <s>sheep</s> <s>grazes</s>(in the meadow.)

churches need
9. The <s>church</s> <s>needs</s> a new paint job.

Mice live
10. A <s>mouse</s> <s>lives</s>(in the basement.)

policies are
11. The U.S. economic <s>policy</s> <s>is</s> complicated.

deer   *are*
12. The <s>deer</s>(at the zoo)<s>is</s> very tame.

13. The ~~doctor works~~ *doctors work* (on cars) (in the evenings.)

14. The stained-glass ~~window~~ *windows* (in that old building) ~~is~~ *are* beautiful.

15. My ~~tax seems~~ *taxes seem* high.

16. The ~~child~~ *children* (on the bicycle) ~~likes~~ *like* to play tag.

17. The ~~leaf falls~~ *leaves fall* (from the tree) (onto the sidewalk.)

18. My ~~cat likes~~ *cats like* to climb (on the roof.)

19. The ~~box~~ *boxes* (on the top) (of the table) ~~weighs~~ *weigh* ten pounds.

20. The ~~horse~~ *horses* leisurely ~~grazes~~ *graze* (in the meadow.)

Checking for Subject-Verb Agreement

1. **Identify all prepositional phrases;** place them in parentheses.

2. **Identify the subject and verb** of each sentence; underline the subject once and the verb twice.

3. **Check whether the verb agrees in number with its subject.**

4. **If not, change the verb** to agree in number with the subject.

EXERCISE **7**

Put parentheses ( ) around each prepositional phrase. Underline each subject once. Then find the verb in each sentence, and, if necessary, correct it to agree in number with the subject. Write "C" to the left of the number if there is no error.

Example:

The children (in the preschool) ~~sings~~ *sing* happily.

1. The trees (by the lake) ~~provides~~ *provide* shade (for the campground.)

2. Blackberry bushes (with juicy fruit) ~~provides~~ *provide* food (for the animals.)

C 3. A <u>snake</u> moves (over the fallen leaves.)

4. A <u>squirrel</u> (with a mouthful)of nuts) *snatches* ~~snatch~~ one more (in her paws.)

5. (From high (in the trees,) <u>birds</u> continuously *sing* ~~sings~~ a cheerful song.

C 6. The <u>squirrels</u> drink (from the birdbath)under the trees.)

C 7. Heavy <u>rains</u> come occasionally (to the forest.)

C 8. Five <u>deer</u> walk (by the stream.)

9. Blue <u>herons</u> *are* ~~is~~ abundant (on the lakes)of northern Colorado.)

C 10. The changing <u>seasons</u> affect all (of the animals.)

11. <u>Hummingbirds</u> (with their long beaks) *drink* ~~drinks~~ (from feeders)suspended (between trees.)

12. <u>Pigeons</u> *feast* ~~feasts~~ (on the crumbs)left (on the ground.)

13. The blue <u>jays</u> *quarrel* ~~quarrels~~ (with one another.)

14. The <u>turtles</u> *walk* ~~walks~~ freely (through the forest.)

C 15. <u>Ferns</u> (of different shades)of green)grow wild.

16. The <u>coyote</u> *helps* ~~help~~ maintain the balance (of nature.)

17. (From inside the cabin,) a <u>child</u> *asks* ~~ask~~ to go outside.

C 18. The <u>people</u> (in the cabin)cause no alarm (to the young skunks.)

19. Not far away, <u>streams</u> (with clear water)*offer* ~~offers~~ a home (to trout.)

C 20. The baby <u>squirrels</u> race (up and down the trees.)

■ Recognizing Singular and Plural Pronouns

Because pronouns can be the subject of a sentence, it is helpful to know which pronouns are singular, which are plural, and which can be either singular or plural.

- **Some indefinite pronouns are always singular, even though we often think of them as plural.**

anybody	everybody	no one
anyone	everyone	nothing
anything	everything	somebody
each	neither	someone
each one	nobody	something
either		

```
s          v  v
```
Everything is working out quite well.

```
    s      v
```
No one wants to work late.

```
       v  s
```
There is something on the table for you.

- **When "each," "every," and "any" modify the subject, the verb is singular.**

```
     n         v  v
```
Each person is asked to contribute to the United Way.

```
     n            v
```
Any carpenter knows the answer.

- **Some pronouns are always plural.**

few

many

```
    s            v
```
A few of my friends are happy about the decision.

```
s       v
```
Many are willing to work.

- Some pronouns may be singular or plural. When these pronouns are immediately preceded by a prepositional phrase, the verb agrees with the prepositional phrase.

all	most
any	part
half	some

       s   v
Some (of the books) are very old.

       s   v
Some (of the candy) is on the table.

      s   v v
Most (of my homework) is finished.

      s   v
Most (of the boys) live in the dorm.

    s   v v
All (of the work) is completed.

    s   v v
All (of the assignments) are completed.

> *Noun:* name of a person, place, or thing
>
> *Pronoun:* word that takes the place of a noun
>
> *Verb:* word that tells what the subject of a sentence does
>
> *Subject:* word that tells who or what to the main verb in the sentence

EXERCISE 8

In the following sentences, put parentheses ( ) around the prepositional phrases. Then underline the subject once and fill in the blank with the verb that agrees in number with the subject.

Example:

Everyone (at the park) ___*endures*___ **the hot, humid weather.**
(endure, endures)

1. <u>Each</u> (of the players) ___*brings*___ a different strength (to the team.) (bring, brings)

2. Every <u>American</u> probably ___*watches*___ some kind (of baseball game) (during the year.) (watch, watches)

3. Each person (on the team) _____ *is* _____ expected to perform well. (is, are)

4. It seems as though everybody _____ *comes* _____ (to the fireworks display.) (come, comes)

5. Many (of the players) _____ *are* _____ paid well (for their work.) (is, are)

6. Someone (in the stands) _____ *yells* _____ (at the pitcher.) (yell, yells)

7. Few (of the fans) _____ *realize* _____ the pressure players are under. (realize, realizes)

8. Hundreds (of fireflies) _____ *glow* _____ in the evening. (glow, glows)

9. Some (of the players) actually _____ *feel* _____ underpaid. (feel, feels)

10. All (of the players) _____ *know* _____ the rules. (know, knows)

11. People _____ *enjoy* _____ baseball whether (at the ballpark) or (at home in front (of the television set.) (enjoy, enjoys)

12. Each play _____ *makes* _____ a difference (in the outcome (of the game.) (make, makes)

13. Nobody _____ *completes* _____ a task as well as Dan does. (complete, completes)

14. Nothing _____ *makes* _____ a team happier than winning. (make, makes)

15. Each one (of the students) _____ *completes* _____ the assignments (without problems) (complete, completes)

16. There _____ *is* _____ something special (about this team.) (is, are)

17. Few (of the fans) _____ *feel* _____ hostility (toward the players.) (feel, feels)

18. Most (of the players) _____ *practice* _____ many hours each day. (practice, practices)

19. Single parents _____ *need* _____ quiet time (for only themselves.) (need, needs)

20. Some (of the outfielders) _____ *cover* _____ a large area. (cover, covers)

EXERCISE 9

Put all prepositional phrases in parentheses ( ). Underline each subject once. Then find the verb in each sentence and, if necessary, correct it to agree in number with the subject. Write "C" to the left of the number if there is no error.

Example:

                         is

Each <u>person</u> (on the fishing boat) ~~are~~ guaranteed (at least) one fish.

                  plans

1. <u>Everybody</u> ~~plan~~ time to relax.

                      vote

2. <u>Half</u> (of the employees) ~~votes~~ (for overtime.)

                    is

3. <u>Nothing</u> (behind the fence) ~~are~~ worth keeping.

                 are

4. <u>Children</u> (in the pool) ~~is~~ supervised (by lifeguards.)

C 5. <u>Everyone</u> needs to spend time enjoying life.

C 6. <u>All</u> (of the planning) needs to be done early.

                stay

7. <u>Some</u> (of the campers) ~~stays~~ (in tents.)

                 stick

8. A <u>few</u> (of the blueberry muffins) ~~sticks~~ (to the pan.)

            are

9. <u>All</u> (of my friends) ~~is~~ going (on a picnic) (with their families.)

        spend

10. <u>Others</u> ~~spends~~ the day working (in the yard.)

                thinks

11. (Without a doubt,) <u>someone</u> ~~think~~ (of a good solution.)

C 12. Few <u>people</u> prefer chess (over baseball.)

            enjoy

13. <u>Children</u> often ~~enjoys~~ camping.

14. Nobody ~~enjoy~~ *enjoys* working all the time.

C 15. Many <u>men</u> become gourmet cooks.

16. <u>Each</u> (of the drivers) ~~need~~ *needs* more practice.

17. <u>Bookstores</u> ~~sells~~ *sell* books (for readers) (of all ages.)

C 18. <u>Everything</u> (from that factory) is made (of oak.)

19. Any <u>diversion</u> (from routine activities) ~~are~~ *is* rewarding.

C 20. Many <u>Taiwanese</u> know how to speak English.

EXERCISE 10

Master for the transparencies is in the Instructor's Manual.

Edit the following paragraphs for subject-verb agreement. Underline the subject(s) in each sentence once and the verb(s) twice. Then find any incorrect verb forms and correct them to agree in number with the subject.

Paragraph 1

<u>Kenting Park</u> <u><u>is</u></u> at the southernmost part of Taiwan. <u>It</u> <u><u>is</u></u> <u><u>surrounded</u></u> by a beach and high cliffs. Luxurious, high-priced <u>hotels</u> ~~is~~ *are* <u><u>available</u></u> for those able to afford approximately $200 a day. When beach <u>play</u> ~~are~~ *is* over, vendor <u>markets</u> with sea shells, costume jewelry, hats, and tourist trinkets <u>~~abounds~~</u> *abound*. The <u>park</u> north of the beach ~~have~~ *has* exotic, tropical plants. For example, a 300-year-old Bonsai-like <u>tree</u> with old exposed roots ~~<u><u>illustrate</u></u>~~ *illustrates* the coastal park's antiquity. In addition, a small <u>cave</u> with a stalactite forming an imaginative, fossil-like figure ~~<u><u>bring</u></u>~~ *brings* relief from the sun and ~~<u><u>offer</u></u>~~ *offers* the passing tourist a peaceful rest. <u>Kenting Park</u> <u><u>has</u></u> many attractions for visitors.

Paragraph 2

Early Native Americans used the buffalo wisely. They ate the meat fresh or dried it in strips to use

throughout the year. Some of the dried strips ~~was~~ *were* eaten the way they were, and other times they ~~was~~ *were*

ground into powder to be cooked. When the meat was scraped off the bones, the large bones ~~was~~ *were*

used for tools. Likewise, a few of the small bones ~~was~~ *were* made into needles. The skins of the buffalo ~~was~~ *were*

used for warm clothing, rugs, or coverings for their homes. Some history of the tribe ~~were~~ *was* written on

the dried buffalo skins. Even the sinews were saved to be used as thread, and the Native Americans

boiled the hooves to make glue. Very little of the buffalo was wasted.

Paragraph 3

The people in the jury assembly room ~~reports~~ *report* for jury duty in clothing that they ordinarily ~~wears~~ *wear*

to work. Several ~~looks~~ *look* like students or service workers. They ~~wears~~ *wear* casual dresses or sport shirts and

jeans. Some in work uniforms ~~appears~~ *appear* to be truck drivers or repair people. A large number of profes-

sional men and women ~~sits~~ *sit* in more formal suits. One gentleman apparently does not know the dress

code for jurors, and he ~~walk~~ *walks* around in shorts and a bright blue T-shirt. This scene is a good example of

the variety of people on juries.

Paragraph 4

When Americans visit England, they ~~is~~ *are* surprised to learn the many differences in "Yank" and

"Queen's" English. Britons do not understand the word "hose." Instead they ~~uses~~ *use* only "nylons."

Britons refer to the word "trousers" rather than to "pants." They ~~uses~~ *use* "pants" for "undergarments,"

which Americans call "undershorts." What Americans ~~calls~~ *call* "suspenders," Britons call "braces." A *are*

"T-shirt" is a "vest," and "galoshes" is "Wellingtons." Tourists in London may be astonished to learn

have

they has purchased the wrong garment.

■ Maintaining Consistent Verb Tense

Test over consistent verb tense p. 31 in Instructor's Manual.

Another important skill you can master once you can identify subjects and verbs is keeping verbs consistent in your writing. What does "consistent" mean in this case? Keeping two or more verbs in a sentence or paragraph consistent means keeping them in the same time or "tense"—most of the time, either in the **present tense** or the **past tense**.

Read the following sentences and note the **time** (tense) of each of the verbs.

> The old man **fished** in the lake every day. Even on rainy days, he **walks** to the lake and **throws** out his line at the same spot. He seldom **caught** a fish, but he never **stopped** going until he **broke** his fishing pole.

The description begins in the past tense ("fished") because all the events happened in the past. The last sentence clearly indicates this. The verbs in the second sentence, though, shift to the present tense ("walks" and "throws"). The present tense suggests to the reader that these events are still going on. The last sentence then moves back to the past tense. All the verbs should be in the past tense, so "walks" and "throws" would have to be changed to "walked" and "threw." All the sentences would then be a description of events in the past. Present-tense verbs would not be appropriate in this description because the man stopped going fishing when he broke his pole. These events are *not* happening now.

Here is the easiest revision to make to eliminate the verb shift:

> The old man **fished** in the lake every day. Even on rainy days, he **walked** to the lake and **threw** out his line at the same spot. He seldom **caught** a fish, but he never **stopped** going until he **broke** his pole.

Because all the verbs are now in the past tense, they are *consistent.*

Present-tense verbs are used to describe something that is still true in the present. For example, one way to show activities that are still going on regularly would be to use the present tense consistently to describe these events. If the old man *had not broken* his pole, he might still be fishing *regularly.*

> The old man **fishes** in the lake every day. Even on rainy days, he **walks** to the lake and **throws** out his line at the same spot. He seldom **catches** a fish, but he never **stops** going.

Using the present tense *consistently* in this way would be appropriate. Your writing will be clearer and will convey your ideas more accurately if you make an effort to use the right time signals for your reader. One such signal is consistent verb tense that is appropriate for your intended meaning.

> ### *Checking Consistent Verb Tense*
>
> 1. **Find the first verb in a paragraph**, and determine whether it is in the present tense or the past tense.
>
> 2. **Check whether all other verbs in the paragraph are in the same tense** as the first verb.
>
> 3. **If not, change the verbs** so that they are all in the same tense.

Note   A list of irregular verbs can be found in Appendix C.

E X E R C I S E 11   *Master for transparency is in the Instructor's Manual.*

Identify the tense of the verb in the first sentence as either present or past, and then make the remaining sentences match that tense.

Paragraph 1

Tense: *present*

A computer virus frequently creates many frustrating moments for users. With no better motive

than harassment, a hacker creates just one program that transfers itself onto an unsuspecting person's

floppy disk. Some viruses ~~destroyed~~ *destroy* data files, ~~locked~~ *lock* up computers, ~~made~~ *make* text fall to the bottom of

the screen, or ~~kept~~ *keep* a computer from booting. In any case, viruses often ~~appeared~~ *appear* at the worst time and

rapidly ~~infiltrated~~ *infiltrate* system networks, resulting in great expense. It is unfortunate that a hacker's exper-

tise is put to destructive rather than constructive use.

Paragraph 2

Tense: *present*

David's best friend is Stormy, his pet dog. Every night she goes to bed with him and ~~stayed~~ *stays* with

him until he gets up the next morning. She sits outside the shower door until he is finished. She also

eats breakfast with him and then sees him off at the front door. After school they ~~played~~ *play* catch or ~~raced~~ *race* through the yard. She always knows when things ~~bothered~~ *bother* him, and she gently ~~showered~~ *showers* him with

"kisses." She becomes his audience when he ~~practiced~~ *practices* his piano or his companion as he builds his

Lego structures. They even ~~shared~~ *share* an afternoon snack of cheese and crackers. Best of all, they are

always there for each other.

Paragraph 3

Tense: *present*

Senior citizens receive many recreational opportunities by living in retirement communities.

Retired men and women ~~attended~~ *attend* craft classes that range from needlecraft to woodwork. Community

members ~~frequented~~ *frequent* one or more recreational halls that are usually equipped with pool tables and

shuffleboard courts. In the evenings, they ~~stayed~~ *stay* busy attending dances or parties. They ~~received~~ *receive*

exercise in indoor or outdoor swimming pools, depending on the specific region of the country.

Fervent golfers ~~teed~~ *Tee* off on well-manicured greens or ~~played~~ *play* tennis on clean courts any time of the day.

No matter what activity people enjoy, they find many others who ~~enjoyed~~ *enjoy* doing the same type of

things.

Paragraph 4

Tense: *present*

A large city like San Francisco offers visitors many kinds of exciting activities. If someone ~~wanted~~ *wants*

to attend sporting events, a large city usually has college basketball and football teams as well as

professional basketball and football teams. If visitors ~~did~~ *do* not care for sports, perhaps museums ~~filled~~ *fill*

the bill. A large city usually has art museums as well as historical and scientific museums. For the visitor

who ~~liked~~ *likes* shopping, the large city ~~provided~~ *provides* a range of stores from small specialty shops to large department stores. Since San Francisco is near the water, it ~~offered~~ *offers* fishing, a harbor cruise, surfing, an

aquarium, and other waterfront activities. Theaters and night clubs also ~~gave~~ *give* visitors a chance to

experience evening entertainment they ~~did~~ *do* not have at home. A large city usually gives an out-of-town

visitor a wide range of activities for excitement and fun.

When you edit and revise your writing, do not try to eliminate all the problems at the same time. Read for one kind of difficulty at a time.

To check for verb consistency in your own writing, read the first sentence in your paragraph. What tense is the verb? Are you describing or discussing an event that happened in the past? Are you talking about something in the future or the present? Make the verbs in the rest of the paragraph consistent with the time established in that first sentence.

Concentrate on the time signals as you read from sentence to sentence. Add other appropriate "time" words ("yesterday" or "last week" or "ten years ago" or "tomorrow" or "now" or "currently") that will clarify meaning for the reader.

The extra **time** spent on **tense** will pay off!

WRITING ASSIGNMENT

Freewrite or brainstorm on one of the following activities that you have done. In one paragraph, explain what you like or dislike *about:*

1. Going to a concert
2. Visiting a relative
3. Walking through a cemetery
4. Watching a fireworks display
5. Shopping at the mall
6. Riding a bus
7. Driving a car
8. Eating at home
9. Eating out
10. Playing a musical instrument

Note   Do not narrate a story or explain how to do this activity. Rather, relate what you like or dislike about the activity.

After you draft your paragraph, revise for content and edit for mechanics.

Content

Revise it so it has a clear topic sentence.

Include four to six supporting sentences.

Include a closing sentence.

Mechanics

~~Check for subject-verb agreement.~~

Check for consistent verbs.

UNIT 3

Being a Sensitive Writer

PART 1

PARTS TO WHOLE: INTERACTION OF TOPIC, PURPOSE, AUDIENCE, AND VOICE

OBJECTIVES

- Understand the interaction of topic, purpose, audience, and voice.
- Identify topic, purpose, audience, and voice in a given situation.
- Identify changes in wording needed when writing for different audiences.
- Compose paragraphs with predetermined topic, purpose, audience, and voice.
- Revise a paragraph when one of the four elements has been changed.

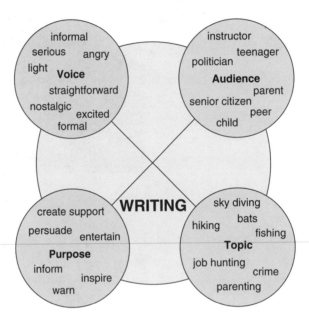

The diagram labeled "writing" shows the interaction of topic, purpose, voice, and audience within your writing. **Topic** is the subject or focus of your paper and helps to establish your **purpose**, which is essentially your reason for writing the paper. The purpose for writing your paper and your **audience**, the intended reader, determine what voice you use. **Voice** is the way the author "sounds" to the reader. If any one of these is ignored, miscommunication occurs, and the message can be misunderstood.

The following example shows how this miscommunication can occur. Dr. Wilson Riles, a well-known California educator, quoted a father who received the following note from his son's principal:

> Our schools' cross-graded, multi-ethnic, individualized learning program is designed to enhance the concept of an open-ended learning program with emphasis on a continuum of multi-ethnic, academically enriched learning, using the identified intellectually gifted child as the agent or director of his own learning.

According to Riles, the father replied with his own note:

> I have a college degree, speak two foreign languages and four Indian dialects, have been to a number of county fairs and three goat ropings, but I haven't the faintest idea as to what the hell you are talking about. Do you?

The principal had a purpose and topic but ignored his voice and his audience. Consequently, misunderstanding and anger occurred. The father also had a topic and purpose, but he considered his voice and audience. He used a straightforward, clear, yet angry voice to achieve his purpose — communicating the principal's failure to explain clearly what his message was.

The note written by the principal seems pretentious and to be written with the purpose of impressing the father rather than communicating with him. The father, on the other hand, responds simply and honestly, and his son's principal probably got the message.

How do you want your reader to respond to what you have to say? If your purpose for writing is to entertain, then you want your reader to react lightheartedly. If your purpose is to inform, you want your reader to take you seriously and to have a clear understanding of your message. If your purpose is to persuade, you may want your reader to take some action or to acknowledge a problem.

To review, then, here are the four elements of writing:

Topic: focus of the paper

Purpose: reason for writing the paper

Audience: intended reader

Voice: way writing "sounds" to the reader

The following situations show how topic, purpose, audience, and voice work together.

Situation 1

Mr. Latham has worked hard at his job as a newspaper editor for six years. He has demonstrated creativity and journalistic talent. In those years, he has received favorable evaluations but not a significant raise. He is writing a memo to his boss to convince him that he deserves a raise.

Topic: Mr. Latham's raise

Purpose: inform and persuade boss to give him a raise

Audience: Mr. Latham's boss

Voice: formal, polite, respectful, yet forceful

Situation 2

Mary Jones is a nurse in an elementary school. Recently a measles epidemic has swept through the community. Ms. Jones is responsible for the health and well-being of the children. Therefore, she is writing a notice to be taken home to explain to the children and their parents why the children must be vaccinated and why it is important not to be afraid to have this done.

Topic: measles vaccination

Purpose: inform them of the facts; persuade them to participate

Audience: children and parents

Voice: simple but serious, knowledgeable

Situation 3

Tessie's friend has just had a skiing accident that has kept her from trying out for the Winter Olympics. Tessie is going to write her friend a note to let her know what has happened at school while she was gone.

Topic: school activities

Purpose: entertain with funny happenings to cheer her up

Audience: Tessie's friend

Voice: humorous, light, sincere, informal

Each of these situations is going to require clear, effective communication to make the writing accomplish the desired purpose. To get the message to the audience, consider how topic, purpose, audience, and voice interact. Try working through the following exercise with this interaction in mind.

EXERCISE 1

Read the following situations and then identify the topic, purpose, audience, and voice. If you wish, use the diagram at the beginning of the chapter for types of words you can use.

Situation 1

A young man has just been offered a job at another company with more benefits and salary. He needs to write a letter to his current employer notifying him of his resignation. However, he wants to leave with an option to return if necessary.

Topic: _resignation_

Purpose: _notification of resignation with option to return to current employment_

Audience: _boss_

Voice: _serious, honest, sincere_

Situation 2

A college student living in a campus dorm has failed one class during her first semester. She has to write a note to her parents because she knows her grade report is being mailed home.

Topic: *bad grades*

Purpose: *appease parents, justify grades*

Audience: *parents*

Voice: *serious, witty, humble, apologetic*

Situation 3

Jane Culver has just learned that her friend recently lost her mother. She sits down to write her a note.

Topic: *death of friend's mother*

Purpose: *show sympathy, understanding*

Audience: *friend*

Voice: *personal, serious, warm, comforting*

Situation 4

Beverly received a ticket for not stopping at a stop sign. Because she lived out of state, she could not conveniently keep the court date, so she wrote to the judge to see if she could settle the matter through correspondence.

Topic: *appearance in court to settle ticket*

Purpose: *settle the situation by mail*

Audience: *traffic judge*

Voice: *factual, sincere, serious, formal*

Situation 5

You have just been hired by a retail store that specializes in compact disks (CDs). The store is expanding its market to include a Filipino store. Your task is to write a simple, brief explanation of what a compact disk is and how much better it sounds than a tape. Your memo will be translated and used to win the Filipino consumer.

Topic: *compact disks*

Purpose: *to sell compact disks*

Audience: *Filipino business dealers and other consumers*

Voice: *persuasive, informative, clear, simple*

Situation 6

Mr. and Mrs. Rosco have just been made directors of an organization called Student Venture. Its mission is to make parents of teens aware of the growing problem of suicide and alcoholism in the neighborhood and to provide assistance for those who feel they need it. They decide to send a letter to parents in the area to invite them for coffee and discussion.

Topic: *the organization*
Purpose: *to discuss problems and organization*
Audience: *parents*
Voice: *factual, serious, concerned, friendly*

As you become a more experienced writer, you will become more aware of how you can adjust your writing to suit topic, purpose, audience, and voice. You will be more aware of how these elements all work together to convey ideas effectively.

Topic and Purpose Influence Voice

Often the **topic** may be given to you, or you may find it fairly soon when brainstorming or freewriting. If so, you might know right away how you want your **voice** to sound to your audience. For example, it would be difficult to write a humorous paper about cancer or AIDS. You would probably want to sound serious so your reader would take you seriously. On the other hand, if you were writing about dieting, you might want to sound lighthearted rather than serious.

Sometimes topic and **purpose** for writing may come to you almost simultaneously. If your topic were cancer, for instance, you might soon discover that you wanted to persuade your audience to have annual physical checkups. To be *persuasive*, you would certainly want your writing voice to sound knowledgeable and convincing. If you wanted to *inform* your reader about facts concerning AIDS, you would want to sound honest and informed. If you were writing about dieting, you might want to *inform and entertain* the reader at the same time. Then your writing voice could be informative as well as humorous. As you gain experience in writing, you will learn to choose a writing voice that is appropriate for the topic and purpose you have identified.

Purpose and Audience Influence Voice

Frequently, purpose and audience seem to interact and become major influences on voice. After you have chosen a topic and have identified a purpose, you should ask yourself, "Who is my **audience**?" If you wanted to persuade children to do something, you would use words that children could understand. If you wanted to entertain your peers, you would choose words that would be appropriate for this situation. If you were writing to someone in authority over you because you needed that person to do something for you, you most certainly would choose your words carefully so that your purpose could be accomplished.

Read the following notes, each written to a different person and with a different audience in mind. In the first note, the topic for the writer is permission to make up a quiz. The audience is the instructor, so the purpose is to persuade the instructor to allow the student to make up the quiz. Consequently, the student's voice is polite, somewhat formal, and respectful. In the student's note to the instructor, the italicized words show how words were chosen that sounded appropriate for the situation.

Note to Teacher

Ms. Mathews:

Please accept my apology for being absent on Friday, November 8. I stayed up very late the night before doing *some homework* that I was having *a hard time understanding*. *Consequently*, I overslept the next morning. *Please allow me* to make up the quiz that was given. *I will try* to catch up with the class by *borrowing the notes* from someone in the class.

Thank you.

In a second note, the purpose is the same—to persuade someone to do something. However, because the topic and the audience are different, the voice has changed to match the situation. The topic is missed lecture notes, and the audience is a fellow student. So the voice is informal, friendly, and honest. In the student's note to a friend, the italicized words show how words were chosen to sound informal—simpler phrasing throughout sounds less formal and more appropriate for the fellow student.

Note to Friend

Carla, I *missed math* yesterday because I overslept. Bill came over, and after he left, I still had to do my biology homework. The *stuff* was so hard I had a hard time reading it, and I stayed up until 2:00 this morning studying. I left a note on Ms. Mathews's door *asking her to let me make up the quiz* we had. *Anyhow*, I told Ms. Mathews I would borrow the notes from someone in the class, *so can you let me borrow yours*?

Word Choice Alters Voice

The preceding two notes show how word choice changed when the audience changed. The note to the student also shows how changing the words made the voice sound very different. Word choice will probably determine whether or not you get your message across. Making poor word choices and not writing for the appropriate audience can distract the reader so much that the message you intended to convey is missed. Recall the earlier situation:

Mr. Latham has worked hard at his job as a newspaper editor for six years. He has demonstrated creativity and journalistic talent. In those years, he has received favorable evaluations but not a significant raise. He is writing a memo to his boss to convince him that he deserves a raise.

Consider the following two memos written by Mr. Latham to his boss. The words used in each memo will affect the boss in very different ways, even though both are written for the same purpose of requesting a raise. The words in italics show how the voice sounds to Mr. Latham's boss.

Memo 1 to Boss

Dear Mr. Stevens,

As you well know, I have worked for this company for six years as a newspaper editor. *Obviously* you haven't *seemed to notice* that *you owe me a raise*. You *can't help but notice* that I have received favorable evaluations, and it is *long past time to give me a raise*. I have gotten awards, but these awards *don't help me pay my bills any easier. I am sick and tired* of watching other people get raises instead of me. Everyone else thinks that I am doing a good job, so *what is wrong with you*?

In this first memo, Mr. Latham uses words like "obviously" and "you owe me a raise" that distract his boss from hearing a fair request for a raise. Instead, Mr. Stevens is going to feel angry and upset that one of his employees has the nerve to use a condescending, demanding voice. Now read the second memo.

Memo 2 to Boss

Dear Mr. Stevens,

I have worked for this company for six years as an *effective newspaper editor* and have devoted these years to quality work. In this time, I have watched the circulation of this newspaper grow tremendously. I have never missed a deadline, and during the time that I have been here, I have received two awards, one of which was authorized by you. My evaluations reflect a *hardworking, serious employee*. I plan to continue with the same dedicated performance. At the same time, I hope that you will *seriously consider my request for a raise in pay*.

In this memo, Mr. Latham has changed his voice by putting in different information. He has used more factual information about his job and about the newspaper. This second memo is directed toward ideas that highlight his own ability or performance. In the first memo, the emphasis was on accusing the boss of wrongdoing. In the second memo, however, word choices like "effective newspaper editor" and "hardworking, serious employee" emphasize Mr. Latham's performance and enhance his image. His voice, then, is polite rather than arrogant or nervy.

Which memo do you think is more likely to accomplish its purpose? Clearly, the second memo is more appropriate for the purpose intended by the writer. It is also important to know that words cannot only create negative feelings but can also create negative images. For instance, if you describe a chair as being a "dull, drab green," the chair may be perceived as being ugly. On the other hand, if you describe the chair as being "bright, leaf-green," the chair is probably perceived as being attractive. These word choices are very important because the negative words result in a negative voice, whereas the positive words result in a positive voice.

A positive voice (like Mr. Latham's in memo 2) is more apt to get the message across because the reader is not distracted by negative or offensive words. Making word changes to suit the purpose and audience is an important goal of revision.

Now it is time to get some practice in creating different voices — whether angry, humorous, sad, or informative.

E X E R C I S E   2

Read the following sentences and then write words to describe the voice or voices reflected by each statement.

Example:

a. Shawn was so perceptive that he understood what I was saying.

Voice/s: *positive, praising*

b. Shawn weaseled the information from me.

Voice/s: *angry, resentful*

c. Shawn obtained the information from me.

Voice/s: *formal, neutral*

1. a. That shirt is yellow.

   Voice/s: *formal, neutral*

   b. That shirt is a bright, sunny color.

   Voice/s: *positive, praising*

   c. That shirt is a drab off-yellow.

   Voice/s: *a put-down, offensive*

2. a. The surfers rode the waves gracefully.

   Voice/s: *pleasant, positive*

   b. Many surfers fought for wave space.

   Voice/s: *negative, intense*

   c. The sunrise caught the patiently waiting surfers.

   Voice/s: *poetic, calm, positive*

   d. At the inept lifeguard's insistence, the surfers dragged their boards from the water and stormed to their cars.

   Voice/s: *angry, hostile*

3. a. Joe was hired for the job.

   Voice/s: *neutral*

   b. Joe's sharp thinking during the interview got him the job.

   Voice/s: *positive, complimentary*

   c. Joe got the job in spite of his muddled answers during the interview.

   Voice/s: *negative, derogatory*

4. a. The master of ceremonies rambled and made few points.

        Voice/s: *negative, critical*

    b. The master of ceremonies was inspirational and motivational.

        Voice/s: *positive, praising*

    c. The master of ceremonies gave a brief talk.

        Voice/s: *neutral, factual*

    d. The master of ceremonies made sarcastic responses to the audience.

        Voice/s: *critical, negative*

5. a. I often think of the kindness that woman extended to me as a child.

        Voice/s: *nostalgic, positive*

    b. That woman took me, a poor child, to her store and helped me select any new clothes I wanted as an Easter gift.

        Voice/s: *complimentary, positive*

    c. When I was a child, the women's organization dumped used, outdated clothes on me.

        Voice/s: *negative, offensive*

    d. On Easter morning, I admired my new clothes in the mirror and then skipped lightly down the hall.

        Voice/s: *light, appreciative, positive*

6. a. The middle-aged woman smiled appreciatively when the award was bestowed on her.

        Voice/s: *positive, happy, proud*

    b. The dumpy-looking woman in her late thirties smiled secretively as she grabbed the award.

        Voice/s: *negative, offensive*

    c. The austere woman tried hard to keep her composure when she realized she had been selected for such a prestigious award.

        Voice/s: *understanding, formal*

7. a. The young people wolfed down their food as though they had not eaten in a week.

        Voice/s: *offensive, rude*

    b. The young people ate heartily, enjoying everything that had been prepared.

        Voice/s: *positive, light, appreciative*

    c. The young people savored the food that had been prepared, much as their parents had done many years before.

        Voice/s: *nostalgic, factual, informative, formal*

    d. The young people had the food thrown at them as if they were animals.

        Voice/s: *negative*

8. a. Robert, stop that nonsense and report to the manager's office immediately.

        Voice/s: *threatening, serious*

    b. Robert, when you finish what you are doing, will you please come to the manager's office?

        Voice/s: *polite, respectful*

c. The crowded, stuffy manager's office reminded me of my cellar.

Voice/s: *factual, negative*

d. The bright, cheery posters on the wall of the manager's office reflect a warm atmosphere.

Voice/s: *inviting, pleasant*

EXERCISE 3

Read the following sentences and then revise them to reflect the new voice given.

Example:

The building was tan. *(neutral)*

The building was painted in earth-tones.

(positive)

The building was painted a boring tan.

(negative)

1. I remember the hillside covered with Texas bluebonnets. *(nostalgic)*

The Texas bluebonnets that covered the hillside made my

(negative) *allergies worse.*

Texas bluebonnets covered the hill.

(neutral)

2. She drove carefully and cautiously. *(positive)*

She skidded down the mountain with her foot on the brake

(negative) *pedal.*

She frantically gripped the steering wheel as the car moved

(scary) *faster and faster down the mountain.*

3. I remember the long, graceful skirts my grandmother wore. *(nostalgic)*

My grandmother's mini-skirt was disgusting.

(negative)

Look at my grandmother's beautiful mini-skirt.

(excited)

4. The people's excited chatter grew louder as the beginning moment for the concert drew near. *(positive)*

The rude concert audience pushed and yelled obscenities.

(negative)

The golden oldies echoed through the park as people recalled college memories.

(nostalgic)

5. The future of our nation depends on the integrity of every citizen. *(formal, serious)*

We are making the world into a stench ball.

(angry)

Don't people realize we have all pitched in to save the environment?

(informal)

6. The food served at that restaurant was moldy and unappetizing. *(negative)*

Umbrella drinks, chopsticks, and exotic flavors bring customers back to the China Inn.

(excited)

The best restaurant in town is the China Inn.

(positive)

7. The blue car had been in the parking lot for three days. *(neutral, informative)*

"Old Blue" rusted away in the corner of the car lot.

(nostalgic)

Please be advised that no cars are allowed overnight in the parking lot.

(polite)

8. The ecstatic players on the soccer team jumped up and down, celebrating victory. *(enthusiastic)*

The opposing team scowled at the referee and angrily shook the hands of their opponents.

(angry)

The game was a show of poor sportsmanship, inept coaching and no game strategy.

(negative)

9. The little boy was covered with gooey chocolate. *(nostalgic, humorous)*

Bratty Johnny deliberately smeared chocolate on himself.
(angry)

The small boy enjoyed the texture and the taste of the chocolate.
(positive)

10. Turn on the light! *(angry)*

Please turn on the light.
(polite)

Hurry and turn on the light!
(frightened)

Maintaining the *same voice* within a paragraph or an entire essay is also an important goal of revision. To help you extend your ability to create and keep a consistent voice, try working through the following exercises to see how all of these elements work together to form a paragraph that will accomplish its purpose.

EXERCISE 4

Read the following paragraphs and identify the topic, audience, and voice. The purpose for each is given.

Paragraph 1

Purpose: to share information about himself and his present conflict

I often wonder what my future life will be. I live on the reservation near Indian Wells, where my little brother and I spend time in the summer taking care of the sheep and the small field of corn that my family owns. In the wintertime, I go to school away from the reservation, and when I am at Lakeside Community College, I still think of the quiet hours we spend watching the sheep eat the little sprigs of grass and weeds. As we work in the corn, we talk about what will happen when I get out of school. He will still be at home and thinks that living in the city all the time will not be good for me. We would have no peaceful times together with the sheep anymore. We couldn't walk down the corn rows and feel the earth. I wish I could live in the city and still have a flock of sheep and a field of corn.

Topic: *personal conflict about the future*
Audience: *counselor, friend, teacher*
Voice: *nostalgic, sad*

Paragraph 2

Purpose: to inform and encourage people not to go to Crestview Mall

For the first time in my life, I feel that writing a letter to a newspaper is necessary. Yesterday I was walking through Crestview Shopping Mall and saw the traditional bell-ringer from the Salvation Army. As I approached, a man suddenly stopped by the woman ringing the bell and told her she would have to leave the mall because no solicitors were allowed there. What is this country coming to when a volunteer seeking help for the less fortunate in our city is not allowed to stand by a store? The bell-ringer represents the spirit of giving that, from my point of view, has just about disappeared from the holiday season. The merchants want all the dollars they can get from us, but they have forgotten the original meaning of Christmas. I for one will not patronize Crestview Mall to buy presents for my family!

Topic: ban on Christmas bell-ringers
Audience: general population
Voice: angry, factual

Paragraph 3

Purpose: to inform and persuade the fire department to admit Shawn Stevens to its training academy

To Whom It May Concern:

Everyone realizes the extreme importance of the qualities a firefighter must possess. On behalf of Shawn Stevens, I would like to make you aware of his ability to do the job of a firefighter. His strongest asset is his dedication. He has shown an ability to commit himself with great self-discipline. For example, five years ago Shawn decided to build his body and has put in the time and energy on a routine basis to achieve that goal. Also, Shawn has experienced panic situations and has remained clear-headed. As a lifeguard for the City of Phoenix, he rescued four near-drowning victims. He knows how to administer CPR and how to react in an emergency. Finally, Shawn has demonstrated leadership. As a swim instructor, he taught approximately two hundred youths to swim, and as a swim coach he directed and inspired several youths on his team to work hard and achieve their swimming goals. Dedication, calmness in an emergency, and leadership are three qualities I imagine you would like your firefighters to possess. I recommend Shawn Stevens because he has proven he has all these characteristics.

Sincerely,
Rebecca Ivans, English Instructor and Counselor

Topic: job recommendation, qualifications of Shawn Stevens
Audience: fire department employer
Voice: formal, perceptive, sincere, persuasive

Paragraph 4

Purpose: to interest people in a vacation to Hong Kong

Have you ever wished to get away from the familiar? Are you ready for an exotic environment full of excitement and cultural diversity? If so, consider visiting beautiful Hong Kong. There, you will find a shopping paradise. Leather, silks, jewelry, and fine china will delight almost anyone's taste. A variety of cuisines including tropical fruits, vegetables, and unusual fish dishes are reminders of how Hong Kong has merged the Far East with the Western world. For an adventure of a lifetime, consider this enchanting city for your next vacation!

Topic: *vacation in Hong Kong*
Audience: *travel customers*
Voice: *excited, positive, upbeat*

Now that you have thought about all the factors needed to get your point across to someone, you are ready to practice writing paragraphs that require thought about topic, purpose, audience, and voice.

EXERCISE 5

Using the topic, purpose, audience, and voice described below, draft a paragraph that reflects the four elements in either A or B. Revise each paragraph to create the most effective voice for the intended purpose. (You may wish to prewrite on other paper first.)

Paragraph 1

A.

Topic:	providing child-care facilities at work
Purpose:	to improve working conditions for parents with small children
Audience:	supervisors
Voice:	honest, factual

B.

Topic:	providing child-care facilities at work
Purpose:	to explain the advantages of these new facilities to parents with small children
Audience:	parents
Voice:	informative, persuasive, upbeat

_____

_____

_____

_____

_____

_____

Paragraph 2

A.

    Topic: improved technology for physically challenged students

  Purpose: to inform the school what they need to provide

Audience: school board

    Voice: authoritative, factual, persuasive

B.

    Topic: improved technology for physically challenged students

  Purpose: to convince citizens that taxes need to be raised

Audience: parents

    Voice: persuasive, factual

_____

_____

_____

_____

_____

_____

_____

Now, as you continue writing, you can be more conscious of and sensitive to your audience so that you can achieve the purpose of your writing. Because voice often determines what kind of attitude the reader has while reading the paper, you can communicate more effectively by selecting the right words.

Collaborative Project: Working and Learning Together

Divide into groups of three. Select one of the following situations. Collaboratively write a short note to the audience based on voice 1, 2, or 3. Then share the notes with the rest of the class.

Situation 1: A company with mandatory overtime for its assembly-line workers has reduced overtime pay from $20 an hour to $15 an hour.

Voice 1: Supervisor to all employees

Voice 2: Supervisor to friend who is scheduled to work twenty hours of overtime

Voice 3: Supervisor to the president

Situation 2: A bond issue for an elementary school district did not pass. Budgets will have to be cut, and the computer labs for the schools will not be completed.

Voice 1: Teachers to students

Voice 2: School board to parents

Voice 3: Parents to the newspaper

Situation 3: A sixteen-year-old borrows her boyfriend's parents' car and dents the fender in an accident.

Voice 1: Young woman to her boyfriend

Voice 2: Young woman to her boyfriend's parents

Voice 3: Young woman to the insurance company

Situation 4: Julie has just moved out of her apartment, and the manager refuses to refund her security deposit even though she has cleaned the apartment thoroughly. She needs the security deposit to buy her college textbooks.

Voice 1: Julie to the apartment manager

Voice 2: Julie to one of her teachers

Voice 3: Julie to the Better Business Bureau

PART 2

SOMETHING TO THINK ABOUT, SOMETHING TO WRITE ABOUT

Getting Off the Roller Coaster

Jerry L. Palmer, *former Utility Worker First-Class, Palo Verde Nuclear Generating Station, presently studying to be a rehabilitation counselor for alcoholics*

1   "Hi, my name is Jerry, and I'm an alcoholic." I'll never forget the day I stood up and said that. It was not easy after twenty years of being an alcoholic to change my life around, yet there I stood at Chit Chat Rehabilitation Hospital saying those words to Group Ten, the support group of twelve people who helped me understand what alcohol did to me. These people, along with the doctor, helped me, a very depressed and insecure person, take the first step on the road back to recovery. However, in order to recover, I had to turn my life completely around emotionally, physically, mentally, and socially.

2   Emotionally, life as an alcoholic is a roller coaster ride. The only problem is the ride never ends. When I was high, I felt more confident, more relaxed, and happier. I could make everyone laugh, and I was always the life of the party. I would never think of going to a party unless I was high on something. But, when I was down, I was very shy, very insecure, and very depressed. I was afraid of life, responsibility, and most people. I needed a crutch in life, and I found it in alcohol. I kept that crutch for twenty years or more. Then on Sunday, April 10, 1986, I found my world closing in around me. I was very unhappy and totally confused about my life. I didn't know which way to turn or whom to turn to. I told my wife I was going to check out of this world and today was just as good as any other day. It was very clear to my wife that I was headed toward a nervous breakdown. The next day my wife had me admitted into Chit Chat Rehab Hospital. Chit Chat was different from the usual twenty-eight-day rehab hospital. At Chit Chat I had to stay until the doctors said I could go home. I didn't know it then, but my life was about to change.

3   When I entered the hospital ward at Chit Chat, the first rule I was taught was that to make the mind healthy, I must first make the body healthy. That meant that before I could start their program and be physically able to handle all the pressure, all the alcohol in my body had to be removed. I spent eight agonizing days in that dreadful hospital ward while my body became accustomed to functioning without alcohol in it. I went through terrible withdrawal (because of the drugs inside me) the first three days, and though I tried, I just could not keep anything down. The fourth day the sweating and shaking stopped, and I had lost eleven pounds. Still I wouldn't eat. All I wanted was a drink of alcohol. I knew without alcohol or drugs in my system I could not function. The doctors told me that alcohol and drugs were the reason that my family put me in there, and if I didn't start eating, they would have no other choice but to force-feed me. I was really determined to get out of that hospital, but at last I realized that no matter what I did or said I wasn't going anywhere. So on the eighth day I stopped fighting them and started eating. I had taken my first step.

4   When I went through detoxification and had all the alcohol and drugs removed from my body, it was like waking up from a twenty-year sleep. Even though the alcohol and drugs were out of my system, mentally I was still sick. When I tried to remember things about my life, I found out I couldn't. I didn't realize that while

I was under the influence of alcohol, I was just existing in this world. Sure, I knew a lot of things, but I didn't know anything about me as a person. When I had started drinking alcohol, I had stopped thinking about myself. All I thought about was getting that next drink; mentally I had stopped growing. I was so thankful that the doctors and the people of Group Ten were there to help me when reality set in and I had that nervous breakdown. Without them, I would have never made it, emotionally or mentally, through one of the hardest times of my life. They helped me turn my life completely around by showing me how to get off and stay off that roller coaster ride, how to believe in myself as a person, how to deal with the pressure when I become nervous and shy around people, and how being myself is more fulfilling than trying to be someone I am not. It took a lot of tears, argument, and hard work to pull me through, but I made it. I was the only black person in that hospital; therefore, I was called "The Soul Survivor." They used a lot of tricks on me that kept me emotionally and mentally strong. They really cared about me, and I knew it.

5   Except for a two-hour visit each Saturday from my family, for seven months the people at Chit Chat were the only people I came in contact with. They told me that changing socially would be very difficult, especially toward family and friends. Socially all my friends were alcoholics. If they didn't drink, I didn't want to hang around them. I have four brothers who are all alcoholics. I knew that if I wanted to stay sober, I had to get away from all of them. It really hurt me to say good-bye to everyone, but I did, and I moved my family out West to Phoenix, Arizona. Out here in Phoenix, I have a new start in life, and my family has adjusted very well to the changes that they had to make. Though I travel back East once a year at Superbowl time to visit Harve, my only friend back home who doesn't drink, I still don't have the confidence in myself to be around my brothers and other friends when they are drinking. So, I sneak in and out of town without anyone knowing I am there. For now, even though it hurts me deep down inside, I know for me to stay sober things must stay this way. Some day, one day, I hope to be able to go home for a visit.

6   Every day I continue to fight a disease that took twenty years out of my life the same way someone would take a bite out of an apple. It is a disease that a lot of people know about, but only a few really understand. I must live with the fact that this disease will never die inside me until the day I die. This disease is called alcoholism. "Hi, my name is Jerry, and I'm an alcoholic, but I've been sober for three years."

▮ Understanding Words

Briefly define the following word as it is used in the above essay.

1. detoxification   *The removal of the effects of poison or drugs*

▮ Something to Write About

Write a paragraph on one of the following topics. Before you draft your paragraph, however, have your purpose clearly in mind. Also, be sure you have identified your audience and considered the voice that will be appropriate for your purpose.

1. In what way has someone you know changed in the last few years?

2. In what way does the author of this essay deserve respect from others?

3. How has your family influenced you positively or negatively?

4. How have your friends influenced you positively or negatively?

5. In what way do people need support from their friends?

6. What kinds of help and support are available to help someone overcome a problem like this?

7. Why is it difficult for people to change?

8. What are the reasons people get involved in drinking?

After you draft your paragraph, do each of the following:

Revise it so it has a clear topic sentence.

Include four to six supporting sentences.

Include a closing sentence.

Check to be sure your voice is appropriate for your purpose and audience.

Then,

Check for unity and a smooth flow of ideas.

Check for subject-verb agreement.

Check for consistent verb tense.

PARAGRAPHS AND ESSAYS FOR DISCUSSION AND ANALYSIS

The Nursing Home

Steve Bostrom, *student*

I love my grandmother very much, but visiting her in the nursing home is a sad and uncomfortable experience. When I walk in, I see many old, sick people who stare or say weird, crude things. They make me feel that I am intruding and do not belong. My grandmother is suffering from Alzheimer's disease, so it always takes a little time to explain who I am. This also gives me time to mentally orient myself after seeing how the disease has taken a toll on her mind and body. Then another problem appears, what to do while I am there. Conversation is hard because she cannot keep her mind on what the conversation is about although sometimes she will get a thought and will not let it go. For example, she will start yelling, "Take me for a walk!" Because she has a broken hip, walking is very painful for her. I will try to get her mind on another subject, but it does not always work. She keeps insisting on going for a walk until I remind her that she has a broken hip. She then will argue about it and tell me that I'm an "asshole" or "full of shit." She never talked like this before she got sick, so I understand, but it still hurts to hear her talk like that. One of the biggest problems is saying good-bye. I know she likes having people there to visit, but I am so uncomfortable I can hardly stand to stay too long. So I leave, knowing that in a few minutes she will forget that I was even there. Going to visit Grandmother is not fun, but I know it is important, so I'll continue to put myself in that uncomfortable position.

Understanding Words

Briefly define the following word as it is used in the above paragraph.

1. Alzheimer's disease *a disease that causes severe mental deterioration*

Answers for Unit 3, Part 3 are in the Instructor's Manual.

Questions on Content

1. Explain the conflict in the author's mind when he visits his grandmother.
2. What disease has changed his grandmother?
3. How is her behavior different now compared to how she acted in her earlier life?

Questions on Form

1. Describe the author's voice.
2. What is the author's purpose?
3. Who do you think is his audience?

Subways

Muriel Gray, *student*

When I was a child, traveling on the New York subway system to and from school was sheer torture for me. I was sure that every insane perverted drunk in the world traveled only by train. It seemed that I would run into one every day. Some would threaten me with bodily harm while others would hound me until I would give them my lunch money. When the train entered a tunnel, the hair stood up all over my body. The lights in each car went completely out, and I was sure that the weirdo in this car had staked me out for this precise moment. My heart pounded wildly until I reached my stop. The torments of the subway system are still vivid in my mind today.

Understanding Words

Briefly define the following word as it is used in the above paragraph.

1. perverted *turned away from what is good or right*

Questions on Content

1. In what city did these incidents take place?
2. What does the author dislike about the subways?
3. What happened when the train entered a tunnel?

Questions on Form

1. What is the author's purpose? How well does she accomplish her purpose?
2. The author has successfully captured a distinct voice in this paragraph. How would you describe it?
3. Why is this experience so easy for the reader to relate to? What phrases or support sentences make this experience believable?
4. Who could be an appropriate audience for this paragraph?

Growing Up Chicana

Eva Montoya, *teacher*

1   In college in 1967, I decided to join my roommate's sorority. It seemed like the thing to do at the time, even though for me it was expensive. So I went through the party invitation process. Rushing a sorority meant that I could attend only those parties whose members, after scrutinizing me, would reinvite me. I made it through all the parties until the last crucial invitation. When I went to the Dean of Women's office, I noticed that I was not reinvited to the particular sorority I wanted. That afternoon, against all Panhellenic rules, my roommate called me in tears, explaining that a sorority alumna would not approve my membership because of my surname. It was Hispanic. I cannot really explain the futile dismay or defenselessness I felt in this experience. In high school, I had been an honor student, a cheerleader, a girls' state representative, a class officer, and a homecoming and prom princess, yet because of my surname, I could not be a Chi Omega. I could control other aspects of my life, but I could not control my heritage. I went through years feeling misfortune until I reached adulthood and realized the beauty of my

Hispanic culture and its influence on my perception: it helped me to gain the strength to be different and to speak a second language, to appreciate people over materials, to make a celebration out of nothing.

2   I was, in today's vernacular, an exceptional or diverse child; however, because I attended a school with a large Hispanic population, I never noticed my "diversification." However, I do remember having my English teacher correct the pronunciation of various words. This guidance was not unusual except that the incorrect pronunciation was correct at home, so I had to learn which pronunciation to use at school and which to use at home. Again, looking back as an adult, I see now that at an early age I unconsciously perceived myself as being different. Fortunately, because I had no control over my uniqueness, I gave myself permission to be unique, and this has, I believe, been a source of later creative individuality for me. Every day, as an educator, I see inflexible minds that have never had the push to be different. Growing up different at times can be difficult, but the distinction remolds perception in an advantageous way, too.

3   "Mi casa es tu casa," is a very familiar "dicho" among Hispanics as well as Gabachos (whites). The phrase denotes an unlimited welcome, an open-door policy, or a boundless generosity. I remember a visit from friends on the Fourth of July. This family had several children, and the mother was pregnant. During the visit, the mother started labor, and my parents, of course, offered their bedroom. Playing the midwife role, my mother assisted in the birth of a baby boy, and because it was July, he was named Julio. The young parents were so indebted that they offered the baby to my parents. My parents appreciated this gracious offer, but they felt they had enough children. This Hispanic hospitality was not an exceptional happening. Almost every Saturday three to four separate family visits were not unusual, and the minute a foot stepped into our home, the hospitality began. Potatoes were peeled. The beans were warmed; the chili was begun, and the tortillas were rolled for a hot meal. Everyone was unconditionally welcomed and fed, and they usually left with the extra tortillas or fresh produce from the garden. As a child, I thought everyone participated in this unlimited giving and sharing, and it wasn't until I left my childhood inner circle that I learned some people do not open their doors in this way.

4   Most families remember get-togethers as quiet meals and conversations. For me, holidays meant about fifteen Hispanics gathering together. Everyone brought a few basic cultural similarities like red or green chili, a pot of beans, or tamales, and each family brought a specialty like a pineapple-upside-down cake. We ate, and, later, adults and children mixed and played baseball or volleyball. Then, as evening neared, guitars and accordions emerged, and we gathered by an open fire and listened to the traditional Mexican songs. Women and men would sing, and some would dance together with the children. I especially have fond memories of my father playing the guitar and being the center of entertainment. As a child, I never really appreciated these times. Not until I became an adult did I realize the wonderful messages that came from those experiences. To this day, I realize that good times do not have to be expensive or involved.

5   I am a product of my past. Growing up Chicana has made me realize that differences are all right and are to be celebrated, not shunned. Whatever material possessions we have should be shared with our friends, relatives, and, yes, even strangers. The best of times can be spontaneous, cheap, and simple, and, most of all, my childhood was extraordinarily wonderful.

Understanding Words

Briefly define the following words as they are used in the above essay.

1. sorority *a club of women with something in common, as in college*
2. scrutinizing *examining or looking at carefully*
3. dismay *discouragement, fear, dread*
4. vernacular *everyday language of common people*
5. denotes *signifies*

Questions on Content

1. What was the biggest hurt the author experienced during her college years?
2. What are the fond memories she has of her dad?
3. What is the source of her later creative individuality?

Questions on Form

1. How old do you think the author was when she wrote this article? Why is this perspective effective?
2. How would you describe the tone of this essay?
3. In what way is this essay forceful for different audiences?
4. For what purpose do you think this essay was written?

My Best Friend

Bill Devere, *student*

1   In times of trouble, many people can't take the stress and strain that result from hard times. Friends either grow apart or grow closer together. In 1986, when I had an accident at work that left my hands severely hurt, I found out who my best friend was. My best friend is always in my heart and in my thoughts and never leaves my side. Although the requirements for being anyone's best friend are tough, the stipulations for being my best friend are the toughest ones that I could ever think of. I feel my best friend will take care of me if I get sick or hurt, understand my problems, and enjoy the same activities I do.

2   After I had my accident, I called my best friend at work and told her that I would need a ride home from the hospital. As soon as I got to the hospital, I could see she was already there waiting for me. I don't know how, but she beat the ambulance there. True friends manage to do things like that. I felt good as soon as I saw her. Up until then, I was really scared, not knowing what was going to happen to me next. However, I knew with her there everything would be okay. Well, I made it through that day; I was relieved. That was before I found out that that was just the start of the many surgeries to come, but she told me that no matter what happened, she would be right beside me through it all. I needed to have eleven more surgeries over the next two years, but about six months after I got hurt, I became sick. That's when I found out that I was a diabetic, and I was admitted to the hospital. After about two days they offered to put another bed in my room. I think it was for my best friend since she was always with me. I had to learn how to give myself shots and check my blood-sugar level. This way I would know how

much insulin I needed to stabilize my blood-sugar level. Well, my friend was right there the whole time beside me, and they were showing her just in case I couldn't do it for one reason or another.

3   I feel that another one of the qualities of a friend is to know how to understand my problems. I have been very lucky to have my friend with me so much in the last two years. Before I had the problems with my hands and the surgeries, I had a trucking company and had three trucks working, and I was also working full-time as an aerospace sheet-metal mechanic. After I had the accident, I lost my company and went through a lot of problems financially and emotionally. My friend was always there and was really interested in me and my life. My friend had the knack of knowing when to push me and when I just needed to be left alone. She let me rant and rave on when I was mad and never had hard feelings. She understood how I have felt since the accident and the changes I have been going through, at times, I think, more than I did.

4   Best of all, she has the same interests that I do. I know that her family is most important to her, and it is the same with me. We have the same tastes in houses and the same feelings about the way a house should look inside and out. I feel that the yard should be nice and green with the right number of flowers and the right number of trees, and so does she. We talk about the changes we want to make before we make them. We talk about any changes she wants to make inside the house before she will make them. The hardest thing for us to agree on is where she wants to go on her vacation and where I want to go. It always seems to be to different spots, but we talk it out. Finally, she and I agree where to go and whether we will fly or drive. Once there, we share the same interests.

5   I wanted to give up a long time ago, but she kept me going when times got really tough and I wanted to quit. I think that by now a person could figure out that my best friend is also my wife. I know that she has always stood by my side. Even though we have been married eighteen years, I feel she is the best friend that I could have ever had. The feeling of having someone that cares that much about me is the best thing that I could ever hope for. No matter how much I told her to leave when times got tough, she knew I really wanted her to stay right next to me, and she did.

■ Understanding Words

Briefly define the following word as it is used in the above essay.

1. stipulations   *conditions, as for a contract*

■ Questions on Content

1. In what year did the author have his accident?
2. At that time, what two occupations did he have?
3. What interests do the author and his wife have in common?
4. What did his wife do when he ranted and raved?

Questions on Form

1. What is the author's purpose?
2. How would you describe the author's voice?
3. What is the topic sentence in each paragraph?

Dear Dad

Excerpt from *Dear Dad* by **Louie Anderson**, *comedian and actor*

God, what I would have given to hear and see you play. I never did, you know. I've never even seen a photo of you playing the horn. I remember a few times when there was a trumpet resting beside the platform rocker in the living room. But you didn't play it. I wonder, though, if when you performed it was the same as when I'm on stage? You're up there in front of the crowd and every moment is very real. Your heart seems connected to a light, and the truer you are to your heart, the brighter the light gets and the stronger your heart feels, and your eyes see the world spinning at its absolute clearest.

Questions on Content

1. What instrument did Louie Anderson's dad play?
2. What did the author wonder about?

Questions on Form

1. How would you describe the voice of the author?
2. What comparison does Louie Anderson make?
3. Who is Louie Anderson's audience?

Space to Sing

Letter by **Dean K. Terasaki**, *Assistant Chairperson, Art/Photography Department*

1   Toward the end of each spring, the art department in which I teach at Glendale Community College (GCC) exhibits perhaps four or five hundred student artworks, in a salon-style exhibition. This year, amid charges of racism that forced the removal of a student's piece, the exhibit was closed down by the art department faculty. The art department faculty voted to close the exhibition as an act of solidarity with Julie Glaze, the first-year sculpture student whose piece was removed. It was closed to honor the contract we had with each student that no piece would be removed before the close of the exhibition. With tremendous sadness, I voted that the show be closed. I write because I am concerned for my community and this conflict between expression and political correctness.

2   I am concerned for my peers who made the charges of racism because I, too, am a person of color. I am concerned for my students because they are the ones I repeatedly ask to show me in their photographs what they passionately believe to be important, to be the truth, to be worth loving. This is not the sentimental task of trying to please a parent; it is the vulnerable task of the creative endeavor. I am concerned that as this semester winds to a close, an opportunity for discussion of race, stereotype, and free expression will evaporate in the long summer heat.

3   I appreciate the expression of outrage toward Julie Glaze's sculpture, "Mother Earth," which was seen as a racist stereotype by some members of the GCC educational community. In the midst of the racist graffiti that has been appearing on campus, this community has been sensitized to racial conflict. It is in

this atmosphere that the artwork was threatened with destruction and subsequently taken from the exhibition. But something very important was lost with the forced removal of this artwork and the subsequent closing of the Student Art Show. Art is about conversation. It is about intercourse. It is about learning what you and I feel. It's about our experience as separate individuals who share a community and walk on the same ground. This breath of life, this exchange of what is personal, these hopes and fears, laughter and anger are the very things that artists hunger for.

4   Glaze's piece was motivated by love. "Mother Earth" is a sculptural portrait of an outgoing, humorous, black woman whom Glaze spoke and laughed with many times as they rode together on an Atlanta city bus. The removal of this piece from the exhibition in essence sends a message to Glaze. The message essentially states that Glaze's memories of this woman, her feelings of love and respect, indeed her own biography are not valid territories for the expression of art. I fear that every time Glaze or any other student moves to create something in the future it will be tempered by her fear that she will anger someone. I'm wondering if castrated might be a better word than tempered because if she decides not to make her vision a reality, then that is, in fact, what will have happened to that thought, that idea, that love which will not be given its artistic manifestation.

5   Notwithstanding this possible future, the issues of free speech and academic freedom, and the problems of having to remove each and every piece that offends someone for its lack of political correctness, because "Mother Earth" was removed, a voice was silenced. There was no discussion. That was to be the end of the story.

6   I can speak from personal experience that racist stereotypes are a fiction, a lie, a blasphemous, scurrilous oversimplification that deny the humanity and the individuality of those they purport to describe. Those stereotypes deny the very things that art and artists seek to reveal. Could there be some irony here? I believe that catalyzed by this work of art, just at the point when discussion about the vicious nature of racial stereotypes could start to take place in the wider arena of this full community, a conversation clearly needed here at GCC, the germinating seed was nipped in the bud.

7   It must be understood that artistic expression is vulnerable. While this student may claim to have made this work out of love, her piece, like any artwork, had a life of its own. Like any child learning to socialize, this piece said something very rude to some although I would argue it was out of pure innocence. However, because of the larger context of the white supremacist graffiti that has been appearing on campus, a state of fear exists for all minority members of the GCC community.

8   That fear turns to anger when given a chance. My experience of going home confused in the second grade to ask my mother, "What's a Jap?" played no small part in forming the rage that is at the core of my being. I believe this rage must be part of my art. I learned of the emotional power of at least one of my pictures this semester when I retrieved from the Faculty Art Exhibition a photograph that had been spat upon twice during the show. Once I got past my anger and powerlessness, I truly felt that my photograph had succeeded. It somehow represented something so strongly to one or two people out there that they were compelled to express themselves as well with my photograph as the target. While I would have preferred a cup of coffee and some conversation, this story will have to suffice.

9   "Mother Earth" was simply a convenient target as well. It was tangible, both ugly and beautiful in its truthfulness. The solution was not to remove it, denying

an innocent voice the space to sing, and forcing the closure of the Student Art Show. The solution was to talk, maybe even scream, to validate Julie Glaze's experience, and at the same time help her understand that she does not live in a vacuum. The solution was to let people know.

"Can't we all just get along?"

Understanding Words

Briefly define the following words as they are used in the above paragraph.

1. solidarity *being strongly united*
2. vulnerable *easily hurt*
3. stereotype *a fixed picture of a person, usually negative*
4. castrate *to remove the vitality or force of*
5. manifestation *real form*
6. blasphemous *lacking respect for anything considered sacred*
7. scurrilous *abusive, as in language*
8. catalyzed *having caused change without changing its own form*

Questions on Content

1. Who is "Mother Earth"?
2. What happened to "Mother Earth"?
3. Why did the author write the letter?

Questions on Form

1. Describe the author's voice.
2. Who is the audience?
3. Find a passage where you think the author's word choice is especially effective.

PART 4

THE WRITER'S TOOLS: CONSISTENT POINT OF VIEW

OBJECTIVES

- Understand point of view.
- Identify shifts in point of view.
- Make point of view consistent in a paragraph or essay.

Point of view is the way you as the writer present ideas in a paragraph or an essay. You can talk from your own experience, can speak directly to the reader (such as giving directions), or can relate someone else's experience.

When you talk from your own experience, the pronouns *I* or *we* can be used. When you speak directly to the reader, *you* is used for either singular or plural. When you relate someone else's experience, *she, he, it,* or *they* is used.

When you use *I* or *we*, you are using **1st person**. When you use *you*, you are using **2nd person**. When you use *she, he, it,* or *they*, you are using **3rd person**.

	Singular	Plural
1st person	I	we
2nd person	you	you
3rd person	she, he, it	they

In other words, information could be written from different **points of view**. 1st person point of view ("I," "we") allows the author to write it as if the experience has directly happened to her or him.

I will take Psychology 201 next semester.

We will take Psychology 201 next semester.

2nd person point of view ("you") gives directions to the reader or allows the author to speak directly to the reader.

You will take Psychology 201 next semester.

You will enjoy Psychology 201 next semester.

3rd person point of view ("she, he, it, they") allows the reader to be less personal and to discuss someone else's experience.

She will take Psychology 201 next semester.

He will take Psychology 201 next semester.

Helen will take Psychology 201 next semester.

They will take Psychology 201 next semester.

They will take **it** next semester.

■ Determining Point of View

Determining person or point of view is very simple. All you have to do is locate the main subject in a sentence and then decide which pronoun can be used in place of this subject.

For example, in the sentence "Bob and his stereo go everywhere together," the subject is "Bob" and "stereo." The pronoun, therefore, that would be used to replace this subject must be "they," so the point of view is 3rd person plural.

In the sentence "Janet and I often go hiking," the subject is "Janet" and "I." The pronoun used to replace this subject must be "we," so the point of view is 1st person plural.

In the sentence "The manager of the company hired new employees," the subject of the sentence is "manager." The pronoun needed to replace this subject must be either "she" or "he," so the point of view is 3rd person singular.

In the sentence "For a high-school graduate, summer work in a large city is generally easy to find," the subject of the sentence is "work." The pronoun needed to replace this subject must be "it," so the point of view is 3rd person singular.

In the sentence "Bill needs to go on a vacation," the subject is "Bill," and if you were speaking directly to Bill, you would use the pronoun "you" instead of "Bill." "You need to go on a vacation" is 2nd person singular.

Now try identifying the point of view in the following exercise.

EXERCISE 1

Underline the subject, and then above the word, put the pronoun that could be used to replace the subject.

Example:

They
~~The children~~ walked home from school every day.

1. *He*
   ~~Sam~~ is doing well in calculus this semester.

2. *It*
   ~~The kitchen table~~ is often used for purposes other than eating.

3. *It*
   ~~Maintaining a consistent point of view~~ is really quite simple.

4. *They*
   ~~The bicyclists~~ moved through the streets at a rapid pace.

5. *It*
   ~~Quarreling~~ is not going to help anyone on the committee.

6. *We*
   ~~Roger, Stephanie, and I~~ watched the Fourth of July parade, and we enjoyed it.

7. *They*
~~The faculty~~ appreciated the new telephone system and used it often.

8. *They*
~~Many people~~ feel pressures in life.

9. *She*
~~Mary~~ returns to the California coast for vacation every summer.

10. *He*
~~Phillip~~ played a difficult role in the school production.

◼ Maintaining Consistent Point of View

Test over consistent point of view p. 32 in Instructor's Manual.

Maintaining a consistent point of view means that you establish the person (1st person, 2nd person, or 3rd person) in the first sentence of your paragraph and then continue to use that same person throughout the paragraph unless there is a logical reason to change. For instance, if you say, ''Parents often are surprised by the many unpredictable games their children play,'' you would establish the person as 3rd person plural because the subject is ''parents'' (they). You would continue to use nouns that could be substituted for by 3rd person pronouns (she, he, it, or they) or any of these pronouns throughout the remainder of the paragraph. As you read through the following paragraph, pay close attention to the 3rd person nouns and pronouns in bold type. Notice that *they are all in the same person.* Not all 3rd person nouns and pronouns have been marked.

> **Parents (they)** often are surprised by the many unpredictable games **their** children play. **Their** children often imitate activities that **they** have seen grownups do, or **they** simply want to be helpful. **Ann and her sister (they)** did just this when **they** decided to improve the neighbor's lawn chairs by covering them in a nice coating of mud. Not only did the **neighbor (she)** get a grand surprise, but so did the girls' **father (he)** when **he** found out that **they** had used his new paint brush. Another time their **brother Bobby (he)** set up a candy shop in the basement where **he** made a fresh batch of divinity with his **mother's (her)** laundry soap. Working hard to be a great chef, **he** whipped the mixture into a smooth consistency with his mother's egg beater. Their **mother (she)** was the one who was upset this time when **she** went to wash **her** clothes and found that the detergent box was empty. The **children (they)** decided to make lemonade one afternoon but used lemon detergent as the base. Fortunately, **their** effort to help was discovered before anybody drank any of this sparkling drink. Though **parents (they)** can be upset and frustrated when the **children (they)** are so helpful, **they** can also appreciate **their** efforts to be grown up.

Occasionally, you might have a logical reason to shift the point of view in your paragraph. However, if you were to change the first sentence in the previous paragraph to ''Parents often are surprised by the many unpredictable games *your* children play,'' you are implying that the readers' children, not the parents' children, are unpredictable. That is probably not what you intended to say in the sentence.

Note   Perhaps the most common writing difficulty you may run into is a shift from 1st or 3rd person to 2nd person. Therefore, be certain that when you use ''you,'' you are really addressing the reader and not just shifting your point of view.

Once again, use the following table to help you examine the preceding paragraph for consistent point of view of each sentence.

The following exercise will help you change point of view so that you can find and change point-of-view shifts in your own paragraphs.

	Singular			Plural		
	SUBJ.	OBJ.	POSSESSIVE	SUBJ.	OBJ.	POSSESSIVE
1st person	I	me	my, mine	we	us	our, ours
2nd person	you	you	your, yours	you	you	your, yours
3rd person	she	her	her, hers	they	them	their, theirs
	he	him	his			
	it	it	its			

EXERCISE   2

Underline the subject and then change the word(s) to a different person or point of view as shown. Refer to the table if necessary. (Be sure to change any pronouns that might follow in the sentence.)

Example:

Change to 3rd person

Their   *their*
~~Your~~ assignments are always typed on ~~your~~ computer.

1. *Change to 1st person*

   My   *my*
   ~~Willie's~~ enthusiasm for life increased ~~his~~ productivity.

2. *Change to 3rd person*

   They   *their*
   ~~My friend and I~~ have always tried to edit ~~our~~ papers carefully.

3. *Change to 3rd person*

   They / Their family.

   ~~Our family~~ went on a picnic.

4. *Change to 1st person*

   We   *our*

   ~~The couple~~ repeated ~~their~~ marriage vows with spiritual inspiration.

5. *Change to 3rd person*

   listens to his

   Henry, ~~listen to your~~ conscience when decisions need to be made.

6. *Change to 1st person*

   I manipulate my

   ~~Pearl Buck manipulates her~~ point of view to conform to various purposes.

7. *Change to 1st person*

   I   *volunteer*

   ~~Christina~~ often ~~volunteers~~ at the school for handicapped adults.

8. *Change to 3rd person*

   They

   ~~Some students~~ have learned excellent time-management skills this semester.

9. *Change to 1st person*

   I

   ~~Others~~ have procrastinated until the last minute.

10. *Change to 1st person*

    I / we

    ~~Robert~~ should consider the detrimental consequences as well as the advantages.

▆ Revising Inconsistent Point of View

In the following paragraph, the point of view shifts several times in a confusing way. These shifts are marked for you in bold type. Read the paragraph. Then study the sentence-by-sentence analysis that follows so that you can understand how and why the point of view should be revised throughout.

UPS

(1) The hardest **job** is working at United Parcel Service. (2) **They** pay well, but **it** is hard work. (3) **You** have to be able to lift seventy pounds into a truck. (4) **They** require that you load up to nine hundred packages an hour. (5) The **hours** I work are weird, and **that** makes it difficult, too. (6) **I** work third shift, which is three to nine in the morning. (7) There are no **breaks**. (8) **You** work until all the work is done. (9) **I** have four trucks to load. (10) **I** have to run and grab as many packages as I can off the slide and load them into the truck. (11) **I** am running constantly. (12) If **it** weren't for the money, there is no way **I** would work that hard.

Sentence 1: The hardest **job** is working at United Parcel Service.

The subject in the first sentence is "job." The correct subject pronoun to use in place of "job" would be "it." By looking at the table, you can find "it" listed as 3rd person singular. Third person singular sets the point of view for this sentence and, consequently, for the entire paragraph. In using this point of view, the writer is speaking *about* something.

Sentence 2: **They** pay well, but **it** is hard work.

The second sentence has used the subject pronoun "they" rather than a noun for a subject, so to determine the point of view for this sentence, you simply have to find the subject pronoun "they" in the table. As you see from the table, "they" is 3rd person, but because it is *plural*, it does not refer to "job" in sentence 1. To clear up the vague reference, "the company" might be used instead because it is more specific.

Revision: The company pays well.

Sentence 3: **You** have to be able to lift seventy pounds into a truck.

In the third sentence, the writer has shifted to the subject pronoun "you." As the table indicates, a major shift has occurred to 2nd person. Now the writer is speaking directly to the reader.

Revision: Jobs require lifting up to seventy pounds into a truck.

Sentences 4 and 5: **They** require that you load up to nine hundred packages an hour.
The **hours** I work are weird, and **that** makes it difficult, too.

The fourth and fifth sentences have shifted back to 3rd person plural. The writer is speaking *about* something.

Revision: Employees are required to load. . . . The work hours are at odd times, too.

Sentence 6: I work third shift, which is three to nine in the morning.

In the sixth sentence, because the subject is "I," the writer has shifted to 1st person and is speaking from a personal perspective.

Revision: The third shift works three to nine.

Sentence 7: There are no **breaks**.

In the seventh sentence, the writer has shifted to the 3rd person *plural* point of view.

Revision: Third shift has no breaks.

Sentence 8: **You** work until all the work is done.

In the eighth sentence the writer has shifted back to *"you"* and addresses the reader directly again.

Revision: Employees are expected to stay until all the work is done.

Sentences 9–12: I have four trucks to load.

I have to run and grab as many packages as I can off the slide and load them into the truck.

I am running constantly.

If **it** weren't for the money, there is no way I would work that hard.

In the remainder of the paragraph the writer has shifted again to "I." The writer shifts the experience from 2nd person (you), which directs the reader, to 1st person ("I"), which indicates that the writer is sharing his/her own personal experience.

Revision: It is not unusual for employees to load four trucks. They have to run and grab. . . . They are running constantly. . . .

The shifting of point of view in the UPS paragraph makes it difficult for the reader to follow. At times, the reader may lose sight of who is doing the speaking and to whom the writer is speaking. The paragraph, in effect, loses an extremely important component — total coherence. Now read a thorough revision of this paragraph and compare it to the first draft.

Consistent 3rd Person Point of View

UPS

Working at United Parcel Service is strenuous, demanding work. The **company** pays well, but the work is hard. First of all, entry-level **jobs** require lifting up to seventy pounds into the bed of a truck. Along with this, **employees** are required to load nine hundred packages an hour. The work **hours** are at odd times, too. The third **shift** works three to nine in the morning with no breaks. In addition, **employees** are expected to stay until all the work is done. It is not unusual for **employees** to load four trucks in one day. **They** have to run and grab as many packages as **they** can off the slide and load them into the truck. If the **money** weren't good, **United Parcel Service** wouldn't be able to find **people** to do this type of demanding work.

By keeping a consistent 3rd person point of view ("she," "he," "it," "they"), the writer was able to use a variety of nouns as well as the four subject pronouns. Also, the voice now sounds more objective and more convincing.

As a contrast to third person point of view, 1st person ("I") point of view allows the writer to personalize his or her experience and make the tone of the writing more informal. Read the following paragraph and notice how the 1st person ("I") point of view helps the reader identify with the writer's experience.

Consistent 1st Person Point of View

UPS

The hardest job I ever had was working at United Parcel Service. I was pleased with my salary, but I thought it was hard work. First of all, I had to be able to lift seventy pounds into a truck and load up to nine hundred packages an hour. Besides this, I had a difficult schedule, too. I worked the third shift, which was from three to nine in the morning, with no breaks. At times I had to stay longer until all the work was done. Often, I had four trucks to load, and I would have to run and grab as many packages as I could off the conveyor and load them onto the transporting truck. I was running constantly. I believe that if I hadn't been getting good money, there is no way I would ever have worked that hard.

This paragraph has maintained 1st person point of view. It allows the writer to identify all the experiences as his or her own. However, note that the ''I'' is repeated quite often, which may sound monotonous in a longer essay.

Now read the same paragraph written in the ''you'' point of view. Generally, the ''you'' point of view is found in papers that give instructions to a reader or in an explanation or discussion (like this textbook) that speaks directly to the reader. Notice how the 2nd person point of view affects the tone of voice of the paragraph.

Consistent 2nd Person Point of View

UPS

If **you** enjoy hard work, **you** might like working at United Parcel Service. **You** will enjoy the salary because it pays well, but the work will probably be demanding for **you**. First of all, **you** have to be able to lift seventy pounds into the bed of a truck, as well as load nine hundred packages an hour. **You** will also discover that the work hours are at very odd times. If **you** are on the third shift, **you** have to come in at three to nine o'clock in the morning with no breaks. In addition, **you** have to stay until all the trucks are loaded. **You** often load four trucks in one day. **You** have to run and grab as many packages as **you** can off the conveyor and load them into the truck. However, the pay is good. If this sounds appealing to **you**, apply at the United Parcel Service.

The preceding paragraph has a consistent 2nd person point of view. Unless you are giving instructions to someone or are speaking directly to your audience, you may want to choose another point of view. Keep in mind that different points of view create different impressions on your reader. Because you can learn to control point of view, you have one more way of controlling how you sound in your own writing. As a result, you can feel more confident about how your reader will react.

Maintaining consistent point of view helps keep your paragraph focused on one main idea and brings your many sentences together as one piece of writing. For longer writing, consistent point of view is essential for clarity. Consequently, you should edit carefully for a consistent point of view that is appropriate for your topic, purpose, and audience.

As a writer, you must decide what your writing purpose is and conform your point of view to that purpose. Do you want to sound more authoritative or more personal? Do you want to inform or entertain? Do you want to remain distant or get close to your reader? Do you want to sound more formal or informal? Answering these questions will determine your point of view and give you greater control over a writing situation.

EXERCISE 3

Read the following paragraphs and identify the shifts in point of view. The first sentence establishes the point of view that should be maintained. Any deviation from the first sentence should be changed to an appropriate subject pronoun or noun that conforms to the point of view of the first sentence. Revise the following paragraphs by making the point of view consistent. When you have finished revising each paragraph, identify the purpose, voice, and audience.

Paragraph 1

I love to haggle every time I go to a border town in Mexico. First of all, I make out a list of the items I would like to have. Then I find a market square that has lots of vendors. ~~Competition~~ *I believe that competition* allows me to do some comparative scouting and may mean lower-priced items. ~~You should~~ *I* always go dressed in older clothes so that ~~you~~ *I* don't look like the rich American tourist. As ~~you~~ *I* enter the store, ~~you should~~ *I try to* not appear anxious. Next, with a maximum price in my mind, I casually saunter to the object that I most want. If the vendor's price is way above my price, I go to the next store. If not, I smile and offer him a price lower than my set price, and we begin haggling from that point. Usually, ~~a~~ *we can* compromise ~~is struck,~~ and we both go away happy.

Purpose: *to explain shopping in Mexico* Voice: *honest, frank* Audience: *general reader*

Paragraph 2

Many people in the late 1800s were forced to be self-reliant. Though ~~you~~ *people* might be poor, ~~you~~ *they* homesteaded an inexpensive piece of land where ~~you~~ *they* could build ~~your~~ *their* own log cabin and grow ~~your~~ *their* own garden. ~~I learned that the~~ *The* garden provided fresh vegetables in the summer and canned vegeta-

bles throughout the other months of the year. Likewise, fruit was eaten in season and canned to

provide a year-round supply. ~~You~~ *People* often had a place to raise ~~your~~ chickens that provided eggs as well

as meat. ~~You~~ *Many people* found rabbits to be a necessary source of food that could be fried, baked, or stewed. ~~You~~ *These homesteaders*

were able to raise or grow ~~your~~ *their* own food and become self-sufficient on ~~your~~ *their* own land.

Purpose: *to explain how homesteaders lived*   Voice: *informative*   Audience: *general reader*

Paragraph 3

Playing golf is a rewarding experience. It can be a time for relaxing and enjoying a beautiful day.

Because many golf courses are located throughout the city, finding an available tee time is also easy

and convenient. When ~~you~~ *golfers* play eighteen holes, ~~you~~ *they* walk approximately four miles and get ~~your~~ *their* day's

exercise. Furthermore, ~~I believe that~~ golf is challenging. *Some* ~~I~~ used to think that golf was an easy game that

did not require any ability, but it does require precision, patience, and skill. In addition, unlike other

high-endurance sports that only younger players can participate in, golf is a lifelong activity. ~~You~~ *Anyone* can

enjoy it at just about any age. Consequently, golf is a sport everybody should consider playing.

Purpose: *to explain why golf is rewarding*   Voice: *informative*   Audience: *anyone thinking of taking up golf*

Paragraph 4

Japan is no longer a smoker's paradise. Trains and train stations now do not allow ~~you~~ free, open,

unrestricted smoking. ~~I find designated~~ *Designated* smoking areas are marked and monitored. Also, work places

are taking ~~our~~ *a* Western approach and are beginning to discourage unrestricted smoking. Until recently

in Japan, the risk of fire, not health, prohibited ~~you from~~ smoking in theaters and other public places.

This movement, at long last, is taking place thirty years after the United States Surgeon General announced the hazards of smoking; however, ~~I find~~ it is a welcomed movement for the nonsmoking Japanese.

Purpose: _to explain Japan's smoking regulations_ Voice: _informative, formal, persuasive_ Audience: _travelers to Japan_

Paragraph 5

The high-tech computer lab at our college is an efficient room. Over one hundred computers are laid out so that maximum room is obtained for traffic flow, comfort, and usability. Students can choose from a variety of hardware, and technicians are available to give help or to answer questions. In addition to this, ~~you~~ _students_ can easily check out the software ~~you~~ _they_ desire and sign in on the computer at the entrance to the room. One thing that ~~I have found in my~~ _students may find in their_ experience in the high-tech centers is that ~~I~~ _they_ can get copies of ~~my~~ _their_ work quickly because all stations are hooked up to printers. ~~You~~ _Students_ might say that the high-tech center is a perfect place for computer business and pleasure.

Purpose: _to express pride in computer facilities_ Voice: _positive, informative_ Audience: _potential users_

WRITING ASSIGNMENT

Using the steps in the writing process, draft a paragraph about one of the following ideas. Decide on a purpose and an audience, and then decide the voice that would be the most appropriate.

1. The best pet I ever had . . .
2. A senior citizen taught me . . .
3. The best neighbor I ever had . . .
4. Visiting a famous monument or building or a national park . . .
5. My brother's/sister's best trait is/was . . .
6. Something I appreciate most about my mother/father . . .
7. Something I dislike most about my mother/father . . .

After you draft your paragraph, revise for content and edit for mechanics.

Content

Revise it so it has a clear topic sentence.

Include four to six supporting sentences.

Include a closing sentence.

Check to see that the voice is appropriate for purpose and audience.

Mechanics

Check for subject-verb agreement.

Check for consistent verbs.

Check for a consistent point of view.

UNIT 4

Organizing Ideas and Writing Them Clearly

PART 1

PARTS TO WHOLE: THE THESIS SENTENCE

OBJECTIVES

- Write a thesis sentence that states the direction of the paper.

- Write a thesis sentence that previews the points to be covered in the paper. Be sure that all divisions are coordinate with each other, are subordinate to the general direction in the thesis sentence, and are parallel to each other.

- Brainstorm to generate ideas.

- Group related ideas.

- Identify and write the divisions in sequential order.

- Include the key word of each division in the topic idea for each support paragraph.

Just as the paragraph depends on a topic sentence to restrict and control the paragraph, so the longer paper depends on a thesis sentence to restrict and control the longer paper. You have just learned that the most general statement in the paragraph is the topic sentence. The most general statement in the longer paper, similarly, is the **thesis sentence**, which directs and determines the topic sentences that will be used to support the thesis sentence. For example, if you say that "learning disabilities can create problems for students in school," you can use supporting details to develop a paragraph. Read the following sample paragraph.

> Learning disabilities can create problems for students. *Often academic problems arise when learning-disabled students have a difficult time reading the textbook because they are reading two or more years below grade level. Also, the students may have trouble putting into writing what they know well. *This can lead to social problems because students with learning disabilities often spend two or three times longer doing their homework than other students do, leaving no time to spend with others. *Personal problems may emerge because they feel inferior to other students who can spell every word right the first time. *The least noticeable of all might be physical problems like coordination or balance that the average person will not even notice. Though these learning disabilities are difficult for others to detect, they certainly can make life difficult for otherwise bright students.

If you wish to expand this paragraph into a longer paper, you must develop the specific ways in which learning disabilities can create problems for students. A thesis sentence helps you organize your discussion.

You may write the thesis sentence in two ways: one that clearly states the direction for the longer paper or one that states the direction and specifies the points to be covered in the paper.

---

*Notice that the sentences in this sample paragraph that are marked with an asterisk could be developed into separate paragraphs for a longer paper.

■ Thesis Sentence that States the Direction

The thesis sentence of the sample paragraph could still be "**Learning disabilities can create problems for students.**" However, specific problems would have to be discussed in a logical, organized manner. Brainstorming could give you these points. Perhaps you would use the four main kinds of problems included in the sample paragraph (academic, social, personal, and physical) and develop each idea in one (or more) support paragraphs. Each support paragraph will need a strong topic sentence clarifying the point being discussed.

Look at the following list of topic sentences for each of the four support paragraphs. Each topic sentence will be the most general statement in the paragraph.

Students with learning disabilities may encounter many academic problems.

Likewise, students with learning disabilities also encounter many social problems.

Other problems that learning-disabled students experience are personal problems.

The least noticeable problems of all might be physical problems.

■ Thesis Sentence that States the Direction and Previews Main Points of the Paper

Test covering thesis sentences in Instructor's Manual pp. 33-34.

If you preview the main points to be covered in the paper, your thesis sentence might read:

#1   #2   #3   #4

Learning disabilities create academic, social, personal, and physical problems for the student.

(Again, the thesis sentence will be the most general statement in the paper.)

From the points previewed in this thesis sentence, you will be able to write a topic sentence for each support paragraph. The same topic sentences presented in the previous list could be used in this paper as well.

Support paragraph 1: **Students with learning disabilities may encounter many academic problems.**

Support paragraph 2: **Likewise, students with learning disabilities also encounter many social problems.**

Support paragraph 3: **Other problems that learning-disabled students experience are personal problems.**

Support paragraph 4: **The least noticeable problems of all might be physical problems.**

Coordinate and Subordinate Ideas in Thesis Sentences

Whether or not you preview the supporting ideas in the thesis sentence, you need to organize your paper logically. To do this, you need supporting ideas that are **coordinate**, which means that the two or more divisions in the paper must be of equal value. This degree of equality is determined by the restriction and direction of the thesis statement. If in one paper you are writing about working in the yard, having a party, sleeping late, and doing homework, your readers might wonder what these activities have in common. However, if you write

"I enjoy spring break because I enjoy

working in the yard

having a party,

sleeping late, and

doing homework."

the reader is then aware that these activities are what you enjoy doing when school is in recess. They are all equal, even though you might enjoy one activity more than the others.

On the other hand, if you write

"I enjoy spring break because I enjoy

working in the yard and

pulling weeds."

then your thesis statement is faulty because pulling weeds is not equal to working in the yard. Rather, it is one of the activities you might do when you work in the yard. Furthermore, if you write

"During my spring break, I enjoyed

my personal life,

my social life,

my spiritual life, and

picking flowers."

it is easy to see that "picking flowers" is too restricted and narrow and, therefore, is not coordinate with the other ideas in the group.

Also, all of these divisions must be **subordinate** to one idea. In this case they must all be activities you enjoy doing during spring break. These divisions might be different for different people. For example, someone else might say, "But I do not enjoy doing homework." Then that person could substitute "working on a car" or "cooking gourmet meals" or "going on a trip." It really doesn't matter as long as all the divisions are *coordinate* (equal) and *subordinate* to (under) the main idea of the paper. Whether or not you preview the points in your thesis sentence, you need to decide on your supporting ideas before writing your paper.

The following exercises will help you determine which ideas are equal to each other and will also help you realize that these coordinate ideas must be subordinate to a more general statement. These exercises will help you think about how ideas fit together into a paper whether or not they are included in the actual thesis statement.

E X E R C I S E   1

Read the following words or phrases that could be generated through brainstorming. First, determine which word or phrase is the most general. Second, decide which words or phrases are coordinate or equal to each other. Finally, decide which words or phrases are unrelated or part of another group.

Example:

a. playing croquet

b. hitting the ball with the mallet   _____*a*_____ is the most general word or statement.

c. going through the wickets   _*b,c,d*_ are equal to each other.

d. hitting the post   _____*e*_____ is unrelated or part of another group.

e. drinking water

1. a. bluegill

    b. trout   _____*c*_____ is the most general word or statement.

    c. fish   _*a, b, d*_ are equal to each other.

    d. bass   _____*e*_____ is unrelated or part of another group.

    e. fishing

2. a. working in a garden

    b. planting carrots   _____*a*_____ is the most general word or statement.

    c. washing hands   _*b, d, e*_ are equal to each other.

    d. hoeing weeds   _____*c*_____ is unrelated or part of another group.

    e. thinning radishes

3. a. pop

    b. drink   _____*b*_____ is the most general word or statement.

    c. coffee   _*a, c, d*_ are equal to each other.

    d. tea   _____*e*_____ is unrelated or part of another group.

    e. sugar

4. a. enrolling in college

   b. completing assignments

   c. being successful in college

   d. attending class

   e. reading the materials

   _____c_____ is the most general word or statement.

   _d, b, e_ are equal to each other.

   _____a_____ is unrelated or part of another group.

5. a. writing letters

   b. mailing packages

   c. mailing letters

   d. buying stamps

   e. using services provided by the post office

   _____e_____ is the most general word or statement.

   _b, c, d_ are equal to each other.

   _____a_____ is unrelated or part of another group.

6. a. cooking

   b. baking

   c. doing dishes

   d. frying

   e. grilling

   _____a_____ is the most general word or statement.

   _b, d, e_ are equal to each other.

   _____c_____ is unrelated or part of another group.

7. a. chewing bubble gum

   b. fielding

   c. playing baseball

   d. batting

   e. catching

   _____c_____ is the most general word or statement.

   _b, d, e_ are equal to each other.

   _____a_____ is unrelated or part of another group.

8. a. translating the text

   b. drawing a picture

   c. learning a language

   d. learning vocabulary

   e. carrying on a conversation

   _____c_____ is the most general word or statement.

   _a, d, e_ are equal to each other.

   _____b_____ is unrelated or part of another group.

9. a. branch

   b. leaf

   c. grass

   d. tree

   e. trunk

   _____d_____ is the most general word or statement.

   _a, b, e_ are equal to each other.

   _____c_____ is unrelated or part of another group.

10. a. sleeping in a tent

b. camping _____*b*_____ is the most general word or statement.

c. roasting marshmallows ___*a, c, d*___ are equal to each other.

d. cooking over an open fire _____*e*_____ is unrelated or part of another group.

e. buying gas

EXERCISE 2

Study the following sentences. First, identify the most general idea in each sentence. Then identify which words are coordinate.

Example:

The mountains are beautiful in the spring because of the new growth, the rains, and the animal activities.

mountains are beautiful in the spring

(most general idea)

new growth, rains, animal activities

(words that are coordinate)

1. Pets aid the elderly by providing security, companionship, and self-esteem.

Pets aid the elderly

(most general idea)

security, companionship, self-esteem

(words that are coordinate)

2. The children enjoyed the pictures that were large, simple, and colorful.

children enjoyed the pictures

(most general idea)

large, simple, colorful

(words that are coordinate)

3. The Iron Man competition includes swimming, biking, and running.

Iron Man competition includes

(most general idea)

swimming, biking, running

(words that are coordinate)

4. Newspapers provide information concerning entertainment, news, and sales.

newspapers provide information

(*most general idea*)

entertainment, news, sales

(*words that are coordinate*)

5. People with diabetes must be concerned with exercise, diet, and stress.

People with diabetes must be concerned with

(*most general idea*)

exercise, diet, stress

(*words that are coordinate*)

6. Having surgery is difficult because it is expensive, painful, frightening, and depressing.

Having surgery is difficult

(*most general idea*)

expensive, painful, frightening

(*words that are coordinate*)

7. Location, price, and size are important when a consumer buys a home.

are important when a consumer buys a home

(*most general idea*)

location, price, size

(*words that are coordinate*)

8. At the fair, the rides, games, food, and exhibits bring enjoyment to children.

bring enjoyment to children at the fair

(*most general idea*)

rides, games, food, exhibits

(*words that are coordinate*)

9. Appetizers, main courses, salads, and desserts are specialties of the chef school.

specialties of the chef school

(*most general idea*)

appetizers, main courses, salads, desserts

(*words that are coordinate*)

10. Swim teams help students develop confidence, coordination, and physical strength.

swim teams help students develop

(*most general idea*)

confidence, coordination, physical strength

(*words that are coordinate*)

11. Hillary Clinton serves as an attorney, a community service worker, and an administrator.

Hillary Clinton serves as

(*most general idea*)

attorney, community service worker, administrator

(*words that are coordinate*)

12. Shopping is mentally, physically, and financially draining.

shopping is draining

(*most general idea*)

mentally, physically, financially

(*words that are coordinate*)

■ Overlapping Coordinate Ideas

Another important idea to keep in mind when you are writing thesis sentences is to be sure that the coordinate ideas do not overlap in meaning. **Overlapping** occurs when two or more coordinate ideas have approximately the same meaning. For example, the following sentence shows two coordinate ideas with similar meanings.

Redecorating a house requires *creativity*, time, *talent*, and money.

"Creativity" and "talent" overlap in meaning. These two italicized ideas are so close in meaning that it would be hard to write separate support paragraphs about them. When you try to write the essay, the two support paragraphs will end up being about the same idea. For example, if people are talented, they are able to figure out color schemes for remodeling a room, or maybe they are able to rearrange the furniture to make the room look more appealing. They might also suggest a few accessories that would accent or highlight the old furniture. If people are creative, they are able to do these same things. Consequently, these supporting ideas would overlap each other. Now consider a less obvious thesis sentence.

While raising children, parents try to be *sensitive, understanding*, and cheerful.

Though not quite as obvious, "sensitive" and "understanding" overlap in meaning. A parent might understand a child's outburst of temper if the parent is sensitive enough to know that the child has just been through a frustrating experience. These two ideas are also so close in meaning that you would have trouble deciding in which support paragraph the ideas should go. As you can see in the model essays in Part 3 of this unit, each support paragraph explains a different coordinate idea in the thesis sentence.

Parallel Grammatical Form in Thesis Sentences

If your thesis sentence previews the points to be covered in your paper, be sure that each point is written using the same grammatical form. This similar grammatical structure is called **parallel form**. You may choose whatever grammatical structure you like, such as nouns, verbs, phrases, or clauses. Study the following list to help you understand parallel form.

- **If an "-ing" verb form is used, all divisions must be in an "-ing" form.**

  For the elderly, having a pet means receiving companionship, getting exercise, having protection, and feeling useful.

  receiving companionship

  getting exercise

  having protection

  feeling useful

- **If the present tense of the verb is used, all divisions must be in the present tense.**

  Elderly people with pets receive companionship, get exercise, have protection, and feel useful.

  receive companionship

  get exercise

  have protection

  feel useful

- **If a noun is used, all divisions must be nouns.**

  Having a pet can provide companionship, exercise, protection, and usefulness to the elderly.

  companionship

  exercise

  protection

  usefulness

- **If "to" is used before the verb, all divisions must have "to" written or understood before the verb.**

  Elderly people often own a pet to receive companionship, get exercise, have protection, and feel useful.

  to receive companionship

  to get exercise

  to have protection

  to feel useful

- **If a prepositional phrase is used, all divisions must be prepositional phrases.** (If the same preposition is used, it does not need to be repeated.)

  Elderly people often own pets for companionship, exercise, protection, and a sense of usefulness.

  for companionship

  for exercise

  for protection

  for a sense of usefulness

It really doesn't matter which form is used; however, the thesis sentence will flow smoothly when all divisions are grammatically equal.

EXERCISE 3

In each group below, some ideas are not in parallel form. Revise the wording in each group to make the parts parallel. Try more than one parallel pattern. You may also change the order of the items within each group.

Example:

a. to eat pie

b. drinking milk

c. read a book

a. *to eat pie, to drink milk, to read a book*

b. *eating pie, drinking milk, reading a book*

c. *ate pie, drank milk, read a book*

1. a. formatting a disk

   b. to check for viruses

   c. ran a program

a. *formatting a disk, checking for viruses, running a program*

b. *to check for viruses, to format a disk, to run a program*

c. *ran a program, formatted a disk, checked for viruses*

2. a. growing wheat

   b. canned wild blackberries

   c. raises chickens

a. *growing wheat, canning wild blackberries, raising chickens*

b. *canned wild blackberries, raised chickens, grew wheat*

c. *raises chickens, grows wheat, cans wild blackberries*

3. a. cooking chicken in the crockpot

   b. steamed rice

   c. to barbecue ribs

   d. make a salad

a. cooking chicken in the crockpot, steaming rice, barbecuing ribs, making a salad

b. steamed rice, cooked chicken in the crockpot, barbecue ribs, made salad

c. to barbecue ribs, to cook chicken in the crockpot, to steam rice, to make a salad

d. make a salad, cook chicken in the crockpot, steam rice, barbecue ribs

4. a. buying stocks and bonds

   b. refinanced the house

   c. to invest in apartments

   d. puts money into a savings account

a. buying stocks and bonds, refinancing the house, investing in apartments, putting money into a savings account

b. refinanced the house, invested in apartments, bought stocks and bonds, put money into a savings account

c. to invest in apartments, to buy stocks, to refinance the house, to put money into a savings account

d. puts money into savings account, buys stocks and bonds, refinances the house, invests in apartments

5. a. to practice long hours

   b. read the directions

   c. talking to experts

a. to practice long hours, to read the directions, to talk to experts

b. read the directions, practice long hours, talk to experts

c. talking to experts, practicing long hours, reading the directions

6. a. reads

   b. studied

   c. take the test

a. reads, studies, takes the test

b. studied, read, took the test

c. take the test, read, study

7. a. to get an education

   b. meeting new friends

   c. prepares for a job

   d. improved self-esteem

a. to get an education, to meet new friends, to prepare for a job, to improve self-esteem

b. meeting new friends, preparing for a job, improving self-esteem, getting an education

c. prepares for a job, improves self-esteem, gets an education, meets new friends

d. improved self-esteem, got an education, met new friends, prepared for a job

8. a. live near mountain streams

   b. owning several horses

   c. enjoyed the outdoors

   d. hikes in the nearby mountains

a. live near mountain streams, own several houses, enjoy the outdoors

b. owning several horses, enjoying the outdoors, hiking in the nearby mountains, living near mountain streams

c. enjoyed the outdoors, hiked in the nearby mountains, lived near mountain streams, owned several horses

d. hikes in the nearby mountains, lives near mountain streams, owns several horses, enjoys the outdoors

9. a. to type materials

   b. making phone calls

   c. filed materials

a. to type materials, to make phone calls, to file materials

b. making phone calls, typing materials, filing materials

c. filed materials, typed materials, made phone calls

10. a. size

   b. colors

   c. of the style

   d. shaped

a. size, color, style, shape

b. colors, sizes, styles, shapes

c. of the style, of the size, of the colors, of the shape

d. shaped, sized, colored, styled

EXERCISE 4

Revise the following thesis sentences so that the points previewed are parallel.

Example:

The flower garden provides a colorful sidewalk border, fresh table arrangements,

and gifts for my neighbors.

~~**and my neighbors enjoy receiving them as gifts.**~~

1. National parks offer opportunities for seeing new places, *having* ~~to have~~ outdoor experiences, and meeting people from other states.

2. My summer spent in Maine brings pleasant memories of socializing with friends, *earning* extra money, and ~~of~~ buying my first car.

3. I enjoy going to that restaurant because the prices are reasonable, the food is excellent, and *the service is* good ~~service~~.

4. Mr. Edmonds was the best speaker I have ever heard because he spoke precisely, made clear points, and ~~a~~ serious *was* ~~speaker~~.

5. On my trip to Shanghai, China, I enjoyed visiting the Friendship House ~~and~~ the Bunde shopping area, and ~~I also enjoyed~~ the Peace Hotel.

6. Playing the piano provides an opportunity to relax, to entertain friends, *to* develop~~ing~~ a musical talent, and to learn new songs.

7. For safe driving, one must drive under control, *obey* ~~obeying~~ the speed limit, and never ~~to~~ drive under the influence of alcohol.

8. Smoking alienates people, costs money, and ~~it~~ is bad for your health, too.

9. Some of the things we take into consideration when planning a vacation are ~~how much~~ money ~~to take~~, interesting places to visit, and ~~are we going to have~~ time.

10. When you go river rafting, you must know how to pack the gear, maneuver~~ing~~ a raft, and ~~to~~ judge the rapids.

11. Before going to college, consider ~~how much~~ money ~~you have to spend~~, time, and attitude.

12. Before quitting college, students must examine their academic goals, their obligations to themselves, and *their ability to* ~~if they can financially~~ make more money with their present educational level.

13. Leaving home was very difficult for me because I had to say goodbye to my family, ~~I have~~ *had* to leave my friends, and ~~I~~ had to break up with my girlfriend.

14. Jellyfish, octopus, and ~~eating~~ fried or pickled eel are common Asian foods.

If you do not preview the subtopics in the thesis sentence, be sure that your subtopics are coordinate and identified clearly in your prewriting before drafting the paper.

Generating a Thesis Sentence

Now that you know what a thesis sentence is, you need to learn how to generate ideas that can be used to formulate this thesis sentence. The following steps can help you generate a thesis sentence.

1. **State your topic.**

2. **Brainstorm to find a direction.** Type or write anything that comes to your mind. This is like a game of free association. Continue to jot down ideas as rapidly as they come to mind. Remember, now is the time to use your resources. Generate ideas that come from your personal experiences. Include your feelings. These feelings may be positive or negative; it really doesn't matter so long as they reflect what you have seen or felt.

3. **Find a direction.** Because it is impossible to write everything you know about a subject, it is important to find the direction you want to take. As soon as you are aware of a direction in your brainstorming, write it

down. If your topic were "divorce," you might write the following entries:

a. My divorce has left me with many problems.
b. My divorce was the best thing that ever happened to me.
c. My divorce changed my life.
d. My parents' divorce created many problems for me.
e. My parents' divorce solved many of my problems.
f. My parents' divorce changed my life.

The direction you choose may be either positive (b,e), negative (a,d), or a combination of both (c,f).

4. **Brainstorm with direction.** Once again, jot down everything that comes to mind; however, this time your entries will be more specific because you already have a direction. Continue to brainstorm until you have ten to twelve entries.

5. **Group entries that fit together.** Carefully look over all entries you made while brainstorming. Combine these entries into groups until you have two to five separate areas that support the focused topic. **The key word and direction with two to five support groups form the thesis sentence.** Even if you do not preview the points of the paper in the thesis sentence, you still have coordinate groups of ideas to guide the paper.

6. **Formulate the thesis sentence.** Write it with a clear direction, or write it with a clear direction and previewed subtopics.

Carefully examine the following examples of stating the topic, finding the direction, brainstorming with direction, and sorting related ideas into groups.

Example 1

Topic: Divorce

Brainstorm to find direction:

my divorce   parents divorced

Being divorced has caused me many problems.

divorce is widespread   sister divorced

Direction: Being divorced has caused me many problems.

Brainstorm with direction:

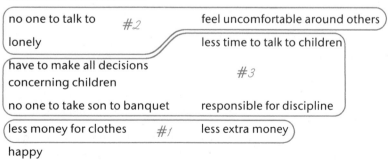

happy

Groups (topic outline):

1. money problems (financial)

2. personal problems (emotional)

3. responsibilities for son (parental)

Thesis sentence with clear direction:

Being divorced has caused me many problems that I did not face when I was married.

Thesis sentence with clear direction and previewed subtopics:

Being divorced has caused me financial, emotional, and parental problems that I did not face when I was married.

Note The groups can serve as a topic outline or as part of the thesis sentence.

Example 2

Topic: pets

Brainstorm to find direction:

dogs	fun for children
need love	good for old people

Direction: beneficial to old people

Brainstorm with direction:

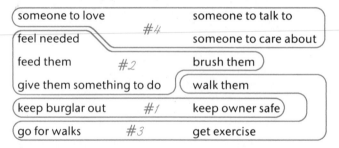

Groups (topic outline):

1. provide protection

2. make them feel needed

3. get exercise

4. have companionship

Thesis sentence with clear direction:

For the elderly, having a pet can be very beneficial.

Thesis sentence with clear direction and previewed subtopics:

For the elderly, having a pet means receiving companionship, getting exercise, having protection, and feeling useful.

Note The groups can serve as a topic outline or as part of the thesis sentence.

EXERCISE 5

Master for transparency is in the Instructor's Manual.

Follow the same process as shown in Examples 1 and 2 in this section to develop a thesis statement for three *of the following subjects:*

tour of your city	*horses*
weight room	*swimming*
football game	*art museums*
a particular restaurant	

1. *Topic:* _____

   Brainstorm to find direction:

   _____

   _____

   _____

   _____

   _____

   Direction:

   _____

   _____

   Brainstorm with direction:

   _____

   _____

   _____

   _____

   _____

   _____

Groups (topic outline):

_____

_____

_____

_____

Thesis sentence:

_____

_____

_____

2. *Topic:* _____

Brainstorm to find direction:

_____

_____

_____

_____

_____

Direction:

_____

_____

Brainstorm with direction:

_____

_____

_____

_____

_____

_____

_____

Groups (topic outline):

_____

_____

_____

_____

Thesis sentence:

_____

_____

_____

3. *Topic:* _____

Brainstorm to find direction:

_____

_____

_____

_____

Direction:

_____

_____

Brainstorm with direction:

_____

_____

_____

_____

_____

_____

_____

Groups (topic outline):

_____

_____

_____

_____

Thesis sentence:

_____

_____

_____

Arranging the Order of Divisions or Subtopics

One last item you need to consider before writing your thesis sentence is the order in which your coordinate ideas are presented. Sometimes there is more than one way to arrange the divisions in a paper, so use your best judgment to decide which order is most effective for the overall development of your essay. Even during drafting, you may discover that you need to rearrange the order of the subtopics. When the thesis sentence does not preview the points to be covered in the paper, the points generated through prewriting can serve as a rough outline. Remember, though, that **the divisions must be presented in some logical order.** Here are some possible arrangements for subtopics.

1. Place the divisions in the order of *increasing importance*, as *you* see them. Put the most important last.

Example: Before buying a used car, a person must consider special features desired, type of car needed, cost, and condition of the car.

Before buying a used car, a person must consider several factors.

1. special features desired
2. type of car needed
3. cost
4. condition of the car

2. Place the divisions in the order of *decreasing importance*, as *you* see them. Put the most important first.

Example: Before buying a used car, a person must consider condition of the car, cost, type of car needed, and special features desired.

Before buying a used car, a person must consider several important factors.

1. condition of the car
2. cost
3. type of car needed
4. special features desired

3. Place the second most important division first and the most important last, as *you* see them. Arrange the weaker points in the middle. This order begins and ends on a strong note.

Example: A nurse must care for patients, fill out charts, and talk to family members.

A nurse has many duties.

1. care for patients
2. fill out charts
3. talk to family members

4. Place in the order of increasing interest, as *you* see them.

Example: Being divorced has caused financial, emotional, and parenting problems.

Being divorced has caused many problems.

1. financial
2. emotional
3. parenting

5. Place in *chronological order*. This is similar to historical progression.

Example: Transportation has progressed from trains to cars to jet planes.

Transportation has progressed rapidly.

1. trains
2. cars
3. jet planes

6. Place in *sequential progression* (one idea naturally follows the other).

Example: To produce good essays, writers brainstorm, sort related ideas into groups, and formulate a thesis sentence.

To produce good essays, writers use an organized process.

1. brainstorm
2. group
3. formulate a thesis sentence

All of these steps will become automatic as you write more and more papers. No one method is used by all writers, and sometimes some steps come more easily than others. Just continue to work hard and have confidence in yourself.

Collaborative Project: Working and Learning Together

Option 1

Divide into groups of three to five. In each group, brainstorm the topic "making a home safe," or "making a home childproof." On self-stick notes, jot down ideas, using only one idea per note. Then, stick the notes on a surface where everybody in your group can see them. Next, group the like ideas together. As a group, compose a thesis sentence that includes a topic and direction. Either preview the main points in the thesis sentence or include a topic outline on a transparency to be shared with the class. Be prepared to discuss each group's thesis sentence.

Option 2

Divide into two age groups: those twenty-five years of age and over and those under twenty-five years of age. Then brainstorm, group, and collaboratively develop a thesis sentence based on the following topics.

Group twenty-five years of age and older: Advantages of going to college right out of high school.

Group under twenty-five years of age: Advantages of going to college after waiting ten or more years.

Then share the thesis sentences with the other group. Discuss the perspective taken by each group.

PART 2

**SOMETHING TO THINK ABOUT,
SOMETHING TO WRITE ABOUT**

Your College Years

Dr. Bob Hartman, *consultant, Student Ministry Department, Baptist Sunday School Board, Nashville, Tennessee*

1   Have you ever considered the changes that are taking place and will take place in your life as a college student? Has it ever occurred to you that your professors and other school personnel have certain goals for your growth and maturity during your college years? Has it ever dawned on you that certain developmental changes will occur in your life as you move from adolescence to young adulthood? Though college students seldom think about them, key changes will probably happen to them during their college years.

2   During this time, students are going through an identity crisis and are endeavoring to find out who they are and what their strengths and weaknesses are. They have, of course, plenty of both. It is important to know how people perceive themselves as well as how other people perceive them. According to Piers and Landau, in an article discussing the theories of Erik H. Erickson in *International Encyclopedia of Social Sciences* (1979), identity is determined by genetic endowment (what is inherited from parents), shaped by environment, and influenced by chance events. People are influenced by their environment and, in turn, influence their environment. How people see themselves in both roles is unquestionably a part of their identity.

3   While students are going through an identity crisis, they are becoming independent from their parents yet are probably still very dependent on them. This independence/dependence struggle is very much a part of the later adolescence stage. In fact, it may be heightened by their choice to pursue a college education. Immediately after graduating from high school, some graduates choose to enter the work world. As a result of this choice, they may become financially independent from their parents. But college students have chosen to grow and learn new skills that take years to develop, so they probably need at least some degree of dependence on their parents.

4   In his April 1984 article "Psychological Separation of Late Adolescents from Their Parents" in the *Journal of Counseling Psychology*, Jeffery A. Hoffman observed that there are four distinct aspects to psychological separation from one's parents. First, there is functional independence, which involves the capability of individuals to take care of practical and personal affairs, such as handling finances, choosing their own wardrobes, and determining their daily agenda. Second, there is attitudinal independence, which means that individuals learn to see and accept the difference between their own attitudes, values, and beliefs and those of their parents. The third process of psychological separation is emotional independence. Hoffman defines this process as "freedom from an excessive need for approval, closeness, togetherness, and emotional support in relation to the mother and father." For example, college students would feel free to select the major that they want to pursue without feeling they must have parental approval. Fourth is freedom from "excessive guilt, anxiety, mistrust, responsibility, inhibition, resentment, and anger in relation to the mother and father." College students need to stand back and see where they are in the independence/dependence struggle.

5   Probably one of the most stressful matters for young college students is establishing their sexual identity, which includes relating to the opposite sex and projecting their future roles as men or women. Each must define her or his sexual
identity in a feminine or masculine role. These are exciting times yet frustrating
times. Probably nothing can make students feel lower or higher emotionally than
the way they are relating to whomever they are having a romantic relationship
with. For example, when I was working with a young college student, he bounced
into my office once with a smile on his face and excitement in his voice. The young
man declared, "I've just had the best day of my life!" He went on to explain how
he had met an extraordinary young woman and how this relationship was all he
had dreamed a romantic relationship should be. That same young man came into
my office less than a week later, dragging his feet with a dismayed, dejected look
on his face. He sat down in the same chair, sighed deeply, and declared, "I've just
had the worst day of my life!" He and the young woman had just had an argument,
and their relationship was no longer going well. Thus, the way students are relating
to those of the opposite sex has a definite influence on their emotions.

6   At the same time, these young adults are learning how to give and receive
affection in the adult world. This aspect of growth deals not only with interaction
with the opposite sex but with friends of both sexes and all ages. As they grow and
reach young adulthood, the way they relate to others changes. It is a time when
they as adults should think about how they relate to and show proper respect for
peers, how they relate to the children and young adolescents in their lives, and
how they relate to their parents and show them affection. For example, when I was
a graduate student at Southwestern Baptist Theological Seminary, I visited my
parents after I had just finished a course in counseling. During the course I had
come to realize that while my world was expanding and new options were opening
for me, my father, who was in his sixties, was seeing his world shrink and his options
narrow. During my visit home, my father and I had several conversations in which
we discussed the content of my course and how it applied to our lives. I found
myself seeing my father in a different way and relating to him as a friend whom I
could encourage. I was consciously encouraging the man who over the years had
encouraged me. I was relating to my father in a different way.

7   Another change for college students is internalizing their religious faith, their
values, and their morals. Since birth, one or more parents have been modeling for
them and teaching them certain beliefs, values, and morals. In their adolescent
years, however, these matters are questioned and in some cases rebelled against.
Now, as young adults, they have the opportunity to decide for themselves what
beliefs, values, and morals they are going to accept for their lives. In the late sixties,
a young woman from a background that was extremely prejudiced against people
from other races came to college convinced that her race was superior. She was
distressed because she had been put into a dorm that had people from a variety of
ethnic backgrounds. Over the next four years, this student, who considered herself
intelligent, found herself in classes and social events in which people of other races
performed as well as or more competently than she did. As she finished her senior
year, she had grown to realize that people of other races were not only equal to
her but were people who could be her friends and from whom she could learn.
These religious, moral, and ethical values that are set during the college years often
last a lifetime.

8   In addition to affirming personal values, college students develop new ways to organize and use knowledge. The challenges of academic life not only introduce them to new knowledge but force them to evaluate how they gather, process, and apply knowledge in their lives. For some, this will be a painful experience, but for all it will be a growing experience. One student with whom I had worked went on to become an English teacher. She shared with me how her attitude toward literature changed during her college years. "In high school I made good grades in English," she observed, "but the material meant very little to me." She then went on to explain how in college she came to realize that literature is one of the best ways to understand a culture. Her way of learning had changed. All students should be aware of how they react to new knowledge and new ways of learning, how they process the knowledge presented to them, and how they organize this knowledge.

9   And last of all, these young adults are becoming world citizens, are becoming aware not only of other groups in their own culture but also of people of other cultures. As they meet these people and interact with them, they find themselves being introduced to new ways of life and new ways of interpreting life. As they do so, they grow and become more mature people. A student attending a community college in his home town explained how as a student he came to know a student from a Third World country—a country he had not even heard of before. The international student, who expected to be appointed to an important governmental position when he returned home, had a brother who taught law at the major university of his country. The American student and the international student became close friends and spent many hours sharing their thoughts and dreams. The American student observed, "Because of our friendship, I have come to understand people of Third World countries in a way I never realized possible. I can no longer read the newspaper or watch a television newscast without seeing the people from other countries in a different light. They are now real people who have dreams, hopes, and struggles, just as I do." Because of the opportunities he had while attending college, this young man, like many other students, experienced a new understanding of the world and of himself.

10   College is designed to be a time of personal growth and expansion. At times it can be threatening. For certain, it is an experience that contributes to young adults' growth and maturity. Not only are they being introduced to new people and new knowledge, but they are also acquiring new ways of assembling and processing information. Just as profoundly, they are growing in their understanding of themselves, others, and the world in which they live.

Understanding Words

Briefly define the following words as they are used in the above essay

1. endeavoring *trying or striving*
2. genetic *related to the science of studying genes*
3. endowment *talent, ability*
4. internalizing *taking in and making an integral part of one's attitude and beliefs*
5. ethical *pertaining to standards of conduct or moral judgment*
6. Third World country *the underdeveloped or emergent countries of the world, especially of Africa and Asia*

Something to Write About

Using one of the assignments listed below, develop a thesis sentence that either states a clear direction or previews the points to be covered in the paper. Then draft your essay.

1. Explain how your life is different now from what it was in high school.
2. Discuss how a friend has changed since graduating from high school.
3. Give the biggest challenges that face college students.
4. Explain qualities that peers most admire in college students.
5. Explain types of support that are important to college students.
6. How is your life different from that of your peers who are working rather than going to college?
7. How has an international student changed your way of thinking?
8. In what ways are you still dependent upon your parents?
9. In what ways are you independent from your parents?
10. How have your values changed in the last few years?

After you draft your essay, revise for content and edit for mechanics.

Content

>   Revise it so it has a clear thesis sentence.

>   Be sure that each support paragraph has a strong topic sentence and ample support sentences.

Mechanics

>   Check for subject-verb agreement.

>   Check for consistent verbs.

>   Check for consistent point of view.

Respect

Phyllis J. Hilding, *student*

1   "I get no respect!" The comedian Rodney Dangerfield has made many of his fans laugh at this famous remark of his. In truth, however, respect for other people and their property is not a laughing matter. In our world as it is today, respect for other people has taken a back seat to flagrant disrespect of people's feelings, their property, and even their very lives.

2   Respect for other people's feelings seems to be out of date in today's world. Children and teenagers are growing into adulthood learning not to "Do unto others as you would wish them to do unto you," but to do unto others before they do unto you. Movies, television, and today's books most probably have all played a part in forming the younger generation's attitudes. Most parents, regardless of how hard it is, have tried to raise their children to be respectful of their elders and their peers. Besides the outside influences like movies, television, and wanting to be like everyone else, being brought up in a disrespectful family environment where family members talk and act badly toward one another can encourage people to grow up without a sense of value and respect for other people. If parents would treat each other and their children in a caring and courteous way, perhaps they could instill in their children a respect for other people's feelings that would stay with them throughout their lives, regardless of what they see or hear in the world at large.

3   Disrespect is shown every day when Americans see or hear of people stealing or damaging other people's property without feeling any guilt. Thievery and vandalism have always existed, but in today's world, they seem to be prevalent, not from need and the frustration of being poor, but because of the current generation's sense of values. Thieves and vandals see no wrong in taking or damaging what does not belong to them because they have never learned to respect people in general.

4   Disrespect for human life seems to be at an all-time high. The movies many kids watch portray cold-blooded killers who take lives without blinking an eye. The so-called good guy in the movie who takes out half a dozen people in the name of justice or retribution is considered an idol by impressionistic children and adults alike, and respect for human life is nowhere to be seen or heard. The television news and the newspapers all tell of murder in the first degree, premeditated killing of human beings without any sense of guilt. Television presents street gangs killing one another without remorse. Killing a person is nothing more to them than swatting at a fly. In stories and in real life, depicted in movies and on television, and in newspapers and magazines, viewers see soldiers or mercenaries nonchalantly standing over the dead bodies of people they have just cold-bloodedly killed, calmly smoking a cigarette, as if the bodies were nothing more than a grease spot in the road. The world must learn to value human life again, whether at war or at peace.

5   If mankind can learn to respect other human beings in thoughts, words, and actions, humanity may survive on this planet, Earth. If parents teach children clearly not only to respect their elders but to treat everyone with respect and courtesy, children may grow up to be responsible adults who influence other people to respect human feelings, rights, and property. They may grow up to cherish human life, not annihilate it. All people want respect, and so they must give it to earn it.

Understanding Words

Briefly define the following words as they are used in the above essay.

1. flagrant *shocking*
2. retribution *deserved punishment*
3. mercenaries *people who will fight wars for any country that will pay them*

Questions on Content

1. In the author's opinion, how do people treat other people today?
2. What do television, movies, and newspapers do that depict a disrespect for human life?
3. How might family life contribute to a loss of respect for human beings?

Questions on Form

1. Identify the thesis sentence.
2. Show how the support paragraphs relate to the thesis sentence.
3. Why does the author use a 3rd person point of view rather than 1st or 2nd person point of view?

Answers for Unit 4, Part 3 are in the Instructor's Manual.

Being a Student

YoungMi Dauer, *student*

1   "I'm so tired of high heels and business suits! I wish I could go back to school," I often grumbled in a cushy chair in my office. My wish came true, and today I once again wear blue jeans and T-shirts, carry a backpack, and hold heavy textbooks in my arms as I had dreamed. But being an older student is not so much fun; socially, financially, and psychologically I am a handicapped person.

2   I used to enjoy the rainy campus in a school cafeteria, hang out with class-mates between and after classes, and go backpacking for a long summer break, experiences that are not available for me any more. Studying time eats most of my day! My social life is zero since I have become a student again. My important assets such as invitations from friends for a party, a potluck, bowling, and camping are now a liability. I can't gladly greet a relative who calls me on the phone to tell me in a bright voice that she will visit me for a week during final exams!!! I murmur for God's mercy on me.

3   I am definitely not ready to be a social butterfly, and I am also limping financially, which is humbling me quite a bit. Without my contribution to the budget, I'm just another item on the expense account. My tuition, expensive books, and other expenses have put my home economy in a recession. Even though I have restrained my personal spending on entertainment, clothing, and gifts for friends, my eyes still flash red lights as chunks of cash fly out for me to buy things. I prefer to be a contributor over being a dependent number on a tax form.

4   An older student isn't a healthy person psychologically; stress, anxiety, confusion, and nervousness are the words that surround my daily life. I can't be just a student as I had dreamed; consequently, my emotions are responsibilities that are

divided between family and student life. Yes, I have things to be faced as a wife at home; I get a headache when thinking about buying a house, dealing with my husband on his bad days, and making a decision on starting a family. On my student side, pressures are not less. Reading the books for each class, meeting the due day for my computer program, doing math homework, and taking the tests make my days pretty rough.

5   School life as an older student isn't as romantic as it was in my old days. Too many responsibilities, pressures, and different priorities are interrupting my concentration just on school work. Maybe I'd rather wear my high heels and business suits than blue jeans and T-shirts.

Understanding Words

Briefly define the following words as they are used in the above essay.

1. assets *things of value*
2. liability *a disadvantage*

Questions on Content

1. How has the author cut down on spending?
2. What pressures does she refer to?
3. What new expenses does she have?

Questions on Form

1. Where is the thesis sentence located?
2. How does the author support the thesis sentence?
3. What makes this essay enjoyable to read?

Golf

Kathy Bagby, *student*

1   "I can't believe anyone would even want to try to hit a dumb little golf ball with one of those skinny little sticks, much less chase it all around a golf course." These were the exact words I had used before the summer I decided to take golf lessons. My daughter was playing on the junior golf team, and I thought it would be nice if we could play together. Much to my surprise and delight, after the first lesson I was hooked! I learned golf can be a terrific challenge, a very humbling game, and, most of all, a great family sport.

2   First of all, I learned that in playing golf, it is me against the course and Mother Nature. Naturally, it's great fun to play the game with friends; however, the real challenge comes when I tee off. I must tackle a fairway covered with innumerable obstacles such as hills, sand traps, rough grassy areas, and ponds. To make matters worse, I usually have only three or four chances to "plunk" the ball into a hole on the green if I want to make par. Then, of course, there is the weather. On a windy day my ball can be thrown in an off-direction or slowed down. Then there are the sandstorms that blind me or perhaps the up-and-coming rainstorm that I'm trying desperately to beat as I race to the ninth hole. It seems the challenges are never-ending, making the game so addictive.

3   Next, golf is a humbling game! I'll never forget the time I set up to tee off. I took my practice swing, stepped up, took form, felt confident, brought down my swing, and hit the ball, only to watch it go a foot! My face was as red as the ball I had just hit. Another example of humility came the day I was playing the front nine at the Bellair Golf Course. I had just birdied my first hole. It was hole seven. I must

have jumped ten feet in the air. I let everyone near and far know what I had done! I was ready for the pro circuit now! Then came the ninth hole with a long, tough par 4. "A cinch for this old pro," I thought to myself as I stepped up to tee off — 1st stroke, 2nd stroke, 3rd stroke, etc., etc., etc. With ten strokes on my card and my head between my knees, I headed for the ninth hole. In addition to these kinds of things, I've had my humbling moments at the water hole. I hit one ball after another, trying any way possible to get over or around the water, only to end up in it. I have definitely eaten a few pieces of humble pie playing this game!

4   The most important part of golf, however, is the pleasurable time I'm able to spend with my family playing together. As an example, we have found it is a great time to share our thoughts and ideas with each other as we walk the course. We will sometimes laugh, tell jokes, or just tease each other. My nine-year-old son loves to show off to his dad just how far he can hit the ball with his custom-made club. My husband and I enjoy moments of closeness as we just walk together quietly. Watching the beautiful grace and form with which my daughter plays swells up a pride within me. Playing together has really helped knit a special closeness in our family.

5   In conclusion, I have found playing golf to be a very positive and rewarding experience. It has taught me many things, such as patience, humility, and perseverance. To anyone who has never given the game a fair chance, I say, "Don't knock it until you try it!"

Understanding Words

Briefly define the following words as they are used in the above essay.

1. innumerable *countless*
2. perseverance *persistence in spite of difficulty*

Questions on Content

1. What do sandstorms do to the player?
2. At Bellaire Golf Course, how did the author do on hole seven? on hole nine?
3. How old is her son?
4. Does it appear as if the writer is a beginning golfer or an experienced player?
5. What does the author mean when she writes, "With ten strokes on my card and my head between my knees, I headed for the ninth hole"?

Questions on Form

1. This essay on golf is well written. However, of the three parts of the essay — introduction, support, and conclusion — which part could use a bit more development? What would you suggest to the writer?
2. Does the essay have a distinct thesis sentence? What makes it effective?

Building a Better Home

John K. Terres, a roving editor for *National Wildlife*

1   A bird's nest is its home — a house without a mortgage, as one ornithological wag said. Products of avian ingenuity and tireless labor, nests and nesting places come in a bewildering variety of sizes, shapes, and styles; each is a marvel of

longtime evolution and adaptation of birds in response to the basic need to protect their eggs and young.

2   The most obvious difference between nests is size, which usually varies in proportion to the size of the builder. Two- to three-inch long calliope humming-birds, the smallest birds in temperate North America, build tiny cups of mosses and lichens only about one and a half inches across, balanced on small dead pine twigs up to 70 feet above the ground. Even more delicate is the tiny spoonlike nest of the Asiatic crested swift. It is made of bark and glued with the swift's saliva to the side of a lofty, slender forest limb.

3   Compare these with nests of larger birds. A bald eagle's nest in the upper branches of a longleaf pine near St. Petersburg, Florida, was the largest known nest ever built in a tree by a single pair of birds. Sticks, grasses, and debris were added annually for many years by the adult eagles. The nest grew to be 20 feet deep and 9½ feet across—and was estimated to weigh several tons.

4   The tall, stately white storks of Europe and Asia construct huge stick nests, usually on roofs or chimney tops. One nest in Holland, built on a huge wagon wheel atop a stable, blew down in a high wind. It was 12 feet across, weighed several thousand pounds and could easily have accommodated six storks standing along the rim of one side of the nest. It was so tightly woven that it could not be torn apart but had to be burned to be disposed of.

5   The largest bird nests in the world, however, are built on the ground by Australasian megapodes—hen to turkey-sized "incubator birds." Using their big feet to scratch up leaves, sticks, and earth from the forest floor, they fashion huge, conical mounds, 5 to 7 feet high and 20 to 50 feet across. Large mounds may weigh up to five tons. The birds' eggs are incubated by the internal heat of the decom-posing litter in the mounds. . . .

6   The African hammerhead, a storklike bird only 12 inches tall, builds a massive, ball-shaped, clay-lined nest of sticks, usually low in the fork of a tree. Six feet deep and six feet across, the nest is so well built it can bear the weight of a man. Building takes six weeks; one pair watched by an American ornithologist made more than 8,000 trips carrying nesting material in their bills.

7   A tropical Wagler's oriole observed in a Panama tree colony took nearly four weeks to weave its three-foot long, pouchlike nest. In contrast, most small Ameri-can songbirds—bluebirds, wrens, catbirds, cardinals, robins, warblers—need a few days to a week to build their nests. Natural selection seems to have speeded up nest-building in temperate regions where the nesting season is shorter and most nests are simpler.

8   Yet some birds labor much longer than seems necessary. Energetic male house wrens, marsh wrens, and prothonotary warblers, as part of their courtship, build extra "dummy" nests—up to six or more in marsh wrens. Each male displays his nests to a female, allowing her to choose among them.

9   One of the most astonishing examples of extra nest building has been shown by the American robin. A pair in Willoughby, Ohio, once decided to nest on a long girder in a partly finished factory building. The problem was that the girder had 26 identical openings. The birds' solution? They began building 26 nests. The pair finally finished one of the nests and successfully raised a brood.

10   Another pair of robins built nine partly finished nests on nine successive steps of a fire escape at the Bronx Zoo. One local newspaper called it the "Case of the Confused Robin." The birds began by bringing nesting material to each of the steps. Then, explained the zoo director, "when the female robin sits on her nest, she looks up, sees those other nests over her head, and flies off for mud and straw to finish them." . . .

11   Some birds nest together, apartment style. In one tree, a flicker, bluebird and a kestrel (sparrow hawk) live harmoniously in separate nesting holes, even though the hawk is normally a predator of the other two birds. House sparrows, night herons, and grackles that nest in the lower parts of the nest of eagles apparently gain protection from the large, fierce raptors.

12   Perhaps the most spectacular nests of all are the gigantic apartment-style structures of the sociable weavers of Africa. Up to 30 feet long, with thatched roofs of grasses and twigs that are 3 to 6 feet thick, the enormous nests are usually found high on the branches of isolated trees in open grassland. From a distance, they are sometimes mistaken for native huts. From 100 to 300 pairs of the sparrow-sized birds work together to build the dwelling in which they live throughout the year and sleep in at night. . . .

13   Normally, nest building ends once the eggs are laid. But some birds continue to add to the nest, especially the lining. Female Costa's hummingbirds often build up the sides of their nests while incubating their eggs. Chimney swifts even continue to gather twigs and glue them in place on the nests with sticky saliva. They stop only after the young have made their first flight from the nest. Such behavior is just one of the many marvels of birds and their nests.

Understanding Words

Briefly define the following words as they are used in the above essay.

1. ornithological *having to do with the study of birds*
2. avian *pertaining to characteristics of birds*
3. ingenuity *cleverness*
4. megapodes *certain birds in Australia and the South Pacific*
5. predator *hunter of prey*

Questions on Content

1. What is the most obvious difference among nests?
2. How much did the largest known nest ever built in a tree by a single pair of birds weigh?
3. When does nest building usually end?

Questions on Form

1. Where does the author state the thesis sentence? What is the thesis sentence?
2. Does each paragraph stay with one idea?
3. Does the entire essay stay with the main idea?

THE WRITER'S TOOLS: ELIMINATING FRAGMENTS, RUN-ON SENTENCES, AND COMMA SPLICES

OBJECTIVES

- Recognize and correct fragments.
- Recognize and correct run-on sentences.
- Recognize and correct comma splices.

To be clearly understood, writing is organized into sentences. Each sentence must be complete, which means that it must contain at least a main subject and a main verb. If a sentence does not have these basic parts, it is a **fragment**.

Sentences must also be separated from each other by being clearly punctuated. If sentences are not properly separated from one another, **run-on sentences** and **comma splices** are created. These sentence problems can confuse and distract the reader from the content of your writing.

Fragments, run-on sentences, and comma splices are major sentence-structure problems that you can learn to eliminate from your writing. Following are explanations, examples, and exercises to help you identify and revise your own writing so that you can write clearly on your job or for your college classes.

■ Fragments

Test covering fragments, run-on sentences, and comma splices p. 35 in Instructor's Manual.

A sentence is a group of words that has a main subject and a main verb and states a complete thought. If a group of words lacks one of these parts, it is a **fragment**.

Types of Fragments

1. fragments that contain no subject
2. fragments that have no verb
3. fragments with verb forms that cannot be the main verb
   "-ing" form of the verb used alone
   "to" before a verb
4. fragments that have both a subject and a verb but are preceded by a subordinator

Fragments that Contain No Subject

Examples: Runs two miles every morning. (fragment)

Ate all of the pizza herself. (fragment)

To add clarity, you can change the fragment to a sentence simply by *adding a subject*—someone who "runs" or someone who "ate."

Steve runs two miles every morning. (sentence)

Theresa ate all of the pizza herself. (sentence)

Note   A command is a sentence, not a fragment, although the subject "you" is not stated.

(You) close the door, please.   (sentence)

EXERCISE 1

Change the following fragments to sentences by adding a subject.

Example:

> *hand, Ellen often*
> **On the other ~~hand, often~~ waited for class to begin.**

1. *we*
    In addition, ~~went~~ on a family vacation.

2. *Phil*
    Then left the car in the middle of the road.

3. *he*
    Suddenly and frantically, searched for his girlfriend.

4. *Mike walked*
    ~~Walked~~ all the way to the gym.

5. *His talk also*
    ~~Also~~ gave us a new perspective on life.

Fragments that Have No Verb

Some fragments have no verb and can often be thought of as "tag-ons" or "afterthoughts."

> *Examples:* The soft, furry kitten.   (fragment)
>
>   The soft, furry kitten in the basket.   (fragment)

To correct these fragments, you can **add a verb** (and other words, if needed).

> The soft, furry kitten in the basket **cried**.
>
> The soft, furry kitten **was** in the basket.

Very often when you are writing, these fragments without a main verb become "tag-on" thoughts that belong with another sentence. The words in bold type in the following examples are fragments and could easily be added to the previous sentence.

He did not give us a number.   **An exact number.**

The child looked longingly at the kitten.   **The kitten in the basket.**

Rusty opened a store.   **Her own store.**

The best way to correct these fragmented "tag-on" thoughts is to **combine the fragment with a complete sentence** (usually the one before or after it).

He did not give us **an exact number.**

The child looked longingly at the soft, furry **kitten in the basket.**

Rusty opened **her own store.**

Note Eliminating these fragments also eliminates a kind of wordiness that distracts from your writing.

EXERCISE 2

Revise the "tag-on" thoughts in the following paragraphs by combining them with another sentence.

Paragraph 1

Citizens can do their part to help the environment. They can crush, save, and take aluminum cans to centers. ~~To recycling centers.~~ [*recycling*] In addition, people can reuse [*glass and plastic*] containers rather than throw them away. ~~Glass and plastic containers.~~ Gardeners can use natural ecological defenses such as lady bugs, water sprays, and beer solutions, ~~Rather~~ [*rather*] than pesticides, ~~Harmful pesticides~~ [*harmful*] to eliminate insects. Car owners who service their own cars should properly dispose of used oil and filters. ~~Motor oil and oil filters.~~ [*motor oil*] Saving the Earth is like preserving America's future.

Paragraph 2

I felt excited as I entered my ~~spot. My~~ favorite spot. I plucked ripe blackberries, ~~Blackberries~~ from the heavy vines. Nearby, I heard a stream flowing. Overhead, [*white, billowy*] clouds comforted me as they appeared in the sky. ~~White, billowy clouds.~~ Oak trees and pine trees provided shade as I sat on the soft pine needles, ~~Needles~~ on the gently sloping ground. I ate the blackberries still in my hands, and as I ate them, I saw the stains. ~~Stains~~ left by the purple, juicy berries. But I didn't care, for I was surrounded by

the freshness. ~~The freshness~~ of nature.

Fragments with Verb Forms that Cannot Be the Main Verb

Some verb forms cannot be used as main verbs in a sentence. If you use them as main verbs, you will create fragments.

Verb Forms that Cannot Be Main Verbs

the "-ing" form of a verb used alone

"to" before a verb

- **The "-ing" form of the verb used alone cannot be the main verb in a sentence.**

    Bill going to the gym after school.   (fragment)

    Going to the yogurt shop.   (fragment)

To be used as a main verb, this "-ing" form must be linked to some "be" verb.

"Be" Verbs			
is	are	were	has been
am	was	had been	have been

For example, if you convert the fragment "Bill going to the gym after school" to "Bill *is* going to the gym after school," you have a complete sentence, and the fragment has been eliminated.

These fragmented sentences can be corrected in a variety of ways. The choice of how to revise them depends on the meaning you would like to communicate in your sentence. Here are some ways to correct the fragment "Going to the yogurt shop."

First, you could **add a subject and some form of the verb "be."**

Bill is going to the yogurt shop.

You could **make the fragment the subject and add a main verb.** (You may want to add other words to make the meaning clear.)

Going to the yogurt shop **makes** the children happy.

Or you could **add a complete sentence (subject and a verb) after the "-ing" verb phrase**.

Going to the yogurt shop, **Bill met his girlfriend**.

Note In the above example, the "-ing" verb form must refer to the subject in the sentence that it is linked to.

EXERCISE 3

Revise the following fragments using these same patterns.

Example:

Walking to the bus stop.

Lori is walking to the bus stop.

Add a subject and some form of the verb "be."

Walking to the bus stop invigorates me.

Make the fragment the subject and add a main verb. (Add other words if needed.)

Walking to the bus stop, I counted six rabbits.

Add a sentence (subject and a verb) after the fragment.

1. Caring for a sick friend.

Randy is caring for a sick friend.

Add a subject and some form of the verb "be."

Caring for a sick friend is rewarding.

Make the fragment the subject and add a main verb. (Add other words if needed.)

Caring for a sick friend, I learned nursing skills.

Add a sentence (a subject and a verb) after the fragment.

2. Collecting aluminum cans.

Harvey is collecting aluminum cans.

Add a subject and some form of the verb "be."

Collecting aluminum cans can be a profitable hobby.

Make the fragment the subject and add a main verb. (Add other words if needed.)

Collecting aluminum cans, Pete found a diamond ring.

Add a sentence (a subject and a verb) after the fragment.

3.   Becoming older.

My dog is becoming older.

Add a subject and some form of the verb "be."

Becoming older is simply part of life.

Make the fragment the subject and add a main verb. (Add other words if needed.)

Becoming older, I appreciate life more.

Add a sentence (a subject and a verb) after the fragment.

4.   Running for political office.

My neighbor is running for political office.

Add a subject and some form of the verb "be."

Running for political office requires a lot of money.

Make the fragment the subject and add a main verb. (Add other words if needed.)

Running for political office, my neighbor goes from house to

Add a sentence (a subject and a verb) after the fragment.   *house talking to people.*

5.   Typing a research paper.

Joe is typing a research paper.

Add a subject and some form of the verb "be."

Typing a research paper is easier on the computer than on the

Make the fragment the subject and add a main verb. (Add other words if needed.)   *typewriter.*

Typing a research paper, Tony spent hours in the lab.

Add a sentence (a subject and a verb) after the fragment.

6.   Welcoming his friends.

Danny was welcoming his friends.

Add a subject and some form of the verb "be."

Welcoming his friends turned out to be easy for Danny.

Make the fragment the subject and add a main verb. (Add other words if needed.)

Welcoming his friends, Danny seemed at ease.

Add a sentence (a subject and a verb) after the fragment.

- **"To" plus a verb cannot be the main verb in a sentence.**

  To fish at the lake.   (fragment)

Based on your sentence meaning, you may revise these types of fragments in any of the following ways.

First, you could **link the fragment to a complete sentence.**

To fish at the lake, **Rene bought a fishing license**.

You could **add both a subject and a verb.**

Bill likes to fish at the lake.

Or you could **make the fragment the subject and add a verb**. Be sure to add any other needed words.

To fish at the lake **is** relaxing.

E X E R C I S E   4

Revise the following fragments using these same patterns.

Example:

To get the work done.

To get the work done, Ralph hired new men.

Link the fragment to a complete sentence.

Ralph worked to get the work done.

Add both a subject and a verb.

To get the work done cost a lot of money.

Make the fragment the subject and add a verb. (Add other words if needed.)

1. To collect baseball cards.

To collect baseball cards, she must be informed.

Link the fragment to a complete sentence.

Sara liked to collect baseball cards.

Add both a subject and a verb.

To collect baseball cards is a profitable hobby.

Make the fragment the subject and add a verb. (Add other words if needed.)

2.   To say a kind word.

To say a kind word, Mary made a special trip to her neighbor's house.

Link the fragment to a complete sentence.

He was not reluctant to say a kind word.

Add both a subject and a verb.

To say a kind word is easy.

Make the fragment the subject and add a verb. (Add other words if needed.)

3.   To win the lottery.

To win the lottery, the secretaries bought ten tickets each.

Link the fragment to a complete sentence.

The secretaries wanted to win the lottery.

Add both a subject and a verb.

To win the lottery seemed hopeless.

Make the fragment the subject and add a verb. (Add other words if needed.)

4.   To watch Michael Jordan.

To watch Michael Jordan, the crowd came to the arena early.

Link the fragment to a complete sentence.

The youngsters stayed late to watch Michael Jordan.

Add both a subject and a verb.

To watch Michael Jordan was worth the price of admission.

Make the fragment the subject and add a verb. (Add other words if needed.)

5.   To sleep late in the mornings.

To sleep late in the mornings, John turned off his alarm.

Link the fragment to a complete sentence.

John liked to sleep late in the mornings.

Add both a subject and a verb.

To sleep late in the mornings was difficult for John.

Make the fragment the subject and add a verb. (Add other words if needed.)

6.   To master the keyboard.

To master the keyboard, James practiced many hours.

Link the fragment to a complete sentence.

James worked to master the keyboard.

Add both a subject and a verb.

To master the keyboard required long hours of practice.

Make the fragment the subject and add a verb. (Add other words if needed.)

Fragments that Have Both a Subject and a Verb but Are Preceded by a Subordinator

Some fragments have both a subject and a verb but are preceded by a subordinator.

Example: **When** I get my paycheck.   (fragment)

This fragment does not state a complete thought. For example, if you walked into a room and said to a friend, "When I get my paycheck," the person you are speaking to would expect to know "what about 'when I get my paycheck'?"

However, if you complete this thought by adding a sentence, your meaning will be clear.

When I get my paycheck, **we will go shopping.**   or

We will go shopping when I get my paycheck.

("We will go shopping" is a complete sentence that can stand alone.)

In these fragments, the subordinator makes the thought incomplete. (You will learn more about subordinators later in this unit.) Here is a list of subordinators that change a complete sentence into a fragment:

Subordinators

after	in order that	whether
although	since	which
as	so that	whichever
as if	that	who
as long as	though	whoever
as soon as	till	whom
as though	unless	whomever
because	until	whose
before	what	whosoever
even though	whatever	why
how	when	
if	where	

EXERCISE 5

Revise the following fragments by linking them to a complete sentence.

Example:

When I go on a diet, *I am grumpy.*

1. Before we go on vacation, *we must get traveler's checks.*

2. Even though the movie was long, *we never lost interest in the story.*

3. Unless I can fix my car, *I will not be able to go to school.*

4. Even though his birthday is on Saturday, *John will have to work.*

5. Until you buy insurance for your car, *you cannot drive it.*

6. Because my neighbor had an abundance of pecans, *she shared them with me.*

7. So that I can go to the movies, *I will do my homework.*

8. As soon as the rain stopped, *the children ran out to play.*

9. If Randy will send us the information, *we will respond.*

10. After I learn to cook, *I will make lasagna.*

The best practice for revising fragments is to work on your own paragraphs. However, you can practice by correcting the following sample paragraphs and then applying the practice to your own paragraphs.

EXERCISE 6

Master for transparency is in the Instructor's Manual.

For the following sample paragraphs, do one or more of the following: (1) add a subject, a verb, or both a subject and a verb, or (2) combine the fragment with a sentence before it or with a sentence after it.

Paragraph 1

Diabetes is a disease that requires *dietary* control. ~~Dietary control.~~ People with diabetes need to balance the insulin and sugar level in their blood. Most of the time, they need to avoid foods that contain sugar. They also need to eat smaller meals more often throughout the day. However, if they have not eaten enough and their insulin level rises, ~~Must~~ *, they must* eat or drink something with sugar so that the insulin level in their blood will be balanced. For example, when they feel shaky~~.~~ ~~They~~ *they* may eat a candy bar or drink a soda pop. Diabetics can be healthier~~,~~ ~~If~~ *if* they watch their diet.

Paragraph 2

   I found that setting up an aquarium is expensive. After buying the tank, light, filter, and ~~heater. I~~ *heater, I* had other initial expenses. I needed to purchase chemicals, ~~Chemicals~~ to eliminate chlorine and to reduce the acidity. I made the tank attractive, ~~Adding~~ *by adding* colored gravel and plants, ~~Adding~~ *, adding* ceramic figures, ~~Placing~~ *, and placing* a nice background behind the glass. ~~To~~ *Next, I needed to* test the water and to keep the tank water at the right temperature. Adding a variety of fish with beautiful colors ~~,~~ *also helped.* When everything was set up, I *,* had fun. The aquarium can provide a center of enjoyment.

■ Run-On Sentences

   A second type of sentence-structure problem is the **run-on sentence**. The term ''run-on'' explains the mistake; two sentences have been run together. In other words, no punctuation mark separates the independent thoughts.

   The assignment was easy it took only a couple of hours to complete.
   (run-on sentence)

   In this run-on sentence there are two independent thoughts about the assignment. One is that it was easy, and the other is that it took only a couple of hours to complete. Two sentences have been written as one sentence. Here is one way these two thoughts could be written:

   The assignment was easy. It took only a couple of hours to complete.

   One misunderstanding that some writers have is that if ideas are related to each other, they should be written as one sentence. Look at the following ideas.

   My cousin is coming to Arizona she wants to visit the Grand Canyon.
   (run-on sentence)

These two ideas (coming to Arizona and visiting the Grand Canyon) are related, but they should be two separate sentences. Each idea has a subject and a verb and is an independent thought:

My cousin is coming to Arizona. She wants to visit the Grand Canyon.

Another misunderstanding writers have concerning run-on sentences is that if the idea is short, it cannot be two sentences. However, sentences are determined by whether or not they have a subject and a verb, not by length.

If you say "We should hurry we are late," you have two sentences. "We should hurry" is one sentence with its own subject and verb. "We are late" is another sentence with its own subject and verb.

We should hurry. We are late.

It is important that your writing is free of run-on sentences because if you have not identified where one sentence ends and another begins, your reader may misinterpret your thoughts. These run-on sentences may be revised in several ways.

Ways to Revise Run-On Sentences

Add a period at the end of each complete thought.

Use a comma and a connecting word called a coordinate conjunction.

Use a semicolon.

Use a semicolon, a connecting word called a conjunctive adverb, and a comma.

Use a subordinator.

Note   A list of conjunctive adverbs precedes Exercise 10, and a list of subordinators precedes Exercise 5.

Adding a Period at the End of Each Complete Thought

The simplest way of dealing with this problem is to add a period at the end of each complete thought. For practice, complete the following exercise.

EXERCISE 7

Identify the place where the first sentence ends and the second sentence begins. Then revise each run-on sentence by adding a period after the first sentence and by beginning the second sentence with a capital letter.

Example:

                    chores. They
The girls chose their ~~chores they~~ did them rapidly.

1. Humor is important to people's ~~health without~~ *health. Without* it, they become tired and depressed.

2. Father came ~~home we~~ *home. We* watched television.

3. My cat had ~~kittens we~~ *kittens. We* had to find homes for them.

4. Building houses requires licensed ~~contractors they~~ *contractors. They* know regulations and codes.

5. Michelle sang in the talent ~~show she~~ *show. She* danced, also.

6. Collecting antiques requires ~~knowledge it~~ *knowledge. It* can be expensive, too.

7. The phone ~~rang it~~ *rang. It* was in the other room.

8. Sam came ~~over we~~ *over. We* played football.

9. We went to the ~~store we~~ *store. We* bought bread.

10. He wanted to ride his ~~bike she~~ *bike. She* wanted to walk.

Using a Comma and a Coordinate Conjunction

Another way of revising run-on sentences is to connect them with a comma and an appropriate coordinate conjunction.

Coordinate Conjunctions

for	but
and	or
nor	yet
	so

I enjoy my job the rewards are great.   (run-on sentence)

I enjoy my job, **and** the rewards are great.   (correct)

Note   The first letters of the coordinate conjunctions spell "fan boys."

EXERCISE	8

Revise each of the following sentences by finding the place where the sentences should be separated. Then add a comma and a coordinate conjunction between the two sentences.

Example:

lunch, and they

The boys ate pizza for ~~lunch they~~ enjoyed it.

1. Firefighters spend many hours training for emergencies ^*, so* they are well qualified.

2. A leader sees the long-range picture ^*, but* a manager oversees the daily business operations.

3. Classes are over for the day ^*, so* we can go home.

4. Jack walked to the library ^*, but* he forgot his library card.

5. The men placed third overall ^*, and* the women placed second overall.

6. Wayne is an engineer ^*, and* he won the engineer-of-the-year award.

7. A frost came in May ^*, so* many fruit trees didn't blossom.

8. We can go to the football game ^*, or* we can go to the school play.

9. The track team traveled to the conference meet ^*, and* they won second place.

10. Hank found a lost kitten ^*, and* he wanted to keep it.

Using a Semicolon (;)

You may also revise run-on sentences by separating the complete thoughts with a semicolon.

I enjoy my job the rewards are great.   (run-on sentence)

I enjoy my job; the rewards are great.   (correct)

EXERCISE 9

Revise each of the following sentences by finding the place where the sentences should be separated. Then add a semicolon to separate the sentences.

Example:

me; I
Seven cars were in front of ~~me I~~ needed to turn left.

1. Farmers depend heavily on nature; weather conditions are important to them.

2. Working after school is hard; I need to do my homework.

3. Automobile technicians require specialized training; they must know computers and other electronic equipment.

4. The bus arrived on time; I was waiting to get on.

5. His class is very interesting; I am learning a lot.

6. Planning a vacation takes time; you want to be sure you do not forget anything.

7. Audrey is a good nurse; I would recommend her.

8. I bought a new computer; now I need a printer.

9. Airplane travel is safer than automobile travel; air accidents are just more publicized.

10. Football players have employment benefits; their jobs can be very exciting, too.

Using a Semicolon, a Conjunctive Adverb, and a Comma

Run-on sentences may also be revised by joining the two complete thoughts with a semicolon, a conjunctive adverb, and a comma.

Most Frequently Used Conjunctive Adverbs

as a result	moreover
consequently	nevertheless
furthermore	otherwise
however	therefore
in addition	thus
in fact	

I enjoy my job the rewards are great.   (run-on sentence)

I enjoy my job; **moreover**, the rewards are great.   (correct)

EXERCISE 10

Revise each of the following sentences by finding the place where the sentences should be separated. Then add a semicolon, a conjunctive adverb, and a comma between the two sentences.

Example:

delicious; in fact, it

The spaghetti was ~~delicious it was~~ homemade.

1. I lost my traveler's checks *; consequently,* I had to go to the bank to replace them.

2. Owning a new car can be exciting *; however,* driving a new car can be expensive.

3. A free trade zone provides many jobs *; moreover,* the benefits profit the entire city.

4. Keeping rivers clean should be a priority *; in fact,* children can get involved.

5. Working is good for teenagers *; in fact,* they learn responsibility.

6. Justine hiked through the woods *; consequently,* she picked many colorful flowers.

7. Sailing is a relaxing sport *; moreover, / in fact,* a weekend sailor can escape reality.

8. Peanuts are high in protein *; in addition,* they are high in calories.

9. The road was winding *; nevertheless,* it was several lanes wide.

10. Nursing can be a rewarding profession *; however,* it can also be stressful.

Using a Subordinator

Another way to revise run-on sentences is to join them by using a subordinator. You can easily achieve sentence variety in this way.

I enjoy my job the rewards are great.   (run-on sentence)

I enjoy my job **when** the rewards are great.   (correct)

EXERCISE 11

Revise each of the following sentences by finding the place where the sentences should be separated. Then add a subordinator from the list that precedes Exercise 5 of this unit. (Use a comma when needed.)

Example:

I want to go to the ~~store I~~ *store because I* just got paid.

1. People might like to move to a cold climate *if* they like winter sports.

2. Playing chess can improve a person's mind *because* most moves are based on strategy.

3. I finished all my homework *so that* I could go to the movies.

4. People should not live in a desert climate *unless* they enjoy the heat.

5. We ate the fruit *although* it was sour.

6. The occupational therapist put in long hours *until* he had seen everyone.

7. The children played on the swings *before* they were called in to dinner.

8. The dog knocked over the lamp *when* he ran into the room.

because

9. I enjoy fishing ̭it is relaxing.

because

10. Food manufacturers are producing healthier foods ̭consumers do not want to eat much sugar

and fat.

▪ Comma Splices

Another sentence structure problem similar to the run-on sentence is the **comma splice.**

We spent the day at the beach, we came home sunburned.   (comma splice)

In this case, the writer has separated two sentences with a comma. Using only a comma, however, is *not* an acceptable way to divide two independent thoughts. The easiest way is to substitute a period for the comma and begin the next word with a capital letter.

We spent the day at the beach. We came home sunburned.   (correct)

Sometimes this method creates too many short sentences in a row. In such cases, other kinds of revision can help your sentences flow better. To correct comma splices and still retain sentence variety, do the following:

- **Use a comma and a coordinate conjunction.**

  We spent the day at the beach, **and** we came home sunburned.   (correct)

- **Use a semicolon.**

  We spent the day at the beach; we came home sunburned.   (correct)

- **Use a semicolon and a conjunctive adverb.**   (See the list that precedes Exercise 10 in this unit.)

  We spent the day at the beach; **as a result,** we came home sunburned.

  (correct)

- **Use a subordinator that logically links the two sentences.**

  Because we spent the day at the beach, we came home sunburned.

  (correct)

Note   When the subordinator is added to the first sentence, this introductory idea is separated from the rest of the sentence with a comma. For more detailed explanation, see Unit 6, Part 4.

EXERCISE 12

Revise the following comma splices. Try using several of the methods explained in the text.

Example:

cats. Then
cats, and then

Mary often took in hungry, stray ~~cats, then~~ she tried to find homes for them.

1. Father's Day is as important as Mother's Day, ^*but* it does not get as much publicity.

2. The turtle hibernated for many months, ^*; consequently,* he emerged famished and began to eat his way through the garden.

3. When a tornado touches down, it may destroy everything in its path, ^*; however,* the American Red Cross assists the victims.

4. When we arrived at the beach, we headed for the water, ^*and* then we took off our shoes and waded in the surf.

5. The children ended the school year with a swim party, *;* they had a wonderful time.

6. *Because living* ~~Living~~ in a houseboat can be a confining experience, people are then generally happy to return home.

7. While we were on the beach, we collected shells, *. Then* ~~then~~ we built a sand castle.

8. Inside the registration building, students made out their schedules for next year, *. They* ~~they~~ checked the computers to see which classes were open.

9. In the springtime, the trees were covered with green leaves, ^*and* the shrubs were covered with lavender blossoms.

10. Harry read the three articles about drug abuse in the newspaper; in addition, he took notes for his history report.

Note If you want further practice on these types of combinations, review the materials in Units 5 and 6, Part 4.

EXERCISE **13**

Master for transparency is in the Instructor's Manual.

Revise the fragments, run-on sentences, and comma splices in the following paragraphs. Be creative by using as many different methods as possible.

Paragraph 1

The forest service is becoming more sensitive to the needs of the physically challenged outdoors person. Braille camping trails offer a way for the visually impaired to tramp through America's remarkable forests without fear. ~~America's remarkable forests.~~ Blind hikers can begin to experience what others take for granted. Braille signs identify the surrounding trees and plants, as well as mark the trails. These trails are carefully constructed and twist their way through wooded valleys, and onto safe hillsides. Some paths are only a quarter of a mile; others stretch for almost a mile, so that hikers can choose a long or a short route. Some campgrounds have wheelchair accessible paths throughout the area, and some even include ramps to lakes where the campers can fish from the bank. Each campground is calm, serene, and accommodating to the physically challenged.

Paragraph 2

Because pizza is so versatile, it is no wonder that it is one of America's favorite foods. Pizza is available frozen at the grocery store or piping hot from a variety of pizza restaurants. It can be bought with thin crust ~~or~~ thick crust, or ~~it can be~~ sandwiched between two crusts. Plain pizza crust can be bought frozen~~or~~ already baked in packages much like bread, or mixed at home. Almost every person's

individual taste can be satisfied because of the variety of toppings, ~~Toppings~~ spread on the sauce.

Pepperoni leads the list for favorites, but jalapeño, anchovies, olives, and sausages are some of the

other options, ~~even~~ sausage comes in different types. For a real "like-home" Italian taste, ~~The~~ pizza

can be topped with garlic bits and a little Parmesan cheese without the sauce. Since pizza can be

varied, almost everyone can be satisfied.

Paragraph 3

Owning cats can be a frustrating experience. Sometimes they want to be affectionate and even

sit in their owner's lap, ~~other~~ times, they treat their owner like a second-class citizen and turn away,

~~Turn away~~ saucily. A person who does not know cats may be frustrated by their cautiousness, ~~And~~

mistake it for a lack of affection. For example, a lazy-looking cat gazing out the window may really be

a lonesome pet, ~~he~~ may really be eagerly waiting for the owner to come home. When the owner does

come home, ~~The~~ cat probably will not immediately jump down like a dog and run to greet the owner.

~~the~~ cat may cautiously turn his head and look the other way. He is not ignoring his owner but just

showing caution in case the owner may ignore him. This is the kind of lukewarm "hello" that frustrates

people who do not understand, ~~Understand~~ cats.

It is easy to identify fragments, run-ons, and comma splices when the sentences have been isolated and you are looking for a specific kind of sentence-structure problem. However, in your own writing this major problem may be hidden within your ideas and may be overlooked. If you seem to be having a problem identifying run-ons, comma splices, or fragments, read backwards through your paper. Going backward through your paper will help you concentrate on the structure of your sentences rather than on the ideas.

EXERCISE 14

Practice identifying the sentence-structure problems in the following paragraph. Start with the last sentence and read each sentence individually, moving backward *through the text. Identify each sentence as a fragment (F), a comma splice (CS), a run-on sentence (RO), or a proper sentence (OK) in the blanks provided after the paragraph.*

(1) Alamogordo, New Mexico, and its outlying area offer its residents a variety of experiences. (2) The image of a sleeping lady is carved by the sloping Sacramento foothills this image identifies from a distance the location of Alamogordo. (3) Located ninety-five miles north of the Texas/Mexican border in the south-central part of the state. (4) Consequently, it has a rich Hispanic influence that is reflected in its architecture, history, and people. (5) Approximately fifty miles north in the beautiful Sacramento Mountains with tall pines, noisy streams, and wild horses is the Mescalero Apache Indian Reservation. (6) Also adding another ethnic exposure to the city. (7) Twenty miles west is White Sands National Monument, dunes of snow white gypsum provide a unique place for sand surfing, picnicking, or sunset viewing. (8) Twenty miles northeast is a village called Cloudcroft. (9) A quaint little village. (10) Because of its 5,000-foot elevation and its rustic shops. (11) This area resembles the Swiss Alps instead of New Mexico. (12) Despite Alamogordo's hidden location, it is a progressive city. (13) A city of approximately 45,000 people. (14) Holloman Air Force Base is located outside the city, it adds many talented people from all corners of the United States. (15) Presto and Levi Strauss have factories in the city, and the Space Hall of Fame shows that technology and advancement have also added their mark to Alamogordo, New Mexico.

15. __OK__	10. __F__	5. __OK__
14. __CS__	9. __F__	4. __OK__
13. __F__	8. __OK__	3. __F__
12. __OK__	7. __CS__	2. __RO__
11. __OK__	6. __F__	1. __OK__

WRITING ASSIGNMENT

Using the steps of the writing process that you are familiar with, draft an essay explaining what a person must consider before undertaking one of the following actions:

1. Moving out on one's own
2. Moving back in with parents
3. Moving back with a mate or roommate
4. Becoming a college student
5. Participating in extracurricular activities in school
6. Playing sports in school

Or, draft an essay discussing the advantages or disadvantages of one of the following:

7. Jobs on campus
8. Minimum wage
9. A hobby
10. Breakfast

After you draft your essay, revise for content and edit for mechanics.

Content

Essay

Check to see that the thesis sentence states a clear direction or previews the points to be covered in the paper.

Check to see that the voice is appropriate for your purpose and audience.

Paragraphs

Revise so each has a clear topic sentence that develops an idea suggested by or previewed in the thesis sentence.

Include four to six supporting sentences.

Include a closing sentence.

Mechanics

Check for subject-verb agreement.

Check for consistent verbs.

Check for a consistent point of view.

Check for fragments, run-on sentences, and comma splices.

UNIT 5

Writing with More Depth and Variety

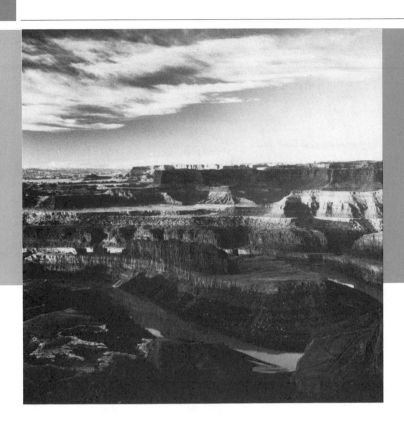

187

PARTS TO WHOLE: WRITING WITH EXAMPLES

OBJECTIVES

- Understand the purpose of an example.
- Recognize sources of examples.
- Generate examples through freewriting or brainstorming.
- Recognize and write both extended and short, interrelated examples.
- Use only relevant examples.
- Determine number of examples needed to clarify topic idea.

In composition writing, an **example** is a specific reference to an experience or experiences that you have had, have witnessed in person, have read about, or have seen in a movie or on television. Such a reference helps you clarify or illustrate a point, fact, or opinion you wish to make in your paper.

◼ The Purpose of Examples

Just as your paragraphs need specific details for good, solid support, they also can be more fully developed through relevant, well-selected examples. Examples in writing are based on life experiences that can be used to support your focused thesis, and by presenting selected examples, you add more credibility to your writing. Think of examples as "defense for your case" as you stated it in your thesis and as ways you are going to win your reader and present your essay as trustworthy rather than as weak and unbelievable.

As you learned in Unit 2 on topic sentences and paragraphs, the following sentences would not be sufficient for a paragraph.

> Even though collies are beautiful dogs, they are also known to be protectors. They seldom harm other animals and often turn guardian of their charges.

These two sentences express the main idea, but you still need more information:

> Even though collies are beautiful dogs, they are also known to be protectors. They seldom harm other animals and often turn guardian of their charges. **They have been known to protect small children and other pets and can keep them from being harmed. When someone tries to commit a crime against the owners, collies come to the rescue.**

Notice that the two sentences added (in bold type) give support to the paragraph, but you might want to "show" how this is true through *specific examples* that clarify the point being made. What is needed is one or more detailed examples—*incidents* or *pictures*—to show the topic idea. Now read the following revised paragraph. Two specific **examples** have been added.

> Even though collies are beautiful dogs, they are also known to be protectors. They seldom harm other animals and often turn guardian of their charges. They have been known to protect small children and other pets and can keep them

from being harmed. When someone tries to commit a crime against the owners, collies come to the rescue. For example, when Charlie was a child, he had a collie that often helped catch loose rabbits when they got out of their cages. One evening she barked at the back door until someone came. She had found a baby rabbit who had fallen out of the wire cage, had picked it up gently in her mouth, and had brought it to the house unharmed. Another time, when a strange man tried to break into the house, she positioned herself between the family members and the stranger. Baring her teeth and growling deeply, she stopped him. The family always felt everything was under control as long as they had their "best friend" close by.

This paragraph shows the reader "in what way" collies are protectors by stating that "they seldom harm other animals and often turn guardian of their charges." This statement is explained and then clarified by two supporting examples. One is the experience in which the collie brought the baby rabbit to the owners, and the other is when the collie protected the family from the strange man. In your writing you, too, can relate specific examples that help the reader understand your main idea.

Sources of Examples

Finding appropriate examples for your writing involves discovering sources through freewriting, brainstorming, or other prewriting activities.

Sources that Provide Examples

personal experiences

personal observations of other people

short stories, novels, television, or movies

facts, statistics, or reports from authoritative sources

Personal Experiences

A personal experience can add convincing information to support your thesis. Frequently, personal experiences that you can recall in detail can help you clarify the main point for the reader. The more specific the example is, the clearer the topic idea becomes to the reader. Freewriting and brainstorming can help you remember details of events in your life. If these events are important enough for you to remember, then perhaps your reader will also be able to relate to these examples. Suppose your topic idea for a paragraph is the following:

Topic: Taking a child shopping can be embarrassing.

Perhaps during freewriting or brainstorming, you remember the following incident:

When I took my four-year-old child shopping at Metrocenter, he decided to "check out" the mannequin with a beautiful black slinky dress, and somehow he managed to knock it over with a thud. Instantly a salesperson appeared to see if my child was hurt. He wasn't hurt, but he was scared. People began to gather from all directions. I wasn't sure what to do, so we quietly slipped away.

Notice that the above incident "shows" the reader "in what way" taking a child shopping can be embarrassing. This *incident* or *picture* that you have created for the reader is a strong, *specific example*.

Realistic examples make the topic idea clearer to the reader. Made-up stories often have a fake sound that do little or nothing to add credibility to your writing. It is much easier to remember the time your child knocked over the mannequin than it is to make up an example that never happened. In the earlier paragraph, it would be very difficult to make up a story about a collie that picked up a newborn rabbit and brought it safely to the owner. Therefore, by recalling real events that have happened to you, you can "show" what it is you want to prove. "Showing" makes writing stronger and more interesting than "telling about" an idea.

Observations of Other People

Observations that you have made of other people can illustrate the topic you are discussing and add more credibility to your paragraphs. Perhaps you are writing about fatherhood, but you are not a father. Maybe your brother, husband, or neighbor is a father, and you have observed him with his children. After freewriting or brainstorming, you might have decided to begin with this topic idea:

Topic: Many fathers in the United States are becoming involved in all aspects of their children's lives.

During additional freewriting or brainstorming, you might remember when you saw a father becoming involved in his children's lives:

Last summer I always knew it was 5:30 P.M. because I could see Hugh Dobson and his son, equipped with a bat, gloves, and a baseball, emerge from their front door. Sometimes they would practice catching, sometimes pitching, and other times batting.

Even though these are not your personal experiences, they are events that you have witnessed. They will sound more convincing to your reader than a made-up incident.

Short Stories, Novels, Television, or Movies

Examples that come from short stories, novels, television, or movies can also support or "show" topic ideas. This extensive source for examples can include characters and events from stories that you have read in books or seen in the movies or on television.

If you are writing an essay about how the meaning of life can change for a person, you might use an incident from Orwell's *1984* as an example. The change Winston feels regarding sex could be an example of your topic idea. You could summarize the incident and use it to support your topic idea:

> Winston's sexual encounter with a prostitute is very degrading to him. The prostitute is repulsive, and he feels that the sexual act itself has been lowered to only a mechanical act. Winston feels no love as he performs a loveless, almost disgusting act.   (This would be considered one example.)

Or if you are writing an essay about the realistic depiction of the Vietnam War, you might draw from a movie like *Platoon*. The topic idea might be that young men would do anything to get home from the war, and you might use specific examples as follows:

> One of the soldiers stabbed himself in the knee so he could go home. Another soldier put a solution on the bottoms of his feet so that they would be severely cracked and look as if he couldn't walk.

(This would be considered two examples.)

Or if you are writing a paper about humorous events in family life, you could use a current television program for appropriate examples.

Facts, Statistics, or Reports from Authoritative Sources

Research studies, verifiable facts, or current news stories can provide examples to support your thesis. To use these kinds of examples, you might have to read material in the library or talk to someone who is an expert on your topic. If you want to write a paper about aquariums but do not have one, you can still write about them if you take the time to read books or articles about aquariums or if you go to a fish store and talk to someone who is knowledgeable in the field. You would want to know if this "authority in the field" is or has been a breeder and/or has been working with fish for a long time. You need this background to decide if you can trust the source of your information, whether it comes from a book or from a personal interview.

Once you have read about or talked to someone about your topic, your freewriting or brainstorming might have given you this topic idea for one paragraph in your essay:

Topic: When an aquarium is set up correctly, a natural balance results.

Your conversation at a fish store with an expert has given you a specific example of a natural balance. You could use the information like this:

> According to the owner of the Coral Reef fish store, catfish clean up the waste from the bottom of the fish tank. In this way, the catfish help to create a natural balance.

The catfish would be only one specific example for your paragraph. Your reading and your conversation with the store owner would give you other specific examples for your paragraph.

In a different essay, you might be working on one paragraph to support the topic idea that a person might make a profit by investing in a home. You could recall some factual information you have read, or you could go to the library to do research. As a result of your reading in the June 1989 issue of *Reader's Digest*, you find an article by Sonny Bloch and Grace Lichtenstein about affording homes. This article has a great example you might decide to use. You could write something like this in your paragraph:

> In the June 1989 issue of *Reader's Digest,* an article titled "Afford a Home of Your Own" includes the story of a young couple who bought an old home for $61,000. They did a lot of work fixing it up, and in less than three years they sold the home for $127, 500.

This specific example could be used in your paragraph; however, as you can see, you do need to let the reader know where you got the information. This is one kind of authoritative example that can give credibility to your writing.

In each of the previous writing situations, you would also need other examples in each paragraph to support the topic idea. These examples could come from your personal experience or from observations of other people you know. As you have already learned, one of your goals in each paragraph is to support the topic sentence with enough specific information to convince your reader.

Generating Examples Through Freewriting and Brainstorming

As you have already learned, freewriting and brainstorming are important steps in the writing process that you can use at different times. You can freewrite or brainstorm to get started in a writing situation. You can also use these strategies to help you think of or "discover" more or better examples needed to support your thesis sentence and/or topic sentences.

Suppose you have developed the following thesis sentence:

> Returning to school has been a rewarding experience because I have found that I have abilities I never knew I had before, have changed the way I dress, and have met new friends.

In looking over the freewriting or brainstorming you have already done, you probably realize that you may not have enough specific information to write strong paragraphs. Using each topic idea previewed in the thesis sentence, then, do more freewriting and/or brainstorming to find the examples you need. For instance, freewriting and brainstorming on "I have found that I have abilities I never knew I had before" might produce the following ideas. (Remember that in freewriting or brainstorming you do not stop to correct errors!)

Freewriting for Examples

> Going to school can be rewarding. I need to come up with some examples of times when I found I had new abilities I didn't know I had before. There are many times that I have found that I could things that I didn't think I could do before. I

haven't been to school in ten years and I thought that the kids just out of high school would do circles around me or make me feel inferior. I still think it is hard. But I am really not in that bad of shape. I am doing <u>pretty good in my English class and in my Psychology class.</u> I hope that my grade point average is an A. I am more concerned about learning though. I studied for my grammar test. It came out pretty good too. <u>I made 95 percent on that test. It was on consistent point of view.</u> Most of the kids made around 70 percent, so that really made me feel like I could do alright. Noone has made fun of me yet. Some of the younger kids think I am an old lady, but that is ok. Jim didn't seem to think I was so dumb when <u>the teacher asked me to help him with the topic sentence. He began to get it too.</u> I felt real proud when I could show him how to write one. You know, it made it easier for me too. I guess showing someone else how to do things is good for me. It made me feel better, and now I think I'll make it. Maybe I'll even decide to be a teacher. I had a little trouble when I wrote my first essay. <u>The next time I wrote one the teacher told me I had an effective thesis sentence and that my support was good.</u> That really made me feel good. I wasn't sure I could do all that when I came back to school.

When you reread the freewriting, you can see three distinct examples of the way you are doing well in your English class. By using these examples, you can *show* "in what way" you discovered abilities that you didn't know you had. These three examples would help you write a strong support paragraph for this part of your essay.

Study the following list to see how the ideas underlined in the previous freewriting have been rewritten as specific examples that support the topic sentence "I have abilities I never knew I had before." The topic sentence, in turn, clearly relates to the main idea in your thesis sentence.

Thesis sentence: Returning to school has been a rewarding experience because I have found that I have abilities I never knew I had before, have changed the way I dress, and have met new friends.

Topic sentence: I have found that I have abilities I never knew I had before.

Linking sentence: I did well in my English class.

Specific example 1: When I wrote my second essay using my job as the topic, my instructor told me that my thesis sentence was well written and that I had followed through well on my paragraphs.

Specific example 2: My English instructor asked me to help a student who was having trouble with the topic sentence, and as I helped him, I felt good because he understood what I was saying.

Specific example 3: I took my first grammar test on consistent point of view and scored ninety-five percent on it.

Notice that a linking sentence, "I did well in my English class," has been put in. Sometimes in the freewriting you can also find a suitable sentence to link the examples to the topic sentence. Also notice that a lot of unnecessary or "warm-up" information has been left out.

Brainstorming for Examples

Topic sentence: I have abilities I never knew I had before.

> did well on grammar test: 95 percent
>
> helped other student with topic sentence
>
> wrote good essay
>
> did well in English class

Sometimes it is easier to freewrite before you brainstorm and then pull the ideas from the freewriting. Others prefer just to brainstorm in order to generate ideas.

The other two support paragraphs can also be developed through freewriting or brainstorming. The choice is yours.

How Finding Examples Fits into the Writing Process

At this point, you might find it helpful to review the writing process. Study the following review of the writing process for a longer paper — from selecting a topic to finding examples.

Steps in the Writing Process to Generate Ideas for a Paper

selecting a topic

freewriting/brainstorming for direction

identifying direction

freewriting/brainstorming and grouping for thesis sentence

writing the thesis sentence

freewriting/brainstorming again to recall specific examples

Suppose you have selected "driving on ice" as the topic for your longer paper, and you decide to use brainstorming to help you find a direction and develop a thesis sentence. Now follow this process from selecting the topic of "driving on ice" to writing one of the support paragraphs in a longer paper.

Choose a topic:	driving on ice
Brainstorm for direction:	hazardous
	dangerous
	could get hurt
Identify direction:	hazards of driving on ice
Brainstorm and group for thesis sentence:	

black ice is scary	braking
nothing can be done to prevent it	weather conditions
causes skidding	driving too fast

shiny, clear, invisible	drive slower
freezes at 32 degrees F	chains
learn from experienced driver	warnings
salt on road	

Next, group similar ideas, rewrite them, and give each group a "label."

learning to control the car

> realize that braking causes the skid
>
> know how to bring the car out of a skid
>
> > turn in the direction of a skid
>
> drive with someone who is used to driving in icy weather

understanding dangerous conditions

> shiny, clear, invisible
>
> occurs at 32 degrees F

following safety precautions

> using chains
>
> driving only on roads that have been salted
>
> obeying warnings
>
> listening to weather reports
>
> driving at slower speeds

Write the thesis sentence: Driving safely on ice involves learning to control the car, understanding dangerous conditions, and following safety precautions.

At this point in the process, you know that you need more specific examples to write strong paragraphs, so you may either freewrite or brainstorm to find these examples.

Freewrite to recall specific example(s):

I need to remember examples that show driving on ice safely involves learning to control the car. I am a pretty good driver but ice still scares me. I guess it scares me because of the time that time I almost hit another car because I put on the brakes and went into a skid. That was really scary. I remember that I was near my house and since I thought I was a pretty good driver in winter weather, I wasn't paying too much attention to how fast I was going. It is a good thing I did know how to bring the car out of a skid. I remembered Mr. Lopez, but that really didn't have anything to do with controlling the car. That was more because he didn't have time to bring his car out of a skid.

Brainstorm to recall specific example(s):

Mr. Lopez, who was fatally injured

the time I almost got into a wreck

Either of these two incidents, whether generated through freewriting or brainstorming, could provide convincing details. You may choose one or both of them to support your topic idea. Each incident you select would be *one detailed example* that helps you develop the topic idea that learning to control the car is important when driving on ice. You might write the paragraph this way:

> Being able to control the car is important when I drive on dangerous ice. Being a native of Colorado, I am comfortable with my ability to drive in the winter months, but each year I get shocked into reality. This winter was no different. A week after the worst snow storm, I thought things were getting better because the snow was beginning to melt. Suddenly, without warning, a cold night froze the melting snow at a busy intersection close to my house. As I came to the stop sign, I applied the brakes as usual, but my Bronco seemed to accelerate into the flow of traffic. I quickly took my foot off the brake and concentrated on turning into the skid. Thanks to my guardian angel, I barely missed an innocent motorist. Next year I hope I can remember this near-miss as vividly as I do now and can avoid an ice accident.

The following exercise will give you practice in generating examples to support a topic idea. Either freewrite or brainstorm to find these ideas.

EXERCISE 1

Master for transparency is in the Instructor's Manual.

Using the following topic ideas, write a personal example, a personal observation of someone else, a fictionalized example, and a fact, statistic, or incident from an authoritative source. (In order to obtain an authoritative example, you might need to go to the library or talk to an expert on your topic.)

1. Pets comfort their owners.

_____

(personal example)

_____

_____

_____

_____

(personal observation of someone else)

_____

_____

_____

(example from a short story, novel, television show, or movie)

_____

_____

_____

_____

(fact, statistic, or incident from an authoritative source)

_____

_____

_____

_____

2.   Gangs have changed American neighborhoods.

_____

(personal example)

_____

_____

_____

_____

(personal observation of someone else)

_____

_____

_____

_____

(example from a short story, novel, television show, or movie)

_____

_____

_____

_____

(fact, statistic, or incident from an authoritative source)

3. Big cities can be filled with many activities.

(personal example)

(personal observation of someone else)

(example from a short story, novel, television show, or movie)

(fact, statistic, or incident from an authoritative source)

Extended Examples and Shorter, Interrelated Examples

Examples can appear in basically two forms:

1. extended examples

2. series of shorter, detailed, interrelated examples

Extended Examples

An extended example illustrates one person, one experience, or one significant incident developed fully so that the reader has not only a clear picture of the example but also its relationship to the topic idea. An extended example appears in the following paragraph.

> **Driving on ice can be dangerous because it is invisible and can catch motorists unaware.** Mr. Lopez was one of these unsuspecting motorists. As a UPS inspector, he had to take his turn on the graveyard shift. When he drove to work in the early evening, the roads were fine, but when he left at 2:00 in the morning, black ice had formed. Because he was anxious to get home to his warm bed and no traffic slowed him down, he came upon an unexpectedly busy intersection too rapidly. As he applied the brakes, his tires slid on the ice, and his car slammed into a big diesel. Mr. Lopez, who never knew what had hit him, died unnecessarily.

The above paragraph uses an **extended example** to support the topic sentence in bold type. The second sentence—"Mr. Lopez was one of these unsuspecting motorists"—is the link between the topic idea and the extended example of Mr. Lopez's accident.

You do not need to relate everything that you know about Mr. Lopez, only the information that supports the topic sentence. Your reader does not need to know if Mr. Lopez was single or married, if he was rich or poor, if he liked to fish or play football. That information is irrelevant to the topic sentence.

Remember the pattern:

topic sentence

linking sentence

extended example

The following exercise will help you write extended examples and their linking sentences.

EXERCISE 2

Master for transparency is in the Instructor's Manual.

For each topic sentence given, write a sentence that links the topic idea to an appropriate extended example. Then write an extended example that clarifies the topic sentence. (You may find it easier to write the example first and then think of an appropriate linking sentence.)

1. *Topic sentence:* Motherhood/fatherhood can be a frustrating experience.

_____

(linking sentence)

_____

_____

(extended example)

_____

_____

_____

2. *Topic sentence:* Saving money can be done in many ways.

_____

(linking sentence)

_____

_____

(extended example)

_____

_____

_____

3. *Topic sentence:* Student athletes or working students must organize their time carefully.

_____

(linking sentence)

_____

(extended example)

_____

_____

_____

_____

4. *Topic sentence:* Looking at a family photo album brings back memories.

_____

(linking sentence)

_____

_____

(extended example)

_____

_____

_____

5. *Topic sentence:* A college library has many resources.

_____

(linking sentence)

_____

_____

(extended example)

_____

_____

_____

After you have recalled the extended example by freewriting/brainstorming, you need to decide how much of the freewriting/brainstorming you actually need to use in the paragraph. Sometimes in freewriting, you might get carried away and put in details that are not related to the topic sentence. You may remember many more details than you need to use. Just keep in mind the requirements for a good paragraph: topic sentence, related support sentences, and a related concluding sentence.

The following exercise will help you sort out unrelated details in an extended example.

E X E R C I S E   3

Read the following paragraphs and decide if there is any extra information that is not needed to support the topic idea. First, underline the topic sentence and the linking sentence. Then strike out the sentences in each extended example that do not support the topic sentence.

Paragraph 1

When my child first learned to read, short-term rewards were often more important than the actual ability to read. He wanted to be a good reader. When he realized he needed to work hard and practice, he wasn't sure reading was as important as watching "Mr. Wizzard's World" to obtain his knowledge about the scientific world. However, he was willing to sit down and plan a strategy. Because he also wanted to set up an aquarium that had been unused for many years, together we decided that for every fifty pages he read aloud to me, he could either buy a fish or have two dollars of in-store credit. ~~He had two other pets.~~ With this agreed upon, he assembled the aquarium, filled it with water, and went to the fish store to wish. As soon as we got home and he walked through the door, he said, "Let's read." And read we did. Even though the first book was below his grade level, it took him four days to finish fifty pages. However, it only took twenty minutes to get the first inhabitant for his tank. That one fish looked lonely, and the only solution was to read another fifty pages. Soon he had earned another fish and another fish. ~~The fish cost me anywhere from eighty-nine cents to two dollars.~~ Moving up to grade-level books brought a little resistance because there were NO pictures. But soon these books, too, seemed easier and easier until he was able to select books way above grade level. Now he was enjoying reading for the sake of reading, and he began to read extra books on his own. ~~Of all the books he read, he enjoyed the one about a kid who ended up with jars and jars of goldfish with no place to put them.~~ As he earned fish, he began to love reading for the sake of knowledge, but he had seldom found reading a chore because every page had brought him closer to a new fish.

Paragraph 2

Being hospitalized for an illness can cause a person to suffer a financial setback. The extensive bills can mount up. Bo Lewis suffered a severe financial setback when he spent several weeks in the hospital. The seven days in intensive care and four additional weeks in the hospital resulted in astronomical costs. Even though he had insurance, he had to pay a $100 deductible and 20 percent of the bill. Because the hospital bill alone was over $14,000, his responsibilities were $2,800. ~~Also, his wife went on a shopping spree for new summer clothes.~~ On top of this, he had to purchase several hundred dollars worth of medicine. He also had to purchase medical supplies that were not covered by insurance. Because Bo Lewis was unable to work, he was eligible for disability, but this amount was much less than his regular salary. ~~Before his illness, he smoked only one carton of cigarettes a week, but because of the stress during and after his illness, he smoked two cartons.~~ In just a few weeks, he found himself owing $6,000 in medical expenses. It is scary to think how fast medical bills can accumulate when an extended illness occurs.

Shorter, Detailed, Interrelated Examples

In addition to one extended example to develop a whole paragraph, your brainstorming may give you a series of shorter, detailed, interrelated examples that can be used in your support paragraphs. Here is a paragraph that uses these shorter, detailed, interrelated examples.

When an aquarium is set up correctly, a natural balance results. Choosing the correct plant and animal life provides an opportunity for these two forces to live harmoniously. Not only do plants put oxygen into the water, but they also provide a place for baby fish to hide so they won't be eaten. Selection of animal life is just as important to the owner of the aquarium. Catfish are scavengers that clean up the waste from the bottom and sides of the fish tank. Plecostomus, which are a type of catfish, even clean plants that have become slimy from algae. Snails can be seen removing the algae and slime or eating fish that have died and settled on the bottom of the tank. At the same time, all of these fish return carbon dioxide to the water. If proper thought is put into starting an aquarium, a harmonious balance can be achieved.

The above paragraph has a clear topic sentence and a linking sentence to introduce the short, interrelated examples. Four separate examples support the topic sentence: (1) plants, (2) catfish, (3) plecostomus, and (4) snails.

The following exercise will give you practice in generating short, interrelated examples and the appropriate linking sentences.

EXERCISE 4

Master for a transparency is in the Instructor's Manual.

Using each topic sentence given, write a sentence that links the topic idea to appropriate short, interrelated examples. You may use the same linking sentences that you wrote in Exercise 2. Then write the short interrelated examples that clarify the topic sentence. If it is easier for you, write the series of short examples first; then write a sentence to link them to the topic sentence.

1. *Topic sentence:* Motherhood/fatherhood can be a frustrating experience.

_____

(linking sentence)

_____

_____

(short, interrelated examples)

_____

_____

_____

2. *Topic sentence:* Saving money can be done in many ways.

_____

(linking sentence)

_____

_____

(short, interrelated examples)

_____

_____

_____

3. *Topic sentence:* Student athletes or working students must organize their time carefully.

_____

(linking sentence)

_____

_____

(short, interrelated examples)

_____

_____

_____

4. *Topic sentence:* Looking at a family photo album brings back memories.

_____

(linking sentence)

_____

(short, interrelated examples)

_____

_____

_____

_____

5. *Topic sentence:* A college library has many resources.

_____

(linking sentence)

_____

_____

(short, interrelated examples)

_____

_____

_____

Stressing Relevance in Short, Interrelated Examples

You have already learned that strong paragraphs are unified, that all the sentences relate to the topic sentence. Whenever you use examples to develop your paragraph, be sure that every example is related to the topic idea.

In the previous paragraph about setting up a balanced aquarium, all of the sentences support one topic idea. Suppose, in further reading, you find that ''Dojos are Chinese weather fish that change color with the weather'' and that ''African frogs are nocturnal aquatic creatures that come out to play at night when the fish are sleeping.'' This information sounds so interesting that you decide to include it. Here is your new paragraph:

> When an aquarium is set up correctly, a natural balance results. Choosing the correct plant and animal life provides an opportunity for these two forces to live harmoniously. Not only do plants put oxygen into the water, but they also provide a place for baby fish to hide so they won't be eaten. Selection of animal life is just as important to the owner of the aquarium. Catfish are scavengers that clean up the waste from the bottom and sides of the fish tank. Plecostomus, which are a type of catfish, even clean plants that have become slimy from algae. Snails can be seen removing the algae and slime or eating fish that have died and settled on the bottom of the tank. At the same time, all of these fish return carbon dioxide to the water. **Dojos are Chinese weather fish that change color with the weather, and African frogs are nocturnal aquatic creatures that come out to**

play at night when the fish are sleeping. If proper thought is put into starting an aquarium, a harmonious balance can be achieved.

Even though these two new examples are appealing, you cannot add them to the paragraph because they do *not* support the topic idea of a balanced aquarium. When you are drafting or revising a paragraph, you have time to think through how well your examples support the topic sentence. Do not hesitate to cut examples that are interesting but are not directly related to the topic idea.

The following exercise will give you practice in finding examples that are not relevant to the topic sentence.

EXERCISE   5

Read the following paragraphs, and in each paragraph decide which examples are relevant to the topic sentence and which examples are not. Then cross out the examples that do not support the topic idea.

Paragraph 1

Early Americans had to rely on their own ingenuity to make life comfortable or even to survive. They turned survival skills into a type of art that was passed down from generation to generation. Some of these art forms, which may no longer be practical in today's society, were a part of living for our great-grandparents. In the West, sturdy houses could be made from adobe brick, but first the brick had to be made from mud and straw. Making clothes was also an art of the past that few people could accomplish today. Even buying material for clothes was a luxury few knew. The process of making a new dress or shirt or pants involved shearing sheep, carding wool, spinning yarn, and weaving cloth. Sometimes the clothing maker dyed the yarn different colors, using natural materials like walnut shells. ~~The women enjoyed growing flowers to make the home look more attractive.~~ Tatting — making lace by hand — became an art form that was used to decorate collars or to bring beauty to something as necessary as pillowcases. ~~People loved to get together in the evenings and have dances.~~ Since there were no refrigerators, families found making beef jerky was a way of preserving meat that provided a year-round supply. And if they wanted to take a bath, they needed soap, but making soap at home, an art almost unheard of today, was required before that bath could take place. When the supply of candles, the source of night light, became low, there was one solution — making more from melted lard. ~~Sometimes the men and women would work from sunup to sundown so they could take a day off for celebration.~~ Today, we talk of "the good old days" when life was simple, but maybe we should say when families were resourceful and used art in order to survive.

Paragraph 2

Many farmers and gardeners have tried creative methods to eliminate garden pests organically and safely, without the use of insecticides. Some American gardeners are said to harvest pesky tomato worms, put them into a blender, and then spray the mixture onto the healthy plants. The tomato bugs smell death and depart as quickly as they arrived. ~~Farmers in the southwestern part of the United States depend on irrigation for good crops.~~ In China, farmers build little hibernation huts to encourage spiders to build webs in their rice fields, so when the spiders "wake up" or hatch, they are ready to harvest the bugs that are so damaging to the rice crops. ~~Most American farmers also rotate crops. One season they might plant alfalfa to replenish the soil, and the next season they will plant a different crop like cotton.~~ Cotton farmers in the southwestern parts of the United States are said to have dumped millions of woolyworms into the cotton fields to eat the boll weevils before they could destroy the cotton crop. After a fine feast, the woolyworms marched off, and the cotton crops were saved. All of these solutions to insect problems did not use any lethal sprays that could be passed on to humans.

Deciding How Many Short Examples to Use

Usually after you have drafted your paragraph, you need to decide how many short, interrelated examples are needed to clarify the topic sentence. This is something you have to think through logically. You want to provide as many different types of examples as you can. You do not, however, want to refer to the same types of examples over and over again. Read again the sample paragraph about the balanced aquarium:

> When an aquarium is set up correctly, a natural balance results. Choosing the correct plant and animal life provides an opportunity for these two forces to live harmoniously. Not only do plants put oxygen into the water, but they also provide a place for baby fish to hide so they won't be eaten. Selection of animal life is just as important to the owner of the aquarium. Catfish are scavengers that clean up the waste from the bottom and sides of the fish tank. Plecostomus, which are a type of catfish, even clean plants that have become slimy from algae. Snails can be seen removing the algae and slime or eating fish that have died and settled on the bottom of the tank. At the same time, all of these fish return carbon dioxide to the water. If proper thought is put into starting an aquarium, a harmonious balance can be achieved.

Catfish are chosen as an example because they clean up the wastes. Plecostomus are added because they do one additional thing — they clean the algae slime from the plants. There are many more varieties of algae eaters, but they are not needed to make the point that an aquarium that is set up properly can result in a natural balance between plants and animals. The four examples clearly and forcefully support the topic idea. All four add something *different* to the supporting details.

Look at the following paragraph on special-interest classes offered by a community college.

> Special-interest classes are offered by many community colleges to meet the needs of all members of a society. The classes are often varied in scope and content depending on the population living around the college. "Remodeling Your Own Kitchen" offers an opportunity for people to become equipped with information before investing thousands of dollars on a remodeling job. "Quilting for Fun" can enable men and women to learn an art that is no longer passed down from generation to generation. "Making Animals from Balloons" is a course offered to children and should provide hours of creative enjoyment. "Living with an Elderly Parent or Handicapped Child" could ease the responsibility felt by adults in charge. These courses are as varied as the community itself and are intended to provide community enrichment for the public.

Four *different types* of courses are included. More examples could have been added. You would not, however, add an example like "Remodeling Your Bathroom" or "Simple Needlecraft" because these types of examples have already been used. You might, though, use a different type of example, such as "Camping Made Easy."

Deciding how many examples to use is up to you. Three or four is usually a good number to put into each paragraph. Remember, though, that each one should add something different to support the topic sentence. Each one should show in a different way "how the topic sentence is true."

The following exercise will give you practice in finding duplicate examples in a paragraph that is developed with a series of short, interrelated examples.

EXERCISE 6

Read the following paragraphs carefully. Then decide which examples duplicate a type of example already used and which examples show different ways in which the topic idea is true. Strike out any example that duplicates a type already used. Be prepared to explain how it duplicates another example.

Paragraph 1

In order to avoid the high costs of living, many retired couples have become full-time recreational vehicle travelers ("RVers"). After selling or renting their homes, they literally spend their time traveling. One couple sold their home and bought a fully equipped van. They now pull a boat that provides recreation, and, when the boat is not being used on the water, it provides storage. Another couple sold their home and now spend several months in an Indiana resort area trading a few hours of work for a place to stay and free hookups. When summer comes, they do the same thing in an RV resort in Florida. Another retired couple spend their time working at national and state parks in exchange for a place to live and modest pay. ~~Likewise, a couple who lived in New Mexico now spend all their time moving from one national park to another serving as a host to the RV campground.~~ In this way, these retired people reduce their living costs and are able to live on moderate retirement funds.

Paragraph 2

Today in America, medical researchers are realizing the many ways pets are helping physically handicapped adults. These pets are an extension of these adults, as they perform tasks that are often impossible for the handicapped adult to do alone. Seeing Eye dogs are being used to guide visually handicapped people so that these individuals can experience the freedom their blindness has taken from them. Trained monkeys are being used to perform simple manual tasks like turning light switches on and off or holding the telephone receiver for adults with limited or no use of their hands and arms. Parrots are being used to bring companionship to handicapped adults who are confined to their homes. The parrot and master can sing songs together and can even talk to one another. ~~Cats are also being used for companionship so that the handicapped adult doesn't feel so lonely.~~ All of these pets and their owners become great friends as they lean on each other for support.

When adding examples to your writing, use your own judgment to decide whether you want one longer, extended example or many shorter examples. Remember, *both* types of development are effective because they contain specific details that provide strong support for a topic idea.

EXERCISE 7

Read the following paragraphs and decide whether each one is developed by using several short, interrelated examples or one longer, extended example. Identify the kind of example that is used by writing "SIE" (short, interrelated example) or "Ext" (extended) in the margin to the left of the paragraph.

Paragraph 1

SIE When families travel, they often find that fast-food restaurants come in handy. If they are traveling with children, they can often find fast-food restaurants that have play areas where children can get a little exercise when they stop. At least one McDonald's restaurant has a "dog rest area" where owners can water and feed their dogs who rest in runs while their owners eat. Places like Kentucky Fried Chicken allow families to pick up a complete meal that can be taken to a rest area and enjoyed. Many places have food packaged so that travelers can pick up their food at the drive-through window and then eat in the car as they travel. Some of the restaurants have outside tables where families can keep their dogs with them as they eat instead of leaving their pets in the car. Many of these restaurants have clean, large rest rooms because they want to accommodate customers. These restaurants provide convenient services for customers.

Paragraph 2

Ext The persecution of Jewish children was a tragedy that has been captured in the Holocaust Museum in Washington, D.C. The museum features a thought-provoking exhibit entitled, "Remember the Children." It is the story of Daniel, which dramatizes one child's life as it changed from freedom to a Polish ghetto to Auschwitz, a concentration camp. Daniel's life is pictured in a series of rooms with excerpts from his diary to show his life's progressive deterioration. The first room illustrates Daniel's home full of bright lights, laughter, and good food. Daniel's displayed diary shows how the persecution of Jews increased. Daniel, his mother, and his sister were moved to a Polish ghetto. Through Daniel's diary, the exhibit shows that his father was sent away to a camp. Daniel's life then became barren and more difficult. The last phase of Daniel's life was depicted by a dark, silent room with a dirt floor closed in by barbed wire. His life portrayed a part of history that many Jewish children experienced.

Paragraph 3

Ext Cats are bright animals. Most people consider them fur-brained, but if closely observed and nurtured, a household cat can demonstrate intelligence. A precocious pet named Ashes knows how to communicate and assert herself. When she's hungry and her bowl is empty in the morning, she patiently stands at the foot of the bed and eyes her owner. She doesn't meow until she hears her friend stir. She then knows that her owner is awake. At other times, if Ashes can't make eye contact, she sounds a particular cry for help. She has learned where to find her owner, what tone to use, and when to speak, and this learning has been reinforced — a remarkable feat for a being that can't talk. Because cats are subtle, quiet creatures, people fail to recognize their intellect.

Paragraph 4

SIE

Throughout the history of our nation, the wives of the presidents of the United States have often made a lasting impact on America. Eleanor Roosevelt is often considered the most active first lady of the White House. She traveled all over the world as a goodwill ambassador and was even named a delegate to the United Nations General Assembly. Most important, she made a determined effort to break down discrimination against blacks. Another important first lady, Jacqueline Kennedy, brought continuity to the hodgepodge of decor of the public rooms of the White House through remodeling and refurnishing these rooms to recapture the authentic look of the White House. Lady Byrd Johnson launched an extensive campaign to clean up America by enlisting the aid of Americans in removing the litter from the sides of the roads and in getting rid of tacky billboards that destroyed the scenic beauty of the land. She is still involved in encouraging people through her personal example to make use of wildflowers in landscaping. Nancy Reagan initiated a program aimed at drug control. Her main emphasis was aimed at stopping drug abuse in the schools. Nancy Reagan's antidrug campaign is still going on, even though she no longer resides at the White House. These first ladies all were energetic women who made preserving America's values their number one goal.

Paragraph 5

SIE

Many times students think teachers are callous and don't care when the students have problems. Teachers may not be callous or uncaring. They simply may have been taken in by one too many sob stories. For example, a student came in after missing a test plus two other days of class. He said he had had some personal problems — his mother had died. The teacher began to worry about him, and the next day she called to see if there was anything she could do. His mother answered the phone. Another time a student left a message telling his teacher that he was too sick to come to class. Later that afternoon when the teacher was working out at the fitness center, she saw the student working out there, too. When she asked him how he was feeling, he looked embarrassed. Another time a student came in to say that he hadn't been to class the week before because it was raining too hard for him to catch the bus. The teacher thought he might have some special type of problem and asked why he couldn't ride the bus when she had seen other students getting off the same bus. These teachers are not callous, but rather they do not want to be unfair to the rest of their students by giving a special privilege to an irresponsible student.

Paragraph 6

Ext

Gabriel Garcia Marquez's characters in his novel *Love in the Time of Cholera* dedicate their entire lives to fulfilling their commitments. The reader can imagine what it would be like to be able to live this kind of life or to sacrifice a lifetime for a value or purpose. Florentino Ariza is just such a character. Florentino loves Fermina Daza for fifty-one years. He first sees her when he is a delivery boy and is asked to take a telegram to her father. She is unaccessible because of a watchful aunt, yet he knows her route to church, and as he pretends to read a book, he watches her pass every Sunday. He courts her briefly but so does an affluent doctor's son. She feels something for Florentino but chooses money over love. He watches her marry the doctor's son and remains single, waiting for the death of her husband. He thinks of her obsessively. To ease his pain, he fantasizes the smallest details of intimate encounters. Suddenly, Fermina's husband dies, and Florentino now has his long-awaited opportunity. Of course, these events may seem unrealistic, but the reader is swept away and can experience, at least in the reading of the novel, a true, undaunted love.

EXERCISE 8   *Master for transparency is in the Instructor's Manual.*

Carefully consider each of the following thesis sentences. Then develop a topic sentence for each division in the thesis sentence. Brainstorm on a separate sheet of paper to generate examples. Decide whether an extended example or several shorter examples would be most effective for the development of each paragraph. Then write each paragraph, using one extended example or several short, interrelated examples.

1. *Thesis sentence:* Throughout my years as a college student, I have experienced many enjoyable times by meeting new people, participating in student activities, and acquiring knowledge.

Paragraph 1

_____

(topic sentence)

_____

(extended example or several shorter examples)

_____

_____

_____

_____

Paragraph 2

_____

(topic sentence)

_____

(extended example or several shorter examples)

_____

_____

_____

_____

_____

Paragraph 3

_____

(topic sentence)

_____

_____

(extended example or several shorter examples)

_____

_____

_____

_____

2. *Thesis sentence:*   Zoos provide opportunities for people to observe animals in their natural habitat, for children to pet and feed animals, and for all people to become aware of endangered species.

Paragraph 1

_____

(topic sentence)

_____

_____

(extended example or several shorter examples)

_____

_____

_____

_____

Paragraph 2

_____

(topic sentence)

_____

_____

(extended example or several shorter examples)

_____

_____

_____

_____

Paragraph 3

_____

(topic sentence)

_____

_____

(extended example or several shorter examples)

_____

_____

_____

_____

3. *Thesis sentence:* I have experienced satisfaction at work because of my new skills, my supportive boss, and my friendly coworkers.

Paragraph 1

_____

(topic sentence)

_____

_____

(extended example or several shorter examples)

_____

_____

_____

_____

Paragraph 2

_____

(topic sentence)

_____

_____

(extended example or several shorter examples)

_____

_____

_____

_____

Paragraph 3

_____

(topic sentence)

_____

(extended example or several shorter examples)

_____

_____

_____

_____

_____

■ Collaborative Project: Working and Learning Together

In groups of three, discuss one major problem on your campus. Then brainstorm as many examples as possible that illustrate the problem. Generate short, interrelated examples that come from personal experience, observation, or authoritative sources. Have one person from each group report the results of the discussion.

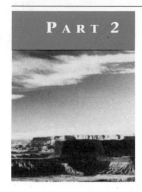

SOMETHING TO THINK ABOUT, SOMETHING TO WRITE ABOUT

Would You Know a Computer if You Met One?

Alicia Ottenberg, *professor of computer information systems, Glendale Community College*

1   If someone were to ask you if you have ever used a computer before, you might answer "No," or, perhaps, "only in school." You may not realize just how many computers you use directly on a regular basis and how many more you use indirectly.

2   Before identifying the computers you have probably used, it might be useful to describe just what a computer is. In his book, *Introduction to Computers and Information Systems*, Robert Szymanski defines a computer as "a device that accepts data, performs certain functions on that data, and presents the results of those operations." Accepting data means that there has to be a way to get the data into the computer. The input device used might be a keyboard or a floppy-disk drive, or perhaps a light pen! There are many ways to get data into a computer.

3   Performing certain functions on that data is accomplished within the computer itself. The functions may include anything from calculating your grade point average to determining when to fire a booster rocket on the Space Shuttle. A set of instructions, called a program, is used to tell the computer just what functions are to be performed.

4   Finally, there must be a way to present the results of the operations. Common output devices include monitors and printers, but there are also many others. All of the input and processing that is done would not be useful unless there was a way to use the results.

5   Some computers that you have used are more obviously identifiable than others, usually because there is a keyboard, a monitor, and, often, a box that has slots for disks. When you registered for school, you probably recognized that the registrar used a keyboard to enter the information regarding your chosen classes. He or she may have been able to tell you if the classes were closed by looking at the results of the inquiry on the monitor. If everything was in order, a registration slip was printed on a special form. Think about what happened: Your personal and course data were entered into the computer; your tuition and fees were calculated according to the instructions in the program; and these results were printed on a special registration form.

6   You need to do a little shopping, but you're short of cash and the bank is already closed. This is no longer a problem. Many banks have automatic teller machines, or ATMs, that are "open" twenty-four hours a day, seven days a week. The ATM is another computer that you may have recognized. There are really two input devices here: a specialized one to read your bank card and a keyboard for you to type in your individual identification number and dollar amounts. There are also two output devices: the monitor that displays instructions and information, and a mechanical device that distributes money if appropriate. "Banker's hours" are definitely not the obstacle they used to be!

7   Now that you have money to spend, go to the supermarket. Many stores now use computers to help keep track of prices and inventory. They use a bar code that represents each item's unique identification number that can be input using a light

pen or a laser device like those found in grocery stores. Once the unique number is read, the program matches it with price and inventory information already stored in the computer. The price is then output onto the cash register and the tape, and the inventory count for that item is adjusted. This is why many stores now no longer have a sticker price on each item; price changes are simply input into the computer instead of being redone on all of the items. This lowers labor costs and, it is hoped, your final total.

8   Before you leave the grocery store, put a quarter in the video game. Your quarter starts a program running on this very specialized computer. You recognize the screen as being an output device, but where's the keyboard? There is none; instead, you input data by pushing buttons and moving the joystick. Each of your actions is processed by the program, and the results are shown on the screen as graphic movements of the video characters. Unfortunately for many inexperienced players, the computer does *exactly* what you tell it to do; so, often, the games are very short!

9   As you step out into the parking lot, you may not realize that you are probably surrounded by many computers. Late-model cars have not one, but multiple computers controlling various functions. Mechanical gauges provide the input that enables the computers to adjust fuel intake, display warning signals, and do many other jobs. You may have been surprised the first time you heard a car say, ''Please fasten your seat belt.'' The voice was produced from a special output device when the input from the seat-belt sensor revealed that the seat belt was not fastened. Not only are there computers operating in the car itself, but the engineers who planned the car used computers to design and test it for efficiency and safety. It's less expensive to see how a computer model will perform under normal and adverse conditions than to build an actual car. And, as you can imagine, alterations to improve the design are made more easily on a computer model than on a real car!

10   Look around town. There is a movie theater across the street; many visual and audio sequences would not be possible without the use of computers. Computer-generated graphics and audio have become so sophisticated that many viewers cannot tell that the spaceship battle they are watching wasn't photographed with actual models or that the sound of the helicopter approaching was never made by a real whirlybird! The newspaper available at the corner stand was created and printed using computers. The hospital down the street uses computers to monitor patients, to perform specialized tests, to aid in diagnosis, and of course, to calculate the bill!

11   Look up. The jet flying overhead has computers controlling every aspect of the flight. The train you hear in the distance is on a computer-controlled route. The ingredients to make the candy bar in your pocket were measured by a computer, and the finished product was packaged and shipped with the aid of more computers. How about a glass of milk with that candy bar? The milk was produced by dairy cows whose amount and type of feed was controlled by a computer and was processed and packaged with equipment monitored by computers. Virtually everything available for purchase has probably been ''touched'' by a computer in some way.

12   Go home and put away the groceries. Hungry? Why don't you pop a frozen dinner in the microwave? As you press the numbers on the touch-pad, you realize that you are using another input device to give information to this specialized computer. The performance of the appliance is the output, although you might think the output is your dinner!

13   Many aspects of your home are smoothly controlled by computers without your having to think about it. The letter you put in the mail today has a good chance of reaching its destination because computers help route the millions of pieces properly. The electricity, gas, and water you used in your home this morning were there because computers made them possible. The phone call you need to make could not be accomplished without computers to direct it. Think about how many homes across the nation are enjoying these same benefits, benefits we would simply not have without the aid of computers.

14   At this time, many people are working with computers on your behalf, hoping to improve the quality of life through medical research, product testing, scientific exploration, and education. In most instances, these accomplishments can only be attained because of computers, those marvelous tools.

15   Now, if someone asks you if you have ever used a computer, you can smile and answer, "Of course, every day! Doesn't everybody?"

Understanding Words

Briefly define the following words as they are used in the above essay.

1. gauges *devices for measuring something*
2. whirlybird *helicopter*

Something to Write About

Using one of the topics listed below, develop a strong thesis sentence. Then draft your essay.

1. How has technology (any use of machines) made your life different from your grandparents' lives?
2. How has television changed people's life-styles?
3. How have home computers made life easier for people?
4. Give reasons people do not need computers.
5. How have computers helped people with disabilities?
6. Why do people resist change?
7. How have video games affected you?
8. How is playing Nintendo beneficial or harmful?

After you draft your essay, revise for content and edit for mechanics.

Content

    Revise it so that is has a clear thesis sentence.

    Be sure each support paragraph has a strong topic sentence and ample supporting examples.

    Check for unity and a smooth flow of ideas.

Mechanics

    Check for subject-verb agreement.

    Check for consistent verbs.

    Check for consistent point of view.

    Check for fragments, run-ons, and comma splices.

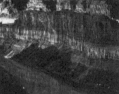

Legacy

Renee Robbe, *student*

1   I had a wonderful friend who was older than I was, but that was all right with me. I had been with her ever since I could remember, so I watched my best friend grow up through the years. I thought of her as my role model, and she thought of me as her little sister. Why was she my role model? I admired her because she was smart, artistic, and determined.

2   Everything came easy to my sister; therefore, I thought she was very smart. She had no problems in school; in fact, she was a straight "A" student. I always asked her for help with my homework because she explained it better than my teachers; as a result, I became a "B" student. Not only that, but my sister had a job working with computers, and she was very good at using them. Because I did not even know how to turn a computer on, she taught me the basics about computers, but I am still not as expert at them as she was. I admired the knowledge she had about computers because computers are the way of the future. My sister was smart in another way that helped me to solve my problems because she gave smart advice. She was like my own personal psychiatrist, but she did not charge me by the hour. I often wish I had my sister's brain.

3   Another quality I liked about my sister was her artistic talents. She was great at drawing cars, landscapes, and portraits. I was jealous of her drawing abilities because when I was little, I wanted to be an artist; however, I was never any good at art. Because decorating was something that she also loved to do, she wanted to open her own interior design business. It was amazing how she could put together colors to make a room have its own personality. I was inspired to follow in her footsteps and make interior design my career. Her artistic ability also appeared in her talent for sculpting nails. It might look easy, but if a person does not have a steady hand and is not artistic, the nails will look fake. My sister had the talent to make the nails look real. I know from experience because she used to do my nails. I have always admired my sister because she had so much artistic talent.

4   Having determination helped my sister get through life. When she found out that she had cancer, she was determined to survive it. She went through several operations, and no matter how much pain she had to endure, she held on. After seeing what my sister had to go through, I do not think that I could even try. Even though my sister had cancer, she was determined to live a normal life. She lost all her hair due to radiation; therefore, she wore a wig, but it never bothered her. She even went bald sometimes. She had made up her mind that she was not going to hide in her bedroom just because she had no hair. My sister was also determined to follow through with school. She knew she was going to die, but she did not let that stop her from living the rest of her life fully. My sister taught me that having determination will get a person through life, good or bad.

5   My sister taught me many things in her lifetime. She gave me knowledge about things I never knew about, and she taught me a little about art, but most important she taught me never to give up on life. I think I was lucky to have a role model like my sister to watch and learn from while I was growing up.

▣ Understanding Words

Briefly define the following word as it is used in the above essay.

1. legacy *inheritance*

▣ Questions on Content

Answers to
Unit 5, Part 3
are in the
Instructor's
Manual.

1. What did the author learn from her older sister?
2. What artistic talents did her sister have?
3. What was the older sister's reaction to her illness?

Questions on Form

1. In paragraph 3, what kinds of examples are used?
2. Describe the voice in paragraph 4.
3. What is the purpose of the essay?

Cigarette, Anyone?

JoAnn Baugh, *student*

1   Every year hundreds of people light up their first cigarette, and every year hundreds of people die from the effects of smoking cigarettes. The risks outweigh the benefits of smoking, and yet the cigarette industry flourishes. However, a trend has begun to reverse the attractiveness of smoking. Cigarette advertisements have been banned from television, and more statistics are showing the hazards of smoking. Society has become more health conscious, and over the last few years, people have become more aware of the reasons why they should not smoke. The facts that cigarette smoking is expensive, causes addiction, and is harmful to people's health are just a few incentives to keep them from smoking.

2   Cigarette smoking is not cheap. The cost of a pack of cigarettes is about $1.75. If the average smoker goes through two packs a day, then spending over $100 a month is easy. Also, a smoker most often marries another person who smokes, which would most likely double the cost of supplying their habits. Other times, costly furniture can be left with cigarette burns that cannot be repaired. The expenses also escalate when falling cigarette ashes burn holes in favorite clothes. This cigarette money can put a pinch on any budget, especially when people consider that this money is going "up in smoke."

3   It is a known fact that cigarette smoking causes addiction. Smoking the first cigarette may be a simple act. It probably makes people feel that they are fitting into the crowd, or perhaps it is calming to them. They are unaware at this time of the path of dependency ahead of them if they continue to smoke. Their lives will revolve around the cigarettes. They will be in situations in which they are not allowed to smoke, and that urge of dependency will no longer be a calming influence to them but will become a burden. People would probably never take that first cigarette if they could travel ahead in time and see what this addiction could do to their lives.

4   Health factors are the main reason why a person should not smoke. Every pack of cigarettes sold has a warning label by the Surgeon General of the hazards of smoking cigarettes. But this warning seems to be overlooked. Unfortunately, it is not easy to overlook hundreds of people dying from lung cancer each year.

Smokers can also develop many other high-risk conditions such as emphysema, high blood pressure, or heart disease. The people suffering from the ill-effects of smoking would have a stronger, more effective warning to share with those people about to take up smoking.

5   The trend has begun to help people recognize the reasons they should not smoke. Although it is unlikely that this trend will bring about the extinction of cigarettes, there has been a decrease in the number of people who smoke. If this trend continues and more people are educated about the risks, then it is safe to say that people suffering from the ill-effects of cigarette smoking are doing so by their own foolishness.

■ Understanding Words

Briefly define the following words as they are used in the above essay.

1. flourishes *thrives*
2. incentives *things that make someone want to work or try hard*
3. escalate *grow or expand*
4. emphysema *a lung disease that causes labored breathing*
5. extinction *putting out of existence*

■ Questions on Content

1. What reasons are given to convince readers not to smoke?
2. What is the main reason?
3. What does the author call the dependence on smoking?

Questions on Form

1. How many examples are given to support the idea that smoking is not cheap?
2. What do you think is the strongest paragraph?
3. Identify the supporting examples in paragraph four.

Responsibility

Charles Marchbanks, *student*

1   Recently, I spent four years living with my uncle. I was a little apprehensive about living with him because I had not met him, and I had heard that he was very mean and nasty. My first encounter with him proved no different. I was sleeping, and a rude voice came bellowing down the hallway. "Wake up! Get up!" I had a feeling that I was about to come face to face with my uncle for the first time. He walked into my room screaming, "You better get out of that bunk before I drop you." I was so startled that I didn't know what to think. Meanwhile, he continued to yell and scream, and I was wishing that I could transform into a speck of dust and blow away. The first impression I received of my uncle was not very good; however, I later found him to be very fair and giving. My uncle has altered my life in a positive way. He has done this by instilling in me discipline, self-pride, and responsibility.

2   While staying with my uncle, I received a fair amount of what he called justice and I called punishment. When I graduated from high school, I thought that I was

ready for the world; I thought incorrectly. I had a fair amount of discipline while growing up, but I totally lacked self-discipline. Well, my uncle filled in the void. If I got into trouble, I was disciplined, and the discipline was strictly enforced. Staying with my uncle, I found there was no room for slack. For instance, I accidentally called my uncle "Dude." He didn't like that; consequently, I was outside for fourteen days painting curbs, trimming bushes, and sweeping rocks. The discipline was effective to say the least.

3   Self-esteem is also a quality that I did not possess before living with my uncle. It was something that I had to work on, and my uncle helped me a great deal. He helped me by rewarding and praising me for doing a good job. I remember the first time that he ever praised me. It was when I had stayed late at work while all my coworkers had gone home. I had done this because there was a piece of equipment that was broken, and it needed to be fixed as soon as possible. Well, I stayed there until I had repaired it. My uncle was very pleased, and he praised me for my work. Through his encouragement and positive reinforcement on this and other occasions, I was able to build confidence and pride.

4   Responsibility is one of the major attributes that were implanted in me. I was fortunate to have an uncle that was more than happy to force responsibility on me. He always gave me a job that was a challenge, and he would see how well I could perform the task. If I didn't perform to his satisfaction, he did not give me any responsibilities for a long time. I can see now why he tried so hard to make me more responsible. He knew that if I was irresponsible in the future I could not make it in the job market. Now I accept responsibility with the greatest of ease. Being with my uncle gave me a chance to accept responsibilities that might not have come my way. I find that being a responsible person can make a job or even my life a lot easier to handle.

5   In summary, these three attributes—discipline, pride, and responsibility—are qualities that will make my life flow a little more smoothly. I now feel that my decision to live with my uncle was one of the wisest that I have made, and if I had the choice, I would do it all over again.

▊ Understanding Words

Briefly define the following words as they are used in the above essay.

1. apprehensive   *anxious, uneasy, fearful*
2. void   *vacant, not occupied*
3. attributes   *natural qualities of a person*

▊ Questions on Content

1. What was the author's first impression of his uncle?
2. What did he learn from his uncle?
3. Why did his uncle stress responsibility?

Questions on Form

1. Identify the topic sentence in paragraph 2.
2. Which paragraph, in your opinion, has the strongest support?
3. Do the support paragraphs contain short, interrelated examples or an extended example?

Cooking

Maria Palomino, *student*

1   When I think of ways to entertain and get acquainted with someone, my thoughts turn to cooking. There are many reasons why people like to cook. For some, it is a hobby; for others, it is a way to relieve stress; and, I think, for most people, cooking is a way to express love and appreciation for family or friends.

2   Cooking as a hobby can be fun, rewarding, and creative. I viewed cooking as a hobby when I took a natural-foods cooking class. I would attend once a week and experiment with new recipes. I found it to be fun, and at the same time it developed my creativity. For example, one day I decided to follow a recipe for bran muffins. The recipe sounded flat to me because all it called for was bran, oil, water, and honey. I decided to experiment with other ingredients, so I added what I thought would improve the taste of the muffins. I added two ripe bananas, molasses, vanilla, eggs, and some sunflower seeds. I was so pleased when they were done. They came out delicious. The muffins were a great success because of their good taste and my fun in creating the new version.

3   I also find that, for me, cooking relieves stress because there are days when I need to take the focus off the demands and pressures of the week. That is when I decide to cook something. Depending on how ambitious I'm feeling, I might decide to try a new recipe. For instance, one day I came home from a hard day at school. I had taken a long and difficult test. I was still feeling wound up and stressed out, so I decided to tackle a new cheesecake recipe. Well, fifteen minutes into the recipe, I was so immersed in what I was doing that I forgot about all the pressures of the day. The aroma of the cheesecake baking was overwhelming. After having a piece of cheesecake, I had a new and refreshing outlook on my problems. They did not seem so pressing.

4   Finally, one of the most wonderful reasons to cook is to express love and appreciation for someone. Preparing a meal for someone is a special way of showing that I care for and value that person. I am giving a part of myself in a nonthreatening manner. When I cook for people and serve them, I am nurturing and providing them pleasure. I don't believe I have to prepare an elaborate meal for them to know how much I care. The "tender loving care" I put into the cooking will be a clear indication of my love. For example, one day my daughter and I had a disagreement. Her feelings were hurt, and she and I didn't have a chance to resolve the problem. I decided to invite her over for dinner. She was reluctant to come until I told her I was preparing her favorite meal. When she arrived for dinner, I could tell that she enjoyed the aroma when she said, "It sure smells good." That seemed to break the ice. She sat down to dinner, and I served her, telling her that we needed to talk. Well, the evening ended with us laughing and enjoying one another's company. She knew that cooking the meal for her was a way to let her know I loved her and wanted to nurture and provide pleasure with her favorite dish.

5   I'm glad God made food for us to eat and cook because cooking provides not only a creative hobby but also therapy for relieving stress and anxiety. One of the most important reasons for cooking, for me, is to show love and appreciation for another person.

■ Understanding Words

Briefly define the following words as they are used in the above essay.

1. immersed *profoundly involved*
2. aroma *a pleasant, often spicy odor*
3. nurturing *training, bringing up, caring for*

■ Questions on Content

1. In the author's opinion, why do people like to cook?
2. How can cooking be creative?
3. For what special reason did the author cook her daughter's favorite meal?

Questions on Form

1. In each support paragraph, does the author use short, interrelated examples or an extended example?
2. Point out effective details in the examples used.
3. Why does the author discuss the "love and appreciation" reason last?

Wandering Through Winter

Excerpt from *Summer in January* by **Edwin Way Teale**

In the folklore of the country, numerous superstitions relate to winter weather. Back-country farmers examine their corn husks — the thicker the husk, the colder the winter. They watch the acorn crop — the more acorns, the more severe the season. They observe where white-faced hornets place their paper nests — the higher they are, the deeper will be the snow. They examine the size and shape and color of the spleens of butchered hogs for clues to the severity of the seasons. They keep track of the blooming of dogwood in the spring — the more abundant the blooms, the more bitter the cold in January. When chipmunks carry their tails high and squirrels have heavier fur and mice come into country houses early in the fall, the superstitious gird themselves for a long, hard winter. Without any scientific basis, a wider-than-usual black band on a wooly-bear caterpillar is accepted as a sign that winter will arrive early and stay late. Even the way a cat sits beside the stove carries its message to the credulous. According to a belief once widely held in the Ozarks, a cat sitting with its tail to the fire indicates very cold weather is on the way.

■ Understanding Words

Briefly define the following words as they are used in the above paragraph.

1. folklore *traditional beliefs*
2. severity *gravity or seriousness*
3. credulous *easily convinced*

■ Questions on Content

1. What does the author call the ideas that farmers and country people have about judging a coming winter?

Questions on Form

1. What makes the paragraph well developed?
2. Identify the kinds of examples used.

2. What kind of "basis" or proof is lacking for these ideas?
3. In what part of the United States was there a belief about cats sitting close to the fire?

Overheard on a Train Trip Through England

Excerpt from *Kingdom by the Sea* by **Paul Theroux**

Once, from behind a closed door, I heard an Englishwoman exclaim with real pleasure, "They are *funny*, the Yanks!" And I crept away and laughed to think that an English person was saying such a thing. And I thought: They wallpaper their ceilings! They put little knitted bobble-hats on their soft-boiled eggs to keep them warm! They don't give you bags in supermarkets! They say sorry when you step on their toes! Their government makes them get a hundred-dollar license every year for watching television! They issue drivers' licenses that are valid for thirty or forty years — mine expires in the year 2011! They charge you for matches when you buy cigarettes! They smoke on buses! They drive on the left! They spy for the Russians! They say "nigger" and "Jewboy" without flinching! They call their houses Holm-leigh and Sparrow View! They sunbathe in their underwear! They don't say "You're welcome"! They still have milk bottles and milkmen, and junk-dealers with horse-drawn wagons! They love candy and Lucozade and leftovers called bubble-and-squeak! They live in Barking and Dorking and Shellow Bowells! They have amazing names, like Mr. Eatwell and Lady Inkpen and Major Twaddle and Miss Tosh! And they think *we're* funny?

Understanding Words

Briefly define the following word as it is used in the above paragraph.

1. flinching *drawing away or moving away from as in pain*

Questions on Content

1. What two nationalities are the focus of this paragraph?
2. What is the author replying to in the paragraph?
3. What is the author really saying in the question in the end?

Questions on Form

1. What makes the supporting examples effective in this paragraph?
2. How many examples are given?
3. What is the implied topic sentence?

Courtship Through the Ages

Excerpt from *My World and Welcome to It* by **James Thurber**

1   Surely nothing in the astonishing scheme of life can have nonplussed Nature so much as the fact that none of the females of any of the species she created really cared very much for the male, as such. For the past ten million years Nature has

been busily inventing ways to make the male attractive to the female, but the whole business of courtship, from the marine annelids up to man, still lumbers heavily along, like a complicated musical comedy. I have been reading the sad and absorbing story in Volume 6 (Cole to Dame) of the *Encylopaedia Britannica*. In this volume you can learn all about cricket, cotton, costume designing, crocodiles, crown jewels, and Coleridge, but none of these subjects is so interesting as the Courtship of Animals, which recounts the sorrowful lengths to which all males must go to arouse the interest of a lady.

2   We all know, I think, that Nature gave man whiskers and a mustache with the quaint idea in mind that these would prove attractive to the female. We all know that, far from attracting her, whiskers and mustaches only made her nervous and gloomy, so that man had to go in for somersaults, tilting with lances, and perform-ing feats of parlor magic to win her attention; he also had to bring her candy, flowers, and the furs of animals. It is common knowledge that in spite of all these "love displays" the male is constantly being turned down, insulted, or thrown out of the house. It is rather comforting, then, to discover that the peacock, for all his gorgeous plumage, does not have a particularly easy time in courtship; none of the males in the world do. The first peahen, it turned out, was only faintly stirred by her suitor's beautiful train. She would often go quietly to sleep while he was whisking it around. The *Britannica* tells us that the peacock actually had to learn a certain little trick to wake her up and revive her interest: he had to learn to vibrate his quills so as to make a rustling sound. In ancient times man himself, observing the ways of the peacock, probably tried vibrating his whiskers to make a rustling sound; if so, it didn't get him anywhere. He had to go in for something else; so, among other things, he went in for gifts. It is not unlikely that he got this idea from certain flies and birds who were making no headway at all with rustling sounds.

3   One of the flies of the family Empidae, who had tried everything, finally hit on something pretty special. He contrived to make a glistening transparent balloon which was even larger than himself. Into this he would put sweetmeats and tidbits and he would carry the whole elaborate envelope through the air to the lady of his choice. This amused her for a time, but she finally got bored with it. She demanded silly little colorful presents, something that you couldn't eat but that would look nice around the house. So the male Empis had to go around gathering flower petals and pieces of bright paper to put into his balloon. On a courtship flight a male Empis cuts quite a figure now, but he can hardly be said to be happy. He never knows how soon the female will demand heavier presents, such as Roman coins and gold collar buttons. It seems probable that one day the courtship of the Empidae will fall down, as man's occasionally does, of its own weight.

4   The bowerbird is another creature that spends so much time courting the female that he never gets any work done. If all the male bowerbirds became nervous wrecks within the next ten or fifteen years, it would not surprise me. The female bowerbird insists that a playground be built for her with a specially con-structed bower at the entrance. This bower is much more elaborate than an ordi-nary nest and is harder to build; it costs a lot more, too. The female will not come to the playground until the male has filled it up with a great many gifts: silvery leaves, red leaves, rose petals, shells, beads, berries, bones, dice, buttons, cigar bands, Christmas seals, and the Lord knows what else. When the female finally condescends to visit the playground, she is in a coy and silly mood and has to be chased in and out of the bower and up and down the playground before she will quit giggling and stand still long enough even to shake hands. The male bird is, of course, pretty well done in before the chase starts, because he has worn himself out hunting for eyeglass lenses and begonia blossoms. I imagine that many a

bowerbird, after chasing a female for two or three hours, says the hell with it and goes home to bed. Next day, of course, he telephones someone else and the same trying ritual is gone through with again. A male bowerbird is as exhausted as a night-club habitué before he is out of his twenties.

5 The male fiddler crab has a somewhat easier time, but it can hardly be said that he is sitting pretty. He has one enormously large and powerful claw, usually brilliantly colored, and you might suppose that all he has to do was reach out and grab some passing cutie. The very earliest fiddler crabs may have tried this, but, if so, they got slapped for their pains. A female fiddler crab will not tolerate any caveman stuff; she never has and she doesn't intend to start now. To attract a female, a fiddler crab has to stand on tiptoe and brandish his claw in the air. If any female in the neighborhood is interested — and you'd be surprised how many are not — she comes over and engages him in light badinage, for which he is not in the mood. As many as a hundred females may pass the time of day with him and go on about their business. By nightfall of an average courting day, a fiddler crab who has been standing on tiptoe for eight or ten hours waving a heavy claw in the air is in pretty sad shape. As in the case of the males of all species, however, he gets out of bed next morning, dashes some water on his face, and tries again.

6 The next time you encounter a male web-spinning spider, stop and reflect that he is too busy worrying about his love life to have any desire to bite you. Male web-spinning spiders have a tougher life than any other males in the animal kingdom. This is because the female web-spinning spiders have very poor eyesight. If a male lands on a female's web, she kills him before he has time to lay down his cane and gloves, mistaking him for a fly or a bumblebee who has tumbled into her trap. Before the species figured out what to do about this, millions of males were murdered by ladies they called on. It is the nature of spiders to perform a little dance in front of the female, but before a male spinner could get near enough for the female to see who he was and what he was up to, she would lash out at him with a flat-iron or a pair of garden shears. One night, nobody knows when, a very bright male spinner lay awake worrying about calling on a lady who had been killing suitors right and left. It came to him that this business of dancing as a love display wasn't getting anybody anywhere except the grave. He decided to go in for web-twitching, or strand-vibrating. The next day he tried it on one of the nearsighted girls. Instead of dropping in on her suddenly, he stayed outside the web and began monkeying with one of its strands. He twitched it up and down and in and out with such a lilting rhythm that the female was charmed. The serenade worked beautifully; the female let him live. The *Britannica*'s spiderwatchers, however, report that his system is not always successful. Once in a while, even now, a female will fire three bullets into a suitor or run him through with a kitchen knife. She keeps threatening him from the moment he strikes the first low notes on the outside strings, but usually by the time he has got up to the high note played around the center of the web, he is going to town and she spares his life.

7 Even the butterfly, as handsome a fellow as he is, can't always win a mate merely by fluttering around and showing off. Many butterflies have to have scent scales on their wings. Hepialus carries a powder puff in a perfumed pouch. He throws perfume at the ladies when they pass. The male tree cricket, Oecanthus, goes Hepialus one better by carrying a tiny bottle of wine with him and giving drinks to such doxies as he has designs on. One of the male snails throws darts to entertain the girls. So it goes, through the long list of animals, from the bristle worm and his rudimentary dance steps to man and his gifts of diamonds and sapphires. The golden-eye drake raises a jet of water with his feet as he flies over a lake; Hepialus has his powder puff, Oecanthus his wine bottle, man his etchings. It

is a bright and melancholy story, the age-old desire of the female to be amused and entertained. Of all the creatures on earth, the only males who could be figured as putting any irony into their courtship are the grebes and certain other diving birds. Every now and then a courting grebe slips quietly down to the bottom of a lake and then, with a mighty "Whoosh!," pops out suddenly a few feet from his girl friend, splashing water all over her. She seems to be persuaded that this is a purely loving display, but I like to think that the grebe always has a faint hope of drowning her or scaring her to death.

8   I will close this investigation into the mournful burdens of the male with the *Britannica*'s story about a certain Argus pheasant. It appears that the Argus displays himself in front of a female who stands perfectly still without moving a feather. . . . The male Argus the *Britannica* tells about was confined in a cage with a female of another species, a female who kept moving around, emptying ashtrays and fussing with lampshades all the time the male was showing off his talents. Finally, in disgust, he stalked away and began displaying in front of the water trough. He reminds me of a certain male (*Homo sapiens*) of my acquaintance who one night after dinner asked his wife to put down her detective magazine so that he could read a poem of which he was very fond. She sat quietly enough until he was well into the middle of the thing, intoning with great ardor and intensity. Then suddenly there came a sharp, disconcerting slap! It turned out that all during the male's display, the female had been intent on a circling mosquito and had finally trapped it between the palms of her hands. The male in this case did not stalk away and display in front of a water trough; he went over to Tim's and had a flock of drinks and recited the poem to the fellas. I am sure they all told bitter stories of their own about how their displays had been interrupted by females. I am also sure that they all ended up singing "Honey, Honey, Bless Your Heart."

▨ Understanding Words

Briefly define the following words as they are used in the above essay.

1. nonplussed   *astonished or shocked*
2. condescends   *takes a step down to another level*
3. coy   *shyly flirtatious*
4. habitué   *one who frequents a certain club, restaurant, etc.*
5. brandish   *to wave in a threatening way*
6. badinage   *light or playful joking*
7. rudimentary   *elementary*
8. etchings   *drawings*

▨ Questions on Content

1. What is the meaning of courtship?
2. What are some ways males attract females?
3. How does the author let us know he is talking about people?
4. What, in your opinion, is a vivid example of courtship?

Questions on Form

1. Does the author use an extended example or short, interrelated examples?
2. Identify the main idea of the essay.
3. What is the voice of the author?

| **PART 4** | **THE WRITER'S TOOLS: SENTENCE VARIETY —**
FORMING AND PUNCTUATING
COMPOUND SENTENCES |

OBJECTIVES

- Combine simple sentences using coordinate conjunctions.
- Combine simple sentences using conjunctive adverbs.
- Combine simple sentences using a semicolon.

Test over compound sentences, p. 36–38 in Instructor's Manual.

One of the first steps of good revision is to change short, choppy sentences into compound sentences. You may write good compound sentences now but may not be aware of them. On the other hand, perhaps you could strengthen your writing by learning to revise short, choppy sentences into effective compound sentences. In this way, you will achieve some sentence variety. Additional types of sentence patterns will be covered in Unit 6.

A **compound sentence** is two or more simple sentences combined in a variety of ways. They may be joined by a comma and a coordinate conjunction, a semicolon followed by a conjunctive adverb and a comma, or just a semicolon.

Using a Comma and a Coordinate Conjunction

Coordinate conjunctions join two sentences that are of equal value or are "coordinate" with each other. The coordinate conjunctions you choose depend upon the meaning you want to achieve in your writing.

Coordinate Conjunctions

for	but
and	or
nor	yet
	so

Note Remembering the words "fan boys" can help you memorize the list of coordinate conjunctions.

Here are some examples of the use of coordinate conjunctions to join two simple sentences.

and (adds)

Mike enjoys his job.

He performs well.

Mike enjoys his job, **and** he performs well.

but (contrasts)

Mike enjoys his job.

He has a long drive each day.

Mike enjoys his job, **but** he has a long drive each day.

229

for (gives a reason)

Mike enjoys his job.

It offers a challenge.

Mike enjoys his job, **for** it offers a challenge.

nor (adds another negative idea)

Mike does not enjoy his job.

He does not perform well.

Mike does not enjoy his job, **nor** does he perform well.

or (gives a choice)

Mike can choose to work four ten-hour days.

He can work five eight-hour days.

Mike can choose to work four ten-hour days, **or** he can work five eight-hour days.

so (shows result)

Mike enjoys his job.

He works hard.

Mike enjoys his job, **so** he works hard.

yet (shows change or contrast)

Mike works hard.

He also enjoys life.

Mike works hard, **yet** he also enjoys life.

EXERCISE 1

Combine the two simple sentences into one compound sentence by adding a comma and a coordinate conjunction. Make the revisions above the sentences.

Example:

The day was cool and <u>refreshing. We</u> went on a picnic.
(revision above: refreshing, so we)

1. Tourists on Virginia Beach watched fireworks on Thursday. ~~They~~ went sailing on Friday.
(revision above: , and they)

2. Jeremy finished repairing the car. ~~He~~ filled it with gas.
(revision above: , so he)

3. I did not enjoy the food. ~~I did not~~ care for the entertainment either.
(revision above: , nor did I)

4. They enjoyed playing basketball. ~~They~~ seldom went to any professional games.
(revision above: , yet they)

5. Robert exercises regularly, *, yet he* ~~He~~ has trouble losing weight.

6. We lived in Germany for six years, *, for my* ~~My~~ wife was in the service.

■ Using a Conjunctive Adverb

You can combine two simple sentences by placing a conjunctive adverb between them. Place a semicolon at the end of the first sentence to separate the two sentences, and then put a comma after the conjunctive adverb.

> The clerk offended the customer; **consequently,** the customer did not shop at that store again.

When you put a conjunctive adverb *within* a sentence rather than between two simple sentences, put a comma *before and after* the conjunctive adverb.

> The clerk offended the customer. The customer, **consequently,** did not shop at that store again.
>
> Helen hates the heat; she, **however,** is coming to Phoenix in July.

Note In the second example, which is a compound sentence, a semicolon still separates the two complete sentences.

Conjunctive Adverbs

as a result	moreover
consequently	nevertheless
furthermore	otherwise
however	therefore
in addition	thus
in fact	

Just as you choose a coordinate conjunction to express a particular meaning you want in your writing, so you must pay close attention to the conjunctive adverb you select. Here are some examples of conjunctive adverbs in compound sentences.

as a result (shows a result)
> Mike enjoys his job; **as a result,** he works very hard.

consequently (shows a result)
> Mike does not enjoy his job; **consequently,** he does not work very hard.

furthermore (shows an additional idea)
> Mike plans to quit his job; **furthermore,** he plans to change his career.

however (shows a contrast)
> Mike likes his job; **however,** he plans to find a better one.

in addition (adds an equally important idea)

    Mike likes his job; **in addition,** he likes his coworkers.

moreover (adds an equally important idea)

    Mike likes his job; **moreover,** he likes his coworkers.

nevertheless (shows a contrast)

    Mike enjoys his job; **nevertheless,** he finds time for other things.

otherwise (indicates a result if the first idea did not occur)

    Mike enjoys his job; **otherwise,** he would look for a new job.

therefore (shows a result)

    Mike wants more money; **therefore,** he will ask his boss for a raise.

thus (shows a result)

    Mike has saved money from his job; **thus,** he will be able to go to school.

EXERCISE 2

Combine each of the following pairs of simple sentences into one compound sentence by adding a semicolon, a conjunctive adverb, and a comma. Make the revisions above the sentences.

Example:

salty; however, we

The stew was too ~~salty. We~~ ate it anyway.

; therefore,

1.   The toll charge was a quarter, Frank paid it as he entered the freeway.

Minutes"; consequently, she

2.   Her favorite program is "60 ~~Minutes." She~~ watches it every Sunday evening.

; however, it

3.   Traveling can be a pleasant experience, ~~It~~ can be stressful for a large family.

; otherwise, she

4.   Chris read the entire book, ~~She~~ would not have known the answers.

; nevertheless, the

5.   Many people give to charity, ~~The~~ food bank needs more canned goods.

; in addition, he

6.   Danny graduated from college, ~~He~~ got a job working for Motorola.

Using a Semicolon

    Two simple sentences can also be connected by using a semicolon. However, when they are joined by a semicolon, the second sentence does *not* begin with a capital letter.

The clerk offended the customer.

The customer did not shop at that store again.

The clerk offended the customer; the customer did not shop at that store again.

EXERCISE 3

Combine the two simple sentences into one compound sentence by adding a semicolon. Remember to begin the second sentence with a lowercase letter. Make the revisions above the sentences.

Example:

females; two

Five of the puppies were ~~females. Two~~ were males.

1. We enjoyed going to the ocean *; the* ~~. The~~ children collected seashells.

2. We laughed *; we* ~~. We~~ cried *; we* ~~. We~~ shared memories.

3. Mark was hungry *; he* ~~. He~~ snacked on peanuts.

4. Seventy percent of the work was done *; only* ~~. Only~~ 30 percent was left to complete.

5. The dog barked loudly *; soon* ~~. Soon~~ it stopped.

6. They stocked the shelves *; they* ~~. They~~ cleaned up the aisles.

EXERCISE 4

Master for transparency is in the Instructor's Manual.

For each of the following items, combine the two simple sentences into one compound sentence as indicated. Punctuate correctly.

Example:

Sara trains dogs well. She is always busy.

Sara trains dogs well, so she is always busy.

(coordinate conjunction)

Sara trains dogs well; she is always busy.

(semicolon)

Sara trains dogs well; consequently, she is always busy.

(conjunctive adverb)

1. Maria rolled her own tortillas. She made fresh green chili.

Maria rolled her own tortillas, and she made fresh green chile.

(coordinate conjunction)

Maria rolled her own tortillas; she made fresh green chile.

(semicolon)

Maria rolled her own tortillas; in addition, she made fresh green chili.

(conjunctive adverb)

2. Pete does excellent carpentry work. He receives many jobs.

Pete does excellent carpentry work, so he receives many jobs.

(coordinate conjunction)

Pete does excellent carpentry work; he receives many jobs.

(semicolon)

Pete does excellent carpentry work; therefore, he receives many jobs.

(conjunctive adverb)

3. Brenda is an excellent secretary. She works well with people.

Brenda is an excellent secretary, and she works well with people.

(coordinate conjunction)

Brenda is an excellent secretary; she works well with people.

(semicolon)

Brenda is an excellent secretary; in addition, she works well with people.

(conjunctive adverb)

4. Keta and Bede live in Alaska. They often fish for salmon.

Keta and Bede live in Alaska, so they often fish for salmon.

(coordinate conjunction)

Keta and Bede live in Alaska; they often fish for salmon.

(semicolon)

Keta and Bede live in Alaska; consequently, they often fish for salmon.

(conjunctive adverb)

5. The child got out the peanut butter and jelly. He made a sandwich.

The child got out the peanut butter and jelly, and he made a sandwich.
(coordinate conjunction)

The child got out the peanut butter and jelly; he made a sandwich.
(semicolon)

The child got out the peanut butter and jelly; thus, he made a sandwich.
(conjunctive adverb)

6. The attorney worked hard on the divorce case. He won it.

The attorney worked hard on the divorce case, so he won it.
(coordinate conjunction)

The attorney worked hard on the divorce case; he won it.
(semicolon)

The attorney worked hard on the divorce case; consequently he won it.
(conjunctive adverb)

7. Randi has an extensive doll collection. She attends many doll shows.

Randi has an extensive doll collection, so she attends many doll shows.
(coordinate conjunction)

Randi has an extensive doll collection; she attends many doll shows.
(semicolon)

Randi has an extensive doll collection; as a result, she attends many doll shows.
(conjunctive adverb)

8. The man was working hard all morning. He went swimming.

The man was working hard all morning, yet he went swimming.
(coordinate conjunction)

The man was working hard all morning; he went swimming.
(semicolon)

The man was working hard all morning; nevertheless, he went swimming.
(conjunctive adverb)

9. Dusty won the national roping contest. He won $2,000.

Dusty won the national roping contest, and he won $2,000.
(coordinate conjunction)

Dusty won the national roping contest; he won $2,000.
(semicolon)

Dusty won the national roping contest; in fact, he won $2,000.
(conjunctive adverb)

10. Angelina works full time. She goes to school.

Angelina works full time, yet she goes to school.
(coordinate conjunction)

Angelina works full time; she goes to school.
(semicolon)

Angelina works full time; in addition, she goes to school.
(conjunctive adverb)

EXERCISE 5   *Transparency can be made p. 67.*

Revise the following paragraphs by changing the short choppy sentences into compound sentences. Use a variety of ways to combine the sentences.

Paragraph 1

Throughout their adult years, people often need to adjust to many changes in their lives. Technology may require people to retrain for a new job. *, and often* ~~Often~~ company restructuring causes change, Sometimes promotion causes change. *; sometimes* ~~Sometimes~~ job loss causes change. Other major changes occur in people's personal lives, too. For various reasons, some married adults are separated from their mates. *, so they* ~~They~~ must take on the total responsibilities for the household. Many adults must deal with having the last child leave home. *; however, some* ~~Some~~ people must cope with adult children returning home. Sometimes they return alone. *, and other times* ~~Sometimes~~ they return with children. Once in a while, they may return with a

, or they
mate. ~~They~~ may return with a mate and children. All these situations can cause adults to make shifts in

their life-styles.

Paragraph 2

; nevertheless, they
American people do not want to eat less. ~~They~~ want to consume fewer calories. Food companies

, and they
know this. ~~They~~ are coming out with reduced- or low-calorie food products. Powdered "butter"

; furthermore, ice
substitutions boast of having the same taste as real butter with a fraction of the calories. ~~Ice~~ cream is

appearing in "light" form ~~also~~. Producers use fat substitutes and sugar substitutes that add up to fewer

calories but have "the same great taste" for the consumer. Even potato chips come with the "light"

option. Not only single items but many prepackaged microwave meals specialize in meals with under

, and the
three hundred calories. ~~The~~ meal can be topped off with a variety of pastries with "less than half the

, so consumers
calories of other baked goods." Food producers keep churning out new alternatives. ~~Consumers~~ keep

"eating them up."

Paragraph 3

Today, more than ever, people are realizing the need to conserve our resources, especially water.

, but every   *, for these*
This effort can be effective. ~~Every~~ American must be willing to make adjustments. ~~These~~ adjustments

will save this essential resource. Anne is one person who has done her part to help in this effort. Inside

, and then
her house, she always fills her dishwasher. ~~Then~~ she runs it. She always washes a full load of clothes.

; as a result, each
She has also placed a water saver in her toilet tank. ~~Each~~ flush takes less water. She never leaves the

water running while she brushes her teeth. Outside, she has installed a drip-water system to keep her

, so this
plants wet. ~~This~~ way she does not lose water to evaporation. She has also landscaped her yard with

; moreover, she

plants that require little water, ~~She~~ never uses the hose to wash off the sidewalk or driveway. If every

American will try to follow this example, millions of gallons of water will be saved every day.

Paragraph 4

Dyslexia is a learning disability that may be overcome through compensation. Many times people

, and they   ; however, they

with dyslexia are extraordinarily intelligent, ~~They~~ show no outward signs of this disability, ~~They~~ often

have difficulty performing certain tasks such as learning to read. They become frustrated when they

; nevertheless, she

attempt these tasks that are simple to other people. For example, Dr. Marie Xavier is a dyslexic, ~~She~~

, so she

learned to cope with her learning disability. She was a rebellious teen, ~~She~~ did not take an interest in

, and she

school. Later she was inspired, ~~She~~ excelled. She overcame her reading problem by using a patch over

, but her

one eye and special reading glasses, ~~Her~~ study time was always at least double that of her classmates.

; as a result, she

She went on to medical school, ~~She~~ graduated with honors. She could more keenly relate to those

, and she

who were suffering, ~~She~~ became a doctor and an advocate for dyslexics. She proved that dyslexia can

, and in

be overcome, ~~In~~ this way, she set an example for Americans everywhere.

WRITING ASSIGNMENT

Using the steps of the writing process that you are familiar with, draft an essay on one of the following topics.

1. Qualities that make a perfect mate
2. Reasons people buy clothes
3. Issues facing your city government, state government, or federal government
4. Reasons cars are important to people
5. Reasons a particular vacation was exciting or boring
6. Information people can learn by reading a newspaper
7. Reasons children or adults find television appealing
8. Reasons music appeals to people
9. Reasons people ride bicycles rather than drive cars
10. Reasons people drive cars rather than ride bicycles
11. Characteristics of memorable birthday celebrations

After you draft your essay, revise for content and edit for mechanics.

Content

   Essay

      Check to see that the paper has a strong thesis sentence.

      Check to see that the voice is appropriate for purpose and audience.

   Paragraphs

      Revise so that each has a clear topic sentence that develops an idea suggested in the thesis sentence.

      Include four to six supporting sentences that are developed using short interrelated examples or an extended example.

      Include a closing sentence in each paragraph.

Mechanics

   Check for subject-verb agreement.

   Check for consistent verbs.

   Check for a consistent point of view.

   Check for fragments, run-on sentences, and comma splices.

   Check punctuation of compound sentences.

Sentence variety

   Revise short sentences into compound sentences.

UNIT 6

Reaching an Audience by Creating Interest

PART 1

PARTS TO WHOLE: INTRODUCTORY AND CONCLUDING PARAGRAPHS

OBJECTIVES

- Understand the purpose of introductions.
- Recognize the parts of an introductory paragraph.
- Understand the types of hooks used in introductory paragraphs.
- Be aware of audience and purpose in relation to hook.
- Write an introductory paragraph that has a hook, transition, and a thesis sentence.
- Understand the purpose of conclusions.
- Recognize and revise a weak conclusion.
- Recognize and write a strong conclusion.

After you are able to write both a thesis sentence and the support paragraphs necessary for the longer paper, you need to add an effective introductory paragraph. Because you already know how to write a thesis sentence, you only need to add a hook and a smooth transition to that thesis sentence.

Parts of an Introductory Paragraph

hook

transition

thesis sentence

■ The Purpose of Introductory Paragraphs

The purpose of an introductory paragraph is to get the reader's attention and to let the reader know what will be covered in the essay. Very often, it sets the tone for the entire essay. While reading your introduction, your audience might think, "This paper really sounds good," or "I can't figure out what this person is talking about." The first response is what you want from your reader. The introduction gives you a chance to "hook" your audience right away.

■ Developing Introductory Paragraphs

Writing an introductory paragraph can be simplified if you follow a step-by-step process.

Compose the thesis sentence.

Decide on the type of hook that is most effective.

Write the hook.

Write the transition.

Draft these three parts into an introductory paragraph.

Composing the Thesis Sentence

Although the same process does not always work for everyone, the part of the introductory paragraph that you write first is the thesis sentence. As you recall, the thesis sentence consists of either the topic and a clear direction, or a topic, a clear direction, and a preview of the points to be covered in the paper. Because the thesis sentence keeps you on track, it is composed first; however, it will be the *last* sentence in the introductory paragraph.

Developing the Hook

Transparency can be made of types of hooks and examples: pp. 68 - 70 in Instructor's Manual.

After you have composed your thesis sentence, you need to write a strong hook. Even though the hook is usually the second part you write, it comes *first* in the actual introductory paragraph; consequently, it should be strong and should make the reader keep on reading. There are several ways to get the reader's attention, and your job is to be creative in finding the best way for each specific essay that you write. An effective introduction may contain *one or more* of the following hooks.

Types of Hooks

1. personal examples
2. quotations
3. facts or statistics
4. rhetorical questions
5. current events
6. contrast to the thesis sentence

Using Personal Examples Examples can be either a personal experience or an experience that you witnessed happening to someone else.

Personal experience usually provides strong, maybe even dramatic incidents to use. Writing about personal experiences may be difficult for some people, but if you are honest in expressing your thoughts and feelings, you will establish a real connection with your reader. Sharing with the reader can create interest and form a healthy bond that will last throughout the paper. The reader will want to read further because you are sharing a part of yourself, and that is what communication is all about. This personal experience should have really happened to you. If you make up the experience and the reader discovers you are pretending, you have lost your credibility as a writer, and you have lost your reader as an audience.

Another type of hook can come from **personal observation** of an experience that you saw happening to someone else. It must be something that really impressed you when you saw it, or it will not impress anyone else. For example, if you see a terrible accident, recalling facts or observations from this experience may be appropriate to grab the reader's attention for a paper you are writing.

The following introductory paragraphs effectively use personal examples to hook the reader. In each paragraph the hook is in bold print and the thesis sentence is underlined. First, read this example that uses a personal experience as a hook.

On February 19, 1982, life changed for an eighteen-year-old young man. He became very ill from a bacterial infection. His body could not fight the infection. Why? After a week of tests and examinations by several specialists, the diagnosis was made. He had leukemia, a cancer in the bone marrow. I am that young man. When a person finds out that he has cancer, just as I did, his whole world changes. A cancer patient is affected physically, psychologically, and socially by the impact of cancer.

This paragraph captures the reader's attention immediately. Credibility is established when the author states the exact date, February 19, 1982, and when he notes that the specific type of infection was bacterial. The audience is taken by surprise to read "I am that young man." Probably every reader would be affected by this dramatic statement and would identify with the writer. (A shift in point of view is permissible if it is used for special effect.)

Anytime someone is told about a serious, life-threatening illness, the situation is emotional. Telling this incident in a straightforward way, however, makes the information all the more moving. Readers of all ages are able to identify with the young man and will listen to his ideas. The reader knows from this introduction that the experiences and ideas in the paper are real and believable.

Now read the following example showing a personal observation of someone else's experience used as a hook.

One morning a young mother had her seven-month-old son in his stroller under the peach tree near their family swimming pool. She walked to her kitchen to get a knife so she could peel a peach for him. Ten seconds later, she found him face down with the stroller at the bottom of the pool. She immediately pulled him out and administered artificial respiration to her son. If she had been gone any longer, he might have become one of the statistics that plague our country every year when many children die needlessly in water-related accidents. These child drownings could, however, be greatly reduced if parents never left their children unattended around water, if pools were properly fenced, and if other safety devices were installed in or by the pool.

This example is also very moving because the writer saw and remembered the scene vividly. It helps the reader recognize the fear that comes with a near-tragedy and identify with the memory of an unforgettable trauma. This example brings home the reality of the dangers of a swimming pool. The incident is very appropriate to get the reader interested in ways to keep children from drowning or from becoming permanently disabled in family swimming-pool accidents.

You may think that you do not have experiences as dramatic and emotionally appealing as these, but you do. Be detailed and thorough when you think about ways to get your audience caught up in your topic, and you will discover effective experiences.

The following exercise will help you use a personal experience to create a hook for an introductory paragraph.

EXERCISE **1**

Using the thesis sentences that follow the blanks given, write a personal example that you feel would get the reader's attention. You may use either a personal experience or a personal observation.

1. _____

_____

_____

_____

Mom's Country Kitchen offers tasty food, entertainment for children, and quick service.

2. _____

_____

_____

_____

Helping a son or daughter plan a wedding can create family unity, leave pleasant memories, yet create unexpected expenses.

3. _____

_____

_____

_____

Attending college allows students to learn new information, make lifetime friends, and prepare for a career.

Using Quotations Another way to get your reader's attention is to quote an effective line or two from someone famous or even someone not so famous. Just as the personal examples were dramatic or surprising, the content of the **quotation** should also be dramatic or in some way emotionally appealing, surprising, or humorous. You might choose a humorous quotation from Ben Franklin, like "Fish and visitors smell in three days." Or perhaps you might choose a line of poetry, like "Come live with me and be my love,/and we will all the pleasures prove. . . ." Another might be a phrase like "Born in the USA." If the quotation is relevant to the thesis sentence and the connection between the quotation and the thesis sentence is established, the reader will be not only willing but eager to continue.

Look at another sample introductory paragraph. This time the student writer began with the topic "facing life." After freewriting/brainstorming, the following thesis sentence was composed: "We can control the way we face life through our attitude, determination, and ability." The student then wanted to use a quotation to get the attention of the reader and found one in a book of famous quotations. The student writer knew he wanted to stress how a person's mental outlook can bring success or failure, so he looked up "mind" in the book of quotations. He found a sentence with a "ring" to it. Notice how the student then put the introductory paragraph together, starting with the quotation.

> **"The mind is its own place, and in itself can make a heaven of hell, a hell of heaven."** This thought by John Milton was recorded over four hundred years ago, but it is still timely for us today. He seems to be saying that we are the ones to control our lives. We can be miserable when things are going well, just as we can be happy when things are going wrong. With this thought in mind, we can control the way we face life through our attitude, our determination, and our ability.

The quotation is effective because it is thought-provoking. Although it was said many years ago, it is still applicable to most people today. Also, the writer is quoting a famous man, John Milton, a great English poet. We always seem to pay attention to intelligent, profound comments made by famous people.

Sometimes a quotation used with a personal example can make both more effective. To see how this can be so, first look at the use of a personal example without a quotation as the hook in a paragraph.

> **Parents of children with learning disabilities have often felt unprepared to help their children with their handicaps and frustrated with attempts to seek the proper placement of them in the public-school system.** The experience of school can be overwhelming for any children who have trouble learning. The learning-disabled student in the public educational system must deal with academic, social, and emotional problems.

The previous paragraph uses only a personal example for the hook, but the following paragraph is stronger because it combines a quotation with a personal example.

> **"I am stupid. I am never going back to school."** These are the words spoken by a learning-disabled child when he was in the first grade. He cried as he slowly walked to his bedroom, shredding his schoolwork into small pieces. This was the first of many times when he and his parents would feel frustrated because there was nothing that they could do. Parents of children with learning disabilities have often felt unprepared to help their children with their handicaps and frustrated with attempts to seek the proper placement of them in the public-school system. The experience of school can be overwhelming for children who

have trouble learning. <u>The learning-disabled student in the public educational system must deal with academic, social, and emotional problems.</u>

This quotation will attract anyone who has had to cope with a disability of any type or anyone who has had a family member with a disability. It will also help arouse sensitivity in a person who has had no direct experience with a disability. The quotation makes the personal example even more effective.

EXERCISE 2

Using the thesis sentences given, write a direct quotation that you think would get the reader's attention. You may use either a quotation that you can remember hearing or a quotation that you looked up in a book of quotations. If you wish, you can combine it with a personal example.

1. _____

   _____

   _____

   _____

   Healthy dieting requires accurate medical information, appropriate exercise, and nutritious food.

2. _____

   _____

   _____

   _____

   A teenager's sexual behavior can be altered by movies, a fear of AIDS, and peer pressure.

3. _____

   _____

   _____

   _____

   Smoking is detrimental because it costs money, creates pollution, and results in medical problems.

Using Facts or Statistics To generate interest, you may also use a fact or a statistic as your hook. To be effective, the fact or statistic must be startling or unusual. You do, however, need to be sure that it really is a fact and that it comes from a credible source. When you are reading the newspaper or reading for your other classes, you could be alert for information that catches your attention. If you are keeping a journal, you could jot these facts down to use in future writing.

The following introductory paragraphs begin with a fact or statistic to hook the reader. The first hook contains a fact that is fairly well known to people who live in the Southwest.

> **In the desert regions of Arizona, solar homes date back to the pre-Columbian Indians. These people carefully designed their homes in the recesses of south-facing cliffs to receive the warmth of the winter sun. In the summer, shade was provided by the overhanging cliffs.** Today, as then, <u>the desert-region solar home must be carefully designed to use the sun efficiently in the orientation, the exterior, and the interior.</u>

In the previous paragraph, the hook creates curiosity because it brings out a fact that is probably not known to most people outside the Southwest. Because the student lived in the Southwest, she knew that solar homes date back to pre-Columbian times. This association between the ruins of ancient Indian homes and modern solar homes makes this introduction unique and effective.

In the next example, the student writer quotes some statistics gathered from outside reading.

> **According to an article in *Family Safety & First Aid* published by Berkley Books, ". . . every 45 seconds a fire breaks out in an American home — 700,000 residences aflame each year. And 16 times a day somebody dies in one of these burning homes."** These statistics are frightening and should not be taken lightly. The best way to deal with the possibility of loss from fire is to plan ahead before it happens. Otherwise, it is too late. In order not to become one of these statistics, <u>Americans need to equip their homes with safety devices, set and adhere to safety rules, learn safety procedures in case of a fire, and practice a family escape plan.</u>

Such statistics are shocking, and they get the reader's attention because these fires happen so often, every 45 seconds, and to so many people, 700,000 homes a year. These statistics should make the reader stop and think about how prevalent fires are and would, therefore, make the reader more willing to listen to the advice given in the thesis sentence.

In another example, the writer combines citing a personal experience with quoting some statistics:

> **According to Burt Hood, manager of health services for the Central Arizona Chapter of the American Red Cross, "In the first six months of 1989, the City of Phoenix responded to fifty-six calls of water-related accidents, and of the fifty-six, twelve were fatalities." He went on to say that of these near drownings, approximately "30 percent never really recover." Neighborhood drownings occur often. Just yesterday a seven-month-old child fell into a swimming pool, but he was pulled out a few seconds later when his mother found him.** He was lucky, but what about the many other children who die or are permanently disabled needlessly in water-related accidents? <u>The number of child</u>

drownings and near-drownings could, however, <u>be greatly reduced if parents</u> <u>never left their children unattended around water, if pools were properly fenced,</u> <u>and if safety devices were installed in or by the pool.</u>

The writer has experienced firsthand what it feels like to see a small body being given artificial respiration. In addition, the writer has taken time to check out the facts from a very creditable source, the manager of health services for the Central Arizona Chapter of the American Red Cross.

EXERCISE 3

Using the thesis sentences given, write a fact or statistic intended to get the reader's attention. You may use either something that you recently heard or something that you took time to look up in a book or periodical. If you wish, you can combine it with a personal example.

1. _____

_____

_____

_____

Women who enter politics are usually socially conscious, extraordinarily bright, and self-directed.

2. _____

_____

_____

_____

Small businesses usually succeed when the owners are adventuresome, creative, and well organized.

3. _____

_____

_____

_____

Visitors to foreign countries can experience new foods, a different language, and unique architecture.

Using Rhetorical Questions Rhetorical questions are asked for effect or for emphasis because no answer is actually expected. However, you can present the answer in the thesis statement. The purpose of these rhetorical questions is to generate thought about an idea before it is presented in the thesis sentence.

In the following introductory paragraph, the student writer effectively uses several questions to hook the reader.

> **When people think ahead to the year 3000, many different questions come to mind. What new inventions will be in use in the common household? How much will the world of transportation be advanced? What type of weaponry will have been invented? In what type of environment will people be living?** All of these questions indicate that <u>in the year 3000 there will be major differences in science, in transportation, and in people's life-styles.</u>

In the hook, the author asks rhetorical questions and provokes curiosity about possible changes made by the year 3000. These questions have inspired the reader to think about how different life might be in 1,000 years. The thesis then connects these questions with major ideas to be presented in the paper.

EXERCISE 4

Using the thesis sentences given, write one or more rhetorical questions that you think will get the reader's attention.

1. _____

   _____

   _____

   _____

   Old automobiles can be costly and dangerous.

2. _____

   _____

   _____

   _____

   Heavy flooding can drive people from their homes, destroy crops, and interrupt business activities.

3. _____

_____

_____

_____

America's war on drugs has been strengthened by education, the media, and the government.

Using Current Events   A **current event** is a recent, important incident or a series of incidents made public by newspapers, magazines, television, or radio. Everyone who reads newspapers or watches television should then be familiar with this current event. Your job is to use this occurrence to lead into the thesis sentence.

In the following introductory paragraph, the student writer effectively uses two current events to hook the reader.

> **This morning's newspaper reported a man who had shot his twenty-three-year-old girlfriend and her nine-month-old child because he believed his girlfriend had transmitted AIDS to him. In 1984, a nurse in Kokomo, Indiana, refused to go into 13-year-old Ryan White's hospital room because he had just been diagnosed with AIDS, and in 1987, a bullet shattered his home's picture window, forcing Ryan and his family to move to Cicero, Indiana, a community twenty miles south.** Though these incidents seem bizarre in 20th-century civilized America, <u>many people fear AIDS because of the consequences of the disease, the misinformation concerning the disease, and the increasing number of cases of the disease.</u>

The hook in the preceding introductory paragraph contains two different examples related to AIDS, a current topic that is prevalent in the news today. The examples startle the reader because they show how fear makes people behave illogically and violently. Because the reader becomes involved emotionally, the hook works effectively.

If you wish, you may use only one example related to a current event. But keep in mind that you might need more than one brief example to reach your audience immediately, especially if you have access to several examples that do not duplicate one another. You will need to rely on your own judgment to decide how many examples would be effective.

EXERCISE   5

Using the thesis sentences given, briefly describe a current event that you think would get the reader involved right away. If you wish, this current event can be combined with one of the other hooks explained previously.

1. _____
   _____
   _____
   _____

Irresponsible and illegal activities of athletic role models usually involve illicit drugs, illegal gambling, and socially unacceptable life-styles.

2. _____
   _____
   _____
   _____

Camcorders have brought pleasure to families, have provided hobbies for people, and have even made law-enforcement officers more accountable.

3. _____
   _____
   _____
   _____

Coming to a decision about the abortion issue includes legal, physical, and mental considerations.

Using Contrast to the Thesis Sentence   Sometimes the thesis sentence contains an idea that might be surprising to the reader or might be different from what is expected. An introduction can be effective when the hook contains information that is in direct **contrast to the main idea in the thesis sentence**.

In the following introductory paragraph, the student writer uses contrast to hook the reader.

> **Since the middle of the 1940s, the female *Cannabis sativa* plant, commonly known as marijuana, has been classified by the United States government as a Schedule I drug. This classification recognizes marijuana as a dangerous narcotic, similar in potency to heroin and possessing no redeeming medicinal qualities.** Research in the last few years, however, has brought many new discoveries in medicine relating to the possible uses of marijuana to treat many different illnesses, including glaucoma, cancer, asthma, and phantom limb pain suffered by paraplegics and amputees.

The hook in the previous paragraph reaffirms the reader's opinion because most people think of marijuana as an illegal drug that causes problems. The general public often identifies marijuana use with negative results. Because the main idea in the paper is that this drug may be *useful* in treating certain health problems, the hook directly contrasts with what the reader expects.

EXERCISE 6

Using the thesis sentences given, write a contrasting idea for a hook that you think will get the attention of the reader. If you wish, you can combine it with one of the other types of hooks.

1. _____

   _____

   _____

   _____

   Having out-of-state guests can be enjoyable because of the excitement of planning for their arrival, the opportunity for catching up on each other's lives, and the fun of breaking the normal routine.

2. _____

   _____

   _____

   _____

   Self-awareness, information about particular job skills, and knowledge of future job opportunities help people choose careers.

3. _____

   _____

   _____

   _____

   Having a family member in a hospital can be stressful, expensive, and frightening.

As you have seen in this unit, an effective introduction may contain one type of hook or may contain a combination of hooks. Use the hook that will be most appealing to your audience and most appropriate to help you meet your purpose.

Creating Transition to the Thesis Sentence

Regardless of what you use, the hook must be clearly connected to the thesis sentence in your essay. Nothing jars a reader more than a disjointed introduction—one with no connection between the hook and the thesis sentence. The hook will seem mechanical and artificial if it is not clearly related to the thesis sentence.

Transition is the clear *connection* between the hook and the thesis sentence and is the part of the introduction that you write *last*. The transition may be a word, a phrase, or a sentence or sentences between the hook and the thesis sentence that clearly shows the relationship of the hook to the broader thesis so that the reader understands the connection.

For instance, if you use a specific quotation as your hook, you will need to take the reader from that specific quotation to a more general thesis sentence. Look at the following introductory paragraph. The specific quotation is about one person, whereas the thesis statement is about a larger group of people.

> "Why try? The white kids get all the jobs!" That is what Ken used to say whenever he tried to find a job.
>
> Current research indicates that black unemployment is a result of racial discrimination, economic conditions, and the educational system.

Remember, the thesis sentence was written first and the hook second. Now a logical transition is needed to bridge the gap from the quotation, "Why try? The white kids get all the jobs!" to the broader thesis sentence about black unemployment. The sentences in bold type in the following paragraph show how one student bridged this gap.

> "Why try? The white kids get all the jobs!" That is what Ken used to say whenever he tried to find a job. **It seemed that the jobs were out there, but only the white teenagers, not the black teenagers, got those jobs. This problem could not be something that developed overnight but rather evolved over many years.** Current research indicates that black unemployment is a result of racial discrimination, economic conditions, and a failure in the educational system.

Each of the introductory paragraphs presented earlier has logical transition that shows the relationship between the thesis sentence and the hook. Note the transitions in the following introductory paragraphs to see how those transitions tie the paragraphs together. The transitions are highlighted in bold type.

Transition from Personal Example to Thesis Sentence

> On February 19, 1982, life changed for an eighteen-year-old young man. He became very ill from a bacterial infection. His body could not fight the infection.

Why? After a week of tests and examinations by several specialists, the diagnosis was made. He had leukemia, a cancer in the bone marrow. I am that young man. **When a person finds out that he has cancer, just as I did, his whole world changes.** A cancer patient is affected physically, psychologically, and socially by the impact of cancer.

In one simple sentence, this transition transfers the reader from one specific personal example of a young man who discovers he has cancer to all cancer patients.

Transition from Quotation to Thesis Sentence

"The mind is its own place, and in itself can make a heaven of hell, a hell of heaven." **This thought by John Milton was recorded over four hundred years ago, but it is still timely for us today. He seems to be saying that we are the ones to control our lives. We can be miserable when things are going well, just as we can be happy when things are going wrong.** With this thought in mind, we can control the way we face life through our attitude, our determination, and our ability.

The transition in the previous paragraph contains the author's explanation of the meaning of the quotation and its relationship to the thesis sentence. The author also bridges the gap between today and four hundred years ago. The transition between a quotation and the thesis almost always begins with a phrase like "this quotation" or "this thought" (as underlined above).

Transition from Fact to Thesis Sentence

In the desert regions of Arizona, solar homes date back to the pre-Columbian Indians. These people carefully designed their homes in the recesses of south-facing cliffs to receive the warmth of the winter sun. In the summer, shade was provided by the overhanging cliffs. **Today, as then,** the desert-region solar home must be carefully designed to use the sun efficiently in the orientation, the exterior, and the interior.

The student used "Today, as then," to draw a parallel between the construction of homes in pre-Columbian times and the construction of homes today.

Transition from Statistic to Thesis Sentence

According to an article in *Family Safety & First Aid* published by Berkley Books, ". . . every 45 seconds a fire breaks out in an American home — 700,000 residences aflame each year. And 16 times a day somebody dies in one of these burning homes." **These statistics are frightening and should not be taken lightly. The best way to deal with the possibility of loss from fire is to plan ahead before it happens. Otherwise, it is too late. In order not to become one of these statistics,** Americans need to equip their homes with safety devices, set and adhere to safety rules, learn safety procedures in case of a fire, and practice a family escape plan.

The transition in the previous paragraph interprets the meaning of the statistics and makes a suggestion about preventing this disaster. "These statistics" starts the shift that the reader must make to understand the connection between the startling numbers and the conclusion that the author is going to state in the thesis sentence—if we plan correctly, we will not become part of these statistics of disaster.

EXERCISE 7

Transparencies can be made, pp. 71-72 of Instructor's Manual.

The following introductory paragraphs lack a transition from the hook to the thesis sentence. Try to bridge the gap logically so that your reader understands the connection between the hook and the thesis sentence.

Paragraph 1

According to Richard Alfred in his article titled "Positioning Alternatives and New Partnerships," a worker entering the labor force "would have to relearn his job seven times in a forty-year career."

_____

_____

_____

To aid students who are retraining, community colleges offer assessment and advisement, financial aid, and updated curricula.

Paragraph 2

Last year I lost my driver's license. I planned to get another one the next day. However, a week later, when I got a ticket for speeding, I realized that I had not yet gotten another driver's license. Instead of just one ticket for speeding, I got two tickets, one for speeding and one for driving without a driver's license. Instead of paying $45 for one ticket, I had to pay $95 for two tickets.

_____

_____

_____

Putting responsibilities off can be expensive, inconvenient, and embarrassing.

Paragraph 3

In this morning's mail was a brown envelope with the following message written in large type: "R. E. Benson, you have won $50,000 if you subscribe to this magazine and mail in your money within 20 minutes!"

_____

_____

_____

Misleading mail advertisements play on people's emotions, have hidden loopholes, and cheat individuals out of thousands of dollars.

Paragraph 4

"Mitch Singer, a former Valley restaurant owner, has been indicted by a federal grand jury on drug charges. . . . A Mesa businessman missing for more than a week surfaced in Indio, California, . . . telling police he escaped a cocaine-snorting kidnapper. . . ."

_____

_____

_____

Cocaine use in America is still a concern, is usually crime-related, and still reaches all social levels in America.

Paragraph 5

"Mom, Dad, will you please play a game of Risk™ with us?"

_____

_____

_____

Playing board games with your family can create a challenge, encourage family unity, and bring excitement.

EXERCISE 8

In the following introductory paragraphs, underline the hook, circle the transition, and underline the thesis sentence.

Paragraph 1

Williamsburg, Virginia, offers a time-travel visit to 1775, a year before the American Revolutionary War. The city was restored in the 1930s to its 1775 appearance, so it resembles the town as it was in the 18th century. The governor's palace that housed the royal ruling power exhibits impressive 18th-century guns and swords on the walls and ceiling in organized, decorative patterns. In another historic area, near Gentryville and Dale, Indiana, the Lincoln Boyhood National Memorial contains a log cabin that is an approximation of the original log cabin where Lincoln once lived. The area also includes a living historic farm where early 19th-century life is portrayed. Such realistic depictions and information that take people back to earlier times can be obtained by visiting restored historic landmarks. Through these moving re-creations, visitors can obtain historical information and gain a feeling for bygone times.

Paragraph 2

Why are some people self-directed, confident, and personable? Why do some people have high standards and honorable values? Why are some people optimists and others pessimists? The answers to these questions are complex. Home environment, socioeconomic level, and genetic background are some of the factors that make people what they are. However, one constant in all of these influences is parents. Parents affect children's self-confidence, attitude toward others, and general outlook toward life.

Paragraph 3

"Reading is to the mind, what exercise is to the body," Sir Richard Steele wisely stated. Steele's quotation draws an analogy between the importance of exercise to tone the body and reading to stimulate the mind. If people do not exercise, they become fat, sluggish, unhealthy, and weak, and this condition is readily visible. When people do not exercise their minds, they become mentally unhealthy and weak, yet this situation is even more dangerous because it is not noticeable. This is especially true for children in their formative years when habits are developing. Reading can make the difference between a strong or weak mind. Encouraging children to read improves vocabulary, expands understanding, and increases their creativity.

EXERCISE 9

Using the topics listed below, write introductory paragraphs that include a hook, a logical transition, and a thesis sentence. You may use several types of hook in your beginning. Develop the thesis sentence first, the hook second, and the transition third.

food   self-defense
music   weight training
insects   political movements
shopping   water sports

Paragraph 1

_____

_____

_____

_____

_____

_____

_____

Paragraph 2

_____

_____

_____

_____

_____

_____

_____

Paragraph 3

_____

_____

_____

_____

_____

_____

_____

Here is one final piece of advice: For successful introductory paragraphs, **do not**

repeat the wording the instructor has used for the assignment

apologize for your paper

claim a disinterest in the topic

use an inappropriate tone

write ''In this essay, I will. . . .''

▮ The Purpose of Concluding Paragraphs

The last part of your essay is the concluding paragraph. This final paragraph gives you a chance to reemphasize the thesis you have supported throughout the paper. The conclusion should be thorough, not just cut off prematurely. At the end of the paper, the reader should *not* ask "Where is the rest of the paper?" or "What did the author mean?" Rather, the reader should say, "Now I see how nicely everything fits together and how it applies to me."

The purpose of the introduction is to get the attention of the reader; the purpose of the support paragraphs is to focus on the thesis and develop that main idea thoroughly. The purpose of the conclusion is unique. Its task is to bring all of the thesis points together in a reflective way. In your concluding paragraph, you don't have to worry about building up lots of support. For this reason, conclusions are fun to write because most of the work has been done. Your only concerns are blending together the main points, providing a feeling of closure, and reinforcing your main points. If your reader has drifted away at any time during the paper or lost his or her concentration, you can recap the main points.

▮ Recognizing Weak Conclusions

After you have finished writing the support paragraphs in your paper, it is not time to ease up. It is time to be forceful to keep the reader with you. Sometimes you might feel rushed when you get to the end of your paper and be tempted just to finish it in a hurry so you can turn it in. This is like constructing a beautiful house and then deciding that you do not have time to put on a roof because you want to move in "right now."

The following essay includes an introductory paragraph and three support paragraphs but no conclusion. Read the essay and then read the conclusions that follow. All four illustrate weaknesses to avoid.

Family Weekend Vacations

1   "More than 2.1 million children from ages 5 to 13 have no adult supervision after school, and many are alone at other times of the day and night," according to a column by Abigail Van Buren. These children come from families in which both parents work or there is only one parent, and that one parent must work full-time. Even though these children must come home alone after school each day, the parents are often home on the weekends. If everyone is willing to cooperate and get the work done during the week, these weekends can be filled with short vacations that can help family members come together whether the household is headed by two parents or one parent. These weekend vacations can provide many rewarding activities for family members, including family togetherness, knowledge, and exercise.

2   Family togetherness is strengthened when the members participate in weekend vacations. Before families go away for the weekend, they often spend time planning what they are going to be doing for the next two days. When a weekend trip includes sight-seeing, family members have time to

communicate with one another as they go from place to place. When camping, families often hike together, exploring rivers or streams as they share their thoughts with one another. When visiting relatives, families experience a broader sense of togetherness as time is shared "catching up" with cousins, grandparents, and other relatives, or finding out what mom and dad did when they were young. When it is time for dinner, everyone sits down together and discusses the comedies or tragedies of the day. Whether they have been camping, sight-seeing, or seeing relatives, they become a stronger unit.

3   While family members are sharing themselves, they often find themselves sharing knowledge that is obtained on these treasured weekend vacations. Combing the beach in the early morning as the light slowly appears, children and adults alike realize that shells that are washed onto the shore are more than treasures to be taken home. They bring food to the many sea gulls and other birds that live there. In addition, visiting Indian ruins can teach how the early inhabitants lived on the land that we now enjoy. Visiting Amish villages can help each member of the family see what America was like before it became so technologically oriented. There is no end to the educational opportunities offered by simple weekend vacations.

4   An additional benefit that cannot be overlooked is the exercise obtained during these weekend vacations. Many occasions require more physical activity than just spending time at home being a couch potato. Amusement parks like Disneyland are large and keep everyone walking from one attraction to another. Jet skiing or waterskiing seems to work every muscle of the body. Surfing in the ocean or simply swimming in the salt water provides an extensive workout. Some of the beaches like Laguna Beach are equipped with gymnastic apparatuses that let adults and children test muscles as they fly through the air. Even shopping at resorts or quaint towns or ghost towns like Jerome requires a lot of walking, if no more than simply window shopping or sight-seeing. The best part of all is that all of these activities can be shared by all members of the family.

Following, you will find several weak conclusions that add little to the effectiveness of the essay.

These weekend vacations can provide many rewarding activities for family members, including family togetherness, knowledge, and exercise.

Notice how this conclusion does not do anything for the essay. It simply repeats the thesis sentence and leaves the reader hanging.

These weekend vacations can provide many rewarding activities for family members, including family togetherness, knowledge, and exercise. First, family togetherness is strengthened. Second, family members learn a lot on these trips. And last of all, these same family members get a lot of exercise.

This conclusion shows no creativity. It simply copies the thesis sentence and mechanically repeats what has already been said in the essay. It appears artificial and redundant.

So guys, let's put our heads together and chat about ways to spend the weekends. Well, you only live once, so why not forget the dishes and floors. The dirt won't go away. Just party long and hard. The weekends will be so much fun that you may never want to come back home or back to the drudgery of work and school.

This conclusion has thrown the reader off because instead of ending on a serious note that was consistent throughout the essay, it attempts to be humorous and flippant. The point that should be stressed in the conclusion is lost. Consequently, the unity of the entire essay has been destroyed. If you are ironical throughout an essay, you might want to make the most biting statement in the conclusion. If you are humorous, end on a humorous note. For best effect, do not change to a different tone of voice in the concluding paragraph.

Time is a precious commodity, and certainly mom and dad can find other tasks to do instead of taking the family out for a weekend trip. However, these weekend trips are important for unifying the family, educating the family, and keeping the family physically active. If this is done, many problems are avoided, like juvenile delinquency and divorce. Consequently, this time is worth it.

This conclusion also throws the reader off. It does reiterate the main points of the essay; however, it then goes off on a tangent about major problems like delinquency and divorce. These issues can be mentioned in the conclusion only if they have been mentioned in the introduction and discussed in the paper. Also, this type of ending leaves the reader with the feeling that the writer is not clear about the point to be made. A strong conclusion does not suddenly introduce a new idea.

The Conclusion Should *Not*

repeat the thesis sentence exactly as it appeared in the introduction

repeat the thesis sentence and mechanically repeat the topic sentences

change the tone of the essay

introduce a new idea in the conclusion

Recognizing and Writing Strong Conclusions

Just as a weak conclusion can leave the reader confused and cheated, a strong conclusion can leave the reader informed and emotionally gratified. You have flexibility in writing a conclusion because many choices are available.

The Conclusion *Should*

summarize main points made in the paper and creatively restate the ideas in the thesis sentence

end with an obvious closure that leaves the essay with a sense of completeness

Read the following concluding paragraph, which includes both a summary and an obvious closure.

> The mind, the body, and the soul of a family unit can be invigorated simply by spending precious days together taking weekend vacations. Teenagers, small children, and adults have quality time together as they share the many opportunities offered simply by being alive and enjoying each other's company doing little things. While these family members are strengthening the bond they feel for one another, they are also gaining valuable knowledge and healthy exercise. Weekend vacations provide this for them.

This concluding paragraph shows creativity. The writer has addressed the family as if it is a living being when she identifies the family as having "The mind, the body, and the soul." Family members are identified in "Teenagers, small children, and adults." The thesis idea is repeated but is not redundant because the author has chosen different words. This conclusion links to the introduction as well as to the support paragraphs. It is not rushed and does not cut off abruptly. The writer shows sincerity and maintains a consistent tone.

Additional strategies, however, can be used to add to or enhance a conclusion.

Strong Conclusions

refer to an example, fact, or statistic mentioned in the introduction

end with a question that leaves the reader thinking about what was said

comment about the future

- **For added emphasis, recall an example, fact, or statistic mentioned in the introduction.**

> The mind, the body, and the soul of a family unit can be invigorated simply by spending precious days together taking weekend vacations. Teenagers, small children, and adults have quality time together as they share the many opportunities offered simply by being alive and enjoying each other's company doing little things. While these family members are strengthening the bond they feel for one another, they are also gaining valuable knowledge and healthy exercise. **Even though nothing can be done about the fact that so many children from ages five to thirteen are getting home from school before their parents get home, something can be done about the weekend that will leave lasting memories for these children.** Weekend vacations can provide these memories for them.

The idea in bold type adds to the effectiveness of this conclusion because it goes back to and enforces the emotional appeal that was made in the introductory paragraph. The statistic that "children from ages five to thirteen are getting home from school before their parents" is smoothly linked to the thesis sentence that "these weekend vacations can provide many rewarding activities. . . ." Without introducing any new ideas, the conclusion is uplifting and optimistic because it reassures the reader that something can be done about the future.

• **Use an appropriate question to leave the reader thinking.**

> The mind, the body, and the soul of a family unit can be invigorated simply by spending precious days together taking weekend vacations. Teenagers, small children, and adults have quality time together as they share the many opportunities offered simply by being alive and enjoying each other's company doing little things. While these family members are strengthening the bond they feel for one another, they are also gaining valuable knowledge and healthy exercise. Even though nothing can be done about the fact that so many children from ages five to thirteen are getting home from school before their parents get home, something can be done about the weekend that will leave lasting memories for these children. **What kind of memories are these parents leaving for their children?**

The preceding paragraph ends with a different kind of emotional reaction. It causes the reader to search her/his conscience. This emotional strategy might cause some parents to stop and think and, as a result, begin spending time with their children.

• **Comment about the future.**

> The mind, the body, and the soul of a family unit can be invigorated simply by spending precious days together taking weekend vacations. Teenagers, small children, and adults have quality time together as they share the many opportunities offered simply by being alive and enjoying each other's company doing little things. While these family members are strengthening the bond they feel for one another, they are also gaining valuable knowledge and healthy exercise. Even though nothing can be done about the fact that so many children from ages five to thirteen are getting home from school before their parents get home, something can be done about the weekend that will leave lasting memories for these children. What kind of memories are these parents leaving for their children? **Instead of checking out the TV schedule this weekend, maybe more families should be checking out the adventurous opportunities waiting to be taken.**

This concluding paragraph ends with a recommendation for the future. Parents are being called upon to make a change in their lives. Instead of being vague, this conclusion gives the reader a definite action to take.

EXERCISE 10

Each introduction below is followed by a weak conclusion. Revise each conclusion. Use a combination of strategies.

1. **Introduction**

According to an article in *Family Safety & First Aid* published by Berkley Books, "... every 45 seconds a fire breaks out in an American home—700,000 residences aflame each year. And 16 times a day somebody dies in one of these burning homes." These statistics are frightening and should not be taken lightly. The best way to deal with the possibility of loss from fire is to plan ahead before it happens. Otherwise, it is too late. In order not to become one of these statistics, Americans need to equip their homes with safety devices, set and adhere to safety rules, learn safety procedures in case of a fire, and practice a family escape plan.

Conclusion

Americans need to equip their homes with safety devices, set and adhere to safety rules, learn safety procedures in case of a fire, and practice a family escape plan. If these things are done, maybe we will not have as many people killed in fires.

---

2. **Introduction**

"Why try? The white kids get all the jobs!" That is what Ken used to say whenever he tried to find a job. It seemed that the jobs were out there, but only the white teenagers, not the black teenagers, got those jobs. This problem could not be something that developed overnight but rather evolved over many years. Current research indicates that black unemployment is a result of racial discrimination, economic conditions, and the educational system.

Conclusion

In conclusion, black unemployment is an obviously bad condition. The first reason is all the racial discrimination in society. Another reason is the economic conditions that blacks are subjected to. The third reason is the educational system. All these reasons together result in black unemployment.

---

3. **Introduction**

When people think ahead to the year 3000, many different questions come to mind. What new inventions will be in use in the common household? How much will the world of transportation be advanced? What type of weaponry will have been invented? In what type of environment will people be living? All of these questions indicate that in the year 3000 there will be major differences in science, in transportation, and in people's life-styles.

Conclusion

The future is important to everyone, and in some small way, all people mold the future. There will be lots of differences in sciences, in transportation, and in people's life-styles. There will be differences in clothing, too.

_____

_____

_____

_____

_____

4. **Introduction**

This morning's newspaper reported a man who had shot his twenty-three-year-old girlfriend and her nine-month-old child because he believed his girlfriend had transmitted AIDS to him. In 1984, a nurse in Kokomo, Indiana, refused to go into 13-year-old Ryan White's hospital room because he had just been diagnosed with AIDS, and in 1987, a bullet shattered his home's picture window, forcing Ryan and his family to move to Cicero, Indiana, a community twenty miles south. Although these incidents seem bizarre in 20th-century civilized America, many people fear AIDS because of the consequences of the disease, the misinformation concerning the disease, and the increasing number of cases of the disease.

Conclusion

AIDS is the tragedy of the century. It is sweeping the country and killing thousands of innocent victims. The most tragic of all are the small children who are coming into this world already affected by the AIDS virus. Hospitals need to require their health care workers, including doctors, to be screened for the HIV virus.

_____

_____

_____

_____

_____

_____

EXERCISE 11

Write an effective conclusion for each of the following introductions. Use a combination of strategies.

1. **Introduction**

   Williamsburg, Virginia, offers a time-travel visit to 1775, a year before the American Revolutionary War. The city was restored in the 1930s to its 1775 appearance, so it resembles the town as it was in the 18th century. The governor's palace that housed the royal ruling power exhibits impressive 18th-century guns and swords on the walls and ceiling in organized, decorative patterns. In another historic area near Gentryville and Dale, Indiana, the Lincoln Boyhood National Memorial contains a log cabin that is an approximation of the original cabin where Lincoln once lived. The area also includes a living historic farm where early 19th-century life is portrayed. Such realistic depictions and information that take people back to earlier times can be obtained by visiting restored historic landmarks. Through these moving re-creations, visitors can obtain historical information and gain a feeling for bygone times.

   Concluding paragraph

   _____

   _____

   _____

   _____

   _____

2. **Introduction**

   Why are some people self-directed, confident, and personable? Why do some people have high standards and honorable values? Why are some people optimists and others pessimists? The answers to these questions are complex. Home environment, socioeconomic level, and genetic background are some of the factors that make people what they are. However, one constant in all of these influences is parents. Parents affect children's self-confidence, attitude toward others, and general outlook toward life.

Concluding paragraph

_____

_____

_____

_____

_____

3. **Introduction**

"Reading is to the mind, what exercise is to the body," Sir Richard Steele wisely stated. Steele's quotation draws an analogy between the importance of exercise to tone the body and reading to stimulate the mind. If people do not exercise, they become fat, sluggish, unhealthy, and weak, and this condition is readily visible. When people do not exercise their minds, they become mentally unhealthy and weak, yet this situation is even more dangerous because it is not noticeable. This is especially true for children in their formative years when habits are developing. Reading can make the difference between a strong or weak mind. Encouraging children to read improves vocabulary, expands understanding, and increases their creativity.

Concluding paragraph

_____

_____

_____

_____

_____

Collaborative Project: Working and Learning Together

As a class, select a thesis sentence from any of the examples given in the exercises in Unit 6. Then divide into six groups. Within each group, using the same thesis sentence, select a different type of hook from the following list to compose an introductory paragraph:

1. personal example

2. quotation

3. fact or statistic

4. rhetorical question

5. current example

6. contrast to the thesis sentence

Share the introductions, and post them on a bulletin board for future reference as a reminder of the many choices you have for possible introductions to the same thesis sentence.

**SOMETHING TO THINK ABOUT,
SOMETHING TO WRITE ABOUT**

Women in Science and Engineering

Shyrl Emhoff, *retired aeronautical engineer, instructor of technical writing at Glendale Community College*

1   Throughout history, and even as we approach the 21st century, women have not been given credit for possessing any technical ability. However, records reveal that in the 19th century, and more so in the 20th century, the achievements of women particularly merit recognition equivalent to their male colleagues' in science and engineering. Moreover, during the first 100 years of recorded patents, more than 8,000 patents were issued to women. Among the awards was a patent to Margaret Knight who, although she had only a high school education, designed and made a mechanism for paper-feeding machines to fold square-bottomed paper bags. This device was just one of her many inventions that involved heavy equipment and won her the accolade of being called the "Woman Edison." There are many other role models for women in science and engineering whose names are not recognized as well as those of their male colleagues but who have been in the forefront of extending the frontiers of science and engineering during the past 100 plus years.

2   Among those women in the 1800s was Emily Roebling. When the Brooklyn Bridge was opened May 24, 1883, Emily Roebling should have been given at least some credit for the design and construction supervision of the 1,595-foot suspension bridge across the East River in New York City. A few days into the project, her husband became paralyzed, and Emily assumed full responsibility. The construction crews were fully aware of her achievement, but the public and politicians never gave her the recognition she deserved.

3   On the other hand, the name Marya Sklodovska, for most people, would not project an image of anyone of importance. Now add the title Professor at the Sorbonne, and the receipt of a Nobel prize in physics and a Nobel prize in chemistry, and you have the only woman who has won two Nobel prizes—Madame Marie Curie. Her work with her husband Pierre in the discovery of radium is well known, but lesser known, until you think about the second Nobel prize, is her discovery of the 84th element in the periodic table—polonium, which is named after her native country Poland.

4   Again, among those distinguished women in science in the early part of the 20th century was one of the atomic pioneers. Lise Meitner was the first woman to earn a Ph.D. in physics from the University of Vienna. She devoted her life to the exploration of the elements, and working with the famous German scientist, Dr. Otto Hahn, they discovered a new element—the 91st element in the periodic table, now known as protactinium. But Dr. Meitner's work, accomplished while in exile in 1938 in Sweden, deserves the most attention. Without her discovery of the loss of mass in the splitting of an atom, the United States would not have been able to complete the atomic bomb in the time frame that it did. It all began while Hitler was in power. Through her correspondence with Hahn who, because he was not Jewish, remained at the Kaiser Wilhelm Institute in Germany experimenting with uranium, she learned about his experiment of obtaining barium from uranium. This experiment prompted Lise to calculate the conversion of a particular loss of

mass into energy. The result of her reasoning and analysis was the stepping stone that provided Bohr and Fermi the key to perform the simple experiment that would show them fission. From that point, Fermi was able to continue his research and see something related to fission that proved to be more important than splitting the atom — chain reaction. This, of course, led to the atomic bomb for which Lise Meitner claimed no part, but when asked what peaceful purposes could be served, she was quick to reply "for driving submarines, aircraft, and industrial power." Her predictions have proven true.

5   And then in 1963, an educator and nuclear physicist, Maria Goeppert Mayer, who had been born in Poland but became an American citizen in 1933, was the first American woman to win the Nobel prize in physics. The concept of the atom at that time was based on her research in quantum mechanics. She developed the nuclear shell theory, which detailed the activity inside the nucleus of an atom.

6   Diverging from physics and chemistry, and looking at the field of industrial engineering in the early 1920s, one name stands out — Dr. Lillian Moller Gilbreth. She is recognized immediately when *Cheaper by the Dozen* is mentioned. As the parents of twelve children, she and husband Frank planned the operation of their household according to the efficiency procedures they recommended to their industrial clients. Five days after Frank's death in 1924, Dr. Gilbreth attended the First International Management Congress in Prague, Czechoslovakia, which they had helped organize. Not only did she read the paper he was to present, but she presided over the sessions he was assigned. Upon returning home, she assumed the presidency of their company, and Gilbreth, Inc., subsequently became highly respected in the field of time and motion study. Among her other notable achievements was the instigation of the formation of the Society of Women Engineers (SWE). In 1946, while a member of the faculty at Purdue University, and with the approval and full support of Dr. Andre A. Potter, Dean of Engineering, Dr. Gilbreth and a nucleus of thirteen women engineering students formed the engineering group known as Pi Omicron. Thus, when she returned to her home in New Jersey with this recent achievement fresh in her mind, she set into motion the formation of a national organization (later to become international) based on some of the ideas promulgated at Purdue University. There were forty-eight charter members, with Dr. Gilbreth listed as an honorary member, and four charter sections: Boston, New York, Philadelphia, and Washington, D.C.

7   Today there are more than ten thousand students and members of SWE throughout the fifty states. Although composed predominantly of women, SWE now boasts of nondiscrimination by having men among its membership; Dr. Gilbreth would certainly approve wholeheartedly. Besides all her accomplishments, perhaps the culminating recognition of her contribution to engineering and society in general is her appearance on the forty-cent stamp in the Great American Series.

8   Many, many young women today are finding exciting careers in the field of computing, but in the 1950s the situation was different. Nevertheless, in the early fifties, Grace Murray Hopper, whose career within the computer science field is legendary, developed the world's first compiler and Common Business Oriented Language (COBOL). She was the last World War II WAVE to leave active duty. Moreover, after having been recalled twice by the U.S. Navy because of her expertise in computing, she retired as a rear admiral. Her departure at the age of seventy-nine was an auspicious occasion aboard the *USS Constitution* in August 1986.

9   Although the Soviets can claim to have had the first woman in space in 1963, when Valentina Tereshkova flew a 48-orbit mission in Vostok-6, twenty years later, the youngest American astronaut to go into orbit was Dr. Sally Ride. The five other

women admitted to the U.S. space program in 1978 with Sally, who has her doctorate in astrophysics, were Anna Fisher and Rhea Seddon, both medical doctors; Kathryn Sullivan, marine geophysicist; Shannon Lucid, chemist and biochemist; and Judith Resnik, electrical engineer. Dr. Resnik became the second American woman in space in May 1984 aboard the space shuttle *Discovery*. Tragically, she was one of the crew on the *Challenger* when it exploded after it left the launch pad on January 28, 1986. However, she left a legacy behind for all women when she stated in *U.S. Woman Engineer* (April 1984) that "women who make breakthroughs in space or other horizons must pursue their endeavors to the end of full equality."

10   Because women make up more than 50 percent of today's population and little more than 10 percent of women are working scientists and engineers in the United States, the bank of talent offered by women has hardly been tapped. Probably the greatest obstacle to their underutilized talent is the ancient mental attitude of a "woman's place." This attitude was addressed beautifully by the late Dr. Gilbreth, who in 1967 set the tone for SWE's Second International Conference at Cambridge University, England, with these words:

> The world needs the contribution that women engineers and scientists are able to make, and we, in turn, need to be needed. . . . It is a universal need. People of all ages, all walks of life, and every country on earth need to be needed. Life becomes exciting and worthwhile when our skills are applied to needed tasks. . . .

Understanding Words

Briefly define the following words as they are used in the above essay.

1. patents *rights given by a government to an inventor to make, use, or sell an invention*
2. accolade *approval or praise*
3. exile *banishment*
4. fission *splitting apart*
5. nucleus *a central thing or part around which other parts or things are grouped*
6. instigation *bringing about the start of something*
7. culminating *reaching highest point or climax*
8. auspicious *favorable*

Something to Write About

Using one of the ideas or questions listed below, develop either a thesis sentence that states a clear direction or a thesis sentence that previews the points to be covered in the paper. Then draft your essay.

1. Write about someone you know who has had the courage to pursue a difficult career.
2. What makes a person outstanding?
3. What have you accomplished in the last five years?
4. What do you plan to accomplish in the next five years?
5. Describe your role model.
6. How has the role of women changed in the last twenty years?
7. How has the role of men changed in the last ten years?

8. Why is it difficult to be a woman today?

9. What are the advantages of being a woman today?

10. What can schools do to encourage young women to pursue careers in technical fields?

After you draft your essay, do each of the following:

Revise it so that it has an effective introduction that includes a hook, a transition, and a thesis sentence.

Be sure that each support paragraph has a strong topic sentence and ample supporting examples.

Check for unity and a smooth flow of ideas.

Revise to include a strong concluding paragraph.

Check for subject-verb agreement.

Check for consistent verbs.

Check for consistent point of view.

Check for fragments, run-ons, and comma splices.

Check punctuation of compound sentences.

PART 3

ESSAYS FOR DISCUSSION AND ANALYSIS

Dancer

Nancy Chandler, *student*

1   "She is the fool who ruined our recital" are the words that rang in my ears as I looked up to see the whole dressing room looking at my nakedness as Margaruite Swartz pointed her finger at me. At nine years old, I felt that I was never going to dance again in a group. But twenty years later, that's exactly what I was doing professionally. In fact, I was not only dancing but creating dances and leading a troupe. Leading, choreographing, and dancing in a troupe were rewarding for me emotionally, physically, and personally.

2   The emotional stimulation of creating, teaching, and performing dance numbers was the most uplifting experience in my life. I especially enjoyed choreographing the dance routines that our troupe performed because of the recognition I got from my fellow dancers and the management. I remember one time in particular when this was true. The manager of the club in which we performed had given me a song, a favorite of his, to create a dance number with. When I performed this number for him and the dancers so it could be critiqued, they gave me a standing ovation. They also said that if we chose this particular number in a competition we were considering entering, we would surely win. The feeling of accomplishment and respect I got from my colleagues is one of my most cherished memories.

3   The physical benefits of performing regularly in a dance troupe were an outstanding plus for my physical being. I do not think I have ever been in such top shape as when I was dancing professionally. The troupe not only performed on Friday and Saturday nights, but we also practiced Monday through Friday for about five hours. I never needed to worry about dieting in my days of dance. Even teaching aerobics, as I had in the past, did not sculpture my body in quite the manner that dancing did. Performing regularly in a troupe was definitely the most physically demanding and physically beneficial job I have ever been involved in.

4   Not only was my physical body in shape, but my personal life was also becoming more satisfying as a direct result of being involved in the troupe. The troupe itself had become more like a family to me than anything else. They were a support system for me because I was going through a hard time in my marriage. I remember an especially memorable time when one of my dancers came to my rescue on a particular evening when I was in need of a hero. I had had a bad fight with my husband, and he had thrown me out of the house into the rain. I did not know what to do, so I called Raynard, one of the dancers, and he was there in a flash. Raynard was so understanding and diplomatic when it came to getting my daughter out of the house that my husband let me back into the house and apologized. I never knew what the conversation was between the two men, but my husband was much more civil to me for quite a while afterward. There are many benefits I got as a result of being involved with the dance troupe, such as courage, self-respect, and self-assurance, but most of all it was the friendships that I cherished.

5   Dancing in a troupe was definitely my favorite job, but it did not seem like a job at all to me. Dancing was an outlet for my inner emotions and my physical expression, and a social activity for me. When I was nine years old and red-faced with embarrassment, I would have never guessed that I would end up becoming a dancer and falling so much in love with it as I did.

Understanding Words

Briefly define the following words as they are used in the above essay.

1. troupe *company or group of actors or singers or dancers*
2. choreographing *planning the dance steps and movement of the ballet*
3. critiqued *analyzed and judged*
4. ovation *enthusiastic outburst of applause or public welcome*
5. diplomatic *tactful*

Questions on Content

1. How many hours a day did the author practice dance?
2. What happened when she performed a special number?
3. What was the most physically demanding thing she had ever done?

Questions on Form

1. What makes the introduction so effective?
2. What is effective about the conclusion?

Collecting Sports Cards

Joseph Mata, *student*

1   "Oh, yes! I have just attained the rookie-of-the-year rookie card, and it is going for $200 and rising." This is what anyone would say who had just opened a dollar packet of fifteen sports cards that had in it a player card of this value. It would be a moment in a person's lifetime to share with everyone and remember forever. Many people could have a moment like this if they chose to have a hobby like sports card collecting that can offer many advantages. For instance, people may be drawn into card collecting because of pride, profit, or the enjoyment of keeping up with player statistics.

2   Sports card collecting can bring pride to collectors. Being the proud owner of some rare, vintage cards can put a smile on any collector's face. A collector is gratified when cards of rookie players, which usually sell for a moderate price, eventually become collector's items when the players excel in their professional sports. Also, collectors can be very pleased when buying complete sets that are only made in short prints; as a result, certain cards as well as the whole set can become scarce items that can bring pleasure just in owning the collection. Limited edition cards, cards that are available in a small number and may be available to the public only for a short period of time, make collecting more gratifying because everyone else will not have these cards. The longer people collect cards, the more they may feel satisfaction with their hobby.

3   From another viewpoint, people can also get involved for profit making. For instance, selling cards from home on the weekends can be profitable if the collector advertises a yard sale with a variety of merchandise including the sports memorabilia. Collectors can also make a profit by getting a dealer's license and buying in quantity directly from the warehouses at a lower cost than is available to the public. Also, a collector can make money by entering sports card shows at different stores and malls where they can sell their cards. Furthermore, people may even decide to own a shop or a small chain of card shops someday. The earnings of card collectors are only enhanced by their creativity.

4   Fascination with player statistics is probably the most common reason people become interested in card collecting. Perhaps they look up last year's statistics for a certain player who might have an outstanding upcoming year. Since baseball cards often include batting averages, home runs, runs batted in, and positions played, a card collector might compare the strengths and weaknesses among players to decide which cards will become valuable in the upcoming year. These statistics help the collector know what is going on. Also, if collectors are fascinated with certain players, they might enjoy reading the cards to find out such biographical information as where a player was born, when his birthday is, and where he lives during the off season. Some cards might even go back to the player's rookie year and give information about the different teams he played on. Being able to collect this information from season to season is what adds to the fun and interest of card collecting.

5   Whatever route people choose in getting involved in an avocation like this, whether it is for recreation or business, card collecting should always remain an enjoyable and relaxing amusement. Once they find a valuable card like the $200 rookie card for only a dollar, they are on the way to searching for more valuable cards. This hobby brings not only monetary rewards but also self-satisfaction and knowledge of the world of sports.

Understanding Words

Briefly define the following words as they are used in the above essay.

1. rookie *first-year player*
2. vintage *characterized by special value, old, one-of-a-kind*
3. avocation *hobby*

Questions on Content

1. According to the author, how can collectors make money?
2. How much did the package of fifteen sports cards cost?
3. List the examples given in paragraph 2.

Questions on Form

1. What kind of hook is used?
2. What is the transition in the introduction?
3. How does the conclusion add to the effectiveness of the essay?

A Good Manager

Marlene Reed, *student*

1   What qualities make a good manager? Should a manager be a "good buddy" or be stern and strict? Should a manager have a combination of these traits? Because the majority of the population is working-class, many may work under the authority of a manager. They certainly hope to work under managers who know their jobs and know how to work with people. Paul Eweres, a manager at Safeway, is an excellent manager because he is disciplined, intelligent, and fair.

2   There is a special, admirable quality in Mr. Eweres: his self-discipline. Mr. Eweres is one of the most disciplined people that anyone could work for. Safeway managers must work with district managers, the constant threat of losing their

jobs, and very long hours. Many managers with pressures such as these lose their cool—not Mr. Eweres. He can take all that the job dishes out, get the work done, and not once blame his problems on someone else, much less take these problems out on the employees. This is a sign of considerable maturity, and more managers should have self-discipline such as this.

3   Of equal importance, a manager needs to be intelligent. Without knowing his I.Q., one can tell that Mr. Eweres is very bright. The ease with which he solves complex problems is noteworthy. For example, when his store recently received new scanner registers, Mr. Eweres had no problems adjusting to the new system, as most managers might. Any problem that came up he knew instantly how to fix. In addition, Mr. Eweres knows how to make a schedule that works well. This has proven to be a problem for many managers because it takes considerable savvy to know when help is needed and to keep hours within the amount allotted. Managers most often do not schedule enough help at the right times, or they schedule too much help when it is not needed, yet this has never been a problem for Mr. Eweres. His schedules are accurate, and his store runs smoothly because he has the needed intelligence.

4   Above all else, Mr. Eweres is fair. He does not let his personal preferences guide his decisions, and he always tries to work with his employees. Managers sometimes use intimidation to get work done. Though the use of intimidation might get the job done, it only breeds contempt and ill feelings. When people are treated like animals, they grow to hate their jobs and begin to call in sick. Paul Eweres doesn't use intimidation because he does not have to. His employees respect him; therefore, they not only do their jobs, but they do their best. He makes employees feel important to the store, not like cogs in a machine.

5   It is the opinion of this writer that, without these three qualities—discipline, intelligence, and fairness—the manager at Safeway on 19th Avenue and Northern would be just a manager, nothing special. Yet, because he possesses these qualities he is so much more effective. No, Paul Eweres is not just a manager; he is the best manager Safeway has.

Understanding Words

Briefly define the following words as they are used in the above essay.

1. intimidation *deterring with threats or fear*
2. contempt *feeling someone has toward someone considered to be lower, scorn*

Questions on Content

1. What does Mr. Eweres manage?
2. What does Mr. Eweres do that illustrates his intelligence?
3. Why does he not have to rely on intimidation to get employees to work?

Questions on Form

1. What is the hook used in the introduction? Is it effective?
2. Comment on the force of the conclusion. Is it consistent with the rest of the essay?
3. Has the student used any specific examples to support her opinion of Mr. Eweres's character? If so, what are they?

The Right Thing to Do

Jeff Collins, *student*

1   I had to think for a long time before getting married; however, many people didn't understand the thought and preparation it took to decide I could not live with my wife anymore. How would my son handle it? Was it the right thing for my child? When my marriage broke up, the right thing to do for my son took a great deal of thought, some value arranging, and not doing necessarily what everyone else wanted me to do.

2   When my marriage broke up, the toughest decision to make was doing the right thing for my son — for example, deciding with whom, when, and where my child was going to live. This decision took a long time because sometimes I did not like this answer. A change in this decision could have left my son misunderstanding the entire situation and put him in a tailspin for the rest of his life. The last thing I wanted my child thinking was he was not loved or did not belong anywhere. He had to know where he lived was his home, and his home was where he should go if he had any problems. I had to decide who could make a better home for my son — my ex-spouse or me? Should both of us be able to visit our son? Should I move far away and keep visitation limited? I personally had to make these decisions, and they took a large toll in my life.

3   In deciding the future of my son, I needed to do some value rearranging. I needed to set goals and decide what I was going to do for the rest of my life, what I wanted for my son, and what means were needed to provide the things I wanted for my son. The hardest decision I have ever made was to decide I could not provide for my son as well as my ex-spouse could. She had a house for the two of them to live in, a good job to fall back on, and parents that lived nearby for support. These assets were the origin for the decision I had to make for my son. It took months of thought and many sleepless nights before I decided to give up my son. I was his father, but a court battle for custody was not going to be good for anyone. I gave him a home and sense of belonging I never had, a chance to be happy with life, and a strong home to build his future with.

4   The decisions I made for my son were not necessarily what everyone else wanted me to do. These decisions took away my right to be part of my family and my right to take part in my son's growing up. My mother, whom I was very close to, had disowned me. My father decided I was wrong to give up my son and did not think I was doing the right thing for him, although I think he understood the pain I was going through. My mother decided I was no longer part of the family if I could give up her first grandson. This was heartbreaking to me, and it will take years for me to understand her selfishness.

5   I missed being able to see my son and watch him learn new things, but I know down deep in my heart I did the right thing for him, and it may take a long time for everyone to understand the parts of my life I had to give up in doing so. But the boy now has the chance to grow up in a strong home with parents who love him and a chance to figure out the tough things, like which shoe to put on which foot and whether to be right handed or left. I gave him the chance I never had, a chance to grow up on his own.

Questions on Content

1. What major decision did the author have to make?
2. Why was this decision so hard for him?
3. What was one negative result for the author?

Questions on Form

1. The author is very honest and feeling in this essay. How does this add to the effectiveness of the essay?
2. In what way is the concluding paragraph effective?

The Car of Tomorrow

Terry M. Donaldson, *student*

1   With the frenzied pace of rapidly advancing technology, the possibilities of the future seem limitless. Even the vague concept of perfection may someday be a part of daily routine. With a vivid (and moderately warped) imagination, anyone can envision some wild and futuristic example of technological advancements making something perfect. One example could be a perfect car. The idea may strike terror into the hearts of automotive engineers now, but future technologies may prove that the perfect car is simply a combination of versatility, performance, and economy.

2   Versatility is an important feature of the perfect car. Why should a driveway be cluttered with two cars, a truck, and a boat when one car can do it all? Impossible, some people say, but that is nonsense! The same technology that gave the Concord SST jetliner a pivoting cockpit and retractable wings has led to the expandable car! The next time a little leaguer volunteers to give his whole baseball team a ride home from practice, it will be no problem. In just a few minutes, the new two-passenger coupe will stretch into a multipassenger bus with the flip of a switch. With the flip of another switch, the sporty little coupe converts into a motorboat for those times that a person "really would rather be skiing." New lighter materials can even make it possible for new cars to fly. Is that versatility or what? The new Vertical Take Off & Landing (V.T.O.L.) option can be an accessory with the new car. Traffic jams will be no problem. A simple flip of a switch and the driver can fly off, leaving the traffic behind. Of course, this option is NOT recommended for use in tunnels or on covered bridges. It surely is exciting to imagine so much versatility wrapped in one perfect little package! The driver must, however, be sure to watch the control panel carefully! Inadvertently flipping the wrong switch could convert the bus back into a two passenger coupe and put twenty screaming ten-year-olds into the driver's lap, and if the person happens to be out on the lake . . . Let me put it this way. How long can a person tread water?

3   Performance is another feature of the perfect car. New discoveries in nuclear fusion have made the hazardous nuclear-fission–based atomic generators and gas-guzzling performance engines of the past obsolete. The advent of this technology, electricity, has replaced gasoline as the fuel of choice for maximum performance from the family car. These new nuclear-fission–based reactors are powerful, safe, compact, and do not produce the hazardous atomic wastes now polluting the country, so an owner need not learn thermonuclear physics just to own and operate a powerful new car. The compact design and light weight of these new reactors make them very conducive to the popular aerodynamically superior sports

car styling people know and love. In common layman's terms, people DO NOT have to ride around in cars that look like giant potatoes on wheels! Every high-performance automobile should look as powerful as it is, and improving the aerodynamics of a car also improves its high-speed performance and handling. Maneuverability and speed are absolute necessities for a truly perfect car, so they are included at no extra charge. The high energy output of technology's newest generators translates into plenty of power for those last minute "banzai" runs downtown. Just how fast will it go? With the V.T.O.L. option, air speeds in excess of Mach 2 are easy. To satisfy a person's curiosity about that speed reference, Mach 2 is twice the speed of sound. A few sharp turns and dives should be a blast at that speed. That kind of performance may sound impossible now, but walking on the moon was impossible once.

4   An additional attraction of the perfect car is economy. The same feature that gives the power, styling, and versatility also make this car extremely economical to operate. Because the perfect car has so few moving parts, the only maintenance it should ever need is a routine lubrication and radiation detoxification. Expensive automobile breakdowns and repairs are things of the past. Just like the dinosaurs, auto repair bills were BIG and DUMB! The atomic power plants used in new cars are eradicating the monstrous repair bills, and they also have an exciting added feature. They will convert any organic material into a radioactive fuel supply that will last for months. Filling up is never a problem. Any plant or stray debris will give a needed refill. Once stuffed into the tank, the car is ready to go. This could be a very useful way of dealing with a neighbor's garbage that ends up in the wrong place. Operating an automobile has never been more economical than this.

5   Everyone has a version of perfection, so my idea of a perfect car may differ slightly from someone else's. A car that can grow into a bus and then sink to the bottom of the lake sounds incredibly versatile to me. Performing like a jet and economically feeding on carefully chosen plants could have a beneficial effect on the environment. Think about it. The possibilities really do seem limitless. What kind of car would you call perfect?

Understanding Words

Briefly define the following words as they are used in the above essay.

1. frenzied *wildly excited, hilarious*
2. versatility *ability to serve many functions*
3. inadvertently *unintentionally*
4. advent *coming or beginning*
5. eradicating *wiping out*

Questions on Content

1. What will the car of the future be able to do?
2. What will the car of the future *not* look like?
3. What could provide fuel for the car?

Questions on Form

1. What does the author do in the introduction to lead to the thesis sentence?
2. What is the thesis sentence?
3. How does the author conclude his essay?

Influence

Brian Barnes, *student*

1   It was the morning of August 13, 1986, when my wife said those famous two words, "It's time," so off we went to the hospital. A few hours later I became a father. Watching and participating in my child's birth was a miraculous experience. It was wonderful to think that my wife and I created this beautiful and perfect little person. It was so wonderful that we created two more. It has only been five years since our first child was born, but watching all of them grow and learn has influenced me in many ways, but my speech, my thoughts, and my whole way of life have been affected.

2   My children have influenced my speech because I find myself speaking to them in a different language called "baby talk." I am able to talk normal English in a normal voice all day, but when I come home and see my kids, something happens to me, and what normally would be my daughter's name, "Brandi Jean," comes out of my mouth as "Bani Bean," or "Doer" for "Daniel" and "Betum" for "Bethani." There are a whole string of words and sounds that I make now that I didn't make before they were born.

3   They also have influenced my thoughts. I think about three more people than I did before, and I wonder if they are OK when I am not with them. When I am away from my children, I think of them all the time. It is so great that I can be driving down the road and think of something they did or said, and it will bring a smile to my face. I also think about their future and what things I can do to make things better or easier for them.

4   Last, my children have influenced me in my way of life. When I wake up in the morning, I have three people to feed and to get dressed. I also have to clean up after them and wash their clothes, give them baths, comb their hair, change diapers, and watch them closely all day to make sure nothing happens to them. Before they came into my life, all I had to worry about was me. I love being a father, and it is a job, but it has its rewards also. When I get angry at them and start to yell at them, all they have to do is look at me with those big sad eyes and say, "I love you, Daddy," and it melts me right away. I have responsibility to be an example to my children. Because they mimic everything I do or say, I have to be careful because they always repeat the bad stuff at the wrong time. I always want to better myself for them, and I want them to grow up to be better than I am.

5   I am very thankful for the children I have, for the conversations we have had that have influenced my speech, for the thoughts about them that enter my mind and bring a smile to my face, and for the ways they have influenced my way of life to make it more fulfilling and exciting. They have influenced me for the better.

■ Questions on Content

1. How do the children influence his thinking when he is away from them?
2. In paragraph 4, what responsibility does he feel for his children?
3. What is the major change in his life because of his children?

Questions on Form

1. What hook does the author use?
2. What is the transition between the hook and the thesis?
3. How effective is the conclusion?

Why Don't We Complain?

Originally published in *Esquire* by **William F. Buckley, Jr.**,
editor of *National Review*

1   It was the very last coach and the only empty seat on the entire train, so there was no turning back. The problem was to breathe. Outside, the temperature was below freezing. Inside the railroad car the temperature must have been about 85 degrees. I took off my overcoat, and a few minutes later my jacket, and noticed that the car was flecked with the white shirts of the passengers. I soon found my hand moving to loosen my tie. From one end of the car to the other, as we rattled through Westchester County, we sweated; but we did not moan.

2   I watched the train conductor appear at the head of the car. "Tickets, all tickets, please!" In a more virile age, I thought, the passengers would seize the conductor and strap him down on a seat over the radiator to share the fate of his patrons. He shuffled down the aisle, picking up tickets, punching commutation cards. *No one addressed a word to him.* He approached my seat, and I drew a deep breath of resolution. "Conductor," I began with a considerable edge to my voice. . . . Instantly the doleful eyes of my seatmate turned tiredly from his newspaper to fix me with a resentful stare: what question could be so important as to justify my sibilant intrusion into his stupor? I was shaken by those eyes. I am incapable of making a discreet fuss, so I mumbled a question about what time we were due in Stamford (I didn't even ask whether it would be before or after dehydration could be expected to set in), got my reply, and went back to my newspaper and to wiping my brow.

3   The conductor had nonchalantly walked down the gauntlet of eighty sweating American freemen, and not one of them had asked him to explain why the passengers in that car had been consigned to suffer. There is nothing to be done when the temperature *outdoors* is 85 degrees, and indoors the air conditioner has broken down; obviously when that happens there is nothing to do, except perhaps curse the day that one was born. But when the temperature outdoors is below freezing, it takes a positive act of will on somebody's part to set the temperature *indoors* at 85. Somewhere a valve was turned too far, a furnace overstocked, a thermostat maladjusted: something that could easily be remedied by turning off the heat and allowing the great outdoors to come indoors. All this is so obvious. What is not obvious is what has happened to the American people. . . .

4   As I write this, on an airplane, I have run out of paper and need to reach into my briefcase under my legs for more. I cannot do this until my empty lunch tray is removed from my lap. I arrested the stewardess as she passed empty-handed down the aisle on the way to the kitchen to fetch the lunch trays for the passengers up forward who haven't been served yet. "Would you please take my tray?" "Just a *moment*, sir!" she said, and marched on sternly. Shall I tell her that since she is headed for the kitchen *anyway*, it could not delay the feeding of the other passengers by more than two seconds necessary to stash away my empty tray? Or remind her that not fifteen minutes ago she spoke unctuously into the loudspeaker the words undoubtedly devised by the airline's highly paid public relations counselor: "If there is anything I or Miss French can do for you to make your trip more enjoyable, *please* let us —" I have run out of paper.

5   I think the observable reluctance of the majority of Americans to assert themselves in minor matters is related to our increased sense of helplessness in an age of technology and centralized political and economic power. For generations, Americans who were too hot, or too cold, got up and did something about it. Now we call the plumber, or the electrician, or the furnace man. The habit of looking after our own needs obviously had something to do with the assertiveness that characterized the American family familiar to readers of American literature. With the technification of life goes our direct responsibility for our material environment, and we are conditioned to adopt a position of helplessness not only as regards the broken air conditioner, but as regards the overheated train. It takes an expert to fix the former, but not the latter; yet these distinctions, as we withdraw into helplessness, tend to fade away.

6   Our notorious political apathy is a related phenomenon. Every year, whether the Republican or the Democratic Party is in office, more and more power drains away from the individual to feed vast reservoirs in far-off places; and we have less and less say about the shape of events which shape our future. From this alienation of personal power comes the sense of resignation with which we accept the political dispensations of a powerful government whose hold upon us continues to increase.

7   An editor of a national weekly news magazine told me a few years ago that as few as a dozen letters of protest against an editorial stance of his magazine was enough to convene a plenipotentiary meeting of the board of editors to review policy. "So few people complain, or make their voices heard," he explained to me, "that we assume a dozen letters represent the inarticulated views of thousands of readers." In the past ten years, he said, the volume of mail has noticeably decreased, even though the circulation of his magazine has risen.

8   When our voices are finally mute, when we have finally suppressed the natural instinct to complain, whether the vexation is trivial or grave, we shall have become automatons, incapable of feeling. When Premier Khrushchev first came to this country late in 1959 he was primed, we are informed, to experience the bitter resentment of the American people against his tyranny, against his persecutions, against the movement which is responsible for the great number of American deaths in Korea, for billions in taxes every year, and for life everlasting on the brink of disaster; but Khrushchev was pleasantly surprised, and reported back to the Russian people that he had been met with overwhelming cordiality (read: apathy), except, to be sure, for "a few fascists who followed me around with their wretched posters, and should be horsewhipped."

9   I may be crazy, but I say there would have been lots more posters in a society where train temperatures in the dead of winter are not allowed to climb to 85 degrees without complaint.

▮ Understanding Words

Briefly define the following words as they are used in the above essay.

1. virile *masculine*
2. sibilant *hissing*
3. stupor *a partial or complete loss of the senses*
4. discreet *reserved or modest*

5. gauntlet *challenge*
6. consigned *turned over to the control or power of someone else*
7. phenomenon *observable fact or event*
8. vexation *disturbance or annoyance, especially in little things*
9. automatons *things that can move or act themselves*
10. apathy *lack of feeling, indifference, lack of interest*

▪ Questions on Content

1. Although the temperature outside was below freezing, what was the temperature inside the train?
2. What were the author and many of the train passengers trying to do?
3. Where was the author when he was drafting this essay?
4. What does the author feel is the cause for Americans' reluctance to speak up?
5. What is a "related phenomenon"?

Questions on Form

1. What kind of hook does the author use?
2. What method of development does the author use to clarify his main idea?
3. Why is the conclusion effective?

THE WRITER'S TOOLS: SENTENCE VARIETY—USING COMPLEX SENTENCES

OBJECTIVES

- Combine simple sentences using subordinators.
- Get additional practice revising sentences.

Sometimes writing can become less interesting to the reader if the sentences are all too much alike. A series of short, simple sentences will seem monotonous to the reader. Even too many sentences joined with ''and'' or ''but'' will seem monotonous.

The following draft paragraph contains only simple sentences.

> All the players in the basketball game played very hard. They ran up and down the court. They frequently jumped and moved around quickly. They dodged back and forth. The guards dribbled the ball all around the court. They also passed the ball hard to other members of their team. Sometimes the players even knocked opposing team members to the floor. They twisted, turned, and bumped into each other. Occasionally, they ran into the referees. All the activity caused the players to exert lots of energy throughout the game.

As you learned earlier, one way to make writing more interesting is to combine simple sentences into compound sentences.

> They ran up and down the court, **and** they frequently jumped and moved around quickly.

Too many compound sentences can also sound monotonous, though, and somewhat elementary. When you revise a draft, you may want to use other kinds of connecting words to combine ideas in a paragraph. For instance, if one sentence gives a reason for something, a word like ''because'' can be used to make one stronger sentence out of two shorter related sentences.

> Sometimes the players even knocked opposing team members to the floor **because** they twisted, turned, and bumped into each other.

This kind of sentence is called a **complex sentence**. The simple sentence ''They twisted, turned, and bumped into each other'' has now become an idea that is *dependent* upon the idea in the first part of the sentence. So that you can understand more clearly how complex sentences are used, a simple discussion follows.

Test covering complex sentences pp. 39-41 in Instructor's Manual.

Independent and Dependent Clauses

A complex sentence contains two kinds of clauses: one independent clause and one or more dependent clauses.

A **clause** is a group of words with a subject and a complete verb. An **independent clause** can stand by itself and be a sentence because it contains a complete idea. A **dependent clause** cannot stand by itself and cannot be a sentence. Combining two independent clauses with "because" makes one of them dependent on, or *subordinate to*, the other. The word "because" is called a subordinator. Thus, the new sentence formed has become a complex sentence. It now has two clauses — one independent and one dependent. The "because" idea now has become a dependent clause subordinate to the other idea in the sentence. The idea in a subordinate clause receives *less emphasis* than the idea in the independent clause. Consider the same complex sentence again:

> Sometimes the players even knocked opposing team members to the floor **because** they twisted, turned, and bumped into each other.

Now, "because they twisted, turned, and bumped into each other" can no longer stand by itself as a sentence. The word "because" makes this part a dependent clause, and it also clearly shows why players are sometimes knocked down in a basketball game.

Many common words are used to combine ideas into more mature sentences. Most of these connecting words you probably already know and use. These words are called **subordinators**. Here is a list of subordinators (you may already have studied them in Unit 4, Part 4 concerning fragments).

Subordinators

after	in order that	whether
although	since	which
as	so that	whichever
as if	that	who
as long as	though	whoever
as soon as	till	whom
as though	unless	whomever
because	until	whose
before	what	whosoever
even though	whatever	why
how	when	
if	where	

Using Subordinators to Form Complex Sentences

Even more important, however, is knowing how to use the subordinators to combine simple sentences into stronger, more mature ideas. These stronger, revised sentences clearly show how ideas relate to each other. Consider the following list of uses of subordinators.

after

> I will finish this chapter.
>
> I will treat myself to some fudge cake.
>
> *After* **I finish this chapter,** I will treat myself to some fudge cake.*
>
> I will treat myself to some fudge cake *after* **I finish this chapter.**

Note   When the dependent clause is an introductory expression in the sentence, put a comma after it.

as soon as

> John is coming.
>
> I am leaving.
>
> *As soon as* **John comes,** I am leaving.*
>
> I am leaving *as soon as* **John comes.**

before

> Rick needs to study.
>
> He needs to take his test.
>
> Rick needs to study *before* **he takes his test.***
>
> *Before* **he takes his test,** Rick needs to study.

when

> The river dries out.
>
> The fish will die.
>
> *When* **the river dries out,** the fish will die.
>
> The fish will die *when* **the river dries out.**

while

> The bride walked with her father.
>
> The groom waited.
>
> *While* **the bride walked with her father,** the groom waited.
>
> The groom waited *while* **the bride walked with her father.**

where

> The students stood there.
>
> There was shade.
>
> The students stood *where* **there was shade.**
>
> The students stood *where* **the shade was.***

*You might need to make changes in wording when you build complex sentences.

as

> She took the medicine.
>
> The doctor had prescribed it.
>
> She took the medicine *as the doctor had prescribed it.**

if

> We will not have the picnic.
>
> It might rain on Saturday.
>
> We will not have the picnic *if* it rains on Saturday.
>
> *If* it rains on Saturday, we will not have the picnic.

although

> The coach had a winning season.
>
> He cut six players.
>
> *Although* the coach had a winning season, he cut six players.
>
> The coach cut six players *although* he had a winning season.

because

> We needed the extra money.
>
> Mom decided to get a job.
>
> Mom decided to get a job *because* we needed the extra money.
>
> *Because* we needed the extra money, Mom decided to get a job.

so that

> Mary raked the leaves.
>
> Clay could burn them.
>
> Mary raked the leaves *so that* Clay could burn them.
>
> *So that* Clay could burn the leaves, Mary raked them.

as long as

> The girls were content.
>
> They had games to play.
>
> The girls were content *as long as* they had games to play.
>
> *As long as* the girls had games to play, they were content.

as well as

> Mary Duncan did not run well.
>
> She could have run better.
>
> Mary Duncan did not run *as well as* she could have.*

*Sometimes it does not sound natural to put the dependent clause first.

EXERCISE 1

Using words from the list, choose a subordinator that will logically connect each pair of the following simple sentences. Then combine each pair of sentences into a complex sentence. More than one subordinator may fit, depending upon the meaning you want to express. Also, you may need to make some changes in wording. Reminder: When the dependent clause is an introductory expression in the sentence, put a comma after it.

Example:

The game was over.

The players went into the locker room to change clothes.

The players went into the locker room to change clothes after the game was over.

After the game was over, the players went into the locker room to change clothes.

1. The manager resigned his position.
    It created too much stress in his life.

    The manager resigned his position because it created too much stress in his life.

2. The pitcher threw a wild pitch.
    The manager took him out of the game.

    After the pitcher threw a wild pitch, the manager took him out of the game.

3. The students went to the library to do some research.
    Their classes were over for the day.

    The students went to the library to do some research as soon as their classes were over for the day.

    As soon as their classes were over for the day, the students went to the library to do some research.

4. Maria will be going to Australia.
    She wants to learn about its varied culture.

    Maria will be going to Australia because she wants to learn about its varied culture.

5.   You will not have difficulty making a good grade on the test.
     You can study very hard and work with a tutor.

You will not have difficulty making a good grade on the test if you study very hard and work with a tutor.

6.   The cocker spaniel ran home.
     His owner whistled loudly.

The cocker spaniel ran home when his owner whistled loudly.

Words like "who," "whose," "whom," "which," and "that" are also subordinators and can be used to combine simple sentences into more mature sentence patterns. These more mature sentences are also complex sentences because they have an independent clause and one or more dependent clauses. These connecting words are probably familiar to you.

Cindy saw the herd at the gate.

The gate had been left open.

Cindy saw the herd at the gate *that* **had been left open.**

Jason admires Mr. Winters.

Mr. Winters requires his teams to train hard for their games.

Jason admires Mr. Winters, *who* **requires his teams to train hard for their games.**

The sentences may not always fit end to end. To combine them logically, you may have to put one idea inside the other and make changes in wording. More than one revision may be possible, depending upon the idea you want to emphasize. The important point to remember is that you are revising to make stronger sentences.

The car was stolen from the driveway.

The car belonged to my mother.

The car *that* **belonged to my mother** was stolen from the driveway.

Joseph was the best qualified candidate.

The company hired him after one interview.

Joseph, *who* **was the best qualified candidate**, was hired after one interview.

Note   The commas are required because the "who" clause does not identify Joseph. If the man's name had not been given, no commas would be used, as in this sentence: The man who was the best qualified candidate was hired after one interview.

Joseph, *who was hired after one interview*, was the best qualified candidate.

Joseph, *whom the company hired after one interview*, was the best candidate.

Note   This is a more formal sentence. To learn how to use "whom" appropriately, see the special section later in this unit called "Choosing Who or Whom."

EXERCISE   2

Practice combining simple sentences using "who," "whose," "which," or "that." You may have to make some changes in wording to construct the sentences smoothly and logically.

Example:

The novel was *Moby Dick*.

We all liked that book the best.

The novel that we all liked the best was Moby Dick.

Moby Dick was the novel that we all liked the best.

1.   George Washington was the first president of the United States.
     He was the only president voted in unanimously.

   George Washington, who was the first president of the United States, was the only president voted in unanimously.

2.   The television program will be on tonight.
     It got the highest award.

   The television program which got the highest award will be on tonight.

3.   The book was my favorite novel.
     My brother borrowed it yesterday.

   The book that my brother borrowed yesterday was my favorite novel.

4. Kana learned to cook chocolate cake.
    His dad liked this cake the best.

    Kana learned to cook the chocolate cake that his dad loved best.

5. The tools for the job were listed in the memo.
    The supervisor sent the memo yesterday.

    The tools for the job were listed in the memo that the supervisor sent yesterday.

6. The children are afraid to stay alone in their house.
    The children's parents work.

    The children whose parents work are afraid to stay alone in their house.

Putting the Dependent Clause First

Once in a while for variety, you may even want to use a sentence in which the dependent clause comes first and actually functions as the subject of the sentence. Try varying your sentence patterns by using this kind of sentence. The words that begin these dependent clauses are also in the previously used list of subordinators. Each new, revised sentence will be stronger than the original sentences. Here are some examples showing possible revisions:

You are going on vacation.

Where, depends on you.

Where you go on vacation depends on you.

People watch that program.

It is a mystery to me.

Why people watch that program is a mystery to me.

The committee will vote on the proposal.

It must be reported to the public.

How the committee votes on the proposal must be reported to the public.

EXERCISE 3

Use "who," "why," "how," or "that" to combine each pair of simple sentences into a stronger, complex sentence. To make your revised sentences clear and logical, make any changes in wording you think are necessary. Put the dependent clause at the beginning of the sentence, and eliminate vague words at the same time.

Example:

I want to buy a motorcycle.
It does not thrill my mom.

Why I want to buy a motorcycle does not thrill my mom.

That I want to buy a motorcycle does not thrill my mom.

1. I earn my own money.
   It is my business.

   How I earn my own money is my business.

2. That decision still bothers me.
   We made the decision to buy the car.

   That we made the decision to buy the car still bothers me.

3. That house is deteriorating.
   It is beyond me.

   Why that house is deteriorating is beyond me.

4. It is the wrong way to start a business.
   They did not plan.

   That they did not plan is the wrong way to start a business.

5. It is up to the voters.
    Someone will be elected.

    Who will be elected is up to the voters.

6. The little girl likes to wear her mom's high heels.
    It is amusing to her parents.

    That the little girl likes to wear her mom's high heels is amusing to her parents.

Putting the Dependent Clause Last

When revising a paragraph or an essay, you may want to eliminate short, ineffective sentences in other ways. Try putting the dependent clause at the end of the sentence and eliminate vague words at the same time.

The director's employees can solve the problem.

He has learned this.

The director has learned *how* **his employees can solve the problem.**

We know the answer.

At least, we could find it at the library.

We know *that* **we could find the answer at the library.**

EXERCISE 4

Use "who," "why," "how," or "that" to combine each pair of simple sentences into a stronger, complex sentence. Again, to make your revised sentences clear and logical, make any changes in wording you think are necessary. Put the dependent clause at the end of the revised sentence, and eliminate vague words at the same time.

Example:

The attorney recalled the information.

Her client told her the facts.

The attorney recalled what her client told her.

The attorney recalled the information that her client told her.

1. They understood.
   I could not go the wedding.

   They understood why I could not go to the wedding.

2. The archeologists discovered the answer.
   Something was missing from the ancient ruins.

   The archeologists discovered that something was missing from the ancient ruins.

3. We know the difficulties.
   They can be overcome by hard work.

   We know that the difficulties can be overcome by hard work.

4. We know the possibilities.
   We can finish the task today.

   We know that we can finish the task today.

5. The books were shelved in the wrong place.
   The librarian realized the situation.

   The librarian realized that the books were shelved in the wrong place.

6. We know the outcome.
   The issue was decided.

   We know how the issue was decided.

Choosing *Who* or *Whom*

Occasionally you may have difficulty knowing whether to use "who" or "whom" in your writing. If the subordinator is used as the subject of your dependent clause and it refers to a person, you should select the subject pronoun "who."

> Bob will marry Marsha next June.
>
> Marsha is an airline pilot.
>
> Next June, Bob will marry Marsha, *who* **is an airline pilot.**

In the previous sentence, "who" refers to a person and acts as the subordinator and the subject of the dependent clause. However, if the dependent clause already has a subject, then the subordinator has to be "whom."

> Bob will marry an airline pilot.
>
> He met the airline pilot in Peru.
>
> Bob will marry an airline pilot *whom* **he met in Peru.**

An easier way that might help you choose between "who" or "whom" is a simple substitution.

- **If you can substitute "he" or "she" into the sentence, use "who."**

- **If you substitute "her" or "him" into the sentence, use "whom."**

  Who (he) is coming for lunch?

  Josh, **who** (he) is my good friend, will be here soon.

In these examples, you would not use "whom" because neither "him is coming" nor "him is my good friend" is correct.

> Josh is the person **whom** (him) we selected for the job.

Note At times you may have to rearrange the dependent clause to see how the substitution works. Thus, in the previous example, "whom we selected for the job" becomes "we selected whom for the job"; using "whom" is correct because you would say "we selected *him*," not "we selected he."

You can remember whether to use "who" or "whom" more easily if you remember that the two words that end in "m" substitute for each other:

her/him ⟷ whom

she/he ⟷ who

EXERCISE 5

Note: Review of sentence combining can be put on transparency, p. 74. Transparency can be made, p. 72.

Revise the following draft paragraphs by combining simple sentences into complex sentences. Try to use a variety of complex sentences.

Paragraph 1

Basketball requires a variety of physical skills. ~~Stamina~~ *Because stamina* is a stringent requirement for this highly active sport~~,~~ *, many* ~~Many~~ times the victory goes to the team with the greatest physical endurance. Agility is another important factor for basketball players~~,~~ ~~They~~ *because they* must be able to move smoothly and quickly~~,~~ ~~They~~ *so that they* can coordinate their moves. Scottie Pippen's finesse on the court is a great example of winning, aerobic-like moves. Sheer aggression defines the dribbling path of his drives to the basket. ~~Players~~ *If players* have peripheral vision~~,~~ *, they* ~~They~~ can pass without looking at the players receiving the ball. ~~Jumping~~ *Because jumping* ability is important~~,~~ *, great* ~~Great~~ basketball players can slam dunk and get many rebounds. These physical skills can lead to a winning team.

Paragraph 2

Bodybuilding is a sport that demands discipline. Bodybuilders *who* push themselves until their muscles won't work anymore~~,~~ ~~They~~ build muscle mass. Serious athletes must work out at the gym five to seven hours a day~~,~~ *until they* ~~They~~ feel a burning sensation in their muscles. *If the* ~~The~~ muscles are sore the next morning~~,~~ *they* ~~They~~ know they had a good workout. Athletes must also have the willpower to adhere to a strict diet~~,~~ *in which they* ~~They~~ eat no fatty foods, especially hamburgers and french fries. ~~They~~ *When they* need to cut fat~~,~~ *, they* ~~They~~ must stay on an even stricter diet than normal. They also must get plenty of sleep. ~~They~~ *When they* are at a party with their friends and everyone else wants to stay late~~,~~ *, dedicated* ~~Dedicated~~ athletes will have enough control to go home early. This dedication, however, will result in a body they can take pride in.

Paragraph 3

Although there are many educational toys in the store today, I didn't have an opportunity to

learn from them as a child. However, I did learn from simple items. ~~They~~ *that* were free for the taking. ~~I had~~ *After*

I had mastered the fine art of making bows and arrows~~,~~ *, I* ~~I~~ learned the types of tree branches that made

strong yet flexible bows. Then I learned by trial and error~~, I learned~~ how tight the string should be to

make the arrow "sing." *When I* ~~I~~ needed a fishing pole~~,~~ *, I* ~~I~~ learned which pieces of wood would stay strong

against the pull of a hungry fish. I learned to braid bracelets from long strands of grass. I learned to

take a simple piece of wood and carve it into a gun. Most educational of all, I learned to paint pictures~~,~~

that were made from natural dyes.

~~I made natural dye from various items.~~ For example, I crushed blackberries to get a deep purple and

used natural coal for black. These "toys" gave me amusement, but, more important, they gave me

knowledge~~,~~ *that I* ~~I~~ still possess ~~this knowledge~~ today.

Paragraph 4

Cheerleading helps people build confidence needed to become outgoing. *Though many* ~~Many~~ people try out

for a cheer position~~,~~ *, very* ~~Very~~ few make the line. ~~Some~~ *Those who* succeed~~, They~~ then feel proud of themselves~~, They~~ *because they*

have accomplished something~~,~~ *that not* ~~Not~~ everyone can do ~~this.~~ *this. Since cheerleaders* ~~Cheerleaders~~ are in front of a lot of people

at one time~~, They~~ *, they* build confidence about themselves by performing well. ~~They gain this confidence~~ *This confidence that they*

gain by performing in front of small groups~~,~~ *This confidence* helps them when they go to state meets and

have to lead cheers in front of thousands of people. Self-esteem grows~~, Other~~ *when other* students come up to talk

to them or tell them that they did a nice job. This confidence helps them shake a bad mood and

become more outgoing and positive around other people.

WRITING ASSIGNMENT

Using the steps of the writing process that you are familiar with, draft an essay on one of the following topics:

1. The most surprising, pleasant experience that has happened to you
2. The most surprising, negative experience that has happened to you

Explain at least three results that occurred because of this experience. Include an introductory paragraph that creates interest (hook) by briefly setting up the experience you remember. End the introductory paragraph with a thesis sentence that focuses on the results of the experience.

After you draft your essay, revise for content and edit for mechanics.

Content

Essay

Check the introductory paragraph for an effective hook.

Check for a smooth transition between hook and thesis.

Check to see that the thesis sentence states a clear direction and, if you wish, previews the points covered in the paper.

Check to see that the voice is appropriate for purpose and audience.

Paragraphs

Revise so that each has a clear topic sentence that develops an idea suggested in the thesis sentence.

Include four to six supporting sentences that are developed using short interrelated examples or an extended example.

Include a closing sentence in each paragraph.

Mechanics

Check for subject-verb agreement.

Check for consistent verbs.

Check for a consistent point of view.

Check for fragments, run-on sentences, and comma splices.

Check punctuation of compound sentences.

Check punctuation of complex sentences.

Sentence variety

Revise short sentences into compound sentences.

Revise sentences to include complex sentences.

UNIT 7

Making Ideas Flow Clearly

PART 1

PARTS TO WHOLE: COHERENCE

OBJECTIVES

- Realize the importance of transition.
- Realize that repeated key words add coherence.
- Realize that time words and other transitional words add coherence.
- Realize that pronouns can add coherence.
- Revise a given paragraph using appropriate transitional words and phrases.
- Recognize how the divisions in the thesis sentence provide the key words for transition in the topic sentences.
- Given a thesis sentence, write topic sentences containing appropriate key words.
- Add coherence within and among paragraphs in an essay.

Clear and interesting writing has logical connections between sentences and between paragraphs, and these clear connections make the writing flow smoothly. Sometimes the relationship is so obvious to you that you do not think that it is necessary to make the connection obvious for the reader; however, it is necessary. Writing that flows smoothly contains specific words that make the connections between ideas so the reader does not have to fill in the gaps. These connections help to clarify meaning.

Creating Coherence Within Paragraphs

The following paragraph does not have clear connections between the sentences and is choppy.

> When I was growing up, I had many responsibilities around my house after school and on Saturdays. I took care of my cats. I picked up the fallen sour oranges from the front yard. Trimming the juniper bushes in the back was my job. Cleaning my room was something I did once a week. Working around the house is one of my clearest memories of growing up.

Each sentence is *isolated* from the next. The sentences might just as well be in a list:

1. When I was growing up, I had many responsibilities around my house after school and on Saturdays.
2. I took care of my cats.
3. I picked up the fallen sour oranges from the front yard.
4. Trimming the juniper bushes in the back was my job.
5. Cleaning my room was something I did once a week.
6. Working around the house is one of my clearest memories of growing up.

What idea ties all of these sentences together? Sentences 2, 3, 4, and 5 are all "responsibilities around my house" referred to in the topic sentence, but the sentences have no obvious connections to each other. If the connections were clearer, the information would be more meaningful to the reader.

Clear connecting words can make these sentences flow more smoothly. A revised paragraph might read as follows:

> When I was growing up, I had several responsibilities around the house. I took care of my cats every day. After school each day in the spring, I had to pick up the fallen sour oranges from the front yard. I usually had to do this chore first because my mom wanted the front yard clean. In addition to these jobs, I spent most Saturday mornings trimming the juniper bushes in the back. After finishing the trimming (or any other work I had to do), I would then clean my room. Working around the house is one of my clearest memories of growing up.

Specific words and phrases have been added to the first draft to make clear *when* the activities occurred in relation to each other, to establish a coherent sequence of events.

These additional words and phrases are called **transitions**. When you write, select the ones that make clear, logical connections between sentences.

There are several kinds of words and phrases that can be used to create **coherence** in a paragraph:

1. **repeated key words** that refer to the *topic* idea in the paragraph: "responsibilities," "this chore," "these jobs," "the trimming."

2. special **time words** and other **transitional words** or phrases that add definite meaning to link sentences logically into a coherent whole: "every day," "after school each day in the spring," "in addition," "then."

3. **pronouns**, including possessive pronouns ("my" mom) and **words that point out** ("this" and "that"). Avoid "it," "they," and "this" whenever they do not refer to specific nouns in the paragraph.

The following paragraph lacks coherence.

> **Learning how to drive a car with a stick shift is difficult.** The location of each gear and the best speed to drive in for each gear must be learned. How to push in the clutch and change the gear to obtain the best speed can be tricky until the driver discovers just where the clutch accelerates the gear speed. Bouncing and jerking can occur until this maneuver is mastered. This "sweet spot" is different in all cars. Down-shifting has to be learned to allow for turns and slowing. The clutch and gear speed work together again, but the gear is shifted to slow down, not to speed up. When shifting and down-shifting are learned, usually driving is easy.

Now consider the following steps for creating coherence within paragraphs.

Repeating Key Words

Repeating **key words** that refer to the topic idea and direction is the easiest way to create coherence in a paragraph. You may want to list words that come to you or refer to a dictionary or thesaurus for variations of the key words. You do not want to look for more complicated words but simply for other common words that will repeat the topic idea without repeating the same word over and over.

The key words in the topic sentence are "learning how to shift a car" and "difficult." Here are other words that could replace "learning how to shift a car":

    shifting

    changing speeds

    changing gears

    slowing down

    procedure

Other words could replace "difficult":

    hard

    frustrating

    demanding

    complicated

    tiring

    bothersome

Look at the paragraph after it was revised by adding new key words:

Learning how to drive a car with a stick shift is difficult. The location of each

gear and the best speed to drive in for each gear must be learned. How to push

tricky and frustrating until

in the clutch and change the gear to obtain the best speed can be ~~tricky until~~ the

driver discovers just where the clutch accelerates the gear speed. Bouncing and

this complicated maneuver   *To make matters more*

    challenging, this

jerking can occur until ~~this maneuver~~ is mastered. ~~This~~ "sweet spot" is different

Though down-shifting is bothersome, it

in all cars. ~~Down-shifting~~ has to be learned to allow for turns and slowing. The

the procedure is harder because the

clutch and gear speed work together again, but ~~the~~ gear is shifted to slow down, not

to speed up. When shifting and down-shifting are learned, usually driving is easy.

Using Time Words and Transitional Words

Special **time words and other transitional words** or phrases add definite meaning to link sentences logically into a coherent whole. Here are some examples of time words and other transitional words that add coherence to the paragraph:

To add something:	also, too, in addition, equally important, furthermore, similarly, again, besides
To show a contrast:	but, yet, however, in contrast to, on the other hand, nevertheless
To give an example:	for example, for instance, thus, in particular, in other words
To compare or show similarity:	similarly, in the same way
To show time sequence:	then, next, first, second, later, finally, previously, afterward, after, yesterday, today, the day (or week or year) before, as, now
To emphasize:	in fact, indeed, to repeat
To show space relationship:	above, beyond, below, near, next to, here, there, to the left, to the right, behind, in front of
To acknowledge a point that may be the opposite of the one you are making:	although, though, even though, in spite of, no doubt, of course
To summarize:	finally, in conclusion, in summary, consequently, thus, therefore, as a result, on the whole, to conclude

Here is the paragraph after revision using time and transitional words:

Learning how to drive a car with a stick shift is difficult. The location of each

before changing   *learned first.*

gear and the speed to drive in ~~for~~ each gear must be ~~learned.~~ How to push in the

clutch and change the gear to obtain the best speed can be tricky and frustrating

until after the   *Furthermore, bouncing*

~~until the~~ driver discovers just where the clutch accelerates the gear speed. ~~Bounc-~~

~~ing~~ and jerking can occur until this complicated maneuver is mastered. To make matters more challenging, this "sweet spot" is different in all cars. ~~Though~~ down- *In addition,*

shifting is bothersome, ~~it~~ has to be learned to allow for turns and slowing. ~~The~~ *but it* *In the same way, the*

clutch and gear speed work together, but the procedure is harder because the

gear is shifted to slow down, not to speed up. When shifting and down-shifting

are learned, usually driving is easy.

Using Pronouns and Words That Point Out

Pronouns, including possessive pronouns, **and words that point out** also create coherence. Possessive pronouns are words like "our," "my," "his," or "their." Words that point out are "this," "that," "these," and "those."

Now look again at the fully revised paragraph. (All the words that point out are highlighted in bold italics.) This paragraph is now coherent.

Learning how to drive a car with a stick shift is difficult. The location of each gear and the speed to drive before changing each gear must be learned first. How to push in the clutch and change the gear to obtain the best speed can be tricky and frustrating until after the driver discovers just where the clutch accelerates the gear speed. Furthermore, bouncing and jerking can occur until *this* complicated maneuver is mastered. To make matters more challenging, *this* "sweet spot" is different in all cars. In addition, down-shifting is bothersome, but *it* has to be learned to allow for turns and slowing. In the same way, the clutch and gear speed work together, but the procedure is harder because the gear is shifted to slow down, not to speed up. When shifting and down-shifting are learned, usually driving is easy.

EXERCISE 1

Transparency of #1 and #2 can be made p. 75 in Instructor's Manual.

Revise the following paragraphs by adding key words derived from the topic idea, time and other transitional words, and pronouns that will make each paragraph a coherent whole.

Paragraph 1

A small park can be a haven for children. ~~Swings~~ *The park swings* are big and sturdy so children can swing,

seemingly to the tops of trees. ~~Ducks~~ *Children love to feed the ducks that* swim close to the shore to eat whatever the small visitors bring.

At the same time, older *while others* *safely* ~~Older~~ children canoe through rippling water, ~~Others~~ stand or sit at the edges of the lake and throw

are content to   *They feel*

out fishing lines complete with worms. The children wait for some hungry fish to bite the hook. ~~Parents~~

comfortable knowing their parents are relaxing or napping

~~of the children relax or nap~~ under the shade of nearby trees. Here the world feels safe as children

watch other families enjoying the park.

Paragraph 2

For example, prepackaged

Prepackaged, microwavable dishes are a way of life for people on the go. ~~Prepackaged~~ entrees

for babies help working mothers serve nutritional meals for small members of the family. Older

soon learn to

children can microwave their own dinners. When mom and dad are unable to prepare lunch, children

then   *Also, entrees*

can heat up such items as spaghetti and meatballs or chicken and rice. ~~Entrees~~ that appeal to the

whole family can be stored in the freezer and popped into the microwave while the cook throws

together a quick salad and sets the table. Chicken and dumplings, vegetable lasagna, or pork back

of these dishes   In addition, evening

ribs are a few of the many varieties available. ~~Evening~~ snacks can include popcorn in minutes or milk

Therefore, people

shakes that defrost in seconds. ~~People~~ with a microwave oven no longer have a reason for skipping

a meal.

Paragraph 3

Making a quilt takes some planning. The most important part of making a quilt is selecting a

After choosing the design, it is also   In addition, adding

design for the quilt. ~~It is~~ important to buy materials that look nice together. ~~Adding~~ some materials

with different textures makes the quilt more appealing. A place to work that has lots of room helps

make the work more pleasant   *too, just as a*

when putting the quilt pieces together. Planning a quilting pattern that looks good helps. ~~A~~ tight

Moreover, setting

quilting frame makes the job easier. ~~Setting~~ up the frame close to other family members or near the

When all the phases of the project are

planned

television set makes the quilting seem less boring. ~~A~~ beautiful quilt can be created. *carefully, a*

Paragraph 4

Driving a school bus is a very responsible job. ~~The~~ *Before starting, the* driver may be expected to make all the safety checks to see that the bus is in top shape. ~~Tires all~~ *a dependable driver knows that tires* need to be checked for proper inflation. ~~Making sure~~ *Another important safeguard is making sure* all the children are safely seated ~~helps~~ *to* prevent falls and tumbles. ~~If~~ *In addition, if* seat belts have been installed, all children should be properly secured. ~~The~~ *In fact, the* driver needs to be alert at all times to prevent accidents and injuries. Responsible people ensure safety for school children *who ride the bus.*

Paragraph 5

Running a lawn service can help teenagers acquire business skills. ~~Meeting~~ *The teenagers learn that meeting* people and keeping people happy are part of the job. Bills must be sent and accounts must be kept *also*. ~~New~~ *In addition, new* customers who are added must be worked into the schedule. ~~When~~ *Moreover, when the lawn* equipment wears out, it must be repaired or replaced. Getting each lawn done properly and rapidly helps ~~business skills~~ *a teenager to become a dependable worker.* These business skills can be acquired on the job *and can be applied to future jobs.*

Creating Coherence Between Paragraphs

Just as the sentences within each paragraph must be connected smoothly, so the paragraphs within an essay must be connected smoothly to each other. Each paragraph must flow logically to the next one.

When you write an essay, you can use the three previously explained methods for connecting ideas: **key words** (repeated topic words or ideas), appropriate **time** and **transitional words** and **phrases**, and **pronouns**.

Read the following thesis sentence and topic sentences for an essay on what can be experienced at the beach. Notice the coherence provided by the words in bold type: key words (KW), time (T), other transitional words (TW), and pronouns (P).

Thesis sentence:

My family and I always look forward to going to the beach at Oceanside because of the many smells, sights, and sounds that abound there.

Topic sentence for the first support paragraph:

          P   *KW*   *P*

As soon as **we** walk onto the **beach, we** notice a multitude of both good

    KW

and bad **smells**.

Topic sentence for the second support paragraph:

TW   *KW*   *KW*   *P* *TW*   *KW*

In addition to fragrances and **odors, we also** observe unusual **sights** —
especially people.

Topic sentence for the third support paragraph:

    KW   *KW* *TW*   *KW*

Our **memories** of the **beach also** include a whole array of **sounds** — from
small, insignificant ones to the pounding roar of the waves.

Concluding sentence:

T   *T*   *P*   *KW*

Over the years, whenever we have stayed at **Oceanside**, we have come away

    TW

with memories of our vacation **there**.

EXERCISE 2

*Using the thesis sentences given, construct three topic sentences with key words that will provide transition.
Then construct an appropriate concluding sentence.*

1.   Neighborhood parks provide places to play, picnic, exercise, and read.

   Topic sentence 1:

_____

_____

_____

   Topic sentence 2:

_____

_____

_____

   Topic sentence 3:

_____

_____

_____

Topic sentence 4:

_____

_____

_____

Concluding sentence to begin the last paragraph:

_____

_____

_____

2. Even though visiting a zoo can be educational and relaxing, it can be expensive.

    Topic sentence 1:

    _____

    _____

    _____

    Topic sentence 2:

    _____

    _____

    _____

    Topic sentence 3:

    _____

    _____

    _____

    Concluding sentence to begin the last paragraph:

    _____

    _____

    _____

3. Graduating from college requires intelligence, perseverance, and adequate finances.

Topic sentence 1:

_____

_____

_____

Topic sentence 2:

_____

_____

_____

Topic sentence 3:

_____

_____

_____

Concluding sentence to begin the last paragraph:

_____

_____

_____

EXERCISE 3

Read the following essays and add coherence in the form of key words, time and other transitional words, and pronouns.

Essay 1

During my morning jog, I stopped and talked to a man who was carefully tending his garden.

When I expressed interest in the luscious garden, he replied, "I got over five, five-gallon buckets of

strawberries alone this summer." I was taken by surprise because the strawberry patch was only about six feet by five feet. His green-bean vines that were growing along the fence were loaded with long, healthy beans, and I could only wonder how many of those he had harvested. Seeing his garden made me think of all the benefits that gardening can bring to anyone who is willing to put in the time and effort. Although having a small garden can be hard work, it can result in pleasure and savings.

The benefits of a garden *, however,* do not come without work. *First, the gardener* ~~S/he~~ must select a location for the garden. *After the plot of ground is selected, it* ~~It~~ needs to be dug out and loosened. *Next, sawdust,* ~~Sawdust,~~ peat, and fertilizer mixed and added will allow the seeds to grow easily. *Just as important, growing* ~~Growing~~ instructions need to be followed when the seeds are planted. *Finally, the* ~~The~~ garden must be watered, weeded, and debugged daily. Watering at the correct time of day *sometimes can be difficult but* is necessary. Keeping the weeds to a minimum *is hard work but* makes the garden vegetables stronger. A good gardener prepares a good place and watches the plants as if they were helpless, defenseless creatures.

With a little dirt, water, and sunshine, a ~~A~~ garden can bring many pleasures. The sight of small sprigs reaching up through the soil toward the sun gives the feeling of capturing a small part of nature and getting in touch with the earth. What greater satisfaction is there for the gardener than to know that s/he has used the elements to produce food? *Usually, more* ~~More~~ than enough is produced, and the gardener can proudly share the crisp flavor of fresh produce with a neighbor. In view of the much-publicized insecticides on commercial produce, the gardener can use natural combatants such as ladybugs or praying mantis or ingenuity to preserve the vegetables and feel comfortable knowing the products from the garden are healthy. A garden can be the source not only of food and pride, but also of peace of mind.

After the initial work is done, having ~~Having~~ a small garden to bring in fresh vegetables provides a savings. Each year grocery prices slowly creep up unnoticeably on such items as lettuce and tomatoes. *For example, tomatoes* ~~Tomatoes~~ that last year cost 49 *now*   *Likewise, lettuce*   *These*

cents a pound, cost 59 cents. ~~Lettuce~~ is sold at 69 cents a pound instead of 69 cents each. ~~The~~ gradual

increases make   *The savings are easy*
                                                     to see because a

price ~~increase makes~~ one wonder if the consumer will ever see the end. ~~A~~ pack of tomato or lettuce

seeds costs about 70 cents total, and these seeds can provide enough tomatoes and lettuce for an

Moreover, extra

entire summer. ~~Extra~~ vegetables can be frozen or canned to provide a year-round supply of fresh food.

Additional savings occur when   *The gardener also saves*
                                      money by trading

~~Surplus~~ vegetables can be sold to bring in extra money. ~~Trading~~ produce with other gardeners ~~pre-~~

to prevent

~~vents~~ buying so much at the grocery store. Gardens can add much-needed pocket change and give

the feeling of defeating the inflationary war.

Work, time, and patience

~~One~~ can transform a tiny seed into baskets of delicious, healthy food. By gardening, a person can

Though a

experience a miracle of nature and can save money at the same time. ~~A~~ person may not be able to get

the twenty-five gallons of strawberries in a five-by-six plot of ground, ~~but~~ that same person may be

able to have as many strawberries as can be eaten and still have some left over. The only way to find

out is to try.

Essay 2

"I would like to take good pictures, but I am not sure if I can learn what is necessary." This

statement is frequently made by people who would like to take good pictures. They may want to have

family pictures or have a visual record of favorite vacation spots, but they do not feel good about their

ability. Confidence can easily be built, however, since learning to use a camera is not hard, especially

if the beginning photographer can watch someone explain the fundamentals. To take good photo-

graphs, a beginning photographer needs some technical knowledge, a little artistic judgment, and

patience with beginning errors.

Learning to be a photographer means that some technical knowledge of basic camera functions

is needed. Using a camera is more than just looking through the viewfinder and pressing the shutter. ~~It~~ *At the beginning, it* is important to know how shutter speed and the amount of light going through the lens work

together to produce a picture. ~~Different~~ *To take a good picture, the beginner learns that different* shutter speeds and different amounts of light produce different

kinds of pictures. ~~The~~ *Also, the* camera must be focused correctly. ~~The~~ *However, the* beginning photographer can buy a fully

automatic camera and not have to learn about shutter speed, light, or focusing. ~~Letting~~ *In this way, letting* an automatic

camera do its own thing can produce good pictures. ~~Greater~~ *On the contrary, however, greater* satisfaction comes from having the

knowledge to choose camera functions rather than letting the camera choose the basics. ~~Acquiring~~ *After gaining technical knowledge, a beginning photographer needs* artistic skill *, which* means that the photographer can judge or "see" a picture even before

looking through the camera. ~~Looking at~~ *The photographer learns to visualize that* the particular way objects or people are placed affects the

finished picture. ~~Knowing~~ *Also, the photographer should know* that the center of interest should not go right in the middle of the frame ~~will~~ *to*

create a more pleasing design. ~~A~~ *For example, a* picture of a cat sitting in a window will look better if the cat is either

up or down from center and left or right of center. ~~The~~ *The photographer learns to see that the* window can provide a nice frame for the

picture. The photographer should be able to see the cat within the window frame even before looking *also*

through the viewfinder. ~~Looking~~ *In addition, looking* beyond the cat at what is in the background will affect the finished

product. It takes some creative power of observation to arrange a background that will emphasize the

center of interest rather than detract from it. If the background behind the cat shows a cluttered back

porch, the cat will no longer be the main part of the picture. ~~Composing~~ *Overall, composing* a picture is a skill that can be

learned.

While acquiring these skills, potential photographers
can experience satisfaction
~~Much satisfaction can come to beginning photographers~~ if they are patient with their first

Very often, the
errors — pictures that they really do not want to show to anybody. ~~The~~ most common mistakes might

be to cut off the top of people's heads, or their legs, or to lop off the beautiful bushy tail of the cat in

Similarly, a
the window. ~~A~~ beautiful red mountain might reflect the setting sun and create a spectacular scene —

only to have the picture spoiled by power lines cutting through the middle. Patience with the first bad

, though,
pictures will help the inexperienced photographer learn to overcome whatever problems created the

poor photographs.

All in all, technical
~~Technical~~ skill and artistic judgment will help a photographer take personally satisfying pictures.

Also, patience
Patience will allow the person to acquire these skills gradually. ~~Patience~~ will help the photographer

learn from the first mistakes and have confidence in a slowly developing ability. A person can learn

Simply, a
enough to take good pictures but must not expect too much too soon. ~~A~~ wish can turn into a reality if

someone takes the first step, having faith in the ability to learn the skill needed.

■ **Collaborative Project: Working and Learning Together**

Read the essay by Cynthia L. Vinzant (in Part 3 of this unit), and in groups of four, evaluate two paragraphs for coherence. Mark the words or phrases that provide coherence. Return to the class as a whole and share your findings.

**SOMETHING TO THINK ABOUT,
SOMETHING TO WRITE ABOUT**

"This Is Going to Help Me More Than It Helps You!"

Patrick Haas, *English instructor and perennial searcher for the fountain of youth, Glendale Community College*

1   When I was a young man, my father, a veteran of World War II, told me, "Never volunteer, Son. That's one thing my hitch in the Army taught me." Considering the circumstances of his enlistment in the army during a world war and my own experience in the United States Navy Seabees during the Vietnam War, volunteering did seem to be rather foolhardy, to say the least. However, time passed, and my youthful reluctance to give freely of myself for the benefit of others slowly evolved into a willingness to take the leap and to volunteer. This has been a necessity in some cases because my three children attend a Catholic school that by its very nature exists only through the benefit of volunteerism from the parents of school-aged children. However, the most striking impact of volunteerism in my life is evident through my son's involvement in the Glendale Recreational Baseball Program. In this instance, a healthy and necessary symbiotic relationship exists between team and volunteer coach.

2   In the baseball program, all coaches are volunteers. All teams are selected by a draft process, but each team is built around a core of "good" players. My job as a volunteer coach is to instruct and cajole my charges in the necessary skills of baseball. This, of course, involves countless hours running players through countless series of repetitive skill-building drills. Hitting, fielding, and throwing—the drills change, but the tedium doesn't. I can only hope that my unbridled enthusiasm is enough to maintain the interest of my better players and to boost the lagging or nonexistent interest of the unskilled or marginal players. For example, all the players like to bat, but very few enjoy playing the outfield during batting practice because so few balls are hit their way. By putting on a glove and playing the outfield with them while either drilling them on skills necessary to this position or joking with them, I hope to keep their heads in the game. Usually this works.

3   On game day, the hours, days, and weeks of unselfish giving are put to the test, sometimes with the reward of a game well played and sometimes with the feeling of "Where did these players come from? They can't be the same players I've been working with the past weeks. They don't remember a thing I tried to teach them." In some games against easy teams, even good players make mental errors I never expect them to make. On the other hand, in games against good teams, sometimes even the weakest player will grab a catch, get a hit, or make a throw that seems totally out of character. These are the consequences and rewards for the volunteer coach trying to instruct the young player.

4   And in this last sentence lies one of the basic tenets of volunteering: to help teach the youthful players. All volunteer coaches share at least one desire, and that is the desire to teach. Inherent in this desire are several factors. One is that, as a coach, I feel I have something important to pass on to my players. This important factor can be the skills of the game, the value of team play, the joy of playing, or simply the fulfillment of doing something with my child who plays on the team. This is its own reward. Another factor is the value to society at large. I know that several players on my baseball team come from neighborhoods where gangs are

very influential. And I am grateful that for the several hours a week they are with me, they are away from the bad influences of these gangs. Therefore, by spending so much time with these young people, I hope I can, in some way, instill some sense of the importance of a healthy body and the benefit of being able to rely on this body when a burst of speed, or a long accurate throw, or a diving catch, or a hit in the bottom of the last inning is needed. Almost all players, even the very youngest, and certainly all the coaches know about the devastating effects of drug abuse often associated with gang involvement, and this may be one of the reasons I work so long and so hard with the youngsters who go out for my teams.

5   Perhaps the least-likely-to-be-voiced reason for being a volunteer coach, but a factor nonetheless, is my desire to be involved with "youth." Many parents try to relive their youth through their children. I believe volunteer coaches aren't much different. One major advantage that I have as a coach is that I can relive the "thrill of victory" through all my players, thus magnifying this job, and I can diffuse "the agony of defeat" through all the members of the team, thus reducing the pain. I like to win, and I know my players do, also. However, losses in life are a reality, too. So I can share these ups and downs with my players while maintaining the same calm, positive attitude of playing the best game possible. All I ask is that my players give me their best efforts. This, to me, is the real victory.

6   A volunteer coach is not, as one mother once told me, "One of those sainted men who work with our children." More often than not, these coaches are more sinners than saints. I know I am often angry and upset and use questionable language with my players. These feelings are not what I seek in return for my volunteer time. However, the payoff for me as a volunteer coach is that undeniable sense of pride I feel when my team presents me with a certificate of appreciation or a small plastic plaque at the end of the season. At that moment, I feel that I have received more out of our times together than they. The sense of "Well, I guess I did something right" is enough motivation to bring me back again for another season, the wins and losses of the past season long forgotten in the eternal optimism of a job well done and yet another new beginning.

7   When I brag that a player is a graduate of the Pat Haas School of Baseball when he does something exceptionally well, I am only half joking. Perhaps, by chance, it was my desire to teach this player, my determination to maintain a positive attitude, my unwavering sense of humor, my firm belief that knowing how to play is essential to knowing how to live that contributed to the player's accomplishment. That, in itself, acknowledged or not, is what keeps me volunteering my time season after season. So my father in all his acquired wisdom may not have been completely correct because through my experiences as a volunteer coach, I have discovered the intrinsic reward that all volunteers must feel: "I may be helping someone else, but by gosh, the payoff for me seems to be many times what I am giving."

Understanding Words

Briefly define the following words as they are used in the above essay.

1. hitch *military slang for a period of enlistment*
2. symbiotic *pertaining to two or more people who are closely dependent on each other*
3. cajole *coax with flattery*
4. tedium *monotony or boredom*

5. tenets *principles or doctrines*
6. inherent *inborn*
7. instill *put an idea or feeling into*
8. intrinsic *coming from the inside, real*

Something to Write About

Using one of the ideas or questions listed below, develop either a thesis sentence that states a clear direction or, if you wish, a thesis sentence that previews the points to be covered in the paper. Then draft your essay.

1. Recall the qualities of a volunteer who helped you.
2. Why do people volunteer in hospitals, in schools, in jails, or in charitable organizations? (choose one)
3. What have you done to help someone? (elderly person, child, parent, or other relative)
4. What do you respect about volunteers?
5. How can organized sports activities help children?
6. How do organized sports harm children?
7. Why do children or teenagers join gangs?
8. How do gangs hurt children or teenagers?

After you draft your essay, do each of the following:

Revise it so that it has an effective introduction that includes a hook, a transition, and a thesis sentence.

Be sure that each support paragraph has a strong topic sentence and ample supporting examples.

Check for unity and a smooth flow of ideas.

Revise to include a strong concluding paragraph.

Check for subject-verb agreement.

Check for consistent verbs.

Check for consistent point of view.

Check for fragments, run-ons, and comma splices.

Check punctuation of compound sentences.

Check punctuation of complex sentences.

Home: Just How Safe Is It?

Cynthia L. Vinzant, *student*

1   According to an article in *The Front Page*, "An estimated four of five sexual-abuse victims know their abusers, who often are their fathers, mothers, uncles, grandparents, clergy, or family friends." This statement made by Ward Harkay is also supported by statistics, which show that one of every three girls and one of every four boys are sexually molested before the age of eighteen. In order to begin addressing the enormous problems associated with sexual abuse of children, Americans must recognize the denial that fuels it, educate themselves on the problems that victims develop, and develop programs that will prevent further abuse as well as aid those already afflicted.

2   Denial is the fuel upon which sexual abuse of children is based. Reports, statistics, and case histories have proven, with shocking detail, the existence of such crimes. And yet the cycle continues, often passing from one generation to the next. In one case history, a woman reported that she was sexually molested by nine members of her family by the age of fifteen. During five years of recovery work, including therapy and twelve-step programs, she reported discovering many more sexual abuse victims within her family. All four siblings that she was raised with, two girls and two boys, were molested as well. Her mother also reported having been molested as a child. One of her brothers in turn molested a niece and nephew. Yet the majority of her family members continue to minimize or deny the sexual-abuse cycle within the family. Once at the age of fourteen, she said she reported the abuse to juvenile authorities. Besides not believing her, they sent her back home assuming that it was a safe place. This is only one of many case histories where denial allowed the abuse to continue.

3   In order to cope with sexual abuse, victims often develop survival skills that can lead to further emotional and mental problems. While aging chronologically, emotionally they remain fixed at their current developmental level. Not having been protected, trusted, or validated, they develop several defense mechanisms in order to survive their traumatic childhood. One common defense mechanism of such victims is depersonalization. In depersonalization, the victim temporarily experiences loss of reality including "feelings of being in a 'dreamlike state,' 'out of the body,' 'mechanical,' or 'bizarre' in appearance," according to *Basic Concepts of Psychiatric–Mental Health Nursing*. It may take years or even decades for such victims to get to the place where they can reach out for help in dealing with their problems.

4   Programs and treatment centers are clearly needed not only to aid those already afflicted but to aid in the prevention of further abuse as well. Perhaps such programs could be modeled after the widespread drug-prevention programs currently sweeping the country. Children who chant, "Just say no" to drugs could also be taught to chant, "Just don't touch" to perpetrators. Prevention has always been the most effective weapon against crime. However, emergency centers and foster home care can provide support services to abusive families within the community. Treatment centers must be concerned with the entire family unit, not just the victims of abuse.

5   Since sexual abuse is so widespread, it is imperative that individuals become united in a mass effort to wake themselves from the perpetuating fuel of denial, begin taking aggressive action to assist those already victimized, and implement effective prevention programs in order to protect the children of tomorrow from becoming sexual-abuse victims.

Understanding Words

Briefly define the following words as they are used in the above essay.

1. perpetrators *offenders*
2. imperative *urgent, necessary*
3. perpetuating *constant*

Questions on Content

1. How does the author think denial harms families?
2. How do victims cope with sexual abuse?
3. What will provide support services to abusive families?

Questions on Form

1. Give examples of good sentence variety.
2. Give examples of words or phrases that create coherence.
3. What is the purpose of this essay?

Education

Jan-Georg Roesch, *student*

Transparency of Education can be made pp. 76-77 in Instructor's Manual.

1   Only fifteen months ago I was sitting in a typical German classroom day-dreaming through the lecture and hoping for a miracle that my grades would improve. All the help I got came too late because I had already wasted too much time in the first semester. My goal was to finish *Abitur* and then continue going to a university. The goal just seemed to vanish in thin air, and how was I going to do my master's degree? Fortunately, my father was going to retire soon, and plans were made to make a permanent settlement in Phoenix because my grandmother lived there. Hence, I was given the opportunity to continue my educational goal in America, skip the draft in Germany, and enjoy the warm Arizona climate.

2   In Germany, I would have to complete thirteen years of school and attain the diploma in order to go to a university. I had completed twelve of the thirteen years and didn't have enough points to get into the last year. Furthermore, the conditions I was facing made it more or less impossible for me to repeat the class, and I did not want to take the risk of losing the prediploma. The only solution left was to come to the United States and try to finish my educational goal. Again, I was very fortunate to have friends in Phoenix who made my entrance into Arizona State University very easy. Although I knew that much of what I had learned over the past two years was going to be repeated, I accepted the challenge because I did not really have a choice.

3   Yet, finishing the educational goal was not the only reason for my coming here. At the age of eighteen every male teenager who had completed school was picked for the draft. This meant I had to serve for fifteen months and receive a wage of $70 a month. The alternatives were either to sign up for a longer period, either

for four or six years, or do social work for the same period. I was not too crazy about the idea of serving fifteen months; I felt that it was a waste of time because the program does not offer any real educational use. Of course, the service does provide people with good educational service; however, I would have to sign up for a longer time period.

4   Finally, my last criterion for coming to Phoenix was the warm climate. I had spent over eighteen years of my life living in countries where the climate was mild, damp, wet, and sometimes very cold. Having the flu five times a year was nothing uncommon and seemed more or less to be part of daily life. In addition, it would sometimes rain for days nonstop and flood all the rivers, which normally resulted in flooding the cellar or creating total chaos in the streets. The so-called summer was usually brief. The warm weather might have stayed for two weeks when the next rain clouds were already expected. The winter period was mainly characterized by residents watching tourists streaming out to see warmer places or sitting next to the warm fireplace and sipping hot chocolate.

5   It is close to one year now since I moved, and I do not regret living the eighteen years in countries with colder climates. However, I also feel that moving to Phoenix will bring me new experiences that I could not have encountered if I had stayed in Germany. I will learn new cultural traits and behaviors that differ from the European heartland. Yet, most important of all, I can finish achieving my educational goal that I once dreamed of fifteen months ago.

■ Understanding Words

Briefly define the following word as it is used in the above essay.

1. criterion *standard, rule, or test by which a judgment can be formed*

■ Questions on Content

1. Why could the author not go to a university in his native country?
2. What were two reasons for his move to Phoenix?
3. How long has he lived in the United States?

Questions on Form

1. What key words from the thesis sentence does the author use for coherence in each topic sentence?
2. What is the transition that links paragraphs 2 and 3?
3. How does the author use time words to provide coherence in paragraph 4?

A Bad Experience

Dominique Charpentier, *student*

1   In January 1966, my eldest brother was hospitalized for a detachment of the retina, and he stayed a long month lying in obscurity, with the fear of remaining with a blind eye. A few months before, he was still a very athletic and hard-working student preparing for his bachelor's degree. On a fall day, as he was playing volleyball, the ball hit his face, causing trauma and the progressive loss of sight. The surgical operation and the hospitalization significantly altered my brother's life, leading to drastic, though temporary, changes in his character, his education, and his relationships.

2   After this stay in the hospital and the obligation to keep quiet at home during two more months, it was easy to notice an obvious change in my brother's character. He knew that in the future he could not continue to practice sports with the same fervor he enjoyed so much, and he became bitter. His sight became weak, and he was afraid of the possibility of injury to the other eye or another injury to his face. What a change for the so active and lively young man he was before! He became worried about his sight, fearing a new operation or new failing vision. He had lost his constant optimism and, in a way, something from his youth.

3   If this operation changed my brother's character and behavior, it also involved the necessity to choose a different way of education. For him it was the important year of the General Certificate of Education, and, of course, he failed his examination. He then had to stay in this class for a second year, and he understood easily that this additional year in school would keep him from joining the engineering college he yearned for. He had to reexamine his plans and his desires according to the new possibilities offered to him. Finally, one year later, he registered in a college specializing in computers. The college was four hundred kilometers away from home. That was very different from his first ambition, but it was the start of a new direction for him.

4   As a result of this trauma, not only did my brother's character and his education change but his personal relationships gradually changed directions. As he began again in the same class, he had to leave his former classmates, losing sight of his best friends. One year later, the break was still worse between him and his friends. He had to go away from home to a distant college, leaving his family and his friends. There, in a way, a new life was beginning for him. Some months later, of course, he had made new friends. He entered into friendships with very interesting teachers and kept in touch with them for many years. At last, it was the place where he met his intended wife and where he settled down to start a family.

5   Today my brother is an engineer in an important computer firm. He enjoys his work, and he loves his family. From his accident he learned that nothing is determined once and for all. An operation in 1966 forced him to change his way of life. He came out of this turmoil more mature and more open-minded. As he says often, it is no good to feel regret. The best thing to do is to turn over the page.

Understanding Words

Briefly define the following words as they are used in the above essay.

1. obscurity *darkness*
2. trauma *an injury violently produced*
3. fervor *passion, great strength of feeling*
4. turmoil *commotion*

Questions on Content

1. How did her brother's character change?
2. What year did he undergo surgery?
3. Why did he have to have surgery?

Questions on Form

1. What key words are used in the topic sentences to add coherence?
2. What time words and phrases are used?
3. What other transitional words are used?

The Strategy of Futureness

Excerpt from *Future Shock* by **Alvin Toffler**

1   Three hundred fifty years after his death, scientists are still finding evidence to support Cervantes' succinct insight into adaptational psychology: "Fore-warned fore-armed." Self-evident as it may seem, in most situations we can help individuals adapt better if we simply provide them with advance information about what lies ahead.

2   Studies of the reactions of astronauts, displaced families, and industrial workers almost uniformly point to this conclusion. "Anticipatory information," writes psychologist Hugh Bowen, "allows . . . a dramatic change in performance." Whether the problem is that of driving a car down a crowded street, piloting a plane, solving intellectual puzzles, playing a cello or dealing with interpersonal difficulties, performance improves when the individual knows what to expect next.

3   The mental processing of advance data about any subject presumably cuts down on the amount of processing and the reaction time during the actual period of adaptation. It was Freud, I believe, who said: "Thought is action in rehearsal."

4   Even more important than any specific bits of advance information, however, is the habit of anticipation. This conditioned ability to look ahead plays a key role in adaptation. Indeed, one of the hidden clues to successful coping may well lie in the individual's sense of the future. The people among us who keep up with change, who manage to adapt well, seem to have a richer, better developed sense of what lies ahead than those who cope poorly. Anticipating the future has become a habit with them. The chess player who anticipates the moves of his opponent, the executive who thinks in long range terms, the student who takes a quick glance at the table of contents before starting to read page one, all seem to fare better.

5   People vary widely in the amount of thought they devote to the future, as distinct from the past and present. Some invest far more resources than others in projecting themselves forward—imagining, analyzing and evaluating future possibilities and probabilities. They also vary in how *far* they tend to project. Some habitually think in terms of the "deep future." Others penetrate only into the "shallow future."

6   We have, therefore, at least two dimensions of "futureness"—how much and how far. There is evidence that among normal teenagers maturation is accompanied by what sociologist Stephen L. Klineberg of Princeton describes as "an increasing concern with distant future events." This suggests that people of different ages characteristically devote different amounts of attention to the future. Their "time horizons" may also differ. But age is not the only influence on our futureness. Cultural conditioning affects it, and one of the most important cultural influences of all is the rate of change in the environment.

7   This is why the individual's sense of the future plays so critical a part in his ability to cope. The faster the pace of life, the more rapidly the present environment slips away from us, the more rapidly do future potentialities turn into present reality. As the environment churns faster, we are not only pressured to devote more mental resources to thinking about the future, but to extend our time horizon—to probe further and further ahead. The driver dawdling along an expressway at twenty miles per hour can successfully negotiate a turn into an exit lane, even if the sign indicating the cut-off is very close to the exit. The faster he drives, however, the further back the sign must be placed to give him the time needed to read and

react. In quite the same way, the generalized acceleration of life compels us to lengthen our time horizon or risk being overtaken and overwhelmed by events. The faster the environment changes, the more the need for futureness.

8   Some individuals, of course, project themselves so far into the future for such long periods that their anticipations become escapist fantasies. Far more common, however, are those individuals whose anticipations are so thin and short-range that they are continually surprised and flustered by change.

9   The adaptive individual appears to be able to project himself forward just the "right" distance in time, to examine and evaluate alternative courses of action open to him before the need for final decision, and to make tentative decisions beforehand.

10   Studies by social scientists like Lloyd Warner in the United States and Elliot Jaques in Britain, for example, have shown how important this time element is in management decision-making. The man on the assembly line is given work that requires him to concern himself only with events close to him in time. The men who rise in management are expected, with each successive promotion, to concern themselves with events further in the future.

11   Sociologist Benjamin D. Singer of the University of Western Ontario, whose field is social psychiatry, has gone further. According to Singer, the future plays an enormous, largely unappreciated part in present behavior. He argues, for instance, that "the 'self' of the child is in part feedback from what is toward what it is becoming." The target toward which the child is moving is his "future focused role image"—a conception of what he or she wishes to be like at various points in the future.

12   This "future focused role image," Singer writes, "tends . . . to organize and give meaning to the pattern of life he is expected to take. Where, however, there is only a hazily defined or functionally non-existent future role, then the meaning which is attached to behavior valued by the larger society does not exist; school-work becomes meaningless, as do the rules of middle-class society and of parental discipline."

13   Put more simply, Singer asserts that each individual carries in his mind not merely a picture of himself at present, a self-image, but a set of pictures of himself as he wishes to be in the future. "This person of the future provides a focus for the child; it is a magnet toward which he is drawn; the framework for the present, one might say, is created by the future." . . .

14   Society has many built-in time spanners that help to link the present generation with the past. Our sense of the past is developed by contact with the older generation, by our knowledge of history, by the accumulated heritage of art, music, literature, and science passed down to us through the years. It is enhanced by immediate contact with the objects that surround us, each of which has a point of origin in the past, each of which provides us with a trace of identification with the past.

15   No such time spanners enhance our sense of the future. We have no objects, no friends, no relatives, no works of art, no music or literature, that originate in the future. We have, as it were, no heritage of the future.

16   Despite this, there are ways to send the human mind arching forward as well as backward. We need to begin by creating a stronger future-consciousness on the part of the public, and not just by means of Buck Rogers comic strips, films like *Barbarella*, or articles about the marvels of space travel or medical research. These make a contribution, but what is needed is a concentrated focus on the social and personal implications of the future, not merely on its technological characteristics.

17   If the contemporary individual is going to have to cope with the equivalent of millennia of change within the compressed span of a single lifetime, he must carry within his skull reasonably accurate (even if gross) images of the future. . . .

18   When millions share this passion about the future we shall have a society far better equipped to meet the impact of change. To create such curiosity and awareness is a cardinal task of education. . . .

19   Education must shift into the future tense.

Understanding Words

Briefly define the following words as they are used in the above essay.

1. succinct *clearly and briefly stated*
2. maturation *becoming mature, ripening*
3. dawdling *wasting time or loitering*
4. tentative *uncertain*
5. heritage *something handed down from one's ancestors, culture handed down from the past*
6. millennia *thousands of years*

Questions on Content

1. Why are certain individuals frustrated and confused by change?
2. What happens when people project too far into the future?
3. What pictures of themselves do coping people carry in their heads?
4. What are "time spanners"?

Questions on Form

1. How does the author use repeated key words to link paragraphs together?
2. How does the author use pronouns to achieve coherence?
3. In paragraph 7, what does the author use to clarify his main idea?

THE WRITER'S TOOLS: REVIEWING PUNCTUATION

OBJECTIVES

- Review the uses of the comma.
- Learn the proper use of quotation marks.
- Learn the use of the apostrophe.
- Learn the use of underlining.
- Learn the use of parentheses.
- Review ways of marking sentences.

Mastering the art of written communication means being able to use appropriate punctuation. Think of appropriate punctuation as traffic signals guiding you through a city. The traffic signs help you to know when to stop or slow down, when to be aware of dangers, when to pause, and when to go on. By not having accurate road signs, your journey through the city would be dangerous. Reading compositions with inappropriate or confusing punctuation makes understanding just as risky.

■ Using Commas

Test covering punctuation, p. 42 in Instructor's Manual.

Using a comma correctly is *not* a matter of guess work. If you follow some very simple rules and use commas only when you know the rules, you will be able to use commas correctly.

Uses of Commas

items in a series

introductory expressions

clarity
    identifying and nonidentifying expressions
    interrupters
    misunderstandings

addresses and dates

direct address

Items in a Series

- **A comma is used to separate three or more items in a series of words, phrases, or clauses.**

A series uses the same grammatical construction—for example, three or more nouns, verbs, phrases, or dependent clauses.

Series of Words

John had a **hamburger, french fries, and a milk shake** for lunch.

Jerry noticed that the dog was **cold, wet, and hungry.**

Books, pens, and papers must be brought to class.

The **blue, yellow, and green** tablecloth is new.

Series of Phrases

People brought aid **to the elderly, to the homeless, and to the sick.**

Playing blackjack, eating Chinese food, and sleeping late in the morning are all activities that Trent enjoys.

The child was guilty of **kicking the nurse, biting the thermometer, and writing on the wall.**

Series of Dependent Clauses

Because the weather turned bad, because the park became crowded, and because we had no more money, we left Disneyland.

I know **why you came, who sent you, and when you will leave.**

The quality of a product is judged by **how long it will last, what it is made out of, and who makes it.**

- A comma is *not* used between two words, two phrases, or two dependent clauses that are joined by a coordinating conjunction.

  Randy received a raise in pay and better working hours.

- A comma is *not* used to separate three or more items in a series if a coordinating conjunction is used to separate these items.

  My date stated that he did not like my hairstyle or my makeup or my dress.

EXERCISE 1

Punctuate the following sentences by adding the necessary commas. Look for items in a series. If no punctuation is needed, write "none" beside the sentence.

Example:

The material was written to be read to be absorbed and to be understood.

1.   The shelties ate their food played together and then slept for two hours.

none   2.   My ex-husband did not care for my cooking or my housekeeping or my job.

none   3.   The playful mule needs to be fed and watered.

4.   We can record a song if you get here by 7:00 P.M. if you bring your guitar and if the

microphone works.

5.   The small sparkling odd-shaped rock was discovered by the farmer taken to the appraiser and sold

for a lucrative price.

6.   Richard fed the dog in the backyard the horse in the south field and the cat by the barn.

EXERCISE 2

Punctuate the following paragraphs by adding commas where necessary. Look for items in a series. Do not remove any commas already in the paragraphs.

Paragraph 1

Grandparents aunts uncles and cousins gathered for the annual picnic at the park. Together they

ate the attractive and well-prepared food that smelled delicious tasted great and satisfied everyone.

Then the older children took turns playing volleyball tennis and tetherball. Some of the grandparents

spread blankets on the green grass for the little ones to take their bottles to nap or just to rest.

Sometimes the adults, too, fell asleep. Later they took turns riding on the park's train looking through

the model-train exhibits and reading about the history of trains. Soon, however, everyone returned to

the picnic tables to munch on leftovers and talk about last year's picnic.

Paragraph 2

The cavy or guinea-pig breeder took excellent care of her animals. Every morning she gave them pellets water carrots and alfalfa. Every day she also checked the hutches for newborn babies for any signs of illness and for any guinea pigs that needed to be put into different cages. Every other day she cleaned each hutch and put in new bedding. Once a week she added vitamin C to their water bottles to make sure there were no pigs with a vitamin-C deficiency. Because she did not want young boars to create problems in the hutches, she separated them at four weeks of age from the females from the older boars and from the young babies. Customers who bought pets from her knew that they had purchased guinea pigs that had healthy coats were free from disease and would tame easily.

Introductory Expressions

- Use a comma to set off introductory expressions which may be single words, phrases, or dependent clauses.

Single Words

Silently, the man walked through the park.

Effortlessly, the ice skaters performed their new routine.

Phrases

In the morning, I will work in the yard.

Running in the yard, the puppy stumbled over her own feet.

Stung by the bee, the child began to cry.

Dependent Clauses

When I get to the lake, I will put up the tent.

After he got to work, he realized he had left the papers at home.

Because I am not hungry, I will not go out to eat.

Note If the expression is placed somewhere else in the sentence, it is not set off by a comma.

The man walked **silently** through the park.

He will work in the yard **in the morning**.

I will put up the tent **when I get to the lake**.

EXERCISE 3

Punctuate the following sentences by adding commas where necessary. Look for introductory expressions. If no comma is needed, write "none" beside the sentence.

Example:

Carefully the father placed the baby in her crib.

1. After Jason polished his car he took his girlfriend for a ride.

2. In June the locusts began their chatter.

3. Quickly Phil jumped out of the shower to answer the phone.

4. Although the weather was cold the children went out to play.

none 5. Becky was on a diet because she had gained too many pounds over the summer.

6. In a matter of minutes the teenager ate four hamburgers and two orders of fries.

EXERCISE 4

Punctuate the following paragraphs by adding commas where necessary. Look for introductory expressions first, and then look for items in a series. Do not remove any commas already in the paragraph.

Paragraph 1

According to Luigi Ciulla the biggest challenge he faced when he came to America in 1961 was to find a job. Because he had trouble filling out an application people would say, "I'm sorry. We don't have a job for you. When you learn to speak English then we can hire you." Just to work on an assembly line employees had to pass required IQ tests. Because the tests were in English and because they were timed it was almost impossible for a person who spoke very little English to pass them. Luigi said that even though some words are learned by studying books some words just cannot be learned without living in a country. He also said that he didn't know anyone, so it was hard to find people to use as references on application forms. Because he had never worked in this country he had no references from previous employers either. One other obstacle in finding a job was lack of any "connections." There was no one who could help him get a "foot in the door." He also had to face the reality that many jobs were far away and transportation to these jobs was hard. He said, "Even if I knew how to drive it was hard to pass the written test for a driver's license." That was twenty-nine years ago, and today he is hiring people to work for him in his own business.

Paragraph 2

Fly-fishing is a combination of luck knowledge and experience. The angler has to have the correct combinations of flies for the correct lake. Sometimes, however, a person can cast out use the right fly yet still not catch any fish. Other times he can be at the wrong lake use the wrong flies and catch fish. A little knowledge about nature, however, helps the angler pick the right night to "pull in that big one." From experience the expert angler knows that windy weather stirs up the lake and makes the water cloudy, and, as a result, the fish do not see the flies and do not bite. This also helps to explain why the fish feed at night when the moon is bright and why these same fish choose to feed during the day if there is very little or no moon to give light during the night. Experience comes in handy when the angler knows the precise second to jerk on the line to hook the fish. No matter how a person looks at it know-how makes a difference in fishing, but a person can't discount other factors.

Commas for Clarity

The need for a clear set of road signs referred to previously really becomes evident when you want to be sure your meaning is clearly understood by the reader. Knowing for sure whether or not to use commas helps you to write exactly what you mean. As a result, your reader is more likely to understand your meaning right away and not stumble and reread your sentences several times.

Identifying and Nonidentifying Expressions

- **If an expression is necessary to identify the noun that comes before it, it is called an identifying expression, and no commas are used to set it off.**

  The dogs **that have had their shots** will be allowed in the mall.

  The chickens **that got out of their pen** laid eggs all over the yard.

  The elephant **with twins** is in the next exhibit.

No commas are used because each expression in bold type identifies the noun before it. The expression could not be left out without creating confusion or changing the meaning entirely.

- **If the noun is already specifically identified, the expression that comes after it is nonidentifying, and commas are used to set it off.**

Using commas means that this nonidentifying expression adds more information to the sentence and could be left out without creating confusion. Names (proper nouns) provide specific identification.

  Lester, **who left town yesterday,** took my fishing rod with him.

  Leroy, **my cousin,** will be in town tomorrow.

However, if you put "cousin" first, *no* comma is used because Leroy identifies which cousin.

  My cousin Leroy will be in town tomorrow.

Interrupters A comma is used before and after an expression that is not really a part of the sentence structure. If the word or expression is not part of the basic structure, the expression is probably an **interrupter**. Taking these interrupters out of the sentence would still leave a complete idea. However, these interrupters often serve as transition and can be necessary for clarity and a smooth flow of ideas.

  Yes, I finished a long time ago.

  I will, **of course,** be on time.

"Yes" and "of course" could be left out, leaving complete sentences, but these interrupters would help these sentences connect more smoothly with others in a paragraph.

Words or Phrases Often Used as Interrupters

as a matter of fact	no
for example	of course
for instance	well
however	yes
nevertheless	

Misunderstandings In some sentences, commas are necessary to prevent confusion and misunderstanding. Without a comma, the exact meaning of the following sentence is not clear.

Besides Mary Lou Anne is the only experienced driver.

Notice how adding a comma not only makes the meaning clear right away, but also changes the meaning in each sentence.

Besides, Mary Lou Anne is the only experienced driver.

Besides Mary, Lou Anne is the only experienced driver.

Besides Mary Lou, Anne is the only experienced driver.

EXERCISE 5

Punctuate the following sentences by adding commas where necessary. Look for nonidentifying expressions, interrupters, and possible misunderstandings. If no comma is needed, write "none" beside the sentence.

Example:

none **The employee who received the award has a special parking space.**

Zebras on the other hand were feisty.

1. I will as a matter of fact complete the project on time.

2. Macon, Georgia which I visited last summer is a friendly town.

3. The pecans for instance that I bought at the stand were old.

4. The museum was filled with outstanding exhibits some more valuable than others.

5. The book is I believe the leading authority on genetics.

6.   My brother Jim as a matter of fact lives in Aspen during the winter months.

none 7.   The girl who is a gymnast is from Salt Lake City.

8.   Rochester for instance is known for its cool summers.

EXERCISE 6

Punctuate the following paragraphs by adding commas where necessary. Look first for interrupters, nonidenti-fying expressions, and expressions that can only be understood with commas. Then look for items in a series and introductory expressions. Do not remove any commas already in the paragraph.

Paragraph 1

The sign reads "No skating biking running or loud music." A granite wall progressively emerges from the ground. From one-sixteenth of an inch and one name the wall grows to one-half inch then to a foot. Two names appear, then three five ten. With no logical mathematical sequence the names increase on the wall until at midpoint it reaches approximately eight feet tall with hundreds of names tightly embedded one after another. The time depicted by the wall was of course the 1960s and the names represent the soldiers killed or missing in Southeast Asia during the Vietnam War. The visual representation of heartfelt American deaths turns the tourist chatter to silence. Experiencing the Vietnam Veterans Memorial it seems makes visitors realize the sacrifices of American youth.

Paragraph 2

The trend of the 1980s to rely heavily on "disposables" has created a throwaway society. Everywhere we look trash that has to be disposed of is piling up. Americans litter the countryside with plastic aluminum cans and glass bottles. At home disposable plates cups plasticware and of course diapers are filling the plastic bags that must be transported to the local landfill. At hospitals paper gowns disposable thermometers towels used in surgery and miles of plastic tubing cannot be resterilized and reused and as a result are being sent to special landfills for medical wastes. Though it takes many years for the paper products to break down in the landfills scientists predict that the plastics will take several hundred years to break down. Styrofoam especially could take an inordinately long time to degrade. These nonbiodegradable plastics are petroleum-based and keep us importing oil to make them. Making aluminum cans likewise uses up our natural resources. Not only does it use up natural resources to make new plastic products aluminum cans and bottles, but it takes energy to manufacture these products. Reusing aluminum cans and glass bottles will save resources and energy. Recycling can help cities and towns that are filling up their landfills and running out of room to construct more. Fortunately we as Americans are trying to make an effort to reverse the trend and use products more than once before throwing them away.

Addresses and Dates

- A comma is used to set off the name of a city, county, state, and zip code in a sentence. There is, however, *no* comma between the state and zip code.

  His work in **Phoenix, Arizona,** was of monumental value to all.

  Jason's home at 2482 North 16th Street, **Phoenix, Arizona 85521,** burned to the ground.

- A comma is used to set off the month, day, and year in a sentence. However, when the day is omitted, a comma is not used.

  On **June 4, 1990,** I fell in love.

  I went to Rocky Point in **July of 1990.**

  The company opened for business in **November 1991.**

Direct Address

- Use a comma when you use a name in speaking directly to someone.

  "Dave, will you please finish this work?"

  "When, Theresa, do you think this work will be done?"

- **Do not use a comma when you are speaking about someone.**

  Sam wants to try out for the elite soccer team.

Punctuate the following sentences by adding commas where necessary. Look for addresses, dates, and direct address. If no punctuation is needed, write "none" beside the sentence.

1. What I want to know Ruby is how you do your art so well.

2. Address the card to 138 West Maple Drive Portland Oregon 94031.

3. The letter sent to 316 West Dove Drive Loganville Georgia 31624 was returned to the sender.

none 4. July 4th is a national holiday.

5. On November 8 1993 the nine black lab puppies were born on the corner of a farm in Loveland Colorado.

6. The baby ducks hatched on April 15 1990 on my parents' farm.

7. Sondra when did you visit your cousin in Nashville Tennessee?

8. June 18 1971 is my birthday Jim.

Punctuate the following paragraphs by adding commas where necessary. Look first for addresses and dates. Then look for items in a series, introductory expressions, interrupters, and nonidentifying expressions. Do not remove any commas already in the paragraphs.

Paragraph 1

On September 1 1939 Germany invaded Poland and started World War II. Beginning in 1940 Hitler invaded Belgium Luxembourg Denmark Norway and France. On April 9 1940 the Germans seized Denmark and invaded Norway. Just one month later on May 10 1940 Germany invaded Belgium. Just a few days later on May 14 1940 the Netherlands surrendered. Because England had treaties with France she made good her commitment, and on September 3 1940 Great Britain and France declared war on Germany. On May 26 1940 the Allied Powers began their heroic evacuation at Dunkirk, a seaport in northern France. By 1940 the entire European continent was at war. Then on June 22 1941 Germany invaded the Soviet Union. On December 7 1941 Japan attacked Pearl Harbor bringing the United States into the war. By now almost all countries in the world were involved in this devastating war.

Paragraph 2

During my childhood I moved many times. On July 2 1968 my family and I moved to El Paso Texas where my mother attended the nursing program at the university. When she graduated on June 2 1971 we moved to Lubbock Texas where she got a job working for the hospital there. However we moved again in March of 1974 because my mom got a better job. We stayed there for a little over two years, and on November 7 1976 we moved to W. Frier Drive Plainville Texas. We stayed in that house for a year and a half but moved for what I hoped would be the last time when my mom remarried on May 14 1978. But as fate would have it only a few months later we moved again, and on October 3 1978 we moved to a house in the country.

▩ Using Quotation Marks

- Use quotation marks to enclose the exact words (direct quotation) of a speaker. A comma is used to set the direct quotation off from the rest of the sentence.

Tom said, "**The house that I like is for sale.**"

"**The house that I like,**" Tom said, "**is for sale.**"

However, if you are summarizing or using the word "that," quotation marks are *not* used.

Tom said **that we could move in tomorrow.**

Mom said **that we would be going on vacation soon.**

Other Punctuation with Quotation Marks

- Periods and commas are *always* placed *inside* the quotation marks.

  Margarita said, "I want a hot fudge sundae."

  "I want a hot fudge sundae," Margarita said.

- Semicolons are *always* placed *outside* the quotation marks.

  Janice said, "I believe we will buy that house"; then she left.

- Question marks and exclamation points are placed inside or outside the quotation marks. Place them *inside* if the direct quotation is the question or exclamation.

  Tom asked, "When can we move into the house?"

  Place them *outside* if the entire sentence is the question or exclamation.

  Did Tom say, "We can move in in three weeks"?

Quotations Within Quotations

- Single quotation marks are used inside the double marks when a quotation exists within another quotation.

  "I heard Keith say, '**Be careful,**' before the board fell," said Stan.

  Stan said, "Before the board fell, I heard Keith say, '**Be careful.**'"

Words or Phrases That Require Special Attention

- Quotation marks or italics are used to set off words that are referred to as words and are not a part of the basic sentence structure.

  When you use the word "**clever,**" use it carefully.

  Try not to use "**very**" too often.

- Quotation marks are used to set off words that are slang or that are used ironically.

  That was a "**rad**" movie.

  Would you like to drive the "**green bomber**"?

Titles Contained Within Larger Works

- Use quotation marks around the title of any selection that has been published within a larger work. Underline or italicize the name of the larger work.

  "**Learning to See**" is the title of the second chapter in Eudora Welty's book <u>One Writer's Beginnings</u>.

  "**On His Blindness**" is a poem that has been included in many anthologies.

■ Using Apostrophes

An apostrophe is used to show ownership. An apostrophe is also used in contractions, which are informal.

Possessive Nouns

- **Form the possessive of singular nouns by adding an apostrophe and -s.**

  Put **John's** book on the **car's** fender.

- **Plural nouns that end in -s form the possessive by adding just an apostrophe.**

  The **books'** edges have been torn.

  The **students'** assignments were all completed on time.

- **Plural nouns that end in any letter other than -s form the possessive form by adding an apostrophe and -s.**

  The **workmen's** wages were paid by the company.

  The puppy played with the **children's** toys.

Note Do not confuse a possessive noun with a plural noun that ends in -s.

  The **books** (plural noun) have not been torn.

  (The books do not own anything.)

  The **books'** edges (ownership) have not been torn.

  (The edges belong to the books; therefore, an apostrophe is used.)

Possessive Pronouns

- **An apostrophe is *not* used to form the possessive of personal pronouns.**

  His book was left on the floor.

  This book is **hers**.

  It's time for us to look at **its** internal structure.

Note "**It's**" with an apostrophe is a contraction for "it is." The "**its**" (without an apostrophe) is a possessive pronoun.

However, an apostrophe *is* used to form the possessive form of indefinite pronouns.

One's work must be done well.

He is **everybody's** favorite trumpet player.

The smoke from **somebody's** barbecue drifted through the neighborhood.

Contractions

- In contractions, an apostrophe indicates that one or more letters have been left out.

  He'll have to get there early to get a parking spot.

  That's a nice place to go on vacation.

■ Using Underlining

- The title of any piece of writing that has been published by itself should be underlined or put into italics. If it has been published within a larger collection or magazine, use quotation marks.

  I read the article "Building Solar Homes" that appeared in the Builders' Guide.

  Of Mice and Men is a novel that appeals to many people.

  I enjoy reading New Times.

■ Using Parentheses

- Parentheses are used to enclose expressions or sentences that are separate from the main thought of the writing. If the entire sentence is set off by parentheses, the end punctuation mark is inside the closing parenthesis. If the expression is part of a sentence, the punctuation is outside the closing parenthesis.

  (The first part needs to be read carefully.)

  Please read all of the first chapter carefully (especially the first part).

EXERCISE   9

Punctuate the following sentences by adding the necessary punctuation. Look for missing quotation marks, for words showing ownership, and for contractions. Add any other punctuation marks that are needed.

1. "If I can get off work early," said Kevin, "we'll go to the lake."

2. "Everybody's favorite dessert is homemade ice cream," said Susan's mother.

3. The sophomore class chose "Go for it" as the motto on their T-shirts.

4. "Where the Red Fern Grows is my favorite book," said Stewart.

5. The poem "The Horses" is in the book To Read Literature by Donald Hall.

6. "Close the window, Kim," Chuck said, "or Joe's camping gear will get wet."

none 7. Keith said that he needs to get his car inspected as soon as he gets home from work.

8. According to the book Sheltie Talk, it's important to brush the dog's coat well.

EXERCISE 10

Punctuate the following paragraphs. Look first for quotations, words that show ownership, titles, and contractions. Then insert any other commas that are needed. Do not remove any punctuation marks already in the paragraphs.

Paragraph 1

My family's trip to the Grand Canyon northwest of Flagstaff, Arizona, was an unforgettable experience. On June 17, 1993, we boarded the steam train in Williams, Arizona, and headed for the Canyon. The train moved across the Kaibab Plateau, which was rolling hills covered with scrub cedar. Once there, we got off the train and walked to Bright Angel Lodge where we bought a lunch that we enjoyed under a tree at the South Rim of the Canyon. There we could see the colorful layers of rock, shadows made by clouds, and distant evergreen trees. We were impressed by the vastness of the Canyon, and from the Canyon's edge, we could see part of Bright Angel Trail. Soon, however, we needed to walk back to the train for the trip back to Williams. Although we were tired, we were inspired by what we had seen.

Surgeons who operate on patients who are not put to sleep sometimes say things that can upset their patients. They forget that the patients are already anxious about having surgery. When Dr. Madox operated on a patient he tuned in some fast music and jokingly commented "There, that's good. It helps me cut faster." When he started sewing up the incision before getting the lab results the patient asked if he had gotten all of the cancer. He replied "I hope so." Later on when he was putting in the sutures he stated "Oh no the nurse is going to be upset with me when she takes this stitch out. I snipped the ends too close." He then headed for the door and said "I'll see you later." The patient asked him if he was coming back, and he just bounced on out the door. Fortunately one of the nurses told the patient that the doctor was going to the lab to get the results. Although the surgery was over the patient dreaded the return visit to the doctor's office to have the surgeon's "closely snipped" sutures removed.

■ Punctuating Sentences

To maintain clarity, you must mark your sentences clearly. Though all sentences in a paragraph revolve around one main idea, you must separate ideas into sentences.

Simple Sentences

- **All simple sentences must end with an end mark like a period, exclamation point, or question mark.**

  We went to the store.

  We bought new school clothes.

  We bought the best school clothes ever!

  Would you like to go shopping with us?

Compound Sentences

- **Simple sentences are combined into compound sentences by using a semicolon, a comma and a coordinate conjunction, or a semicolon followed by a conjunctive adverb and a comma.**

A Semicolon

We went to the store; we bought new school clothes.

A Comma and a Coordinate Conjunction

We went to the store, and we bought school clothes.

A Semicolon Followed by a Conjunctive Adverb and a Comma

We went to the store; therefore, we bought new school clothes.

Compound-Complex Sentences

- Complex sentences can also be joined to simple sentences by using a comma and a coordinate conjunction or by using a semicolon followed by a conjunctive adverb and a comma.

A Comma and a Coordinate Conjunction

After we got paid, we went to the store, and we bought school clothes.

A Semicolon Followed by a Conjunctive Adverb and a Comma

After we got paid, we went to the store; consequently, we bought new school clothes.

EXERCISE 11

Transparency of #1 and #2 can be made, pp. 78-79 in Instructor's manual.

Using all the punctuating skills covered in this section, punctuate the following paragraphs. Do not remove any punctuation marks already in the paragraphs.

Paragraph 1

During World War II average American citizens experienced many difficulties buying products they wanted or needed. The ability just to be able to buy products was restricted by monthly ration stamps for such items as gasoline shoes sugar and meat. Though people had ration stamps meat was especially hard to find because it was put into products like Spam and sent to the men overseas. Even with stamps citizens might not be able to buy the products they wanted. Often the shelves were empty because it seemed as though everything was channeled into America's defense system. For example shoes were difficult to obtain because the shoe producers needed to supply boots for the army.

Likewise material was difficult to purchase because fabrics were shipped to factories to make uniforms

for the Armed Forces. Jim and Alice Basham who owned their own upholstery business said We could

not buy goods to upholster furniture because material was shipped to the Armed Forces. They also

said that women were unable to buy nylons because the fabric needed to make them went into

making parachutes to be used in the war. Imported items like coffee tea sugar and rubber were scarce.

The little rubber that the United States could import went into the production of tires for the Armed

Forces. For four years no automobiles were made because all American energies were channeled into

the production of military vehicles. American citizens who lived through World War II will always

remember those hard times.

Paragraph 2

Summertime offers many opportunities for children of all ages with extra time on their hands.

Kids can spend their days at the Boys' or Girls' Club where they can swim play supervised sports and

even go on field trips. If there is no Boys' Club or Girls' Club for a small fee they can swim in public

pools. There they can join swim teams take swim lessons or just swim for pleasure. Often libraries that

are equipped with reading programs are close by. There children can attend story time to hear such

storybooks as <u>Bears on Wheels</u> or <u>The Honey Hunt</u> check out videotapes or books or leisurely look

through magazines. In the evenings these same children can play Little League baseball or watch

other children play ball. If they want to earn extra money they can collect aluminum cans glass plastic

or paper to recycle. Also a great potential exists for a lawn service that can bring in money for school.

Older children can also earn extra money babysitting or working for the city supervising younger children in recreational programs. Opportunities abound for kids everywhere therefore all they need

to do is look around.

Paragraph 3

Poetry is an art form that can be enjoyed sometimes because of the meaning sometimes because

of the way it is written and other times because of both. Can anyone read Walt Whitman's Leaves of

Grass without saying That is nice really nice Lines that seem to stick in the mind are often written with

a strong message. For instance the lines from Anne Sexton's poem The Abortion Somebody who should

have been born is gone stay in the mind long after the poem has been read. Whenever the question

of abortion arises these lines are recalled in the mind again and again. Thomas Hood wanted to change

labor laws in England. In his poem The Song of the Shirt he wrote With fingers weary and worn, / With

eyelids heavy and red, / A woman sat, in unwomanly rags, / Plying her needle and thread — John Milton,

married but miserable, spent much effort inserting lines about divorce into his poetry in an attempt to

change the laws that forbade divorce. Some poets however do not moralize but simply present things

the way they are. James Dickey a well-known American poet wrote of adultery objectively without

making any judgment of its wrongness or rightness. On the other hand Joyce Peseroff expresses her

ideas in The Hardness Scale in which she seems to be relating a woman's feelings about a man who is

not such a perfect man. Diane Wakoski writes of revenge in her poem You, Letting the Trees Stand as

My Betrayer In this poem nature will pay back someone who loved her and then left her. The meaning

is there in these and many other poems but the way they are written makes the lines occur over and

over in the reader's mind.

WRITING ASSIGNMENT

Freewrite or brainstorm to generate ideas that can be used to analyze or explain the reasons why you enjoyed one of the following. (Do not retell the story.)

1. A movie
2. A play
3. A book

After you draft your essay, revise for content and edit for mechanics.

Content

Essay

Check introductory paragraph for effective hook.

Check for a smooth transition between hook and thesis.

Check to see that your paper has a strong thesis sentence.

Check to see that the voice is appropriate for purpose and audience.

Paragraphs

Revise so that each has a clear topic sentence that develops an idea suggested in the thesis sentence.

Include four to six supporting sentences that are developed using short interrelated examples or an extended example.

Include a closing sentence in each paragraph.

Mechanics

Check for subject-verb agreement.

Check for consistent verbs.

Check for a consistent point of view.

Check for fragments, run-on sentences, and comma splices.

Check for correct punctuation.

Sentence Variety

Revise short sentences into compound sentences.

Revise sentences to include complex sentences.

Check for coherence between and within paragraphs.

UNIT 8

Composing with Effective Alternate Patterns

PART 1

PARTS TO WHOLE: MODES OF DEVELOPMENT

OBJECTIVES

- Develop an essay by using illustration.
- Develop an essay by using comparison/contrast.
- Develop an essay by using classification.
- Develop an essay by using definition.
- Develop an essay by using cause/effect analysis.
- Develop an essay by using process.
- Develop an essay by using argumentation.

When you master the multiparagraph essay using examples, you are well on your way to becoming an effective writer. You have learned a basic skill. However, it is vital that you understand the *connection between the precise form of this essay*, as you have practiced it, *and the other types of writing* that you will need to do.

Mastering a basic plan for a multiparagraph essay is similar to mastering the art of home building because becoming a good builder requires certain skills, just as becoming an effective writer requires precise skills. The following chart shows how both building a house and writing an essay are similar.

Building a Home	Writing an Essay
Planning	Planning
gather house-plan ideas	prewrite
design home for owner	consider audience and purpose
make drawings	outline
Building	Writing
pour foundation	draft a thesis sentence
erect frame	draft support paragraphs
put on roof	draft an introduction and a conclusion
Putting on the finishing touches	
add finishing touches	revise and edit

If you want to be able to write an effective essay, then you need to understand each step of the process. You might think of these components of the essay as a building code to be followed. This building code keeps you from doing shoddy work; however, it does not keep you from being creative and adding variety to your writing. If you drove into a town and saw that every house was built exactly alike, you might wonder what was wrong with the people who lived there and whether they possessed any creativity at all. Similarly, if you learned to write a multiparagraph essay using examples and never learned to go beyond that point, people might wonder whether you, too, lacked creativity. Always remember, though, that *every* completed house has a foundation, a frame, a roof, and finishing touches. It may also have a fireplace, an upper story, picture windows, or whatever the builder wanted to add to make the house more appealing. You, too, will want to have that something extra in your essays, even though *every* essay that you write needs an introduction, support paragraphs, a conclusion, and finishing touches.

Once you have learned to write a thesis sentence and support it with examples, you can learn other methods to organize ideas in an essay. You always begin a paper by planning first, using freewriting, brainstorming, or another prewriting activity to generate ideas. Then the organization, no matter what pattern you select, will include an introduction, support, and a conclusion.

Developing a paper can be done in different ways that are usually called **modes of development**. These modes are ways of developing and organizing the support paragraphs that explain a thesis sentence in an essay. The word "mode" can also mean "method." There are many modes of development; all of the following modes are important for basic writers to learn.

Modes of Development

illustration

comparison/contrast

classification

definition

cause/effect analysis

process analysis

argumentation

Your purpose for writing a paper will determine the mode you select to develop your essay. If your purpose is to show how home builders can create energy-efficient homes, you could **illustrate** the way different houses are built to conserve energy. If you are writing an article for home buyers, your purpose might be to **compare/contrast** two different kinds of homes available so that the reader can then decide which home is better. If your purpose is to inform the population about the types of homes available to them, your job would be to **classify** the types of homes available in a certain area. If you wanted to **define** a home, you might include not just the physical structure but the emotions associated with a home. If you want to explain *why* someone wanted to build a home, your purpose would be to explain the **causes** of that event. If you want to discuss remodeling parts of an existing home rather than buying a new home, your purpose would be to explain *how to* remodel or the **process** of remodeling. If you are a person who sells homes, your purpose might be to use an **argument** that would persuade a first-time home buyer that purchasing a repossessed home in need of repair would be more advantageous than buying a new home.

This unit shows how the general subject "homes" can be developed into different kinds of essays, depending upon the particular purpose of the essay. Using the same topic, homes, each of the seven modes of writing is explained and illustrated.

Illustration

In Unit 5, "Writing with More Depth and Variety," you studied how to use examples to clarify and support topic ideas in paragraphs and essays. This use of examples is also a mode of development called **illustration**. Previously, you practiced writing paragraphs and essays by supporting a topic sentence or a thesis sentence with clarifying details and examples. These examples were also illustrations.

To use illustration well in writing a longer paper, you do not need to learn a new way of generating ideas. The simple writing process you used earlier in this text is appropriate in this part, too.

Freewrite/brainstorm your topic.

Group ideas to find a direction or point of view for your topic.

Freewrite/brainstorm again for more details and examples.

Arrange similar details and examples into groups and compose your thesis sentence.

Begin drafting the support paragraphs for your essay.

Draft an introduction and a conclusion.

Revise and edit.

The *purpose* of an illustration paper is to explain or clarify by giving specific examples that show the reader "in what way" the topic idea is true. If you say that "when building a new home, structural changes can be made to make the home energy-efficient," then you need to follow up with specific examples that illustrate structural changes. The entire paper should contain the examples and illustrations that would show how structural changes make the home more energy-efficient.

The *topic* for an illustration paper can be any subject you could convincingly explain by giving examples or illustrations. It is one of the most frequently used modes of writing.

Basically, the pattern of *organization* for this mode of development looks like this:

1. The introductory paragraph includes a hook, a transition, and a thesis sentence.

2. Each support paragraph includes a topic sentence and examples or illustrations.

3. The conclusion includes a restatement of the main idea that the examples have illustrated.

When you use this pattern for a multiparagraph essay, each supporting paragraph is developed with examples or illustrations. During drafting, you could choose short, interrelated examples or a single, extended example or illustration.

In this section, you are *not* learning a new mode or pattern of development. You are learning that you can use a process and pattern that you have already practiced in many writing assignments. You have just learned a new descriptive phrase for it — *development by illustration.*

Suppose you want to write a paper to explain or illustrate to a homeowner the ways in which a house can be energy-efficient. Through brainstorming/ freewriting you have written the following possible thesis sentence:

> A homeowner can have an energy-efficient home by changing certain features in construction, installing energy-efficient devices inside the home, and planning landscaping to control the amount of heat or cold coming into the home.

The following essay shows how you could use illustrations to support this thesis.

A Home for the 1990s

<table>
<tr>
<td>hook</td>
<td>1</td>
<td>Thirty years ago, homeowners believed that there were no limits to the energy needed for them to live a comfortable life. They assumed their American Dream to be the right to own a home without even thinking about how much energy the house required. For most Americans today, part of the American Dream still includes owning a home complete with modern appliances.</td>
</tr>
<tr>
<td>transition</td>
<td></td>
<td>This dream, however, can turn into a financial nightmare if careful attention is not given to using energy wisely. Having a home that uses too much energy can be a financial drain for the owner and, in the long run, for the country.</td>
</tr>
<tr>
<td>thesis sentence</td>
<td></td>
<td>However, a homeowner can have an energy-efficient home by making certain changes in construction, by installing energy-efficient devices inside the home, and by planning landscaping to control the amount of heat or cold coming into the home.</td>
</tr>
<tr>
<td>topic sentence #1
illustration #1</td>
<td>2</td>
<td>When the house is built, the homeowner can have certain features changed or added so that the home will be energy-efficient. For example, in the desert Southwest the roof overhang should be large enough to keep the high summer sun from shining on most of the walls. In the winter, because of the changing position of the sun, the low winter sun can warm the house by shining on the walls under the overhanging roof.</td>
</tr>
<tr>
<td>illustration #2</td>
<td></td>
<td>When plans are being made for the house, the owner can consider block or brick construction.</td>
</tr>
<tr>
<td>illustration #3
illustration #4
concluding sentence</td>
<td></td>
<td>Also, good insulation in the walls and attic can save energy in both summer and winter. Although they may cost more money to put in, special double-paned windows and weather stripping will save energy, too. All these structural features add up to long-range energy savings.</td>
</tr>
<tr>
<td>topic sentence #2
illustration #1
illustration #2
illustration #3</td>
<td>3</td>
<td>If saving energy in the 1990s is important, one of the best ways is to install energy-efficient devices inside the house. Even small changes can be made, such as adding an insulating blanket to the hot-water tank. Putting up drapes with a thermal lining will also help save energy. The most energy can be saved, however, by the type of heating-cooling unit installed in the home. Most recently, the "seasonal energy efficiency ratio" (SEER) provides the best</td>
</tr>
</table>

guide as to the type of unit to install for heating or air conditioning. These ratios are given in numbers like 9, 10, or 11, and by selecting a unit with a high number, the homeowner can save energy as well as money. A new kind of compressor called a scroll compressor is now available for air-conditioning units. This new unit can provide a SEER as high as 12. According to James Dulley (in an article in *The Arizona Republic*, June 11, 1989), this new scroll compressor uses so much less energy than older units that the cooling costs

concluding sentence

will be cut in half. Installing energy-efficient devices like these can help a homeowner conserve energy.

topic sentence #3   4   After considering these ways of conserving energy in a home, the owner should also plan the landscaping so that it helps the house become energy

illustration #1
illustration #2

efficient. If the house is new, the owner can plant trees and shrubs around the home so that they shade the walls and the roof from the sun. Grass that requires little water can be planted close to the house to absorb heat from

illustration #3
illustration #4

the sun. In the wintertime, people who live in the desert should trim their trees and shrubs to allow the sun to shine on the house. In colder parts of the country, landscaping should be planted to give shade in the summer, but trees and shrubs that lose their leaves in the winter should be chosen so that the sun can shine into the house. Landscaping provides more than an attrac-

concluding sentence

tive appearance for a home. It becomes one more way for the homeowner to save money in day-to-day operating costs and, at the same time, to save energy for the country.

concluding paragraph   5   In the 1960s Americans used as much energy as they wanted without concern for the future. In the 1990s, though, Americans have learned that sources for energy are limited and that some kind of conservation is needed if they are going to have enough energy in the future to live in the same kinds of comfortable homes they have always dreamed about. Owning a home today carries the responsibility to reduce the amount of energy required to operate a house and live a comfortable life at the same time. By paying attention to the energy-saving devices now available, homeowners can save money for today and natural resources for tomorrow.

WRITING ASSIGNMENT

Write an essay developed through illustration. Use one of the following topics. During revision and editing, refer to the checklist in the inside back cover.

1.   Problems with transportation in your city
2.   Ways to keep a body healthy
3.   Factors to consider before buying a puppy
4.   Summer projects for the family
5.   Reasons people enjoy vacationing in national parks
6.   Reasons people dread or look forward to holidays
7.   Reasons discipline is important at home or at school

■ Comparison/Contrast

Another useful way to present information is to explain how two items relate to each other. This kind of essay is called a **comparison/contrast** paper. The *purpose* of a comparison/contrast paper is to show how two things are alike or different. A paper may be primarily a comparison (how two items are alike) or primarily a contrast (how two items are different).

The *subject* for a comparison/contrast paper is two people, objects, or places that have both similarities and differences. Two children, two lakes, or two types of flowers would probably be contrasted because their similarities are obvious. A donkey and a person or a flower and a person would probably be compared because it is not so easy to see how they are alike. There would be no point in contrasting two objects if there was no way that they were alike. Likewise, there would be no point in comparing two objects that had no differences. In your other college classes, you may be asked to explain the similarities or differences between ideas: two opinions, two philosophical theories, two personalities, or two political candidates.

In a true comparison/contrast essay, both sides are treated fairly, with equal amounts of information given for each side. However, one side may appear to have the advantage over the other. If one side does have an advantage, it should be discussed *last*. The side with more disadvantages should be covered *first* or should start the discussion. For instance, if you were to write a paper about presidents Nixon and Kennedy, you would want to start your essay with Nixon because he lacked the glamour and prestige of Kennedy and because Nixon was forced to resign.

If the paper is a true comparison/contrast, it will present the same characteristics for both sides. For example, if you talk about Nixon's appearance, you must also talk about Kennedy's appearance. If you talk about Nixon's family, you must talk about Kennedy's family, also. In this way, the paper is balanced equally between the two sides.

The pattern for multiparagraph essays that you have learned can be modified to satisfy the *organization* for this comparison or contrast paper. Your freewriting or brainstorming is done in two separate parts. One section should be labeled "comparisons" or "similarities." The other section should be labeled "contrasts" or "differences."

Suppose you were writing an essay comparing and contrasting the costs of buying either a new or a "fix-up" home. In this case, "item #1" under consideration might be "fix-up homes," and "item #2" might be "new homes." Your brainstorming might be done in lists like the ones that follow.

Similarities

Item #1 (fix-up homes) and Item # 2 (new homes)

_____

_____

_____

Differences

Item #1 (fix-up homes)   **Item #2 (new homes)**

_____   _____

_____   _____

_____   _____

The next step is to *group* ideas and decide whether the information you have generated could be explained best in a paper that presents contrasts (differences) between the two items or in a paper that presents comparisons (similarities) between the two items. The clustering of ideas should lead to an outline that includes a thesis sentence and a preview of the main points to be covered in the paper. There is no definite, correct number of similarities or differences, but the more points you have, the more paragraphs you will have and the better your thesis will be supported.

If the paper is a *comparison*, it will focus primarily on *similarities*, but to be realistic and effective, it may begin and end with significant differences. Or if the paper is a *contrast*, it will focus primarily on *differences*, but, again, to be realistic and effective, it may begin and end with significant similarities.

You now have one more decision to make: how to present your explanation. Choose one of the following patterns:

1. items discussed in alternate paragraphs

2. items discussed in two distinct parts within each paragraph

3. items discussed in alternate sentences within each paragraph

On the following pages are outlines of these patterns; each pattern is then followed by a draft of an essay written according to that pattern.

Items Discussed in Alternate Paragraphs

1. The introductory paragraph previews major differences (with brief reference to a major similarity) *or* previews major similarities (with brief reference to a major difference).

2. Support paragraphs include points of contrast (or comparison) in an alternating pattern.

    First point
        Paragraph 1: Item #1 (fix-up homes)
        Paragraph 2: Item #2 (new homes)

    Second point
        Paragraph 3: Item #1
        Paragraph 4: Item #2

    Third point
        Paragraph 5: Item #1
        Paragraph 6: Item #2

Fourth point (if needed)
   Paragraph 7: Item #1
   Paragraph 8: Item #2

3. The concluding paragraph reemphasizes major differences (with a brief reference to a major similarity referred to in the introduction) *or* reemphasizes major similarities (with a brief reference to a major difference referred to in the introduction).

Read this example of an essay with paragraphs that alternate between the items.

Saving Money on a New Home

<table>
<tr><td>hook</td><td>1</td><td>Jason and Jennifer had been married for two years when they decided that they were ready to start a family. But they decided that they should buy a house before they had children. On their combined income of $42,000 a year, they felt they could afford a home of their own. After they contacted a real estate agent and read articles about home buying, they narrowed their options to buying a new home or a "fix-up" home. The decision would be difficult because both options would result in an investment with a guaranteed return. As many other Americans have learned, the initial money invested, the continual costs, and the return for the investment would vary according to the option selected.</td></tr>
</table>

brief reference to similarity

thesis sentence

first point of contrast
item #1 discussed

2   **Probably the most marked difference between buying a new home and a "fix-up" home is the initial costs involved.** A "fix-up" home does not always have a fixed down payment and sometimes can be purchased at the rate of interest paid by the previous homeowners. The cost of a "fix-up" home is set by the current homeowner, but many times an offer of a few thousand dollars less will be accepted. A "fix-up" home is often sold "as is" with an opportunity for the buyer to check everything out before signing the closing papers. Anything that is defective can be negotiated to be repaired or to lower the cost to the buyer. Anything that breaks after the final papers are signed, though, becomes the responsibility of the new owner. A "fix-up" home often needs landscaping but usually has grass, shrubs, and trees that are already established.

first point of contrast

item #2 discussed

3   **On the other hand,** a new home has higher initial costs and often requires a 10–20 percent down payment with interest rates set by current bank regulations. The initial cost of a new home is set, and an offer at a few thousand dollars less will be met with rejection or even laughter from the salesperson. A new home is not equipped with all of the appliances that will be needed, for example, a washer and dryer, and purchasing new appliances may also mean paying extra for extended warranties. Another initial cost could be upgrading any standard feature that comes with the home, including carpeting or even paint and roofing materials. A new home may be sold with standard landscaping that includes leveling the yard, seeding the lawn, and planting one or two trees, but the buyers may find that they have to spend additional money in the beginning for landscaping.

second point of contrast item #1 discussed	4	**Once the house is purchased, the costs do not end. There are still payments to be made each month.** Buying a "fix-up" house means that payments are less than they would have been had the home been purchased new at the current house prices. In addition to house payments, owners of "fix-up" homes often need to spend money on major renovations, such as restoration of walls or replacement of plumbing lines. Remodeling, however, is done to please the owners, and they can often save money by doing the work themselves or getting several bids to keep costs down. Another cost would be taxes, but they may be lower on a "fix-up" home.
second point of contrast item #2 discussed	5	**In contrast,** when a new home is purchased, house payments are generally higher by at least 10–15 percent over house payments for "fix-up" homes, which might amount to several hundred dollars. However, owners of new homes seldom need to spend additional money repairing fixtures or appliances for the first five to six years, nor do they usually spend money altering the structure of the new home. Buyers of brand new homes do spend money decorating their homes; however, the decorating is not so extensive or so expensive as the remodeling that is needed in a "fix-up" home. Owners of new homes also pay taxes, which may be higher than the taxes on a "fix-up" home.
third point of contrast item #1 discussed	6	**Though there are many costs, these homes also represent a return to buyers because they both appreciate in value within a certain time frame and they both bring satisfaction.** A "fix-up" house, especially an ugly duckling among swans, can appreciate rapidly following, repairs. If the home is bought at half the going price of the surrounding homes, it can equal or surpass the other homes within a year. Owners of "fix-up" homes often need to spend months cleaning up and fixing both the interior and exterior of their new home but are able to give the home a distinct personality that is its own.
third point of contrast item #2 discussed	7	**During the same time frame,** a new home will appreciate slowly at the same rate as the other homes in the neighborhood. The home is bought at the same price as the other homes in the neighborhood, and its value will not change substantially unless it is abused. Buyers of brand new homes are often pleased with their home when they move in and can enjoy it immediately. They do need to spend time and money, though, getting a lawn started and caring for the outside of the home.
concluding paragraph brief reference to similarity	8	Both types of homes are available in a wide range of sizes, styles, and locations that appeal to many people. Some people enjoy spending their spare time working on their homes, whereas others do not. Whether buying a new home or a "fix-up" home, all new homeowners can feel a sense of pride in their investment. And, like Jason and Jennifer, they have an ideal place to raise a family.

Items Discussed in Two Distinct Parts Within Each Paragraph

1. The introductory paragraph previews major differences (with brief reference to a major similarity) *or* previews major similarities (with brief reference to a major difference).

2. Support paragraphs include points of contrast (or comparison) in an alternating pattern.

First point
> Paragraph 1: Item #1 (fix-up homes)
> > Item #2 (new homes)

Second point
> Paragraph 2: Item #1
> > Item #2

Third point
> Paragraph 3: Item #1
> > Item #2

Fourth point (if needed)
> Paragraph 4: Item #1
> > Item #2

3. The concluding paragraph reemphasizes major differences (with a brief reference to a major similarity referred to in the introduction) *or* reemphasizes major similarities (with a brief reference to a major difference referred to in the introduction).

Saving Money on a New Home

hook

1   Jason and Jennifer had been married for two years when they decided that they were ready to start a family. But they decided that they should buy a house before they had children. On their combined income of $42,000 a year, they felt they could afford a home of their own. After they contacted a real estate agent and read articles about home buying, they narrowed their options to buying a new home or a "fix-up" home. The decision would be difficult because both options would result in an investment with a guaranteed return. As many other Americans have learned, the initial money invested, the continual costs, and the return for the investment would vary according to the option selected.

brief reference to
similarity
thesis sentence

first point of contrast
item #1 discussed

2   **Probably the most marked difference between buying a new home and a "fix-up" home is the initial costs involved.** A "fix-up" home does not always have a fixed down payment and sometimes can be purchased at the rate of interest paid by the previous homeowners. The cost of a "fix-up" home is set by the current homeowner, but many times an offer of a few thousand dollars less will be accepted. A "fix-up" home is often sold "as is" with an opportunity for the buyer to check everything out before signing the closing papers. Anything that is defective can be negotiated to be repaired or to lower the cost to the buyer. Anything that breaks after the final papers are signed, though, becomes the responsibility of the new owner. A "fix-up" home often needs landscaping but usually has grass, shrubs, and trees that are already established. **On the other hand,** a new home has higher initial costs and often requires a 10–20 percent down payment with interest rates set by current bank regulations. The initial cost of a new home is set, and an offer at a few thousand dollars less will be met with rejection or even laughter

item #2 discussed

from the salesperson. A new home is not equipped with all of the appliances that will be needed, for example, a washer and dryer, and purchasing new appliances may also mean paying extra for extended warranties. Another initial cost could be upgrading any standard feature that comes with the home, including carpeting or even paint and roofing materials. A new home may be sold with a standard landscaping that includes leveling the yard, seeding the lawn, and planting one or two trees, but the buyers may find that they have to spend additional money in the beginning for landscaping.

second point of contrast

item #1 discussed

3 **Once the house is purchased, the costs do not end. There are still payments to be made each month.** Buying a "fix-up" house means that payments are less than they would have been had the home been purchased new at the current house prices. In addition to house payments, owners of "fix-up" homes often need to spend money on major renovations, such as restoration of walls or replacement of plumbing lines. Remodeling, however, is done to please the owners, and they can often save money by doing the work themselves or getting several bids to keep costs down. Another cost would be taxes, but they may be lower on a "fix-up" home. **In contrast,** when a new home is purchased, house payments are generally higher by at least 10–15 percent over house payments for "fix-up" homes, which might amount to several hundred dollars. However, owners of new homes seldom need to spend additional money repairing fixtures or appliances for the first five to six years, nor do they usually spend money altering the structure of the new home. Buyers of brand new homes do spend money decorating their homes; however, the decorating is not so extensive or so expensive as the remodeling that is needed in a "fix-up" home. Owners of new homes also pay taxes, which may be higher than the taxes on a "fix-up" home.

item #2 discussed

third point of contrast

4 **Though there are many costs, these homes also represent a return to buyers because they both appreciate in value within a certain time frame and they both bring satisfaction.** A "fix-up" house, especially an ugly duckling among swans, can appreciate rapidly, following repairs. If the home is bought at half the going price of the surrounding homes, it can equal or surpass the other homes within a year. Owners of "fix-up" homes often need to spend months cleaning up and fixing both the interior and exterior of their new home but are able to give the home a distinct personality that is its own. **During the same time frame,** a new home will appreciate slowly at the same time as the other homes in the neighborhood. The home is bought at the same price as the other homes in the neighborhood, and its value will not change substantially unless it is abused. Buyers of brand new homes are often pleased with their home when they move in and can enjoy it immediately. They do need to spend time and money, though, getting a lawn started and caring for the outside of the home.

item #1 discussed

item #2 discussed

concluding paragraph

brief reference to similarity

5 Both types of homes are available in a wide range of sizes, styles, and locations that appeal to many people. Some people enjoy spending their spare time working on their homes, whereas others do not. Whether buying a new home or a "fix-up" home, all new homeowners can feel a sense of pride in their investment. And, like Jason and Jennifer, they have an ideal place to raise a family.

Items Discussed in Alternate Sentences Within Each Paragraph

1. The introductory paragraph previews major differences (with brief reference to a major similarity) *or* previews major similarities (with brief reference to a major difference).

2. Support paragraphs include points of contrast (or comparison) in an alternating pattern.

   First point
   > Paragraph 1: Item #1 (fix-up homes)
   >   Item #2 (new homes)
   >   Item #1
   >   Item #2

   Second point
   > Paragraph 2: Item #1
   >   Item #2
   >   Item #1
   >   Item #2

   Third point
   > Paragraph 3: Item #1
   >   Item #2
   >   Item #1
   >   Item #2

   Fourth point (if needed)
   > Paragraph 4: Item #1
   >   Item #2
   >   Item #1
   >   Item #2

3. The concluding paragraph reemphasizes major differences (with a brief reference to major similarity referred to in the introduction) *or* reemphasizes major similarities (with a brief reference to a major difference referred to in the introduction).

Saving Money on a New Home

hook

1 Jason and Jennifer had been married for two years when they decided that they were ready to start a family. But they decided that they should buy a house before they had children. On their combined income of $42,000 a year, they felt they could afford a home of their own. After they contacted a real estate agency and read articles about home buying, they narrowed their options to buying a new home or a "fix-up" home. The decision would be

brief reference to similarity

thesis sentence

difficult because both options would result in an investment with a guaranteed return. As many other Americans have learned, the initial money invested, the continual costs, and the return for the investment would vary according to the option selected.

first point of contrast

item #1 discussed

item #2 discussed

2 **Probably the most marked difference between buying a new home and a "fix-up" home is the initial costs involved.** A "fix-up" home does not always have a fixed down payment and sometimes can be purchased at the rate of interest paid by the previous homeowners. A new home has higher

initial costs and often requires a 10–20 percent down payment with interest rates set by current bank regulations. The cost of a "fix-up" home is set by the current homeowner, but many times an offer of a few thousand dollars less will be accepted. The initial cost of a new home is set, and an offer at a few thousand dollars less will be met with rejection or even laughter from the salesperson. A "fix-up" home is often sold "as is" with an opportunity for the buyer to check everything out before signing the closing papers. Anything that is defective can be negotiated to be repaired or to lower the cost to the buyer. Anything that breaks after the final papers are signed, though, becomes the responsibility of the new owner. A new home is not equipped with all of the appliances that will be needed, for example, a washer and dryer, and purchasing new appliances may also mean paying extra for extended warranties. Another initial cost could be upgrading any standard feature that comes with the home, including carpeting or even paint or roofing materials. A "fix-up" home often needs landscaping but usually has grass, shrubs, and trees that are already established. A new home may be sold with standard landscaping that includes leveling the yard, seeding the lawn, and planting one or two trees, but the buyers may find that they have to spend additional money in the beginning for landscaping.

3   **Once the house is purchased, the costs do not end. There are still payments to be made each month.** Buying a "fix-up" house means that payments are less than they would have been had the home been purchased new at the current house prices. When a new home is purchased, house payments are generally higher by at least 10–15 percent over house payments for "fix-up" homes, which might amount to several hundred dollars. In addition to house payments, owners of "fix-up" homes often need to spend money on major renovations, such as restoration of walls or replacement of plumbing lines. Remodeling, however, is done to please the owners, and they can often save money by doing the work themselves or getting several bids to keep costs down. However, owners of new homes seldom need to spend additional money repairing fixtures or appliances for the first five to six years, nor do they usually spend money altering the structure of the new home. Buyers of brand new homes do spend money decorating their homes; however, the decorating is not so extensive or so expensive as the remodeling that is needed in a "fix-up" home. Another cost would be taxes, but they may be lower on a "fix-up" home. Owners of new homes also pay taxes, which may be higher than the taxes on a "fix-up" home.

4   **Though there are many costs, these homes also represent a return to buyers because they both appreciate in value within a certain time frame and both bring satisfaction.** A "fix-up" house, especially an ugly duckling among swans, can appreciate rapidly, following repairs. If the home is bought at half the going price of the surrounding homes, it can equal or surpass the other homes within a year. A new home will appreciate slowly at the same rate as the other homes in the neighborhood. The home is bought at the same price as the other homes in the neighborhood, and its value will not change substantially unless it is abused. Owners of "fix-up" homes often need to spend months cleaning up and fixing both the interior and exterior

(margin annotations:)

item #1 discussed

item #2 discussed

item #1 discussed

item #2 discussed

item #1 discussed
item #2 discussed

second point of contrast
item #1 discussed

item #2 discussed

item #1 discussed

item #2 discussed

item #1 discussed
item #2 discussed

third point of contrast

item #1 discussed

item #2 discussed

item #1 discussed

item #2 discussed

of their new home but are able to give the home a distinct personality that is its own. Buyers of brand new homes are often pleased with their home when they move in and can enjoy it immediately. They do need to spend time and money, though, getting a lawn started and caring for the outside of the home.

concluding paragraph

brief reference to
similarity

5   Both types of homes are available in a wide range of sizes, styles, and locations that appeal to many people. Some people enjoy spending their spare time working on their homes, whereas others do not. Whether buying a new home or a "fix-up" home, all new homeowners can feel a sense of pride in their investment. And, like Jason and Jennifer, they have an ideal place to raise a family.

The previous patterns reflect a paper that is primarily a contrast. A *comparison* paper would also follow one of the same patterns; however, it would begin and end with differences, and the support paragraphs would *focus on similarities*.

WRITING ASSIGNMENT

Write an essay developed through comparison/contrast. Using the list below, decide what two specific items you plan to compare or contrast. During revision and editing, refer to the checklist in the inside back cover.

1. Show how two holidays are alike or different.
2. Show how physical and mental abuse are alike or different.
3. Show how a vacation in the city and a vacation at a national park are alike or different.
4. Show how a living pet and a stuffed animal are alike or different to a child.
5. Show how two children are alike or different.
6. Show how competitive swimming and football are alike or different.
7. Show how owning an old car or owning a new car are alike or different.

Classification

Another method of organizing information is called classification. **Classification** means grouping objects, people, or events on the basis of similarities or characteristics they have in common. Each of the groups formed on this basis would be a *category*.

For example, if you wanted to open a small clothing store, it would be much easier for your customers to find what they wanted to buy if items were first grouped in logical categories. Your customers would understand categories like children's clothing, women's clothing, and men's clothing. If you did not form these categories or groups, your customers would have to hunt for a boy's shirt among dresses, men's shirts, ties, or women's shoes — and go searching on and on for what they needed to buy. One way, then, to *classify* the items in the store would be by the age and/or sex of the people the clothing is appropriate for. Other logical categories within each of these groups would be underwear and sportswear. By providing your customers with logical categories or groups of items, they could find their way around and you could manage the store better.

Classification can be a useful way of presenting information clearly, but it is not really new for you. When you learned to group the items in your brainstorming, you were also classifying them into groups that have characteristics in common. Classifying and grouping, then, are two words for the same kind of thinking.

The *purpose* for classifying items in a paragraph or an essay works in two ways. First, classification can help you, as the writer, clarify for yourself and explain in writing what many separate items have in common. Second, your reader can in turn better understand the information you are presenting.

One important point to remember about classification, however, is that it is a way of thinking about *similar* characteristics of objects or people or events. The items within each category should have many characteristics in common if the groups are to be useful in your writing. The categories, however, should not ignore so many differences that the groups become illogical.

The *topic* for a classification paper is any group of things that have characteristics in common and can be put into categories. You can classify people by age, sex, occupation, and interests. You can classify cities by size or location. You can classify schools by size or types of programs.

Here are the distinct parts of a classification paper:

1. The introduction contains the thesis sentence, which includes the categories to be discussed in the essay and establishes the basis for the classification.

2. Each support paragraph discusses a separate category established in the introduction. (Each paragraph explains how the items in each category are alike. Each paragraph may also explain how each category is different from the other categories rather than having the reader figure out what the differences are.)

3. The conclusion reaffirms the categories established in the thesis sentence.

The following essay shows how *classification* has been used to organize the information needed by someone who is going to buy a house for the first time.

Buying a House for the First Time

hook

1   Why in the world do so many people every year want to buy a home? Why do they want to take on the often difficult-to-reach goals of paying for and maintaining their own homes? Well, the answers are related to "being a success" or "having a real part of the American Dream" or "always wanting to own a home of their own." Whatever the reasons are at the beginning, people thinking about buying a home for the first time usually begin to try to find out what kinds are available and how much they cost. If they know very little about real estate, they may soon become overwhelmed by the whole

transition

thesis sentence

process. If they start with some basic knowledge, however, they can find the process of buying a home to be fun and educational. The basic knowledge that the first-time buyer should have is an understanding of the three main categories of homes available for purchase — town houses, condominiums, and single-family residences.

support paragraph 1; discusses category #1

2   When a young person or a young couple starts thinking of buying a home, the idea of owning a town house seems appealing. Town houses are places of residence where the owner buys not only the building but also the land the building sits on. They are not like houses, though, because there is usually only a very small patio or terrace or courtyard that goes with the building. Some town houses may have only a small plot of ground for a little flower garden by the front door. If there is a community pool or TV satellite dish, it is usually there when a person purchases the town house. Town-house owners do not have to belong to an association that requires fees and monthly meetings. In size, town houses can be as small or as large as other medium-sized houses. They can contain a living and/or dining room, one or more bedrooms, a kitchen, and various storage areas like closets and cupboards. In one way, having a town house can seem like being in an apartment, but the town-house buyer owns the property, is responsible for its upkeep, and has a solid, long-term investment.

support paragraph 2; discusses category #2

3   The first-time buyer might also consider currently popular residences called condominiums. The condominium owner buys the building walls, floors, and ceilings but, unlike the town-house buyer, does not own the land the building sits on. In contrast to owning a town house, owning a condo, as they are frequently called, means that the owner must belong to an association that requires monthly fees for exterior maintenance and for the support of group recreational facilities, such as a pool or tennis or racquetball courts. If the association does not own a pool or a TV satellite dish, the members must vote on the purchase of these items, which then belong to the association rather than to an individual owner. The owner of the condo does not have any exterior piece of ground for flowers or a small yard. Instead, the condo may be one of several built like apartments in a high rise. Although there is no beautiful yard around their individual home, condo owners may still find that living in a condominium is also a glamorous, carefree life that provides a long-term investment and pride of ownership.

support paragraph 3; discusses category #3

4   The third option a first-time buyer may consider is a single-family residence because, in most cases, it provides a feeling of more privacy and space for the money invested. Buying a single-family residence means buying the land under and around the house as well as the house itself. Decisions like putting in a swimming pool or a TV satellite dish are made by the individual home-owner, who would then own them. A single-family residence includes a living room, a dining room, perhaps a family room, as many bedrooms as the owner needs or can afford, a kitchen, and various storage areas including either a carport or a garage. The house can be as large as the owner wishes. The owner of this type of house does not belong to an association requiring fees for upkeep. Rather s/he is responsible for maintaining the yard as well as any other purchased land surrounding the house. S/he may have more responsibilities than the owner of a town house or condominium, but s/he enjoys more privacy and space.

concluding paragraph

5   When the first-time home buyer finally decides to go house shopping, knowing the basic kinds of homes available will make the process easier and less frustrating. Regardless of what the outcome is — town house, condominium, or single-family residence — the new owner will have made an informed decision.

Write an essay developed through classification. Classify and explain one of the following. During revision and editing, refer to the checklist in the inside back cover.

1. Types of transportation for the elderly
2. Types of transportation in the city
3. Types of transportation in the country
4. Types of pets
5. Special uses for pets
6. Types of activities to keep children busy
7. Sports activities for children
8. Sports activities for handicapped adults
9. Sports activities for college students
10. Sports activities for people who work

Definition

Your *purpose* in writing a **definition** paper is to explain what you mean by a certain word or concept that could have more than one meaning. When you establish the definition in the beginning of the paper, the reader understands how your definition is different from those of others. You want the reader to understand your definition, which is based on your own experiences or thoughts.

In your college courses, you will need to write definitions that are primarily objective and based on a dictionary meaning. You may also be asked to write definitions that are subjective or based on your own feelings or experiences. These two types of definitions, with which you need to be familiar, are *denotation* and *connotation*.

The **denotation** of a word is a *general, objective definition* that might be found in a dictionary or in a science class like biology or chemistry.

A house is a building used as a place to live by one or more people.

An apple is the fruit of any *Pyres malus* tree.

The **connotation** of a word is a more *subjective, emotional definition* of a word or concept whose meaning may differ among people. To one person, an ''educated person'' might be someone who has read the *Encyclopaedia Britannica* from A to Z. But, certainly, few people would agree with this definition, and this definition would not exist in the dictionary. Another person might consider an ''educated person'' to be someone who has a degree from a university, and someone else might consider an ''educated person'' one who has acquired knowledge through experimentation and experience. It would be your job, as the writer, to let the reader know what your definition of ''educated person'' is. If you were to write an essay defining ''educated person,'' here is a possible thesis sentence: ''An educated person is one who has attained knowledge through study, experimentation, and experience and is able to relate it to other people.''

The *subject* for a definition paper, then, is any word or concept that has or can have more than one definition.

Here are the distinct parts of a definition paper:

1. The introduction gives the denotation of a word and your own personal connotation of the word. (This connotation either limits the denotation or extends the denotation.)

2. Support paragraphs contain example(s) that clearly show the difference between the denotation and connotation of the word. (The emphasis is placed on the connotation because this clarifies the writer's definition.)

3. The conclusion reinforces the distinction between the denotation and connotation of the word or concept.

The following essay develops a definition of the word ''home.'' It includes both the denotation and the connotation of the word.

A Home

denotation

1   When many people think about a home, they think about the physical place where they live. This definition restricts a home to a mere physical setting where people reside. Those who consider a home to be a place filled with possessions used solely to impress other people become ''married to their home'' and forget that a home should be a place where they can retreat from the pressures in life. A home is more than just a place in which to dwell.

connotation

Instead, it is a physical place with a psychological feeling that allows a person or people to feel comfortable and safe from the outside world, whether they live in a hogan or in the house next door. This place allows people to enjoy life by themselves or with other members of their family.

2   All members of a family should feel they belong in a home and are free to do the things they enjoy. A home is not a place where the children are forbidden to go into the living room for fear they will mess things up or where they are unable to play with their toys anywhere except in their own rooms.

examples that emphasize what a home is **not**

Nor is it a place where children are always asked to play outside or at a neighbor's home. Rather, it is a place where people are able to do the things that they enjoy doing, whether working on a model airplane or painting on canvas. A home is not a residence with gold-plated bathroom fixtures that no one is allowed to touch. This is not to say that the home cannot be expensive or that it should become a pigpen. Members of a home learn to take care of their sanctuary and treat it with great love and respect.

3   Some Native Americans living on reservations in the Southwest still live in the most cherished homes of all — hogans. Because the hogan has only one room, all activities center in this room. Here the family members cook, converse with each other, and enjoy life with one another. They are protected from the outside world and find safety around a warm stove. When evening comes, they spread their thick blankets on the floor and sleep close to one another. There is great love and camaraderie in this one room that is home. Though the physical surroundings are limited, the psychological feeling of

specific example of a home

spaciousness exists, and the family members experience a harmony with the natural world.

example of an ideal home

4   Sometimes the house right next door is a wonderful home because it is more than just a physical structure. Whenever there are family gatherings, everyone prefers to go to this home. The children are provided with art items and are allowed to cut, paste, and paint to create anything they wish. Their efforts never go unnoticed and are rewarded with praise. When they finish, they clean everything up and then head for the pool table. The smell of food is present as the adults cook, play cards, and share parts of each other's lives. Someone who drives by the home might say that it is an ordinary home in a middle-class neighborhood, but this home is anything but ordinary. The remarkable part of this home is not the physical boundaries but the psychological freedom that provides the love and concern that seem to be everywhere.

conclusion that reinforces distinction between denotation and connotation

5   A home is not just a physical structure where people reside, but rather it is also a place where people feel comfortable and can enjoy doing "their own thing." Here they experience freedom and security in their own sanctuary.

WRITING ASSIGNMENT

Write an essay developed through definition. Show how your meaning is different from the dictionary meaning for one of the following words. During revision and editing, refer to the checklist in the inside back cover.

1. Discipline
2. Loyalty
3. Religion
4. Brother/sister
5. Creativity
6. Beauty
7. Sincerity

Cause/Effect Analysis

This may be the first time you see or hear the term **cause/effect analysis**; however, you use this type of reasoning every day. You get up in the morning and may ask yourself, "Why does it have to rain today of all days?" If your car doesn't start, you mentally question, "I wonder why it isn't starting?" As you rush through traffic, an unconscious thought may be, "Why do I live in such a busy city?" You may also think about the effects of these events: "What will happen next because it is raining?" "What are the results of my having a stalled car?" "What are the effects of my living in such a busy city?" Almost everyone instinctively analyzes day-to-day problems to find the causes and effects. This type of reasoning is similar to the kind of thinking you will do when you write a cause/effect paper. The *purpose*, then, is to explain causes or effects of something that happens.

The *topic* for a cause/effect analysis is any event or occurrence for which you want to find all the causes or effects. For example, if you want to build a custom home, you might want to examine the underlying reasons. Your examination will show that some causes uncover other causes. At times, reasons can be hidden, so when you are analyzing a complex question, spend time seeking all the reasons. Careful thinking and brainstorming will pay off. If you want to examine the effects of an event, you must also do thorough thinking and brainstorming.

For a causal analysis paper, the *thesis sentence* can start as a question but must be in statement form when you draft your paper. For instance, if you want to write an analysis of the causes for the subject "why build a custom home," the thesis sentence, to start with, could be "Why would anyone want to build a custom home?"

Next, *gather information* to help you discuss and explain the reasons discovered in your brainstorming. In your paper, you want to provide your reader with examples, statistics if needed, and authoritative verification of the causes. Then, *draft your paper.*

The pattern of *organization* for a cause/effect paper follows:

1. The introductory paragraph summarizes the causes (or effects) of the subject being analyzed.

2. Support paragraphs clearly explain the causes (or effects) of the event or occurrence being analyzed. (Each support paragraph usually explains one cause or one effect.)

3. The concluding paragraph reinforces the main idea.

For the purpose of illustration, only causal analysis will be shown here. For an example of an essay that discusses *effects*, see the model essay "Parenting: Singular" on page 388.

To Build or Not to Build

hook   1   Building permits, water and sewer taps, architectural drawings, delayed schedules, construction mishaps, and disreputable builders are a few horrors that race through a person's mind when thinking of building a house. Those who have never tried it would probably hesitate or at best think it over for several days. Some people who have dared to build their own homes swear that they would never do it again. So then, why is it that some still choose to enter into this uncelebrated, unfamiliar experience? The reasons vary, but the common ones are that building a home may be a necessity, may have a financial advantage, and can provide personal satisfaction in a unique design.

transition
thesis sentence

necessity   2   In some cases, one major cause, necessity, underlies the decision to build one's own home. Unless people have beautiful property and plenty of money, they purchase a preconstructed home when they are in the market for a house. However, when the housing market does not offer the house they want or need, then potential buyers may be forced to construct the house for themselves. For instance, if one is moving to a small town where land is reasonable and the housing market is poor, building is the only choice. Or if a family has a special need like four baths or a walk-out basement for a business, there is no alternative but to build. If a person wants to move into a certain area where the choice of homes is limited, then construction of a custom home becomes unavoidable.

financial causes

3   Another important reason for building a home may be financial. Building a home keeps an owner from paying a large real-estate commission. Currently, a real estate commission is 7 percent, so if someone buys a ready-made $70,000 home, the buyer will be paying close to $5,000 in real-estate fees. Also, a prospective home builder has some flexible control over the total cost of the construction. "Sweat equity" is a term that means that the home-owner and the home builder enter into a partnership in which the owner can do some of the labor to defray costs. Painting, tiling, landscaping, or any labor the owner chooses can be done on weekends to save dollars. In the same way, if the builders have plenty of time and flexible taste, they can find bargains for lumber, concrete, appliances, carpet, or any other major items. The buyers have no control over most of these items in an already-constructed house. More control over finances can be a significant underlying reason for deciding in favor of building a home instead of purchasing a preconstructed home.

personal/psychological causes

4   Other important reasons for building a home are psychological. The challenge of accomplishing a major project can bring a person satisfaction when the job is completed. Also, the prospective home builders feel as though they are the creators of the home and immediately take on the pride of ownership. Because they have a better idea of the struggle and time that went into the home, they have a deep sense of appreciation. Another emotion that might cause a person to build a home is obtaining a sense of individualism. Because the homeowner-builders have the opportunity to create and change the floor plan, they know that no other home exists that is exactly like their own. To those people who feel strongly about having a unique design, this motive may be a very strong incentive for building. Even though emotional causes may not be very obvious at first, they are usually very strong influencing forces.

conclusion

5   A person's home is an extremely important place. It represents not only shelter but personal tastes and satisfactions. It is also the most valuable item a person ever owns. Deciding to build this valuable possession can be frightening and frustrating. Many people would never choose to take on such a major responsibility and task. However, some people are forced into the decision and find that there are advantages. Financial benefits, an opportunity to exhibit creativity, and a deep enjoyment and satisfaction in having a unique design can cause people to undertake this creative and satisfying project.

WRITING ASSIGNMENT

Write an essay developed through cause/effect analysis on one of the following topics. During revision and editing, refer to the checklist in the inside back cover.

1. Why we have funerals
2. Results of a particular disappointment
3. Reasons for being successful in an activity

4. Results of being successful in an activity
5. Reasons people get a divorce
6. Reasons cities levy taxes
7. Reasons the state government or federal government levies taxes
8. Impact (effects) of taxes on citizens
9. Reasons people change jobs
10. Reasons young people move away from parents
11. Effects of moving away from parents

■ Process Analysis

Many times in your life, both in and out of school, you are going to be asked to explain how something is done or how to do something. How well you handle this request will depend on how clearly you can sort out the steps of a process or procedure and present them in a clear, logical way. Your audience, whether listening to you or reading your explanation, needs to be able to understand your information clearly and, if necessary, follow your directions precisely. The easiest way to practice these skills is to think through and write a **process** essay.

The *purpose* of a process essay is to tell how to do something (give a set of directions) or how something occurs or how something works.

These are important skills in school because your instructors expect you to show how well you understand basic concepts in your classes. Sometimes they want you to demonstrate that you can do something, telling on paper how to go through a particular procedure if that skill is part of your learning in the class. You could be asked to write about a variety of *topics*. For example, you may be asked in your environmental-geology class to explain the process of topsoil erosion in the West. Your history professor may ask you to explain how a tax bill becomes law in the U.S. Congress. Your automotive-technology professor may ask you to explain how to overhaul a carburetor.

These kinds of thinking and writing skills are also important in the world outside of school. In the business world, you could not become a supervisor, a manager, or a director if you could not understand and explain how processes work and be able to explain them to someone else. You might be asked to explain a procedure to a superior or to someone under you. For example, if a vice-president asked you to make a presentation to new employees summarizing how your department works within the entire operation of the company, you would be able to do that if you had practiced these kinds of thinking and writing skills beforehand. Or, if you were responsible for training new employees, you would be able to explain clearly and logically what they should do by giving them clear directions to follow. You might even be so good at this that you could become the head of an entire department devoted to training.

Regardless of what the project or assignment is, before you start, be sure you know the parts of the process you are going to explain. You know the process because you have either read about it or you have done the process yourself. Most of the time, there is no substitute for firsthand information, information gained from your own hands-on experience. Being able to explain a process or give directions means that you must first break down the process into steps to be sure you understand all that is involved and to see which steps are most important. Breaking down the process or procedure into steps also helps you to decide the best order to put them in to explain them clearly. Again, you will not be able to explain anything that you do not know thoroughly.

Be prepared to do some careful thinking to get the information in clear, logical order and write a paper that can be understood easily. As for any kind of paper, producing a process paper follows a series of steps. The following discussion pertains to explaining how to do something.

Decide the purpose of the essay.

Brainstorm or **list the steps** as they occur to you.

Rearrange the list in the order in which the steps must be done.

Draft your paper, using command verbs.

With respect to the essay's purpose, decide what you want the reader to understand clearly. The reader should be able to follow the steps you explain and undertake the project you are giving directions for. The reader should know what to do to get the desired results. If your topic were "remodeling a kitchen," then your reader should learn how to make an efficient, new kitchen with new appliances—carefully and professionally done.

Looking at the rearranged list, begin thinking about drafting support paragraphs for your main idea. Write a *topic sentence* for each major step, and use command verbs to tell the reader clearly what to do at each stage of the process. You will stay on track, and your reader can follow you clearly. Obviously, the number of topic sentences you write will also be the number of support paragraphs for your paper.

Here is the pattern of *organization* for this kind of process paper:

1. The introduction clearly states that this paper will give directions for doing something.

2. Support paragraphs guide the reader step-by-step through the process. (Each paragraph is a separate step.)

3. The concluding paragraph completes the process.

The following essay shows the steps that can be followed to remodel a kitchen.

How to Remodel Your Kitchen

hook

1   After several years of living in the same house, people find that remodeling must be done if the house is to be kept in "livable" condition. The one room that many people decide to remodel first is the kitchen. Many times all the appliances go at once: the refrigerator leaks when it defrosts; the dishwasher does not get the dishes clean; the thermostat in the oven does not work; and

transition

thesis sentence

the garbage disposal quit years ago. The kitchen suddenly seems too small for the family. It is time to remodel. Remodeling to have the kitchen of your dreams can be done without disappointments if you follow some simple steps.

first major step

2   Before you do anything else, **gather information from all available sources**. Purchase a book on kitchen remodeling or go to the library to check out a book or gather magazine articles on the subject. Take a class on remodeling a kitchen. One very valuable resource is stores that specialize in custom kitchen cabinets. Talk to the people at the stores' showrooms. Remember, though, you are still gathering information at this time, so do not sign any contracts. Another excellent source for getting ideas is to look at model homes, so look at as many as possible. Also talk to friends who have remodeled their kitchens recently. Ask them for their ideas or biggest regrets. Profiting from other people's mistakes can often be valuable. When you feel you know everything about kitchens, move on to the next step.

second major step

3   This next step is to **decide on exactly which new appliances to buy**. Usually stoves, refrigerators, and dishwashers are replaced. Decide if you want a built-in stove or a drop-in stove. Also consider a range top built into an island and an oven and microwave built into the wall. Because refrigerators come in many sizes and varieties, choose the size and brand you plan to buy before you go on. Also, consider whether or not you want it built into the wall. After looking at the different kinds of dishwashers available, choose one that will not only clean the dishes well, but is energy-efficient. Get the exact measurements of the stove, refrigerator, and dishwasher you have selected and move on to the next step.

third major step

4   Now the fun begins. **Get a visual idea of your new kitchen.** Buy a package of graph paper and draw the dimensions of your kitchen walls to scale. Be accurate because appliances and cabinets need to fit snugly. Then, using the same scale, cut out a paper representation of each appliance, including the sink. Once this is done, rearrange the appliances on the piece of graph paper, mentally adding possible counter spaces as you go. If you plan to include an island, be sure that the dishwasher door or refrigerator door can swing open easily and that the traffic pattern meets your needs. It could be disastrous if you planned the kitchen so the back door opened into the refrigerator or dishwasher. Also, be sure you have ample counter space near the refrigerator and stove. Then keep shuffling the "puzzle" pieces until you are satisfied with the outcome.

fourth major step

5   Possibly, the least enjoyable but most profitable part comes next: getting the bids and choosing the contractor or subcontractors. **Get bids from at least three different sources.** Of course, if you have one company responsible for all of the remodeling, go to at least three different companies and ask for comparable bids on your scale drawing. If possible, do the subcontracting yourself. Hire your own cabinetmaker, carpenter, electrician, and tile person. The price on any specific job can vary greatly. For instance, three licensed electricians may bid on the needed electrical work. They could bid $1,200, $800, and $400. Before you decide on which bid to take, however, ask for and check out references for their previous jobs, and check with the local registrar of contractors. If possible, look at some work that s/he has done. Though this step is time-consuming, you will be glad that you took the effort to do this evaluation.

conclusion   6   The final step is the simplest. **Sign the contract or subcontracts with the most qualified bidders and relax.** In a matter of weeks, your inadequate kitchen will be transformed into a functional, beautiful kitchen that will be enjoyed by every member of the family. The refrigerator will bring forth ice cubes rather than leak on the floor; the oven will cook without burning; and the dishwasher will get the dishes clean. Ask yourself, "Can I afford to put this off any longer? Is it time to 'go for it'?"

WRITING ASSIGNMENT

Write an essay developed through process analysis. Show how to do one of the following activities successfully. During revision and editing, refer to the checklist in the inside back cover.

1. Eat well.
2. Discipline children.
3. Raise a puppy.
4. Celebrate a holiday.
5. Choose a mate.
6. Put on a play.
7. Keep peace in a family.
8. Prepare for a vacation.
9. Vacation with children.

■ Argumentation

The *purpose* of an **argumentative paper** is to persuade the reader to your way of thinking. Your audience is usually the uncommitted reader, the one who is not strongly committed to one side or the other. You probably would not even attempt to convince a presidential campaign manager to move to the other side in an election. You do not want to alienate anyone who is committed to the other side, but you do want to appeal to someone who is willing to listen to what you have to say. You would try hardest, though, to appeal to the many people from the general population who are uncommitted or not strongly affiliated with the other side.

The *topic* for an argumentative paper must be an issue that has two sides. If your topic involves homes, one side might be that "buying a new home is advantageous to young people" and the other side might be that "owning a foreclosed, 'fix-up' home is the best choice for young people just starting out." After reading and researching, you must decide what your position will be and what the opponent's position will be.

Here are the *distinct parts* of an argumentative paper:

1. The introduction states the writer's position and the opponent's position objectively.

2. Support paragraphs include statistics and authorities in the field to support each point in the argument.

3. The conclusion includes a restatement of the writer's position.

The writer's position and the opponent's position may function as the introductory paragraph for the argumentative paper. The important part to remember is that you as the writer need to be fair in presenting both positions. You may *not* set up the opponent unfairly. Sometimes a writer will deliberately set up a "straw man," or someone presented just so he or she can be knocked down. For instance, you might state your position as "Buying a new home is advantageous to a young couple just starting out." If you state the opponent's position as "Young people who buy new homes right after they start out are greedy and impatient for the good life," you are being unfair and distracting the reader from the real issue. The real issue for the opponent should be that "For young people just starting out, renting a home is more practical than buying a home."

The introduction, then, consists of objectively presenting both the writer's position and the opponent's position (in one or two paragraphs). There is no room to be unfair or to present the introduction from a distorted viewpoint.

Some instructors will require you to preview your main arguments when you state your position in your thesis sentence. Others do not require you to do this. Previewing the main points will help you know in your own mind what your arguments are before you begin the paper.

If you take the position that "buying a 'fix-up' home is advantageous to individuals," you might preview the main points by adding "because it allows them to qualify for a home, to buy a home that appreciates rapidly, and to feel pride in their own creative abilities." This maps out your entire argument, and each paragraph that follows will prove these points.

The next part of the argumentative paper is the support paragraphs. These paragraphs need to persuade the reader that what is presented in the introduction is true. In order to be persuasive, you must avoid using your own opinion anywhere except in stating your own position. Because the thesis sentence (position) is your opinion, the support paragraphs establish that this opinion is valid. You can do this by using statistics or direct quotations from authorities in the field. An authority in the field is someone who has studied the field thoroughly, has received recognition for her/his ideas, and has experience working in the field.

An example of a way to support your position would be to use a quotation like the following: "Used houses cost 15 percent less than comparable new ones." The readers should know that this quotation came from William C. Banks in an article published in *Money* in April 1986. His statement would be considered a credible statistic. If you do not name your source, you could be accused of plagiarism, which means that you have used someone else's ideas as though they were your own.

After you feel you have supported your thesis idea convincingly, you are ready to end your paper. This last part of the argumentative paper is a simple restatement of your position. You have the opportunity to reinforce your opinion (position) given in the thesis sentence.

The following argumentative paper shows how the author has achieved a specific purpose by using arguments to convince the reader to accept the position (opinion) of the writer.

Foreclosed Homes

hook   1   On August 1, 1989, the National Association of Realtors stated that "an index measuring the ability of the typical American family to buy a home fell

opponent's position

in June to its lowest level in three years." They went on to point out that an average family cannot afford to buy a moderately priced home. This is because many people feel the only way to own a home is to buy it new. But in reality, this is not true if people are willing to take advantage of the resources within the community. One of these often unrecognized resources is a foreclosure home. Many foreclosure homes, even if "neglected" or "run-down," can be transformed into attractive, comfortable homes if someone is willing

thesis sentence

to take the time to find one available and is willing to fix it up. These foreclosure homes that often need a little fixing up are advantageous to individuals because they allow them to afford a home, to buy a home that often appreciates rapidly, and to experience independence in ownership and in their creative abilities.

support paragraph 1   2

Many American families who find it almost impossible to buy a new home can often afford a foreclosure home. Individuals who are looking for a home can prequalify for a loan and, in this way, know what their price boundaries are. Individuals who prequalify for a $39,000 mortgage would have a hard

authoritative source

time finding a new home in this price range. Phyllis Booker, a real-estate specialist who has dealt with foreclosure homes for many years, believes that "FHA, VA, and banks who find themselves holding foreclosure homes are not interested in making a profit. They simply want to get the money that is owed to them and then get out." One of Booker's clients was a young man who prequalified for a $42,000 home. With her help, he bid on four foreclosure homes before he was the top bidder on a home and was able to move into one.

support paragraph 2   3

Another way to purchase a foreclosure home is to catch it before the foreclosure papers have gone through. In this way, the prospective buyers can put in a bid and many times can bargain with the owners. Both buyer

authoritative source

and owner stand to gain. An article in the June 1989 issue of the *Reader's Digest* by Sonny Bloch and Grace Lichtenstein gave an example of just such a case. The couple noticed that a home in a nice neighborhood "appeared to

facts

be abandoned." After locating the owners and finding that the home was in preforeclosure, they found that the owner still owed only $17,000 on the home. They offered him "$6,000 in cash in exchange for title to the property." They paid $4,000 in closing costs and assumed the $17,000 unpaid balance. The home was later appraised at $67,000. The house continued to increase in value following repairs. But initially, the buyers were able to purchase the home at 60 percent below its value.

support paragraph 3   4

Once a foreclosure home that is in need of repair is purchased, the appreciation rate can increase rapidly. A home is assessed in line with the other homes in a neighborhood. Therefore, a home that is run-down and in need of repair can often be purchased at a bargain price. According to Susan Givens

statistic and quotation from authoritative source

in an article in *Money*, "You may be able to purchase a dilapidated house for 20 percent to 50 percent below the value it will be after you've put work into it." According to Booker, one of her clients, a single parent, "bought a three-bedroom foreclosed home for $63,000 in a neighborhood where the median home was $85,000." The parent fixed up the house that did not need any major repairs and almost four years later sold the home for $86,000. The appreciation was much greater than it would have been had the woman bought a new home. The bottom line, though, is that she would never have been able to afford an $85,000 home at the time.

support paragraph 4
authoritative source

5   Buying a foreclosure home gives the owner a chance to experience independence through applying creative abilities. In the article "Buying a House That Needs Paint," published in April 1986 by *Money*, William Banks relates the experience of a divorced mother of three who bought a home that needed fixing up. Though the house "lacked space to handle her six-foot-wide grand piano," she purchased it because "she figured that she could enlarge and remodel the house to suit her requirements." He went on to say that she "has

authoritative source

since added . . . a music alcove and library. . . ." In another article that appeared in the August 3, 1987, issue of *U.S. News and World Report*, a Rockford, Ill., interior designer was quoted as saying that "fixing leaky faucets gives me a sense of real independence." Turning something mediocre into something beautiful can build pride not only in owning a home but in a person's ability to accomplish this feat.

concluding paragraph

6   Homes are not out of reach for individuals within our society. With planning and hard work, individuals can own their own homes and turn them into whatever they wish. If people have the discipline to proceed slowly and

restatement of position

methodically, they can afford a home today — maybe not a brand new home but one that can be turned into a beautiful dwelling place that reflects the personality of the owners.

WRITING ASSIGNMENT

Write an essay developed through argument. Persuade a particular audience that:

1. Taxes are necessary.
2. Taxes make people poorer.
3. Divorce is harmful to children.
4. Divorce is good for children.
5. Nursing homes meet the needs of the elderly.
6. Nursing homes do not meet the needs of the elderly.
7. Photo radar should be used by police.
8. Photo radar should not be used by police.
9. Savings accounts should be started when children are young.
10. Mandatory use of seat belts saves lives.
11. Marriage should be abolished.
12. Marriage should be discouraged until both people graduate from college.
13. Custody of children should be given to fathers more often than currently occurs.
14. Custody of children should be equally split between parents.
15. Sex should be reserved for a permanent relationship.

One of the most important skills you need is being able to decide which mode of development is most effective for your topic. The possibilities are as varied as the number of people writing the essays. There is no one correct mode of development. Choose the mode that helps you achieve your purpose and seems the most interesting. Sometimes the assignment specifies the mode; at other times, depending upon your purpose, you will need to think about how the subject can be explained in different ways.

The following list shows how different modes can be used to write about the same subject but with different purposes.

Topic: The Circus

reasons people should not attend a circus: argument

kinds of events at a circus: illustration

types of animals at a circus: classification

types of people at a circus: classification

how to enjoy a circus: process

ways a dog act is different from a tiger act: contrast

Sometimes you can write about a topic by using a combination of several modes within one essay. When your writing project does not specify the pattern of development or organization to be used, you might discover that a blend of patterns will express your ideas more convincingly. The commencement address "Did You Do Your Best?" (in Part 2 of this unit) illustrates how the author achieved his purpose with more than one mode.

Collaborative Project: Working and Learning Together

Read the selection by Dr. Reed, "Did You Do Your Best?" (Part 2 of this unit). Then break into small groups and identify the different modes used in this selection. Be prepared to share your findings with the class.

WRITING ASSIGNMENT

Using the topics given, decide on a particular mode and then develop an essay. Decide what points you want to express. Then choose the method of development that permits you to do this most effectively.

1. Garbage
2. Recycling
3. Historic buildings
4. Movies
5. Custom cars
6. Dates
7. Jobs
8. Gambling
9. Art
10. Investments

After you draft your essay, revise for content and edit for mechanics. Check to see that method (mode) of development is appropriate for topic, purpose, and audience.

Content

   Essay

      Check the introductory paragraph for an effective hook.

      Check for a smooth transition between the hook and thesis.

      Check to be sure the thesis sentence states a clear direction or previews the points to be covered in the paper.

      Check to see that the voice is appropriate for purpose and audience.

   Paragraphs

      Revise so that each has a clear topic sentence that develops an idea suggested in the thesis sentence.

      Include four to six supporting sentences that are developed using short interrelated examples or an extended example.

      Include a closing sentence in each paragraph.

Mechanics

   Check for subject-verb agreement.

   Check for consistent verbs.

   Check for a consistent point of view.

   Check for fragments, run-on sentences, and comma splices.

   Check for correct punctuation.

Sentence variety

   Revise short sentences into compound sentences.

   Revise sentences to include complex sentences.

   Check for coherence between and within paragraphs.

Did You Do Your Best?

James W. Reed, Ph.D., *commencement address given on May 18, 1990, at Glendale Community College's 25th Anniversary*

1   On behalf of the faculty here at Glendale Community College, I want to congratulate each of you this evening on your achievement.

2   While putting this talk together, I began to suffer much the same flight behavior I experienced while writing as an undergraduate. And I found myself doing several of the things I did as a freshman and sophomore — walking back and forth to the refrigerator, tidying my apartment, and looking at *Auto Trader*. Because I've always loved Corvettes — the dream of owning one is probably why I initially enrolled in college — before long my eyes were scanning that section. One ad for a '78 'Vette caught my eye, and I called the owner. As the phone rang, I felt the air blowing through my hair; I smelled the salt air of the surf; and I accelerated out of a curve on Highway 1 south of Carmel, California. Well, we talked for a few minutes. He told me about all the options, including special Indy 500 Pace Car paint. I then asked, "Well, how much do you want for it?" As he gave me the figure, the sleek little car — which was running full throttle across a beautiful suspension bridge — immediately turned into my little red Jeep. I asked the gentleman why he wanted so much, and he simply said, "Don't you understand how special this car is? It's a Silver Anniversary Edition." Today, I want you to know that you're making history. You see, you're GCC's silver anniversary edition as well, and for that reason alone you'll always be a little bit special. Anniversaries make people reflect and reminisce. When you have a chance to look back at your own past, you may understand why it is important to think about what kind of purpose you want for your life and how you work to fulfill that purpose.

3   As faculty, we have recently been looking back to our world twenty-five years ago. Our world's been full of surprising changes. As I sat looking at the silver anniversary pictures, during our celebration several weeks ago, my mind traveled back to that world, a world where we sang about our cars — 409's, GTO's, and little deuce coupes. We could still romanticize with Rock Hudson and Doris Day, and many of us pursued that dream through marriage before ever reaching our twentieth birthday. Terror for us was a memory of a small roadside motel run by Anthony Perkins, which, I might add, made taking a shower a near impossibility for years. We started to see some new attitudes, too. No one over thirty was to be trusted, and people began chanting slogans such as "Black is Beautiful!" Many were admonished for letting their hair grow over their ears and for acting so crazy about John, Paul, George, and Ringo. While some moved in this direction — peace signs, love beads, and turtlenecks — others said goodbye to school, donned military uniforms, and prepared to defend freedom in the tiny and little-known country of Vietnam. That was the world of Glendale Community College twenty-five years ago.

4   That was indeed quite a different world from yours today, one in which television shows arrange dates and people later return telling Chuck every detail — right down to their making love at the end of the evening. In today's world, an unemployed man can scrape together a couple of bucks and win a twenty-million-

dollar jackpot. (We counted on a visit from Michael Anthony.) Or, just think about how Japanese sports cars are everywhere, and the people who drive them are actually proud. We've come a long way, baby, all the way from the world of Donna Reed to that of Roseanne Barr and from "I wanna hold your hand" to "I want your sex."

5   I hesitate to generate any earthshaking contrasts between these two cultures, but if you were to look back at those slides of twenty-five years ago, we were a naive, funny-looking bunch. Hawks and doves alike—we went out into the world to change it, to make it a better place in our own individual way. Reading "Dear Abby" recently (April 29)—I believe in heavy research—I thought I had returned to that era. A St. Cloud University undergraduate wrote the following: "Hundreds upon thousands of men, women, and children die anonymously each and every day in heaps of bloated stomachs and brittle bones for want of food. The industrialized nations continue to belch noxious filth into the air and water of Mother Earth. The rain forests are dying. The oceans are dying." He then moves into the area of racial and class discrimination, talks about the "haves" and "have-nots," and concludes by asking readers to open their eyes regarding future generations. I couldn't help thinking how his message seemed a little out of date, his concern most unlike what I hear from many of you as I move across campus.

6   In order to get a little better handle on just how GCC students view the world, as well as what they plan to do with their future, I began asking several classes questions that addressed their reasons for attending college. Here's what I got. Many want a home—the favorites were Continental Homes at Arrowhead Ranch complete with Paddock Pools and 103 degree Jacuzzis. For cars, I heard the names Lexus, Infiniti, and BMW. There were others equally expensive. For a family, the goal was two to three children enrolled at a preschool. Tickets seemed to be a hot item—season tickets to the Suns, the Phoenix Open, and The Tradition. (I didn't know this one until my poll.) Technology was extremely popular. There was a lot of call—no pun intended—for cellular phones, personal fax machines, modems linking into office computers. Some, believe it or not, can't wait to wear their own beeper. Memberships scored equally high, with the Arrowhead Country Club and the local Rotary ranking highest. As far as recreation goes, a Winnebago, a cabin in Prescott, and a week each year in places like Aspen, Tahoe, and Puerto Vallarta represent the run-of-the-mill answers. Some were not, however, without altruism because quite a few wanted to buy a home for mom and dad in Sun City—two even specified that it be close to Boswell Hospital.

7   I don't doubt for a second that you can have this life-style. You've been exposed to a tremendous learning opportunity. During your days here at GCC, you've written papers—some of them quite good—worked in groups, discussed philosophical concepts, studied the natural and behavioral sciences, and read many of the great books. However, as I talk to many of you, I often feel that the purpose for understanding Maslow's hierarchy of needs has been reduced to simply answering a true-false or essay question—and its application to your lives remains relatively untapped. NO, I'm not going to ask you to join the Peace Corps, go into community legal service, or become a teacher. That was another era. But, I do ask that you reflect the liberal arts education you've been exposed to. There's more to life than earning a living. You serve a higher purpose, I believe, than just to eat, sleep, have sex, and die.

8   When many of us graduated from college, "liberal arts" meant that we were liberated from being a cog in an organizational machine. We stood up straight—

unlike our prehistoric forerunners — we looked around, our minds liberated, and we decided to use our education to do more than forage for food day in and day out. Instead of going into plastics, an offer made to Dustin Hoffman in *The Graduate*, we set out to right the world, *to create positive change*. Some of us even left the United States and went to remote parts of the earth. Now I'm not so sure how well we did. The Hunger Project hasn't been an overwhelming success. We still catch too many dolphins for each tuna, and we continue to make an unforgivable mess of the environment. We committed way too many errors — even though we were well intentioned, and, in the end, I guess many of us have become at least part-time foragers.

9   So where does that leave you? Well, I've got some good news and some bad news. The bad news is — we've got some mighty tall problems, maybe bigger than when we graduated twenty-five years ago. But the good news is — you won't have to leave the area if you want to do something about them. I can't wait to hear the nation's news each morning or read the paper to learn how we Arizonans have distinguished ourselves most recently. I read last week that we graduate fewer individuals from high school than most other states. Imagine that. We're not a dumb lot, though, especially when you consider land acquisitions by elected officials. They seem to know just where and when to make purchases so as to realize tremendous windfall profits. In private industry, we seem to be right in the middle of the savings-and-loan boondoggle. And in the nation's newest "off the record" business — drugs — we rank fourth from the top in cocaine usage.

10   When I told a colleague about my talk, he remarked, "That's not only undignified, it's depressing. I thought you were a motivational speaker." Well, I do motivational speaking, but I see motivation a little differently from most. It's best defined, I believe, as providing someone with a motive to act. If what you've heard here isn't motive, I don't know what is. But frankly, I'm somewhat excited about the future. You are the ones who will be building the homes, arranging the loans, investigating "drive-by" shootings, serving in elected office, and working in our educational system. Whatever your career, you will be involved in the picture, our picture. And you will be called upon to make decisions, *choices*. What will you do?

11   I always turn to philosophers for answers to such questions, and the one I want to turn to this evening is Norda Ramona — that's my mother. As I was getting dressed one morning — while yet in high school — I began to put on a pair of underwear I found on the floor of my bedroom. Not certain if I'd worn them the day before, I yelled to my mother at the other end of the house, "Mama, are these shorts dirty?" She hollered back, "Yes!" At breakfast, I sat across from her wondering how she knew so much — she wasn't even in my room where she could see them. How did she know without even being there whether they were clean or dirty? When I finally asked her this question, she sat up straight, looked at me, and said, "James, if there's ever any question, they're dirty." And that's what I have to say to you this evening. If there's ever any question at all about the choice, it's dirty. You may not be carrying the torch of the sixties, I understand. But you may have an opportunity to carry a few tools home from work. After all, you've been there for five years. Or give someone an unearned grade, maybe fix a smog certificate, mistreat the ones you love, or show a gift to a nonexistent charitable organization on your IRS return. I hope each of these actions would make you pause and ask a question because they're all dirty.

12   A number of years ago, Admiral Rickover was interviewing candidates to head the nuclear submarine program. During a two-hour discussion with one of the officers he asked, "How did you stand in your class at the Naval Academy?" "Sir, I

stood fifty-ninth in a class of 820!" The young officer sat back to wait for the congratulations, but they never came. Instead, the question, "Mr. Carter, did you do your best?" The soon-to-be senior officer of the Sea Wolf gulped and said, "No, sir, I didn't always do my best." Admiral Rickover then shifted in his chair, looked the young Carter in the eyes, and asked one final question: "Why not?"

13   During the time I was reading the Rickover autobiography, I paid a visit to my dentist. When I sat down in his chair, he must have detected my terror — I hate to go there — and began engaging me in a rather long and anxiety-relieving conversation. During our discussion he related that he was a graduate of GCC, and I wouldn't be editorializing too much to say that only a few years ago he was sitting where you are tonight. Finally, needle in hand, he became a man with a purpose. As he drew closer to inject the novacaine, I looked up into his eyes and wondered if he had done his best. Did he attend his classes, do his own work, respond with his own answers, and was he now keeping abreast of the latest techniques? I hoped he wasn't in practice because of a long-term friendship with the State Examiner.

14   As I, along with so many others, look into your eyes tonight, next week, next year — our Silver Anniversary Edition — we ask you the same question. Yes, we want you to have it all, but only if you've gone about it in the right way. We'll no doubt continue to have problems. *However, it's not so much the circumstances that count, but it's how you react to them. We're living in a world where your answer will probably not be heard through your individual expressions but through the community your choices help to create. Only through your making enough of the right choices will we reunite here to celebrate tomorrow's gold.*

15   My colleagues and I congratulate you on being an important part of the GCC tradition. We look forward to the community you will create and to reminiscing with you in 2015. Oh, one final word: *Do your best!*

Understanding Words

Briefly define the following words as they are used in the above essay.

1. reminisce *to call past events to mind*
2. admonished *scolded*
3. naive *innocent, childlike*
4. noxious *harmful, unhealthy, poisonous*
5. altruism *unselfishness*
6. editorializing *expressing an opinion, sometimes inappropriately*

Something to Write About

Write an essay on one of the following questions. Before you draft your essay, however, be sure you have your audience and purpose clearly in mind so that you can select an appropriate mode.

1. What do you plan to accomplish after you graduate from college?
2. What do you think is right with the world today?
3. What do you think is wrong with the world today?
4. What is meant by "underhanded" actions?
5. What makes an effective employee?

6. How does college prepare a person for the future?

7. What do you consider before you have to make a serious decision?

8. Who influences the way people think about what is right and wrong?

9. Are people more or less materialistic than they have been in the past?

10. How have morals changed in the last few years?

After you draft your essay, do each of the following:

Revise it so that it has an effective introduction that includes a hook, a transition, and a thesis sentence.

Be sure that each support paragraph has a strong topic sentence and ample supporting examples.

Check for sentence variety.

Check for unity and a smooth flow of ideas.

Revise to include a strong concluding paragraph.

Check for subject-verb agreement.

Check for consistent verbs.

Check for consistent point of view.

Check for fragments, run-ons, and comma splices.

Check punctuation of compound sentences.

Check punctuation of complex sentences.

PART 3

PARAGRAPHS AND ESSAYS FOR DISCUSSION AND ANALYSIS

■ Illustration

Heroes — "Sung" and "Unsung"

Lorena Acosta, *student*

1   Every nation, every family, every individual has heroes. These people have done something so outstanding that they are admired and respected for their actions. Usually, they have saved a life or lives, or they have done something else that has profoundly affected the beliefs and values of the people who look upon them as heroes. Most of the time these outstanding individuals get wide public recognition for their acts. Sometimes, though, heroic people may not receive any recognition for what they have done. These unrecognized heroes are called the "unsung heroes" of our time. Whether they are publicly acknowledged or not, however, heroes are special people because of their ability to react quickly, calmly, and unselfishly.

2   People who become heroes may have saved someone's life by reacting quickly in circumstances that could lead an ordinary person to freeze or not react in time. Perhaps one of the best illustrations would be a drowning child at the beach or in a swimming pool. The child might be struggling and crying for help or might not be making a sound. A person who can quickly evaluate the situation and dive into the surf or the pool to save the child would certainly be a hero in the eyes of the public. Recently, a five-year-old child jumped into a swimming pool at an apartment complex because he had seen other children doing the same thing. The children at the other end of the pool noticed that he was floating below the surface of the water and quickly pulled him out. The child did not drown or sustain permanent damage because the rescuers were able to see quickly what was happening to the child and, instead of calling out for someone else to help, jumped in and did the job.

3   Sometimes, heroes are those who not only react fast but also calmly under terrifying circumstances. In a 1989 airliner crash landing in Sioux City, Iowa, there were several heroes, one in particular. When the DC-10 crash-landed, it broke apart and caught fire. Although many people died, more than half of the passengers lived. Twenty-five or thirty lived because of one passenger who calmly took charge of one section of the burning plane. Without panic, he helped many people unbuckle their safety belts. He stood calmly and held up out of the way a heavy tangle of cables and wires blocking their way out of the plane. He gave directions to some who could not see because of the smoke, and he had to drop the cables to help some elderly people who fell while trying to get to the opening. After he had them on their feet, he pushed up the cables high enough so the people could get out. Although this hero was one of the "unsung" variety, he certainly deserves the name.

4   The pilot and the crew of the DC-10 described above are prime illustrations of the unselfish hero, who may be the first to deny any heroics. They reacted quickly, calmly, and—most important—unselfishly. They had to fly the large airliner after it had been fatally crippled by a blown engine that had destroyed all the plane's hydraulic systems. While receiving as much help as possible from other

experts and from the controllers at the Sioux City airport, the pilot repeatedly asked for instructions to help him keep the plane away from the city itself. Miraculously, having lived through the crash landing, the pilot said several times afterwards that they were not heroes, having done just what they had to do under the circumstances. From the point of view of many, the public and other professional pilots, getting the plane to the end of the runway was a clear example of calm, unselfish heroism.

5   Whether "sung" or "unsung," special heroes save many lives in America every year. Not all heroes become well known, but they are heroes just the same. Their heroic actions display unselfish actions.

Understanding Words

Briefly define the following word as it is used in the above essay.

1. hydraulic *operated by the force of liquid*

Questions on Content

1. What makes heroes special people?
2. What happened to the five-year-old child who jumped into a swimming pool?
3. What did the hero in paragraph 3 do to save lives?

Questions on Form

1. What mode of development is used in this essay?
2. Where is the thesis sentence?
3. Does paragraph 2 have short interrelated examples or one extended example? Paragraph 3? Paragraph 4?

Comparison/Contrast

Rabbit or Parakeet?

Jason Herrington, *student*

1   There are many people who own either a parakeet or a rabbit (or perhaps both) as a pet, and a new pet owner may wonder which of the two animals makes the better pet. While there are many differences in physical appearance, the care they require, and the rewards an owner would receive from them, both the parakeet and the rabbit make splendid pets.

2   A parakeet and a rabbit show many differences in physical appearance. A parakeet is obviously a bird with wings instead of arms and two spindly legs, each equipped with four long toes used to perch upon a limb. A parakeet has no visible ears and no teeth and must use his beak to crack open seeds. A parakeet is feathered with brightly colored green, red, blue, orange, or purple. In contrast, a rabbit is a mammal with four legs, two short ones in front and two longer ones in back used for hopping. A rabbit has long ears and strong teeth with a double cutting edge on the upper front teeth to cut and grind food. Rabbits are furred in earth-toned colors of white, grey, brown, or black. Because of their physical appearance, it is quite easy to tell the two apart.

3   Because of these physical differences, pet owners should be aware of the differences in care these pets require. Because parakeets are birds, they must be kept in suitable cages with perches and have plenty of room to flutter about. These birds must have a cuttle bone and beak conditioner available to keep their beaks worn down so they can eat properly. Because a parakeet has feathers, its wings must be clipped to keep it from flying away, and special care must be taken when it molts. Rabbits are diggers by nature and must be kept in a cage that reflects this. Wood must be made available for them to gnaw on and to scratch on to keep their teeth and claws worn down. Because a rabbit has fur, it must be brushed and kept clean. Both require care but care in moderation.

4   Finally, the rewards an owner would receive by owning one of these pets also differ. The sweet song of a parakeet on a sunny afternoon has delighted many a parakeet owner. With a little training, a bird can perform tricks on its perch and learn to talk. Rabbits, while they make few noises, are warm and affectionate, and they love contact. With encouragement, rabbits can be housebroken and will hop to meet the owner when called.

5   It is obvious that many differences occur in physical characteristics, the work involved in taking care of these pets, and the satisfaction a person receives by owning them. Yet these differences seem insignificant compared to the fact that both are small animals that make excellent pets for an owner, and they bring love and enjoyment.

Understanding Words

Briefly define the following word as it is used in the above essay.

1. spindly *long and thin*

Questions on Content

1. What physical differences are given between a bird and a rabbit?
2. What keeps a parakeet from flying away?
3. How does a parakeet delight its owner?
4. How does a rabbit delight its owner?

Questions on Form

1. What mode of development is used in this essay?
2. Why doesn't the author state whether a parakeet or a rabbit is a better pet?
3. How does the thesis sentence help the author organize his essay?

Classification

Which One Are You?

Kristi Von Aspen, *student*

1   Midterms! Midterms! Midterms! The mere sound of that word sends chills down most spines. Why? Well, midterms translate into tests and tests require studying—not the most favorable extracurricular activity on a student's agenda.

But no matter what the subject may be, a person acquires certain methods of preparation over the years. I have observed these habits and concluded that there are three major types of students: The Perfectionists, the Naturalists, and the Procrastinators.

2   First of all, the Perfectionists are methodical people. They are always calculating and planning ahead for events in the future. One can usually find them making lists of things to do and then carefully arranging those items into well-thought-out time schedules. For example, if a test is to be given in two weeks and there are 140 pages of material to be covered, the Perfectionist immediately divides the days into the pages. The answer will give him the average number of pages he will need to read each night. There's even a good chance that this person will finish in advance and move on to something else. Perfectionists are high achievers and, on the whole, earn better grades than the other two groups.

3   The second category of students is the carefree spirits I like to call Naturalists. These people possess a casual, happy-go-lucky kind of attitude that reflects in every aspect of their lives. For instance, when it comes to schoolwork, Naturalists study only when it is convenient for them. Their motto is, "If it gets done, it gets done." Don't get me wrong. Most Naturalists do have a conscience; in the back of their minds they know what they have to do, but they do their work in a nonconformist manner. They just refuse to allow academics to dominate their world.

4   Finally, there are the Procrastinators—the obvious choice to discuss last. Waiting until the final hour to study for that big test is one of the main traits of these people. As a result of their postponements, Procrastinators sometimes have to resort to cheating as a means of receiving an acceptable grade. Mothers of these students often have hoarse voices from constantly yelling at their children to do homework. Usually, a person of this nature never learned how to manage time and probably never will. Occasionally, some are able to break out of this rut and begin to lead normal lives.

5   Everyone, at one time or another, has experimented with all three of these studying methods. It's just a matter of discovering what works best for the individual and how to adapt to it. In the meantime, good luck on those midterms!

Understanding Words

Briefly define the following word as it is used in the above essay.

1. procrastinators *people who put off doing something until later*

Questions on Content

1. Who are the methodical people?
2. What characterizes the naturalists?
3. What does a procrastinator sometimes do to pass a test?

Questions on Form

1. What is the basis for the classification, and where is it made clear to the reader?
2. Where does the supporting information come from?
3. Identify a shift in point of view in the conclusion. Does it seem to work in this essay?

Definition

Wealth

Andrea Gonzales, *student*

Wealth is quite often defined as a great quantity or store of money or property of value. However, wealth can be a great quantity of many other things acquired, not just material items. There are those who have had the good fortune to have seen many beautiful places throughout their lives. They have acquired many price-less memories. There is the man who is wealthy because he has many friends who are loyal and true, and to acquire friends like these makes a man rich. Perhaps the most wealthy man of all is the man who has a loving family around him. This alone can bring great happiness, which no amount of money can buy. Wealth is so much more than a great store of money. It can be any possession that is priceless to its owner.

Questions on Content

1. Who is perhaps the wealthiest person of all?
2. What is the denotation of wealth?
3. What is the connotation of wealth?

Questions on Form

1. What did the author do to make the connotation of wealth clear?
2. What makes the end of the paragraph effective?

Winter

Joan Papke, *student*

The meaning of winter according to the dictionary is a period of inactivity and decay. However, to a desert dweller like me, it is not a time of inactivity and decay, but a time of new activities and growth. Many of the summer-scorched desert plants spring to new life from the gentle winter rains, and new species of desert growth bloom only in winter. To me it means the bright green of winter lawns and more traffic on the streets of Phoenix, more hustle and bustle in the stores, elbow-to-elbow crowds, and no room to park at the malls. To me it means people enjoying the park on weekends, jogging, playing handball, and trying unsuccessfully to get a tee time. It means thousands of "snowbirds" and many real snowbirds like mallards and pintails who also make their winter home here. No, to me, winter is not a time of inactivity and decay, but instead is a time of new activity and a resurgence of life.

Understanding Words

Briefly define the following word as it is used in the above paragraph.

1. resurgence *rebirth, forceful coming again*

Questions on Content

1. What is one dictionary meaning of winter?
2. What does winter mean to a desert dweller?
3. What do people in the desert enjoy doing in the winter?

Questions on Form

1. What kind of development does the author use to make the definition clear?
2. In what two places does the author state the denotation?

A Run

Tim Darcy, *student*

1   "I've decided to go on a run over the holiday weekend." This statement is simple enough and would be understood perfectly by millions of bikers and motorcycle enthusiasts throughout the English-speaking world. Why then, out of no less than thirty-two noun definitions of the word "run" in one dictionary, do none of them apply? Apparently, lexicographers don't have the same kind of fun that bikers have because fun is what runs are all about. For the benefit of the uninitiated, a run is a planned motorcycle trip or destination that is meant to be attended by a group of riders.

2   It is interesting to wonder about how the word "run" came to be used by motorcyclists as it is today. The mere thought of a bunch of bearded, beer-bellied bikers in running shorts and Nikes, huffing and puffing down the road, is enough to rule out the most obvious literal connotation. Parallels could be drawn, if rather facetiously, to several standard uses of the word: "a run of good luck," "a dog run," "a beer run," and probably as many more as the imagination would allow. None of these meanings, however, really fit, so the question of why these events are called runs will just have to remain unanswered.

3   A run, as stated above, can be either a trip or a destination, and motorcycles are the common denominator. There are poker runs, in which riders stop at predetermined points along the way to pick up a playing card, and at the last stop, the rider with the best poker hand wins a prize. There are memorial runs, which bring people together to remember and honor departed friends. There are benefit and charity runs, in which bikers ride to bring toys, food, clothing, or money to try to help the needy. Finally, there is the classic run, which is really nothing more than an outdoor party. To qualify as a run, though, the party really should be an overnighter, and there must be travel involved. Riding to the local tavern and passing out in the alley until morning just doesn't constitute going on a run.

4   So what makes a run different from any other motorcycle ride or trip? First, a run is a planned happening; a spur-of-the-moment ride really couldn't be called a run. Runs are not something that are to be done alone, either. Individuals might ride to a run alone, but there must be a group at the destination. A ride to Florida from Colorado could be a mighty long trip, but unless there is a purpose that is shared with other riders, it just isn't a run. In short, a run differs from any other type of ride because, large or small, far away or close by, it is a social event.

5   When a motorcycle enthusiast says that he is going on a run, he is not going for the aerobic exercise and he is not in training for a marathon. When he says that the run is five hundred miles, it is not a five-hundred-mile race. He is going for a ride, very probably with friends, and there is a definite purpose for that ride, even though that purpose may not be obvious to everyone.

■ **Understanding Words**

Briefly define the following words as they are used in the above essay.

1. lexicographers *those who compile dictionaries*
2. literal *concerned with facts, word for word*

■ **Questions on Content**

1. What is the author's definition of a run?
2. Where could he not find an appropriate definition?
3. Why aren't all motorcycle trips runs?

■ **Questions on Form**

1. Identify the hook in the introduction.
2. Describe the voice in this essay.
3. What transitional phrase links paragraph 3 to paragraph 2?

■ **Cause and Effect Analysis**

Parenting: Singular

Jenefer Radas, *student*

1   "Single parents" is a term that we are hearing more about every day. Statistically, the number of single-parent families is rising at the same rate as the divorce rate. The percentage of single-parent families may be as high as 50 percent in some areas of our country. The majority of single parents are women, even though in single-parent families, men have recently had to raise their children on their own also. For many reasons, single parents are in this predicament. Alcohol and drug abuse can cause a parent to leave the children. Also, unwed mothers decide not to marry. With all that is known about single parents, however, the number one reason for a parent to raise a family alone is divorce. Regardless of the causes, the effects on both the parents and the children are serious. The effects of single parenthood can be felt financially, physically, and sociologically.

2   As a country, we know about financial instability. Our economy experiences ups and downs, but the financial stability of single parents is even worse. On the average, single parents are in the lower-income group, yet they are willing to work hard for their family's existence. Not all single parents are able to work. Some are home with infants while others simply do not have the educational background for well-paying jobs. Single parents who have high-paying employment may also have serious financial obligations to meet, which create financial tensions. These obligations can be a high house payment or car payment. In the movie *Baby Boom*, Diane Keaton is a businesswoman with an infant. Her male partner chooses not to help raise the child, leaving Diane alone to support and raise her. Even with Diane's well-paying job, she is almost left bankrupt because of her home repair costs. Eventually, Diane is asked to resign because of her parental responsibilities, leaving her to reevaluate her employment opportunities. This movie example gives a clear picture of a single parent's loss in financial status. A single parent, like the one played by Diane Keaton, can lose financial security and can become destitute very quickly. The finances of a single-parent family can drop dramatically, within a few weeks of onset. Consequently, because of the financial strains put on single-parent

families, many children are poorly fed, poorly dressed, and shunned by those more affluent. Furthermore, many single-parent families must depend on welfare or food programs for their mere existence. Because single parent families make up such a large percentage of families in our country, their needs should be more seriously considered than they are now.

3   The physical effects of being a single parent are another serious issue. To look at many single parents, a person would not know that they were in pain. Chances are those parents are hurting inside. Physical problems in these men and women can be caused by many different factors, but a major problem that exists for many single parents is depression, which leads to physical problems. Doctors found that infants who were refused any physical touch or intimate love became listless and depressed. After a time, the babies refused to eat and became catatonic. Depression in the single parent is brought about in the same manner. These adults that had loving relationships are now without any physical touch or love. This experience has left them in a state of loneliness, which is the cause of the debilitating illness, depression. This physical illness causes a feeling of exhaustion, anxiety, and tension that leaves them feeling listless. Single parents are vulnerable human beings that are more susceptible to all forms of illness. There are other physical effects of single parenthood. Compared to single adults without children, single parents usually contract many more of the childhood illnesses than the single person. They are exposed to these illnesses around the clock. Consequently, single parents put their health needs second to their children. This causes the parent to be sick longer and more frequently than a non-single parent. Single parents carry the weight of the world on their backs. With all that weight there is no wonder they are affected physically.

4   Equally important, the sociological effects on the single parent's life can be the hardest to overcome. Our society dictates what it considers a normal family. A normal family under these prejudiced guidelines is a mother and father and 2.5 children. The single-parent family consists of a mother or father and any number of children. On a daily basis, single parents are painfully reminded of this cultural ideal. These unusual families are looked on as different; they are usually excluded from neighborhood gatherings because of this presumed oddity in their family structure. Single-parent families are what society considers outcasts. Their children are reminded in storybooks and role playing that they are missing a mother or father in their home. Children from two-parent families tell their mommy and daddy stories with proud exuberance. Quietly, one-parent children sit and listen to their stories but feel ashamed to tell their own stories. These feelings of inadequacy and humility in the single-parent family are brought about by society. Even with this stigma toward single-parent families, society is slowly turning around. Single-parent families are being recognized by many as the strength and hope for the children growing up with only one parent. The strength that a single-parent must possess to raise children alone is far greater than the bellows and complaints of a blinded, backward society.

5   Parenting is not for everyone. It takes a strong person to raise a family alone with the financial, physical, and sociological pressures that exist. The parent may fall short of perfection but keeps working to make a good life for the children. Regardless of the causes of single-parent families, the impact on the family is serious and should be given more priority. These families are willing to overcome their problems but must be given a chance to do so.

Understanding Words

Briefly define the following words as they are used in the above essay.

1. statistically *pertaining to a numerical calculation of a group of people*
2. predicament *a distressing situation*
3. destitute *living in complete poverty*
4. affluent *rich or wealthy*
5. listless *without energy*
6. catatonic *immobile, in a stupor*
7. debilitating *making weak*
8. vulnerable *easily hurt*
9. susceptible *easily affected*
10. exuberance *overflowing joy or enthusiasm*
11. stigma *a mark of disgrace or disrepute*

Questions on Content

1. Why is the number of single-parent families increasing?
2. What is the ideal family in our culture?
3. How are children from single-parent families made to feel inferior?

Questions on Form

1. Why are causes given in the introduction even though the paper is about effects?
2. How are the effects organized for the reader?
3. What provides support for each effect?
4. Is the conclusion effective? Why or why not?

Process Analysis

Reducing Fear of a Hospital Stay for a Child

Eric Beach, *student*

1   Years ago, children were taken to the hospital, strapped down on a stretcher, and told to be good while the nurse slapped a gas mask on and the parent disappeared to another room. Little thought was given to the terrified child who didn't have the slightest idea what was going on. Those terrifying experiences do not have to happen. A caring parent can easily prepare a child for a surgical procedure. Though the process of getting a child ready for a hospital stay for the first time can still be scary for both the adult and the child, the stay can be made easier and much less stressful if some careful planning is done beforehand. Role playing, discussion with honest responses, and access to factual information help the child understand what is going on and, thus, keep her from imagining all sorts of scary experiences.

2   Tension can be reduced when preparation involves role playing. First, the child can pretend to be in the hospital and the adult can pretend to be the nurse or doctor. As a "nurse," the adult can fluff up the pillow, take the child's temperature, and take the child's blood pressure—all with a play doctor's kit. Then the

"pretend" nurse can show the child how to ring for help or turn on the television set. The "nurse" can then set up a tray for lunch and say, "This is the way you will be served lunch in the hospital." The "nurse" can be resourceful by finding items around the house that they can pretend with. Then the adult and child might reverse the roles, with the child becoming the nurse and the adult becoming the patient. Then, when it is time for the child to check in at the hospital, she will have some idea of what to expect.

3   The most important part of the process might be to discuss with the child the fact that she will not be left alone in a strange place and forgotten. The child can be encouraged to take a favorite stuffed animal with her or maybe even her special blanket. The child needs to know that after she falls asleep for surgery, someone will be there waiting when she wakes up. The child needs to know that she will not be dropped off in a strange environment with no familiar items or faces. Rather, mom, dad, grandma, sister, or brother will be there as much as possible. Also, this is a good time to let the child know that a nurse will always be there when she needs anything and the stuffed animal can stay right there in bed with her the whole time.

4   Equally important is to allow the child the chance to ask questions. The adults should answer questions as honestly as possible. If the child wants to know if "it" will hurt, the adult should respond by saying, "Yes, it may hurt a little bit, but the nurse or doctor will be as gentle as possible." Then the benefits of the procedure should be explained. If it is the appendix that is being removed, then the adult can say, "But it won't hurt here (touching child's side) as much as it does now." If it is to repair a heart, then the adult might say, "But then you can play more. Remember how tired you get now?" The adult must be honest with the child. If the child asks, "Will I have to have a shot?" the adult should answer by saying, "Yes, and I am sorry." It is important for the child to know that the adult cares.

5   If time allows, the adult and child might visit a library and/or hospital for more specific information. At the library they can read children's books and view simple videos about hospitals. At the hospital, they might pick up a pamphlet that would show the child pictures of what to expect once in the hospital. A book that shows the internal parts of the body can also be useful. If a child is to have tonsils removed, a picture of the tonsils can be found. If the procedure is to be a complicated one, like heart surgery, the adult might show the child what will be fixed. The adult only needs to explain what the child is old enough to understand.

6   Following this process of preparing a child for surgery can have benefits for both the child and the adult. In today's world, it is unforgivable not to give the child information that she can understand and that will reduce anxiety and fear. Hospital stays do not need to be nightmares that are relived over and over again.

Questions on Content

1. What process is being explained?
2. What can the adult do to make this process easier?
3. What are the benefits of planning ahead?
4. What can a child take to the hospital with him or her?

Questions on Form

1. How does the writer organize the process?
2. What point of view is being used?
3. What makes the introduction effective?

■ Argumentation

The Human Genome Initiative

Joy Osterberg, *student*

1   The Human Genome Initiative is a massive project reminiscent of the space program when it was preparing to put a man on the moon. The United States Congress is presently considering legislation that would establish a committee comprising several government agencies, including the Department of Energy and the National Institute of Health, to organize the effort to map and sequence the human genome, the entire sequence of three billion base pairs of DNA that are in twenty-three pairs of chromosomes. Workshops and symposia are being held to gather the leading scientists together in hopes of creating a consortium of government agencies, universities, and private industry to implement the Initiative. Support of this program is very critical because the benefits derived from it would include advancing technology, supplying new information for the studies of evolution and molecular biology, and allowing biomedical researchers to concentrate on the diagnosis and treatment of health problems.

2   Many scientists are concerned that the cost of such a large program might drain funds from other biological research. The article by Jeffrey L. Fox "Contemplating the Human Genome" in the July/August 1987 issue of *BioScience* says that "some biologists argue that sequencing the entire genome is an impractical approach for answering questions about human genetics. Within the genome, only about three percent of the sequence encodes protein." This small percentage, they assert, is the most important genetic material to investigate. Mapping the genome, in their opinion, would not be the best use of money available for biological research.

3   Great technological advances have been made in molecular biology during the past decade. Cloning techniques have made possible the first attempts at mapping the genome. The article "Genes for Sale" in the January 1988 issue of *Discover* tells of a new automated system called the DNA Sequencer, invented by the Caltech biologist Leroy Hood, that is "reading up to 13,000 [nucleotide] pairs every 24 hours." The article goes on to say that "one sign of how fast the field is moving . . . is that there are already new devices in the works that will make Hood's DNA Sequencer look 'like a Model T.'"

4   Analysis of the human genome would supply new information that could enhance such fields of study as evolution and molecular biology. Robert A. Weinberg, a professor of biology at the Massachusetts Institute of Technology and a member of the Whitehead Institute for Biomedical Research, wrote in an essay for the November 1988 issue of *Scientific American* that "within the sequence lie many clues to our origins and our complex function." He continues, further in the article, by saying, "Most of the genome seems to represent evolutionary detritus — the discarded drafts of essays that lost any meaning 100 or 1,000 million years ago." Even though this genetic material may not sequence for proteins today, it may be useful in establishing evolutionary branches to the Tree of Life. In the field of molecular biology, knowing the structure of a protein is only the first step to finding

its function within the cell. Weinberg explains that "a single protein functions in the context of a complex interacting network of other proteins." The knowledge of how a protein is made is scratching the surface of how a cell works.

5   Mapping and sequencing the human genome would allow biomedical researchers to concentrate on the diagnosis and treatment of health problems. The article in *BioScience* states, "In addition to purely scientific analysis, information on the human genome could be used for diagnosing genetic diseases and for monitoring chemical or radiation damage to genes, a powerful tool for enforcing health and safety regulations." Weinberg supports this idea: "The availability of a complete map of the human genome will enormously facilitate the identification of genes responsible for a thousand diseases such as cystic fibrosis and Huntington's disease as well as for susceptibility to cancer." Once the genes are located on the map, the research for a cure will be that much further along.

6   The Human Genome Initiative is one of the most important scientific projects of this century. Like the space program, its benefits will far outreach its immediate goal of mapping and sequencing the human genome. The technological advances have already started and will continue as effort is directed toward the human genome project. And the new technology will most likely spill over into other fields of research and even everyday life. The information that the map will provide those studying evolution is just starting to be recognized as important. The approach of matching amino-acid sequences in different species has already started, and this project would intensify the effort. Biomedical researchers would have vital information available to help them focus their attention on diagnosis and treatment of genetic disease, cancer, and radiation damage. Support of the Human Genome Initiative would greatly benefit us individually, our country, and the world as a whole.

◼ Understanding Words

Briefly define the following words as they are used in the above essay.

1. genome *a complete, normal set of chromosomes*
2. reminiscent *remembering*
3. symposia *meetings or conferences for the discussion of the same topic*
4. consortium *a partnership or an association of groups having extensive financial resources*
5. molecular *of or pertaining to a molecule, the smallest particle of a substance*

◼ Questions on Content

1. What is the human genome project?
2. What are the diseases that cures might be found for once the genes have been mapped?
3. What type of support does the author use?

◼ Questions on Form

1. What device is used in the first two sentences of the introduction to get the reader's attention?
2. Where is the position of the author stated?
3. Where is the main opposition to the author's position stated?

Confusing Words

This appendix is designed to help you clarify and eliminate misunderstood words. These errors may often seem minor to you, but they can distract the reader or change the meaning of a sentence.

Similar Words Misused

Some words are pronounced so similarly to another word or words that they are misspelled. You may want to learn and practice one or two a day or practice only those that are troublesome to you. To learn the slight differences in the pairs of words, study the meanings; then look at the spelling or construction of the word. Finally, by practicing the correct use of these words in sentences, you will be ready to use them properly in your writing. If you still have difficulty with a pair of words, write them down and restudy them.

Definitions and Practice Sentences

Read the following short definitions and examples of confusing words. Work through the practice sentences by striking through the word errors. Then write the correct form above the words that are wrong. Write "C" if the sentence contains no errors.

Pair 1

a lot: an acceptable (but overused) form meaning many or much (You may want to consider alternate words that say the same thing, such as "many," "frequently," "much," or "often.")

A lot of my friends enjoy dancing.

alot: incorrect form, often a misspelling for "a lot"

allot: to give or assign as one's portion

He did not allot enough time to do the job properly.

1. Steve often has alot of figs on his tree.

2. The employer will not alot any money for repairs.

a lot

3. Sonja often caught ~~alot~~ of fish at that lake.

allot

4. I was hoping he would ~~alot~~ us more time to get the work done.

Pair 2

accept: receive

I accept your apology for not calling.

except: excluding

Everyone except Jason came home.

C 1. She accepted my apology and walked away with a frown on her face.

except

2. Everyone went to the ball ~~accept~~ Cinderella.

C 3. She accepted the money greedily.

except

4. When Natalie arrived in class, everyone was present ~~accept~~ Maria.

Pair 3

adapt: to adjust or change to make usable (often followed by "to")

Often students must learn to adapt to different instructors.

adopt: to accept as one's own

The mother dog adopted both litters of puppies.

C 1. When people move to a new country, they must adapt to new customs.

adopted

2. The organization ~~adapted~~ the constitution the way it was originally written.

adopt

3. They hoped to ~~adapt~~ the little girl.

adapt

4. They needed to ~~adopt~~ to the changing weather conditions.

Pair 4

advise: (verb) to give valuable information

Please advise John of the change.

advice: (noun) valuable information given

John followed the advice.

C 1.   John advised Butch not to hike the steep mountain.

advice

2.   Take the lifeguard's ~~advise~~ and don't swim while it is raining.

advised

3.   I ~~adviced~~ her to do her house chores early.

advice

4.   Margaret refused to take my ~~advise~~.

Pair 5

affect: (verb) to change or influence

effect: (noun) a result

(verb) to accomplish or bring about

affect

1.   His action cannot ~~effect~~ us.

effect

2.   One ~~affect~~ of staying up late can be having a headache in the morning.

C 3.   His honesty affected everyone around him.

C 4.   His response effected mass hysteria.

Pair 6

all ready: fully or completely ready
We are all ready for finals.

already: something completed previously
Finals are already over.

all ready

1.   Are you ~~already~~?

already

2.   She is ~~all ready~~ at the soccer game.

C 3.   When she got to the party, everyone was already there.

all ready

4.   I was not ~~already~~ for the English exam.

Pair 7

all together: to indicate a group who performed an action collectively (''All together'' can be used only if ''all'' and ''together'' can be separated in the sentence.)

The Club members work all together.
All the club members work *together.*

altogether: completely, wholly (Always use ''altogether'' except in the above situation.)

Altogether, it was a strange event.
He was altogether surprised by the outcome of the election.

altogether

1. Sharon was ~~all together~~ surprised by his comment.

Altogether

2. ~~All together~~, I put in two weeks on that job.

C 3. All together, we worked for at least two weeks on that job.

C 4. That summer, the young people were all together.

Pair 8

among: (preposition) separates three or more things

The tasks were divided among all five of the employees.

between: (preposition) separates two objects in space, time, or degree

The tasks were completed between two and six o'clock.

between

1. She divides her time ~~among~~ job and family.

among

2. I hope you will share the information ~~between~~ all employees.

C 3. That item was among the first ones to be considered.

between

4. I parked my boat ~~among~~ the house and the oak tree.

Pair 9

are: (verb) form of ''be''

My friends are usually willing to help me.

our: (pronoun) showing ownership

Our family enjoyed life.

Our
1. ~~Are~~ children are ready to go to the zoo.

are
2. When ~~our~~ you going to visit me?

are
3. The trees ~~our~~ growing faster than we had hoped.

C 4. Who is responsible for our future?

Pair 10

brake: act of stopping or the device for stopping
I brake for animals.

break: separate into parts
I do not want to break the dishes.

brake
1. The bus driver slammed on the ~~break~~, and the passengers flew forward.

C 2. How did you break the lamp last night?

brake
3. When the car in front of us stopped, I hit the ~~break~~ with my foot.

break
4. The karate expert will ~~brake~~ twenty boards in twenty-five seconds.

Pair 11

by: a preposition indicating near, through, during, no later than, or respect to
He parked his car by a fire hydrant.

buy: to purchase
I want to buy a new car.

buy
1. Mrs. Smith needed to ~~by~~ detergent for her washing machine.

C 2. The fishing gear is by the car in the garage.

C 3. Mick needs to be at church by 8:30 A.M.

C 4. Who put the *TV Guide* by the lamp?

Pair 12

capital: punishable by death; excellent; place where the government is located; money or property

> That was a capital offense.
> The drama department put on a capital performance.
> He did not have enough capital.

capitol: building where a legislature meets

> We visited the state capitol.

1. The field trip included a visit to the ~~capital~~ *capitol* building.

C 2. Capital punishment is rare in all states.

C 3. When he gets enough capital, he plans to start his own business.

C 4. That was a capital performance.

Pair 13

cite: to quote or mention

> She cited Shakespeare in her talk.

sight: refers to seeing

> I did not sight any new cars.

site: location

> We particularly enjoyed that vacation site.

1. This is a wonderful ~~cite~~ *site* for the new building.

2. Which ~~sight~~ *site* would you prefer for the housing development?

3. I was unable to catch any ~~site~~ *sight* of him.

4. I would like to ~~site~~ *cite* your book in my next article.

Pair 14

coarse: rough; not refined

> The boards were too coarse to use.

course: mental or physical path going from one point to another; complete series of studies

> His course in life was a challenge.

of course: as one expects

> Of course, I can be there on time.

C 1. The course I liked the best was not necessarily the easiest.

2. Of ~~coarse~~ *course*, I enjoyed the play.

3. The ~~coarse~~ *course* he took was a challenge.

4. The woman at the ball park appeared ~~course~~ *coarse*.

Pair 15

conscience: (noun) moral value that guides behavior

His conscience bothers him when he lies.

conscious: (adjective) aware

He was conscious of his mistake.

C 1. The crowd sighed in relief when she became conscious.

2. My ~~conscious~~ *conscience* forced me to return the lost wallet.

C 3. I didn't want to study, but my conscience reminded me of the importance of making good grades.

4. My grandmother is always ~~conscience~~ *conscious* of my birthday.

Pair 16

could of, must of, might of, should of: These are all incorrect forms and should not be used. Instead, use "could have," "must have," "might have," and "should have."

I could have gone to the lake today.

1. Everyone at the lake should ~~of~~ *have* used sunblock.

2. My parents must ~~of~~ *have* cut the grass.

C 3. The street leading to the city could have been blocked off.

4. When he fell asleep, he must ~~of~~ *have* left the television on.

Pair 17

council: group of persons, assembly

  The council will convene shortly.

counsel: advice or attorney

  He provided effective counsel for the young man.

counsel

1. The ~~council~~ for the defense was an inexperienced attorney.

C 2. Every year the student body elects a new council.

counsel

3. The father gave ~~council~~ to his son.

C 4. The city council voted on new ordinances.

Pair 18

forth: forward

  We must continue to move forth.

fourth: referring to the number four

  She was only the fourth person to come into the store this morning.

C 1. He ate his fourth poppy-seed muffin.

fourth

2. This is the ~~forth~~ time I have lost my keys.

forth

3. The prime minister must continue to move ~~fourth~~.

fourth

4. Chip is working on his ~~forth~~ assignment.

Pair 19

good: (adjective) better than average

  The president did a good job.

  "Good" is used when the verb refers to the senses (taste, feel, smell).

  Jessica feels good about her recent victory.

well: An adverb

  Sontos hit the ball well.

  "Well" used to introduce a sentence adds little meaning to your sentences. It is an expression that should not be used in more formal writing. It is frequently used in informal speech.

  Well, I'm broke.

1. The flowers smell ~~well~~. *good*

2. The little boy wrote the story ~~good~~. *well*

3. The apple pie was ~~well~~. *good*

4. The apple pie was made ~~good~~. *well*

Pair 20

hear: ability to pick up sounds with one's ears

    She hears what she wants to hear.

here: location

    We can all gather here for lunch.

1. Didn't you ~~here~~ the car honking? *hear*

C 2. Come here and write your paper.

3. From our kitchen, we could ~~here~~ birds singing. *hear*

C 4. Here is my assignment.

Pair 21

hole: an opening in something

    I have a hole in my shoe.

whole: entire

    He ate the whole pie.

1. Be careful; I think there's a ~~whole~~ around here. *hole*

2. The ~~hole~~ house was a mess. *whole*

3. Tall, yellow weeds covered the ~~hole~~ field. *whole*

4. The yard was filled with small prairie-dog ~~wholes~~. *holes*

Pair 22

imply: to suggest or hint

The president implied that we need to save money.

 infer: to conclude, based on what a speaker or writer says

I inferred that he was talking about my department.

infer

1.   What did you ~~imply~~ from the speech?

implied

2.   The evidence ~~inferred~~ that she was guilty.

implied

3.   From what he ~~inferred~~, did you infer the right answer?

inferred

4.   She ~~implied~~ from the information provided that we had made the wrong decision.

Pair 23

 its: ownership or possession (3rd person singular)

Its water bowl is empty.

it's: contraction for it is, it has

It's been a long time since they visited Hawaii.

it's

1.   I believe ~~its~~ going to be a rainy day.

Its

2.   ~~It's~~ only purpose is to give directions.

its

3.   It's been a long time since ~~it's~~ beginnings.

it's

4.   I wonder if ~~its~~ in good shape.

Pair 24

knew: understood

We thought we knew the answers.

 new: not old

The puppy liked his new bed.

C 1.   The meteorologist knew it was going to rain Wednesday.

new

2.   Mary was disappointed because she ripped her ~~knew~~ red dress.

knew

3. I ~~new~~ the test would be difficult.

C 4. The new peach sweater looked terrific on Olivia.

Pair 25

know: to understand

I know what you are thinking.

no: a response in the negative

There are no raisins in the oatmeal.

know

1. Don't you ~~no~~ not to stick a fork into the toaster?

no

2. ~~Know~~, you cannot play on the computer.

C 3. I know I shouldn't watch TV when I have homework.

C 4. Margaret asked her dad for $200, but he said, ''No.''

Pair 26

lie: to recline or rest; to tell an untruth

Please do not lie on the table.

lay: to put or to place (takes a direct object)

Please lay the child on the table.

(The child receives the action of being placed on the table.)

Dr. Dries laid the child on the table.

Note: ''Lay'' is also past tense of ''lie.''

Yesterday, Scott lay in bed all day.

Present	Past	Past Participle	Present Participle
lie	lay	lain	lying
lay	laid	laid	laying

C 1. The young man continued to lie throughout the investigation.

laid

2. The contractor ~~lay~~ the brick according to code.

lie

3. The doctor advised Chad not to ~~lay~~ in the sun.

C 4. We must lay a foundation before we can build the gazebo.

Pair 27

lose: (verb) misplace or not win

They managed to lose only the last game.

loose: (adjective) not bound, free, not tight

The children were turned loose after school.

1. Mom didn't want to ~~loose~~ *lose* Amy in the crowd, so she held her hand tightly.

2. The fashion today is ~~lose~~ *loose* clothing.

C 3. The knot Bob made was too loose to hold the calf.

4. Louise lost the ~~lose~~ *loose* ring Friday.

Pair 28

passed: (verb) successfully completed; handed to; filed by or went by

She passed the bar exam.

past: time gone by, yesterday

In the past five years, they moved twice.

1. My teammate ~~past~~ *passed* the ball to me, and I made a touchdown.

2. Susie was dreaming about her ~~passed~~ *past* when she was awakened.

C 3. Mr. Van passed out the test at 8:00.

C 4. Karen sprinted past Matt to win the 50-meter dash.

Pair 29

peace: quiet and calm

It is hard to keep world peace.

piece: a section or part

He ate a piece of fudge cake.

1. Pass Julio a ~~peace~~ *piece* of cherry pie.

2. The Protestants made ~~piece~~ *peace* with the Catholics in Ireland.

3. Roger lost a ~~peace~~ *piece* of my science project, but I passed anyway.

4. The ~~piece~~ *peace* symbol was part of the sixties generation.

Pair 30

principal: main; head of a school (Note: They usually are "pals," which is part of the word.)

Money was his principal reason for quitting the job.
The school principal called a meeting.

principle: rule, law, or regulation

His answer was based on a simple principle.

1. Our ~~principle~~ *principal*, Ms. Jones, is a sensitive woman.

C 2. We learned the principles of good marketing.

3. I called her and explained the new club's ~~principals~~ *principles*.

C 4. As a matter of principle, I defended the child.

Pair 31

quiet: calm, peaceful

The baby was finally quiet.

quite: very, to a great extent

He was quite sure of himself.

1. Laura is ~~quiet~~ *quite* a pretty girl.

2. Grand Lake is always calm and ~~quite~~ *quiet*.

3. The Russians were ~~quiet~~ *quite* surprised that they came in second in the gymnastics events.

4. After the children are put to bed, the Wagners' house is ~~quite~~ *quiet*.

Pair 32

right: correct or opposite of left

> He always seems to know the right answer.

  rite: ceremony

> They participated in the rite of matrimony.

write: communicate with written words

> She likes to write her thoughts in her journal.

write
1.   Beatrice started to ~~rite~~ her essay but was interrupted by another phone call.

right
2.   Henry turned ~~rite~~ at the intersection.

right
3.   I broke my ~~rite~~ hand when I fell.

rite
4.   Some communities have a ~~right~~ of passage into adulthood.

Pair 33

than: used in comparisons

> It is later than you think.

then: at that time; next in order; in that case

> Then we can order two more books.

C 1.   We will be through by then.

than
2.   I have more homework ~~then~~ I can complete.

than
3.   He has more money ~~then~~ I do.

C 4.   If we go then, we can get a discount.

Pair 34

 there: location

> He left his papers there.

  their: ownership

> Their papers were all turned in on time.

they're: contraction of "they are"

> They're determined to finish first.

their
1. They left ~~there~~ book in their car.

C 2. They're making excellent grades.

C 3. The puppy is hiding there in the grass.

        they're   *their*
4. Sam said ~~their~~ going to ~~there~~ favorite spot.

Pair 35

though: (even), (although), however, nevertheless

He wants to buy a car even though he cannot afford one.

thought: thinking or an idea

I thought you would never ask.

C 1. Though Juana was tired, she stayed up and baked bread.

        thought
2. The ~~though~~ of cooking another meal depressed the cook.

C 3. The Comets lost the game though they played their best.

C 4. Her thought was to plan a surprise party for Jim.

Pair 36

threw: tossed in air (past tense)

He threw the ball into the net.

through: from one side to the other

They passed through the city.

        through
1. Sarah climbed ~~threw~~ the tunnel and ran for the slide.

                    threw
2. The muscular football player ~~through~~ a bullet pass to the receiver.

        through
3. Ann ran ~~threw~~ the woods, jumping over logs and stones.

                            through
4. Janice accidentally poked the sharp pencil ~~threw~~ the soft Styrofoam.

Pair 37

> **to:** a preposition that shows direction toward or part of an infinitive (to sing, to act)
>
> Sara wanted to go to the fair.

> **too:** also, more than enough
>
> Sharon wanted to go, too.

> **two:** number two
>
> The two women enjoyed the same types of activities.

two

1. The final score was three to ~~too~~.

to

2. The Fishers love ~~too~~ swim at night in the summer.

too

3. Nicki finished her paper, ~~to~~.

Too

4. ~~Two~~ many people were at the party in the small house.

Pair 38

> **wander:** to go from place to place aimlessly
>
> He tends to wander in the summertime.

> **wonder:** feel surprise, amazement; have doubts about; question mentally
>
> I wonder if he will get off work on time.

wanders

1. He ~~wonders~~ from one city to another.

wonder

2. I will always ~~wander~~ about his decision.

C 3. I often wonder how my family is doing.

wander

4. I like to ~~wonder~~ down the beach.

Pair 39

> **weak:** not strong
>
> Sara is still weak from having the flu.

> **week:** seven days
>
> Eric stayed for three weeks.

weak
1. Is she too ~~week~~ to go shopping?

weak
2. Al's knee has been ~~week~~ since he broke it.

week
3. The child gets an allowance every ~~weak~~.

weeks
4. Every six ~~weaks~~, she goes to the doctor for a checkup.

Pair 40

weather: outside temperature and conditions

The weather is beautiful.

whether: if, in case of

She wanted to know whether or not she needed to take a sweater.

weather
1. The ~~whether~~ is great in Colorado in the summer.

C 2. Whether or not you apologize, Tracey's feelings are hurt.

C 3. The weather for tomorrow is predicted to be beautiful.

whether
4. Tom was sorry ~~weather~~ he could admit it or not.

Pair 41

were: past tense verb

Six flowers were placed in the vase.

where: place

Where can we find a good place to eat?

Where
1. ~~Were~~ were you when I needed help?

were
2. Fifteen of the students ~~where~~ going on a hike.

where
3. Tanya went ~~were~~ the other students were playing volleyball.

C 4. They were moving into a new apartment.

Pair 42

who's: contraction for who is or who has

Who's responsible for the vase of red roses?

whose: relating to possession of an object, frequently in a question

Whose pie is in the refrigerator?

1. ~~Whose~~ *Who's* at the door, John?

C 2. I forgot whose keys these are.

3. ~~Whose~~ *Who's* at the other end of the phone?

4. ~~Whose~~ *Who's* done the most work?

Pair 43

who: refers to people (usually used in formal writing)

The people who live here are energetic.

which: should not be used to refer to people

We finished the assignment, which the teacher made on Monday.

that: can refer to people or things

The soup that I like is all gone.

1. Cecil threw out the food ~~who~~ *that* was spoiled.

2. We like the neighbor ~~which~~ *who or that* moved in across the street.

3. The people ~~that~~ *who* came late to the concert could not get in.

4. The programs ~~who~~ *that* received the awards were purchased by the library.

Pair 44

woman: one adult female human

She was the woman of his dreams.

women: two or more adult female humans

The women shared their concerns with one another.

women
1. The three ~~woman~~ went through nurse's training together.

woman
2. The ~~women~~ Jason married was his childhood sweetheart.

C 3. The most prestigious award was given to an outstanding woman student.

women
4. Of all the ~~woman~~ he dated, that woman stole his heart.

Pair 45

your: ownership or possession (2nd person singular or plural)

Janet, your speech was well received.

you're: contraction for "you are"

You're not feeling well, are you?

you're
1. Jesse said that ~~your~~ not going.

C 2. Would you be willing to move your car?

you're
3. I'm sorry, Jane, but ~~your~~ not going to be able to swim today.

C 4. Your assignment is not due until next Monday.

Keeping a Journal

Journal writing serves several purposes, none of which should be overlooked. It helps you

Transparencies can be made from sample journal entry p. 49 and journal log p. 50.

work through emotions

make the words flow more freely

communicate with others

remember events in the past

make class notes clearer

Journal writing helps you *work through emotions* so you can back off and then deal objectively with whatever was bothering you. Someone once said that you can become a journal writer only after you have written about the thing that hurt the most, and as you release your feelings on paper, you also release the tears that have been long overdue. For example, a man in his forties had not spoken to his mother and father for twenty years. He filled two journals in which he communicated with them only on paper. Eventually he wrote his mother and initiated some type of interaction. Though he could not change what had happened in his childhood, he was able to begin a new relationship with his parents.

When Ivan Lacore, a serious journal writer, was asked if journal writing helped him cope with life, he said, "Writing in my journal helps me face the future without the anger of the past."

One bonus to journal writing is that it *makes the words flow more freely*. The more you write, the easier it becomes. This can be compared to walking. If you stayed in bed for six weeks and did not once walk, you would lose that ability to walk and would have to "learn" to walk all over again. Elementary school teachers often remind us that children who do not read over the summer cannot read as well in September as they did in June. Whether walking, reading, or writing, the more you do of it, the better you become at it. As you began this course, it might have been an effort to write one paragraph. However, by the end of the term you may be able to write a multiparagraph essay in the same length of time you once needed for one paragraph.

Journal writing can also help you *communicate with others*. What you write in your journal often involves your feelings about other people. Sometimes you may choose to write a letter to someone. Another time you may want to take

414

parts of your journal to share with another person or with many people. Then editing and reworking the material becomes an important part of the writing. One lady wrote her memories of her childhood and her daughter's childhood. She then typed her journal and presented it to her grandchild. This journal became a treasure that will most likely be passed down from generation to generation.

Journal writing often allows you to *remember events in the past* that you have blocked from your mind, but when you begin writing about these things, details surface and memories are renewed.

Another important purpose of journal writing is to *make class notes clearer.* Sometimes you may want to rework the notes that you took in this class or in another class. This reorganizing helps you understand ideas and concepts that your instructor wants you to grasp. Notes are often taken so rapidly in class that rewriting and reworking your notes immediately after class can make the concept "stick" in your mind.

Some instructors think that a notebook should be turned in and graded. Others think that these notebooks can be checked without the teacher reading the entries at all. These instructors do not check the entries because they feel that students should be able to write about their most personal feelings without worrying about an audience. For instance, if your instructor were to say that the journal is to be read and graded for grammar, you would be concerned with both form and content. On the other hand, if your instructor were to say that he or she would only flip through the pages without reading the contents, you would feel assured that you could write about anything you wanted to without worrying about form.

The actual journal may be a special composition book your instructor requires you to buy at the book store, a leather-bound book that might cost twenty dollars, or a spiral notebook you bought for twenty-five cents on sale. Whatever you use really does not matter. Unless your instructor requires a special type of writing instrument, you should use anything that feels comfortable. You can use a pencil, a pen, a typewriter, or a word processor. You can write in neat lines and will want to if your instructor is going to read your journal. If not, you might find yourself writing from corner to corner, in circles, or whatever feels right. Likewise, you might have a special desk you like to sit at when you are writing, or you might like to sit on the floor. You might like everything quiet, or you might like both the radio and the TV going.

One last thought about journals is that you are not just meeting a requirement to pass a course. You are learning to feel on paper. Though writing about how you feel about what is happening in your life may seem strange at first, you may be willing to keep a journal years after this course is finished. This journal can help you improve your writing and thinking skills for many years to come.

WRITING ASSIGNMENT

1. Try writing in your journal about the most wonderful place you can remember as a child. Close your eyes until you can reenter this place. Then let the reader enter this place with you. What do you see, feel, touch, taste, smell? What is above you? What is around you? Begin to write when your mind can reenter this place and continue to write as long as you can.

2. Try writing in your journal about the last time you got mad. Describe how you felt. Why did you feel that way? Who made you angry? Why were you angry? (Just continue to write until nothing more comes.)

3. In your journal, write a letter that is overdue. Perhaps you can write a letter to someone who might have reason to be upset with you. Or perhaps you can write a letter to someone whom you really dislike or like. (There is no need to mail this letter.)

4. In your journal, rework your notes in this class or another class immediately after the class is over.

5. In your journal, write about anything that bothers you. This can be prejudice, frustration, homelessness, your classes, or anything else. Try to recall a particular event that bothered you.

Irregular Verbs

Irregular verbs may cause a few problems because they have many different forms. Feel confident, however, that you probably use most of these verbs correctly.

You may find that you do not know some of the forms. Perhaps, in addition to not knowing them, you may *say* the verb forms correctly but not *spell* them correctly when you write them. In either case, you may need to refer to the following list.

What makes a verb "irregular"? It is irregular if it forms the past tense in any of the following ways.

Ways Verbs Are Irregular in the Past Tense

By changing the internal sound and/or spelling

I *speak* now. I *spoke* yesterday.

I *write* now. I *wrote* yesterday.

By changing most of the sound and most of the spelling

I *bring* my lunch on Mondays.

I *brought* it yesterday.

By changing to a different word

I *go* today. I *went* yesterday.

I *am* here now. I *was* here earlier.

You do not need to know these changes by name. Being able to use the verbs is much more important. Do not try to memorize all the forms in the following table; instead, use it as a reference when you are revising your writing.

IRREGULAR VERBS

PRESENT	PAST	PAST PARTICIPLE*	PRESENT PARTICIPLE*
am	was	been	being
become	became	become	becoming
begin	began	begun	beginning
bite	bit	bitten	biting
blow	blew	blown	blowing
break	broke	broken	breaking
bring	brought	brought	bringing
buy	bought	bought	buying
catch	caught	caught	catching
choose	chose	chosen	choosing
come	came	come	coming
dig	dug	dug	digging
draw	drew	drawn	drawing
drink	drank	drunk	drinking
drive	drove	driven	driving
eat	ate	eaten	eating
fall	fell	fallen	falling
fight	fought	fought	fighting
fly	flew	flown	flying
freeze	froze	frozen	freezing
get	got	gotten	getting
give	gave	given	giving
go	went	gone	going
grow	grew	grown	growing
hang†	hung	hung	hanging
have	had	had	having
hear	heard	heard	hearing
hide	hid	hidden	hiding
know	knew	known	knowing
lay (set something down)†	laid	laid	laying
lead	led	led	leading
lie (recline)‡	lay	lain	lying
lie (tell untruth)	lied	lied	lying
pay	paid	paid	paying
read	read	read	reading
ride	rode	ridden	riding
ring	rang	rung	ringing

* When the past participle or present participle is used as a complete verb, a *helping verb* is always used.
† Takes a direct object.
‡ Does not take a direct object.

PRESENT	PAST	PAST PARTICIPLE*	PRESENT PARTICIPLE*
rise‡	rose	risen	rising
run	ran	run	running
see	saw	seen	seeing
set (put something down)†	set	set	setting
shine‡	shone	shone	shining
sing	sang	sung	singing
sit‡	sat	sat	sitting
speak	spoke	spoken	speaking
sting	stung	stung	stinging
steal	stole	stolen	stealing
swear	swore	sworn	swearing
swim	swam	swum	swimming
take	took	taken	taking
think	thought	thought	thinking
throw	threw	thrown	throwing
wake	woke	woken	waking
wear	wore	worn	wearing
win	won	won	winning
write	wrote	written	writing

*When the past participle or present participle is used as a complete verb, a *helping verb* is always used.
†Takes a direct object.
‡Does not take a direct object.

Answers to Odd-Numbered Exercises (Including Appendix A)

UNIT 2 / Part 1

EXERCISE 1 (Page 25)

1. *Topic:* Doing well in college
   Direction: requires organization

3. *Topic:* School board meetings
   Direction: inform parents about the school

5. *Topic:* Enrolling in college
   Direction: can be a surprising experience

7. *Topic:* Riding in an airplane
   Direction: can be stressful

9. *Topic:* Walking to school in the spring
   Direction: saves money

11. *Topic:* Going out to eat
    Direction: can be a cultural experience

13. *Topic:* The birthday party
    Direction: was a great success

15. *Topic:* Character
    Direction: can be built through studying karate

17. *Topic:* Owning a car
    Direction: can be expensive

19. *Topic:* Writing a research paper
    Direction: takes preparation

EXERCISE 2 (Page 27)

Answers will vary.

EXERCISE 3 (Page 29)

TS   1. The Mayan Indians of South America contributed many common food products.

broad   3. The causes of world hunger are complicated.

broad   5. Many varieties of aquatic life can be found in the ocean.

TS   7. Ralph's room is a disaster.

___*broad*___   9. Children are a mystery.

___*TS*___   11. Swimming provides great exercise.

___*TS*___   13. Yard work can be fun.

___*fact*___   15. My math book is on the floor.

___*fact*___   17. Three fish share the aquarium.

___*broad*___   19. Pollution causes many environmental problems.

EXERCISE 4 (Page 31)

1. Fans can be installed.

   Some shade screens reduce the sun's glare by 20 percent.

   Large trees on the west side shield a house from the afternoon heat.

   Insulation in attics helps keep a house cool in the summer.

   <u>Tips for keeping a home cooler in the summer heat are helpful.</u>

3. Contrasts in landscape range from beautiful deserts to majestic mountains.

   Native American and Hispanic cultures are reflected in the architecture of many cities in New Mexico.

   Carlsbad Caverns is a breathtaking sight to take in.

   <u>As the license plate boasts, New Mexico is the "Land of Enchantment."</u>

   The weather is varied but not extreme.

5. Cleaning up after the puppies is a never-ending job.

   Seeing that they are all fed is a major responsibility.

   <u>Raising puppies is time consuming.</u>

   Finding good homes for them is also a part of the job.

   Housebreaking them takes patience.

   Playing with them keeps the owners busy.

7. He appointed his wife to chair a national health care task force.

   <u>President Clinton made several important decisions in his first days as president.</u>

   He nominated the first woman attorney general to take charge of national law enforcement.

   He proposed economic reforms.

9. Some people fear flying.

   <u>Phobias are varied.</u>

   Acrophobes get nervous when they are looking down from great heights.

   Agoraphobia causes people to withdraw and remain indoors for years.

   People who feel anxiety in closed spaces are claustrophobic.

11. Small cars are easy to park.

    <u>Many advantages result from owning and operating small cars.</u>

    Small cars usually run on three or four gallons of gas per week, depending on the miles driven.

    Cleaning small cars does not take much time.

    Small cars are easier to drive in traffic.

13. Many types of jobs are usually available.

Entertainment can be found in many places.

<u>Living in a city has advantages.</u>

Medical facilities are readily available.

Shopping centers provide a variety of stores.

15. Richard really likes Philip Marlowe.

The Maltese Falcon is one of his favorites.

<u>Richard enjoys American detective fiction.</u>

He has read several of Raymond Chandler's books.

Of current writers, he enjoys Robert B. Parker and Tony Hillerman.

He especially likes Ross Macdonald's detective stories.

EXERCISE 5 (Page 38)

Answers will vary.

EXERCISE 6 (Page 40)

Answers will vary.

EXERCISE 7 (Page 41)

Additional support sentences in each paragraph will vary. In each paragraph, the first sentence is the topic sentence, and the last sentence is the conclusion.

EXERCISE 8 (Page 45)

1. _____1_____ The roof on Frank's house leaked.

   _____2_____ He called a roofer to have it fixed.

3. _____1_____ Sammy and his mother bought dog food at the store.

   _____3_____ Sammy put the food down for his puppies at three o'clock.

   _____2_____ Sammy got the food ready with his mom's help.

5. _____3_____ Ruth attended classes.

   _____2_____ Ruth paid her registration fees for two classes in the fall.

   _____1_____ Ruth took a hundred dollars from savings for her fees.

7. _____4_____ Harry deposited his paycheck in the bank.

   _____2_____ Harry walked to the personnel office to pick up his paycheck.

   _____1_____ Harry cleared his desk for the day at 4:30.

   _____3_____ Harry filled out the deposit slip on the way to the bank.

9. _____4_____ Tosha removed the old filter and put in the new one.

   _____2_____ She bought oil and an oil filter from the automotive store.

   _____3_____ Tosha drained the oil from her car.

_____5_____ Tosha put the new oil in her car.

_____1_____ Tosha decided to change the oil in her car.

EXERCISE 9 (Page 48)

1. _____S_____ George bought a Ford.

   _____TS_____ George admires American cars.

   _____U_____ He needs a new lawn mower.

3. _____TS_____ Raising children can be a wonderful experience.

   _____S_____ Cathy has three children.

   _____U_____ Clothes for both boys and girls can be costly.

5. _____TS_____ The football training program is strenuous.

   _____U_____ The quarterback is an education major.

   _____S_____ The runningbacks have to run many wind sprints.

7. _____S_____ The librarian ordered fifteen new American novels.

   _____TS_____ The library has an extensive collection of American literature.

   _____U_____ The library's art collection is outstanding.

9. _____S_____ John wrote a research paper for Biology 101.

   _____TS_____ The biology class required several lab and writing assignments.

   _____U_____ John missed two biology lectures.

11. _____S_____ The rose quartz was one of the best pieces displayed.

    _____U_____ Kim liked to go rock hunting on weekends.

    _____TS_____ The school library had a special rock and gem collection.

13. _____S_____ The dishes need to be done.

    _____U_____ I finally hired a gardener to do the yard work.

    _____TS_____ Housekeeping can be a never-ending job.

15. _____TS_____ Swimming provides an excellent source of exercise.

    _____S_____ Swimming develops upper-body muscle tone.

    _____U_____ Many cities offer swimming classes during the summer.

17. _____U_____ John wants to run for public office.

    _____S_____ Two or three hours a day can be spent giving speeches.

    _____TS_____ Running for public office can be demanding.

19. _____U_____ Michael Jackson has his own private Ferris wheel on his estate.

    _____TS_____ Eli Bridge Company is America's foremost builder of Ferris wheels.

    _____S_____ The company has built approximately 1,400 Ferris wheels.

EXERCISE 10 (Page 50)

Paragraph 1

Adult reentry students often have special needs. They may have time restraints caused by families and jobs as well as by school. <u>Reentry students are willing to put in the extra time to be successful.</u> Since they sometimes work more slowly than younger students, they may require more time to complete tasks. As adults grow older, their vision is not as keen, so classrooms need excellent lighting with little glare. <u>They have more experiences than younger students.</u> Also, reentry students may experience hearing problems, making it hard for them to hear everything that is said in the classroom. These problems, although serious, do not need to be a barrier to education.

Paragraph 3

People from other countries have different reasons for wanting to come to live in the United States. For example, some might want higher-paying jobs than they can get in their own countries. Some want the freedom to change jobs or professions. Some might want the chance to get more education for themselves and their families. <u>Church groups often sponsor people coming to America.</u> Perhaps one of the most important reasons would be the desire to own and operate a business. <u>Many people wait a long time for the chance to live in the United States.</u> Every year, regardless of the reasons, many more people come to live in America.

EXERCISE 11 (Page 52)

Topic sentences with key words or phrases circled are given. Answers will vary for the rest of each paragraph.

Paragraph 1

Jason enjoys card games.

Paragraph 3

My favorite birthday present was a trip through the zoo.

UNIT 2 / Part 4

EXERCISE 1 (Page 68)

1. The Florida Everglades have a wide variety of beautiful birds.
3. Jill went home early because of the rain.
5. Jim leaned against the table for support.
7. The participant in the Iron Man contest continued beyond human limits.
9. Without thinking, the man spent his entire paycheck.
11. During the winter we enjoy traveling to a warmer climate.
13. We floated down the river on an inner tube.
15. One of my favorite sights is the Arizona sunset.
17. The child behind the tree is looking for her kitten.
19. The children staying at the lake preferred swimming in the pool.

EXERCISE 2 (Page 68)

Paragraph 1

Parenting requires major changes(for young couples). They must take the responsibility(for someone)(besides themselves). Staying(at home)and caring(for a new infant)twenty-four hours a day are two major changes. Parents are required to spend their money(on the child's needs)rather than(on their own needs). They need to be able to function(on less sleep)and be prepared to get up several times each night to feed, change, and comfort a small one. This commitment continues(for many years).

EXERCISE 3 (Page 70)

1. The <u>pizza</u>, <u>bread sticks</u>, and <u>salad</u> were her favorite meal.
3. The little <u>girl</u>(on the tricycle)ran(into the rose bushes).
5. (You)Please close the door.
7. The <u>man</u> and his <u>wife</u> discussed the various tours(of China).
9. The young <u>woman</u> took her book(off the shelf)and read it.
11. The <u>dog</u> and the <u>cat</u> are playing together.
13. The <u>students</u>(in the classroom)brought paper and pencils(to class).
15. <u>Josh</u> is the smartest person(in the world).
17. The <u>bride</u> and <u>groom</u> had a wonderful day.
19. The <u>water</u>(in the swimming pool)is clear and blue.

EXERCISE 4 (Page 71)

Paragraph 1

<u>Libraries</u> have many activities(for children)(in the summer). <u>Many</u> offer movie schedules (with educational, nonviolent classics). (Because of donations)(from public and private organizations), reading <u>programs</u> that award prizes can also motivate young readers.(For excitement), <u>goals</u> are made, and <u>prizes</u> can be won.(In most cases), <u>everyone</u> is a winner.(During many hot days), happy <u>children</u> are found browsing (through books), looking (at special displays), or watching fish(in the library aquarium). Cool, quiet learning <u>environments</u>(in a library)can be appealing(to children).

EXERCISE 5 (Page 77)

1. The <u>flowers</u>(in the vase) *need* water. (need, needs)
3. The <u>lady</u>(at the information booth)usually *knows* the answers. (know, knows)
5. The <u>circus</u> *brings* enjoyment(to all). (bring, brings)
7. The <u>leader</u>(of the group)*speaks*(at 7:00)tonight. (speak, speaks)
9. The <u>parents</u>(of young children)*have* many responsibilities. (have, has)
11. All <u>phases</u>(of production)*are done*(by the students). (is done, are done)
13. <u>Steve</u> *enjoys* going(to the lake) (enjoy, enjoys)
15. The <u>president</u>(of the college)*speaks*(at 6:00)tonight. (speak, speaks)
17. The <u>puppies</u> *play*(with each other). (play, plays)
19. The <u>bags</u>(of groceries)*need* to be put away. (need, needs)

EXERCISE 6 (Page 78)

1. A goose *Geese* <u>swims</u> *swim* (in the pond).

3. The <u>elephant</u> *elephants* (at the circus) <u>eats</u> *eat* hay.

5. The <u>man</u> *men* (at the counter) <u>donates</u> *donate* many extra hours (of work).

7. The <u>child</u> *children* (in the classroom) <u>listens</u> *listen* (to instructions).

9. The <u>church</u> *churches* <u>needs</u> *need* a new paint job.

11. The U.S. economic <u>policy</u> *policies* <u>is</u> *are* complicated.

13. The <u>doctor</u> *doctors* <u>works</u> *work* (on cars) (in the evenings).

15. My <u>tax</u> *taxes* <u>seems</u> *seem* high.

17. The <u>leaf</u> *leaves* <u>falls</u> *fall* (from the tree) (onto the sidewalk).

19. The <u>box</u> *boxes* (on the top) (of the table) <u>weighs</u> *weigh* ten pounds.

EXERCISE 7 (Page 79)

1. The <u>trees</u> (by the lake) ~~provides~~ *provide* shade (for the campground).

C 3. A <u>snake</u> moves (over the fallen leaves).

5. (From high (in the trees), <u>birds</u> continuously ~~sings~~ *sing* a cheerful song.

C 7. Heavy <u>rains</u> come occasionally (to the forest).

9. Blue <u>herons</u> ~~is~~ *are* abundant (on the lakes) (of northern Colorado).

11. <u>Hummingbirds</u> (with their long beaks) ~~drinks~~ *drink* (from feeders) suspended (between trees).

13. The blue <u>jays</u> ~~quarrels~~ *quarrel* (with one another).

C 15. <u>Ferns</u> (of different shades) (of green) grow wild.

17. (From inside the cabin), a <u>child</u> ~~ask~~ *asks* to go outside.

19. Not far away, <u>streams</u> (with clear water) ~~offers~~ *offer* a home (to trout).

EXERCISE 8 (Page 82)

1. <u>Each</u> (of the players) ~~bring~~ *brings* a different strength (to the team). (bring, brings)

3. Each <u>person</u> (on the team) *is* expected to perform well. (is, are)

5. Many (of the players) _are_ paid well (for their work) (is, are)

7. Few (of the fans) _realize_ the pressure players have. (realize, realizes)

9. Some (of the players) actually _feel_ underpaid. (feel, feels)

11. People _enjoy_ baseball whether (at the ballpark) or (at home) (in front) of the television set) (enjoy, enjoys)

13. Nobody _completes_ a task as well as Dan does. (complete, completes)

15. Each one (of the students) _completes_ the assignments (without problems) (complete, completes)

17. Few (of the fans) _feel_ hostility (toward the players) (feel, feels)

19. Single parents _need_ quiet time (for only themselves) (need, needs)

EXERCISE 9 (Page 84)

1. Everybody ~~plan~~ _plans_ time to relax.

3. Nothing (behind the fence) ~~are~~ _is_ worth keeping.

C 5. Everyone needs to spend time enjoying life.

7. Some (of the campers) ~~stays~~ _stay_ (in tents)

9. All (of my friends) ~~is~~ _are_ going (on a picnic) (with their families)

11. Without a doubt, someone ~~think~~ _thinks_ (of a good solution)

13. Children often ~~enjoys~~ _enjoy_ camping.

C 15. Many men become gourmet cooks.

17. Bookstores ~~sells~~ _sell_ books (for readers) (of all ages)

19. Any diversion (from routine activities) ~~are~~ _is_ rewarding.

EXERCISE 10 (Page 85)

Paragraph 1

Kenting Park is at the southernmost part of Taiwan. It is surrounded by a beach and high cliffs. Luxurious, high-priced hotels ~~is~~ _are_ available for those able to afford approximately $200 a day. When beach play ~~are~~ _is_ over, vendor markets with sea shells, costume jewelry, hats, and tourist trinkets ~~abounds~~ _abound_. The park north of the beach ~~have~~ _has_ exotic, tropical plants. For example, a 300-year-old Bonsai-like tree with old exposed roots ~~illustrate~~ _illustrates_ the coastal park's antiquity. In addition, a small cave with a stalactite forming an imaginative, fossil-like figure

brings   *offers*
bring relief from the sun and offer the passing tourist a peaceful rest. Kenting Park has many

attractions for visitors.

Paragraph 3

report
The people in the jury assembly room reports for jury duty in clothing that they ordinarily

wear   *look*   *wear*
wears to work. Several looks like students or service workers. They wears casual dresses or

appear
sport shirts and jeans. Some in work uniforms appears to be truck drivers or repair people.

sit
A large number of professional men and women sits in more formal suits. One gentleman

walks
apparently does not know the dress-code for jurors, and he walk around in shorts and a

bright blue T-shirt. This scene is a good example of the variety of people on juries.

EXERCISE 11 (Page 88)

Paragraph 1

Tense: present

A computer virus frequently creates many frustrating moments for users. With no better

motive than harassment, a hacker creates just one program that transfers itself onto an

destroy   *lock*
unsuspecting person's floppy disk. Some viruses destroyed data files, locked up computers,

make   *keep*
made text fall to the bottom of the screen, or kept a computer from booting. In any case,

appear   *infiltrate*
viruses often appeared at the worst time and rapidly infiltrated system networks, resulting

in great expense. It is unfortunate that a hacker's expertise is put to destructive rather than

constructive use.

Paragraph 3

Tense: present

Senior citizens receive many recreational opportunities by living in retirement commu-

attend
nities. Retired men and women attended craft classes that range from needlecraft to wood-

frequent
work. Community members frequented one or more recreational halls that are usually

stay
equipped with pool tables and shuffleboard courts. In the evenings, they stayed busy

receive

attending dances or parties. They ~~received~~ exercise in indoor or outdoor swimming pools,

tee

depending on the specific region of the country. Fervent golfers ~~teed~~ off on well-manicured

play

greens or ~~played~~ tennis on clean courts any time of the day. No matter what activity people

enjoy

enjoy, they find many others who ~~enjoyed~~ doing the same type of things.

UNIT 3 / Part 1

EXERCISE 1 (Page 94)

Situation 1

Topic:	resignation
Purpose:	notification of resignation with option to return to current employment
Audience:	boss
Voice:	serious, honest, sincere

Situation 3

Topic:	death of friend's mother
Purpose:	show sympathy, understanding
Audience:	friend
Voice:	personal, serious, warm, comforting

Situation 5

Topic:	compact disks
Purpose:	to sell compact disks
Audience:	Filipino business dealers and other consumers
Voice:	persuasive, informative, clear, simple

EXERCISE 2 (Page 99)

1. a. formal, neutral
   b. positive, praising
   c. put-down, offensive

3. a. neutral
   b. positive, complimentary
   c. negative, derogatory

5. a. nostalgic, positive
   b. complimentary, positive
   c. negative, offensive
   d. light, appreciative, positive

7. a. offensive, rude
   b. positive, light, appreciative
   c. nostalgic, factual, informative, formal
   d. negative

EXERCISE 3 (Page 101)

Answers will vary.

1. negative   The Texas bluebonnets that covered the hillside made my allergies
                worse.
    neutral   The Texas bluebonnets covered the hillside.

3. negative   My grandmother's miniskirt was disgusting.
    excited   Look at my grandmother's beautiful miniskirt!

5. angry   We are making the world into a stench ball.
    informal   Don't people realize we have all pitched in to save the environment?

7. nostalgic   "Old Blue" rusted away in the corner of the car lot.
    polite   Please be advised that no cars are allowed overnight in the parking lot.

9. angry   Bratty Johnny deliberately smeared chocolate on himself.
    positive   The small boy enjoyed the texture and the taste of the chocolate.

EXERCISE 4 (Page 103)

Paragraph 1

Topic: personal conflict about the future
Audience: counselor, friend, teacher
Voice: nostalgic, sad

Paragraph 3

Topic: job recommendation, qualifications of Shawn Stevens
Audience: fire department employer
Voice: formal, perceptive, sincere, persuasive

EXERCISE 5 (Page 105)

Answers will vary.

UNIT 3 / Part 4

EXERCISE 1 (Page 120)

1. ~~Sam~~ *He* is doing well in calculus this semester.

3. ~~Maintaining a consistent point of view~~ *It* is really quite simple.

5. ~~Quarreling~~ *It* is not going to help anyone on the committee.

7. ~~The faculty~~ *They* appreciated the new telephone system and used it often.

9. ~~Mary~~ *She* returns to the California coast for vacation every summer.

EXERCISE 2 (Page 122)

1. ~~Willie's~~ *My* enthusiasm for life increased ~~his~~ *my* productivity.

3. ~~Our family~~ *They/Their family* went on a picnic.

5. Henry, ~~listen to your~~ *listens to his* conscience when decisions need to be made.

7. ~~Christina~~ *I* often ~~volunteers~~ *volunteer* at the school for handicapped adults.

9. ~~Others~~ *I* have procrastinated until the last minute.

EXERCISE 3 (Page 127)

Paragraph 1

I love to haggle every time I go to a border town in Mexico. First of all, I make out a list of the items I would like to have. Then I find a market square that has lots of vendors. ~~Competition~~ *I believe that competition* allows me to do some comparative scouting and may mean lower-priced items. ~~You~~ *I* should always go dressed in older clothes so that ~~you~~ *I* don't look like the rich American tourist. As ~~you~~ *I* enter the store, ~~you should not~~ *I try not to* appear anxious. Next, with a maximum price in my mind, I casually saunter to the object that I most want. If the vendor's price is way above my price, I go to the next store. If not, I smile and offer him a price lower than my set price, and we begin haggling from that point. Usually, ~~a~~ compromise ~~is struck~~ *we can*, and we both go away happy.

> *Purpose:* to explain shopping in Mexico
> *Voice:* honest, frank
> *Audience:* general reader

Paragraph 3

Playing golf is a rewarding experience. It can be a time for relaxing and enjoying a beautiful day. Because many golf courses are located throughout the city, finding an available tee time is also easy and convenient. When ~~you~~ *golfers* play eighteen holes, ~~you~~ *they* walk approximately four miles and get ~~your~~ *their* day's exercise. Furthermore, ~~I believe that~~ golf is challenging. ~~I~~ *Some* used to think that golf was an easy game that did not require any ability, but it does require precision, patience, and skill. In addition, unlike other high-endurance sports

that only younger players can participate in, golf is a lifelong activity. ~~You~~ *Anyone* can enjoy it at just

about any age. Consequently, golf is a sport everybody should consider playing.

>   *Purpose:* to explain why golf is rewarding
>   *Voice:* informative
> *Audience:* someone thinking of taking up golf

Paragraph 5

The high-tech computer lab at our college is an efficient room. Over one hundred com-

puters are laid out so that maximum room is obtained for traffic flow, comfort, and usability.

Students can choose from a variety of hardware, and technicians are available to give help

or to answer questions. In addition to this, ~~you~~ *students* can easily check out the software ~~you~~ *they* desire

and sign in on the computer at the entrance to the room. One thing that ~~I have found in my~~ *students may find in their*

experience in the high-tech center is that ~~I~~ *they* can get copies of ~~my~~ *their* work quickly because all

stations are hooked up to printers. ~~You~~ *Students* might say that the high-tech center is a perfect place

for computer business and pleasure.

>   *Purpose:* to express pride in computer facilities
>   *Voice:* positive, informative
> *Audience:* potential users

UNIT 4 / Part 1

EXERCISE 1 (Page 135)

1. ___*c*___ is the most general word or statement.

  ___*a,b,d*___ are equal to each other.

  ___*e*___ is unrelated or part of another group.

3. ___*b*___ is the most general word or statement.

  ___*a,c,d*___ are equal to each other.

  ___*e*___ is unrelated or part of another group.

5. ___*e*___ is the most general word or statement.

  ___*b,c,d*___ are equal to each other.

  ___*a*___ is unrelated or part of another group.

7. _____*c*_____ is the most general word or statement.

   _____*b,d,e*_____ are equal to each other.

   _____*a*_____ is unrelated or part of another group.

9. _____*d*_____ is the most general word or statement.

   _____*a,b,e*_____ are equal to each other.

   _____*c*_____ is unrelated or part of another group.

EXERCISE 2 (Page 137)

1. *most general idea:* Pets aid the elderly
   words that are coordinate: security, companionship, self-esteem

3. *most general idea:* Iron Man competition
   words that are coordinate: swimming, biking, running

5. *most general idea:* People with diabetes must be concerned with
   words that are coordinate: exercise, diet, stress

7. *most general idea:* are important when a consumer buys a home
   words that are coordinate: location, price, size

9. *most general idea:* specialties of the chef school
   words that are coordinate: appetizers, main courses, salads, desserts

11. *most general idea:* Hillary Clinton serves as
    words that are coordinate: attorney, community service worker, administrator

EXERCISE 3 (Page 141)

1. a. formatting a disk, checking for viruses, running a program
   b. to check for viruses, to format a disk, to run a program
   c. ran a program, formatted a disk, checked for viruses

3. a. cooking chicken in the crockpot, steaming rice, barbecuing ribs, making a salad
   b. steamed rice, cooked chicken in the crockpot, barbecued ribs, made salad
   c. to barbecue ribs, to cook chicken in the crockpot, to steam rice, to make a salad
   d. make a salad, cook chicken in the crockpot, steam rice, barbecue ribs

5. a. to practice long hours, to read the directions, to talk to experts
   b. read the directions, practice long hours, talk to experts
   c. talking to experts, practicing long hours, reading the directions

7. a. to get an education, to meet new friends, to prepare for a job, to improve self-esteem
   b. meeting new friends, preparing for a job, improving self-esteem, getting an education
   c. prepares for a job, improves self-esteem, gets an education, meets new friends
   d. improved self-esteem, got an education, met new friends, prepared for a job

9. a. to type materials, to make phone calls, to file materials
   b. making phone calls, typing materials, filing materials
   c. filed materials, typed materials, made phone calls

EXERCISE 4 (Page 143)

1. National parks offer opportunities for seeing new places, ~~to have~~ *having* outdoor experiences, and meeting people from other states.

3. I enjoy going to that restaurant because the prices are reasonable, the food is excellent, and ~~good service~~ *the service is good*.

5. On my trip to Shanghai, China, I enjoyed visiting the Friendship House, ~~and the~~ Bunde shopping area, and ~~I also enjoyed~~ the Peace Hotel.

7. For safe driving, one must drive under control, ~~obeying~~ *obey* the speed limit, and never ~~to~~ drive under the influence of alcohol.

9. Some of the things we take into consideration when planning a vacation are ~~how much~~ money ~~to take~~, interesting places to visit, and ~~are we going to have~~ time.

11. Before going to college, consider ~~how much~~ money ~~you have to spend~~, time, and attitude.

13. Leaving home was very difficult for me because I had to say goodbye to my family, I ~~have~~ *had* to leave my friends, and ~~I~~ had to break up with my girlfriend.

EXERCISE 5 (Page 147)

Answers will vary.

UNIT 4 / Part 4

EXERCISE 1 (Page 164)

1. In addition, ^*we* went on a family vacation.

3. Suddenly and frantically, ^*he* searched for his girlfriend.

5. ~~Also~~ ^*His talk also* gave us a new perspective on life.

EXERCISE 2 (Page 165)

Paragraph 1

Citizens can do their part to help the environment. They can crush, save, and take aluminum cans to ~~centers. To~~ recycling centers. In addition, people can reuse containers ^*glass and plastic* rather than throw them away. ~~Glass and plastic containers.~~ Gardeners can use natural

ecological defenses such as lady bugs, water sprays, and beer solutions. ~~Rather~~ than pesti-
                                                                            rather *harmful*
                                                                              ^   ^

~~cides. Harmful~~ pesticides to eliminate insects. Car owners who service their own cars should
                                                                  motor
properly dispose of used ~~oil and filters. Motor~~ oil and oil filters. Saving the Earth is like
                              ^

preserving America's future.

EXERCISE 3 (Page 167)

1. Caring for a sick friend

   Randy is caring for a sick friend.

   Add a subject and some form of the verb "be."

   Caring for a sick friend is rewarding.

   Make the fragment the subject and add a main verb. (Add other words if needed.)

   Caring for a sick friend, I learned nursing skills.

   Add a sentence (subject and a verb) after the fragment.

3. Becoming older

   My dog is becoming older.

   Add a subject and some form of the verb "be."

   Becoming older is simply part of life.

   Make the fragment the subject and add a main verb. (Add other words if needed.)

   Becoming older, I appreciate life more.

   Add a sentence (subject and a verb) after the fragment.

5. Typing a research paper

   Joe is typing a research paper.

   Add a subject and some form of the verb "be."

   Typing a research paper is easier on the computer than on the typewriter.

   Make the fragment the subject and add a main verb. (Add other words if needed.)

   Typing a research paper, Tony spent hours in the lab.

   Add a sentence (subject and a verb) after the fragment.

EXERCISE 4 (Page 169)

1. To collect baseball cards

To collect baseball cards, she must be informed.

Link the fragment to a complete sentence.

Sara liked to collect baseball cards.

Add both a subject and a verb.

To collect baseball cards is a profitable hobby.

Make the fragment the subject and add a verb. (Add other words if needed.)

3. To win the lottery

To win the lottery, the secretaries bought ten tickets each.

Link the fragment to a complete sentence.

The secretaries wanted to win the lottery.

Add both a subject and a verb.

To win the lottery seemed hopeless.

Make the fragment the subject and add a verb. (Add other verbs if needed.)

5. To sleep late in the mornings

To sleep late in the mornings, John turned off his alarm.

Link the fragment to a complete sentence.

John liked to sleep late in the mornings.

Add both a subject and a verb.

To sleep late in the mornings was difficult for John.

Make the fragment the subject and add a verb. (Add other words if needed.)

EXERCISE 5 (Page 172)

1. Before we go on vacation, *we must get travelers' checks.*
3. Unless I can fix my car, *I will not be able to go to school.*
5. Until you buy insurance for your car, *you cannot drive it.*
7. So that I can go to the movies, *I will do my homework.*
9. If Randy will send us the information, *we will respond.*

EXERCISE 6 (Page 172)

Paragraph 1

Diabetes is a disease that requires control. *dietary* ^ Dietary control. People with diabetes need to

balance the insulin and sugar level in their blood. Most of the time, they need to avoid foods that contain sugar. They also need to eat smaller meals more often throughout the day.

However, if they have not eaten enough and their insulin level rises. ~~Must~~ *, they must* eat or drink

something with sugar so that the insulin level in their blood will be balanced. For example,

when they feel shaky. ~~They~~ *, they* may eat a candy bar or drink a soda pop. Diabetics can be

healthier. ~~If~~ *if* they watch their diet.

EXERCISE 7 (Page 174)

1. Humor is important to people's ~~health without~~ *health. Without* it, they become tired and depressed.

3. My cat had ~~kittens we~~ *kittens. We* had to find homes for them.

5. Michelle sang in the talent ~~show she~~ *show. She* danced, also.

7. The phone ~~rang it~~ *rang. It* was in the other room.

9. We went to the ~~store we~~ *store. We* bought bread.

EXERCISE 8 (Page 176)

1. Firefighters spend many hours training for emergencies *, so* they are well qualified.

3. Classes are over for the day *, so* we can go home.

5. The men placed third overall *, and* the women placed second overall.

7. A frost came in May *, so* many fruit trees didn't blossom.

9. The track team traveled to the conference meet *, and* they won second place.

EXERCISE 9 (Page 177)

1. Farmers depend heavily on nature *;* weather conditions are important to them.

3. Automobile technicians require specialized training *;* they must know computers and other electronic equipment.

5. His class is very interesting *;* I am learning a lot.

7. Audrey is a good nurse *;* I would recommend her.

9. Airplane travel is safer than automobile travel *;* air accidents are just more publicized.

EXERCISE 10 (Page 178)

1. I lost my traveler's checks *; consequently,* I had to go to the bank to replace them.

3. A free trade zone provides many jobs *; moreover,* the benefits profit the entire city.

5. Working is good for teenagers *; in fact,* they learn responsibility.

7. Sailing is a relaxing sport *; moreover/in fact,* a weekend sailor can escape reality.

9. The road was winding *; nevertheless,* it was several lanes wide.

EXERCISE 11 (Page 179)

1. People might like to move to a cold climate *if* they like winter sports.

3. I finished all my homework *so that* I could go to the movies.

5. We ate the fruit *although* it was sour.

7. The children played on the swings *before* they were called in to dinner.

9. I enjoy fishing *because* it is relaxing.

EXERCISE 12 (Page 181)

1. Father's Day is as important as Mother's Day *, but* it does not get as much publicity.

3. When a tornado touches down, it may destroy everything in its path *; however,* the American Red Cross assists the victims.

5. The children ended the school year with a swim party *;* they had a wonderful time.

7. While we were on the beach, we collected shells *. Then* ~~then~~ we built a sand castle.

9. In the springtime, the trees were covered with green leaves *and* the shrubs were covered with lavender blossoms.

EXERCISE 13 (Page 182)

Paragraph 1

The forest service is becoming more sensitive to the needs of the physically challenged outdoors person. Braille camping trails offer a way for the visually impaired to tramp through America's forests without fear. ~~America's~~ *remarkable* ~~remarkable~~ forests. Blind hikers can begin to experience what others take for granted. Braille signs identify the surrounding trees and plants. ~~As~~ *as* well as mark the trails. These trails are carefully constructed and twist their way

through wooded valleys. ~~And~~ *and* onto safe hillsides. Some paths are only a quarter of a mile ;

others stretch for almost a mile. ~~So~~ *so* that hikers can choose a long or a short route. Some

campgrounds have wheelchair accessible paths throughout the area, *and* some even include

ramps to lakes where the campers can fish from the bank. Each campground is calm, serene,

and accommodating to the physically challenged.

Paragraph 3

Owning cats can be a frustrating experience. Sometimes they want to be affectionate

and even sit in their owner's lap, ~~other~~ *Other* times, they treat their owner like a second-class

citizen and turn away. ~~Turn away~~ saucily. A person who does not know cats may be frus-

trated by their cautiousness. ~~And~~ *and* mistake it for a lack of affection. For example, a lazy-

looking cat gazing out the window may really be a lonesome pet, ~~he~~ *. He* may really be eagerly

waiting for the owner to come home. When the owner does come home. ~~The~~ *, the* cat probably

will not immediately jump down like a dog and run to greet the ~~owner the~~ *owner. The* cat may cau-

tiously turn his head and look the other way. He is not ignoring his owner but just showing

caution in case the owner may ignore him. This is the kind of lukewarm "hello" that

frustrates people who do not understand. ~~Understand~~ cats.

EXERCISE 14 (Page 184)

15. OK   13. F   11. OK   9. F   7. CS   5. OK   3. F   1. OK

UNIT 5 / Part 1

EXERCISE 1 (Page 196)   **EXERCISE 2 (Page 200)**

Answers will vary.   *Answers will vary.*

EXERCISE 3 (Page 202)

Paragraph 1

When my child first learned to read, short-term rewards were often more important than
the actual ability to read. He wanted to be a good reader. When he realized he needed to

work hard and practice, he wasn't sure reading was as important as watching "Mr. Wizard's World" to obtain his knowledge about the scientific world. However, he was willing to sit down and plan a strategy. Because he also wanted to set up an aquarium that had been unused for many years, together we decided that for every fifty pages he read aloud to me, he could either buy a fish or have two dollars of in-store credit. ~~He had two other pets.~~ With this agreed upon, he assembled the aquarium, filled it with water, and went to the fish store to wish. As soon as we got home and he walked through the door, he said, "Let's read." And read we did. Even though the first book was below his grade level, it took him four days to finish fifty pages. However, it only took twenty minutes to get the first inhabitant for his tank. That one fish looked lonely, and the only solution was to read another fifty pages. Soon he had earned another fish and another fish. ~~The fish cost me anywhere from eighty-nine cents to two dollars.~~ Moving up to grade-level books brought a little resistance because there were NO pictures. But soon these books, too, seemed easier and easier until he was able to select books way above grade level. Now he was enjoying reading for the sake of reading, and he began to read extra books on his own. ~~Of all the books he read, he enjoyed the one about a kid who ended up with jars and jars of goldfish with no place to put them.~~ As he earned fish, he began to love reading for the sake of knowledge, but he had seldom found reading a chore because every page had brought him closer to a new fish.

EXERCISE 4 (Page 203)

Answers will vary.

EXERCISE 5 (Page 206)

Paragraph 1

Early Americans had to rely on their own ingenuity to make life comfortable or even to survive. They turned survival skills into a type of art that was passed down from generation to generation. Some of these art forms, which may no longer be practical in today's society, were a part of living for our great-grandparents. In the West, sturdy houses could be made from adobe brick, but first the brick had to be made from mud and straw. Making clothes was also an art of the past that few people could accomplish today. Even buying material for clothes was a luxury few knew. The process of making a new dress or shirt or pants involved shearing sheep, carding wool, spinning yarn, and weaving cloth. Sometimes the clothing maker dyed the yarn different colors, using natural materials like walnut shells. ~~The women enjoyed growing flowers to make the home look more attractive.~~ Tatting—making lace by hand—became an art form that was used to decorate collars or to bring beauty to something as necessary as pillowcases. ~~People loved to get together in the evenings and have dances.~~ Since there were no refrigerators, families found making beef jerky was a way of preserving meat that provided a year-round supply. And if they wanted to take a bath, they needed soap, but making soap at home, an art almost unheard of today, was required before that bath could take place. When the supply of candles, the source of night light, became low, there was one solution—making more from melted lard. ~~Sometimes the men and women would work from sunup to sundown so they could take a day off for celebration.~~ Today, we talk of "the good old days" when life was simple, but maybe we should say when families were resourceful and used art in order to survive.

EXERCISE 6 (Page 208)

Paragraph 1

In order to avoid the high costs of living, many retired couples have become full-time recreational vehicle travelers ("RVers"). After selling or renting their homes, they literally spend their time traveling. One couple sold their home and bought a fully equipped van.

They now pull a boat that provides recreation, and, when the boat is not being used on the water, it provides storage. Another couple sold their home and now spend several months in an Indiana resort area trading a few hours of work for a place to stay and free hookups. When summer comes, they do the same thing in an RV resort in Florida. Another retired couple spend their time working at national and state parks in exchange for a place to live and modest pay. ~~Likewise, a couple who lived in New Mexico now spend all their time moving from one national park to another serving as a host to the RV campground.~~ In this way, these retired people reduce their living costs and are able to live on moderate retirement funds.

EXERCISE 7 (Page 209)

Paragraph 1 SIE

Paragraph 3 Ext

Paragraph 5 SIE

EXERCISE 8 (Page 211)

Answers will vary.

UNIT 5 / Part 4

EXERCISE 1 (Page 230)

1. Tourists on Virginia Beach watched fireworks on Thursday. *, and they* ~~They~~ went sailing on Friday.

3. I did not enjoy the food. *, nor did I* ~~I did not~~ care for the entertainment.

5. Robert exercises regularly. *, yet he* ~~He~~ has trouble losing weight.

EXERCISE 2 (Page 232)

1. The toll charge was a quarter. *; therefore,* Frank paid it as he entered the freeway.

3. Traveling can be a pleasant experience. *; however, it* ~~It~~ can be stressful for a large family.

5. Many people give to charity. *; nevertheless, the* ~~The~~ food bank needs more canned goods.

EXERCISE 3 (Page 233)

1. We enjoyed going to the ocean. *; the* ~~The~~ children collected seashells.

3. Mark was hungry. *; he* ~~He~~ snacked on peanuts.

5. The dog barked loudly. *; soon* ~~Soon~~ it stopped.

EXERCISE 4 (Page 233)

1. *Maria rolled her own tortillas, and she made fresh green chili.*
   (coordinate conjunction)

   Maria rolled her own tortillas; she made fresh green chili.
   (semicolon)

   Maria rolled her own tortillas; in addition, she made fresh green chili.
   (conjunctive adverb)

3. *Brenda is an excellent secretary, and she works well with people.*
   (coordinate conjunction)

   Brenda is an excellent secretary; she works well with people.
   (semicolon)

   Brenda is an excellent secretary; in addition, she works well with people.
   (conjunctive adverb)

5. *The child got out the peanut butter and jelly, and he made a sandwich.*
   (coordinate conjunction)

   The child got out the peanut butter and jelly; he made a sandwich.
   (semicolon)

   The child got out the peanut butter and jelly; thus, he made a sandwich.
   (conjunctive adverb)

7. *Randi has an extensive doll collection, so she attends many doll shows.*
   (coordinate conjunction)

   Randi has an extensive doll collection; she attends many doll shows.
   (semicolon)

   Randi has an extensive doll collection; as a result, she attends many doll shows.
   (conjunctive adverb)

9. *Dusty won the national roping contest, and he won $2,000.*
   (coordinate conjunction)

   Dusty won the national roping contest; he won $2,000.
   (semicolon)

   Dusty won the national roping contest; in fact, he won $2,000.
   (conjunctive adverb)

EXERCISE 5 (Page 236)

Paragraph 1

Throughout their adult years, people often need to adjust to many changes in their lives.

, and often

Technology may require people to retrain for a new job. ~~Often~~ company restructuring

; sometimes

causes change. Sometimes promotion causes change. ~~Sometimes~~ job loss causes change.

Other major changes occur in people's personal lives, too. For various reasons, some mar-

, so they

ried adults are separated from their mates. ~~They~~ must take on the total responsibilities for

; however, some

the household. Many adults must deal with having the last child leave home. ~~Some~~ people

, and other times

must cope with adult children returning home. Sometimes they return alone. ~~Sometimes~~

, or they

they return with children. Once in a while, they may return with a mate. ~~They~~ may return

with a mate and children. All these situations can cause adults to make shifts in their life-

styles.

Paragraph 3

Today more than ever, people are realizing the need to conserve our resources, especially

, but every

water. This effort can be effective. ~~Every~~ American must be willing to make adjustments.

, for these

~~These~~ adjustments will save this essential resource. Anne is one person who has done her

, and then

part to help in this effort. Inside her house, she always fills her dishwasher. ~~Then~~ she runs it.

She always washes a full load of clothes. She has also placed a water saver in her toilet tank.

; as a result, each

~~Each~~ flush takes less water. She never leaves the water running while she brushes her teeth.

, so this

Outside, she has installed a drip-water system to keep her plants wet. ~~This~~ way she does not

lose water to evaporation. She has also landscaped her yard with plants that require little

; moreover, she

water. ~~She~~ never uses the hose to wash off the sidewalk or driveway. If every American will

try to follow this example, millions of gallons of water will be saved every day.

UNIT 6 / Part 1

EXERCISE 1 (Page 245)

Answers will vary.

EXERCISE 2 (Page 247)

Answers will vary.

EXERCISE 3 (Page 249)

Answers will vary.

EXERCISE 4 (Page 250)

Answers will vary.

EXERCISE 5 (Page 251)

Answers will vary.

EXERCISE 6 (Page 253)

Answers will vary.

EXERCISE 7 (Page 256)

Answers will vary.

EXERCISE 8 (Page 258)

Paragraph 1

Williamsburg, Virginia, offers a time-travel visit to 1775, a year before the American Revolutionary War. The city was restored in the 1930s to its 1775 appearance, so it resembles the town as it was in the 18th century. The governor's palace that housed the royal ruling power exhibits impressive 18th-century guns and swords on the walls and ceiling in organized, decorative patterns. In another historic area near Gentryville and Dale, Indiana, the Lincoln Boyhood National Memorial contains a log cabin that is an approximation of the original cabin where Lincoln once lived. The area also includes a living historic farm where early 19th-century life is portrayed. Such realistic depictions and information that take people back to earlier times can be obtained by visiting restored historic landmarks. Through these moving re-creations, visitors can obtain historical information and gain a feeling for bygone times.

Paragraph 3

"Reading is to the mind, what exercise is to the body," Sir Richard Steele wisely stated. Steele's quotation draws an analogy between the importance of exercise to tone the body and reading to stimulate the mind. If people do not exercise, they become fat, sluggish, unhealthy, and weak, and this condition is readily visible. When people do not exercise their minds, they become mentally unhealthy and weak, yet this situation is even more dangerous because it is not noticeable. This is especially true for children in their formative years when habits are developing. Reading can make the difference between a strong or weak mind. Encouraging children to read improves vocabulary, expands understanding, and increases their creativity.

EXERCISE 9 (Page 259)

Answers will vary.

EXERCISE 10 (Page 265)

Answers will vary.

EXERCISE 11 (Page 268)

Answers will vary.

UNIT 6 / Part 4

EXERCISE 1 (Page 290)

1. The manager resigned his position because it created too much stress in his life.

   Because it created too much stress in his life, the manager resigned his position.

3. The students went to the library to do some research as soon as their classes were over for the day.

   As soon as their classes were over for the day, the students went to the library to do some research.

5. You will not have difficulty making a good grade on the test if you study very hard and work with a tutor.

   If you study very hard and work with a tutor, you will not have difficulty making a good grade on the test.

EXERCISE 2 (Page 292)

1. George Washington, who was the first president of the United States, was the only president voted in unanimously.
3. The book that my brother borrowed yesterday was my favorite novel.
5. The tools for the job were listed in the memo that the supervisor sent yesterday.

EXERCISE 3 (Page 294)

1. How I earn my own money is my business.
2. Why that house is deteriorating is beyond me.
5. Who will be elected is up to the voters.

EXERCISE 4 (Page 295)

1. They understood why I could not go to the wedding.
3. We know that the difficulties can be overcome by hard work.
5. The librarian realized that the books were shelved in the wrong place.

EXERCISE 5 (Page 298)

Paragraph 1

Basketball requires a variety of physical skills. *Because stamina* ~~Stamina~~ is a stringent requirement for this highly active sport. ~~Many~~ *, many* times the victory goes to the team with the greatest physical endurance. Agility is another important factor for basketball players. ~~They~~ *because they* must be able to move smoothly and quickly. ~~They~~ *so that they* can coordinate their moves. Scottie Pippin's finesse on the court is a great example of winning, aerobic-like moves. Sheer aggression defines the dribbling path of his drives to the basket. ~~Players~~ *If players* have peripheral vision. ~~They~~ *, they* can pass without looking at the players receiving the ball. ~~Jumping~~ *Because jumping* ability is important. ~~Great~~ *, great* basketball players can slam dunk and get many rebounds. These physical skills can lead to a winning team.

Paragraph 3

Although there are many educational toys in the store today, I didn't have an opportunity to learn from them as a child. However, I did learn from simple items. ~~They are~~ *that were* free for the taking. I had mastered the fine art of making bows and arrows. ~~I~~ *After* had learned the types of *, I* tree branches that made strong yet flexible bows. Then I learned by trial and error. ~~I learned~~ how tight the string should be to make the arrow "sing." ~~I~~ *When* needed a fishing pole. ~~I~~ *, I* learned which pieces of wood would stay strong against the pull of a hungry fish. I learned to braid bracelets from long strands of grass. I learned to take a simple piece of wood and carve it into a gun. Most educational of all, I learned to paint pictures. ~~I made natural dye from various items.~~ *that were made from natural dyes.* For example, I crushed blackberries to get a deep purple and used natural coal for black. These "toys" gave me amusement, but, more important, they gave me knowledge. ~~I~~ *that I* still possess ~~this knowledge~~ today.

UNIT 7 / Part 1

EXERCISE 1 (Page 306)

Paragraph 1

The park swings

A small park can be a haven for children. ~~Swings~~ are big and sturdy so children can

Children love to feed the ducks that

swing, seemingly to the tops of trees. ~~Ducks~~ swim close to the shore to eat whatever the

At the same time, older   while others   safely

small visitors bring. ~~Older~~ children canoe through rippling water. ~~Others~~ stand or sit at the

are content to

edges of the lake and throw out fishing lines complete with worms. The children wait for

They feel comfortable knowing their parents are relaxing or napping

some hungry fish to bite the hook. ~~Parents of the children relax or nap~~ under the shade of

nearby trees. Here the world feels safe as children watch other families enjoying the park.

Paragraph 3

Making a quilt takes some planning. The most important part of making a quilt is

After choosing a design, it is also

selecting a design for the quilt. ~~It is~~ important to buy materials that look nice together.

In addition, adding

~~Adding~~ some materials with different textures makes the quilt more appealing. A place to

make the work more pleasant

work that has lots of room helps when putting the quilt pieces together. Planning a quilting

too, just as a   Moreover, setting

pattern that looks good helps. ~~A~~ tight quilting frame makes the job easier. ~~Setting~~ up the

frame close to other family members or near the television set makes the quilting seem less

When all phases of the project are planned carefully, a

boring. ~~A~~ beautiful quilt can be created.

Paragraph 5

The teenagers learn that meeting

Running a lawn service can help teenagers acquire business skills. ~~Meeting~~ people and

also

keeping people happy are part of the job. Bills must be sent and accounts must be kept.

In addition, new   Moreover, when the lawn

~~New~~ customers who are added must be worked into the schedule. ~~When~~ equipment wears

out, it must be repaired or replaced. Getting each lawn done properly and rapidly helps

a teenager to become a dependable worker.   and can be applied to future jobs.

~~business skills.~~ These business skills can be acquired on the job.

EXERCISE 2 (Page 309)

Answers will vary.

EXERCISE 3 (Page 311)

Essay 1

During my morning jog, I stopped and talked to a man who was carefully tending his garden. When I expressed interest in the luscious garden, he replied, "I got over five, five-gallon buckets of strawberries alone this summer." I was taken by surprise because the strawberry patch was only about six feet by five feet. His green-bean vines that were growing along the fence were loaded with long, healthy beans, and I could only wonder how many of those he had harvested. Seeing his garden made me think of all the benefits that gardening can bring to anyone who is willing to put in the time and effort. Although having a small garden can be hard work, it can result in pleasure and savings.

The benefits of a garden *, however,* do not come without work. ~~S/he~~ *First, the gardener* must select a location for the garden. ~~It~~ *After the plot of ground is selected, it* needs to be dug out and loosened. ~~Sawdust~~ *Next, sawdust,* peat, and fertilizer mixed and added will allow the seeds to grow easily. ~~Growing~~ *Just as important, growing* instructions need to be followed when the seeds are planted. ~~The~~ *Finally, the* garden must be watered, weeded, and debugged daily. Watering at *sometimes can be difficult but* the correct time of day is necessary. Keeping the weeds to a minimum *is hard work but* makes the garden vegetables stronger. A good gardener prepares a good place and watches the plants as if they were helpless, defenseless creatures.

With a little dirt, water, and sunshine, a A garden can bring many pleasures. The sight of small sprigs reaching up through the soil toward the sun gives the feeling of capturing a small part of nature and getting in touch with the earth. What greater satisfaction is there for the gardener than to know that s/he has used the elements to produce food? ~~More~~ *Usually, more* than enough is produced, and the gardener can proudly share the crisp flavor of fresh produce with a neighbor. In view of the much-publicized insecticides on commercial produce, the gardener can use natural combatants such as ladybugs or praying mantis or ingenuity to preserve the vegetables and feel comfortable knowing the products from the garden are healthy. A garden can be the source not only of food and pride, but also of peace of mind.

After the initial work is done, having
~~Having~~ a small garden to bring in fresh vegetables provides a savings. Each year grocery

For example, tomatoes
prices slowly creep up unnoticeably on such items as lettuce and tomatoes. ~~Tomatoes~~ that

now   *Likewise, lettuce*
last year cost 49 cents a pound, cost 59 cents. ~~Lettuce~~ is sold at 69 cents a pound instead of

These   *increases make*
69 cents each. ~~The~~ gradual price ~~increase makes~~ one wonder if the consumer will ever see

The savings are easy to see because a
the end. ~~A~~ pack of tomato or lettuce seeds costs about 70 cents total, and these seeds can

Moreover, extra
provide enough tomatoes and lettuce for an entire summer. ~~Extra~~ vegetables can be frozen

Additional savings occur when
or canned to provide a year-round supply of fresh food. ~~Surplus~~ vegetables can be sold to

The gardener also saves money by trading   *to prevent*
bring in extra money. ~~Trading~~ produce with other gardeners ~~prevents~~ buying so much at

the grocery store. Gardens can add much-needed pocket change and give the feeling of

defeating the inflationary war.

Work, time, and patience
~~One~~ can transform a tiny seed into baskets of delicious, healthy food. By gardening, a

Though a
person can experience a miracle of nature and can save money at the same time. ~~A~~ person

may not be able to get the twenty-five gallons of strawberries in a five-by-six plot of ground,

~~but~~ that same person may be able to have as many strawberries as can be eaten and still

have some left over. The only way to find out is to try.

UNIT 7 / Part 4

EXERCISE 1 (Page 327)

1. The shelties ate their food, played together, and then slept for two hours.
None 3. The playful mule needs to be fed and watered.
5. The small, sparkling, odd-shaped rock was discovered by the farmer, taken to the appraiser, and sold for a lucrative price.

EXERCISE 2 (Page 328)

Paragraph 1

Grandparents, aunts, uncles, and cousins gathered for the annual picnic at the park.

Together they ate the attractive and well-prepared food that smelled delicious, tasted great,

and satisfied everyone. Then the older children took turns playing volleyball, tennis, and

tetherball. Some of the grandparents spread blankets on the green grass for the little ones to take their bottles^, to nap^, or just to rest. Sometimes the adults, too, fell asleep. Later they

took turns riding on the park's train^, looking through the model-train exhibits^, and reading

about the history of trains. Soon, however, everyone returned to the picnic tables to munch

on leftovers and talk about last year's picnic.

EXERCISE 3 (Page 330)

1. After Jason polished his car^, he took his girlfriend for a ride.
3. Quickly^, Phil jumped out of the shower to answer the phone.

None 5. Becky was on a diet because she had gained too many pounds over the summer.

EXERCISE 4 (Page 330)

Paragraph 1

According to Luigi Ciulla^, the biggest challenge he faced when he came to America in

1961 was to find a job. Because he had trouble filling out an application^, people would say,

"I'm sorry. We don't have a job for you. When you learn to speak English^, then we can hire

you." Just to work on an assembly line^, employees had to pass required IQ tests. Because

the tests were in English and because they were timed^, it was almost impossible for a person

who spoke very little English to pass them. Luigi said that even though some words are

learned by studying books^, some words just cannot be learned without living in a country.

He also said that he didn't know anyone, so it was hard to find people to use as references

on application forms. Because he had never worked in this country^, he had no references

from previous employers either. One other obstacle in finding a job was lack of any "con-

nections." There was no one who could help him get a "foot in the door." He also had to

face the reality that many jobs were far away and transportation to these jobs was hard. He

said, "Even if I knew how to drive^, it was hard to pass the written test for a driver's license."

That was twenty-nine years ago, and today he is hiring people to work for him in his own

business.

EXERCISE 5 (Page 333)

1. I will, as a matter of fact, complete the project on time.
3. The pecans, for instance, that I bought at the stand were old.
5. The book is, I believe, the leading authority on genetics.

None 7. The girl who is a gymnast is from Salt Lake City.

EXERCISE 6 (Page 334)

Exercise 1

The sign reads "No skating, biking, running, or loud music." A granite wall progressively emerges from the ground. From one-sixteenth of an inch and one name, the wall grows to one-half inch, then to a foot. Two names appear, then three, five, ten. With no logical mathematical sequence, the names increase on the wall until at midpoint it reaches approximately eight feet tall with hundreds of names tightly embedded one after another. The time depicted by the wall was, of course, the 1960s, and the names represent the soldiers killed or missing in Southeast Asia during the Vietnam War. The visual representation of heartfelt American deaths turns the tourist chatter to silence. Experiencing the Vietnam Veterans Memorial, it seems, makes visitors realize the sacrifices of American youth.

EXERCISE 7 (Page 336)

1. What I want to know, Ruby, is how you do your art so well.
3. The letter sent to 316 West Dove Drive, Loganville, Georgia 31624, was returned to the sender.
5. On November 8, 1993, the nine black lab puppies were born on the corner of a farm in Loveland, Colorado.
7. Sondra, when did you visit your cousin in Nashville, Tennessee?

EXERCISE 8 (Page 336)

Paragraph 1

On September 1, 1939, Germany invaded Poland and started World War II. Beginning in 1940, Hitler invaded Belgium, Luxembourg, Denmark, Norway, and France. On April 9, 1940, the Germans seized Denmark and invaded Norway. Just one month later, on May 10, 1940,

Germany invaded Belgium. Just a few days later, on May 14, 1940, the Netherlands surrendered. Because England had treaties with France, she made good her commitment, and on September 3, 1940, Great Britain and France declared war on Germany. On May 26, 1940, the Allied Powers began their heroic evacuation at Dunkirk, a seaport in northern France. By 1940, the entire European continent was at war. Then, on June 22, 1941, Germany invaded the Soviet Union. On December 7, 1941, Japan attacked Pearl Harbor, bringing the United States into the war. By now, almost all countries in the world were involved in this devastating war.

EXERCISE 9 (Page 340)

1. *"If* I can get off work *early,"* said *Kevin, "we'll* go to the *lake."*

3. The sophomore class chose *"Go for it"* as the motto on their T-shirts.

5. The poem *"The Horses"* is in the book To Read Literature by Donald Hall.

None 7. Keith said that he needs to get his car inspected as soon as he gets home from work.

EXERCISE 10 (Page 341)

Paragraph 1

My family's trip to the Grand Canyon northwest of Flagstaff, Arizona, was an unforgettable experience. On June 17, 1993, we boarded the steam train in Williams, Arizona, and headed for the Canyon. The train moved across the Kaibab Plateau, which was rolling hills covered with scrub cedar. Once there, we got off the train and walked to Bright Angel Lodge where we bought a lunch that we enjoyed under a tree at the South Rim of the Canyon. There we could see the colorful layers of rock, shadows made by clouds, and distant evergreen trees. We were impressed by the vastness of the Canyon, and from the Canyon's edge, we could see part of Bright Angel Trail. Soon, however, we needed to walk back to the train for the trip back to Williams. Although we were tired, we were inspired by what we had seen.

EXERCISE 11 (Page 343)

Paragraph 1

During World War II, average American citizens experienced many difficulties buying products they wanted or needed. The ability just to be able to buy products was restricted by monthly ration stamps for such items as gasoline, shoes, sugar, and meat. Though people had ration stamps, meat was especially hard to find because it was put into products like Spam and sent to the men overseas. Even with stamps, citizens might not be able to buy the products they wanted. Often the shelves were empty because it seemed as though everything was channeled into America's defense system. For example, shoes were difficult to obtain because the shoe producers needed to supply boots for the army. Likewise, material was difficult to purchase because fabrics were shipped to factories to make uniforms for the Armed Forces. Jim and Alice Basham, who owned their own upholstery business, said, "We could not buy goods to upholster furniture because material was shipped to the Armed Forces." They also said that women were unable to buy nylons because the fabric needed to make them went into making parachutes to be used in the war. Imported items like coffee, tea, sugar, and rubber were scarce. The little rubber that the United States could import went into the production of tires for the Armed Forces. For four years, no automobiles were made because all American energies were channeled into the production of military vehicles. American citizens who lived through World War II will always remember those hard times.

Paragraph 3

Poetry is an art form that can be enjoyed sometimes because of the meaning, sometimes because of the way it is written, and other times because of both. Can anyone read Walt Whitman's "Leaves of Grass" without saying, "That is nice"? Lines that seem to "stick in the mind" are often written with a strong message. For instance, the lines from Anne Sexton's poem "The Abortion," "Somebody who should have been born/is gone," stay in the mind long after the poem has been read. Whenever the question of abortion arises, these lines are recalled in the mind again and again. Thomas Hood wanted to change labor laws in England. In his poem "The Song of the Shirt," he wrote, "With fingers weary and worn,/With eyelids heavy and red,/A woman sat, in unwomanly rags,/Plying her needle and thread—" John Milton, married but miserable, spent much effort inserting lines about divorce into his poetry in an attempt to change the laws that forbade divorce. Some poets, however, do not moralize but simply present things the way they are. James Dickey, a well-known American poet, wrote of adultery objectively without making any judgment of its "wrongness" or "rightness." On the other hand, Joyce Peseroff expresses her ideas in "The Hardness Scale," in which she seems to be relating a woman's feeling about a man who is not such a perfect man. Diane Wakoski writes of revenge in her poem "You, Letting the Trees Stand as My Betrayer." In this poem, nature will pay back someone who loved her and then left her. The meaning is there in these and many other poems, but the way they are written makes the lines occur over and over in the reader's mind.

Answers to Confusing Words (Appendix A)

PAIR 1 (Page 395)

1. Steve often has ~~alot~~ _a lot_ of figs on his tree.

3. Sonja often caught ~~alot~~ _a lot_ of fish at that lake.

PAIR 3 (Page 396)

C 1. When people move to a new country, they must adapt to new customs.

3. They hoped to ~~adapt~~ _adopt_ the little girl.

PAIR 2 (Page 396)

C 1. She accepted my apology and walked away with a frown on her face.

C 3. She accepted the money greedily.

PAIR 4 (Page 396)

C 1. John advised Butch not to hike the steep mountain.

3. I ~~adviced~~ _advised_ her to do her house chores early.

PAIR 5 (Page 397)

1. His action cannot ~~effect~~ *affect* us.

*C*3. His honesty affected everyone around him.

PAIR 7 (Page 398)

1. Sharon was ~~all together~~ *altogether* surprised by his comment.

*C*3. All together, we worked for at least two weeks on that job.

PAIR 9 (Page 398)

1. ~~Are~~ *Our* children are ready to go to the zoo.

3. The trees ~~our~~ *are* growing faster than we had hoped.

PAIR 11 (Page 399)

1. Mrs. Smith needed to ~~by~~ *buy* detergent for her washing machine.

*C*3. Mick needs to be at church by 8:30 A.M.

PAIR 13 (Page 400)

1. This is a wonderful ~~cite~~ *site* for the new building.

3. I was unable to catch any ~~site~~ *sight* of him.

PAIR 15 (Page 401)

*C*1. The crowd sighed in relief when she became conscious.

*C*3. I didn't want to study, but my conscience reminded me of the importance of making good grades.

PAIR 6 (Page 397)

1. Are you ~~already~~ *all ready*?

*C*3. When she got to the party, everyone was already there.

PAIR 8 (Page 398)

1. She divides her time ~~among~~ *between* job and family.

*C*3. That item was among the first ones to be considered.

PAIR 10 (Page 399)

1. The bus driver slammed on the ~~break~~ *brake*, and the passengers flew forward.

3. When the car in front of us stopped, I hit the ~~break~~ *brake* with my foot.

PAIR 12 (Page 400)

1. The field trip included a visit to the ~~capital~~ *capitol* building.

*C*3. When he gets enough capital, he plans to start his own business.

PAIR 14 (Page 400)

*C*1. The course I liked the best was not necessarily the easiest.

3. The ~~coarse~~ *course* he took was a challenge.

PAIR 16 (Page 401)

1. Everyone at the lake should ~~of~~ *have* used sunblock.

*C*3. The street leading to the city could have been blocked off.

PAIR 17 (Page 402)

counsel
1. The ~~council~~ for the defense was an inexperienced attorney.

counsel
3. The father gave ~~council~~ to his son.

PAIR 18 (Page 402)

C 1. He ate his fourth poppy-seed muffin.

3. The prime minister must continue to
forth
move ~~fourth~~.

PAIR 19 (Page 402)

good
1. The flowers smell ~~well~~.

good
3. The apple pie was ~~well~~.

PAIR 20 (Page 403)

hear
1. Didn't you ~~here~~ the car honking?

hear
2. From our kitchen, we could ~~here~~ birds singing.

PAIR 21 (Page 403)

hole
1. Be careful; I think there's a ~~whole~~ around here.

whole
3. Tall, yellow weeds covered the ~~hole~~ field.

PAIR 22 (Page 404)

infer
1. What did you ~~imply~~ from the speech?

implied
3. From what he ~~inferred,~~ did you infer the right answer?

PAIR 23 (Page 404)

it's
1. I believe ~~its~~ going to be a rainy day.

its
3. It's been a long time since ~~it's~~ beginnings.

PAIR 24 (Page 404)

C 1. The meteorologist knew it was going to rain Wednesday.

knew
3. I ~~new~~ the test would be difficult.

PAIR 25 (Page 405)

know
1. Don't you ~~no~~ not to stick a fork into the toaster?

C 3. I know I shouldn't watch TV when I have homework.

PAIR 26 (Page 405)

C 1. The young man continued to lie throughout the investigation.

lie
3. The doctor advised Chad not to ~~lay~~ in the sun.

PAIR 27 (Page 406)

lose
1. Mom didn't want to ~~loose~~ Amy in the crowd, so she held her hand tightly.

C 3. The knot Bob made was too loose to hold the calf.

PAIR 28 (Page 406)

passed
1. My teammate ~~past~~ the ball to me, and I made a touchdown.

C 3. Mr. Van passed out the test at 8:00.

PAIR 29 (Page 406)

1. Pass Julio a ~~peace~~ *piece* of cherry pie.

3. Roger lost a ~~peace~~ *piece* of my science project, but I passed anyway.

PAIR 30 (Page 407)

1. Our ~~principle~~ *principal*, Ms. Jones, is a sensitive woman.

3. I called her and explained the new club's ~~principals~~ *principles*.

PAIR 31 (Page 407)

1. Laura is ~~quiet~~ *quite* a pretty girl.

3. The Russians were ~~quiet~~ *quite* surprised that they came in second in the gymnastics events.

PAIR 32 (Page 408)

1. Beatrice started to ~~rite~~ *write* her essay but was interrupted by another phone call.

3. I broke my ~~rite~~ *right* hand when I fell.

PAIR 33 (Page 408)

C 1. We will be through by then.

3. He has more money ~~then~~ *than* I do.

PAIR 34 (Page 408)

1. They left ~~there~~ *their* book in their car.

C 3. The puppy is hiding there in the grass.

PAIR 35 (Page 409)

C 1. Though Juana was tired, she stayed up and baked bread.

C 3. The Comets lost the game though they played their best.

PAIR 36 (Page 409)

1. Sarah climbed ~~threw~~ *through* the tunnel and ran for the slide.

3. Ann ran ~~threw~~ *through* the woods, jumping over logs and stones.

PAIR 37 (Page 410)

1. The final score was three to ~~too~~ *two*.

3. Nicki finished her paper, ~~to~~ *too*.

PAIR 38 (Page 410)

1. He ~~wonders~~ *wanders* from one city to another.

C 3. I often wonder how my family is doing.

PAIR 39 (Page 410)

1. Is she too ~~week~~ *weak* to go shopping?

3. The child gets an allowance every ~~weak~~ *week*.

PAIR 40 (Page 411)

1. The ~~whether~~ *weather* is great in Colorado in the summer.

C 3. The weather for tomorrow is predicted to be beautiful.

PAIR 41 (Page 411)

Where
1. ~~Were~~ were you when I needed help?

where
3. Tanya went ~~were~~ the other students were playing volleyball.

PAIR 43 (Page 412)

that
1. Cecil threw out the food ~~who~~ was spoiled.

who
3. The people ~~that~~ came late to the concert could not get in.

PAIR 45 (Page 412)

you're
1. Jesse said that ~~your~~ not going.

you're
3. I'm sorry, Jane, but ~~your~~ not going to be able to swim today.

PAIR 42 (Page 412)

Who's
1. ~~Whose~~ at the door, John?

Who's
3. ~~Whose~~ at the other end of the phone?

PAIR 44 (Page 412)

women
1. The three ~~woman~~ went through nurse's training together.

C 3. The most prestigious award was given to an outstanding woman student.

Index

Instructor's Manual for
WRITING PARAGRAPHS AND ESSAYS

Integrating Reading, Writing, and Grammar Skills

Second Edition

Joy Wingersky
Glendale Community College, Glendale

Jan Boerner
Glendale Community College, Glendale

Diana Holguin-Balogh
Front Range Community College, Colorado

WADSWORTH PUBLISHING COMPANY
Belmont, California   A Division of Wadsworth, Inc.

Contents

Introduction

Teaching writing to basic writers is often a challenge, not necessarily because learning to write is difficult for them, but rather because they have often experienced failure as writers. This failure has left students with the feeling that writing is easy for others but not for themselves. As the instructor, therefore, you can help your students understand that writing is a skill that can be learned. Your students will gain confidence along with their skills if you simplify the process by beginning with one simple concept and adding other skills one at a time so that writing becomes cumulative. When you give students one task at a time rather than many all at once, you and your students will experience less frustration. For this reason, we have sequenced the writing process into concepts that your students can understand and practice one at a time. Unit I shows various means of prewriting to generate ideas for writing. The remaining seven units all follow the same arrangement. Part 1 in each unit shows the student how to do one step of the writing process and gives exercises for practicing that skill, including collaborative exercises. Part 2 in each unit is an article by a professional that can be a model of writing as well as a means for generating ideas for writing assignments that follow. Part 3 in each unit consists of model paragraphs and/or essays that demonstrate the skill explained in Part 1 of the same unit. Part 4 in each unit consists of a grammar component that is related to the writing skill taught in Part 1 of the same unit or in previous units. Part 4 ends with suggested writing assignments that encourage revision but, at the same time, stress only the particular concepts taught and illustrated in that unit. Unit 8 has no new grammar component; it has extensive writing assignments throughout.

We believe that a major goal of an instructor is to help students build confidence by showing them in one-on-one writing conferences what they have done correctly and then what needs to be done next for them to gain greater control of the concept being practiced. The organization of *Writing Paragraphs and Essays* promotes this type of learning. Since the focus of the text is learning one skill at a time, you might consider having students rewrite their assignments until they are "acceptable," without assigning any letter grades. Classroom research has demonstrated that students have a greater chance of succeeding if they do not go on to the next writing assignment until they are ready. "Succeeding" means only that the student can do those skills that have been practiced. Your students will revise a writing assignment one or more times until they have done it correctly. Therefore, by the time they go on to the next writing assignment, they understand what needs to be done and can apply what they have learned to the next assignment. For example, students rewrite the first writing assignment until they have a topic sentence and until all sentences in the paragraph support the topic sentence. Students must be able to accomplish this before moving on to the next writing concept. Students progressing slowly can easily work collaboratively with other students who have already finished that writing assignment, or you can work individually with them. One-on-one writing conferences, which can be very brief, help you monitor individual student progress.

Because some students will need longer than others to complete an assignment, you might consider self-pacing the classroom. After the first three or four writing assignments, some students are able to work ahead while others are not ready to do so. Self-pacing makes it easy for you to work one-on-one with each student. If you spend half of the class time in an in-class lab/workshop setting, with students either working on computers, writing out the assignments by hand, or bringing in typed drafts of their assignments for you to look at, you can give more individualized instruction. Since few students finish at exactly the same time, you will be free to help students during the process of writing by explaining quite rapidly what needs to be done to accomplish the goal of each assignment. The students can then immediately revise the paper because they understand what needs to be done. On the other hand, if the paper is acceptable, students may go on to the next writing assignment, work with someone else, write in journals, or read ahead in the text about the next concept to be studied. Often you may refer students to a particular section of the text for review. Though this workshop approach is very demanding and requires keen concentration from both you and your students, you can feel certain that students understand what is required of them. You also never have to wonder if you are wasting your time writing comments that students might not read or understand.

Being self-paced does not mean that the class has no structure. On the contrary, a self-paced class must be highly structured and organized so the students know everything that must be completed throughout the course. Each student, however, may meet objectives at different times.

One of the most important concepts to get across to students is that effective writing means hard work and revision. However, students who work hard consistently and fairly rapidly should not have to wait for other students to catch up before they can continue with additional assignments. If your course is self-paced, you can allow your students to take their final examination (which should be a writing assignment) as soon as they have completed all assignments. Also, if your department/division policy allows some flexibility, you might consider allowing the students to take the final more than once to receive a grade of "C" or better. (A suggestion for giving finals is included on page 28 in this Instructor's Manual.)

We realize that self-pacing is not desirable for all instructors. Because *Writing Paragraphs and Essays* was written for different classroom formats, it can be used successfully in classes that are not designed around in-class writing workshops. You may assign reading and exercises as homework to be discussed during the next class or you may assign exercises to be done independently as you wish. If you would like to include a testing component in your class, an A and B version of nine tests are included (18): six grammar concepts, one for punctuation review, and two for writing sections are included in this instructor's manual. If you wish to use small-group work, you will find many exercises in **Writing Paragraphs and Essays** that are suitable for collaborative activities. (See section on collaborative learning on page 4 of this manual.)

Proficiency Examinations

Writing Paragraphs and Essays provides practice in both "local" and "global" skills required for students to pass proficiency tests in usage, sentence skills, and paragraph and essay writing. It provides exercises that are suitable for individual, small-group, and whole-class practice. An instructor is free to choose whatever will give students the best pre-test preparation.

Usage and grammar exercises are integrated into writing sections; however, exercises stressing individual skills can be assigned and discussed as needed. For example, *Writing Paragraphs and Essays* covers the following individual grammar and usage points: subject-verb agreement; consistent verb tense; fragments, run-ons, and comma splices; consistent point of view; and a thorough review of punctuation. The paragraph exercises (throughout the book) requiring editing for these "local" problems also provide extensive practice for students who need these skills to pass an essay proficiency test. In addition, an appendix gives simple explanations and exercises in using commonly confused words, such as "their," "there," and "they're." Exercises at the sentence-level include parallel structure.

Writing Paragraphs and Essays provides practice in the skills students need to write and revise an essay for a proficiency test. Students consider purpose, audience, and voice in a writing situation. They generate ideas and examples suitable for the topic chosen. In addition, they organize and think through the relationships of ideas, then draft, revise, and edit both paragraphs and multi-paragraph essays. Moreover, the unit on generating and writing topic sentences includes exercises designed to help students discriminate between general (main) and specific (supporting) ideas. Exercises in this unit also help students think through the logical arrangement of ideas within paragraphs. Because variety in sentence structure is one of the major criteria used to evaluate student essays, *Writing Paragraphs and Essays* also includes major sections on sentence combining to achieve sentence variety. Exercises stress more mature simple sentences (with little abstract grammar terminology), compound sentences, and complex sentences.

Furthermore, *Writing Paragraphs and Essays* includes an entire unit on the rhetorical modes of development. If students are required to pass a proficiency test by writing an essay using one of these modes, this section would give them many examples and much practice in these more advanced skills. This unit would be an excellent review for students who already have adequate writing skills but need a simple review of the rhetorical modes. *Writing Paragraphs and Essays* covers the following rhetorical modes: illustration, comparison-contrast, classification, definition, cause-effect analysis, process, and argument.

Another strength of *Writing Paragraphs and Essays* lies in its many student and professional models that require students to read, answer comprehension questions, and analyze the reading to understand how it incorporates the writing skills being discussed in each unit. The unique sections "Something to Think About, Something to Write About" also encourage students to write in response to thoughtful, well-written essays.

Collaborative Learning

Current research supports the value of collaborative learning in the classroom; therefore, we have added collaborative activities throughout the text. Collaborative learning increases the student's opportunities to learn and practice skills in situations like those they may encounter in life outside the classroom. To be successful though, you must plan carefully so that you keep the class organized and on task. You want every activity to be productive for both you and your students. As your class becomes actively involved in group work, your class will move away from a teacher-centered classroom to a student-centered classroom where students think and learn through participation in small groups.

If you are experienced at using collaborative techniques, you already know the benefits as well as the responsibilities, but if you are new to this kind of teaching, a list of benefits might be helpful. Collaborative learning

encourages students to become involved in the learning process and, thereby, take responsibility for their own learning

helps students utilize ideas and experiences from other students

creates a need for students to cooperate with each other to achieve success

prepares students for working as part of a team to solve problems in other classes and in the work place beyond school

makes thinking and writing more exciting

fosters respect for the ideas and culture of other people

The following suggestions are designed to help you plan collaborative activities for your classes:

Consider the number of students in each group, for example, two to five. Decide how the groups will be formed: at random in class by the "count-off method," at random by student choice, or arranged by you ahead of time. Advantages and disadvantages exist for all these methods, but after trying a few collaborative activities, you will arrive at the best arrangements for your class. Part of collaborative learning is modifying procedures based on the particular characteristics of each class.

Decide on the responsibility of each group member: to ask questions, to take notes, to contribute a definite number of ideas, to keep track of time, or to report to the class later for the group, etc. If you decide to have students work in larger groups, you might want to have the students select a group leader whose job is to keep the group on task.

Develop ahead of time, the written materials the students will need and/or the transparencies you want. You might want to model a collaborative exercise by having the class as a whole perform the activity while you assume the role of the group leader.

Anticipate how long each activity should take based on the importance of the skills or concepts being learned and practiced. A

20-minute exercise allows ample time for other activities. Decide on the specific outcomes for the activity. For example, each group might develop topic sentences, define words, brainstorm topics, answer specific questions about someone else's essay, read a model introduction in the text and then collaboratively write a paragraph with the same kind of hook.

At the same time, you must decide if the completed assignment will be written or oral, presented individually or as a group. Finally, decide if you will evaluate each student individually or if the group, as a whole, will receive the same grade.

Unit Notes

Unit 1   Introduction to Writing

Unit 1 is designed to show students how the writing process works. The students are given strategies for prewriting, writing, and rewriting. Emphasis is placed on the thinking that is an integral part of the writing process. No writing assignments are suggested in this part so that students can simply concentrate on ways to generate ideas and can see how a simple version of the writing process works. The emphasis is on showing students that writing is systematic and can be learned. A collaborative exercise is presented to help students think about the writing process. This is an ideal place for you to model this activity with a simple piece of your own writing, like a memo, letter, or note to a colleague.

Unit 2   Writing Sentences and Paragraphs

Part 1   Parts to Whole: Topic Sentences and Paragraphs

Part 1 in Unit 2 explains and gives examples of the elements in strong paragraphs. First, it shows how to tell a topic sentence from other kinds of sentences and how to develop a topic sentence and support sentences for a paragraph. We use a directed writing assignment first and then discuss the text material on the topic sentence. (We sometimes use the first journal writing assignment [Appendix B] for this first writing assignment.) For example, we have students get out a pencil or pen and a piece of paper. Then we ask them to recall the safest, most secure place they can remember from their childhood or where they went when they got into trouble. Before students begin to write, we answer all questions and explain that they should write only for content, ignoring errors or problems in spelling and punctuation. We then have them concentrate on their special place as we prompt them. We ask the students to begin describing that place on paper as soon as they can visualize it in their minds. We ask them to recall what they saw, what they heard, what they smelled, and who was there. We repeat these sensory-provoking questions as students are asked to look into their minds and then share this place on paper. We stop using these verbal prompts only when all students begin writing.

This exercise can easily be done prior to studying the topic sentence because most students will have a usable topic sentence. Many will begin by saying, "The safest place I remember as a child was my bedroom" or "my tree house in the back yard." Many of their memories will be what made this place safe. The prompts we give them to get started help to keep them on the topic. However, if students have not stayed with the idea of a safe place, we help them to see that, during revision, they need to prove "in what way" this place was safe. This freewriting can become the first writing assignment and can provide an opportunity to use a workshop or collaborative approach. For this first writing assignment, we stress only main idea and support for this main idea. When students are asked to concentrate on too many tasks at one time, they may become frustrated and give up.

How should you give feedback to your students about this first writing assignment? You may want to use a sample student paragraph from another class to show how someone else has done this assignment. One strategy is to show two versions of the same paragraph on the overhead projector—one that needs more work and one that has been revised. Before putting up the revised version, you might try to get students to make observations about the paragraph to see if they are understanding the concept of main idea and supporting information. Then show the revised draft so they can see the improvements. We never use a current student's paragraph as an example of poor writing.

If you feel comfortable having the class critique class members' papers as a group, you might then put up a copy of a current student's paper. First, have the class find several good points about the paragraph. Then have students make suggestions on what could be done to strengthen the paragraph. *Do not ever refer to these suggestions as bad points.* Though students may be reluctant at first to have their paragraphs critiqued in front of the whole class, they will soon welcome having the other students help them rewrite their paragraph if a non threatening atmosphere is maintained. During this activity, we stress revising sentences rather than correcting spelling and punctuation. Until students have gained enough skills to know what they should be looking for in papers, we have them comment on papers as a class rather than in small groups. After collaboratively working as a class, students can break into groups to critique each other's papers.

An additional component in Unit 2, Part 1 discusses, gives examples of, and includes exercises for the unity, logical order, and coherence of paragraphs. Sometimes it is difficult to know when to help basic writers with problems in coherence. Because of the various levels of ability and experience, some students will probably have some sense for coherence and effective writing. Others need patient instruction in the most basic skill needed to connect sentences logically. If a student has many problems in writing, it may be best to concentrate first on basic sentence structure and paragraph unity and not try to teach coherence until later in the term. The best way we have found to help students with basic paragraph writing is to work individually with them on their own paragraphs. Coherence is covered in depth in Unit 7, Part 1.

Part 1 of this unit concludes with two collaborative projects: one to help students formulate topic sentences in a group and one to help them evaluate student paragraphs in the text.

Part 2   Something to Think About, Something to Write About

Dr. Coble's article, which discusses childhood memories from the viewpoint of a psychologist, can help students reinforce the value of the past as it provides ideas for writing. The article helps support the idea that students' personal experiences are important and are worth writing about. It may also encourage students to share ideas and feelings. You may want to discuss the article in class as a model for writing because it does exemplify topic sentences and support for paragraphs. Writing assignments suggested directly or indirectly by Dr. Coble's discussion are listed at the end of the article.

This is a good time to introduce *journal writing*, which you may or may not want to require. Much current research indicates that this extra writing practice helps students improve. If you decide to require journal writing, some suggestions are in order to allow students the opportunity to use journals without adding a burden for you. For example, if you require your students to write for one hour a week, a log can be very useful. We ask students to have a separate notebook for journals. Then they write JE1 (Journal-entry 1) at the top of the first page. In the left margin, they enter the time they start, then write for however long they wish, and then, in the right margin, enter the time when they stop. When they have written for a total of one hour (or however long you might require) they begin on JE2. If you wish to use a one-page log for students' journals, one is provided in the instructor's manual. This log can be duplicated so that students can attach it to the inside of the front cover of their journals. All you have to do is check the time entered in the log and initial the end of the entry. You may sign the log and/or assign points for each journal entry completed. (Transparencies for sample journal entry and log can be found on pages 70 and 71 of this Instructor's Manual.)

We think that reading students' journals makes the students write to please their instructors rather than to write what they really think and feel. When the instructor is the audience, students experience inhibitions that defeat the purpose of journal writing of this type. We do not read our students' journals and always inform the class of this procedure, so the students get practice and we are not bogged down by an undue amount of paperwork. We often use the analogy of learning to drive a car to explain this to our students:

If you wanted to learn to drive, you can either get instruction or just get in the car and drive. You will probably learn to drive either way; however, you will learn more easily and more rapidly if you receive both instruction and driving practice. We have provided you with a textbook that will help you learn the basics of driving. In return, we ask that you practice driving. The more you practice, the better you will become. Do not wait until the end of the course to practice driving or you will find the driving test difficult to pass. In the same manner, we ask that you practice writing before you try to pass a final essay in this course.

Part 3   Paragraphs for Discussion and Analysis

Part 3 includes student and professional examples that illustrate topic sentence and support. Each writing model has questions on both content and form that can be used for class discussion. Most writing models include a vocabulary study. You might want to remind students that these are revised versions of paragraphs. (Answers for Part 3 begin on page 19 of this Instructor's Manual.)

Part 4   The Writer's Tools: Basic Sentence Skills

Part 4 deals with basic sentence skills. The most common problems include sentence-structure errors, errors in subject-verb agreement, and inconsistent verb tense. Because eliminating sentence structure errors (fragments, run-on sentences, and comma splices) is so important, we preview them in this chapter but treat them in depth in Unit 4, Part 4, when students are better able to understand these types of errors. If you feel these should be covered in depth at this point, you might want to include Unit 4, Part 4 at this time.

Identifying subjects and verbs is explained simply. We have students identify prepositional phrases first because we find that they often confuse prepositional phrases for the subject of a sentence. Once they can recognize prepositional phrases, we find they can determine subjects and verbs more easily. Also, once they can identify subjects and verbs, we have them check for subject-verb agreement and consistent verb tense. Once they practice on the paragraphs in the text, we have them check their own paragraphs and essays for these problems throughout the term. Though we point out other errors and help the students correct these errors, we keep the emphasis at this time on topic sentence, support sentences, and basic sentence skills. At the end of Part 4 in each unit is an editing checklist. Each checklist includes the current concept being taught as well as those from previous units.

Students will gain skill and confidence if they look for only one new kind of problem at a time. If you see that a student does not have any of these problems, then you probably will not want that student to spend too much time on the text exercises. A self-paced class will allow you to evaluate each student's progress individually. Starting on page 29 of this Instructor's Manual, you will find A and B versions of nine twenty-point tests (eighteen tests) that you may want your students to take. We allow our students to take a test as many times as necessary to understand the concept being taught. If you choose to self-pace your class, you might want to have these tests kept in a learning center or testing center so that students may take them whenever they are ready without taking up class time.

Unit 3   *Being a Sensitive Writer*

Part 1   Parts to Whole: Interaction of Topic, Purpose, Audience, and Voice

Part 1 deals with interaction of topic, purpose, audience, and voice. You probably want to help students be aware that the purpose for writing is not achieved unless it has the appropriate voice to go with it. In this part, students learn to distinguish the elements in a writing situation. Students also need to know that they can control these elements. The exercises help students gain confidence in their ability to control these elements in their writing. You might consider having each student write a letter in response to an injustice that has been done. You might suggest that they write this letter, not in anger, but rather in explanation of what has happened. We encourage students to write a letter to the editor of the local newspaper or to the president of a company with which they have experienced a problem. If a student's letter is published or if a student receives a response from a company, the student can share the response with the class and let the other students discuss it.

Part 1 of this unit concludes with one collaborative project that has several options designed to help students practice writing using a particular voice and audience.

Part 2   Something to Think About, Something to Write About

In "Getting off the Roller Coaster," Jerry Palmer explains how it is possible to recognize a problem and have the stamina to face that problem. His voice is sincere and identifiable as he speaks candidly of his experiences while overcoming alcoholism. This voice allows students to empathize with him.

From this article, students can begin to think about problems that they or someone that they know has had to cope with. Some of these problems they have no control over, but other problems they do have control over. This discussion can lead to writing such meaningful assignments as ways of coping with physical disabilities, family problems, loss of jobs, or drug use. Students can put into practice what they have learned about becoming sensitive writers.

Part 3   Paragraphs and Essays for Discussion and Analysis

Part 3 includes student and professional examples that illustrate the interaction of topic, purpose, audience, and voice. Each writing sample has questions on both content and questions that can be used for class discussion. Most writing models include a vocabulary study.

Part 4   The Writer's Tools: Consistent Point of View

Unit 3, Part 4, shows students the importance of maintaining a consistent point of view. You might want to point out to students how point of view affects voice. For example, first person is more personal just as third person is more formal and detached. You might have students break into small groups and then collaboratively write paragraphs about purchasing books at the bookstore on the first day of class using first person (the participant's point of view). The same paragraph can then be changed to third person (an observer's point of view) simply by changing the pronouns. In this way, students will learn to control point of view by learning to control pronouns.

You might want to mention that point of view can also be changed by changing the speaker. For example, if the paragraph were written from the bookstore manager's point of view, third person would probably still be used. The word choice and perspective, however, would be from a different slant.

You might also point out to students that unintentional mixing up of the point of view is a sure sign of lack of experience in writing and is very distracting to the reader. If the students are aware of point of view and have control over it, then when they intentionally want to shift the point of view, it is possible to do so effectively. The better control they have over their language, the more control they have over situations in which language is needed to solve problems.

Unit 4   *Organizing Ideas and Writing Them Clearly*

Part 1   Parts to Whole: The Thesis Sentence

Once again, students are asked to add only one new skill, the thesis sentence. This section of the text covers both a thesis that simply states the topic and direction and one that states topic, direction, and a preview of the main points of the paper. We find that our students do better when they preview the main points of the paper in the thesis sentence. Another alternative would be to have the students write a thesis that contains only a topic and a direction and then have them include a topic outline with their paper. We find the previewed subpoints easier for students to understand. That is why we ask them to include these points now, though they may do that mentally when they become more experienced writers.

You might want to explain thesis sentence and then put a topic on the board for students to brainstorm as a class. Have them quickly name whatever comes to mind. Then help the students group these ideas together to form a topic outline that could be incorporated into the thesis sentence. After your students do this as a class, have them work in groups creating thesis sentences that preview the main points of the paper. If you do not want them to preview the main points in the thesis sentence, you might want them to include a topic outline. Possible topics might be summer break, dating, good students, and/or eating. You might have the students write on transparencies with felt pens and then put each group's work on the overhead. A positive critique can help students build confidence in writing thesis sentences. Then, during the next class period, have all students begin a writing assignment that requires a thesis sentence. If you wish, you might require each student to have you approve the thesis sentence before writing the essay. For the remainder of the term, you can allow students to check their thesis sentences with you before continuing with any of the remaining writing assignments.

Because this is the first multi-paragraph essay, you will need to show students how each point in the thesis sentence or the topic outline will be used as a topic sentence in the essay.

When the students do their first multi-paragraph essay, we ask the students to put the thesis sentence by itself, separating it from the support paragraphs of the essay. We find that when our students are asked to limit a thesis to one sentence, then later when they add a hook, transition, and thesis to form the complete introductory paragraph, they are familiar with a concise thesis sentence.

Part 1 of this unit concludes with two collaborative projects, both designed to help students formulate thesis sentences.

Part 2   Something to Think About, Something to Write About

In the article "Your College Years," Dr. Hartman deals with changes that students experience while they are attending college and becoming independent from their parents. Dr. Hartman, a psychologist and minister, has focused on the youth who have possibly gone away to college and are thus in transition from their parents' world to their own world. Because there may be parents of teenagers in your class, class discussion might also include parents who have watched or are watching their children move away from home. Your class may also include international students who have experienced new values while living in America.

You might have the students describe the voice in this article and discuss its appropriateness for the topic. You might also point out how his article illustrates a clear thesis sentence with fully developed paragraphs that support that thesis sentence. Dr. Hartman does not preview the main points in the thesis sentence, but he does show "in what way" college students experience change.

Part 3   Essays for Discussion and Analysis

Part 3 includes student and professional examples that illustrate thesis sentence and support. Each writing sample has questions on both content and form that can be used for class discussion. Most writing models include a vocabulary study.

Part 4   The Writer's Tools: Eliminating Fragments, Run-On Sentences, and Comma Splices

Though sentence-structure errors were briefly introduced in Part 4 of Unit 2, Part 4 in this unit deals extensively with fragments, run-on sentences, and comma splices. Although this part contains some sentence-level revision exercises, the emphasis in the text is on editing paragraphs rather than isolated sentences. The text groups fragments into four of the most common types of errors students make. If your students' essays show a repetition of the same types of errors, you might want to point out the type of errors they are making and have them carefully work though the explanation in the text. (See transparencies beginning on page 77 of this Instructor's Manual.)

After covering this concept, you might want to place the greatest emphasis on correcting sentence-structure errors in your students' own assignments. This is a good time to include group editing of each other's papers. Since there is more than one way of correcting an error, the students might suggest different ways to their peers.

Unit 5   Writing with More Depth and Variety

Part 1   Parts to Whole: Writing with Examples

Part 1 of this unit shows development through specific examples. It includes instruction on both short, interrelated examples and extended examples. At this point, students should be able to write a thesis sentence and have support paragraphs. However, they often have a difficult time developing each paragraph without being redundant. By adding examples, they are clarifying the points being made and are developing their paragraphs more fully.

When students are unable to write using specific examples, you might use the following dialogue. When a student says something like, "The managers at fast-food stores don't seem to care about their employees," you might respond by saying, "How do I know they don't care?" The student might reply, "They are always scheduling me to work when I can't." You then might respond by saying, "I don't understand. Please give me an example." The student might say, "Well, I have classes until 1:00 p.m. on Mondays, Wednesdays, and Fridays, and the managers always schedule me to come in at 12:00 p.m. Anyhow, sometimes I have to work until 1:00 a.m. when I should have gone home at 8:00 p.m." This would be a more specific example to explain "in what way the managers don't care about their employees." Students can then get a better idea of using specific examples.

You might also have the students use specific words instead of general words. For example, when they say "song," have them name specific songs. When they say sports, have them name specific sports and even particular teams. Because some students can apply these ideas more quickly than others, one-on-one revision conferences allow you to work with students at their best pace.

Part 1 of this unit concludes with one collaborative project designed to help students generate short, interrelated examples.

Part 2   Something to Think About, Something to Write About

In "Would You Know a Computer If You Met One?" Professor Ottenberg shows how people are not aware of how many times they are dependent upon computers in their everyday lives. Students are able to relate to the many examples and usually can identify them.

Professor Ottenberg uses both extended examples and short, interrelated examples to develop her thesis. Paragraphs 5 and 6 are effective models of extended examples, just as paragraphs 11 and 12 are effective models of short, interrelated examples.

You might also want to ask students to identify the point of view used and explain how it relates to the author's purpose. You might ask the students how the "you" point of view adds to this article. Students will probably understand that this point of view makes the article more personal by involving the reader more closely.

Part 3   Paragraphs and Essays for Discussion and Analysis

Part 3 includes student and professional examples that illustrate writing with examples. Each writing sample has questions on both content and form that can be used for class discussion. Most writing models include a vocabulary study.

Part 4   The Writer's Tools: Sentence Variety—Forming and Punctuating Compound Sentences

Part 4 of this unit shows various ways of combining simple sentences into compound sentences to obtain more maturity in writing. Though this material is important, you might cover it briefly and then stress having students incorporate compound sentences into their next writing assignment. When covering this material, you also might stress punctuating compound sentences correctly. Again, some students need more help than others in applying these concepts. (See transparencies starting on page 87.)

Unit 6   Reaching an Audience by Creating Interest

Part 1   Parts to Whole: Introductory and Concluding Paragraphs

Part 1 of this unit shows students a simple step-by-step approach to writing introductory paragraphs. It stresses having the students write a thesis first, then a hook, and then a transition from that hook to the thesis sentence, which is the last sentence in the introductory paragraph. The text explains and illustrates six types of hooks. (See transparencies.) You might explain these hooks and then write a thesis sentence on the board. Then have students suggest possible hooks that can be used. After working as a class, you might write a different thesis on the board and have students work collaboratively in groups to create possible introductory paragraphs. Students can work on transparency sheets that can then be put on the overhead. The class can easily see different hooks for the same thesis sentence. Exercises for creating and revising introductions in the text can be used for small-group activities.

After students practice writing introductory paragraphs, you will want to teach concluding paragraphs. The text includes what is necessary in concluding paragraphs and gives some options for developing them more fully. You might go through these and then have students practice writing conclusions based on the introductory paragraphs written previously. (See transparencies on pages 90-97.)

Part 1 of this unit concludes with one collaborative project designed to help students understand as well as compose various types of hooks that can be used in writing introductory paragraphs.

Part 2   Something to Think About, Something to Write About

"Women in Science and Engineering," by Professor Emhoff, gives examples of women who are not as well known in their field as their male colleagues even though these women have made significant contributions to science and engineering in the past one hundred years. You might have students discuss what the purpose of this article is and how the author gets her point across. The purpose is stated in the thesis, and she gets her point across through detailed examples.

You might point out to students how the hook used in the introduction to this article is a statistic and a specific example. The introduction prepares the reader for the kind of information the article includes. Though the thesis sentence does not preview the main points of the paper, it is clearly stated and is the last sentence in the introductory paragraph. Since this article is both informative and persuasive, the author comes back to the idea that women's talents have not been recognized and uses a quotation that reinforces the main point.

Part 3   Essays for Discussion and Analysis

Part 3 includes student and professional examples that illustrate introductions and conclusions. Each writing sample has questions on both content and form that can be used for class discussion. Most writing models include a vocabulary study.

Part 4   The Writer's Tools: Sentence Variety—Using Complex Sentences

Part 4 builds on the skill of forming compound sentences. Many times students write short, choppy sentences simply to avoid having fragments in their writing. However, once they can recognize what a complete sentence is, they can combine these sentences in different ways to achieve sentence variety. You might put two short sentences on the board and have students combine them in as many ways as possible using the list of subordinators. Punctuation of complex sentences is also stressed. The sentence combining becomes more difficult as the section progresses.

This is a good time to review all types of sentence combining and/or revision covered in the text. An example is given here of compound, complex, and more sophisticated simple sentences. (Also on transparency, page 100, in this Instructor's Manual.)

The old man enjoyed his garden. He planted many new flowers.

Compound

The old man enjoyed his garden; he planted many new flowers.
The old man enjoyed his garden; as a result, he planted many new flowers.
The old man enjoyed his garden, so he planted many new flowers.

Complex

The old man enjoyed his garden where he planted many new flowers.
Because the old man enjoyed his garden, he planted many new flowers.
The old man enjoyed his garden because he planted many new flowers.
The old man that enjoyed his garden planted many new flowers.
The old man who planted many new flowers enjoyed his garden.
The old man whose garden contained many new flowers enjoyed them.

Simple (From the section on fragments, run-on sentences, and comma splices)

Enjoying his garden, the old man planted many new flowers.
To enjoy his garden, the old man planted many new flowers.
Enjoying his garden caused the old man to plant many new flowers.
Planting many new flowers helped the old man enjoy his garden.

Unit 7   *Making Ideas Flow Clearly*

Part 1   Parts to Whole: Coherence

At this point, students should be able to handle the concepts of *key words, time signals, other transitional words,* and *using pronouns* to make ideas flow smoothly. Although you may have already directed more motivated students to study this section, they could benefit from class discussion of the kinds of transition available to writers.

One strategy is to use sample paragraphs on transparencies. Show the kinds of transition one at a time by underlining the words or phrases on the screen. First, go through the paragraph and show how the *key word* from the topic sentence or a *variation* of the key word is repeated throughout the paragraph. Then, go through the paragraph and point out one at a time each of the other ways of connecting ideas smoothly. Then you might want to show a paragraph that lacks coherence and have the class add coherence as they work in small groups on transparency sheets. (See transparency on page 101 of this Instructor's Manual.)

Part 1 of this unit concludes with one collaborative project designed to help students evaluate paragraphs for coherence.

Part 2   Something to Think About, Something to Write About

In "This Is Going to Help Me More Than It Helps You," Professor Haas discusses the benefits of being a volunteer coach for his son's baseball team. In this article, Coach Haas talks about creating enthusiasm in his players, satisfying his desire to teach, being involved with youth, and feeling pride in his players. This information can lead to a discussion on volunteerism in general.

In this article, Professor Haas uses effective introductory and concluding paragraphs. In the introduction, he uses as the hook a contrast to the thesis sentence when he talks about his reluctance to volunteer and then switches to benefits of being a volunteer. The conclusion has a sense of closure and maintains unity by referring to the hook used in the introduction.

You might want to point out the use of coherence that is evident *between paragraphs*, especially in the first sentence of paragraphs 4, 5, and 6. It is also evident *within paragraphs*, especially paragraph 4, with such phrases as "one is that," "this important factor," "another factor," "therefore," and "and this may be one of the reasons."

You also might want to point out his effective use of sentence variety throughout the article.

Part 3 Essays for Discussion and Analysis

Part 3 includes student and professional examples that illustrate coherence. Each writing sample has questions on both content and form that can be used for class discussion. Most writing models include a vocabulary study.

Part 4 The Writer's Tools: Reviewing Punctuation

Throughout the text, punctuation has been integrated into the writing process. This section, then, simply serves as a review of punctuation for students. It includes uses of the comma, quotation marks, and other punctuation needed by basic writers. (See transparencies, pages 104 and 105, of this Instructor's Manual.)

Unit 8 Composing with Effective Alternate Patterns

Part 1 Parts to Whole: Modes of Development

This last section on writing deals with using modes effectively. The purpose for this section is to show students that no matter what type of pattern is used to develop a topic, all writing has one thing in common—a thesis sentence that restricts and controls the paper. Seven alternate patterns are used and demonstrated. One topic, *homes,* is used to show seven different patterns of development. Illustration (writing with examples) is included first because it has been covered under "Writing With Examples."

An explanation for developing the essay, a model essay, and suggested writing assignments are included for each mode of development. You might decide to use parts of this chapter earlier in your course; you might use this chapter as a brief explanation of what students will learn in freshman-level composition; or you may choose not to teach modes at all.

Part 1 of this unit concludes with one collaborative project designed to give students experience in identifying the blend of rhetorical modes used in one essay.

Part 2 Something to Think About, Something to Write About

In his graduation speech "Did You Do Your Best?" Dr. Reed delivered a motivational speech to the graduating class. In this speech, he uses several different modes for development. He depends very strongly on *illustration* since he includes numerous examples throughout the speech. He also uses *comparison/contrast* to show how life for a college graduate twenty-five years ago was both similar to and different from life for a college graduate today. Dr. Reed includes a *definition* in paragraph 10, the definition of motivation. Another mode Dr. Reed uses is *argumentation* to show that the time in which a person lives doesn't matter, but the fact that people do their best never changes.

Part 3 Paragraphs and Essays for Discussion and Analysis

Part 3 includes student and professional examples that illustrate the various modes. Each writing sample has questions on both content and form that can be used for class discussion. Most writing models include a vocabulary study.

Suggested Writing Assignments

The authors suggest eight writing assignments–three paragraphs and five multi-paragraph essays–each demanding more of the students. Writing assignments are located in two places in each unit: One group of writing assignments follows each "Something to Think About, Something to Write About" section, and another group of writing assignments follows each grammar component. The following eight writing assignments may be given one at a time or may be given to the class all at one time so students can progress at their own speed.

Writing Assignments

WA1:   Page 56. Write one paragraph supporting an identifiable topic sentence.
Unit 2, Part 2

WA2:   Page 90. Write one paragraph that includes a topic sentence and a concluding sentence. Edit for subject-verb agreement and consistent verbs.
Unit 2, Part 4

WA3:   Pages 109-110 or page 129. Write one paragraph that includes a topic sentence and a concluding sentence. Edit for previous skills learned plus voice and audience and consistent point of view.
Unit 3, Part 2 or Unit 3, Part 4

WA4:   Pages 156. Write an essay that includes a thesis sentence and support paragraphs. Edit for previous skills.
Unit 4, Part 2

WA5:   Page 185. Write an essay that includes a thesis sentence and support paragraphs. Check for previous skills plus fragments, run-on sentences, and comma splices.
Unit 4, Part 4

WA6:   Page 218 or pages 238-239. Write an essay that uses extended examples or short, interrelated examples to support the thesis sentence. Edit for previous skills and revise to include compound sentences.
Unit 5, Part 2 or Unit 5, Part 4

WA7:   Pages 273-274 or page 300. Write an essay that includes an introductory paragraph, support paragraphs, and a concluding paragraph. Edit carefully for previous skills and revise to include complex sentences.
Unit 6, Part 2 or Unit 6, Part 4

WA8:   Pages 318 or page 346. Write an essay that includes an introductory paragraph, support paragraphs, and a concluding paragraph. Edit for all aspects of writing. Check punctuation carefully.
Unit 7, Part 2 or Unit 7, Part 4

Answers to Questions on Content/Questions on Form

Unit 2, Part 3

"Summer at Aunt Clara and Uncle Frank's Farm" (p. 57)
Content: 1. to help her aunt and uncle because they had no children of their own; 2. the big boar; 3. a camaraderie among family and friends
Form: 1. Things they did every day were progressive, concluding with what they did every evening; 2. all the details of events that occurred from morning to night, including chores and activities; 3. reemphasizes the nostalgic feelings of the memories of the past

"My Grandmother and Grandfather's House" (p. 58)
Content: 1. the remembrance of the love and warmth of that place; 2. the corner where he slept; 3. the candle's reflection
Form: 1. "The corner of my grandmother and grandfather's house is not an ordinary corner of a house but a very special place to me."; 2. yes; 3. warmth of the blankets, sounds of gas, soft floor, brother's back, the candle's reflection, and the subtle breathing sound

"Concentration Camp" (p. 59)
Content: 1. over fifty years ago; 2. a graveyard by night; 3. cold, indifferent, negative/described echoing footsteps, muffled mumbles, and inexplicable, sharp smell
Form: 1. sight, sound, and smell; 2. clear direction: frightful and thoughtful experience; 3. "The major impact this place had on me was that even the most negative thought could not describe the coldness of this place."

"Fort Leonard Wood" (p. 60)
Content: 1. foreboding; 2. exploding shells; 3. "the parched sand blowing in the wind"; 4. war and its devastating consequences
Form: 1. the use of vivid descriptions and surprising words; 2. specific details that stay with one idea; 3. a thought that leaves the readers with a penetrating message about war

"Munich" (p. 60)
Content: 1. something always going on: "fests," castles, palace, brewery; 2. went shopping at the "marktplatz"; 3. two or three miles
Form: 1. yes; 2. yes, because it has clear direction

"An Eyewitness Account of the San Francisco Earthquake" (p. 61)
Content: 1. absolutely nothing; 2. streets torn apart; walls fallen; steel rails twisted; communication systems disrupted; and water mains burst; 3. 5:15 a.m. on a Wednesday morning
Form: 1. yes; 2. subject-verb reversal in first sentence; 3. yes, it sums up vividly the destruction that occurred in thirty seconds

"Martin Luther King" (p. 61)
Content: 1. in the back of the bus; 2. give up their seats to white people; 3. the South
Form: 1. yes; 2. first sentence; 3. specific details

"Making a World of Difference" (p. 62)
Content: 1. Peace Corps; 2. spicy rice dish; 3. food
Form: 1. in the second sentence; 2. describes a "cultural hurdle" she had to get through; 3. yes

"Subway Station" (p. 63)

Content: 1. the uniqueness of the place; 2. appreciation or enjoyment; 3. the steel tracks

Form: 1. "Standing in a subway station, I began to appreciate the place–almost to enjoy it." 2. the many descriptive images the writer creates for the reader; 3. ends with "experience," a key summary word, and gives a feeling of closure

"Birds of an Old Farm" (p. 64)

Content: 1. a small white butterfly; 2. dropped the stick and quickly flew the other way; 3. disappeared and remained aloof

Form: 1. "Secretiveness is part of the nesting season for many of our birds."; 2. does have closure but is not as obvious as the closure in other selections; though key word is not presented, the paragraph seems to end because the bird thinks it is being secretive

Unit 3, Part 3

"The Nursing Home" (p. 111)

Content: 1. He loves her and wants to go see her, but he feels uncomfortable when he is there; 2. Alzheimer's; 3. She can't carry on a conversation. She yells; she argues; she uses obscenities.

Form: 1. sad, regretful, loving, and caring; 2. explain the need to visit her and explain how uncomfortable it is when he gets there; 3. probably himself or someone who knows and loves her

"Subways" (p. 112)

Content: 1. New York City; 2. fear of being accosted and threatened by "weirdos" riding the subway; 3. the hair stood up all over her body, lights went out in each car

Form: 1. to illustrate the fearful thoughts she had while riding the subway; accomplishes her purpose well; paragraph devoted to hypothetical fears; 2. intense, forboding; 3. similar feeling that many people have about this kind of experience: "sheer torture for me," "hair stood up all over my body," and "my heart pounded wildly"; 4. people who have experienced fear in a place where they do not have control over what is happening

"Growing Up Chicana" (p. 114)

Content: 1. being rejected from a sorority because of her surname and for no other reason; 2. playing the guitar at family gatherings; 3. knowing she was different and giving herself permission to view the world differently

Form: 1. possibly middle-aged; this perspective was more enlightening because, while she was going through the experience, she wasn't able to see the value of her childhood; 2. sincere and open; 3. minorities who might not yet value their cultural environment–able to learn from Eva's experience and develop a new pride in their heritage; those in the majority society–able to gain a new respect and value for differences; 4. to help the author understand herself better; possibly to let go and understand some hidden anger of past years; to let others who had similar experiences gain a new appreciation or understanding of themselves and their backgrounds.

"My Best Friend" (p. 115)

Content: 1. 1986; 2. owned a trucking company and worked full time as an aerospace sheet-metal mechanic; 3. same feeling for family, same tastes in houses and landscape preferences; 4. always stood by his side and encouraged him to go on

Form: 1. to express his appreciation for all the times she stood by him. 2. perceptive, frank, and genuine; 3. paragraph 2 (support #1): "True friends manage to do things like that"; paragraph 3 (support #2): "I feel that another one of the qualities of a friend is to know how to understand my problems"; paragraph 4 (support #3): "Best of all, she has the same interests that I do."

"Dear Dad" (p. 116)

Content: 1. trumpet; 2. if his father felt the same about being on stage as he did

Form: 1. regretful and melancholy; 2. how it must have been like for his father and how it is for him; 3. himself, his father, or other people who have to come to terms with their childhoods

"Space to Sing" (p 118)

Content: 1. an art entry depicting an acquaintance of Glaze, a first year art student; 2. removed from the art show; 3. to explain why he felt it was wrong to remove the student's art work and to express his regret in not being able to discuss or resolve the situation

Form: 1. pensive, emotional, sincere; 2. faculty and students; 3. effective in many places, especially:

paragraph # 6: "I can speak from personal experience that racist stereotypes are a fiction, a lie, a blasphemous, scurrilous oversimplification which deny the humanity and the individuality of those they purport to describe."

paragraph #9: "The solution was not to remove it, denying an innocent voice the space to sing, and forcing the closure of the Student Art Show."

Unit 4, Part 3

"Respect" (p. 158)

Content: 1. disrespectful, angry, mean; 2. show violence including murders, street gangs, and mercenaries killing for money; 3. They do not set the right examples.

Form: 1. The last sentence in the introductory paragraph; 2. The topic sentence in each paragraph uses one of the points previewed in the thesis sentence; 3. The 1st person point of view would have been limited to one viewpoint whereas the 3rd person point of view is more objective and more authoritative.

"Being a Student" (p. 159)

Content: 1. cut down on personal spending on entertainment, clothing, and gifts to friends; 2. buying a house, dealing with husband, making a decision on starting a family, reading books for class, meeting due dates for computer program, doing math, taking tests; 3. tuition, expensive books

Form: 1. last sentence in the introductory paragraph; 2. specific details and examples; 3. her humor

"Golf" (p. 160)

Content: 1. blind her so that she cannot see the ball; 2. hole 7: birdied it; hole 9: 10 strokes; 3. nine years old; 4. beginning player; 5. humorously and graphically describes how she felt after bringing so much positive attention to herself only to fail so dismally on the next hole

Form: 1. the conclusion; should reinforce thesis sentence; 2. yes, last sentence in introduction; provides a distinct direction for the essay

"Building a Better Home" (p. 162)

Content: 1. the size of the nests; 2. approximately several tons; 3. when eggs are laid

Form: 1. in the introductory paragraph: "Products of avian ingenuity and tireless labor, nests and nesting places come in bewildering variety of sizes, shapes and styles; each is a marvel of longtime evolution and adaptation of birds in response to the basic need to protect their eggs and young"; 2. yes; 3. yes

Unit 5, Part 3

"Legacy" (p. 220)

Content: 1. school lessons, new knowledge about computers, art, and the determination "never to give up on life"; 2. "great at drawing cars, landscapes, and portraits," interior design, sculpting nails; 3. She was going to have a normal life in spite of the illness

Form: 1. short, interrelated examples; 2. realistic, honest, and admiring; 3. to honor her sister

"Cigarette, Anyone?" (p. 221)

Content: 1. expense, addiction, and health; 2. health; 3. an addiction.

Form: 1. five: cost of one pack of cigarettes; projected cost per month; cost of a marriage partner's habit; damaged furniture; damaged clothing; 2. various answers possible; 3. lung cancer, emphysema, high-blood pressure, and heart disease

"Responsibility" (p. 222)

Content: 1. an unfair screaming tyrant; 2. to be disciplined, to have pride in himself, and to be responsible; 3. knew his nephew had to be responsible to be able to compete in today's job market

Form: 1. first sentence in paragraph; 2. various answers possible; 3. paragraph 2: one short example; paragraph 3: extended example

"Cooking" (p. 224)

Content: 1. because it is a way to express love and appreciation for family or friends; 2. by experimenting with different recipes and ingredients; 3. as a way of offering a peaceful reunion

Form: 1. an extended example; 2. paragraph 2: exact ingredients added to the bran muffins; paragraph 3: the aroma of the cheesecake; paragraph 4: narrative about the writer and her daughter; 3. is one of the most important to the writer, is strategically placed last for emphasis

"Wandering Through Winter" (p. 224)

Content: 1. superstition; 2. scientific basis or valid research; 3. in the Ozarks

Form: 1. the number of short, interrelated examples; 2. short, interrelated examples using animals

"Overheard on a Train Trip Through England" (p. 225)

Content: 1. English and American; 2. a comment by an English woman that Americans are "funny"; 3. that in reality it is the English that seem peculiar

Form: 1. that they are uniquely idiosyncratic about the English, and that most Americans would find them amusing; 2. approximately seventeen short, interrelated examples; 3. In actuality, the English are funny.

"Courtship Through the Ages" (p. 228)

Content: 1. "the sorrowful lengths to which all males must go to arouse the interest of a lady"; 2. growing whiskers, doing somersaults, tilting lances, performing feats, giving candy, flowers, and animal furs; 3. uses the word "man" and "lady"; has birds and animals doing things only people can do: for example, paragraph 4, lines 14-18; 4. various answers possible

Form: 1. extended examples in most paragraphs; short, interrelated examples in paragraph 7; 2. the cumbersome, ineffective methods of male courtship; 3. satirical and lighthearted

Unit 6, Part 3

"Dancer" (p. 276)

Content: 1. about five hours; 2. standing ovation by the dance troupe; 3. dance regularly in a professional dance troupe

Form: 1. the hook, a quotation that contrasts with the main idea in the thesis; 2. relates back to the hook and gives the essay a sense of unity

"Collecting Sports Cards" (p. 277)

Content: 1. selling cards from home, becoming a dealer and selling at a mall or store, entering shows; 2. one dollar; 3. buying inexpensive rookie-player cards, buying complete sets "made in short prints," and acquiring "limited-edition cards"

Form: 1. quotation; 2. 2nd, 3rd, and 4th sentences plus "For instance," in paragraph 1; 3. It ties it back to the introduction by referring to the hook

"A Good Manager" (p. 278)

Content: 1. the Safeway at 19th Avenue and Northern; 2. is a good problem solver, is quick with new technology, knows how to solve any problem with the new scanner, creates good schedules; 3. because he relies on fairness and respect, makes his employees feel as if their jobs are important

Form: 1. rhetorical questions; yes, because they effectively set up the thesis and the support paragraphs that ultimately answer the questions; 2. reinforces the thesis sentence but could be developed further; yes; 3. no, only example is paragraph 3 about his ability

"The Right Thing To Do" (p. 280)

Content: 1. whom his son would live with after his divorce; 2. knowing he had to give up his future life with his son because he wasn't sure he could offer his son as much as his ex-wife could; 3. not being a part of his son's growing up and having his mother disown him

Form: 1. makes the reader empathetic because the voice is not angry, consequently drawing the reader into understanding and possibly relating to the writer's predicament; 2. presents the final resolutions for the writer, acts as the writer's acceptance of his painful decision

"The Car of Tomorrow" (p. 281)

Content: 1. transform itself into a variety of vehicles, run inexpensively, and travel at Mach 2; 2. a giant potato on wheels; 3. garbage or any organic substance

Form: 1. challenges the reader to imagine the car of the future; 2. "The idea may strike terror into the hearts of automotive engineers now, but future technologies may prove that the perfect car is simply a combination of versatility, performance, and economy"; 3. reiterates the thesis with short examples from his support paragraphs

"Influence" (p. 282)

Content: 1. causes the author to think about his children rather than about himself; 2. not only to provide for their immediate needs and their future but also to be an example for them; 3. have made his life more fulfilling and exciting

Form: 1. example of the birth of his first child plus a quotation; 2. the sentence "It has only been five years since our first child was born"; 3. reinforces thesis sentence but could use more development, could allude to difficulties yet rewards of parenthood

"Why Don't We Complain?" (p. 285)

Content: 1. about 85 degrees; 2. read; 3. on an airplane experiencing the same kind of problem that he did on the train–hesitation to complain; 4. paragraph 5: being overwhelmed with helplessness that comes with technological advances; paragraph 6: strong central government; 5. "political apathy"

Form: 1. extended personal example; 2. other specific examples such as the airplane, magazines, editorials, and visit of Khrushchev; 3. reverts back to the author's original train anecdote and leaves the reader thinking about how the train apathy relates to political apathy

Unit 7, Part 3

"Home: Just How Safe Is It?" (p. 320)

Content: 1. keeps the family from recognizing the problem, and perpetuates the problem from one family to another; 2. through denial and survival skills such as depersonalization; 3. programs and treatment centers, education

Form: 1. throughout essay, especially paragraph 2; 2. The phrase "sexual abuse" in the topic sentence links to the thesis sentence as well as the preceding paragraph. Sentence 2 contains the word "emotionally" that links back to the topic sentence.

The pronoun "they" used in several sentences links back to the word "victims" of sexual abuse. The word "victims" is used in the concluding sentence and links back to the topic sentence. 3. to call attention to the problem of denial by families who experience abusive behavior

"Education" (p. 321)

Content: 1. had not achieved enough points to advance to the university; 2. paternal grandmother who lived in Phoenix and his parents' relocation to the United States; 3. almost one year

Form: 1. paragraph 2 (support paragraph 1): school, diploma; paragraph 3 (support paragraph 2): educational goal, draft; paragraph 4 (support paragraph 3): Phoenix, warm climate; 2. "Yet, finishing the educational goal was not the only reason for my coming here"; 3. to help give a chronology of his whole life in Germany and its contrasts with his life in America

"A Bad Experience" (p. 322)

Content: 1. became bitter, worried, and pessimistic; 2. 1966; 3. to repair detached retina

Form: 1. paragraph 2 (support paragraph 1): obvious change, character; paragraph 3 (support paragraph 2): character, behavior, different, education; paragraph 4 (support paragraph 3): trauma, character, education, change, relationships changed direction; 2. paragraph 2: after, during two more months, before; paragraph 3: then, second year, finally, one year later; paragraph 4: as he began again, one year later, some months later, for many years, at last; 3. paragraph 3: also, of course; paragraph 4: as a result, there, in a way, of course

"The Strategy of Futureness" (p. 325)

Content: 1. their inability to project their thinking very far into the future, to anticipate required actions; 2. become entrapped in fantasies; 3. images of what they want to be in the future; 4. knowledge of music, history, literature, and science that links each generation with the past

Form: 1. by using one idea represented by a key word, such as "future," and carrying the key word or a variation to the next paragraph; 2. paragraph 5: uses various pronouns to refer to "people": they, some, themselves, others; 3. an example that is a comparison: a freeway driver anticipating signs compared to someone traveling through life experiencing changes

Unit 8, Part 3

"Heroes–'Sung' and 'Unsung'" (p. 384)

Content: 1. "their ability to react quickly, calmly, and unselfishly"; 2. floated below the surface of the water and almost drowned; 3. calmly helped other passengers off the plane by holding up obstructing cables and bringing elderly people up on their feet

Form: 1. illustration; 2. the last sentence in the introduction; 3. all extended examples

"Rabbit or Parakeet?" (p. 385)

Content: 1. parakeet: feathers, beak, two spindly legs, and an assortment of bright colors; rabbit: two short legs, two longer back legs, strong cutting teeth, and white, gray, brown, or black fur; 2. clipped wings; 3. sings, performs tricks, and learns to talk; 4. cuddles and responds to its name

Form: 1. comparison/contrast; 2. purpose of author is to remain as objective as possible without being judgmental and to show that both make good pets; 3. indicates the basis of the comparison

"Which One Are You?" (p. 386)

Content: 1. perfectionists; 2. "carefree spirits"; nonchalant people who study only when it is convenient, people who do not let school dominate their lives; 3. cheat

Form: 1. how students study for tests; made clear in the introduction; 2. author's observations of students; 3. ending statement shifts to second person; adds a familiar, warm tone

"Wealth" (p. 387)

Content: 1. anyone who has a loving family around her/him; 2. "great quantity or store of money or property of value"; 3. memories of beautiful places, relationships with loyal friends, and, most important of all, a loving family

Form: 1. contrast the denotative meaning with the connotative meaning; 2. emphasizes that real wealth is more than money

"Winter" (p. 388)

Content: 1. "a period of inactivity and decay"; 2. "time of new activities and growth"; 3. "enjoying the park on weekends, jogging, playing handball, and trying unsuccessfully to get a tee time."

Form: 1. short, interrelated examples; 2. first and last sentences

"A Run" (p. 389)

Content: 1. "a planned motorcycle trip or destination that is meant to be attended by a group of riders"; 2. in any dictionary; 3. because a run specifically has to involve others and is planned

Form: 1. the opening quotation; 2. knowledgeable, informative, informal, humorous; 3. "as stated above"

"Parenting: Singular" (p. 391)

Content: 1. drug and alcohol abuse, unwed mothers, and divorce; 2. "a mother and a father and 2.5 children"; 3. "excluded from neighborhood gatherings"; "reminded in storybooks and role playing"; "ashamed to tell their own stories"

Form: 1. helps establish the problem explained in the paper; 2. in the order of importance according to the author; 3. paragraph 2: extended example from a movie; paragraph 3: information from authorities in the field; paragraph 4: personal experience and a statistic; 4. yes, reinforces thesis, provides unity with a reference to causes

"Reducing Fear of a Hospital Stay for a Child" (p. 392)

Content: 1. preparing a child for a hospital stay; 2. role play activities that will happen in the hospital, allow for special toys and people to be present, and give the child informative and accurate details about the hospital stay and the operation; 3. assurance that a child is less anxious and well prepared for the procedure: 4. a favorite stuffed animal or special blanket

Form: 1. order in which it would be easiest for the child to understand; 2. third person; 3. realistic details of how little people have done in the past to keep children from being afraid of a hospital stay

"The Human Genome Initiative" (p. 394)

Content: 1. "a massive project...to map and sequence the human genome, the entire sequence of three billion base pairs of DNA that are in twenty-three pairs of chromosomes"; 2. "cystic fibrosis," "Huntington's disease," "susceptibility to cancer"; 3. statistics and authorities in the field

Form: 1. definition, current event; 2. in the thesis; 3. paragraph 2

Suggested Schedule of Activities

Week 1   Orientation, Writing Sample
Introduction to Writing: Unit 1
Generating Ideas for Writing

Week 2   Topic Sentences, Paragraphs: Unit 2, Parts 1, 2, 3
Twenty-Point Test over Topic Sentences
Writing Workshop, Writing Assignment (WA) 1
Keeping a Journal, Appendix B
Journal Entry (JE) 1 due

Week 3   Subjects, Verbs, and Prepositional Phrases
Subject-Verb Agreement and Consistent Verb Tense: Unit 2, Part 4
Twenty-Point Test over Subject-Verb Agreement
Twenty-Point Test over Consistent Verb Tense
Writing Workshop, WA2
JE2 due

Week 4   Writing Workshop, Rewrites
Interaction of Topic, Purpose, Audience, and Voice: Unit 3, Part 1
Reading Student and Professional Examples: Unit 3, Parts 2, 3
JE3 due

Week 5   Consistent Point of View: Unit 3, Part 4
Twenty-Point Test over Consistent Point of View
Writing Workshop, WA3
JE4 due

Week 6   Thesis Sentence: Unit 4, Part 1
Twenty-Point Test over Thesis Sentence
Reading Student and Professional Examples: Units 4, Parts 2, 3
Writing Workshop, WA4
JE5 due

Week 7   Fragments, Run-on Sentences, Comma Splices: Unit 4, Part 4
Twenty-Point Test over Fragments, Run-On Sentences, and Comma Splices
Writing Workshop, Rewrites
JE6 due

Week 8   Writing with Examples: Unit 5, Part 1
Reading Student and Professional Examples: Unit 5, Parts 2, 3
Writing Workshop, WA 5
JE7 due

Week 9   Sentence Combining, Compound Sentences: Unit 5, Part 4
Twenty-Point Test over Sentence Combining Using Compound Sentences
Writing Workshop, Rewrites
JE8 due

Week 10   Introductions and Conclusions: Unit 6, Part 1
Writing Workshop, WA6
JE9 due

Week 11   Reading Student and Professional Examples: Unit 6, Parts 2, 3
Sentence Combining, Complex Sentences: Unit 6, Part 4
Twenty-Point Test over Sentence Combining Using Complex Sentences
Writing Workshop, Rewrites
JE10 due

Week 12   Coherence: Unit 7, Part 1
Reading Student and Professional Examples: Unit 7, Parts 2, 3
Writing Workshop, WA7
JE11 due

Week 13   Punctuation Review: Unit 7, Part 4
Twenty-Point Test over Punctuation
Writing Workshop, Rewrites
Confusing Words, App. A
JE12 due

Week 14   Writing Workshop, WA8
JE13 due

Week 15   *Last day* to turn in first draft of any writing assignment
Practice finals
JE14 due

Week 16   *Last day* to complete any assignments.
Practice Finals

Final Exam

We suggest that a multi-paragraph essay similar to writing assignments seven and eight be used as a final exam. We allow our students two to three hours to complete a five-hundred-word essay. If your class is self-paced, students might go to a testing area or a monitored writing center to complete the final exam. As we noted earlier, students could take the final exam as many times as needed, until they are ready to succeed in freshman-level writing.

Some suggested topics to be used as finals:

Advantages/disadvantages of living at home while going to school
Movies are getting too violent and/or graphic
Reasons humanity does/does not need to worry about the
    environment
Reasons people watch television
Reasons people spend so much money
Advantages/disadvantages of eating at a restaurant
Advantages/disadvantages of eating at home
Reasons people have parties or reasons people go to parties
Childproofing a house
Moving
Ways to help people after a disaster
Important qualities to teach children before they are grown
Qualities of a good salesperson
If I won the lottery
Ways of coping with frustration
Results of running
Reasons for telling the truth
Advantages/disadvantages of having siblings
Advantages/disadvantages of running for public office
Ways people can prepare for retirement
Ideal environment for a child
Advantages/disadvantages of living in a city/in the country
Advantages/disadvantages of being a foreign student in America
Qualities of a perfect mate
Reasons people participate in sports
Home activities that children enjoy
Favorite weekend activities
Types of adults who attend college
Ways to make life simpler
Reasons conflicts occur between parents and children

Twenty-Point Tests

The tests referred to in the "Suggested Schedule of Activities" are included here for your convenience. These eighteen tests may be duplicated for use in your classes. (Also, answers to these tests follow.) These tests focus on skills needed by students to edit and revise their own writing. The tests stress thinking skills and paragraph editing/revision rather than correcting isolated sentences.

Topic Sentence A

Twenty points

Part 1

Study each sentence below and decide if it is a simple fact (F), too broad to develop in one paragraph (B), or a suitable topic sentence (TS).

_____   1. World War II provided many lessons for Americans.
_____   2. The book *The Russia House* costs $4.75.
_____   3. Toni Morrison won the Nobel Prize for literature in 1993.
_____   4. The Wolf spiders have interesting web-making habits.
_____   5. The insects of South America are varied.
_____   6. A spider has eight legs.
_____   7. Toni Morrison wrote realistically about Black women.
_____   8. Computers have revolutionized the world.
_____   9. Chess is a challenging game.
_____   10. Waterworld is an exciting place to spend a summer day.

Part 2

Study each group of related sentences. Mark the most general statement that could be a topic sentence for each group.

11. a. Time management is an essential skill for college success.
     b. Active studying should replace nonproductive phone calls.
     c. During commuting time, students can listen to lecture tapes.
     d. Using time between classes for studying can result in free time during weekends.

12. a. Shadow finger puppets are fun.
     b. Play dough can be made easily from plain white flour.
     c. Children can be entertained easily at home.
     d. From an ordinary dish soap, bubbles can be created.
     e. Little gardens can be planted from discarded seeds.

13. a. Rapid body growth is taking place.
     b. Surviving adolescence is difficult.
     c. Insecurities about self-identity can cause acting up.
     d. Peer pressure adds stress and an awareness of differing values.
     e. Teens may want material items but have no way to acquire a job and money.

14. a. Parents can remind children of positive attributes.
     b. Parents can be flexible when making judgments.
     c. Parents can demonstrate that they believe in their children.
     d. Children learn respect and trust from their parents' model, so it is important that parents exhibit these qualities.
     e. Parents can do much to build their children's self-esteem.

15. a. Lasagna is made with wide noodles, Italian meat sauce, and various cheeses.
     b. Spaghetti, a common dish, is made with different kinds of sauces.
     c. Ravioli is a noodle sandwich patty that is filled with meat or cheese.
     d. Fettuccine is a long, narrow noodle served with a red or white Italian sauce.
     e. Italian food has many variations of pasta dishes.

16. a. Shopping without children can save buying unneeded items.
    b. Careful shoppers can save money at grocery stores.
    c. Buying items that are on sale can save money.
    d. Using coupons can reduce the grocery bill total.
    e. Shopping with a list prepared ahead of time can avoid impulse buying.

17. a. Travel benefits are usually available.
    b. Retirees have medical insurance.
    c. Being retired from military service has benefits.
    d. People are often young enough to have second careers.
    e. They have access to all military base stores.

18. a. Atmosphere in a restaurant can increase one's appetite.
    b. Price is always a consideration.
    c. The type of food served is usually a personal preference.
    d. Geographical location of the establishment can be both advantageous and troublesome.
    e. Length of waiting time before being served can affect one's choice of restaurant.
    f. Choosing a restaurant is an important decision.

19. a. Revision is an important part of the writing process.
    b. Revision allows writers to add details to support the topic sentence.
    c. Revision helps writers put ideas in logical order.
    d. Revision helps writers eliminate unrelated ideas.
    e. Revision gives the author pride in the finished paper.

20. a. A mole is usually not more than five to seven inches long.
    b. The animal seldom comes to the surface and is very awkward above ground.
    c. It has a stout body without a visible neck, a small tapering head, strong claws, no external ears, short limbs set far apart, and soft fur.
    d. Moles are unusual animals.
    e. The tail of the mole is three-fourths as long as its body.

Topic Sentence B

Twenty points

Part 1

Study each sentence below and decide if it is a simple fact (F), too broad to develop in one paragraph (B), or a suitable topic sentence (TS).

_____ 1. She threw the ball one hundred feet.
_____ 2. The Democratic and Republican parties have different views.
_____ 3. The car has a flat tire.
_____ 4. Many people enjoy riding bicycles.
_____ 5. Maya Angelou is an excellent poet.
_____ 6. Maya Angelou read a poem at President Clinton's inauguration.
_____ 7. American poets express many ideas.
_____ 8. Baseball is enjoyable to play.
_____ 9. My sister works at a McDonald's restaurant.
_____ 10. McDonald's is an enjoyable place for children.

Part 2

Study each group of related sentences. Mark the most general statement that could be a topic sentence for each group.

11. a. The swamp provides plenty of water.
  b. The Okefenokee Swamp is an ideal habitat for alligators.
  c. Floating islands of peat moss provide privacy for the alligators.
  d. The alligators can find ample food.
  e. Many places are ideal for nests that are safe from other reptiles.

12. a. Advanced medical care ensures good health in later years.
  b. Crafts provide hours of pleasure for retired adults.
  c. Because they have few responsibilities outside the home, they have time to enjoy doing jobs around the house.
  d. They often take enjoyable classes like square dancing.
  e. America's older adults often enjoy retirement.
  f. Condominiums for senior citizens require little maintenance.

13. a. Junior showmanship classes at dog shows are beneficial to young people.
  b. Young handlers learn the responsibility of caring for the dogs.
  c. Junior handlers learn sportsmanship.
  d. Junior handlers meet friends who have the same interests.
  e. These young people must teach their dogs socialization skills.
  f. Junior showers learn to act and dress appropriately.
  g. Junior showers are exposed to future career opportunities by associating with professional handlers.

14. a. Adult reentry students take assignments seriously.
  b. They realize college is a means to a better job.
  c. Adult reentry students seldom miss classes.
  d. Adult reentry students often do well in college.
  e. They learn to balance school and home responsibilities.

15. a. Parents can make books available and can read to their children.
    b. Adults in the household can carefully select television programs to be viewed by children.
    c. Creating a learning environment at home is important for children.
    d. Discussions about current events can help children understand the world they live in.
    e. Parental interest in school and homework can help children realize the importance of an education.

16. a. Less time is spent going to and from work.
    b. When employees need to miss a day of work, they can make up the time on their day off.
    c. Employees have an extra day to do whatever needs to be done at home.
    d. Working a four-day week can be beneficial to employees.
    e. More can be accomplished during a longer work day.

17. a. Students can often skip units that they already understand.
    b. Students can spend more time on one unit if they need to.
    c. Taking self-paced classes can have advantages for students.
    d. Students can work anywhere it is convenient to do so.
    e. Many students learn to manage their time wisely.

18. a. Mentally handicapped people are often discriminated against in our society.
    b. Sometimes they are not allowed to raise their own children.
    c. They often are not given the same service when they go to buy a car.
    d. At times, they are not allowed to get married.
    e. Some have to have legal guardians for their entire lives.

19. a. Campers learn valuable skills.
    b. Family members spend time together.
    c. Being out in nature exposes the campers to a different lifestyle.
    d. Camping can be a good family experience.
    e. Families learn team work.

20. a. People in the military have the opportunity to travel to other countries.
    b. People in the military have the opportunity to take classes and learn new skills.
    c. People in the military learn discipline.
    d. People in the military have many advantages.
    e. People in the military learn team work.

Subject-Verb Agreement A

Twenty points

Part 1

Put all prepositional phrases in parentheses ( ). Underline each subject once. Then find the incorrect verb form in each sentence and correct it to agree in number with the subject. Write C to the left of the number if there is no error. (Keep the present tense.)

1. He do not care for the bicycle in the garage.

2. She is not the first recipient of the Presidential Award.

3. Everybody in the United States need concern for the environment.

4. A few of the people enjoys picking apples in the fall.

5. We was the only ones who took the lesson seriously.

6. The team member with the most points will receive an award.

7. The team are trying hard to win the tournament.

8. Each of the students want an "A."

9. Nobody wants to miss the concert.

10. Patty and Sue was elected to the senate.

Part 2

Edit the following paragraph for subject-verb agreement only. Underline the subject(s) in each sentence once and the verb(s) twice. Then find any incorrect verb forms in each sentence and correct them to agree in number with the subject.

The culture of the Aztec Indians provide us with insight to the people of that region and time. They was an intelligent group with a sophisticated money system. Cocoa beans was used as money in exchange for raw goods. Also, almost everyone were a good farmer who developed an efficient irrigation system to support, in particular, a diet of corn. A government system of a higher-ranking chief and many common laborers prevailed. In addition, they was knowledgeable about architecture and built many pyramids. One aspect of their culture, however, do not appeal to others. Virgins was offered as sacrificial victims to the gods. Though this were a part of the Aztec culture, other people finds human sacrifice barbaric. All in all, the Aztec Indian culture leave us with a legacy of intrigue as well as information.

Subject-Verb Agreement B

Twenty points

Part 1

Put all prepositional phrases in parentheses ( ). Underline each subject once. Then find the incorrect verb form in each sentence and correct it to agree in number with the subject. Write C to the left of the number if there is no error. (Keep the present tense.)

1. The president of the student body always deliver a challenging speech to new students.

2. Honesty, one of his best qualities, make him appealing.

3. Either the husband or the wife arrive late for work.

4. The husband and wife often agree on major decisions.

5. Only a few of my friends goes to parties during the week.

6. Nobody seem to enjoy life as much as Shawn.

7. Each of my puppies have a unique personality.

8. The Student Ambassador program encourage good will among young people from the United States and from other countries.

9. The director of the campus placement service always inform the incoming students of their opportunities.

10. Several courses meets the graduation requirements in mathematics.

Part 2

Edit the following paragraph for subject-verb agreement only. Underline the subject(s) in each sentence once and the verb(s) twice. Find any incorrect verb forms in each sentence and correct them to agree in number with the subject.

Biking can be fun; however, if people does not take proper care of their equipment, bike riding can be dangerous. For example, responsible bikers adjusts brake pads properly and replaces them periodically. Bikers risk injury on mountain trails if the brakes are unreliable. Regular tire inspections for cracks or bubbles mean that the bikers detects defective tires before problems occur. Also, if the gears are not lubricated, they may not work properly, causing hazardous conditions for the biker. Another dangerous situation occur if the chain are not oiled. As a result, the cyclists finds themselves unable to peddle, and the bike chain can break. Unless damaged reflectors is replaced, bikers cannot be seen after dark. Responsible riders who keep their bikes in excellent condition is less apt to have perilous experiences.

Consistent Verb Tense A

Twenty points

Edit the following paragraphs for consistent verb tense only. Identify the tense in the first sentence as present or past, and then make the remaining sentences match that tense.

Paragraph 1

Tense_____

Phi Theta Kappa is an honorary organization for community college students. It is basically devoted to scholarship, fellowship, and community service. All students who have a 3.5 grade point average or above and who have accumulated twelve semester hours of credit were invited to join. After joining, students attended leadership conferences, raised money for service or scholarships, and supported one another. In addition, they are recognized during graduation ceremonies, and their diplomas and transcripts are sealed with a gold Phi Theta Kappa sticker. Usually the group was energetic and creative. At the end of the semester, another group of honor students was invited to join, and the cycle repeated itself.

Paragraph 2

Tense_____

Our Sunday afternoon picnic to Red Feather Lakes brought a typical Colorado experience. Each of the teenagers in the family invites a guest. We pack food, sports equipment, and camping equipment. On the hour drive, we played travel games and listened to tapes. Just as most of us were getting tired, we spot the beautiful lakes. However, when we first arrive, it becomes cloudy. The wind increases, and the area grows cold. Most of us come unprepared for cold weather, so some stayed in the car; a few put up a small tent to protect themselves from the cold wind; others wrap themselves with whatever they could find. In the adverse wind, we cook steaks and chicken, but after we ate, the weather clears and turns sunny. So we pull out our baseball equipment and enjoyed a game. The time to go came too soon. On the return trip, everyone but the driver slept.

Consistent Verb Tense B

Twenty points

Edit the following paragraphs for consistent verb tense only. Identify the tense in the first sentence as present or past, and then make the remaining sentences match that tense.

Paragraph 1

Tense_____

More and more people today find fitness centers are an invaluable opportunity. While working out inside a climate-controlled atmosphere, people were sheltered from natural elements like pollution or severe weather conditions. For example, they left rain, snow, or sleet outside and worked out in comfort. Likewise, if the temperature outside turned hot and humid, they stepped inside to refrigerated comfort. Also, when they jog, biked, or climb stairs, they are not exposed to road hazards such as cars, torn-up roads, potholes, or even acts of violence. These fitness centers were well monitored by knowledgeable personnel who knew how to operate the equipment safely. Often trainers helped newcomers use the equipment with maximum efficiency. Fitness centers seemed to be the answer that many avid exercisers want.

Paragraph 2

Tense_____

The pigeons on our campus fascinated me that fall afternoon as they fed together on the rye grass seed that was intended to produce a nice green winter lawn. First one, then ten, then twenty fly in and share the feast. None made a sound; rather, all are intent on the spread put before them. They neither argue nor chase one another away. They do not have to hurry off to prepare supper or run errands. Plump and healthy, they live year after year as they built nests in palm trees, drink water from puddles on the ground, and ate whatever came their way. In the springtime, baby pigeons hatch from eggs and repeated the cycle, ignoring the humans that lived in the same area. Only the humans hurried here and there, go home, cooked supper, and then returned the next morning to find that the rye grass needed cutting.

Consistent Point of View A

Twenty points

Edit the following paragraphs for consistent point of view only. Using the first sentence as the basis for the point of view, change the rest of the paragraph to maintain a consistent point of view. Do not edit for any other kinds of changes.

Paragraph 1

Breaking my leg was an unpleasant experience for me. Initially the pain, not from the broken bone, but from the strained muscles and ligaments, was excruciating for you. People felt an intense discomfort for two to two and one-half weeks. Simple, ordinary maneuvers suddenly became difficult for you. For example, people found making a simple sandwich a major undertaking and taking a shower a major task. You found driving was possible; however, your physician advised you not to drive. Into the fourth week, you felt an unbearable yet inaccessible itching occurring below the cast. This was maddening. Finally, when the sixth week arrived, I had your leg x-rayed and the cast removed. Still, you needed some rehabilitation because my leg would not be back to normal for about three more months.

Paragraph 2

At amusement parks, people love dressing up in costumes to have their pictures taken. Costumes let you personify a different character momentarily. Women can outfit themselves in large frilly hats, old-fashioned skirts, and parasols, or you can appear in Native American dress. Men can don ten-gallon hats, cowboy shirts, and chaps, or I can try on Mexican sombreros and throw a poncho over my shoulders. The photo models can create a fantasy all our own. Some participants enter a photo session in groups, and we produce a running theme for the picture. We can select a certain culture, and all the members of our group choose clothing of that era and culture. At times, normally light, jovial personalities become serious, stiff-faced models. Other times, your serious models become lighthearted and carefree. No wonder we find these special photo shops fun.

Consistent Point of View B

Twenty points

Edit the following paragraphs for consistent point of view only. Using the first sentence as the basis for the point of view, change the rest of the paragraph to maintain a consistent point of view. Do not edit for any other kinds of changes.

Paragraph 1

Three teenagers, two brothers and one sister, from Bloomington, Indiana, realized that if they worked hard and used ingenuity they could build a successful business. I kept in mind that customers wanted excellent service as well as honest dealings. Of course, you also realized that the key to success started with the realization that a service was needed in an area, and then I went out and aggressively tackled the problem. These college students, who lived just ten miles from Lake Monroe, a resort area, found no pizza parlors near by, so I decided to "zero in" on the opportunity, and I started my own business. I found an old, abandoned building that you could obtain at a reasonable price. With little overhead, I added an attractive deck in front, tables, and chairs. I then purchased used kitchen equipment that produced excellent pizzas. When customers came in, they received exceptional service; therefore, business grew. This is but one example of individuals starting a successful business in the 1990s.

Paragraph 2

Attending college can create stress for students. Taking too many classes and not being able to get homework in on time can create tension for you. As a result, not doing the homework may keep you from learning some of the course content, so you may not do well on tests. To avoid pressure, I must do well on my tests and in other class activities to maintain a high grade point average if I wish to receive credit in the course or even to stay in school. Not only are tests and homework difficult to handle, but if you happen to be taking self-paced courses, finding time to complete these classes on campus can cause more anxiety. These increasing demands on your time are very hard to manage. In addition, when students encounter inflexible deadlines and excessive homework, you might have more stress. Students who stay in school and succeed in your classes have learned, probably above all else, to control the stress that comes with attending college.

Thesis Sentence A

Twenty points

Part 1

Read the following thesis sentences. First, circle the most general idea (topic and direction). Then underline the coordinate ideas that complete the thesis sentence.

1. Restoring an old car can be time-consuming and expensive yet fulfilling.
2. Speaking two languages can be advantageous when a person seeks a job, travels in another country, or assists foreign people.
3. When interacting with a disabled person, one needs to be empathetic, realistic, and knowledgeable.
4. Lungs, heart, and throat are major parts of the body affected by a long-term smoking habit.
5. Learning about our prehistoric past involves studying historical archives, visiting archaeological museums, and interpreting new findings.

Part 2

Carefully read the following thesis sentences. Correct the faulty parallel structure or mark correct if the coordinate ideas are written in parallel form.

6. When buying children's toys, parents need to be sure the toys are safe, appropriate, durable, and have lots of bright colors.

7. Ray spent his life working hard all day, to socialize in the evening, and sleeping well at night.

8. His summers are spent jet-skiing at the lake, surfing at the beach, and he even sails on the ocean.

9. An afternoon in an art museum can be fun, inexpensive, educational, yet tiring.

10. Raising children requires time, having patience, and money.

11. Jerry's retirement years were pleasant because he had bought land, invested in stocks, and saving some money.

12. His knowledge, he had social skills, and his age helped make him successful at his job.

Part 3

Carefully read the following thesis sentences. Some of the coordinate ideas are faulty because they overlap (have almost the same meaning) or are not coordinate (equal). Cross out the overlapping or uncoordinate idea. If the coordinate ideas are logical, mark correct.

13. Eating popcorn, seeing the animals, watching the clowns, enjoying the elephants, and reading a program are memories from the circus.

14. A person running for public office needs money, emotional support from friends and family, personal endurance, and stamina.

15. Jean's favorite activities are collecting coins, painting pictures, restoring old telephones, and painting with oils.

16. After work, Harry drives home safely, watches the news, works in the yard, cooks supper, and watches television.

17. Strength, speed, intelligence, and willingness to cooperate are qualities of a good football player.

18. Addictive eating disorders can destroy a person physically, mentally, socially, and psychologically.

19. Packing a picnic lunch, wearing cool clothing, taking extra drinks, bringing chips, and using sunblock can make a family outing at the lake more fun.

20. A teacher should have patience, sensitivity, tolerance, and knowledge.

Thesis Sentence B

Twenty points

Part 1

Read the following thesis sentences. First, circle the most general idea (topic and direction). Then underline the coordinate ideas that complete the thesis sentence.

1. A company's wellness program offers such benefits as financial incentives, educational seminars, and, as a result, improved health.
2. Artists today may exhibit and sell their work at local fairs, galleries, and private sales.
3. Attending college can be a financial burden; however, a good financial aid package, a part-time job, and a budget can ease the difficulty.
4. Car manufacturers appeal to people's interests in comfort, appearance, and power.
5. Classroom software should be easy to use, relevant to class goals, inexpensive to purchase, and positive in its approach to course content.

Part 2

Carefully read the following thesis sentences. Correct the faulty parallel structure or mark correct if the coordinate ideas are written in parallel form.

6. Adobe buildings are strong, simple, look attractive, and practical.

7. AIDS can be contracted through blood transfusions, irresponsible sexual relationships, and sharing drug needles.

8. Comforting a child, to provide a pleasant home environment, and teaching a child are all aspects of parenting.

9. Disadvantages of shopping at membership warehouse stores include buying large quantities, needing more time to shop, and to experience a limited selection.

10. To eat right, working out hard, avoiding sweets, and sleeping well are important to health-conscious people.

11. Firefighters help society by fighting fires, helping accident victims, and they can volunteer in community organizations.

12. Going on a date requires money, time, and finding a partner.

Part 3

Carefully read the following thesis sentences. Some of the coordinate ideas are faulty because they overlap (have almost the same meaning) or are not coordinate (equal). Cross out the overlapping or uncoordinate idea. If the coordinate ideas are logical, mark correct.

13. Air pollution can irritate eyes and noses, cause lung problems, damage plants, damage buildings, and destroy outer layers of stone buildings.

14. Before buying a computer, people should consider personal needs, expenses, available software, computer capabilities, and costs.

15. Bowl game excitement includes pre-game activities, the game itself, parades, colorful half-time activities, and post-game celebrations.

16. Preparing a meal includes planning the menu, buying the foods, cooking the meal, and buying vegetables.

17. Collectibles can be found at garage sales, antique stores, thrift shops, auctions, and yard sales.

18. Home health aides must be trustworthy, skilled, patient, and honest.

19. Homemade whole-grain bread can be nutritious, flavorful, inexpensive, and tasty.

20. Tour coordinators must consider insurance, accommodations, safety, hotel reservations, and activities.

Fragments, Run-On Sentences, and Comma Splices A

Twenty points

Revise the following paragraphs to eliminate sentence-structure errors.

Paragraph 1

Every summer we look forward to going camping at Big Lake. As soon as we get to the campground. We leisurely set up the tent under the tall, shady trees. Then we organize our fishing gear. And get everything ready for the next few days of fishing. We gather firewood soon we start a campfire and cook juicy hamburgers. That cannot be equaled anywhere else. Later, we enjoy toasted marshmallows. Marshmallows that smell as good as they taste. With stomachs content, we carry our fishing gear to the water's edge we look for that special hole where we caught the "big ones" last year. Shortly, a big moon rises in the sky, millions of stars appear. Though we do not catch any fish. We see trout jumping on top of the water everywhere we relax, knowing that we still have several days ahead to forget our lives. Our busy lives at home.

Paragraph 2

Garage sales that appeal to bargain seekers. Items found at reasonable prices. Items of all kinds. Everything from dog kennels to baby strollers selling at a fraction of their original costs. Collectors often finding old fountain pens or thimbles for their collections. Professional upholsterers who find good, solid pieces of furniture. Furniture that they can recover. Other times, items are in excellent condition they simply need a good scrubbing. Some items might even be unused gifts. Gifts that are still in their original boxes. Some people furnish their entire homes inexpensively. But nicely by shopping at these bargain centers.

Fragments, Run-On Sentences, and Comma Splices B

Twenty points

Revise the following paragraphs to eliminate sentence-structure errors.

Paragraph 1

In today's society, more and more people finding that they can save money by shopping wisely. Shoppers are heading for outlet malls. Where they can purchase quality merchandise at a fraction of its price. Retail price. Some outlet clothing stores carry merchandise. That is exclusively for women. However, other clothing stores carry discounted clothing for all members of the family, some stores carry only baby clothing other shops specialize in toys. Shoppers can also find discount stores. That specialize in linens, crystal, books, or cookware. For additional savings, shoppers often finding end-of-season markdowns at these outlet stores. No matter what shoppers need. They can usually find a store that features these items at reduced prices they can save money.

Paragraph 2

Being a prisoner of war in Vietnam was one of the most dreadful ordeals anyone could experience. According to former prisoners of war. When they arrived at the prisons. Their wounds or injuries were sometimes ignored. Later, if they became ill. They were often refused medical attention. They were in total isolation and were not allowed to talk to anyone they were cut off from any human contact. They were forced to remain in solitary, confined areas. That were so small the prisoners could not exercise or, in some cases, even stand. To add to their torture. Prisoners suffered through winters with no heat or blankets. In the summer, they had to choose between covering themselves to avoid being bitten by mosquitoes. Or being unbearably hot. Also, they were given very little food, the food they were given was almost impossible to eat. Some prisoners of war were tortured. To make false confessions. Each day, trying to remain sane. They remembered their loved ones and families at home.

Sentence Combining Using Compound Sentences A

Twenty points

Combine the two simple sentences into one compound sentence, following directions carefully. Make corrections above the sentences.

1. Combine the two simple sentences by using the coordinating conjunction "and." Punctuate correctly.

   Many community college students have full-time jobs. Most have family responsibilities.

2. Combine the two simple sentences by using a semicolon.

   Many community college students have full-time jobs. Most have family responsibilities.

3. Combine the two simple sentences by using a semicolon and the conjunctive adverb "in addition." Punctuate correctly.

   Many community college students have full-time jobs. Most have family responsibilities.

4. Combine the two simple sentences by using the coordinating conjunction "for." Punctuate correctly.

   Colorado, Arizona, and New Mexico are appealing southwestern states. They all have mountains, large uninhabited spaces, and sun.

5. Combine the two simple sentences by using a semicolon.

   Colorado, Arizona, and New Mexico are appealing southwestern states. They all have mountains, large uninhabited spaces, and sun.

6. Combine the two simple sentences by using a semicolon and the conjunctive adverb "furthermore." Punctuate correctly.

   Colorado, Arizona, and New Mexico are appealing southwestern states. They all have mountains, large uninhabited spaces, and sun.

7. Combine the two simple sentences by using the coordinating conjunction "but." Punctuate correctly.

   Hawaii is a land of paradise. It is extremely expensive to live there.

8. Combine the two simple sentences by using a semicolon.

   Hawaii is a land of paradise. It is extremely expensive to live there.

9. Combine the two simple sentences by using a semicolon and the conjunctive adverb "however." Punctuate correctly.

   Hawaii is a land of paradise. It is extremely expensive to live there.

10. Combine the two simple sentences by using the coordinating conjunction "and." Punctuate correctly.

    Some states have traffic problems. They may also have problems with pollution.

11. Combine the two simple sentences by using a semicolon.

    Some states have traffic problems. They may also have problems with pollution.

12. Combine the two simple sentences by using a semicolon and the conjunctive adverb "as a result." Punctuate correctly.

    Some states have traffic problems. They may also have problems with pollution.

13. Combine the two simple sentences by using the coordinating conjunction "and." Punctuate correctly.

    Movies are very expensive. Many people continue going to them.

14. Combine the two simple sentences by using a semicolon.

    Movies are very expensive. Many people continue going to them.

15. Combine the two simple sentences by using a semicolon and the conjunctive adverb "however." Punctuate correctly.

    Movies are very expensive. Many people continue going to them.

16. Combine the two simple sentences by using the coordinating conjunction "nor." Punctuate correctly.

    The men do not want to join the fraternity. They do not want to participate in intramural sports.

17. Combine the two simple sentences by using a semicolon.

    The men do not want to join the fraternity. They do not want to participate in intramural sports.

18. Combine the two simple sentences by using a semicolon and the conjunctive adverb "furthermore." Punctuate correctly.

    The men do not want to join the fraternity. They do not want to participate in intramural sports.

19. Combine the two simple sentences by using the coordinating conjunction "so." Punctuate correctly.

    The students were hungry after class. They stopped at the pizza place.

20. Combine the two simple sentences by using a semicolon and the conjunctive adverb "therefore." Punctuate correctly.

    The students were hungry after class. They stopped at the pizza place.

Sentence Combining Using Compound Sentences B

Twenty points

Combine the two simple sentences into one compound sentence, following directions carefully. Make corrections above the sentences.

1. Combine the two simple sentences by using the coordinating conjunction "and." Punctuate correctly.

   Rose produced the home video with great care. Everyone enjoyed watching it.

2. Combine the two simple sentences by using a semicolon.

   Rose produced the home video with great care. Everyone enjoyed watching it.

3. Combine the two simple sentences by using a semicolon and the conjunctive adverb "therefore." Punctuate correctly.

   Rose produced the home video with great care. Everyone enjoyed watching it.

4. Combine the two simple sentences by using the coordinating conjunction "for." Punctuate correctly.

   She cherished her dishes. They had belonged to her grandmother.

5. Combine the two simple sentences by using a semicolon.

   She cherished her dishes. They had belonged to her grandmother.

6. Combine the two simple sentences by using a semicolon and the conjunctive adverb "furthermore." Punctuate correctly.

   She cherished her dishes. They had belonged to her grandmother.

7. Combine the two simple sentences by using the coordinating conjunction "yet." Punctuate correctly.

   The trail over the mountain was steep. They enjoyed the climb.

8. Combine the two simple sentences by using a semicolon.

   The trail over the mountain was steep. They enjoyed the climb.

9. Combine the two simple sentences by using a semicolon and the conjunctive adverb "however." Punctuate correctly.

   The trail over the mountain was steep. They enjoyed the climb.

10. Combine the two simple sentences by using the coordinating conjunction "so." Punctuate correctly.

    Consumers are secure in their jobs. They buy more goods.

11. Combine the two simple sentences by using a semicolon.

    Consumers are secure in their jobs. They buy more goods.

12. Combine the two simple sentences by using a semicolon and the conjunctive adverb "as a result." Punctuate correctly.

    Consumers are secure in their jobs. They buy more goods.

13. Combine the two simple sentences by using the coordinating conjunction "so." Punctuate correctly.

    His job performance was outstanding. He continued to improve.

14. Combine the two simple sentences by using a semicolon.

    His job performance was outstanding. He continued to improve.

15. Combine the two simple sentences by using a semicolon and the conjunctive adverb "moreover." Punctuate correctly.

    His job performance was outstanding. He continued to improve.

16. Combine the two simple sentences by using the coordinating conjunction "nor." Punctuate correctly.

    The teenagers did not want to join the gang. They did not want to leave their families.

17. Combine the two simple sentences by using a semicolon.

    The teenagers did not want to join the gang. They did not want to leave their families.

18. Combine the two simple sentences by using a semicolon and the conjunctive adverb "furthermore." Punctuate correctly.

The teenagers did not want to join the gang. They did not want to leave their families.

19. Combine the two simple sentences by using the coordinating conjunction "so." Punctuate correctly.

The members of the bicycle club had scheduled a fifty-mile ride. They got up early in the morning.

20. Combine the two simple sentences by using a semicolon and the conjunctive adverb "therefore." Punctuate correctly.

The members of the bicycle club had scheduled a fifty-mile ride. They got up early in the morning.

Sentence Combining Using Complex Sentences A
Twenty points

Combine the two simple sentences into one complex sentence, following directions carefully. Make corrections above the sentences.

1. Combine the two simple sentences by using the connecting word "because." Use a comma only if the dependent clause comes at the beginning of the sentence.

   I graduated from college. I hope to get a good job.

2. Combine the two simple sentences by using the connecting word "if." Use a comma only if the dependent clause comes at the beginning of the sentence.

   I am paid today. We can go out to eat.

3. Combine the two simple sentences into one sentence by changing the second sentence into the dependent clause "that I liked" and combining it with the first sentence. No commas are needed.

   The sales representative was honest. I liked the representative.

4. Combine the two simple sentences into one sentence by changing the second sentence into the dependent clause "whose car was stolen" and combining it with the first sentence. No commas are needed.

   The student had to ride the bus. The student's car was stolen.

5. Combine the two simple sentences into one sentence by changing the second sentence into the dependent clause "where Rica works out" and combining it with the first sentence. No commas are needed.

   The gym is filled with excellent equipment. Rica works out there.

6. Combine the two simple sentences by using the connecting word "because." Use a comma only if the dependent clause comes at the beginning of the sentence.

   Mr. Jones is a salesman. He is often away from home.

7. Combine the two simple sentences by using the connecting word "when." Use a comma only if the dependent clause comes at the beginning of the sentence.

Maria walked to the store. She found a wallet.

8. Combine the two simple sentences by changing the second sentence into the dependent clause "who are able to preregister" and inserting this clause after the word "students" in the first sentence. No commas are needed.

Continuing students often get the classes they need. They are able to preregister.

9. Combine the two simple sentences into one sentence by changing the second sentence into the dependent clause "that had been found in the attic" and combining it with the first sentence. No commas are needed.

The book was very valuable. The book had been found in the attic.

10. Combine the two simple sentences by using the connecting word "after." Use a comma only if the dependent clause comes at the beginning of the sentence.

The doctor had both back and heart surgery. He decided to retire.

11. Combine the two simple sentences into one sentence by changing the second sentence into the dependent clause "who studied hard" and combining it with the first sentence. No commas are needed.

The student made the highest score on the exam. She studied hard.

12. Combine the two simple sentences into one sentence by changing the second sentence into the dependent clause "where they live" and combining it with the first sentence. No commas are needed.

The house is in the oldest section of town. It is where they live.

13. Combine the two simple sentences by using the connecting word "because." Use a comma only if the dependent clause comes at the beginning of the sentence.

The puppy was barking at her dish. She was hungry.

14. Combine the two simple sentences by using the connecting word "when." Use a comma only if the dependent clause comes at the beginning of the sentence.

The child ate all of his supper. He got dessert.

15. Combine the two simple sentences by using the connecting word "when." Use a comma only if the dependent clause comes at the beginning of the sentence.

    We arrived in El Paso. We found someone to fix the car.

16. Combine the two simple sentences by using the connecting word "as." Use a comma only if the dependent clause comes at the beginning of the sentence.

    The fruit ripened. The birds had a feast.

17. Combine the two simple sentences into one sentence by changing the second sentence into the dependent clause "whose last child moved out of the house" and combining it with the first sentence. No commas are needed.

    The couple went on a trip to Hawaii. Their last child moved out of the house.

18. Combine the two simple sentences by using the connecting word "after." Use a comma only if the dependent clause comes at the beginning of the sentence.

    I finished the yard work. I sat down to enjoy a cold drink.

19. Combine the two simple sentences into one sentence by changing the second sentence into the dependent clause "whose boss did not show up" and combining it with the first sentence. No commas are needed.

    The secretary finished all her work. Her boss did not show up.

20. Combine the two simple sentences by using the connecting words "as soon as." Use a comma only if the dependent clause comes at the beginning of the sentence.

    Ralph graduates from college. He has a job waiting for him.

Sentence Combining Using Complex Sentences B
Twenty points

Combine the two simple sentences into one complex sentence, following directions carefully. Make corrections above the sentences.

1. Combine the two simple sentences by using the connecting word "because." Use a comma only if the dependent clause comes at the beginning of the sentence.

   She was interested in helping people. She completed her paramedic training.

2. Combine the two simple sentences by using the connecting word "because." Use a comma only if the dependent clause comes at the beginning of the sentence.

   The electrician finished the job. He will get paid today.

3. Combine the two simple sentences into one sentence by changing the second sentence into the dependent clause "who was kind to guests" and combining it with the first sentence. No commas are needed.

   The talk-show host had a large audience. The host was kind to guests.

4. Combine the two simple sentences into one sentence by changing the second sentence into the dependent clause "whose surgeons were skilled" and combining it with the first sentence. No commas are needed.

   The patient recovered quickly. Her surgeons were skilled.

5. Combine the two simple sentences into one sentence by changing the second sentence into the dependent clause "that I visited" and combining it with the first sentence. No commas are needed.

   The wildlife preserve was beautiful. I visited the preserve.

6. Combine the two simple sentences by using the connecting word "because." Use a comma only if the dependent clause comes at the beginning of the sentence.

   Tony loves to cook many different types of pasta. He eats well.

7. Combine the two simple sentences by using the connecting word "when." Use a comma only if the dependent clause comes at the beginning of the sentence.

The team scored a basket. The fans cheered them on.

8. Combine the two simple sentences by changing the second sentence into the dependent clause "who use computers" and inserting this clause after the word "students" in the first sentence. No commas are needed.

Students find writing is easy. They use computers.

9. Combine the two simple sentences into one sentence by changing the second sentence into the dependent clause "that I had to update" and combining it with the first sentence. No commas are needed.

The computer was not very powerful. I had to update it.

10. Combine the two simple sentences by using the connecting word "after." Use a comma only if the dependent clause comes at the beginning of the sentence.

The weather turns cold. Plants are in danger of freezing.

11. Combine the two simple sentences into one sentence by changing the second sentence into the dependent clause "who sold his sand paintings" and combining it with the first sentence. No commas are needed.

The old man had a profitable year. He sold his sand paintings.

12. Combine the two simple sentences into one sentence by changing the second sentence into the dependent clause "where they love to eat" and combining it with the first sentence. No commas are needed.

The restaurant serves the most authentic Mexican food in town. They love to eat there.

13. Combine the two simple sentences by using the connecting word "because." Use a comma only if the dependent clause comes at the beginning of the sentence.

Sal's homework was done. He could enjoy his day off.

14. Combine the two simple sentences by using the connecting word "if." Use a comma only if the dependent clause comes at the beginning of the sentence.

The trees are planted in the back yard. They need to be watered

15. Combine the two simple sentences by using the connecting word "when." Use a comma only if the dependent clause comes at the beginning of the sentence.

    The mail arrived. We received wonderful news from home.

16. Combine the two simple sentences by using the connecting word "as." Use a comma only if the dependent clause comes at the beginning of the sentence.

    The sun went down. The puppies fell asleep one by one.

17. Combine the two simple sentences into one sentence by changing the second sentence into the dependent clause "whose baby was born prematurely" and combining it with the first sentence. No commas are needed.

    The chimpanzee rested for several hours. Her baby was born prematurely.

18. Combine the two simple sentences by using the connecting word "after." Use a comma only if the dependent clause comes at the beginning of the sentence.

    I got up in the morning. I repaired my motorcycle.

19. Combine the two simple sentences into one sentence by changing the second sentence into the dependent clause "whose crops were destroyed" and combining it with the first sentence. No commas are needed.

    The farmer faced bankruptcy. His crops were destroyed.

20. Combine the two simple sentences by using the connecting words "as soon as." Use a comma only if the dependent clause comes at the beginning of the sentence.

    Tran turned in his last paper. He decided to celebrate.

Punctuation A

Twenty points (in each paragraph)

Add punctuation to the following paragraphs. Include underlining. (Do not eliminate any punctuation already in the paragraph.)

Paragraph 1

College and university newspapers offer journalism students many opportunities to use their abilities. Student newspapers need editors reporters photographers, and lay-out staff. While working as newspaper reporters students can follow up on leads and interview interesting people. If the newspaper needs current information on particular issues the student reporters can conduct personal-opinion polls of students faculty and administration. Other reporters follow sports events, and they write weekly columns featuring outstanding student achievements in football soccer tennis golf or whatever sport is in season at the time. Because sports provide excellent opportunities for action photos student photographers get lots of hands-on experience and the lay-out people get the practice they need. Still other reporters cover their schools musical calendar and report on concerts recitals and auditions. Although student journalists will not be working in an organization as large as the New York Times or the Chicago Tribune they will receive valuable experience knowledge and contacts for their future careers.

Paragraph 2

Sometimes in the world of raising dogs for the show circuit events do not always turn out as expected. On April 22 1990 in Buffalo New York a litter of Sheltie puppies was born. Out of the litter came two perfectly sized pups one oversized pup and one undersized pup. At the end of six weeks one of the pups with show prospects was sent to a home in Altadena California. The other correctly sized pup was shipped to a home in Clearwater Florida. Because the large puppy could not become a show dog he was sold as a pet. Several people who came to purchase a possible dog for show looked at the small pup but they all said right away "She is pretty but she is just too small. However a young handler said, I will take a chance on her. Amazingly enough after she spent several months with the young handler she grew to fourteen and a half inches and eventually became a fifteen-point champion.

Punctuation B

Twenty points (in each paragraph)

Add punctuation to the following paragraphs. Include underlining. (Do not eliminate any punctuation already in the paragraph.)

Paragraph 1

On October 27 1993 the people of southern California saw one of their worst fears come true: wildfires. North and east of Los Angeles the wildfires began in the hills. Because the hot desert Santa Ana winds were blowing the flames quickly spread through the dry brush on the hills. With the Santa Anas blowing up to fifty miles an hour the flames became a firestorm. Soon brush was not all that fed the flames. One after another homes in Altadena and Laguna Hills burned to ashes. Within a few hours fires started in other parts of southern California roared down the canyons to the sea and took home after home. In the wealthy area of Malibu more blazes appeared. In all these fires people had so little warning that most of them were able to take only whatever they could pack into one or two cars. Firefighters worked constantly but people's homes were lost and, in many cases most of their personal property, such as furniture clothing family heirlooms and photographs, was also lost. Before all the wildfires were extinguished this disaster caused millions of dollars worth of property damage. In addition people suffered overwhelming personal losses that money can never restore.

Paragraph 2

Every year thousands of animal species become extinct. They often lose their natural habitat because of overpopulation natural disasters and development by humans. Incorporated in 1951 the Nature Conservancy, a national nonprofit wildlife organization, pledges to protect both plants and animals in their natural habitat. Today more than 1,300 preserves exist throughout the world. According to the Nature Conservancy, Our goal is to find protect and maintain the best examples of communities ecosystems and endangered species in the natural world. For example a Conservancy in the town of Whiskey Mountain Wyoming has taken on the challenge of the survival of bighorn sheep. Near Pine Butte Montana an 18,000-acre preserve supports watering holes for such animals as the grizzly bear mountain lion bighorn sheep beaver, badger and more than 150 types of birds. In these many preserves both wildlife and their habitats are allowed to remain unspoiled.

60

Answers to Tests

Topic Sentence A

B	1.
F	2.
F	3.
TS	4.
B	5.
F	6.
TS	7.
B	8.
TS	9.
TS	10.

11. a
12. c
13. b
14. e
15. e
16. b
17. c
18. f
19. a
20. d

Topic Sentence B

F	1.
B	2.
F	3.
TS	4.
TS	5.
F	6.
B	7.
TS	8.
F	9.
TS	10.

11. b
12. e
13. a
14. d
15. c
16. d
17. c
18. a
19. d
20. d

Subject-Verb Agreement A

Part 1 (Verbs that need to be changed are in boldface.)
   1. He **does** not care (for the bicycle) (in the garage).
C 2. She is not the first recipient (of the Presidential Award).
   3. Everybody (in the United States) **needs** concern (for the environment).
   4. A few (of the people) **enjoy** picking apples (in the fall).
   5. We **were** the only ones who took the lesson seriously.
C 6. The team member (with the most points) will receive an award.
   7. The team **is** trying hard to win the tournament.
   8. Each (of the students) **wants** an "A."
C 9. Nobody wants to miss the concert.
   10. Patty and Sue **were** elected (to the senate).

Part 2 (Verbs that need to be changed are in boldface.)
     The culture of the Aztec Indians **provides** us with insight to the people of that region and time. They **were** an intelligent group with a sophisticated money system. Cocoa beans **were** used as money in exchange for raw goods. Also, almost everyone **was** a good farmer who developed an efficient irrigation system to support, in particular, a diet of corn. A government system of a higher-ranking chief and many common laborers prevailed. In addition, they **were** knowledgeable about architecture and built many pyramids. One aspect of their culture, however, **does** not appeal to others. Virgins **were** offered as sacrificial victims to the gods. Though this **was** a part of the Aztec culture, other people **find** human sacrifice barbaric. All in all, the Aztec Indian culture **leaves** us with a legacy of intrigue as well as information.

Subject-Verb Agreement B
Part I (Verbs that need to be changed are in boldface.)
1. The <u>president</u> (of the student body) always **delivers** a challenging speech (to new students).
2. <u>Honesty</u>, one (of his best qualities), **makes** him appealing.
3. Either the <u>husband</u> or the <u>wife</u> **arrives** late (for work).
C 4. The <u>husband</u> and <u>wife</u> often agree (on major decisions).
5. Only a <u>few</u> (of my friends) **go** (to parties) (during the week).
6. <u>Nobody</u> **seems** to enjoy life as much as Shawn.
7. <u>Each</u> (of my puppies) **has** a unique personality.
8. The Student Ambassador <u>program</u> **encourages** good will (among young people) (from the United States) and (from other countries).
9. The <u>director</u> (of the campus placement service) always **informs** the incoming students (of their opportunities).
10. Several <u>courses</u> **meet** the graduation requirements (in mathematics).
Part 2 (Verbs that need to be changed are in boldface.)

<u>Biking</u> <u>can be</u> fun; however, if <u>people</u> **do** not <u>take</u> proper care of their equipment, <u>bike riding</u> <u>can be</u> dangerous. For example, responsible <u>bikers</u> **adjust** brake pads properly and **replace** them periodically. <u>Bikers</u> <u>risk</u> injury on mountain trails if the <u>brakes</u> <u>are</u> unreliable. Regular tire inspections for cracks or bubbles **mean** that the <u>bikers</u> **detect** defective tires before problems occur. Also, if the <u>gears</u> <u>are</u> not <u>lubricated</u>, <u>they</u> <u>may</u> not <u>work</u> properly, causing hazardous conditions for the biker. Another dangerous <u>situation</u> **occurs** if the <u>chain</u> **is** not <u>oiled</u>. As a result, the <u>cyclists</u> **find** themselves unable to peddle, and the bike <u>chain</u> <u>can break</u>. Unless damaged <u>reflectors</u> **are** replaced, <u>bikers</u> <u>cannot be seen</u> after dark. Responsible <u>riders</u> who keep their bikes in excellent condition **are** less apt to have perilous experiences.

Consistent Verb Tense A
Paragraph 1 Tense __present__ (Verbs that need to be changed are in boldface.)

Phi Theta Kappa is an honorary organization for community college students. It is basically devoted to scholarship, fellowship, and community service. All students who have a 3.5 grade point average or above and who have accumulated twelve semester hours of credit **are** invited to join. After joining, students **attend** leadership conferences, **raise** money for service or scholarships, and **support** one another. In addition, they are recognized during graduation ceremonies, and their diplomas and transcripts are sealed with a gold Phi Theta Kappa sticker. Usually the group **is** energetic and creative. At the end of the semester, another group of honor students **is** invited to join, and the cycle **repeats** itself.
Paragraph 2 Tense__past__ (Verbs that need to be changed are in boldface.)

Our Sunday afternoon picnic to Red Feather Lakes brought a typical Colorado experience. Each of the teenagers in the family **invited** a guest. We **packed** food, sports equipment, and camping equipment. On the hour drive, we played travel games and listened to tapes. Just as most of us were getting tired, we **spotted** the beautiful lakes. However, when we first **arrived**, it **became** cloudy. The wind **increased**, and the area **grew** cold. Most of us **came** unprepared for cold weather, so some stayed in the car; a few put up a small tent to protect themselves from the cold wind; others **wrapped** themselves with whatever they could find. In the adverse wind, we **cooked** steaks and chicken, but after we ate, the weather **cleared** and **turned** sunny. So we **pulled** out our baseball equipment and enjoyed a game. The time to go came too soon. On the return trip, everyone but the driver slept.

Consistent Verb Tense B
Paragraph 1 Tense__present__ (Verbs that need to be changed are in boldface.)

More and more people today find fitness centers are an invaluable opportunity. While working out inside a climate-controlled atmosphere, people **are** sheltered from natural elements like pollution or severe weather conditions. For example, they **leave** rain, snow, or sleet outside and **work** out in comfort. Likewise, if the temperature outside **turns** hot and humid, they **step** inside to refrigerated comfort. Also, when they jog, **bike**, or climb stairs, they are not exposed to road hazards such as cars, torn-up roads, potholes, or even acts of violence. These fitness centers **are** well monitored by knowledgeable personnel who **know** how to operate the equipment safely. Often trainers **help** newcomers use the equipment with maximum efficiency. Fitness centers **seem** to be the answer that many avid exercisers want.

Paragraph 2 Tense__past__ (Verbs that need to be changed are in boldface.)

The pigeons on our campus fascinated me that fall afternoon as they fed together on the rye grass seed that was intended to produce a nice green winter lawn. First one, then ten, then twenty **flew** in and **shared** the feast. None made a sound; rather, all **were** intent on the spread put before them. They neither **argued** nor **chased** one another away. They **did** not have to hurry off to prepare supper or run errands. Plump and healthy, they **lived** year after year as they built nests in palm trees, **drank** water from puddles on the ground, and ate whatever came their way. In the springtime, baby pigeons **hatched** from eggs and repeated the cycle, ignoring the humans that lived in the same area. Only the humans hurried here and there, **went** home, cooked supper, and then returned the next morning to find that the rye grass needed cutting.

Consistent Point of View A

Paragraph 1 (Words that need to be changed are in boldface.)

Breaking my leg was an unpleasant experience for me. Initially the pain, not from the broken bone, but from the strained muscles and ligaments, was excruciating for **me**. **I** felt an intense discomfort for two to two and one-half weeks. Simple, ordinary maneuvers suddenly became difficult for **me**. For example, **I** found making a simple sandwich a major undertaking and taking a shower a major task. **I** found driving was possible; however, **my** physician advised **me** not to drive. Into the fourth week, **I** felt an unbearable yet inaccessible itching occurring below the cast. This was maddening. Finally, when the sixth week arrived, I had **my** leg x-rayed and the cast removed. Still, **I** needed some rehabilitation because my leg would not be back to normal for about three more months.

Paragraph 2 (Words that need to be changed are in boldface.)

At amusement parks, people love dressing up in costumes to have their pictures taken. Costumes let **people** personify a different character momentarily. Women can outfit themselves in large frilly hats, old-fashioned skirts, and parasols, or **they** can appear in Native American dress. Men can don ten-gallon hats, cowboy shirts, and chaps, or **they** can try on Mexican sombreros and throw a poncho over **their** shoulders. The photo models can create a fantasy all **their** own. Some participants enter a photo session in groups, and **they** produce a running theme for the picture. **People** can select a certain culture, and all the members of **their** group choose clothing of that era and culture. At times, normally light, jovial personalities become serious, stiff-faced models. Other times, ~~your~~ serious models become lighthearted and carefree. No wonder **people** find these special photo shops fun.

Consistent Point of View B

Paragraph 1 (Words that need to be changed are in boldface.)

Three teenagers, two brothers and one sister, from Bloomington, Indiana, realized that if they worked hard and used ingenuity they could build a successful business. **They** kept in mind that customers wanted excellent service as well as honest dealings. Of course, **they** also realized that the key to success started with the realization that a service was needed in an area, and then **they** went out and aggressively tackled the problem. These college students, who lived just ten miles from Lake Monroe, a resort area, found no pizza parlors near by, so **they** decided to "zero in" on the opportunity, and **they** started **their** own business. **They** found an old, abandoned building that **they** could obtain at a reasonable price. With little overhead, **they** added an attractive deck in front, tables, and chairs. **They** then purchased used kitchen equipment that produced excellent pizzas. When customers came in, they received exceptional service; therefore, business grew. This is but one example of individuals starting a successful business in the 1990s.

Paragraph 2 (Words that need to be changed are in boldface.)

Attending college can create stress for students. Taking too many classes and not being able to get homework in on time can create tension for **them**. As a result, not doing the homework may keep **them** from learning some of the course content, so **they** may not do well on tests. To avoid pressure, **they** must do well on **their** tests and in other class activities to maintain a high grade point average if **they** wish to receive credit in the course or even to stay in school. Not only are tests and homework difficult to handle, but if **they** happen to be taking self-paced courses, finding time to complete these classes on campus can cause more anxiety. These increasing demands on **their** time are very hard to manage. In addition, when students encounter inflexible deadlines and excessive homework, **they** might have more stress. Students who stay in school and succeed in **their** classes have learned, probably above all else, to control the stress that comes with attending college.

Thesis Sentence A

Part 1
1. Restoring an old car can be time-consuming and expensive yet fulfilling.
2. Speaking two languages can be advantageous when a person seeks a job, travels in another country, or assists foreign people.
3. When interacting with a disabled person, one needs to be empathetic, realistic, and knowledgeable.
4. Lungs, heart, and throat are major parts of the body affected by a long-term smoking habit.
5. Learning about our prehistoric past involves studying historical archives, visiting archaeological museums, and interpreting new findings.

Part 2 (Words that need to be changed or eliminated are in boldface.)
6. When buying children's toys, parents need to be sure the toys are safe, appropriate, durable, and **colorful**.
7. Ray spent his life working hard all day, **socializing** in the evening, and sleeping well at night.
8. His summers are spent jet-skiing at the lake, surfing at the beach, and **sailing** on the ocean.
C 9. An afternoon in an art museum can be fun, inexpensive, educational, yet tiring.
10. Raising children requires time, ~~having~~ patience, and money.
11. Jerry's retirement years were pleasant because he had bought land, invested in stocks, and **saved** some money.
12. His knowledge, **his** social skills, and his age helped make him successful at his job.

Part 3
13. Eating popcorn, seeing the animals, watching the clowns, ~~enjoying the elephants,~~ and reading a program are memories from the circus.
14. A person running for public office needs money, emotional support from friends and family, ~~personal endurance,~~ and stamina. (or ~~stamina~~)
15. Jean's favorite activities are collecting coins, painting pictures, and restoring old telephones, ~~and painting with oils~~.
16. After work, Harry drives home safely, ~~watches the news,~~ works in the yard, cooks supper, and watches television.
C 17. Strength, speed, intelligence, and willingness to cooperate are qualities of a good football player.
18. Addictive eating disorders can destroy a person physically, ~~mentally,~~ socially, and psychologically. (or ~~psychologically~~)
19. Packing a picnic lunch, wearing cool clothing, taking extra drinks, ~~bringing chips,~~ and using sunblock can make a family outing at the lake more fun.
20. A teacher should have patience, sensitivity, ~~tolerance,~~ and knowledge. (or ~~patience~~)

64

Thesis Sentence B

Part 1

1. (A company's wellness program offers such benefits) as financial incentives, educational seminars, and, as a result, improved health.
2. (Artists today may exhibit and sell their work) at local fairs, galleries, and private sales.
3. Attending college can be a financial burden; however, a good financial aid package, a part-time job, and a budget (can ease the difficulty.)
4. (Car manufacturers appeal to people's interests) in comfort, appearance, and power.
5. (Classroom software should be) easy to use, relevant to class goals, inexpensive to purchase, and positive in its approach to course content.

Part 2 (Words that need to be changed or eliminated are in boldface.)

6. Adobe buildings are strong, simple, ~~look~~ attractive, and practical.
7. AIDS can be contracted through blood transfusions, irresponsible sexual relationships, and ~~sharing~~ drug needles.
8. Comforting a child, ~~providing~~ a pleasant home environment, and teaching a child are all aspects of parenting.
9. Disadvantages of shopping at membership warehouse stores include buying large quantities, needing more time to shop, and ~~experiencing~~ a limited selection.
10. ~~Eating~~ right, working out hard, avoiding sweets, and sleeping well are important to health-conscious people.
11. Firefighters help society by fighting fires, helping accident victims, and ~~volunteering~~ in community organizations.
12. Going on a date requires money, time, and ~~finding~~ a partner.

Part 3

13. Air pollution can irritate eyes and noses, cause lung problems, damage plants, **and** damage buildings, ~~and destroy outer layers of stone buildings.~~
14. Before buying a computer, people should consider personal needs, ~~expenses,~~ available software, computer capabilities, and costs. (or ~~costs~~)
15. Bowl game excitement includes pre-game activities, the game itself, ~~parades,~~ colorful half-time activities, and post-game celebrations.
16. Preparing a meal includes planning the menu, buying the foods, **and** cooking the meal, ~~and buying vegetables~~.
17. Collectibles can be found at ~~garage sales~~, antique stores, thrift shops, auctions, and yard sales. (or ~~yard sales~~)
18. Home health aides must be ~~trustworthy~~, skilled, patient, and honest. (or ~~honest~~)
19. Homemade whole-grain bread can be nutritious, flavorful, **and** inexpensive, ~~and tasty.~~ (or ~~flavorful~~)
20. Tour coordinators must consider insurance, ~~accommodations,~~ safety, hotel reservations, and activities. (or ~~reservations~~)

Fragments, Run-On Sentences, and Comma Splices A

Answers will vary, but one possible revision is shown.

Paragraph 1

Every summer we look forward to going camping at Big Lake. As soon as we get to the campground, we leisurely set up the tent under the tall, shady trees. Then we organize our fishing gear and get everything ready for the next few days of fishing. We gather firewood. Soon we start a campfire and cook juicy hamburgers that cannot be equaled anywhere else. Later, we enjoy toasted marshmallows that smell as good as they taste. With stomachs content, we carry our fishing gear to water's edge, and we look for that special hole where we caught the "big ones" last year. Shortly, a big moon rises in the sky, and millions of stars appear. Though we do not catch any fish, we see trout jumping on top of the water everywhere. We relax, knowing that we still have several days ahead to forget our busy life at home.

Paragraph 2

Garage sales appeal to bargain seekers. Items of all kinds can be found at reasonable prices. Everything from dog kennels to baby strollers sell at a fraction of their original costs. Collectors often find old fountain pens or thimbles for their collections. Professional upholsterers find good, solid pieces of furniture that they can recover. Other times, items are in excellent condition and simply need a good scrubbing. Some items might even be unused gifts still in their original boxes. Some people furnish their entire homes inexpensively but nicely by shopping at these bargain centers.

Fragments, Run-On Sentences, and Comma Splices B

Answers will vary, but one possible revision is shown.

Paragraph 1

In today's society, more and more people are finding that they can save money by shopping wisely. Shoppers are heading for outlet malls where they can purchase quality merchandise at a fraction of its retail price. Some outlet clothing stores carry merchandise that is exclusively for women. However, other clothing stores carry discounted clothing for all members of the family. Some stores carry only baby clothing, yet other shops specialize in toys. Shoppers can also find discount stores that specialize in linens, crystal, books, or cookware. For additional savings, shoppers often find end-of-season markdowns at these outlet stores. No matter what shoppers need, they can usually find a store that features these items at reduced prices, and they can save money.

Paragraph 2

Being a prisoner of war in Vietnam was one of the most dreadful ordeals anyone could experience. According to former prisoners of war, when they arrived at the prisons, their wounds or injuries were sometimes ignored. Later, if they became ill, they were often refused medical attention. They were in total isolation and were not allowed to talk to anyone. They were cut off from any human contact. They were forced to remain in solitary, confined areas that were so small the prisoners could not exercise or, in some cases, even stand. To add to their torture, prisoners suffered through winters with no heat or blankets. In the summer, they had to choose between covering themselves to avoid being bitten by mosquitoes or being unbearably hot. Also, they were given very little food. The food they were given was almost impossible to eat. Some prisoners of war were tortured to make false confessions. Each day, trying to remain sane, they remembered their loved ones and families at home.

Sentence Combining Using Compound Sentences A

1. Many community college students have full-time jobs, and most have family responsibilities.
2. Many community college students have full-time jobs; most have family responsibilities.
3. Many community college students have full-time jobs; in addition, most have family responsibilities.
4. Colorado, Arizona, and New Mexico are appealing southwestern states, for they all have mountains, large uninhabited spaces, and sun.
5. Colorado, Arizona, and New Mexico are appealing southwestern states; they all have mountains, large uninhabited spaces, and sun.
6. Colorado, Arizona, and New Mexico are appealing southwestern states; furthermore, they all have mountains, large uninhabited spaces, and sun.
7. Hawaii is a land of paradise, but it is extremely expensive to live there.
8. Hawaii is a land of paradise; it is extremely expensive to live there.
9. Hawaii is a land of paradise; however, it is extremely expensive to live there.
10. Some states have traffic problems, and they may also have problems with pollution.
11. Some states have traffic problems; they may also have problems with pollution.
12. Some states have traffic problems; as a result, they may also have problems with pollution.
13. Movies are very expensive, yet many people continue going to them.
14. Movies are very expensive; many people continue going to them.

15. Movies are very expensive; however, many people continue going to them.
16. The men do not want to join the fraternity, nor do they want to participate in intramural sports.
17. The men do not want to join the fraternity; they do not want to participate in intramural sports.
18. The men do not want to join the fraternity; furthermore, they do not want to participate in intramural sports.
19. The students were hungry after class, so they stopped at the pizza place.
20. The students were hungry after class; therefore, they stopped at the pizza place.

Sentence Combining Using Compound Sentences B
1. Rose produced the home video with great care, and everyone enjoyed watching it.
2. Rose produced the home video with great care; everyone enjoyed watching it.
3. Rose produced the home video with great care; therefore, everyone enjoyed watching it.
4. She cherished her dishes, for they had belonged to her grandmother.
5. She cherished her dishes; they had belonged to her grandmother.
6. She cherished her dishes; furthermore, they had belonged to her grandmother.
7. The trail over the mountain was steep, yet they enjoyed the climb.
8. The trail over the mountain was steep; they enjoyed the climb.
9. The trail over the mountain was steep; however, they enjoyed the climb.
10. Consumers are secure in their jobs, so they buy more goods.
11. Consumers are secure in their jobs; they buy more goods.
12. Consumers are secure in their jobs; as a result, they buy more goods.
13. His job performance was outstanding, and he continued to improve.
14. His job performance was outstanding; he continued to improve.
15. His job performance was outstanding; moreover, he continued to improve.
16. The teenagers did not want to join the gang, nor did they want to leave their families.
17. The teenagers did not want to join the gang; they did not want to leave their families.
18. The teenagers did not want to join the gang; furthermore, they did not want to leave their families.
19. The members of the bicycle club had scheduled a fifty-mile ride, so they got up early in the morning.
20. The members of the bicycle club had scheduled a fifty-mile ride; therefore, they got up early in the morning.

Sentence Combining Using Complex Sentences A
1. I graduated from college because I hope to get a good job.
   Because I graduated from college, I hope to get a good job.
2. If I am paid today, we can go out to eat.
   We can go out to eat if I am paid today.
3. The sales representative that I liked was honest.
4. The student whose car was stolen had to ride the bus.
5. The gym where Rica works out is filled with excellent equipment.
6. Because Mr. Jones is a salesman, he is often away from home.
   Mr. Jones is often away from home because he is a salesman.
7. When Maria walked to the store, she found a wallet.
   Maria found a wallet when she walked to the store.
8. Continuing students who are able to preregister often get the classes they need.
9. The book that had been found in the attic was very valuable.
10. After the doctor had both back and heart surgery, he decided to retire.
    The doctor decided to retire after he had both back and heart surgery.
11. The student who studied hard made the highest score on the exam.
12. The house where they live is in the oldest section of town.
13. Because the puppy was hungry, she was barking at her dish.
    The puppy was barking at her dish because she was hungry.

14. When the child ate all of his supper, he got dessert.
    The child got dessert when he ate all of his supper.
15. When we arrived in El Paso, we found someone to fix the car.
    We found someone to fix the car when we arrived in El Paso.
16. As the fruit ripened, the birds had a feast.
    The birds had a feast as the fruit ripened.
17. The couple whose last child moved out of the house went on a trip to Hawaii.
18. After I finished the yard work, I sat down to enjoy a cold drink.
    I sat down to enjoy a cold drink after I finished the yard work.
19. The secretary whose boss did not show up finished all her work.
20. As soon as Ralph graduates from college, he has a job waiting for him.
    Ralph has a job waiting for him as soon as he graduates from college.

Sentence Combining Using Complex Sentences B
1. Because she was interested in helping people, she completed her paramedic training.
   She completed her paramedic training because she was interested in helping people.
2. Because the electrician finished the job, he will get paid today.
   The electrician will get paid today because he finished the job.
3. The talk-show host who was kind to guests had a large audience.
4. The patient whose surgeons were skilled recovered quickly.
5. The wildlife preserve that I visited was beautiful.
6. Because Tony loves to cook many different types of pasta, he eats well.
   Tony eats well because he loves to cook many different types of pasta.
7. When the team scored a basket, the fans cheered them on.
   The fans cheered the team on when they scored a basket.
8. Students who use computers find writing is easy.
9. The computer that I had to update was not very powerful.
10. After the weather turns cold, plants are in danger of freezing.
    Plants are in danger of freezing after the weather turns cold.
11. The old man who sold his sand paintings had a profitable year.
12. The restaurant where they love to eat serves the most authentic Mexican food in town.
13. Because Sal's homework was done, he could enjoy his day off.
    Sal could enjoy his day off because his homework was done.
14. If the trees are planted in the back yard, they will need to be watered.
    The trees will need to be watered if they are planted in the back yard.
15. When the mail arrived, we received wonderful news from home.
    We received wonderful news from home when the mail arrived.
16. As the sun went down, the puppies fell asleep one by one.
    The puppies fell asleep one by one as the sun went down.
17. The chimpanzee whose baby was born prematurely rested for several hours.
18. After I got up in the morning, I repaired my motorcycle.
    I repaired my motorcycle after I got up in the morning.
19. The farmer whose crops were destroyed faced bankruptcy.
20. As soon as Tran turned in his last paper, he decided to celebrate.
    Tran decided to celebrate as soon as he turned in his last paper.

Punctuation A
Paragraph 1 (Answers are circled.)

College and university newspapers offer journalism students many opportunities to use their abilities. Student newspapers need editors, reporters, photographers, and lay-out staff. While working as newspaper reporters, students can follow up on leads and interview interesting people. If the newspaper needs current information on particular issues, the student reporters can conduct personal-opinion polls of students, faculty, and administration. Other reporters follow sports events, and they write weekly columns featuring outstanding student achievements in football, soccer, tennis, golf, or whatever sport is in season at the time. Because sports provide excellent opportunities for action photos, student photographers get lots of hands-on experience, and the lay-out people get the practice they need. Still other reporters cover their school's musical calendar and report on concerts, recitals, and auditions. Although student journalists will not be working in an organization as large as the New York Times or the Chicago Tribune, they will receive valuable experience, knowledge, and contacts for their future careers.

Paragraph 2   (Answers are circled.)

Sometimes in the world of raising dogs for the show circuit, events do not always turn out as expected. On April 22, 1990, in Buffalo, New York, a litter of Sheltie puppies was born. Out of the litter came two perfectly sized pups, one oversized pup, and one undersized pup. At the end of six weeks, one of the pups with show prospects was sent to a home in Altadena, California. The other correctly sized pup was shipped to a home in Clearwater, Florida. Because the large puppy could not become a show dog, he was sold as a pet. Several people who came to purchase a possible dog for show looked at the small pup, but they all said right away, "She is pretty, but she is just too small." However, a young handler said, "I will take a chance on her." Amazingly enough, after she spent several months with the young handler, she grew to fourteen and a half inches and eventually became a fifteen-point champion.

Punctuation B

Paragraph 1   (Answers are circled.)

On October 27, 1993, the people of southern California saw one of their worst fears come true: wildfires. North and east of Los Angeles, the wildfires began in the hills. Because the hot desert Santa Ana winds were blowing, the flames quickly spread through the dry brush on the hills. With the Santa Anas blowing up to fifty miles an hour, the flames became a firestorm. Soon, brush was not all that fed the flames. One after another, homes in Altadena and Laguna Hills burned to ashes. Within a few hours, fires started in other parts of southern California, roared down the canyons to the sea, and took home after home. In the wealthy area of Malibu, more blazes appeared. In all these fires, people had so little warning that most of them were able to take only whatever they could pack into one or two cars. Firefighters worked constantly, but people's homes were lost, and, in many cases, most of their personal property, such as furniture, clothing, family heirlooms, and photographs, was also lost. Before all the wildfires were extinguished, this disaster caused millions of dollars worth of property damage. In addition, people suffered overwhelming personal losses that money can never restore.

Paragraph 2   (Answers are circled.)

Every year, thousands of animal species become extinct. They often lose their natural habitat because of overpopulation, natural disasters, and development by humans. Incorporated in 1951, the Nature Conservancy, a national nonprofit wildlife organization, pledges to protect both plants and animals in their natural habitat. Today, more than 1,300 preserves exist throughout the world. According to the Nature Conservancy, "Our goal is to find, protect, and maintain the best examples of communities, ecosystems and endangered species in the natural world." For example, a Conservancy in the town of Whiskey Mountain, Wyoming, has taken on the challenge of the survival of bighorn sheep. Near Pine Butte, Montana, an 18,000-acre preserve supports watering holes for such animals as the grizzly bear, mountain lion, bighorn sheep, beaver, badger, and more than 150 types of birds. In these many preserves, both wildlife and their habitats are allowed to remain unspoiled.

Transparencies

Sample Journal Entry

2:40 I was there — escape from the world. I could leave it all behind — people. As I walked a small opening invited me through. My opening and no one else's. On the other side now quickly another world opens up to me. I move quickly, skipping, listening for the creek that gave me directions. I step across, hopping from one stone to another, crossing as it were to another world. once on the other side it opens up — there is beauty here and noone save the animals. On the ground is small hoof marks. A small rabbit looks at me — not moving — just looking as if to ask where I have been. There are bushes — many many blackberry bushes — each filled with black ripe berries. I am disturbed by noone. There is no noise — just those of my friends. The sounds of water moving across erase all feelings of humans and it is good. Here no one can tell call to me. No one knows where I am. I reach out and touch the berries plucking them from the bush and my fingers turn a red blue and the juice runs over my fingers.

2:55

Journal Log

Date Submitted for Evaluation	Total Time Spent on Journal Ent.	Number of Pages in Journal Ent.	Entry #	Grade
			JE1	
			JE2	
			JE3	
			JE4	
			JE5	
			JE6	
			JE7	
			JE8	
			JE9	
			JE10	
			JE11	
			JE12	
			JE13	
			JE14	

Subjects, Verbs, and Prepositional Phrases

Exercise 4 , Page 71

Identify prepositional phrases in the following paragraphs by enclosing them in parentheses. Underline the subject of each sentence.

Paragraph 1

Libraries have many activities for children in the summer. Many offer movie schedules with educational, non-violent classics. Because of donations from public and private organizations, reading programs that award prizes can also motivate young readers. For excitement, goals are made, and prizes can be won. In most cases, everyone is a winner. During many hot days, happy children are found browsing through books, looking at special displays, or watching fish in the library aquarium. Cool, quiet learning environments in a library can be appealing to children.

Paragraph 2

This spring a mother sparrow with her two young sparrows ventured out of their nest in search of food and water for the first time. As the trio bounced along, it was easy to pick out the baby birds from the mother because the young sparrows fluttered their wings and opened their beaks. Then the mother sparrow inserted a crumb of bread or a little bug into the tiny gaping beaks. In her effort to feed both babies, she quickly hopped from one to the other, attending to both of them. She then slowly drank from a small rain puddle. The babies, however, had nothing on their minds except food. It was a pleasant sight to see.

Subject-Verb Agreement

Exercise 10 , Page 86

Edit the following paragraphs for subject-verb agreement. Underline the subject(s) in each sentence once and the verb(s) twice. Then find any incorrect verb forms and correct them to agree in number with the subject.

Paragraph 2

Early Native Americans used the buffalo wisely. They ate the meat fresh or dried it in strips to use throughout the year. Some of the dried strips was eaten the way they were, and other times they was ground into powder to be cooked. When the meat was scraped off the bones, the large bones was used for tools. Likewise, a few of the small bones was made into needles. The skins of the buffalo was used for warm clothing, rugs, or coverings for their homes. Some history of the tribe were written on the dried buffalo skins. Even the sinews were saved to be used as thread, and the Native Americans boiled the hooves to make glue. Very little of the buffalo was wasted.

Paragraph 3

The people in the jury assembly room reports for jury duty in clothing that they ordinarily wears to work. Several looks like students or service workers. They wears casual dresses or sport shirts and jeans. Some in work uniforms appears to be truck drivers or repair people. A large number of professional men and women sits in more formal suits. One gentleman apparently does not know the dress-code for jurors, and he walk around in shorts and a bright blue T-shirt. This scene is a good example of the variety of people on juries.

Consistent Verb Tense

Exercise 11, Pages 88-89

Identify the tense of the verb in the first sentence as either present or past, and then make the remaining sentences match that tense.

Paragraph 2   Tense_____

David's best friend is Stormy, his pet dog. Every night she goes to bed with him and stayed with him until he gets up the next morning. She sits outside the shower door until he is finished. She also eats breakfast with him and then sees him off at the front door. After school they played catch or raced through the yard. She always knows when things bothered him, and she gently showered him with "kisses." She becomes his audience when he practiced his piano or his companion as he builds his Lego structures. They even shared an afternoon snack of cheese and crackers. Best of all, they are always there for each other.

Paragraph 4   Tense_____

A large city like San Francisco offers visitors many kinds of exciting activities. If someone wanted to attend sporting events, a large city usually has college basketball and football teams as well as professional basketball and football teams. If visitors did not care for sports, perhaps museums filled the bill. A large city usually has art museums as well as historical and scientific museums. For the visitor who liked shopping, the large city provided a range of stores from small specialty shops to large department stores. Since San Francisco is near the water, it offered fishing, a harbor cruise, surfing, an aquarium, and other waterfront activities. Theaters and night clubs also gave visitors a chance to experience evening entertainment they did not have at home. A large city usually gives an out-of-town visitor a wide range of activities for excitement and fun.

Generating a Thesis Sentence

Exercise 5, Pages 147-148

Topic:

Brainstorm to find direction:

Direction:

Brainstorm with direction:

Groups (topic outline):

1.

2.

3.

4.

Thesis sentence with clear direction:

Thesis sentence with clear direction and previewed subtopics:

Fragments

Exercise 6, Pages 172-173

For the following paragraphs, do one or more of the following: (1) add a subject, a verb, or both a subject and a verb, or (2) combine the fragment with a sentence before it or with a sentence after it.

Paragraph 1

Diabetes is a disease that requires control. Dietary control. People with diabetes need to balance the insulin and sugar level in their blood. Most of the time, they need to avoid foods that contain sugar. They also need to eat smaller meals more often throughout the day. However, if they have not eaten enough and their insulin level rises. Must eat or drink something with sugar so that the insulin level in their blood will be balanced. For example, when they feel shaky. They may eat a candy bar or drink a soda pop. Diabetics can be healthier. If they watch their diet.

Paragraph 2

I found that setting up an aquarium is expensive. After buying the tank, light, filter, and heater. I had other initial expenses. I needed to purchase chemicals. Chemicals to eliminate chlorine and to reduce the acidity. I made the tank attractive. Adding colored gravel and plants. Adding ceramic figures. Placing a nice background behind the glass. To test the water and to keep the tank water at the right temperature. Adding a variety of fish with beautiful colors. When everything was set up. I had fun. The aquarium can provide a center of enjoyment.

Run-On Sentences (Explanation pages 173-180)
(Non-text exercise)

The retired gentleman stayed busy helping others. He grew a vegetable garden he shared the vegetables with his neighbors. He kept an eye on neighbors' houses they were at work. The neighbors were on vacation he was always willing to feed his neighbors' dog also he brought in the newspaper for them. Someone's roof needed to be repaired he was ready and willing to help. A stray cat or dog came into his yard he tried to locate the owners his days were busy. Every Monday he picked up his grandchildren from school he took them to their music lessons then they stopped at the park to play on the swings. Every evening he was tired but happy he was glad that he no longer had to get up early the next morning to go to work.

Fragments, Run-On Sentences, and Comma Splices

Exercise 13, Page 182

Revise the fragments, run-on sentences, and comma splices in the following paragraphs. Be creative by using as many different methods as possible.

Paragraph 1

The forest service is becoming more sensitive to the needs of the physically challenged outdoors person. Braille camping trails offer a way for the visually impaired to tramp through America's forests without fear. America's remarkable forests. Blind hikers can begin to experience what others take for granted. Braille signs identify the surrounding trees and plants. As well as mark the trails. These trails are carefully constructed and twist their way through wooded valleys. And onto safe hillsides. Some paths are only a quarter of a mile others stretch for almost a mile. So that hikers can choose a long or a short route. Some campgrounds have wheelchair accessible paths throughout the area, some even include ramps to lakes where the campers can fish from the bank. Each campground is calm, serene, and accommodating to the physically challenged.

Paragraph 2

Because pizza is so versatile. It is no wonder that it is one of America's favorite foods. Pizza is available frozen at the grocery store or piping hot from a variety of pizza restaurants. It can be bought with thin crust or thick crust, it can be sandwiched between two crusts. Plain pizza crust can be bought frozen or already baked in packages much like bread, or mixed at home. Almost every person's individual taste can be satisfied because of the variety of toppings. Toppings spread on the sauce. Pepperoni leads the list for favorites, but jalapeño, anchovies, olives, and sausages are some of the other options, even sausage comes in different types. For a real "like-home" Italian taste. The pizza can be topped with garlic bits and a little Parmesan cheese without the sauce. Since pizza can be varied, almost everyone can be satisfied.

Paragraph Without Examples/Unit 5
(Non-text exercise)

A tiny town in northeast Wyoming has a variety of summer activities for people who live in the town and who live on the ranches in the surrounding county. Since the town is too small for a movie theater, other types of pastimes occur frequently during the summer. Some activities are get-togethers for food and entertainment. Other regular events stress historical and patriotic activities and local talents and skills. In addition to these events, the town still finds time for one-of-a-kind activities of local importance. The most prominent bulletin board in the town, the wall next to the front door of the local cafe, is usually full of announcements for coming events.

Paragraph with Examples (Unit 5)

A tiny town in northeast Wyoming has a variety of summer activities for people in the town and on the ranches in the surrounding county. Since the town is too small for a movie theater, other types of pastimes occur frequently during the summer. Some activities are get-togethers for food and entertainment. Two Fridays in June, in the basement of a town government building, the local cafe hosts a barbecue and square dance, with door prizes for both adults and children. Other regular events stress historical and patriotic activities and local talents and skills. Each July fourth, the entire county gathers for a picnic and fireworks, and a county rodeo is usually organized to begin the day after these celebrations. Later in the month, their annual Western Heritage Days celebration takes place to honor the pioneers who settled the area. Dances, food, arts and crafts, and "homemade" skits recreate their old West heritage. In addition to these events, the town still finds time for one-of-a-kind activities of local importance, such as a "traveling bake sale" to raise money to send a town boy to a regional wrestling tournament. The most prominent bulletin board in the town, the wall next to the front door of the local cafe, is usually full of announcements for coming events.

Generating Examples

Exercise 1, Pages 196-197

Using the following topic idea, write a personal example; a personal observation of someone else; an example from a short story, novel, television show, or movie; and a fact, statistic, or incident from an authoritative source.

Gangs have changed American neighborhoods.

personal example:

personal observation of someone else:

example from short story, novel, television show, or movie:

fact or statistic from an authoritative source:

Adding an Extended Example

Exercise 2, Page 200

For each topic sentence given, write a sentence that links the topic idea to an appropriate extended example. Then write an extended example that clarifies the topic sentence. (You may find it easier to write the example first and then think of an appropriate linking sentence.)

1. Topic sentence:

   Motherhood/fatherhood can be a frustrating experience.

   linking sentence:

   extended example:

2. Topic sentence:

   Saving money can be done in many ways.

   linking sentence:

   extended example:

Adding Short, Interrelated Examples

Exercise 4, Page 203

Using each topic sentence given, write a sentence that links the topic idea to short, interrelated examples. (You may find it easier to write the examples first and then think of an appropriate linking sentence.)

1. Topic sentence:

   Motherhood/fatherhood can be a frustrating experience.

   linking sentence:

   short, interrelated examples:

2. Topic sentence:

   Saving money can be done in many ways.

   linking sentence:

   short, interrelated examples:

Developing an Essay Using Examples

Exercise 8, Page 211

Carefully consider each of the following thesis sentences. Then develop a topic sentence for each division in the thesis sentence. Then write each paragraph, using one extended example or several short, interrelated examples.

1. Thesis sentence:

Throughout my years as a college student, I have experienced many enjoyable times by meeting new people, participating in student activities, and acquiring knowledge.

Paragraph 1
Topic sentence:

Extended example or several shorter examples:

Paragraph 2
Topic sentence:

Extended example or several shorter examples:

Paragraph 3
Topic sentence:

Extended example or several shorter examples:

Sentence Combining: Compound Sentences

Exercise 4, Pages 233-236

For each of the following items, combine the two simple sentences into one compound sentence as indicated. Punctuate correctly.

2. Pete does excellent carpentry work. He receives many jobs.

   (coordinate conjunction)

   (semicolon)

   (conjunctive adverb)

4. Keta and Bede live in Alaska. They often fish for salmon.

   (coordinate conjunction)

   (semicolon)

   (conjunctive adverb)

6. The attorney worked hard on the divorce case. He won it.

   (coordinate conjunction)

   (semicolon)

   (conjunctive adverb)

8. The man was working hard all morning. He went swimming.

   (coordinate conjunction)

   (semicolon)

   (conjunctive adverb)

Sentence Combining: Compound Sentences

Exercise 5, Pages 237-238

Revise the following paragraphs by changing the short choppy sentences into compound sentences. Use a variety of ways to combine the sentences.

Paragraph 2

American people do not want to eat less. They want to consume fewer calories. Food companies know this. They are coming out with reduced- or low-calorie food products. Powdered "butter" substitutions boast of having the same taste as real butter with a fraction of the calories. Ice cream is appearing in "light" form also. Producers use fat substitutes and sugar substitutes that add up to fewer calories but have "the same great taste" for the consumer. Even potato chips come with the "light" option. Not only single items but many pre-packaged microwave meals specialize in meals with under three hundred calories. The meal can be topped off with a variety of pastries with "less than half the calories of other baked goods." Food producers keep churning out new alternatives. Consumers keep "eating them up."

Paragraph 4

Dyslexia is a learning disability that may be overcome through compensation. Many times people with dyslexia are extraordinarily intelligent. They show no outward signs of this disability. They often have difficulty performing certain tasks such as learning to read. They become frustrated when they attempt these tasks that are simple to other people. For example, Dr. Marie Xavier is a dyslexic. She learned to cope with her learning disability. She was a rebellious teen. She did not take an interest in school. Later she was inspired. She excelled. She overcame her reading problem by using a patch over one eye and special reading glasses. Her study time was always at least double that of her classmates. She went on to medical school. She graduated with honors. She could more keenly relate to those who were suffering. She became a doctor and an advocate for dyslexics. She proved that dyslexia can be overcome. In this way, she set an example for Americans everywhere.

Writing Introductory Paragraphs/Unit 6
(Pages 242-253)

Possible types of hooks

Personal examples   Rhetorical questions

Quotations   Current events

Facts or statistics   Contrast to thesis sentence

Personal example (Page 244)

On February 19, 1982, life changed for an eighteen-year-old young man. He became very ill from a bacterial infection. His body could not fight the infection. Why? After a week of tests and examinations by several specialists, the diagnosis was made. He had leukemia, a cancer in the bone marrow. I am that young man. When a person finds out that he has cancer, just as I did, his whole world changes. A cancer patient is affected physically, psychologically, and socially by the impact of cancer.

Quotation (Page 246)

"I am stupid. I am never going back to school." These are the words spoken by a learning-disabled child when he was in the first grade. He cried as he slowly walked to his bedroom, shredding his schoolwork into small pieces. This was the first of many times when he and his parents would feel frustrated because there was nothing that they could do. Parents of children with learning disabilities have often felt unprepared to help their children with their handicap and frustrated with attempts to seek the proper placement of them in the public-school system. The experience of school can be overwhelming for children who have trouble learning. The learning-disabled student in the public educational system must deal with academic, social, and emotional problems.

Fact (Page 248)

In the desert regions of Arizona, solar homes date back to the pre-Columbian Indians. These people carefully designed their homes in the recesses of south-facing cliffs to receive the warmth of the winter sun. In the summer, shade was provided by the overhanging cliffs. Today, as then, the desert-region solar home must be carefully designed to use the sun efficiently in the orientation, the exterior, and the interior.

Rhetorical question (Page 250)

When people think ahead to the year 3000, many different questions come to mind. What new inventions will be in use in the common household? How much will the world of transportation be advanced? What type of weaponry will have been invented? In what type of environment will people be living? All of these questions indicate that in the year 3000 there will be major differences in science, in transportation, and in people's life-styles.

Current event (Page 251)

This morning's newspaper reported a man who had shot his twenty-three-year-old girlfriend and her nine-month-old child because he believed his girlfriend had transmitted AIDS to him. In 1984, a nurse in Kokomo, Indiana, refused to go into 13-year-old Ryan White's hospital room because he had just been diagnosed with AIDS, and in 1987, a bullet shattered his home's picture window, forcing Ryan and his family to move to Cicero, Indiana, a community twenty miles south. Though these incidents seem bizarre in twentieth century civilized America, many people fear AIDS because of the consequences of the disease, the misinformation concerning the disease, and the increasing number of cases of the disease.

Contrast to the thesis sentence (Page 252)

Since the middle of the 1940s, the female Cannabis sativa plant, commonly known as marijuana, has been classified by the United States government as a Schedule I drug. This classification recognizes marijuana as a dangerous narcotic, similar in potency to heroin and possessing no redeeming medicinal qualities. Research in the last few years, however, has brought many new discoveries in medicine relating to the possible uses of marijuana to treat many different illnesses, including glaucoma, cancer, asthma, and phantom limb pain suffered by paraplegics and amputees.

Introductory Paragraph Transition

Exercise 7, Pages 256-257

The following introductory paragraphs lack a transition from the hook to the thesis sentence. Try to bridge the gap logically so that your reader understands the connection between the hook and the thesis sentence.

Paragraph 1

According to Richard Alfred in his article titled "Positioning Alternatives and New Partnerships," a worker entering the labor force "would have to relearn his job seven times in a 40-year career."

To aid students who are retraining, community colleges offer assessment and advisement, financial aid, and updated curricula.

Paragraph 4

"Mom, Dad, will you please play a game of Risk with us?"

Playing board games with your family can create a challenge, encourage family unity, and bring excitement.

Strong Conclusions (Pages 263-264)

The conclusion should not

> repeat the thesis sentence exactly as it appeared in the introduction

> repeat the thesis sentence and mechanically repeat the topic sentences

> change the tone of the essay

> introduce a new idea in the conclusion

The conclusion should

> summarize main points made in the paper and creatively restate the ideas in the thesis sentence

> end with an obvious closure that leaves the essay with a sense of completeness

Strong conclusions

> refer to an example, fact, or statistic mentioned in the introduction

> end with a question that leaves the reader thinking about what was said

> comment about the future

Strong Conclusion (Page 265)

The mind, the body, and the soul of a family unit can be invigorated simply by spending precious days together taking weekend vacations. Teenagers, small children, and adults have quality time together as they share the many opportunities offered simply by being alive and enjoying each other's company doing little things. While these family members are strengthening the bond they feel for one another, they are also gaining valuable knowledge and healthy exercise. Even though nothing can be done about the fact that so many children from ages five to thirteen are getting home from school before their parents, something can be done about the weekend that will leave lasting memories for these children. What kind of memories are these parents leaving for their children? Instead of checking out the TV schedule this weekend, maybe more families should be checking out the adventurous opportunities waiting to be taken.

Sentence Combining: Complex Sentences

Exercise 5, Pages 298-299

Revise the following draft paragraphs by combining simple sentences into complex sentences. Try to use a variety of complex sentences.

Paragraph 1

Basketball requires a variety of physical skills. Stamina is a stringent requirement for this highly active sport. Many times the victory goes to the team with the greatest physical endurance. Agility is another important factor for basketball players. They must be able to move smoothly and quickly. They can coordinate their moves. Scottie Pippen's finesse on the court is a great example of winning, aerobic-like moves. Sheer aggression defines the dribbling path of his drives to the basket. Players have peripheral vision. They can pass without looking at the players receiving the ball. Jumping ability is important. Great basketball players can slam dunk and get many rebounds. These physical skills can lead to a winning team.

Paragraph 2

Bodybuilding is a sport that demands discipline. Bodybuilders push themselves until their muscles won't work any more. They build muscle mass. Serious athletes must work out at the gym five to seven hours a day. They feel a burning sensation in their muscles. The muscles are sore the next morning. They know they had a good workout. Athletes must also have the willpower to adhere to a strict diet. They eat no fatty foods, especially hamburgers and french fries. They need to cut fat. They must stay on an even stricter diet than normal. They also must get plenty of sleep. They are at a party with their friends and everyone else wants to stay late. Dedicated athletes will have enough control to go home early. This dedication, however, will result in a body they can take pride in.

Paragraph 4

Cheerleading helps people build confidence needed to become outgoing. Many people try out for a cheer position. Very few make the line. Some succeed. They then feel proud of themselves. They have accomplished something. Not everyone else can do this. Cheerleaders are in front of a lot of people at one time. They build confidence about themselves by performing well. They gain this confidence by performing in front of small groups. This confidence helps them when they go to state meets and have to lead cheers in front of thousands of people. Self-esteem grows. Other students come up to talk to them or tell them that they did a nice job This confidence helps them shake a bad mood and become more outgoing and positive around other people.

Sentence Combining to Form Compound, Complex, and More Sophisticated Simple Sentences (Non-text Examples)

The old man enjoyed his garden. He planted many new flowers.

Compound

The old man enjoyed his garden; he planted many new flowers.

The old man enjoyed his garden; as a result, he planted many new flowers.

The old man enjoyed his garden, so he planted many new flowers.

Complex

The old man enjoyed his garden where he planted many new flowers.

Because the old man enjoyed his garden, he planted many new flowers.

The old man enjoyed his garden because he planted many new flowers.

The old man that enjoyed his garden planted many new flowers.

The old man who planted many new flowers enjoyed his garden.

The old man enjoyed his garden that contained many new flowers.

Simple

Enjoying his garden, the old man planted many new flowers.

To enjoy his garden, the old man planted many new flowers.

Enjoying his garden caused the old man to plant many new flowers.

Planting many new flowers helped the old man enjoy his garden.

Adding Coherence

Exercise 1, Page 306

Revise the following paragraphs by adding key words derived from the topic idea, time and other transitional words, and pronouns that will make the paragraph a coherent whole.

Paragraph 1

A small park can be a haven for children. Swings are big and sturdy so children can swing, seemingly to the tops of trees. Ducks swim close to the shore to eat whatever the small visitors bring. Older children canoe through rippling water. Others stand or sit at the edges of the lake and throw out fishing lines complete with worms. The children wait for some hungry fish to bite the hook. Parents of the children relax or nap under the shade of nearby trees. Here the world feels safe as children watch other families enjoying the park.

Paragraph 2

Prepackaged, microwavable dishes are a way of life for people on the go. Prepackaged entrees for babies help working mothers serve nutritional meals for small members of the family. Older children can microwave their own dinners. When mom and dad are unable to prepare lunch, children can heat up such items as spaghetti and meatballs or chicken and rice. Entrees that appeal to the whole family can be stored in the freezer and popped into the microwave while the cook throws together a quick salad and sets the table. Chicken and dumplings, vegetable lasagna, or pork back ribs are a few of the many varieties available. Evening snacks can include popcorn in minutes or milk shakes that defrost in seconds. People with a microwave oven no longer have a reason for skipping a meal.

Education (Pages 320-321)
Jan-Georg Roesch, student

Only fifteen months ago I was sitting in a typical German classroom daydreaming through the lecture and hoping for a miracle that my grades would improve. All the help I got came too late because I had already wasted too much time in the first semester. My goal was to finish *Abitur* and then continue going to a university. The goal just seemed to vanish in thin air, and how was I going to do my master's degree? Fortunately, my father was going to retire soon, and plans were made to make a permanent settlement in Phoenix because my grandmother lived there. Hence, I was given the opportunity to continue my educational goal in America, skip the draft in Germany, and enjoy the warm Arizona climate.

In Germany, I would have to complete thirteen years of school and attain the diploma in order to go to a university. I had completed twelve of the thirteen years and didn't have enough points to get into the last year. Furthermore, the conditions I was facing made it more or less impossible for me to repeat the class, and I did not want to take the risk of losing the prediploma. The only solution left was to come to the United States and try to finish my educational goal. Again, I was very fortunate to have friends in Phoenix who made my entrance into Arizona State University very easy. Although I knew that much of what I had learned over the past two years was going to be repeated, I accepted the challenge because I did not really have a choice.

Yet, finishing the educational goal was not the only reason for my coming here. At the age of eighteen every male teenager who had completed school was picked for the draft. This meant I had to serve for fifteen months and receive a wage of $70 a month. The alternatives were either to sign up for a longer period, either for four or six years, or do social work for the same period. I was not too crazy about the idea of serving fifteen months; I felt that it was a waste of time because the program does not offer any real educational use. Of course, the service does provide people with good educational service; however, I would have to sign up for a longer time period.

Finally, my last criterion for coming to Phoenix was the warm climate. I had spent over eighteen years of my life living in countries where the climate was mild, damp, wet, and sometimes very cold. Having the flu five times a year was nothing uncommon and seemed more or less to be part of daily life. In addition, it would sometimes rain for days nonstop and flood all the rivers, which normally resulted in flooding the cellar or creating total chaos in the streets. The so-called summer was usually brief. The warm weather might have stayed for two weeks when the next rain clouds were already expected. The winter period was mainly characterized by residents watching tourists streaming out to see warmer places or sitting next to the warm fireplace and sipping hot chocolate.

It is close to one year now since I moved, and I do not regret living the eighteen years in countries with colder climates. However, I also feel that moving to Phoenix will bring me new experiences that I could not have encountered if I had stayed in Germany. I will learn new cultural traits and behaviors that differ from the European heartland. Yet, most important of all, I can finish achieving my educational goal that I once dreamed of fifteen months ago.

Punctuation

Exercise 11, Pages 343-344

Using all the punctuating skills covered in this section, punctuate the following paragraphs.

Paragraph 1

During World War II average American citizens experienced many difficulties buying products they wanted or needed. The ability just to be able to buy products was restricted by monthly ration stamps for such items as gasoline shoes sugar and meat. Though people had ration stamps meat was especially hard to find because it was put into products like Spam and sent to the men overseas. Even with stamps citizens might not be able to buy the products they wanted. Often the shelves were empty because it seemed as though everything was channeled into Americas defense system. For example shoes were difficult to obtain because the shoe producers needed to supply boots for the army. Likewise material was difficult to purchase because fabrics were shipped to factories to make uniforms for the Armed Forces. Jim and Alice Basham who owned their own upholstery business said We could not buy goods to upholster furniture because material was shipped to the Armed Forces. They also said that women were unable to buy nylons because the fabric needed to make them went into making parachutes to be used in the war. Imported items like coffee tea sugar and rubber were scarce. The little rubber that the United States could import went into the production of tires for the Armed Forces. For four years no automobiles were made because all American energies were channeled into the production of military vehicles. American citizens who lived through World War II will always remember those hard times.

Paragraph 3

Poetry is an art form that can be enjoyed sometimes because of the meaning sometimes because of the way it is written and other times because of both. Can anyone read Walt Whitmans Leaves of Grass without saying That is nice really nice Lines that seem to stick in the mind are often written with a strong message. For instance the lines from Anne Sextons poem Abortion Somebody who should have been born/is gone stay in the mind long after the poem has been read. Whenever the question of abortion arises these lines are recalled in the mind again and again. Thomas Hood wanted to change labor laws in England. In his poem The Song of the Shirt he wrote With fingers weary and worn,/ With eyelids heavy and red,/ A woman sat in unwomanly rags,/ Plying her needle and thread-- John Milton, married but miserable, spent much effort inserting lines about divorce into his poetry in an attempt to change the laws that forbade divorce. Some poets however do not moralize but simply present things the way they are James Dickey a well-known American poet wrote of adultery objectively without making any judgment of its wrongness or rightness. On the other hand Joyce Peseroff expresses her ideas in The Hardness Scale in which she seems to be relating a womans feelings about a man who is not such a perfect man. Diane Wakoski writes of revenge in her poem You, Letting the Trees Stand as My Betrayer In this poem nature will pay back someone who loved her and then left her. The meaning is there in these and many other poems but the way they are written makes the lines occur over and over in the readers mind.